European economic integration

third edition

• •

Frank McDonald
Stephen Dearden

LONGMAN

Pearson Education Limited
Edinburgh Gate
Harlow
Essex CM20 2JE
England
and Associated Companies throughout the world

Visit us on the world wide web at:
http://www.pearsoneduc.com

Published in the United States of America
by Addison Wesley Longman Inc., New York

First edition © Longman Group UK Limited 1992
Second edition © Longman Group Limited 1994
This edition © Addison Wesley Longman Limited 1999

First published 1992
Second edition 1994
Third edition 1999
Reprinted 1999

ISBN 0 582 309174

British Library Cataloguing-in-Publication Data
A catalogue record for this book is available from the British Library

Library of Congress Cataloging-in-Publication Data
European economic integration/edited by Frank McDonald, Stephen
  Dearden. — 3rd ed.
     p. cm.
  Includes bibliographical references and index.
  ISBN 0–582–30917–4 (pbk.)
  1. European Economic Community. 2. European Economic Community
countries—Economic policy. I. McDonald, Frank, 1951– .
II. Dearden, Steven, 1950– .
HC241.2.M227 1999
337.1′42—dc21
                                                        98–27076
                                                        CIP

Set by 35 in 10/12pt New Baskerville
Printed in Great Britain by Henry Ling Ltd., at the Dorset Press, Dorchester, Dorset

European economic integration

For condi

Contents

INTRODUCTION
The origins and development of the European Union 1

Frank McDonald

CHAPTER 1
Market integration in the European Union 34

Frank McDonald

CHAPTER 2

Macroeconomic policy cooperation 73

Nigel Healey

CHAPTER 3

Economic and monetary union 94

Nigel Healey

CHAPTER 4

The budget of the European Union 117

Keith Penketh

CHAPTER 5

The European Union and competition policy 128

John Kemp

CHAPTER 6
Industrial policy in the European Union *156*

Frank McDonald and Margaret Potton

CHAPTER 7
Social policy *180*

Stephen Dearden

CHAPTER 8
Regional policy *209*

Reiner Martin

CHAPTER 9
Environment policy *238*

CHAPTER 10
Transport policy *251*

CHAPTER 11
The Common Agricultural and Fisheries Policies *281*

CHAPTER 12
External trade policy *302*

CHAPTER 13
The European Union and Central and Eastern Europe 314

Andrei Kuznetsov

CHAPTER 14
The European Union and the Third World 332

Stephen Dearden

CHAPTER 15
The European Union and the Triad 357

Frank McDonald

CHAPTER 16

Foreign direct investment and the European Union 384

Adam Cross

CHAPTER 17

The importance of Germany in Europe: Trade and direct foreign investment 407

Heinz J Tuselmann

Contributors

Adam Cross, Lecturer in International Business, Centre for International Business, University of Leeds – Chapter 16.

Stephen Dearden, Senior Lecturer in Economics, Department of Economics, Manchester Metropolitan University – Chapters 7, 10 and 14.

John Gibbons, Senior Lecturer in Politics, Department of Philosophy and Politics, Manchester Metropolitan University – Chapter 11.

John Hassan, Senior Lecturer in Economic History, Department of History, Manchester Metropolitan University – Chapter 9.

Nigel Healey, Professor of Business Economics, Department of Business Studies, Manchester Metropolitan University – Chapters 2 and 3.

John Kemp, Senior Lecturer in Economics, Department of Economics, Manchester Metropolitan University – Chapter 5.

Andrei Kuznetsov, Senior Lecturer in International Business, International Business Unit, Manchester Metropolitan University – Chapter 13.

Frank McDonald, Principal Lecturer in International Business, International Business Unit, Manchester Metropolitan University – Introduction, Chapters 1, 6 and 15.

Reiner Martin, Researcher in the Centre for European Policy Studies, Brussels – Chapter 8.

Keith Penketh, Formerly Principal Lecturer in Economics, Department of Economics, Manchester Metropolitan University (now retired) – Chapters 4 and 12.

Margaret Potton, Formerly Senior Research Fellow in European Studies, International Business Unit, Manchester Metropolitan University (now freelance researcher), with interest in the EU dating from the 1960s when she attended the College of Europe – Chapter 6.

Heinz J Tuselmann, Senior Lecturer in International Business, Manchester Metropolitan University – Chapter 17.

Preface to the third edition

Many changes have taken place in Europe since the second edition of this book was published. The European Union has extended its membership to 15 countries and it is likely that it will soon welcome the first wave of members from Central and Eastern Europe. European monetary union will begin in 1999 with 11 of the member states joining the first wave of countries who will adopt the euro as their currency. The Amsterdam Treaty was signed in 1997 and extended the scope of the work of the European Union. In global terms the European Union has played an increasing role in influencing developments in political matters as well as trade issues.

In the light of these events the editors thought that a third edition should be issued to examine the implications of these changes.

A new author was brought in to write on macroeconomic topics, and this edition has substantially more coverage of integration issues related to macroeconomic affairs than the previous editions. The Regional Policy chapter has also been written by a new author and therefore presents a significantly different view on regional issues from the previous editions. A new chapter has been added on foreign direct investment inflows into the European Union. The chapters on the Customs Union and the Single European Market have been integrated, and the theoretical and empirical material on the process of the integration of markets has been expanded. A section on the Common Fisheries Policy has been added to the chapter on the Common Agricultural Policy. The other chapters have been substantially re-written to reflect the changes that have taken place.

The format of the book has also been altered. Much of the factual material or case illustrations has been placed in boxes. This allows the text to be read separately from long passages of factual or illustrative material. Diagrams with accompanying exposition of economic theory have also been separated from the text. The editors are hopeful that this will help those students who have a limited knowledge of economic theory to understand the text more easily. In most cases the text can be read separately from the economic theory that is attached to the diagrams. The editors are confident that this book could easily be used by students who have a good knowledge of elementary economic theory. However, the book will be useful to students who have a knowledge of advanced economic theory because it gives guidance on more advanced theoretical literature on the subject and the chapters also outline contemporary theoretical work that focuses on economic integration. Moreover, the chapters provide material that is very relevant to an understanding of the economics of integration which are often missing from standard economic theory, for example, the importance of institutional structures, culture, history and geography.

The editors and contributors expect that students of business, economics, economic geography, European studies and politics will find this edition to be a useful tool to aid in their understanding of the process of European integration.

Acknowledgements

The editors would like to thank the contributors for their willingness to conform to the demands placed upon them by the editors. We are also grateful to our students for the valuable information sources that they discovered and passed on to the editors.

We are grateful to the following for permission to reproduce copyright material:

Table 1.3 from *Business Survey*, Table 1.4, 1.5, 1.6 from *Eurostat*, Table 5.1, Figure 5.4 (a) and (b), 5.5 (a) and (b) from *Annual Report on Competition Policy*, DGIV, 1996, Figure 7.1, 7.2, 7.3, 7.4 and 7.5 from *Employment in Europe* 1996, Table 8.1, 8.2, 8.3, 8.4 from *First Report on Economic Cohesion* 1996, Table 8.5 from Agenda 2000 Vol. I Communication: For a Stranger and wider Union, 1997, Table 10.2 from *Second Survey on State Aids*, 1992, Table 14.7 from *Aid Review*, 1992–93 and 1994–95, Table 14.9 and 14.10 from *The Courier*, Table 16.3 and 16.4 from *European Economy* 1996, all the above reprinted with permission from the European Community, Office of Official Publications of the European Communities; Figure 8.2 and 8.4 from *Statistics in Focus*, Eurostat, 1997 reprinted with permission; Figure 14.1 reprinted with permission from World Trade Organisation; Table 14.1 from *Direction of Trade Statistics Yearbook*, 1995 reprinted with permission from International Monetary Fund; Table 14.11 from *World Investment Report*, 1994 UN Transnational Corporations, Employment and Workplace, pp. 409–12 reprinted with permission; Table 16.2 from *Trade and Foreign Direct Investment*, New Report by the WTO, PRESS 57 (October, 1996) reprinted with permission from the World Trade Organisation.

Whilst every effort has been made to trace the owners of copyright material, in a few cases this has proved impossible and we take this opportunity to offer our apologies to any copyright holders whose rights we may have unwittingly infringed.

A	Austria
ACP	African, Caribbean and Pacific countries
AFTA	ASEAN Free Trade Agreement
APEC	Asia-Pacific Economic Cooperation
ASEAN	Association of South East Asian Nations
ASEM	Asia-Europe Meeting
B	Belgium
BL	Economic union of Belgium and Luxembourg
BRIDGE	Biotechnology Research for Innovation and Development in Europe
BRITE	Basic Research in Industrial Technologies in Europe
CAP	Common Agricultural Policy
CCP	Common Commercial Policy
Cedefop	European Centre for the Development of Vocational Training
CEECs	Central and Eastern European countries
CEFTA	Central European Free Trade Agreement
CEN	Comité Européen de Normalisation (European Standards Body)
CENELEC	Comité Européen de Normalisation Electronique (European Standards Body for Electrical Equipment)
CET	Common External Tariff
CF	Cohesion Fund
CFC	Chlorofluorocarbon
CI	Community Initiatives
CM	Common Market
COMECON	Council for Mutual Economic Assistance (also known as CMEA)
COMETT	Community Action Programme for Education and Training for Technology
COREPER	Committee of Permanent Representatives
COST	European Co-operation in the Field of Scientific and Technical Research
CSF	Community Support Framework
CTP	Common Transport Policy
CU	Customs Union
D	Germany
DELTA	Developing Learning through Technological Advance
DG	Directorate General

DK	Denmark
E	Spain
EAGGF	European Agricultural Guidance and Guarantee Fund
EAP	Environmental Action Programme
EBRD	European Bank of Reconstruction and Development
EC	European Community
ECB	European Central Bank
ECJ	European Court of Justice
ECSC	European Coal and Steel Community
ECU	European Currency Unit
EDF	European Development Fund
EEA	European Environment Agency (also European Economic Area)
EEIG	European Economic Interest Group
EFTA	European Free Trade Association
EIA	Environmental Impact Assessment
EIB	European Investment Bank
EMI	European Monetary Institute
EMS	European Monetary System
EMU	Economic and Monetary Union
EP	European Parliament
ERDF	European Regional Development Fund
ERM	Exchange Rate Mechanism
ESCB	European System of Central Banks
ESF	European Social Fund
ESPRIT	European Strategic Programme for Research and Development in Information Technology
ETUC	European Trade Union Confederation
EU	European Union
EURATOM	European Atomic Energy Community
EUR6	Six original members of the EU (B, F, D, I, L and the NL)
EUR12	EUR6 plus Dk, E, Gr, Irl, P and the UK
EUR15	EUR12 plus A, Fin and Sw
EUREKA	European Research Cooperation Agency
EWC	European Works Council
FDI	Foreign Direct Investment
Fin	Finland
FTC	Fair Trade Commission (Japan)
G8	Group of seven largest Western industrial countries plus Russia
GATT	General Agreement on Tariffs and Trade
GDP	Gross Domestic Product
GNP	Gross National Product
GR	Greece
GSP	General System of Preferences
I	Italy
ILO	International Labour Organisation
IMF	International Monetary Fund
IMP	Integrated Mediterranean Programme

Irl	Ireland
IT	Information technology
JRC	Joint Research Centre
L	Luxembourg
LDC	Less developed countries
M	Imports
Marpol	International Convention for the Prevention of Pollution from Ships
MCA	Monetary Compensation Amount
MEP	Member of the European Parliament
MERCOSUR	Agency seeking to create a common market for Argentina, Brazil, Paraguay, Uruguay and Free Trade area with Bolivia and Chile
MES	Minimum Efficiency Scale
MFA	Multi Fibre Arrangement
MFN	Most favoured nation
MITI	Ministry of International Trade and Industry (Japan)
MNC	Multinational company
MTIP	Multi-annual Transport Infrastructure Programme
NAFTA	North American Free Trade Area
NATO	North Atlantic Treaty Organisation
NIC	Newly Industrialised Country
NIP	National Indicative Programme
NL	Netherlands
NTA	New Transatlantic Agenda
NTB	Non-tariff barrier
NUTS	Nomenclature of Territorial Units
OECD	Organisation for Economic Co-operation and Development
OEED	Organisation for European Economic Development
OP	Operational Programmes
P	Portugal
PHARE	Pologne-Hongrie: Actions pour la reconversion économique (Programme for the Reconstruction of Poland and Hungary)
PPS	Purchasing Power Standard
PSO	Public Service Obligation grant
QMV	Qualified majority voting
RACE	Research and Development Programme in Advanced Communications Technologies for Europe
R&D	Research and Development
RECHAR	Fund for the Reconversion of Coal Mining Areas
RENAVAL	Fund for the Reconversion of Shipbuilding Areas
RESIDER	Fund for the Reconversion of Steel Areas
RETEX	Fund for the Reconversion of Textile Areas
ROW	Rest of the World
RPK	Revenue passenger kilometres
RTD	Research and Technological Development
SAS	Structural Adjustment Support
SEA	Single European Act

SEM	Single European Market
SF	Structural Funds
SME	Small and medium-sized enterprises
SPRINT	Strategic Programme for the Transnational Promotion of Innovation and Technology Transfer
STABEX	Fund for the Stabilisation of Primary Product Prices
STC	Specific Transport Instrument
STRIDE	Science and Technology for Regional Innovation and Development in Europe
Sw	Sweden
SYSMIN	Fund for the stabilisation of mineral prices
TACIS	Programme for Technical Assistance to the Commonwealth of Independent States
TEMPUS	Trans-European Mobility Scheme for University Studies
TEU	Treaty on European Union (Maastricht Treaty)
TGV	Train à Grande Vitesse
TIC	Transport Infrastructure Committee
UIC	Union Internationale des Chemins de Fer
UK	United Kingdom
UNCTAD	United Nations Conference on Trade and Development
UNICE	Union of Industrial and Employers' Confederations of Europe
VAT	Value Added Tax
VER	Voluntary Export Restraint
WTO	World Trade Organisation
X	Exports

The origins and development of the European Union

Frank McDonald

Introduction

The moves to complete the Single European Market (SEM) and the progress towards Economic and Monetary Union (EMU) focused attention on the European Union (EU) as the key actor in the process of European integration. The EU has also become involved in a host of policies that affect many aspects of the economic and social activities of the member states. Agricultural matters, especially the Common Agricultural Policy (CAP), were once the only significant policy of the EU. However, the increasing integration of the member states brought competition, social, regional, and environmental policies to the forefront of the activities of the EU.

A number of other factors have contributed to a growing focus on the EU. The Community experienced several enlargements that increased its membership from the original six states to fifteen members. The end of the Cold War, the demise of communism in Central and Eastern Europe, the reunification of Germany and the collapse of the Soviet Union led to the EU becoming the unchallenged centre of economic and business activity in Europe. These developments presented a series of new problems for European integration. One of the main issues that is being faced is the future development of the Community's relations with Central and Eastern European Countries (CEECs) and with the republics of the former Soviet Union. The importance of the EU in world trade has also led to a growing role for the Community in the World Trade Organisation (WTO). Moreover, the Community's links to many Third World countries through special arrangements with developing countries, for example, the African, Caribbean and Pacific countries (ACP), have increased the importance of the EU in development issues. Strong trade links with the USA, Japan and the newly industrialised countries (NICs) have further contributed to the importance of the EU in the important forums of world politics and trade. Therefore, in global forums that discuss problems in areas such as trade, global pollution, organised crime and security matters, the EU has become an important player.

What is the European Union?

The term European Union (EU) came into common usage in 1993 after the Council of Ministers renamed itself the Council of the European Union. This name stems from the Maastricht Treaty (more correctly called the Treaty on European Union) which created the term to encompass the variety of cooperation and integration work that was carried out by the member states. However, the EU did not replace the European Community (EC). The EC is itself a composite term for the European Coal and Steel Community (ECSC) (founded by the Treaty of Paris in 1951), the European Economic Community (EEC) and the European Atomic Energy Community (EURATOM) founded by the Treaty of Rome in 1957. These three entities were merged in 1965 when a common institutional structure to govern the work of these agencies was established. This body was called the European Community (EC) or, more accurately, the European Communities. The Maastricht Treaty created three pillars – the EC, justice and home affairs, foreign and security policy – and called the umbrella structure for these three pillars the EU. The EC is governed by the institutions of that agency (e.g. the European Commission, the European Parliament and the European Court of Justice), while the two other pillars are not subject to these institutions but are governed by the Council of the European Union (ministers from the national governments of the member states). The Amsterdam Treaty transferred immigration and asylum policy to the institutions of the EC, but the complex distinctions and interconnections between the ECSC, EEC, EURATOM and the two other pillars still remain.

The term EU has come to be used as the generic term for all of the agencies of the member states. This has led to mistakes in terminology. For example, reference is made to EU law, but there is no such concept because the EU does not have a legal personality. Furthermore, prior to 1993 the EU did not have any kind of existence. However, reference to the EU as a term for the EC or even the EEC is widespread in newspapers and even in academic journals and books. Indeed, the Commission often uses the term EU when referring to policies or programmes that are related to EC matters. This confusion is understandable given the difficulty of clearly identifying the time period and changing role and names of the various agencies that compose the EU. The use of the EU as a generic term is well established and it is unlikely that greater precision in its use will emerge except by pedants and in areas where distinguishing between the component parts of the EU is important (e.g. in legal matters and when examining the role and functions of the institutions of the different parts of the EU).

This book uses the term EU or Community, except in historical contexts when the terms ECSC, EEC and EC are used. However, as the book is mainly concerned with economic matters, most of the references to the EU should perhaps be to the EC or to the EEC. However, the editors believe that the use of the generic terms EU and Community does not lead to any grave errors and avoids unnecessarily complicated explanations in the text.

The European Unity movement

The origins of what developed into the EU can be traced to the European Unity movement. A full description and analysis of the historical development of the European Unity movement can be found in Nugent (1995), and a review of the main elements in this process is provided in Swann (1996) and Commission (1990). The origins of the move to achieve European Unity stemmed from a desire to avoid the periodic wars between the nation states of Europe. There was also some consideration of the advantages of creating a larger market in Europe to allow economies of scale to be reaped. However, it was political factors that predominated in the early attempts to achieve European Unity. Therefore, although there were economic factors behind this movement, the main objectives were political. When the first steps towards creating the EU were made, specific economic objectives were the main methods advocated to achieve European unity; they were, however, generally regarded as means to an end, and the end was the establishment of some kind of political union.

In the aftermath of the Second World War the countries of Europe were faced with several difficult issues. Much of the continent of Europe was severely war damaged, and a large reconstruction process was necessary. The Cold War was developing, dividing Europe into two opposing camps, with a divided Germany as the potential flashpoint for renewed conflict in Europe. Any such conflict would have been between the two new superpowers of the USA and the Soviet Union and could have involved the use of nuclear weapons. In such circumstances it was not surprising that the Europeans should have looked for some methods to ensure that they had a voice in shaping the dramatic events that were taking place in Europe. The main obstacles to this were that Europe could not speak with one voice because it was composed of a number of sovereign nation states and these states did not have a common view on the solutions to the problems of post-war Europe.

The main powers in Europe were the USA and the Soviet Union. The UK, which was the strongest European power, was not particularly interested in becoming involved in attempts to achieve European unity. In this period the UK was interested in promoting stability in Europe that would allow the UK to concentrate on the creation of zones of influence in the Commonwealth and with developing a 'special relationship' with the USA. Although the UK was not opposed to European unity, it favoured loose inter-governmental arrangements between the countries of Europe where each country retained sovereignty (the right to make decisions independently of other governments or agencies) in the important areas of policy-making. Consequently, the UK was not prepared to become involved in attempts to create any supranational European agencies as they would have powers that would erode the sovereignty of the member countries. Most of the Scandinavian countries were concerned to maintain their neutrality in the face of the growth of the Cold War and wished to retain sovereignty in key economic and political areas. Therefore, they were unwilling to become involved in the creation of supranational European agencies. The countries of Southern Europe were scarcely connected to these events. Spain and Portugal were dictatorships and were not considered to be eligible to join the democratic countries of

Europe in creating new arrangements to forge European unity. Greece was in a state of political flux, with the possibility that it could go communist and forge links with the Soviet Union. Indeed, the main focus of attention on the countries of Southern Europe was to ensure that they were not recruited to the communist side and to enrol them in the defence coalition opposing the Soviet Union.

In the immediate post-war period Europe was divided not only into East and West, but also into those countries that favoured the creation of some kind of supranational European agencies and others who looked for some loose forms of inter-governmental cooperation. There was also division between the democratic countries of Western Europe and the dictatorships of Southern Europe.

By the 1980s the geographically based divisions began to crumble and the division with Southern Europe vanished. The USA no longer dominated Europe economically and the ending of the Cold War reduced American political and military influence in Europe, but there was no consensus on the future role of the USA in European economic, political and military matters. Although Europe largely ceased to be divided into different camps on the basis of ideology, there were still considerable disputes over the characteristics that the European Unity should have. These disputes stem from differences of opinion about the approach that should be adopted to creating European Unity.

The European Unity movement is split into a variety of approaches on how best to achieve viable integration. Three main approaches have emerged.

1. Federalists – This group favours the creation of a political community that is founded on strong constitutional and institutional frameworks. The resulting Federation would have supranational powers that would take precedence over the powers of the member states. Therefore, achieving European Unity is seen as requiring the creation of new federal structures.

2. Functionalists – This group advocates that integration should be based on the 'functional' activities of governments. It regards security, defence and foreign policy as being very 'political' and considers that national governments are reluctant to surrender sovereignty in these areas. However, in less 'political' areas, such as policies towards particular sectors and detailed economic areas such as trade rules, it is easier to obtain agreement to integrate government policies. Neo-Functionalists argue that, as functional areas of governments are integrated, the political and bureaucratic elite that handle these policies will increasingly switch their loyalties, expectations and goals from the national government arena to the overall aims of the integration agencies. In this scenario a Functionalist approach would gradually move the elite towards the goals of European political integration.

3. Nationalists – This group regards the nation state as the prime focus for all government activity, in areas such as trade rules and sectorial policies as well as in the 'big' policy areas such as security and defence. In this view European integration should be based on inter-governmental cooperation in cases where all parties can expect to benefit from such cooperation. Agencies with supranational powers should only be created if the benefits available from such agencies are very large and cannot be captured by some kind of inter-governmental body.

Federalists and Functionalists have a common goal – an integrated Europe based on the creation of new supranational structures. Their only substantial difference is over the means to this end. The Federalists favour a 'big bang' approach based on dramatic constitutional and institutional change. In contrast, the Functionalists work towards a gradual drift into European Unity as the elite become more and more entangled in the functional work of the integration agencies. Nationalists have a very different agenda. They regard integration as primarily a process of inter-governmental cooperation to achieve mutually beneficial outcomes. In their view the integration process is not seen as a method of building European political union, but as a method of collaborating to find solutions to common problems. However, European political union could emerge from the Nationalists' approach if there were overwhelming benefits from such a union.

The Nationalists versus the Federalists and Functionalists battle has had a powerful influence on the development of the EU. The dispute between Federalists and Functionalists has been about the speed and type of change. However, the Nationalists have fought against the direction of integration when it has led towards the growth of supranational governmental structures. These disputes have contributed to the rather strange governmental structures that have been developed in the Community. The institutions of the Community are a mixture of supranational and inter-governmental structures, which reflect the lack of consensus on how best to promote the well-being of European countries. The conflict that arises over the speed and type of reform among the supporters of supranationalism illustrates the continuing debate between the Federalists and the Functionalists.

In spite of these disputes there is a consensus that in economic matters the EU is the key to the development of Europe. In political and even security matters, the EU, or at least institutions with strong connections to it, is seen as the way forward to allow adjustment to the new conditions that prevail in Europe. The European Economic Community (EEC), and its precursor the European Coal and Steel Community (ECSC), always had economic objectives to the fore, and this remains true even though the EU is beginning to expand into more overtly political objectives. Indeed, many of the pressures to move into political areas stem from the need to create the necessary conditions under which economic objectives such as establishing the Single European Market (SEM) and Economic and Monetary Union (EMU) can be achieved. There are also pressures to modify the political structures to aid in the growing role that the EU plays in the world economy. The process of European economic integration is therefore at the heart of the current changes in Europe, and the EU is the key agent in this process.

The origins of the European Union

The origins of the EU stem from the failure in the early post-war period of the main countries of Europe to reach agreement on how European Unity should proceed. France and West Germany formed an alliance to promote European integration to rebuild their shattered economic systems and to foster the conditions that would prevent war between Western European countries. The Franco-German alliance favoured the creation of limited supranational agencies in order to curb the tendency for European countries to develop nationalistic tendencies that could have led to poor relations between European countries. However, in major issues it was considered important to retain power at national government level. This approach gave the Franco-German alliance a major role in defining and developing the European Unity movement. Italy, Belgium, Holland and Luxembourg supported the Franco-German approach and these six countries started the process that ultimately led to the EU. In the UK and the Scandinavian countries the predominant view was that an inter-governmental approach should be taken to rebuilding Europe and to securing stability in the region.

These early developments in the European Unity movement have had long-lasting effects. The Franco-German alliance came to dominate the process of European integration. The Franco-German view has tended to regard Euro-pean Unity as primarily a political issue and that economic considerations are a means to a political end. This end was seen as being primarily the creation of security and prosperity by integration, and that economic efficiency considera-tions were secondary to the goal of achieving unity. The importance of this view can perhaps be best observed in the creation of such policies as the Common Agricultural Policy (CAP), which is very strong on stability, security and the prosperity of farmers, but has little connection with any concept of economic efficiency. The British and Scandinavian views of European integration were based on a more economic and pragmatic view of the need for integration programmes. Therefore, the driving force for integration programmes was very different among the countries of Western Europe.

The EU has developed largely in accordance with the vision of the Franco-German alliance. The alliance has tended to guide the development of the Community, but this has led to resistance by Italy and the smaller member states to the dominance of the Franco-German alliance in the development of the Community. They have sought to curb the power of the alliance by increasing the supranational aspects of the Community. The scepticism of the UK and the Scandinavians towards plans for greater political integration and the extension of supranationalism stems in part from their different perception of the pur-pose of the EU. However, these countries have not been able to steer the Com-munity away from the powerful influence of the Franco-German alliance.

These differences can be seen in attitudes to European monetary union. The Franco-German alliance regarded monetary union largely as a political im-perative to weld the countries of the Community together while allowing the alliance to continue to drive developments in the EU. Italy and the smaller mem-ber states regard it as a means to lessen the power of Germany in monetary mat-ters. The British and the Scandinavians tend to regard the project in a more pragmatic light and consider it to be a potentially beneficial move for some, but not necessarily all, of the member states. However, they also regard monetary union as raising very serious questions about the sovereignty of the member states.

The Franco-German alliance experienced considerable strain over the appoint-ment of the President of the European Central Bank (ECB). The Germans and the other member states favoured the appointment of Wim Duisenberg, the head of the European Monetary Institute (EMI). However, the French insisted that a French candidate Jean-Claude Trichet be appointed to head the ECB. At a summit in Brussels in May 1998 a compromise was reached that allowed Wim Duisenberg to be appointed but he promised to retire after four years (instead of the eight years specified in the Treaty on European Union (TEU)) to allow Jean-Claude Trichet to take over as President of the ECB. The conflict over who should be the President of the ECB indicated that within the Franco-German alliance nationalist agendas have a very strong influence. This dispute also revealed that some of the large member states are unwilling to reduce the influence that they have on major developments in the EU.

In the 1950s matters relating to foreign relations and military arrangements were heavily influenced by the development of the Cold War. The dominance of the USA and the Soviet Union in security and military matters resulted in the setting up of opposing alliances in Europe based on the Warsaw Pact alliance in Eastern Europe, and the North Atlantic Treaty Organisation (NATO) in Western Europe. The former institution was dominated by the Soviet Union and the latter by the USA. The early attempts to establish economic and non-military political arrangements in Western Europe were centred on the Organisation for European Economic Co-operation (OEEC), and the Council of Europe. The OEEC failed to develop because of disputes about the need for some kind of supra-national decision-making powers. It eventually expanded its membership and became the Organisation for Economic Co-operation and Development (OECD). The Council of Europe was not granted any supranational powers and still exists as a forum for inter-governmental discussion on issues of interest to Europe. Its main advantage is that its membership includes most European countries. It has not played a significant role in the integration of Europe.

By the early 1950s a series of inter-governmental agencies existed in Western Europe – the Council of Europe, the OEEC, and NATO. For those countries that favoured more supranational powers for European agencies these institutions did not seem to be capable of integrating Europe. In 1948, Belgium, Luxembourg and the Netherlands agreed to form a Customs Union (CU). This example of the use of specific economic means of achieving European Unity was to come to the fore in the development of the Community. The main political and military issues in Western Europe were heavily influenced by NATO and the Americans, and were firmly based on inter-governmentalism. The European Federalists and Functionalists were therefore unable to expand their ideas into these areas. The involvement of West Germany in any attempt to form a type of supranational agency with responsibility for political and defence issues was restricted by the opposition of the Soviet Union to any German involvement in these matters. In the immediate post-war period there was popular opposition within Western Europe to allowing Germany any such role in these areas. Consequently, the Federalists and the Functionalists were restricted to economic matters in proposals for any supranational agency.

In those countries where Federalist and Functionalist views were strong (France, Germany, Italy, Holland, Belgium, and Luxembourg: the original six), there was a desire to establish agencies with some supranational powers and this led them to establish the ECSC in 1951. One of the motives for this was to integrate the coal and steel industries of Germany, the heart of its war machine, into an interdependent European industrial structure, thereby making war between Western European countries impossible. The ECSC had a High Authority that had some supranational powers in the areas of coal and steel, but the main decision-making powers rested with the Council of Ministers. This Council was composed of the Ministers of the member states and was therefore inter-governmental in character. Nevertheless, the ECSC was an agency that had some supranational powers, and was a kind of cross between an inter-governmental and a supranational agency. This strange mixture was also to characterise the EEC and EURATOM, the agencies that followed the ECSC, and from which the EU arose. Consequently, the origins of the EU led to an institutional structure that was focused on economic matters and was neither a pure inter-governmental nor a supranational agency, but rather a mixture of these forms.

The setting up of the EEC and EURATOM resulted from the Spaak Committee, first convened in 1955. The UK joined with the original six countries represented in this committee, but withdrew when it became clear that the original six wanted new institutional forms based on the model of the ECSC and were also seeking wide-ranging economic integration. Therefore the UK did not join the original six when they established the EEC and EURATOM by the Treaty of Rome, signed in 1957. Instead, the UK formed the European Free Trade Association (EFTA) in 1960 with Austria, Switzerland, Norway, Sweden, Denmark, and Portugal. The arrangements within EFTA were considerably less ambitious than in the EEC. The EEC had elements of supranationality in decision-making and was committed to the establishment of a Customs Union, a Common Market and had vaguely defined objectives to create EMU, while EFTA was purely inter-governmental and was aiming to achieve a free-trade area.

By the early 1960s Europe appeared to have created a new political order that was based on the division of Europe into East and West, with the Soviet Union and the USA largely directing events in this area, and an economic order based on the EEC, EFTA and the Council for Mutual Economic Assistance (COMECON). However, the EEC was soon to emerge as the dominant economic agency in Europe.

The development of the European Union

The EU developed in a series of phases beginning with the enlargement of the original six to nine and then to twelve members. During the 1970s and early 1980s the integration process did not progress until the deadlock was broken by the agreement on the Single European Act (SEA). This led to the Maastricht Treaty and the preparation for EMU. After the Maastricht Treaty the EU has struggled to cope with the problem of high unemployment, the inability to tackle the issue of institutional reform and the efforts to integrate the CEECs into the Community.

The enlargement of the original six

The original six experienced high growth rates in the 1960s which were often attributed to the ambitious programme of economic integration on which the

EEC had embarked. It may, however, have had more to do with the rapid growth of West Germany as it experienced an 'economic miracle' in the post-war reconstruction process. In this period Germany became the leading industrial power in Europe and the other members of the EEC benefited from their growing economic links with this dynamic economy. Whatever the reason for the relative success of the member states of the EEC, certain groups in the UK eventually came to regard the Community as the key to the future economic prosperity of Britain. It had become clear to key decision-makers in the UK that the Commonwealth was not a viable economic bloc and that EFTA was not large enough to provide the necessary market size to allow for the reaping of economies of scale. The EEC, with the new economic power of Germany at the centre, was deemed to be the appropriate vehicle to allow the UK to halt and then reverse its relative economic decline. It was therefore mainly economic reasons that drew the UK towards applying for membership of the EEC. The accession of the UK to the EEC was a long and difficult process because the CAP and the commitment of the EEC to a degree of supranational decision-making ran counter to long-held traditions in the UK. However, after a series of long and complex negotiations (see Swann, 1996 for a survey), the UK, along with Ireland and Denmark, joined the EEC in 1973. This had a profound influence on the development of the EU. The EEC now included the four largest economies in Western Europe – Germany, France, Italy and the UK. There was also an increase in the conflicts within the EEC as the UK had an economic and political structure that did not sit easily with that of the EEC. This became obvious with disputes about the CAP and the connected budgetary problems. The regional problems of the EEC were also brought more sharply into focus as the membership of both the UK and Ireland greatly increased the number of relatively deprived regions in the Community.

The expansion in the membership of the EEC in 1973 was not followed by fast progress in implementing the integration programme of the Community. Indeed, the 1970s was a period of considerable stagnation in the Community. The problems in adjusting to the issues raised by the enlargement were one factor in the lack of progress in developing the necessary policies and programmes to allow greater integration to take place. There were also problems raised by the OPEC oil price increases, and the instability of the international monetary system caused by the ending of the Bretton Woods system. These problems led to poor growth rates in the member states. The EEC did not manage to adopt a united approach to these issues and generally there was a pronounced lack of momentum in the Community. By the 1970s the Community had accomplished the creation of the Customs Union (although a large number of non-tariff barriers remained in place), but was not making much progress to create a Common Market. The CAP was the only significant common policy of the EEC and that was causing considerable problems both within the Community and with the rest of the world. In the movements towards EMU practically no progress was being made. However, this state of affairs was to change dramatically in the 1980s.

A new momentum began to arise with the second enlargement of the EEC when Greece joined in 1981, and Spain and Portugal in 1986. This led to the creation of a potential market of 320 million consumers. This enlargement resulted in few problems in incorporating these countries into the Community, in spite of the large differences in their levels of economic development compared with the rest of the EEC. There were also movements to alter the Treaty of Rome to remove some of the constraints imposed by the cumbersome nature of the decision-making process of the Community. This led to the SEA and the start of the SEM programme. The launching of the European Monetary System (EMS) in 1979, and the implications of the creation of the SEM for monetary and other macro-economic policies, increased pressures for monetary integration in the Community.

The Maastricht Treaty

By the early 1990s the Community had made considerable progress in establishing the SEM. It had also developed detailed plans for the creation of monetary union and there was a growing momentum to increase Community competencies in the social, environmental and regional areas. Furthermore, issues connected with foreign and security policies and other types of political policies increased in importance. The reunification of Germany and the collapse of communism in the CEECs swept away the post-war economic and political order of Europe. These factors led to pressures to increase the integration programmes of the Community. Germany and France, in particular, sought to deepen the integration of the Community. To investigate the means to achieve these aims the Community established two Inter-governmental Conferences (IGCs): one on Economic and Monetary Union and the other on Political Union. The IGCs sought to build upon the changes that the SEA had brought about and to develop the ideas that had been advocated in the Delors report on Economic and Monetary Union (Commission, 1989).

The IGCs led to the negotiations on the Maastricht Treaty, also known as the Treaty on European Union (TEU). The debates and arguments that emerged in the drafting of this treaty clearly indicated that there was little consensus among the member states about how 'federal' the Community should become. The UK made it clear that the concept of a federal Community was not acceptable. France and Germany were also opposed to granting significant new powers to the European Parliament (EP) and the Commission. However, many of the smaller member states were in favour of granting more powers to these institutions. The negotiations consequently proved to be very difficult. Agreement was reached to establish monetary union but the UK and Denmark secured the right to 'opt out' of the process. The Maastricht Treaty also contained a Social Chapter as a basis for expanding EU competencies in the social policy area. However, the UK obtained an 'opt-out' from implementing any legislation that might emerge from the Social Chapter. In the areas of foreign and security policy, and justice and home affairs the TEU created new structures that were separate from the existing institutions of the Community. In these fields any cooperation or co-ordination was to be achieved by inter-governmental procedures (Duff, Pinder and Pryce, 1994).

The difficulties that were encountered in ratifying the TEU further exposed the lack of consensus on the future development of the Community. A referendum on ratification, held in Denmark in 1992, produced a 'no' verdict. This was followed by a narrow 'yes' vote in a referendum in France. In the UK the government faced considerable difficulties in processing the ratification bill through Parliament, and the Conservative Party experienced a deep and damaging split over its European policy. A second referendum in Denmark, in 1993, secured a small majority for ratification. The final obstacle was a referral to the constitutional court in Germany. This followed from a claim, by a former German Commissioner, that the German government could not ratify the TEU because it did not have the right to transfer sovereignty to non-German institutional structures. The court ruled that the TEU could be ratified. The final irony of the ratification process was that Germany, one of the strongest supporters of the Maastricht Treaty, was the last country to ratify the treaty.

In 1992, speculative pressures began to undermine the Exchange Rate Mechanism (ERM) and by the end of 1993 the ERM had effectively ceased to operate as an effective mechanism for managing the exchange rate policies of the member states. By early 1993 both the UK and Italy had withdrawn from the ERM, and Spain, Ireland and Portugal had experienced substantial devaluation of their currencies within the EMS. By the end of 1993 the ERM bands had been widened to ±15 per cent (except for the deutschmark/guilder rate).

The Community also experienced considerable difficulties in reforming the CAP in order to satisfy the conditions for reaching agreement on the Uruguay Round of the General Agreement on Tariffs and Trades (GATT). France caused some concern by refusing to agree to the reform of the CAP that had been agreed between the Community and the USA. Agreement over the reform of the CAP was necessary if the Uruguay Round was to be successfully completed. France also objected to the liberalisation of trade in television programmes and films in the GATT round. Eventually, this area had to be removed from the GATT round in order to allow agreement to be reached. However, the French stance on these issues caused considerable concern in the EU, especially in the UK, Germany and the Netherlands.

Problems such as these led to growing confusion among both governments and citizens as to the future role of the Community. Despite these difficulties the Community reached agreement, in 1993, to establish the European Economic Area (EEA). The EEA was an area composed of the 12 member states and most of the countries of EFTA. In the EEA free movement of goods, services, capital and labour was to be established, and most of the laws relating to the SEM were also accepted by the EFTA members of the EEA. The EFTA members of the EEA also agreed to contribute towards the costs of helping the poorer regions of the Community. However, in March 1994 agreement on conditions for membership was reached with Austria, Finland, Norway and Sweden for these countries to join the Community. This agreement led to full membership for Austria, Finland and Sweden in 1995. Norway decided not to proceed to membership. Switzerland rejected membership of the EEA after a referendum in 1993 and also removed its application for full membership of the EU.

In the early 1990s progress was made to increase the help that was given to the poorer regions of the Community. The structural adjustment funds were considerably expanded and proposals on how to make best use of the 'Cohesion

Fund' and the structural funds were put forward in a package of proposals commonly called Delors II. The 'Cohesion Fund' (founded on the basis of Article 130d of the Maastricht Treaty) is intended to help in the areas of the environment and trans-European networks in transport infrastructures. Delors II (Commission, 1992) recommended that the funds should be concentrated in Objective 1 areas; that is, those regions with a per capita GDP that is less than 75 per cent of the average of the EU, namely Ireland, Northern Ireland, Portugal, Greece, Southern Italy, most of Spain, Corsica and the French Overseas Departments. However, Germany and the UK, the two largest net contributors to the budget of the Community, expressed concern over the cost of the structural funds and the 'Cohesion Fund'. The prospect of some of the countries of Central and Eastern Europe joining the Community caused even more concern about the cost to the richer member states of transferring large amounts of funds to the poorer members. These concerns led to calls for the Community to concentrate on creating an effective SEM as the best method of increasing the living standards of the citizens of the Community. However, the Southern European member states and Ireland regarded the transfer of funds as a crucial component in the attempt to boost the living standards of all of the citizens of the Community. Once again dispute emerged as to the future direction of the Community.

The EU experienced a remarkable change in its fortunes in the early 1990s. It moved from being an agency making seemingly unstoppable progress towards some kind of 'federal' system to an agency that was unclear as to which direction it should take. The Community was very much a child of the Cold War, and consequently a Western European club. The Community found it difficult to develop its role in a Europe that was no longer divided into hostile blocs.

Recession and the third enlargement

In the mid-1990s the EU experienced a series of problems that led to searching examinations of the role and purpose of the Community (see Henning *et al.*, 1994 for a review of these issues). The problems arose from economic conditions in continental Europe, the difficulties of making the institutional structures work effectively, and the issues raised by the desire of many of the CEECs to become full members of the EU.

In the mid and late 1990s continental European economies suffered a prolonged and deep recession. This was related to the aftermath of German reunification and the need to curb government budget deficits in the run-up to European monetary union. The recession added to the problems with high unemployment that had afflicted Europe since the early 1990s. The high levels of unemployment in some of the member states made it difficult for governments to persuade their electorates that European monetary union was beneficial and also to allow them to press ahead with plans to liberalise their national markets in areas such as telecommunication services, energy and airlines.

The enlargement of the EU in 1995 exposed the inadequacies of the institutional structure of the Community. The basic structure of the institutions has not been substantially altered since the formation of the EEC in 1957. The only major changes (agreed in the SEA and the TEU) were to grant some increases in the power of the Commission and the EP to influence legislation and to reduce the power of veto by national governments in some areas of law making. However, the EU had developed from six members to fifteen and had enlarged its policies and legislation from trade and agricultural matters to nearly all aspects of economic life and a substantial part of civic and social life. In these circumstances the institutions of the Community found it difficult to govern effectively the wide range of policies and programmes that had emerged from the integration process.

The desire of many of the CEECs to become full members further increased concerns about the institutional structure of the EU. If the EU found it difficult to govern 15 member states effectively, the prospects of a Community with over 20 member states might prove to be too much for the existing institutional structure. The problems of transforming the CEECs into modern market-based economies were clearly revealed to be a major challenge by the experiences of German reunification. The German economy encountered considerable problems in integrating the former East Germany. These problems arose despite large budgetary transfers from the West to the East. The former East Germany was also one of the most developed of the CEECs, but the problems of modernising such systems were clearly considerable. This experience indicated that the EU would face significant difficulties if the CEECs were to be granted full membership of the Community. Such an enlargement would also put pressure on the financial arrangements of the agricultural and regional policies of the EU.

Widening versus deepening and flexibility

A vigorous debate about the future direction of the EU arose in the light of these problems. The debate focused on the widening versus deepening controversy. Some argued that the EU should concentrate on widening by integrating the economies of the CEECs into the Community and that less emphasis should be placed on developing new agendas such as EMU and Political Union. Others argued that the Community should deepen by developing EMU and Political Union and placing less emphasis on enlargement. A third route was envisaged which involved both widening and deepening simultaneously. This route was usually thought to require a multi-tiered or two-speed approach to integration that would allow member states to opt out of some parts of the integration process (Duff, 1997). The concept of opt-out or two-speed integration had been given a boost by the provisions of the TEU that had allowed for countries to opt out of parts of the integration programme or to join in at a later stage. This type of approach permits a complex and flexible set of linkages to be established and also allows those member states who wish to make faster progress to proceed. The Schengen Agreement is another example of this type of agreement. The Schengen Agreement allows member states to remove all frontier controls on the movement of people within the Schengen area. However, this flexible approach may lead to damaging splits in the EU (e.g. in the case of EMU) and it could allow member states to gain competitive advantage (e.g. the UK opt-out from the Social Chapter of the TEU).

The confusion about how best to proceed was revealed in the negotiations on the Amsterdam Treaty. This treaty does not contain any major changes to the institutional structure of the Community, nor did it resolve the issues connected to widening versus deepening. However, it eliminated one opt-out (the UK opt-out from the Social Chapter of the TEU), and created another one (the opt-out by Denmark, Ireland and the UK from the Schengen Agreement). The Amsterdam Treaty contains provisions on the use of 'flexibility' that might allow for a two- or multi-speed Community to develop. However, the provisions do not provide a firm foundation for the widespread use of the concept of flexibility (Duff, 1997). The Amsterdam Treaty required that these unresolved issues on institutional structure be referred to yet another IGC. The Amsterdam Treaty left a large number of unresolved issues and achieved only minor changes to the institutional structure of the Community. The problems that the member states encountered in the negotiations for the Amsterdam Treaty clearly indicate that a Federalist solution to the problems of integration does not have widespread support across the member states. Equally, the approach of the Functionalists can be seen to have many problems – in particular, frequent recourse to compromise solutions that permit the continuance of ineffective structures that hamper the development of the integration process.

Notwithstanding these problems, the EU continued to press on with its ambitious integration programmes. European monetary union is due to begin in 1999 and will include 11 of the member states. Denmark, Greece, Sweden and the UK who could not, or would not, join may apply for membership of the monetary union early in the next century. The EU has also started another IGC to find a solution to the problems with the institutional structure. Many of the CEECs are also likely to be full members of the EU within the next five to ten years. In order to accomplish this the EU has set up ambitious programmes to reform the agricultural policy and the system of aid to the poorer regions of the Community (Commission, 1997).

Although the EU has experienced a period of pronounced political and economic difficulties in the 1990s it still managed to enlarge the Community from 12 to 15 members, to prepare the way successfully to begin European monetary union and to start the process of accepting some of the CEECs into full membership. These 'successes' say much for the ability of the EU to press on with its integration programmes in the face of complex and uncertain political and economic conditions.

The institutional structure of the European Union

The institutional structure of the EU is determined by the various treaties that have been agreed by the member states. The Treaties of Paris (1951) and Rome (1957), as amended by the SEA (1986) and the TEU (1992), form the current basis of the EU. The Amsterdam Treaty (due to be ratified by the end of 1998) did not alter the fundamental basis of the institutional structure of the EU.

There are five main institutions in the current structure of the EU.

1. The Council of the European Union
2. The European Commission
3. The European Parliament (EP)
4. The European Court of Justice (ECJ)
5. The European Monetary Institute (EMI), to be replaced by the European Central Bank (ECB) in 1999

The Council of the European Union

The Council of the European Union (commonly called the Council of Ministers) is composed of the relevant government ministers of the member states; for example, proposals concerned with agricultural matters are considered by the ministers of agriculture from the member states. The Presidency of the Council of the European Union rotates around the member states every six months. The government of the member state that holds the Presidency has the task of seeking to make progress with proposals that have been held up by disagreements among the member states and to further the objectives that have been agreed by the Council. The Council of Ministers has a standing committee of civil servants, composed of the permanent representatives of the national governments. This committee is called COREPER and it does most of the groundwork on any proposed legislation. The ministers generally become involved at the end stage to settle unresolved problems, or to agree to disagree. In the latter case a proposal can be returned to the Commission and the European Parliament for further consideration, or it can be left on the table until some sort of compromise can be reached. This means that the governments of the member states have considerable powers to prevent, delay or modify any proposal for new Community laws. Voting in the Council of Ministers can be by unanimity (on matters connected to industry, taxation, culture, R&D programmes and regional and social funds) or by qualified majority (on issues related to agriculture, fisheries, the internal market, the environment and transport). It is therefore possible for EU legislation to become Community law against the wishes of a member state. Hence the power that the governments of the member states have to control the legislative programme of the Community depends on how far they are in agreement with each other, and on the extent of qualified majority voting.

The Council of the European Union holds regular meetings of the heads of government of the member states – the European Council. The European Council had no treaty basis until the role of this body was recognised in the SEA. However, since 1974 the European Council has held regular summit meetings of the heads of government of the member states. The summits are chaired by the member state that holds the Presidency of the Council and include the heads of government of the member states, the President of the Commission and the President of the European Parliament, who gives a presentation of the views of the Parliament at the start of summits. European Council meetings are generally strongly influenced by whoever holds the Presidency. The Council is an inter-governmental institution, and often reflects the interests of the country that holds the Presidency. In spite of this some of the most significant steps in the integration process have been initiated by the European Council, such as the SEA and the moves towards EMU. Indeed, no major developments in the integration process would be possible without the approval of the European Council. The European Council therefore plays a key role in the development of the EU and is very clearly under the control of the governments of the member states. This does not mean that the EU has no significant supranational characteristics. Once the European Council decides to establish elements of supranational decision-making into Community policies or programmes, member states effectively lose sovereignty in that area.

The European Commission

The European Commission is a cross between a civil service and an executive body. There are 20 Commissioners, two each from Germany, France, Italy, Spain, and the UK, and one from each of the other member states. Commissioners are appointed by their member states, but are not responsible to them. In principle, they are accountable to the EP. The President of the Commission, who is appointed by governments of the member states and approved by the EP, has considerable influence by way of a seat on the European Council, and in other economic and political forums. In its role as an administrative body it is split into a number of Directorates General (DGs), which have specific areas of responsibility (see Box I.1). The Commission is the guardian of the Treaties and is responsible for monitoring and policing EU law. It does not implement these laws, but depends on the governments of the member states to carry out this function. The Commission has the power to investigate suspected breaches of EU law by governments, companies and individuals, and can impose fines if it considers that the law has been broken. It also has powers to compel changes in the policies of national governments if it considers that they are contrary to Community law. The governments of the member states are obliged to ensure that the decisions of the Commission in these matters are implemented unless they dispute the ruling of the Commission. When this occurs the case is sent to the European Court of Justice (ECJ). The Commission therefore has supranational powers in certain areas. The day-to-day operation of EU policies and programmes, and the administering of the Structural Funds, are also under the control of the Commission. All proposals for new Community legislation must be initiated by the Commission on the basis of the Treaties, or the decisions of the European Council. The Commission also provides help and information on Community matters to companies and organisations of various types.

The European Parliament

The European Parliament is not responsible to, nor appointed by, the governments of the member states. Since 1979 the EP has been directly elected by the citizens of the Community. The number of Members of the European Parliament (MEPs) which a country has depends on the size of the population, the larger countries having more seats than the smaller. The powers of the EP are limited, but have been growing since the SEA. In principle, the EP can dismiss

Box I.1   The Directorates General

The Commission of the EU is split into Directorates General (DGs), which have responsibilities for both the day-to-day administration of Community operations and the framing of proposals for new laws.

The current DGs are:

DGI   External Relations: Commercial Policy and relations with North America, the Far East, Australia and New Zealand

DGIA   External Relations: Europe and the New Independent States, Common Foreign and Security Policy and External Missions

DGIB   External Relations: Southern Mediterranean, Near East, Latin America, South and South-east Asia and North-South Cooperation

DGII   Economic and Financial Affairs

DGIII   Industry

DGIV   Competition

DGV   Employment, Industrial Relations and Social Affairs

DGVI   Agriculture

DGVII   Transport

DGVIII   Development

DGIX   Personnel and Administration

DGX   Audiovisual Media, Information, Communication and Culture

DGXI   Environment, Civil Protection and Nuclear Safety

DGXII   Science, Research and Development

DGXIII   Telecommunications, Information Market and Exploitation of Research

DGXIV   Fisheries

DGXV   Internal Markets and Financial Services

DGXVI   Regional Policies and Cohesion

DGXVII   Energy Policies

DGXIX   Budgets

DGXXI   Customs and Indirect Taxation

DGXXII   Education, Training and Youth

DGXXIII   Enterprise Policy, Distributive Trades, Tourism, and Cooperatives

DGXXIV   Consumer Policy and Consumer Health Protection

the Commissioners and can refuse to approve the budget of the EU. These powers are, however, too great to be used, as they would effectively make the government of the Community impossible. The SEA granted the EP more influence in the process of making EU law in many areas and the TEU extended this by introducing the concept of co-decision making between the Council and the EP. The Amsterdam Treaty simplified and extended the principle of co-decision making (see Box I.2). When the Amsterdam Treaty provisions take effect most of the proposals for new EU law in economic matters will be subject to the co-decision process. The EP also investigates the activities of the Commission by

Box 1.2   **The legislative process of the Community**

The legislative process of the Community is complex. What follows is a simplified outline of this process (for a fuller treatment see Nugent, 1995).

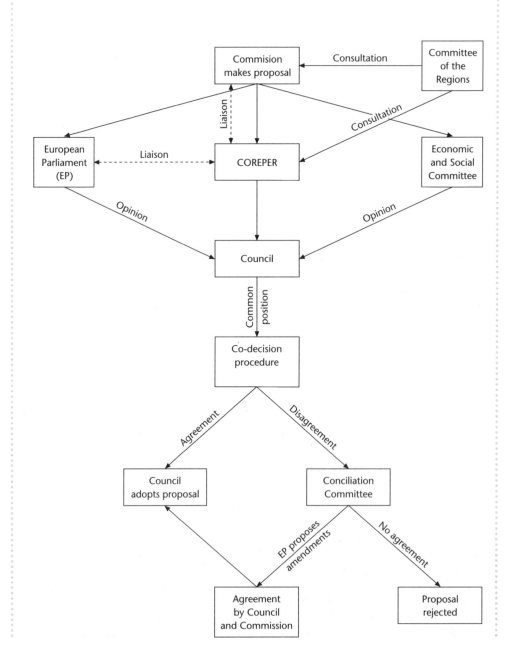

The Community has four main methods of making law and for issuing rules. These are:

1. regulations: these are binding and have direct effect in the member states;

2. directives: these must be incorporated into the law of the member states in accordance with their national legislative practices;

3. decisions: these are binding rulings by the Commission on specific issues and are directly applied to governments, companies, and individuals and must be complied with;

4. recommendations and opinions: these have no legal standing.

In practice most Community law-making consists of issuing directives. The use of regulations and decisions is mainly to govern or amend policies that have already been agreed. The method of issuing directives involves a series of protracted discussions and negotiations between the Commission, the EP and the Council of Ministers. Since the Maastricht Treaty this is primarily done by the co-decision procedure.

means of a series of committees that examine the working of the various policies of the Community. It has influence on the appointment of the Commission and has the right to refuse to accept the nominations for the President of the Commission. The Council of Ministers is not accountable to the EP. Although there are loose arrangements between the political parties in the European Parliament they do not form a coherent European political party system.

The European Court of Justice

The European Court of Justice (ECJ) is composed of 15 judges who are appointed by the member states. It is responsible for interpreting Community law and making judgements when there are disputes on this law. If EU law and national law conflict, then Community law must take precedence. The ECJ is the final court to which disputes on EU law can be brought, and national courts must accept and implement the judgements of the Court. In some respects the ECJ is the most supranational institution in the EU, as it is not accountable to any national government, and the decisions of this Court are influential in the development of national law. The decisions of the ECJ are also important in the operation of Competition Policy as the Court has established many important principles by its judgements on particular cases. Furthermore, decisions of the ECJ are important in establishing principles in the area of employment law and equal opportunities.

The European Central Bank

The Maastricht Treaty called for the creation of two further institutions – the European Monetary Institute (EMI) and the European Central Bank (ECB). The EMI, which began operation in 1994, developed the procedures for strengthening cooperation between the central banks of the member states and monitoring the convergence of the economic and monetary conditions that are necessary to achieve monetary union. (The EMI was replaced by the ECB in May 1998.) The ECB will be a type of federal bank on similar lines to the Bundesbank. The central banks of the members of the monetary union will be reformulated into a new institution – the European System of Central Banks (ESCB). The ESCB will form the operating arm of the ECB in the member states and will help in the construction and implementation of the common monetary policy of the Union. The President of the ECB will be appointed by the European Council for a period of eight years. The technical details of monetary and exchange rate policy will be determined by the ECB and will be independent of national governments and the other institutions of the EU. The prime objective of the ECB, according to the Maastricht Treaty, is the pursuit of price stability.

Other institutions

There are four other major institutions in the Community: the Economic and Social Committee, the European Investment Bank, the Court of Auditors and the Committee of the Regions. The Economic and Social Committee is a forum for interest groups and sectoral interest (e.g. farmers, trade unionists and representatives of employers) to express opinions on proposed legislation. It does not have any powers other than to express opinions on proposed legislation. The European Investment Bank provides loans to finance capital projects that help to develop the process of European integration and which aid in the achieving of the aims of the EU. The main function of the Court of Auditors is to audit the expenditure activities carried out on behalf of the Community. As these activities are often carried out by national governments, this gives it rights to investigate the practices of the governments of member states. The Court of Auditors is generally concerned with the proper use of funds and checking on fraud, rather than value-for-money evaluations. However, the Court of Auditors could in future be used to assess the effectiveness of Community expenditures. At present it may submit reports on the use of Community funds to the institutions of the EU and this could develop into the basis for value-for-money evaluations. A Committee of the Regions composed of representatives from regional and local authorities was established in 1994 in accordance with Article 198a of the Maastricht Treaty. This Committee is appointed by the Council on the recommendation of the national governments of the member states. It may be consulted by the Commission and the Council on matters that affect the regions, but the Committee need not be consulted. In this respect the Committee would appear to have less power than the Economic and Social Committee. It may, however, issue an opinion on its own initiative.

The institutional structure of the EU is complex, with many different bodies responsible for decision-making and for the implementation, monitoring and policing of Community laws. Most of the members of these institutions are appointed by national governments. Furthermore, in the case of directives, the governments of the member states must transpose the objectives specified in the directives into national law. The differences in national institutional structures

Box 1.3	**Interrelationships between Community laws and national systems**

Directives must be transposed into national laws and regulations by national governments. Moreover, national governments and courts are responsible for the monitoring and enforcing of these national laws and regulations to ensure that directives are properly implemented. National institutional frameworks and cultural characteristics influence the way in which directives affect companies, organisations and individuals. For example, some member states have a strong commitment to equal opportunities and have special agencies within their institutional frameworks that seek to promote equal opportunities; other member states have less emphasis on such matters. The Commission has the responsibility to assess if directives have been properly implemented and cases can be referred to the ECJ which makes final judgements on matters related to Community law. These rather complicated procedures mean that a range of bodies affect the manner in which Community laws affect companies, organisations and individuals in the member states. Given the differences in national institutional frameworks and cultural characteristics, it is possible that directives do not have equal effect across the member states. The figure below provides a schematic outline of these factors.

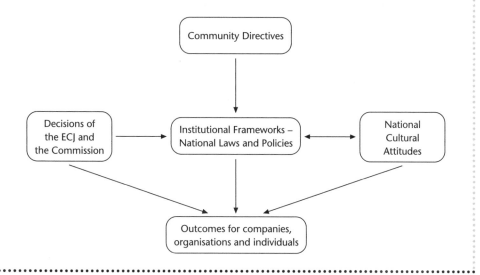

and cultures further complicate the influence that national governments and cultures have on Community laws (see Box I.3).

The democratic deficit

There have been concerns about the 'democratic deficit' in the EU. Only the EP is directly elected and is therefore subject to the choice of the citizens of the Community. However, the Council of Ministers and the Commission take decisions that impinge on many of the activities of the citizens of the Community. Furthermore, the establishment of monetary union will lead to the creation of another powerful Community institution – the ECB. The ECB could develop into the most important economic agency in the EU, but its accountability to the citizens of the Community would be very indirect. These issues have led to pressures to expand the powers of the EP, to reduce the size of the Commission and to develop governmental structures that would be more accountable. The member states of the EU were committed by the Maastricht Treaty to examining these issues. This led to the establishment of an IGC to consider plans to reform the institutional structures of the EU. The IGC led to the negotiations on the Amsterdam Treaty. However, the member states could only agree on a limited number of changes to the institutional structures. The unresolved issues were referred to another IGC that must make proposals before the next enlargement of the Community.

The voting procedures of the Council of Ministers have also caused some problems. The Council can take decisions by unanimity, simple majority vote or qualified majority vote (QMV). The system for QMV allows the smaller member states, in principle, to exercise some power in the decision-making systems of the EU. The four large member states cannot, in cases that require QMV, obtain a winning coalition among themselves, that is, they need the support of some of the smaller member states in order to secure a winning coalition. Furthermore, a coalition of most of the smaller member states can result in a blocking vote, that is a voting bloc that is sufficiently large to prevent the fulfilling of the criteria for QMV – 62 votes. A blocking coalition may also be constructed by an alliance between some of the large member states and a group of smaller states. This ability to use blocking coalitions gives the smaller member states leverage in the decision-making frameworks of the EU. This leverage arises from the process of log-rolling. Log-rolling involves the use of bargaining between parties to use strategic voting to further their objectives (Buchanan, 1978). Thus a group of smaller member states could agree to vote with some of the larger member states on issues in which they have no particular interest, in return for the support of the larger member states on issues in which they do have a strong interest. For example, some of the smaller member states could support France to block a proposal deemed to be against French interests, in return for the support of France against proposals that are regarded as against the interests of the smaller member states.

Such log-rolling behaviour has both advantages and disadvantages. It allows the smaller member states to exercise some degree of power in the EU. Therefore, it helps to overcome some of the problems that may arise from the power of the larger member states. However, log-rolling can allow rejection of proposals that have net benefits for the EU. Outcomes such as this can arise when the benefits of implementing proposals are skewed towards certain member states, but these member states cannot secure a winning coalition because of strategic voting by disinterested parties who are engaged in log-rolling exercises (Buchanan *et al.*, 1990).

The extension of the areas of decision-making that are subject to qualified majority voting has increased the problems that the EU has experienced with the voting procedures of the Council. The possible extension of the Community to include many more smaller member states may well expand opportunities for log-rolling behaviour in the EU.

Political union

The EU has had a long-standing commitment to European Political Cooperation (EPC). This was restricted to a series of meetings of the foreign ministers of the member states to discuss and, where possible, to reach common positions on issues relating to foreign relations and security matters. This was necessary in areas connected with trade as the EU has a great influence in the external economic relations of the member states. There have also been attempts to arrive at common positions on matters concerned with the prevention of terrorism, relations with the former Soviet Union and Eastern Europe, and on the security of Europe in the light of the ending of the Cold War. The Community sought to reach a common position on the Gulf War, and to act collectively in response to the civil war in the former Yugoslavia.

These attempts to act collectively were not successful. During these crises the Community could do little more than reflect the differences in the interests of the member states. The attempts by the Community to act in the civil war in the former Yugoslavia were hampered by the reluctance to become involved militarily to provide a peace-keeping force, and by the failure of the member states to reach agreement on anything other than a minimum intervention by imposing trade embargoes and providing the means for the various parties to negotiate cease-fires with a view to arranging a lasting peace. The disappointment caused by this failure to reach effective common positions resulted in increased calls for a radical restructuring of the political integration programme of the EU.

The SEA contained rather vague statements on the need for closer co-operation on foreign and security matters. There was considerable pressure to move beyond such statements towards a clearer policy on political union. The Maastricht Treaty envisaged a Community with a single currency and with a commitment to establishing a stronger political union. In particular, the member states agreed to use inter-governmental procedures based on general guidelines from the European Council, with the Council of Ministers taking policy decisions. Joint actions (or positions) may be adopted by unanimous decision of the Council of Ministers, and in some cases qualified majority voting could be used. These procedures cover two of the three 'pillars' of the EU (the other 'pillar' being the economic arrangements of the EC). The two new 'pillars' were foreign and security issues; justice, home affairs and immigration. The Amsterdam Treaty made some minor modifications to the three-pillar system, in particular asylum and immigration matters are to be transferred from the third pillar to the EC pillar and QMV can be used in some areas of foreign policy (Duff, 1997).

The political and institutional nature of the Community is becoming more supranational. This prospect has caused some alarm among some politicians and decision-makers, particularly in Denmark, Sweden and the UK. The possible emergence of what would be some sort of federal Europe brings with it the prospect of national governments being little more than regional assemblies, with their legislative programmes constrained by the growing integration of markets that will lead to common or harmonised policies in many areas. The establishment of a common monetary policy would also curtail the taxation and expenditure plans of national governments. If many aspects of foreign policy and security, and justice and home affairs were determined by QMV at the Council of Ministers, the characteristics of national governments would indeed begin to resemble those of regional or local government.

In spite of such reservations there are strong forces at work to enhance the political integration of the EU. In international trade matters the Community is already more important than the member states in negotiations with other countries, and with the WTO. The establishment of monetary union will also require a Community voice in organisations such as the IMF and the G8 group of countries. Many issues of foreign policy and security matters are related to international trade flows. Therefore, growing economic integration of the EU will increasingly require a measure of consistency by the member states in these areas.

The loss of sovereignty (the ability of a state to determine its own policies independently of other governments) is already undermined by the dominance of the Americans in matters related to global political and security issues. The question is whether the Community is in a position to achieve a degree of political integration sufficient to allow a more independent line to be pursued. This would perhaps require a common and effective European foreign policy and security arrangements, and a European defence force. In these circumstances Europeans could exercise a significant counterbalancing force if American policies were considered to be against European interests. Such an outcome would involve a radical revision of the foreign and security policies of the member states, and may not be feasible unless all the major member states come to regard this as a viable and desirable goal.

In political matters more directly related to the economic integration programme the need for some change to the policies and political arrangements of the Community is widely accepted. The granting of new powers for the EU to act in the social area may be necessary to overcome fears that the more competitive conditions induced by the SEM will result in a downward spiral in social and working conditions. There are also growing pressures to grant new competencies to Community institutions in industrial, and research and development policies to help in the restructuring of the economy of the EU induced by the creation of the SEM and move towards EMU.

Some member states seem to want more policy-making to be decided at Community level, while wishing to keep important decisions in the domain of the Council of Ministers, but with the Commission and the EP having more influence in the decision-making process. In the future it is possible that many of the policies that govern economic activity will be decided at Community level by majority voting. An outcome such as this will ultimately lead to changes to the political structure of the EU to ensure that decisions can be made effectively, and to give the system some kind of legitimacy and accountability. The implication is that the Community will evolve into some kind of federal system.

The main challenges facing the European Union

The EU faces a series of challenges to the development of its integration pro-grammes. Two main issues may be identified:

1. the high levels of unemployment that have afflicted the EU in the 1990s;
2. the difficulties of implementing the principle of subsidiarity.

Unemployment

In the 1990s unemployment has clearly been a more serious problem for the EU than for the USA and Japan. Apparently both the Americans and the Japanese seem better able to deal with the problems of unemployment that emerged in the developed economies in the 1990s. The USA was able to gen-erate more jobs from growth than were the Europeans, while the Japanese seem to be more able to retain employment levels in the face of pressures on jobs resulting from recession and structural change. However, in the late 1990s un-employment rose in Japan, although the unemployment rate did not reach the levels experienced in the EU.

Concern over unemployment led to a reappraisal of policies to counter unemployment. At the Edinburgh meeting of the European Council in 1992, an initiative was put forward to coordinate macroeconomic policies to help boost non-inflationary growth in the EU. The prime objective of this initiative was to lower unemployment. However, the initiative envisaged only a small boost to the economy of the EU and was largely based on an aggregation of existing pub-lic expenditure plans by the member states.

The debate on the appropriateness of using the Social Chapter of the Maastricht Treaty to improve working conditions was also brought into ques-tion. The UK government consistently argued that to use EU legislation to improve working conditions would result in higher non-wage costs (and possible wage costs) of hiring labour, and that this would inevitably lead to higher unemployment. The implications of increasing the non-wage costs (or wage costs) of hiring labour are that either such increases are compensated for by higher productivity, or EU-based producers become less competitive. In the latter case the EU would have to protect its industries and/or seek to use depreciation of the currencies of the member states (relative to main trading partners) in order to defend the competitive position of EU-based companies. Outcomes such as these are not attractive because of the problems that would be caused to trading relations, in particular with the USA, Japan and the NICs. Such actions could also harm the allocation of resources within the EU by encouraging production and consumption from high-cost European sources when lower-cost supplies are available from outside the EU. The long-term position of the EU could also be harmed by such policies because they could encourage European producers to maintain production in areas where they do not have comparative advantage.

In 1993 the Commission published a White Paper on Growth, Competitive-ness and Employment (Commission, 1993). The White Paper set a target of 15 million new jobs in the EU by the year 2000. To achieve this objective the member states were encouraged to pursue policies that will deliver non-inflationary growth, create more jobs from growth, and improve the global competitiveness of EU-based companies.

In order to ensure that the growth is non-inflationary, the White Paper argued that the member states should not expand their public sector deficits; the Commission maintained rather that it is important for macroeconomic stability that the current high levels of these deficits should be reduced. This objective is also connected to the plan for the convergence of the economies of the member states in preparation for monetary union. The White Paper therefore did not favour Keynesian type aggregate demand management measures to boost growth rates in order to reduce unemployment.

To encourage the creation of more jobs from growth, the White Paper recommended that the structural problems that have led to unemployment should be addressed. Thus the Commission advocated encouragement of new fast-growing industries such as information technology, telecommunications services and equipment, and biotechnology. This would seem to indicate an increased role for Industrial Policy in the EU.

The problems caused by high non-wage costs were also considered to be a significant obstacle to the creation of jobs, and the White Paper recommended that labour market regulations should be compatible with labour market flexibility. Nevertheless, the Commission made it clear that it did not wish to see a deterioration in working conditions and in the rights of employees. In particular, the White Paper recommended that steps should be taken to avoid the creation of large numbers of low-paid and low-skilled jobs. However, the White Paper advocated that part-time working should be encouraged and that work-sharing might also contribute to the solution of finding ways to lower the unemployment rate. The Commission also recommended the use of government help to lower the costs to companies of hiring the long-term unemployed and young people (these groups constitute the majority of the unemployed in most member states).

The White Paper regarded the creation and maintenance of an open economy for the EU as a crucial requirement for promoting an efficient and dynamic economy. The use of protectionist policies was therefore not advocated as a solution to the high levels of unemployment in Europe. The Commission also maintained that large fluctuations in exchange rates were not conducive to stable and growing world trade. Thus, the White Paper did not advocate the use of depreciation of currencies as a viable solution to the unemployment problem. However, it recommended that the EU adopt a more robust commercial defence in WTO procedures.

The White Paper provided a clear statement that unemployment was the major economic problem facing the EU. On the other hand, it did not provide any significantly new proposals as to how to solve this problem.

For those who favour an EU based on an open trading system with the rest of the world, these proposals were welcome. However, some of the recommendations of the White Paper were less welcome, for example the indications of a need for a more interventionist Industrial Policy and the possibility of a stronger use of the Common Commercial Policy to protect EU industries that faced 'unfair competition'. The indications that the Commission was still committed to using the Social Chapter to improve working conditions by use of laws that may increase the non-wage costs of hiring labour were also not welcomed by free-traders. The free-traders regard the creation of an open and competitive economy as the best method to boost productivity and thereby to tackle the unemployment problem. According to this view, the role of the EU in helping to find solutions to the problem of unemployment are mainly associated with the creation of an effective SEM and the development of an open economy with the rest of the world. Employment may also be generated by the creation of monetary union to eliminate the barriers to free trade (within the EU) caused by exchange rate fluctuations and the transaction costs that result from the existence of different currencies. In the long run it is also possible that monetary union could lead to benefits arising from higher rates of non-inflationary growth and from a more efficient allocation of capital.

The EU faces considerable difficulties in reconciling the opposing views as to the best methods of reducing unemployment in Europe. The free-traders advocate liberalisation of markets, in particular labour markets, and an opening up of Community markets to foreign trade and investments. The free-traders are also reluctant to commit significant funds to Industrial Policy initiatives that seek to identify new and expanding industries: on the whole they would favour the use of market forces to promote the creation of new jobs. The interventionists are keen to promote active government involvement in the encouragement of new industries and to use the law to improve living and working conditions. Indeed, the debate is not unlike the debates that take place within any modern advanced economy between right-wing (or pro-market forces) groups and left-wing (or interventionist) groups.

At a number of meetings between 1993 and 1995 (Edinburgh, Essen and Madrid) the European Council constructed a strategy to combat unemployment. The main elements of the strategy are:

- to complete the Single European Market (SEM) and promote a competitive and dynamic economic environment;
- to encourage small and medium enterprises (SMEs) to develop and adopt new technologies;
- to establish EMU to enhance the ability of the economy to grow and thereby create jobs;
- to take action to reduce the non-wage costs of employing labour;
- to improve education and training to improve the skills of the unemployed;
- to target specific groups to help them to obtain work;
- to concentrate the structural funds on job-creating activities and investments.

The strategy proposes very few concrete plans for reducing unemployment that are not associated with existing programmes of the EU, for example, completing the SEM and establishing EMU. The tone of the strategy is in line with the view that competitive and flexible markets are important for job creation.

This reflects a move away from the development of interventionist legislation in the areas of employment and working conditions. The SEA and the Social Chapter led to a large number of new laws in this area in the early and mid 1990s. However, this type of approach appears to have fallen out of favour and there is a greater focus on avoiding imposing undue costs on employers. In areas where positive policies are advocated, for example education and training and targeting particular groups of the unemployed, the EU has very little influence on the development of policies that may help to reduce unemployment. The strategy adopted an approach that saw the role of government as being primarily to create a low inflation and stable macroeconomic environment together with the fostering of a climate that permits companies to develop productivity. The latter requirement is seen as demanding the need for flexible labour markets and laws and policies that do not burden companies unnecessarily.

The Amsterdam Treaty requires the Council to monitor employment conditions in the member states and, in the light of the information gathered on employment, to make proposals that will help to reduce unemployment in the member states. The Treaty does not envisage that large-scale legislation or new EU policies will be generated by this procedure, rather that information on what is happening in the member states will be shared to help national governments to craft their own responses to their unemployment problems (Duff, 1997).

Attempts to find the means to reduce the high level of unemployment have been given high priority in the EU. However, the most useful approach to this problem, at Community level, is seen as the promotion of integrated and competitive markets. Importance is also being increasingly attached to reducing the costs to employers associated with EU legislation and government policies that affect the cost of employing labour. This does not mean that the EU has abandoned its view that legislation to protect the rights of workers is necessary. A host of such legislation was passed in the 1990s (e.g. the working time directive, a variety of health and safety legislation and equal opportunities directives) and will be developed and possibly extended. However, the thrust of EU policy towards these employment issues has moved towards a less interventionist approach.

The principle of subsidiarity

The inclusion of the concept of subsidiarity in the Maastricht Treaty was an attempt by the EU to tackle the problems of assigning governmental competencies within the Community. Article 3b of the Maastricht Treaty states: 'The Community shall take action, in accordance with the principle of subsidiarity, only if and in so far as the objectives of the proposed action cannot be sufficiently achieved by the Member States and can therefore, by reason of the scale or effects of the proposed action, be better achieved by the Community'. The concept of subsidiarity is therefore concerned with discovering the appropriate tier structure of government. The key is to give to that level of government those functions that would be best performed at that level. The Padoa-Schioppa Report (1987) recommended that the EU should be governed at the local, regional, national or Community level depending on which tier of government could carry out the task most efficiently. This principle is analogous to the recommendations that arise from fiscal federalism (Oates, 1972).

The principle of subsidiarity requires that the EU undertakes only those policies that it would be most efficient in governing. The main issue, if this principle is to be related to efficiency considerations, is to identify those national policies that have significant spill-over effects into other countries.

If the market fails to deliver an optimal allocation of resources, because of externalities or monopoly power, there is a clear case for government action to seek to improve the allocation of resources. Therefore, a case can be made for government policies in areas such as R&D expenditures, education and training, environmental standards and public health. The case for such intervention depends on the existence of the external effects of these activities (i.e. the benefits and/or costs of these activities affecting other agents as well as the producers and/or consumers of such activities). Similarly, the case for government action to create and maintain a competitive environment is a clear requirement for an efficient allocation of resources in a market-based economy.

However, the existence of a rationale for government policies within a country does not necessarily mean that there are good reasons for supranational policies in these areas. Only if national policies have significant spill-overs to other countries do sound reasons exist for supranational policies in these areas. This can be analysed by means of a pay-off matrix (see Box I.4).

Taking account of the policy decision of other countries makes sense only if countries are interdependent with respect to the outcomes of policy actions, that is, they must experience spill-overs. However, the existence of such spill-overs does not mean that common policies are sensible. In some cases coordination of policies to take account of spill-over effects is all that is required. Furthermore, the existence of spill-overs is not a sufficient reason for coordination. If the costs of coordination are greater than the benefits of taking into account spill-over effects, it is not efficient to coordinate policies. Thus in the example overleaf, if the costs of reaching agreement on coordination exceeded 5, the countries would be better off not seeking to reach agreement to coordinate policies. In these circumstances it would be better to find methods of internalising the spill-over effects. This could be achieved by taking action to prevent spill-over from occurring, i.e. retaining all the benefits of the policy within the country. If this proves too costly to achieve, the countries could form one government agency to deal with the policy that is creating the spill-over effects, i.e. adopt a common policy. This analysis suggests that good reasons for common policies in the EU may arise when the costs of reaching coordinated agreements, or preventing spill-overs, are high. In other areas it may be better to seek to coordinate policies, and where there are no (or insignificant) spill-overs, countries should adopt policies independently from other countries.

However, the allocation of government competencies using such criteria requires considerable knowledge (and agreement among affected parties) about the extent and size of spill-overs and about the cost of coordinated or common policy solutions. Also, it is not obvious that the EU is always the appropriate agency to be used for coordinated or common policies. In cases where spill-overs extend beyond the frontiers of the EU, or where the spill-overs affect only parts of the

Box 1.4   Subsidiarity and R&D expenditures

Country X

		A	B
Country Y	A	5, 5	−5, 10
	B	10, −5	0, 0

The matrix illustrates the pay-off for two countries from the various options that are available for a particular policy, for example, help with R&D expenditures.

In case A the country provides help to its companies to cover the external benefits of R&D payments, while in case B the country does not provide help in the R&D area. If both countries adopt policy A, they reap benefits shown by pay-offs of 5 each, shown by the outcome in the top left-hand corner of the matrix. If they both adopt policy B, they end up at the bottom right-hand corner with pay-offs of zero. However, if country X adopts policy A and country Y opts for policy B, the pay-offs will be 10 for country Y and −5 for country X, shown in the bottom left-hand corner. In this situation country X meets the cost of helping with R&D expenditures, while country Y benefits from these expenditures without incurring any expenditures. In other words, country Y benefits from the spill-over effects of the R&D policy of country X. The outcomes of country X adopting B and country Y choosing A are shown in the top right-hand corner of the matrix. In this situation the outcome for each country depends on the choices made by the other country. The two countries are interdependent because of the spill-overs that arise from their policies. If both countries are averse to risk with regard to the costs of policy mistakes, they will both choose policy B (leading to the outcome illustrated in the bottom right-hand corner). This outcome is preferable to policy A because it avoids the risk of a negative outcome. However, if the countries coordinate their policies, to ensure that both countries adopt policy A, they reap the pay-offs shown in the top left-hand corner of the matrix. This is a more desirable outcome than the non-cooperative outcome shown in the bottom right-hand corner of the matrix.

EU, it may be more efficient to have other governmental agencies to determine policies. In these circumstances an agency appointed to find the most efficient solution may be useful. The EU could provide the institutional framework to determine such solutions for the member states. The EU could provide the means to determine whether there should be coordinated policies, common policies for all the Community, common policies that are operative for part of the Community, and policies (coordinated or common) that extend beyond its frontiers.

In such a scenario the EU would assess the costs and benefits of assigning governmental competencies and would seek to find the best solution. However, this would require a federal-type constitution for the EU with clear rules on the powers of the federal government relative to those of the member states. This analysis suggests that the principle of subsidiarity can work efficiently only if the EU develops a federal system of government with a constitution backed by an independent court. In other words, the EU would need to become a federal state not dissimilar to the USA or Germany. Attempts to implement the subsidiarity principle in the present governmental system of the EU are likely (at best) to lead to a good deal of confusion or (at worst) to an inefficient and problematical system for determining governmental competencies.

Conclusion

The EU has achieved a remarkable degree of integration among its member states in the post-war period. It has extended its membership to include the largest economies in Europe and it has become one of the most important economic blocs in the world. In the mid to late 1980s it experienced a surge in implementing its integration programmes, particularly with the SEM programme and the moves towards monetary union. However, in the 1990s the EU has experienced a series of problems that cast doubt on its future development. The end of the Cold War and the collapse of communism did not provide an easy opportunity for the EU to expand its membership, while also deepening its integration programmes. The problems encountered in ratifying the Maastricht Treaty illustrated the difficulties of convincing the citizens of the EU that further integration was in their interests. The crises in EMS and the return to floating exchange rates by some member states were also a disappointment for those who looked to a deepening of the integration programmes of the EU. The growing problem of unemployment in Europe has also made it very difficult for the EU to press on with its integration programmes. The pressures for the EU to become more involved in transferring income from its richer to its poorer regions have also grown, and have added to the difficulties of reaching agreement among the member states on the appropriate development of the EU.

However, despite these problems the EU succeeded in expanding its membership, paving the way for EMU to start in 1999, and has set in motion the process of admitting some of the CEECs into full membership. Although unemployment continued to be a major problem the member states managed to curb government budgets in order to meet the convergence criteria for monetary union. The EU also managed to secure a small measure of reform of the institutional structures of the Community. However, the prospect of further enlargement means that a solution to this problem will have to be found if the EU is to incorporate the CEECs successfully into the Community.

The EU remains at the heart of the process of constructing economic and political frameworks in Europe. Only a few politicians in the British Conservative Party are in favour of a fundamental downgrading of the EU, such that it would become little more than a free-trading area. In world terms the EU plays a major part in global economic arrangements and it may increase its role in political frameworks. The pressures to develop federal types of government in the EU are also growing, and the establishment of monetary union will increase the need to make the institutions more accountable. Nevertheless, the EU is likely to encounter considerable difficulties in finding solutions to the economic and political problems that it faces.

References

Buchanan J 1978 *The Economics of Politics*, Institute of Economic Affairs, London.

Buchanan J, Pöhl K, Curzon-Price V and Vibert F 1990 *Europe's Constitutional Future*, Institute of Economic Affairs, London.

Commission 1989 *Report on Economic and Monetary Union in the European Community*, Office for Official Publications of the European Communities, Luxembourg.

Commission 1990 *European Unification: The Origins and Growth of the European Community*, Office for Official Publications of the European Communities, Luxembourg.

Commission 1992 *From the Single Act to Maastricht and Beyond: The Means to Match our Ambitions*, COM(92)2000, Brussels.

Commission 1993 *White Paper on Growth, Competitiveness and Employment*, COM(93)700 Final, Brussels.

Commission 1997 *Agenda 2000: For a stronger and wider Union*, Communication from the Commission to the Council and the EP, Brussels.

Duff A 1997 *The Treaty of Amsterdam*, Sweet & Maxwell/Federal Trust, London.

Duff A, Pinder J and Pryce R 1994 *Maastricht and Beyond: Building the EU*, Routledge, London.

Henning C, Hochreiter E and Hufbauer C 1994 *Reviving the European Union*, Institute for International Economics, Washington DC.

Nugent N 1995 *The Government and Politics of the European Community*, Macmillan, London.

Oates W E 1972 *Fiscal Federalism*, Harcourt Brace, New York.

Padoa-Schioppa T 1987 *Efficiency, Equity and Stability*, Cambridge University Press.

Swann D 1996 *The Economics of the Common Market*, Penguin, London.

Further reading

Bulmer S 1994 *Economic and Political Integration in Europe*, Blackwell, Oxford.

George S 1996 *Politics and Policies in the European Union*, Oxford University Press, Oxford.

Wallace H 1997 *Participation and Policy-making in the European Union*, Clarendon Press, Oxford.

Pinder J 1995 *The European Community, Building the Union*, Oxford University Press, Oxford.

Many journals have relevant articles on issues related to European Economic Integration, e.g.

European Business Journal
European Economy
Economic Policy: A European Forum
Journal of Common Market Studies
Journal of European Integration
Journal of European Public Policy

For the most recent developments, on the institutional structures, policies and other matters related to the EU see the Europa web site: http://www.europa.eu.int

Good web sites on issues connected to EMU are available at http://www.euro.co.uk and http://www.ecu-activities.be

A good web site that contains material that takes a sceptical view on European integration is http://www.keele.ac.uk/socs/ks40/ceghome

1 Market integration in the European Union

Frank McDonald

Introduction

The Treaty of Rome (1957) commits the member states to creating a Customs Union (CU) and a Common Market (CM). This requires free movement of goods, services, capital and labour to exist among the member states. To achieve this outcome, legal barriers that prohibit or restrict free trade between the members of the Community must be removed. Legal and governmental systems may also need to be modified to allow free movement to exist. Therefore, regional economic integration requires negative policies (the removal of barriers to trade) and it may also need some positive policies (the creation of legal and governmental systems that ensure that effective free movement is possible).

Tariffs, quotas and non-tariff barriers (NTBs) must be removed to establish free movement. However, commercial, competition, environmental and social policies and some sectoral policies (for example, agriculture and transport) may require modification to enable effective free movement to be established. To achieve the latter objective requires a deeper level of integration than simply the removal of barriers to trade. Furthermore, macroeconomic policies may distort free movement because of the effects of national monetary and fiscal policies on interest and exchange rates. Therefore, the establishment of an effective CU and CM may require a fairly high degree of economic and possibly political integration.

Defining economic integration

The foundation of the analysis of various types of regional economic integration was established by economists who investigated the early attempts by West European countries to engineer regional economic integration (Viner, 1950; Tinbergen, 1954 and Balassa, 1961). Five major types of economic integration can be identified.

1. A Free Trade Area – a group of countries where all barriers to trade in goods are removed.
2. A Customs Union – a free trade area with a common external tariff.

3. A Common Market – a CU plus free movement of capital and labour.

4. An Economic Union – a CM with harmonisation of economic and social policies to ensure effective free movement and harmonisation of macroeconomic policies to ensure that they do not distort trade flows.

5. Economic and Monetary Union (EMU) – an Economic Union plus a common monetary policy.

It is possible to regard the above definitions as tracing out a path that ultimately leads to a complete economic integration – that is, EMU. The EU may be regarded as seeking to follow this path, starting with a CU and going progressively towards deeper economic integration. The EU has also developed a clear commitment to progress towards Political Union – the harmonisation or integration of political policies and institutional frameworks. Thus the EU can be viewed as moving towards ever greater economic and possibly political integration.

However, these concepts of integration do not describe a process of self-contained and inevitable steps to EMU, or Political Union. A movement towards Economic or even Political Union can start early in the process of creating free movement. The Treaty of Rome established the European Court of Justice (ECJ) to clarify the meaning of Community laws, and the Commission to propose, implement, monitor and enforce laws and policies to ensure that free movement within the Community was effectively implemented and developed. These institutions have significant implications for the development of legal and governmental systems in the member states (Nugent, 1995). Furthermore, common policies for commercial relationships with third parties and for competition rules together with common policies for agriculture and transport were thought to be essential to allow effective free movement to be established. Therefore, the Community began the process of creating a CU and a CM with institutions that had significant leverage over national legal and governmental systems.

The Community was founded on the basis that some type of Economic Union and possibly Political Union was required to enable it to fulfil its objectives. The Treaty of Rome has been significantly amended to allow for an increase in the number of common policies, for example, environmental, regional and social policies. Monetary integration has also become one of the central concerns of the EU. These amendments to the Treaty of Rome have often been based on arguments that they are necessary to ensure that the conditions for free movement are fully and effectively implemented.

However, it is not clear if free movement requires the type of institutional structures with the accompanying political dynamics that were laid down in the Treaty of Rome. No other regional economic agency has approached the creation of a CU or a CM in the same manner as the Community. Regional economic agencies such as NAFTA or Mercosur do not have elaborate institutional frameworks, and none has a court such as the ECJ. The appropriate institutional frameworks to enable the creation of a single market may be illustrated by analysing existing single markets where the conditions for effective free movement have been established.

Types of single markets

Most nation states are real single markets in the sense that frameworks have been created and developed to allow effective free movement to take place. Nation states provide three main frameworks that affect the operations of markets.

- Legal frameworks that create, develop and maintain the legal conditions that permit free movement to exist.
- Regulatory frameworks that govern taxation, public procurement, and economic and social policies.
- Macroeconomic policy frameworks that seek to secure a stable economic environment.

Legal and government created barriers to free movement exist in some nation states that would be regarded as real single markets. For example, different laws govern the production and sale of goods and services in the states of the USA (Pelkmans and Vanheukelen, 1988). As state laws on technical regulations and environmental standards vary considerably between the states, companies that wish to trade across state frontiers have to conform to the laws in the different states. Taxation systems also vary among the states of the USA. The goods and services that are subject to sales taxes and the level of these taxes differ from state to state. State income tax, and taxes that relate to income from savings are also different. Federal laws in the USA are concerned with ensuring that there are no prohibitions or limitations applied to non-state suppliers simply because the companies are not based in the state. Federal laws also ensure that markets (for inter-state trade) are not distorted by anti-competitive practices by companies. However, there are no federal laws on public procurement contracts issued by state agencies. Therefore, states are free to limit their public procurement contracts to state-based companies. Furthermore, there are no federal laws that restrict the use of government aid by states who wish to subsidise the operations of companies located within their area of jurisdiction.

The EU has advocated a very different approach towards removing barriers to free movement that are thought to arise from such factors as different taxation systems, technical regulations, public procurement and state aid policies. Differences in taxation treatment on the sale of goods and services and on income from savings are considered to be a serious distortion of free movement. Consequently, many plans have been put forward to harmonise the differences in taxation on the sale of goods, services and savings. The Cassis de Dijon case heralded a new approach to removing barriers associated with technical regulations by requiring member states to accept the technical regulations of other member states by using mutual recognition. Laws governing public procurement and government aid are also very different in the EU compared with the USA. The Community has been involved in a long legislative process that seeks to ensure that public procurement contracts are open to Community-wide competition. In the area of state aids the EU has strong treaty-based powers to monitor state aids and the Commission can prevent state aids being used to favour nationally based companies.

The differences between the USA and the EU become more evident when regulatory frameworks that are concerned with the allocation of resources are considered. Some countries adopt an approach that tends more to the market-based approach while others are more geared towards a social market approach.

The market-based approach is based on minimum interference by the state in the working of the market process. This approach has a strong emphasis on anti-trust policies to limit the ability of companies to acquire monopoly power and to use anti-competitive practices. Efficiency considerations are regarded as a separate issue from equity or even considered to conflict with equity concerns. Therefore, the best method of attaining high living standards is seen to stem from concentrating on efficiency issues. The social market approach regards the promotion of competitive markets as important, but also links equity issues to efficiency concerns. Thus policies to promote social cohesion and to help disadvantaged groups are seen as an important function of governments to help the economy to deliver high living standards.

The USA tend to adopt a more market-based approach to regulating the market process than, for example, Germany or France. The UK could be regarded as occupying a position between that of most continental European countries and the USA. These examples demonstrate that the importance of the regulation of the market process relating to efficiency and equity issues varies considerably among existing real single markets.

A remarkably standard condition in all existing real single markets is that they are also economic and monetary unions. The only exceptions to this are those regional economic agencies, such as the EU, that are attempting to create real single markets. Macroeconomic policies affect the operation of markets because monetary, fiscal and exchange rate policies determine the inflation and growth environment in which companies operate. All existing real single markets have common monetary and exchange rate policies. Fiscal policies are normally harmonised such that the central or federal governments have a strong influence on fiscal policy. However, the Federal government of the USA has no power over the taxation and expenditure and borrowing decisions of the states. In contrast, the EU is seeking to impose control over the fiscal policies (particularly government borrowing) of those member states that join European monetary union (see Chapter 3).

The existence of a real single market does not mean that some markets within the area are not fragmented into specific geographic areas. Fragmentation of markets in real single markets arises from economic and social barriers to labour mobility or consumer preferences that require different products and or marketing approaches for the various cultural groupings within the real single market. Many of these cultural groupings are geographically concentrated, therefore fragmentation of markets can have a distinctive spatial character.

Transaction costs and single markets

Real single markets are influenced by the transaction costs that companies incur in complying with the cultural, economic and legal conditions that prevail in the environment in which they operate. Transaction costs arise when companies organise the production, marketing and sale of goods and services. These costs include establishing contracts with suppliers, buyers, labour and other inputs necessary for the company to engage in business activities. Transaction costs also arise from the need to conform to laws and social conventions that govern economic and social interaction (Williamson, 1975). For single market areas three main factors influence the type and significance of the transaction costs that companies face.

1. The characteristics of legal and regulatory frameworks.

2. Macroeconomic policy frameworks.

3. The extent of the fragmentation markets within the single market area.

Fulfilling legal and regulatory conditions can impose transaction costs on companies because they must alter products or marketing policies to conform to different regulations in the states that compose the single market area. Transaction costs may also arise from the obligations to obey the requirements of economic and social policies, for example, legislation that affects employment rights. Macroeconomic policies can lead to transactions costs if the single market area does not have a single currency. In such single markets companies will be faced with exchange rate risk and currency conversion costs. Moreover, in single markets where macroeconomic policies are not harmonised, costs may arise because inflation and growth rates may vary considerably between the members of the single market area, thereby requiring companies to alter their pricing and sales policies in the different parts of the area. Fragmented markets impose costs by requiring companies to adjust their product and marketing policies to accommodate the conditions that prevail in the various parts of the fragmented market. The impact of transaction costs in single market areas is illustrated in Fig. 1.1.

The process of creating the SEM can be viewed as one of reducing the size of the transaction cost box. However, many European companies may already be well within the existing cost box of the EU. A company that faces few transaction costs from fragmented markets, low compliance with laws, and has low costs associated with the lack of monetary integration may be comfortably within the cost box. Efforts to further integrate the SEM will, therefore, bring little benefit to such companies. However, moves to further integrate the SEM could impose costs on such companies because of the need to comply with new laws or to adjust to a new currency (McDonald, 1997).

The evolution of the SEM programme has resulted in a variety of what are often complex and confusing rules (Mayes, 1997). The impact of these rules on the transaction costs of companies has become important because of the growth of legislation associated with the SEM programme, some of which requires companies to adopt new and costly procedures. The impact of these costs, particularly on SMEs, has led to the beginnings of attempts to seek to reduce the transaction costs to companies of complying with EU legislation (Commission, 1996b). The transaction costs of complying with EU legislation may not be uniform throughout the Community because of the manner by which EU

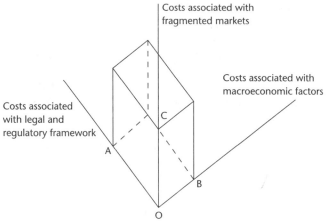

Figure 1.1 Transaction costs and single markets

At point 0 the transaction costs relating to legal, regulatory and macroeconomic frameworks and those associated with fragmented markets are zero. If the maximum costs related to legal and regulatory frameworks are given by 0A, macroeconomic factors by 0B, and fragmented market costs by 0C, the box area within the diagram indicates the maximum possible transaction costs that companies operating in the single market area would face. The position in which companies would find themselves within this cost box would depend upon three factors. First, the level of fragmentation of the market in which the company operates. Secondly, the extent to which companies are subject to costs from the legal and regulatory frameworks that prevail in the single market area. Thirdly, the importance of exchange rate risk and other costs associated with the macroeconomic policies to the operations of the company. A single market area that had a single currency, a low level of market fragmentation, and few economic and social policies that affected the costs of companies would have a smaller cost box than a single market area that did not have these characteristics. Increasing the integration of markets and reducing the transaction costs related to legal and macroeconomic factors would reduce the size of the transaction cost box. The process of creating the SEM can be regarded as attempts to reduce the size of the transaction cost box.

legislation is transposed into national laws. It is possible that EU legislation can be over-implemented by national governments (gold plating of directives) or under-implemented (when the conditions specified in directives are not fully implemented by national governments). The latter is contrary to EU law, but it is probably quite widespread. A large number of complaints have been registered with the Commission on issues connected to recognition of technical regulations (Commission, 1996b). The transaction costs to companies of complying with EU legislation are shown in Fig. 1.2.

It is possible that a single market area such as the USA has lower transaction costs than the EU because the USA has a single currency, fewer cultural differences (therefore, less fragmented markets) and fewer economic and social policies that impact on the transaction costs of companies. However, in some areas the EU may have lower transaction costs than the USA, for example, the use of mutual recognition may reduce the costs associated with conforming to technical regulations. Nevertheless, the characteristics of existing real single markets suggest that the USA is likely to have lower transaction costs than the EU. There

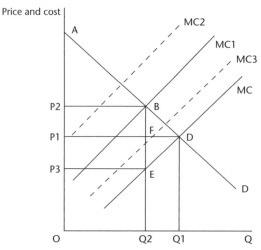

Figure 1.2 Transaction costs and legislation

D = Demand   MC = sum of the marginal costs of companies in the industry

MC1 = marginal cost including the transaction costs of legislation (equal to BE)

P1:Q1 = price and quantity before the imposition of legislation

P2:Q2 = price and quantity after the imposition of legislation

P3 = price received by companies after imposition of legislation (i.e. market price P2 minus transaction costs of legislation BE)

Effects of legislation

Consumer surplus before legislation = P1AD

Consumer surplus after legislation = P2AB

The legislation reduces consumer surplus. The burden of the costs is shared between producers and consumers. Consumers pay an area equal to P1P2BF, while producers pay P3P1FE. The more elastic are demand and supply, the more the transaction cost burden will fall on companies. This analysis suggests that legislation should be carefully framed to minimise the transaction costs burden that will fall on companies and consumers.

   If legislation is over-implemented, the marginal cost curve may shift further to the left (e.g. MC2). This will increase the cost burden of the legislation. However, if the legislation is under-implemented (e.g. MC3), companies located in countries that implement properly or over-implement the legislation will suffer a loss of competitiveness relative to those companies based in countries that under-implement the legislation.

is also some evidence that the single market environment in the USA has delivered an environment that is more conducive to the development of competitiveness by companies (Commission, 1997). However, the cultural differences between the US and the EU are held to require different types of single market environments that will allow European companies to create and maintain competitiveness in a global market (Jacquemin and Pench, 1996). This argument accords with the views of those who regard institutional frameworks as important to the effective working of economies.

The characteristics of real single markets depend to a large extent on the nature of the institutional frameworks of societies. Institutional frameworks are formed by legal and governmental systems and cultural norms that determine the rules of human interaction. Effective institutional frameworks reduce uncertainty and transaction costs in economic and social exchange. Therefore, successful real single markets have succeeded in creating institutional frameworks that effectively reduce uncertainty and transaction costs. However, different societies have different institutional frameworks as a result of their history and their cultural characteristics. Therefore, institutional frameworks are path determined (they emerge from the history of societies) and can not be quickly altered into very different systems (North, 1990). Hence, institutional frameworks that provide the necessary conditions for effective free movement in one society may not be appropriate for another society that has a different history and cultural composition.

The EU is attempting to create an institutional framework that can provide a low transaction cost real single market. However, this process requires the integration of the institutional frameworks of the member states. The member states have a variety of institutional frameworks because their histories are different. If such path determinacy is important, the EU faces considerable problems in its attempt to establish institutional frameworks that can deliver a low uncertainty and transaction cost real single market.

Customs Union

A CU is an area where tariffs and quotas on goods are removed for all intra-Union trade, and where there is a common tariff and quota system for all extra-Union trade. In 1948 the Netherlands, Belgium and Luxembourg formed Benelux, a CU in industrial goods. The Treaty of Paris that established the European Coal and Steel Community (ECSC) required the original six members (Benelux, France, Germany and Italy) to create a CU in coal and steel. The Treaty of Rome extended the CU of the original six to all industrial goods. Article 3 of the Treaty of Rome called for 'the elimination, as between Member States, of customs duties and quantitative restrictions on the import and export of goods, and of all other measures having equivalent effect'. This article requires the removal of NTBs – measures having equivalent effect – as well as tariffs (customs duties) and quotas (quantitative restrictions).

A CU should act as a greater stimulus to intra-Union trade than a free-trade area because the introduction of a common external tariff (CET) should ensure that the same tariff is imposed on imports regardless of the country importing the product. Therefore, the CET ensures that all imports into the CU are treated in the same manner. The CET avoids problems with rules of origin. This problem arises when imports from outside the free-trade area are used as intermediate products in the production of goods that are subsequently exported to another country in the free-trade area. In these cases it is necessary to assess the value of the imported intermediate good in the final good that is exported. This value is required to work out how much of the exported good should be free from customs duties. In the case of products that have large inputs from countries outside the free-trade area the proportion of the final exported goods that was tariff free could be quite small. The Community did not eliminate all rules of origin problems with the introduction of the CET. In the 1980s a series of rules of origin problems arose over the non-Community inputs in the final outputs from Japanese plants that produced output in a member state (see Chapter 15). Nevertheless, on the whole the CU of the EEC did not suffer the same degree of difficulties that free-trade areas such as EFTA encountered with rules of origin problems (Herin, 1986).

The importance of tariffs as a barrier to trade in the EU is influenced by Article 18 of the Treaty of Rome. This article commits the Community to seek to reduce the barriers to trade on the basis of 'reciprocity and mutual advantage to reduce customs duties below the general level of which they could avail themselves as a result of the establishment of a customs union'. This article required the Community to seek to reduce tariffs and quotas against non-member states in the context of world trade negotiations. Membership of the General Agreement on Tariffs and Trade (GATT) also required this undertaking because a CU is against the spirit of the GATT as it does not confer most favoured nations' treatment to non-members. Thus the CU was tolerated by the GATT on the grounds that it would pursue a coherent and sustained attempt to achieve a general reduction in barriers to trade by negotiations.

The Single European Market

The move to establish the Single European Market (SEM) was simply a programme to enable the EU to create a CM. The EU has been committed to establishing a CM since the Treaty of Rome was signed in 1957. Before agreement was reached to establish the SEM by the end of 1992, there had been very little progress towards establishing the CM. The main problem was the difficulty of reaching agreement about eliminating the many NTBs which hindered free movement. A range of NTBs based on diverse national rules, regulations, taxation and subsidies governed the movement of goods, services, capital and labour. Consequently, frontier controls were necessary to ensure that cross-frontier trade in goods adhered to the various national requirements. Cross-frontier trade in some service sectors was rendered impossible by different national rules and regulations. Capital movements were restricted by capital and exchange controls imposed by some member states. Labour mobility was hampered by differences in professional qualifications, and by labour and social security laws and regulations. Before the agreement on the Single European Act (SEA), the EU had attempted to eliminate these NTBs by creating a set of European laws and regulations to govern all aspects of economic activity. This resulted in attempts to determine European standards for a large range of products. Member states could, however, veto any proposal that they thought was detrimental to their economies, therefore very little progress to harmonise common European standards took place. This tendency to protect national interests meant that little progress was made to eliminate the barriers to the free movement of services, capital and labour. Hence the EU did not take any significant steps towards establishing the CM, although the Treaty of Rome clearly committed the member states to achieving this objective.

In the 1980s a process was begun which greatly accelerated the progress towards creating a Common Market. In this period the member states were experiencing lower growth rates and higher unemployment than the USA and Japan. The Japanese were successfully entering many of the most sensitive markets in the EU (e.g. cars, consumer electronic equipment, computing equipment), and the NICs were becoming an increasing threat to many of the industries of the member states. The leading high technology companies tended to be American or Japanese, and many European companies were unable to maintain a presence in these markets. Within the EU continuing conflict over the CAP and associated budgetary problems (see Chapter 11) had diverted the EU from making progress on establishing the Common Market. A view emerged that the EU was stuck in a rut, and was losing its vision and direction.

In spite of these problems there were also signs of the EU making some progress. The European Monetary System (EMS), founded in 1979, had not collapsed as had been predicted in many quarters; rather it had achieved some success in stabilising exchange rate fluctuations and in helping to promote convergence of inflation rates. Greece joined the EU in 1981, and Spain and Portugal joined in 1986, creating a potential market of 320 million consumers. An ECJ ruling in 1978 in the Cassis de Dijon case established the principle of mutual recognition. In this case the ECJ ruled that Germany could not ban the importing of Cassis de Dijon (a French alcoholic drink) on the grounds that it did not conform to German rules and regulations governing the sale of alcoholic drinks. The ECJ established that goods that adhered to the national rules and regulations in the member state in which they were produced should be able to be sold in any member state without need to adhere to the rules and regulations governing the production and sale of the goods in the importing member state. The principle outlined in the Cassis de Dijon case provided an escape route from the long process of establishing common European rules and regulations for all goods. This process could be replaced by the mutual recognition of each other's rules and regulations. The use of mutual recognition was accepted by the EU when the 'New approach to technical harmonisation' was adopted in 1985. The acceptance of the concept of mutual recognition was a major step in the process of removing NTBs caused by differences in rules and regulations. Harmonisation could be limited to essential requirements in order for health and public safety considerations to be accounted for, and to ensure technical compatibility of products. The combination of these factors contributed to the idea that the EU still had potential to be a dynamic body in Europe and the world.

In 1983, at the Stuttgart summit, there was an acknowledgement of the need to take new initiatives to restore some dynamism into the activities of the EU. This took the form of a Solemn Declaration of European Union. There was a growing feeling that the failure to establish the CM (now called the Internal Market) within the EU resulted in major handicaps for EU companies. There was a strong opinion that EU firms faced considerable disadvantages compared with American and Japanese firms. It was noted that American firms had a domestic market of over 200 million consumers, and Japanese firms had a market of 100 million. If the EU were to become a single market it would have a domestic market of 320 million consumers, making it the largest market in the world.

In 1984 the European Parliament issued a draft treaty on European Union. This called for political and economic change, in particular the creation of an internal market and the reform of decision-making procedures of the EU to make them more democratic, or at least more accountable to the European Parliament. At the Fontainebleau summit of 1984, two committees (the Adonnino and the Dooge committees) were set up to consider how the Community might develop. Both of these committees called for institutional change, and the Dooge called for the creation of an Internal Market. In 1985 a White Paper, 'Completing the Internal Market', was published (Commission, 1985). The White Paper called for a programme of legislation to be implemented to create an Internal Market by the end of 1992. At the Milan summit of 1985 all these moves came to a head, and an Inter-governmental Conference was set up to discuss European Union. This resulted in agreement on the SEA that was approved by all member states in 1986, and implemented in 1987.

The SEA was a compromise between those countries such as France and Germany that wanted a new Treaty on European Union, and the UK and Denmark that did not want a new Treaty, but simply the implementation of the White Paper to create an SEM. The SEA allowed for a limited set of changes to the Treaty of Rome that included majority voting in the Council of Ministers in areas related to establishing the Internal Market. The main thrust of the SEA was to establish the SEM by 31 December 1992. When the SEA was approved it was considered to be a poor substitute for a new Treaty on European Union, but given the opposition of the UK and Denmark it was the best that could be achieved. However, the SEA resulted in a dramatic increase in the activities of the EU, and led to a chain of events that focused attention on the EU as being one of the most successful and dynamic economic agencies in the world. At the heart of the 1992 programme was Article 13 of the SEA: 'The internal market shall comprise an area without internal frontiers in which the free movement of goods, persons, services and capital is ensured according to the provisions of this Treaty'.

This was simply a reformulation of the original commitment, in the Treaty of Rome, to establish a CM. The major difference was that there was the political will, and a detailed programme with a practical method of implementation, to achieve this objective. The EU had finally adopted a comprehensive programme to establish a CM. This programme involved the removal of all legal barriers to the free movement of goods, services, capital and labour.

The economic effects of establishing free movement

The early attempts to assess the economic implications of the formation of the CU (Viner, 1950, Meade, 1955 and Lipsey, 1970) continue to influence the type of economic analysis that is used to assess the effects of regional economic agencies. The economic effects of regional economic integration can be classified as arising from either static or dynamic effects of establishing free movement. Static effects are concerned with the allocation of resources when factors of production and technology are fixed, and where the characteristics of the competitive environment are also constant. Dynamic effects arise when regional economic integration induces changes in the quantity and quality of factors of production, improvements in technology and changes to the competitive environment.

Static effects

Viner (1950) showed that the formation of a CU was not necessarily advantageous to all members of a regional economic agency or indeed to the world as a whole. In his analysis he developed the concepts of 'trade creation' and 'trade diversion'. Trade creation arises when a CU leads to the movement of trade from a high-cost to a low-cost producer, whereas trade diversion occurs when the reverse arises. The analysis of trade creation and diversion focuses on the removal of tariffs; however, the basic method of analysis can be extended to cover other barriers to trade, for example quotas and NTBs. Trade creation and diversion effects can arise in any regional economic agency that reduces barriers to trade that are not extended to non-members.

The formation of a CU leads to the elimination of tariffs between members and to the establishment of the CET against all non-members. The removal of tariffs against members will increase imports from the lowest-cost member of the CU to members who have higher-cost producers. If the exporting CU member is also the lowest-cost producer in the world a process of trade creation will arise because imports will come from the least-cost producer in the world. However, if the country with the lowest-cost producers is not in the CU and, if the imposition of the CET results in an import price into the CU that is higher than the price that will be charged by the lowest-cost producer in the CU, trade diversion will result, because imports could be obtained at a lower cost if tariffs had been eliminated against all countries rather than just for the members of the CU. The concepts of trade creation and diversion are illustrated in Figs 1.3 and 1.4.

Trade creation allows resources to be allocated according to comparative advantage. However, even in the case of trade diversion, gains can be reaped by shifting resources to allow specialisation to lower-cost producers within the regional economic agency. This effect is illustrated in Fig. 1.5.

In static terms, a CU is beneficial if trade creation is greater than trade diversion. This outcome is more likely to occur if the CU includes countries that have large numbers of low-cost producers and if the CET is set at a low level. However, in global terms, trade diversion can be avoided if tariff reductions are offered on a most favoured nation basis, that is, the highest level of tariff reductions offered to any nation is made available to all nations. Therefore, the justification for a CU rests on arguments that tariff reductions can be more substantial between a group of countries than if they are granted to all countries.

The case for and against regional economic agencies tends to focus on the overall welfare gains from establishing free movement. However, there are

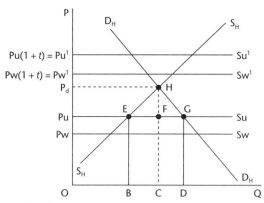

Figure 1.3   Trade creation

D_H and S_H represent the home demand and supply curves for the good. PuSu and PwSw are the CU and rest-of-the-world supply curves. Before membership of the union, both external producers are excluded from the home market by the imposition of a tariff which results in the import supply curves being above the equilibrium price in the domestic economy. The home country is self-sufficient at an equilibrium price of OP_d and quantity of OC. After membership of the CU, the CET does not apply to the union partner, but it applies to the rest of the world. The union partner's supply curve now becomes PuSu, and imports of BD are supplied to the home country. Domestic supply falls from OC to OB, but domestic demand rises from OC to OD. The resource cost of producing BC of the good has fallen from BCHE to BCFE, a saving of EFH. This is beneficial in terms of both CU and world welfare. The home country has gained, for although producers' surplus has fallen by PuEHPd, consumers' surplus has risen by PuGHPd, leading to a net gain of HEG. The gain would have been larger had the home economy adopted a policy of free trade rather than membership of a discriminatory trading regime. However, in terms of welfare gain, participation in the union is obviously a step in the right direction, because there is a gain from free trade. Nevertheless, free trade with all trading partners would lead to greater welfare gains.

distribution effects from the static effects of establishing free movement. The overall effect of reaping comparative advantage is to increase welfare by relocating production to those countries (within the CU) that are relatively most efficient at providing output. However, in those markets where exports rise, the price in the domestic market increases and thereby induces a decline in quantity bought in the domestic market. Thus, consumers in the exporting country suffer a loss of real income because after the rise in exports they must transfer a larger amount of nominal income to receive the same output. Consumers in the importing country face the opposite effects because the supply of the product increases, thereby reducing the price. Producers are also differentially affected by the change in prices induced by the establishment of free movement. In the exporting country they experience higher prices and therefore increased revenues, whereas producers in the importing country face the opposite effect as prices fall in their economies. Furthermore, producers must adjust to the new allocation based on comparative advantage. This may involve temporary unemployment of resources as labour and capital move into those areas in which the country has a comparative advantage.

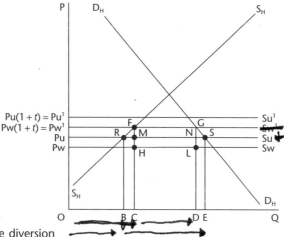

Figure 1.4 Trade diversion

Before participation in a CU and with a tariff level t on potential partner and rest-of-world sup-plies, the lowest priced source of import supply is the rest of the world Pw^1Sw^1. Domestic pro-duction is OC and imports are CD. Tariff proceeds FGLH go to the government of the home economy. The home country joins a CU whose external tariff is identical to that of the home country prior to participation. Domestic production falls to OB but domestic consumption rises to OE; BE imports now come from the union partner at a tariff-free price of OPu. Trade diversion has arisen. The cost of the original quantity of imports CD has risen by HLNM. There is a loss of tariff revenue to the domestic government of FGLH. Moreover, producers' surplus falls by $PuPw^1RF$ and con-sumers' surplus rises by $PuPw^1GS$. The gain in consumers' surplus minus the loss in producers' surplus is RFGS. Part of this – FGNM – is part of the lost tariff revenue, and consequently this reduces the gain of RFGS to the areas RFM and SGN. The other part HLNM (the amount of trade diversion) may be compared with the two triangles RFM and SGN. Clearly, here there is a net trade diversionary loss. The extent of this loss will be the greater, the larger the gap between world prices and union prices.

A fuller account of trade creation and diversion can be found in Hansen and Neilsen, 1997.

Dynamic effects

Three major dynamic effects of regional economic integration can be identified.

- Reducing monopoly power.
- Reducing levels of x-inefficiency – overmanning, excessive holdings of stocks and other types of slack management practices.
- Reaping economies of scale and learning effects.

The removal of barriers to trade can reduce monopoly power by increasing the possible sources of supply from other countries within the regional economic agency. Reductions in monopoly power will lower prices and increase output, thereby leading to net gains for consumers (see Fig. 1.6). Increasing the com-petitive environment may encourage producers to improve non-price competi-tion factors such as the qualities of their products. This may also lead to benefits by increasing the demand for higher quality products (see Fig. 1.7).

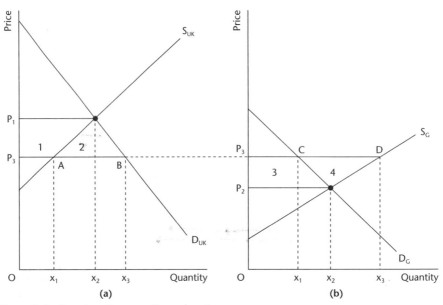

Figure 1.5   Reaping Comparative advantage

In Fig. 1.5(a) the demand and supply conditions for a good in the UK are shown; Fig. 1.5(b) shows market conditions in Germany. The lower equilibrium price in Germany shows that it has a comparative advantage in producing this good. If trade is prevented by the imposition of an NTB, such as rules and regulations after the removal of these barriers, the UK would import the good from Germany. This would result in the price increasing in Germany and falling in the UK. When the price reached the level where imports into the UK were equal to exports from Germany, a new equilibrium price would have been established, i.e. at P_3 where UK imports (AB) equal German exports (CD). This results in a rise in consumer surplus in the UK equal to the areas 1+2. The area 1 is a transfer of producer surplus to consumers; it is not a net welfare gain as it is transferred from producers in the UK to consumers in the UK. The remaining consumer surplus gain of area 2 represents the net welfare gain to the UK. The areas 3+4 represent the gain in producer surplus in Germany. Area 3 is a transfer of consumer surplus to German producers from German consumers. The net gain in Germany is therefore represented by area 4. Therefore, the net gain to both countries is equivalent to areas 2+4.

The removal of trade barriers should lead to the integration of fragmented markets and thereby create a larger market for products. If transport costs are low, it may be possible to serve the integrated market from existing or new plant and thereby allow companies to reap internal economies of scale. The size of the benefits from economies of scale depends upon the nature of the technical relationship between cost and output, in particular the rate at which costs fall as output is increased and by the level of output at which costs are minimised, that is, minimum efficiency scale (MES). Therefore, the magnitude of the benefits from internal economies of scale is determined by the degree of integration of fragmented markets, the significance of transport costs, and the technical relationship between cost and output. If the new larger markets are competitive, prices should be reduced as production costs fall (see Fig. 1.8).

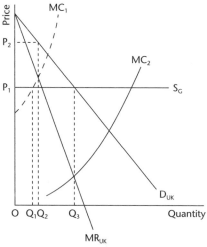

Figure 1.6   Reduction in monopoly power

If the UK had a domestic monopolist totally protected by an NTB, then price would be P_2 and output Q_2 if the monopolist faced the marginal cost curve shown by MC_1. Assuming a perfectly elastic supply of this good from Germany, the ruling market price in the absence of the NTB would be P_1 and the total demand in the UK would be Q_3. If the NTB were removed, the price in the UK would fall to P_1, and the monopolist would be constrained to this price. The monopolist would have to adjust output to Q_1, and the gap in satisfying market demand in the UK at this price would be met by imports from Germany of Q_1–Q_3. There would be benefits in the UK from a lower price and higher output provided that the domestic monopolist's marginal cost curve lay above MC_2. A paper by Jacquemin (1982) shows that this disciplinary effect from foreign competition can also work in oligopolistic markets.

If production in national markets is characterised by large economies of scale, the competitive environment may be strongly oligopolistic if the market is only large enough to sustain a few plants. In these circumstances the creation of a larger market by establishing a CU or a CM may allow an expansion of suppliers to the new larger market and thereby lead to a reduction in price (Krugman, 1988). Thus the establishment of free movement can lead to benefits by increasing the number of suppliers to the market. The emergence of these benefits depends on the existence of a competition policy that is able to stop companies from acquiring control over plants and thereby preventing an increase in the competitive environment.

The integration of fragmented markets may also lead to external economies of scale (Krugman and Obstfeld, 1993). External economies of scale can arise when companies cluster in a specific geographical area and form networks that result in reduced transaction costs in conducting their business. These external economies of scale arise from such factors as the development of a pool of skilled labour, the creation of a network of suppliers and support services etc. Silicon Valley in California is the best known example of a cluster. However, other examples exist – the City of London for foreign exchange dealing, Milan for high fashion, and networks of SMEs that have formed clusters in northern Italy

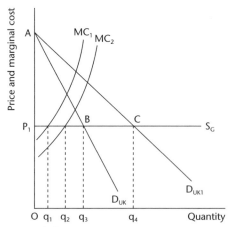

Figure 1.7   X-inefficiency and the SEM

This situation is similar to Fig. 1.6, i.e. a UK monopolist constrained to the price P_1 because of imports from Germany. If this increase in competition is also accompanied by R&D and innovation to improve the non-price characteristics of this good, the demand curve shifts to D_{UK1}. Consumer surplus is increased from P_1AB before the improvements in non-price factors, and to P_1AC after the improvements. Initially, the increase in demand in the UK is met by increased imports from Germany, that is, imports rise from q_1–q_3 to q_1–q_4. If, however, the UK firm responds by reducing X-inefficiency, this could shift the marginal cost to MC_2 and allow the UK firm to increase its share of the market from q_1 to q_2. If the UK firm reduced X-inefficiency without any increase in the non-price characteristics of the good, the result would be that the UK firm would increase market share and its producer surplus. There would be no benefit in terms of increased consumer surplus. This implies that reductions in X-inefficiency do not necessarily lead to net welfare improvements for consumers. Only if the lowering of production costs results in lower prices will there be any benefits to consumers.

(Porter, 1990). The establishment of free movement may allow the market to become large enough to allow for the development of existing clusters or for the emergence of new clusters.

The reaping of both internal and external economies of scale may also further reduce production costs as learning takes place because, as output increases, companies learn how to produce products more cheaply. Learning can also arise from the development of clusters as companies learn how to utilise effectively the networks of business relationships that are at the heart of clusters.

Other effects of establishing free movement

The creation of a CM requires free movement of labour and capital as well as of goods and services. The removal of barriers to movement of factors of production will lead to net benefits and distribution effects that are similar to those that arise from the reaping of comparative advantage (see Figs 1.9 and 1.10).

The increase in the competitive environment that should follow from the establishment of free movement may reduce levels of x-inefficiency and thereby boost

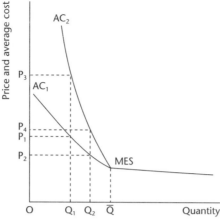

Figure 1.8 Economies of scale

The level of output constrained by the NTB is Q_1, and this results in a price of P_1. If the NTB is removed, the firm could increase exports and thereby expand output to Q_2, which would reduce the price to P_2. This outcome is dependent on the level of competition being sufficient to ensure that firms are constrained to making normal profits, and that they are therefore forced to reduce price when costs are lowered. It is also necessary for the firm to be operating at above minimum efficiency scale (MES), the low point of the average cost curve. If the firm is operating at MES, the opportunity to expand output will not result in lower costs. If the AC curve was given by AC1 (i.e. a steeper AC curve) the reduction in price of the expansion of output from 0Q1 to 0Q2 would be greater. This demonstrates the importance of the technical relationship between cost and output for the magnitude of the cost (and hence possible price reduction) of any increase in output that might arise from economic integration.

the effectiveness of the use of capital and labour in production processes. This will enhance growth because better use will be made of existing production processes. A further expansion of the growth potential will result from the incentive to increase investment to meet the demands of the new larger markets. As income grows, savings will rise, providing the resources for extra investment (Baldwin, 1989). Therefore, the establishment of free movement should have two beneficial effects on growth, arising from the increase in efficiency and from the incentive to invest to benefit from larger markets (see Fig. 1.11).

The adjustment costs of free movement

Economic analysis of free movement implies that the removal of trade barriers offers the potential to reap net benefits. However, these net gains cannot be acquired without changing the distribution of income and they also lead to adjustment costs as companies and individuals respond to changes induced by the establishment of free movement. Adjustment costs are likely to be temporary because in the long run factors of production will relocate, geographically and across sectors, in response to the new market environment. Nevertheless, these costs may be significant and persistent if labour and capital mobility are limited. The

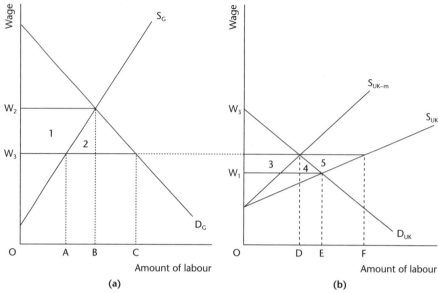

Figure 1.9   Free movement of labour

Before the establishment of free movement of labour in the UK, wage would be W_1 with employment at E, and in Germany the wage would be W_2 and employment at B. When the barriers to labour mobility are removed, a new equilibrium wage will emerge – W_3. At this wage the number of migrant workers from the UK is equal to the inflow to Germany. Employment in the UK would fall to D, with DF of migrant workers. This reduces the supply of labour in the UK to S_{UK-m}, the supply of labour in the UK minus migrants. Employment of German workers would fall to A, with AC of migrant workers from the UK. This leads to gains and losses of economic rent (area above the supply curve of labour, and below the wage line) for labour. Workers in Germany lose an amount equal to area 1, while workers who remain in the UK gain higher wages, leading to economic rent equal to area 3. Migrant workers from the UK would gain the areas 4+5. Employers also make gains and losses (the areas below the demand for labour and above the wage line). In Germany employers gain area 2 from the employment of migrant workers, while in the UK employers lose an amount equivalent to the areas 3+4. The areas 1+3+4 are transfers, area 1 from German workers to German employers, and areas 3+4 from UK employers to UK workers. This leaves areas 2 and 5 as net welfare gains of allowing free movement of labour.

changes in the distribution of income are, in principle, capable of compensation from the net benefits that arise from the establishment of free movement.

These factors are likely to lead to powerful political pressures to redistribute income, geographically, across sectors and among different groups of workers to compensate those who feel harmed by the integration process. Legislation can also be used to limit the scale of changes and to direct the changes in ways that are considered to be less onerous than those that emerge from the unconstrained market process. Furthermore, action to slow down and reduce the impact of trade liberalisation programmes may be adopted by members of regional economic agencies in efforts to mitigate against the cost of adjustment. These

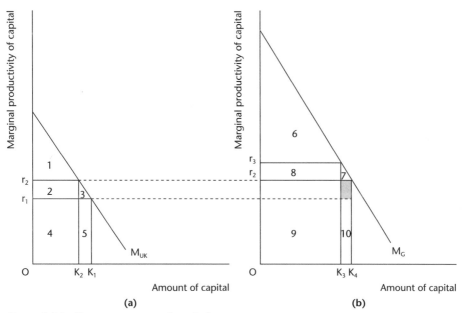

Figure 1.10 Free movement of capital

The stock of capital in the UK is given by K_1 and in Germany by K_3. The marginal productivity of capital is shown by M_{UK} and M_G. The marginal productivity of capital in Germany is higher than in the UK, therefore the rate of return to capital in Germany (r_3) is higher than in the UK (r_1). In the UK, capital receives a total reward equal to the areas 4+5, while labour receives 1+2+3. In Germany the total return to capital is shown by areas 8+9, and area 6 is the payment to labour. If the barriers to capital mobility are removed, capital will flow from the UK to obtain the higher rate of return available in Germany. This will continue until the rate of return is equal in both countries, i.e. at r_2. This results in an export of capital from the UK of K_1–K_2, corresponding to the capital stock increase in Germany of K_3–K_4. This reduces total product in the UK to an amount equal to areas 1+2+4. However, the exported capital results in a transfer of profits to the UK from Germany, equal to area 10. In Germany national product is increased by areas 7+10, leading to a net welfare gain to Germany equivalent to area 7. The shaded part of area 10 is equal to the higher return to UK capital from being invested in Germany. In Fig. 2.6 this area is twice the size of area 3. Hence the net loss of areas 3+5 to the UK is more than compensated for by the remittance of profits from Germany, as area 10 is greater than areas 3+5. So the net welfare gains of allowing free movement of capital are equal to area 7 plus half the shaded area. There are, however, distribution effects to labour resulting from capital mobility. Labour's share in the UK falls by areas 2+3, while in Germany it rises by areas 7+8.

responses have certainly been evident in the EU and have led to a significant amount of redistribution and to slow progress in implementing the programmes to remove barriers to trade effectively.

Problems with empirical studies

Empirical studies on the effects of regional economic integration have taken two main forms.

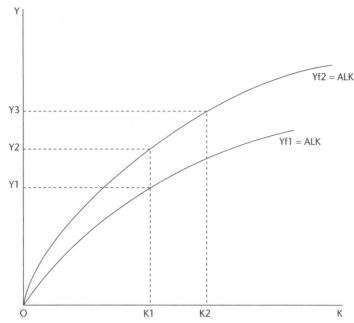

Figure 1.11 The growth effects of free movement

Y = output/income   A = efficiency factor in the use of capital and labour

L = labour   K = capital

Yf = A,L,K (production function, that is Y, is determined by a fixed amount of labour (L) and variable amounts of capital (K) and the efficiency factor)

Creating free movement will improve the efficiency of the use of capital and labour (A) because the increase in competition that follows from free movement will reduce the level of X-inefficiency in the use of capital and labour. This is shown by a shift from Yf1 to Yf2. Therefore, at every level of capital a higher level of output will result. This is the static growth effect.

However, there is another possible growth effect from the establishment of free movement. The boost to the size of the market that follows from the establishment of free movement will stimulate incentives to increase investment, thereby boosting the amount of capital that is employed in the economy. The increase in income from the improvement in the efficiency of the use of capital and labour also leads to an increase in savings which can provide the resources to boost investment (providing that individuals are prepared to sacrifice consumption now for consumption in the future). This is the dynamic growth effect.

If the optimal level of capital is given by K1, the static effect would be to increase Y to Y2. The dynamic effect would result in an increase in the amount of capital employed to, say, K2 leading to an income level of Y3. See Baldwin (1989) for a fuller explanation.

1. Estimating the changes to the size and pattern of trade flows before and after trade liberalisation. This is done by creating a model of what trade would have been if a country had not removed or reduced trade barriers, and comparing that outcome with that which occurred after a country liberalised its trade.

2. Estimating the costs and benefits of the programme as indicated by economic theory. This approach requires clear predictions to be derived

from theoretical models, and access to reliable data that can be used to test the predictions.

Both of these approaches have major conceptual problems. These problems mean that considerable caution has to be exercised in interpreting the meaning of the results of empirical studies on the effects of regional economic integration.

Most studies of the effect of the CU have sought to ascertain the effects of tariff reductions by comparing what the situation would have been if a country had not been a member of a regional economic integration agency (the anti-monde position) with the actual outcome of that country after its participation in such an agency (Mayes, 1978; Winters, 1987). Therefore, an anti-monde model of the determinants of trade flows is constructed and predictions are made on what trade flows would be in this world. These predictions are then compared with actual outcomes to estimate the effects of the regional economic agency.

The main problem with this approach is that it is very difficult to ascribe any observable differences from the anti-monde position to the effects of the elimination of trade barriers. A multitude of factors determines trade flows (for example, growth in income levels among trading partners, reductions in barriers to trade not related to the regional economic agency, and changes in the technological and the competitive environment). If these factors are not accurately captured by the anti-monde model, the comparison with actual outcomes may reflect the factors that are not fully specified in the anti-monde model as well as the effects of the regional economic agency. This problem arises in studies of both the static and dynamic effects of regional economic integration.

Predictive models have also been used to estimate the effects of regional economic integration. The Cecchini Report was an attempt to estimate the net benefits of the creation of the SEM (see Emerson *et al.*, 1988, for a summary of this report). The Cecchini Report was largely based on a statistical estimation of the net benefits of trade liberalisation as indicated by economic theory. The theories used were rather more sophisticated versions of those outlined above, including a general equilibrium approach that was based on an imperfectly competitive model of interaction between firms (Smith and Venables, 1988). The Cecchini Report used a variety of economic models to examine particular aspects of the creation of the SEM – economies of scale (Pratten, 1988; Schwalbach, 1988) and innovation (Geroski, 1988). Surveys and studies by management consultants were also used to assess the potential effects of the creation of the SEM for particular sectors and to obtain data for the statistical estimation of the net benefits – foodstuffs (Group MAC, 1988), road haulage (Ernst & Whinney, 1988), telecommunication services (Muller, 1988) and financial services (Price Waterhouse, 1988).

The main problem with the approach used in the Cecchini Report was that other models may have led to different indications of the likely costs and benefits of trade liberalisation. For example, a model based on external economies of scale and trade (for example, Krugman, 1989) may have focused more on the geographical impact of economic integration such as the incentive to develop clusters of industries in response to the potential to reap external economies of scale. This type of geographical impact was largely missing from the Cecchini Report.

It is very difficult to know which model, or models, captures the major factors that are likely to arise from a wide-ranging economic integration programme such as the SEM. Therefore, it is possible that empirical studies based on such an approach will miss major and fundamental effects of large-scale integration programmes. Moreover, obtaining data to estimate the costs and benefits indicated by the theoretical work and the surveys is not an easy task. Consequently, empirical estimates of the impact of economic integration by agencies like the EU are likely to be subject to wide margins of error.

Some studies seek to assess the costs and benefits to individual member states by including all of the trade effects of regional economic integration by using a rough and ready anti-monde model and the budgetary costs of being a member. These types of studies are heroic attempts to discover the meta effects of membership. A good example of this type of approach is the study on the impact of British withdrawal from the EU (Hindley and Howe, 1996).

The problems of using anti-monde models and Cecchini types of approach mean that it is very difficult to obtain reliable and accurate information on the effects of regional economic integration on major economic variables such as trade flows, growth and employment. Therefore, empirical evidence on the effects of regional economic integration can only provide an indication of the economic gains and losses associated with regional economic integration.

Empirical studies

Numerous studies have attempted to estimate the effects of membership on a country joining the EU. Some studies have concentrated on the CU aspect of membership (Kreinin, 1969, 1972, Resnick and Truman, 1971; Williamson and Bottrill, 1971, and Balassa, 1987). Other studies have cast a wider net to embrace other elements in the balance of payments (Featherstone, Moore and Rhodes, 1979; Mayes, 1978, and Winters, 1987). These studies find little evidence of strong trade diversion effects. However, they do not indicate that the static effects of economic integration are large. Therefore, the main economic benefits of economic integration were thought to arise from the dynamic effects of establishing free movement. The first major study that investigated these dynamic effects was the Cecchini Report (Cecchini, 1988, Emerson *et al.*, 1988).

The Cecchini Report

The Cecchini Report established the main barriers that were to be removed by implementing Article 13 of the SEA. These barriers were identified by reference to those outlined in the 1985 White Paper, 'Completing the Internal Market', and by a series of surveys of businesses in the EU. The White Paper listed three main types of barriers that were to be eliminated.

1. Physical barriers – frontier controls and customs formalities.
2. Technical barriers – restriction on economic activities resulting from national rules and regulations. These include technical specifications

which limit or prevent trade in goods; rules and regulations governing services which hinder non-domestic companies from trading across frontiers; discriminatory public procurement rules which limit tendering for government contracts to domestic companies, and legal obstacles faced by foreign companies seeking to set up subsidiaries in other member states.

3. Fiscal barriers – the need to adjust VAT and excise duties as goods cross EU frontiers. This is necessary as member states operate different coverage, and levy different rates of VAT and excise duties.

The Cecchini Report reclassified these barriers to estimate the benefits of removing these NTBs. Five main barriers were identified – tariffs, quotas, cost-increasing barriers, market-entry restrictions, and market-distorting activities practiced by governments. Tariffs and quotas had largely been eliminated by the CU, but some remained, in particular Voluntary Export Restraints (VERs) relating to cars and electronic equipment, and quotas on textiles associated with the Multi Fibre Arrangement (MFA). These were national quotas and were removed or harmonised to allow frontier controls to be eliminated. The majority of the benefits were thought to arise from eliminating the remaining barriers. Cost-increasing barriers include customs formalities such as VAT and excise duty assessments, verification of technical regulations, and costs incurred by companies in adhering to different technical regulations. These can include modifications to products, changes to packaging, etc. Market-entry restrictions include prohibiting or restricting access by foreign companies to the services sector, and rules and regulations that prevent foreign firms from bidding for public procurement contracts. Market-distorting activities arise from state aids such as subsidies, tax concessions, and other financial help given to domestic companies.

Using this taxonomy of barriers, estimates of the benefits of removing them were made. This was carried out for the EU as a whole; no attempts were made to estimate the redistribution effects of removing these trade barriers. The estimates were based on a four-stage assessment of the effects of creating free movement. Stage I is connected with the benefits from removing barriers affecting trade, i.e. frontier controls. Stage II benefits arise from the removal of technical and regulatory rules that increase the costs of companies. The reaping of economies of scale provides the benefits in Stage III. Finally, Stage IV estimates gains from increased competition leading to reductions in X-inefficiency and monopoly rents. The magnitude of these gains is outlined in Table 1.1.

There is some dispute whether the Cecchini Report attempted to quantify the impact of increased competition on levels of X-inefficiency. In Emerson *et al.* (1988) the tables indicate that estimates of gains from reductions in X-inefficiency were included in the Cecchini study; however, Smith (in Dyker, 1992) maintains that the Cecchini estimates do not include any effects that arise from reductions in X-inefficiency.

These benefits were deemed to stem from three separate but connected effects of removing the barriers to free movement. These were the effects of: (a) reducing frontier controls; (b) reducing market entry barriers; (c) reducing cost-increasing barriers. Effect (a) results from the reduction in the cost of frontier

Table 1.1   Estimates of the benefits of removing barriers to create the SEM

	ECU (bn)		as % of the GDP of the EC	
	(a)	(b)	(a)	(b)
Stage I Barriers affecting trade (frontier controls)	8	9	0.2	0.3
Stage II Barriers affecting production (technical and regulatory rules)	57	71	2.0	2.4
Stage III Barriers preventing the reaping of economies of scale	60	61	2.0	2.1
Stage IV Barriers which allow X-inefficiency and monopoly rents to exist	46	46	1.6	1.6
Total benefits	171	187	5.8	6.4

Notes:
(1) (a) Low estimates (b) High estimates
(2) For the EU6 plus the UK
(3) At 1985 prices
Source: Based on the Cecchini Report, Emerson *et al.*, 1988

formalities, that is delays at frontiers and administration costs of dealing with customs forms. The removal of these would have a small but direct effect by increasing trade between EU countries and would lead to secondary effects of lower prices and incentives to increase investment. Effect (b) arises when barriers are of such a high level as to prevent any entry into the market. Such barriers are common in public procurement where standards and rules and regulations can prevent entry by non-national firms. They are also obstacles to the free movement of labour and capital. The removal of such barriers would increase market entry which would lead directly to an increase in competition, and thereby to reductions in X-inefficiency and monopoly pricing practices. There would also be stimulation of investment to reap economies of scale, and to rationalise production and distribution systems. Effect (c) brings benefits by reducing costs incurred by different technical standards for goods, and by removing the barriers caused by the variety of rules and regulations governing key business and consumer services such as financial, legal, accounting and transport services. The removal of these barriers would lead to a direct lowering of costs by reducing the price of imported goods and services. There would also be secondary effects that would increase the degree of competition and the level of investment.

The bulk of the benefits are seen to derive from the effects of increased competition and lower costs that lead to lower prices, and stimulate investment. New market opportunities allow for increased economies of scale, and the rationalisation of artificially segmented markets. The increase in competition allows for considerable improvements in the effective use of inputs, and reductions in the anti-competitive practices of companies. This process is aided further by reductions

Table 1.2 Macroeconomic benefits of creating the SEM

	GDP (%)	Prices (%)	Employment (millions)	External balance (%) of GDP
Without accompanying measures	4.5	−6.1	1.8	1.0
With accompanying measures				
Public finance	7.5	−4.3	5.7	−0.5
External position	6.5	−4.9	4.4	0.0
Disinflation	7.0	−4.5	5.0	−0.2

Notes:
(1) Estimates for EU12
(2) Time scale 6+ years from full implementation of programme (assumed to be 1 January 1993)
(3) Estimates subject to a margin of error of ±30%
(4) Accompanying measures:
    Public finance – this allows for an expansion of public investment and/or reductions in taxation; if the full room for manoeuvre is used it results in the benefits shown above. External position – the benefits here assume that the Community seeks to maintain a balance of payments equilibrium. This reduces the potential for government-led expansion of the economy. This result is very dependent on the state of the world economy and, in the model used to make these predictions, on the exchange rate of the dollar. Disinflation – this assumes that there would be a utilisation of 30 per cent of the room for expansion of the economy which would be brought by the fall in prices and the improvements in public finances which follow from the creation of the SEM. This option would protect the external balance and would allow for a significant disinflationary effect on the level of prices, and also create more employment than the previous option.
Source: Cecchini Report, Emerson *et al.*, 1988

in the costs of business and consumer services made possible by the liberalisation of the service sector. The creation of the SEM is seen by Cecchini as a programme that boosts the effectiveness of the supply side of the economy. This improvement in the supply side leads to an increase in aggregate demand by increasing real purchasing power, increasing investment, and improving the competitiveness of the EU relative to the rest of the world. These changes to the supply side also lead to improvements in public sector budgetary positions, because of reductions in the costs of public procurement, and the growth of GDP that increases taxation revenues. This could allow for the consideration of a policy of expansion of the economy led by government expenditure. Such an expansion could help with temporary unemployment problems associated with the reconstruction of the economy, which is induced by the creation of the SEM. These supply-side changes improve the productive potential of the economy and enhance the ability to reach higher levels of non-inflationary growth. Such government-led expansion of aggregate demand would need to be coordinated to avoid problems of inconsistent growth levels. The Cecchini Report does not have much to say on this issue, but the implication of such a policy is that monetary policies would need to be coordinated to prevent the growth of monetary instability. Cecchini estimated these accompanying macroeconomic policies to have very significant effects on the overall benefits of creating the SEM (see Table 1.2).

The Cecchini Report was subject to considerable criticism because of its rather rosy view of the benefits and its underplaying of the costs of economic integration (see Davies *et al.*, 1989; Cutler *et al.*, 1989; Grahl and Teague, 1990). However, the report was a brave attempt to estimate systematically the economic effects of establishing the SEM. In 1996 the Commission undertook a large-scale review of the effectiveness of the SEM programme (*European Economy*, 1996; Monti, 1996; Commission, 1996a, 1996b and 1996c).

The Review of the Single European Market programme

The Review included a survey of 20,000 enterprises, a number of specific industry studies, an investigation of particular issues (e.g. public procurement, capital market liberalisation, price convergence, market concentration), and studies on the growth and regional development effects of the SEM programme. The Review concentrated on three main economic effects of the SEM programme.

- Allocation effects – improvements in efficiency in the use of resources.
- Accumulation effects – growth effects.
- Locational effects – geographical implications.

Allocation effects

The allocation effects of the SEM programme arise from the static effects (trade creation and diversion) and dynamic effects (economies of scale and the increase in competition) that were thought to be available from the establishment of the SEM. The Review covered the period 1987 to 1994. This is a relatively short time in which to estimate the effects of the SEM, especially as much of the necessary legislation to establish free movement was not implemented until the early 1990s. Moreover, there were very significant changes that affected the EU economy in this period, for example, German reunification, the transformation of Central and Eastern Europe, recession in continental Europe in the early 1990s. In these conditions, estimates of the effects of the SEM programme are somewhat suspect and should be 'viewed as a highly tentative exercise' (*European Economy*, 1996, p. 2).

The effects of establishing the SEM were examined by considering the implications of:

 (i) the removal of frontier controls;
 (ii) the reductions in costs associated with different technical regulations and standards;
(iii) public procurement liberalisation;
(iv) changes to the level and composition of trade flows;
 (v) developments in the nature of the competitive environment and in price differentials.

Frontier controls

Frontier controls were removed on 1 January 1993. However, due to the failure to harmonise VAT and excise duties and the continuation of the use of the destination principle (i.e. levying VAT and excise duties on exports at zero rate and imposing the relevant VAT and excise duties of the country of destination when the products crossed frontiers), a new taxation system had to be created. This system required companies to keep internal taxation records that allow exports to be zero rated for VAT and excise duties. This system is also used to estimate intra-EU trade flows. The Review estimated that this system costs companies ECU 2.3 billion a year to operate. There were also substantial set-up costs involved because of the need to create new IT accounting systems to record export activity accurately within the EU. Most companies reported that the costs of introducing and operating the new taxation systems were compensated for by the reduced costs of handling frontier formalities. However, some 20 per cent of companies claimed that in 1994 they had still not recovered the costs of introducing and operating the new taxation systems (Monti, 1996).

The costs associated with the VAT and excise duties systems could be substantially reduced if the proposal to move to an origin principle (i.e. charging VAT and excise duties at the rates that prevail in the exporting country) were to be implemented (Commission, 1996c). This proposal, if it were accepted, would allow companies to export within the EU without having to keep special records for taxation purposes. However, this proposal has not been approved by the member states.

Technical regulations

The Cecchini Report argued that the harmonisation of technical regulations and standards and the use of mutual recognition would lead to significant benefits. The survey of enterprises conducted for the Review discovered that some industries had benefited from the reduction in costs associated with different technical regulations (see Table 1.3). However, many enterprises reported that the SEM programme had not had a significant effect on the problems associated with technical regulations (see Tables 1.4 and 1.5). These results indicate that considerable efforts need to be made to create the conditions that will allow enterprises to take full advantage of a single market. The main problems appear to arise with acceptance of the principle of mutual recognition and the slow progress in establishing European standards.

Public procurement

The legislation to liberalise public procurement appears to have been particularly unsuccessful (see Table 1.4). Problems have arisen with implementing the public procurement directives and with the monitoring of the laws on free access to public contracts. The lack of European standards in many areas together with complex administrative conditions for public procurement contracts has resulted in a very low growth in intra-EU trade in the public procurement sector.

The results of the survey of enterprises indicate that there are significant problems with the legislative programme of the SEM. Poor implementation of EU laws and a lack of proper monitoring procedures have contributed to the continuance of costs to companies associated with technical regulations, freedom

Table 1.3 Impact of single market measures aimed at removing technical barriers

	Harmonisation of technical regulations and/or standards				Mutual recognition of technical regulations and/or standards				Conformity assessment procedures			
	positive impact	no impact	negative impact	don't know	positive impact	no impact	negative impact	don't know	positive impact	no impact	negative impact	don't know
Food, beverages & tobacco	35	44	9	12	30	48	8	15	24	52	6	19
Machinery & equipment	45	29	20	5	43	37	11	9	32	50	6	12
Electrical & optical machinery	36	48	9	6	50	36	6	8	31	52	8	9
Chemicals, rubber & plastics	33	47	10	10	35	49	7	10	27	53	6	14
Transport equipment	30	56	11	4	49	39	7	5	24	47	5	24
EUR 12	31	51	9	9	32	49	7	12	23	56	5	15

Source: Business survey, Eurostat, European Commission

Table 1.4 Industrial enterprises

Type of measure	Percentage of enterprises reporting the effect of the European single market as:				Percentage of enterprises, weighted by the number of employees, reporting the effect of the European single market as:			
	Positive	No effect	Negative	No opinion	Positive	No effect	Negative	No opinion
Harmonisation of technical regulations and/or standards	31	51	9	9	40	45	8	8
Mutual recognition of technical regulations and/or standards	32	49	7	12	40	45	5	10
Conformity assessment procedures	23	56	5	15	27	55	4	13
Simplified patenting procedures	13	64	2	21	24	57	1	18
The opening up of public procurement	9	71	4	16	13	68	5	13
The elimination of customs documentation	60	30	5	5	69	23	5	3
Deregulation of freight transport	43	43	3	12	50	38	2	10
The elimination of delays at frontiers	56	35	2	7	63	31	1	5
The change in VAT procedures for intra-EU sales	32	41	15	11	32	37	21	11
The liberalisation of capital movements	23	61	2	14	29	58	1	12
Double-taxation agreements	17	60	2	21	25	55	1	19

Source: Eurostat, European Commission

of establishment and in access to public procurement contracts. These issues require better systems for ensuring that EU laws on free movement are properly
implemented and effectively operated.

Estimates of the effects on trade flows

The Review discovered that intra-industry trade had grown rapidly in the period
1985 to 1994. Intra-industry trade was split into two categories:

(i) intra-industry trade in products with similar price and quality
characteristics;

(ii) intra-industry trade in products with dissimilar price and quality
characteristics.

The latter type of trade is based on competition where there are high, medium or low price and quality characteristics (e.g. low price and quality shirts

Table 1.5   General opinions on the single market programme

Percentage of enterprises agreeing or disagreeing with the following statements on the single market

Statement	Industry			Services (excluding distributive trades)		
	Agree	No opinion	Disagree	Agree	No opinion	Disagree
The single market programme has been successful in eliminating obstacles to EU trade in your sector	41	39	20	22	65	13
The single market programme has been successful in creating a genuine internal market in your sector	23	43	35	6	67	26
Additional measures are needed to eliminate obstacles to EU trade	27	61	12	18	75	7
Additional measures are needed in this sector to create a genuine internal market	25	61	14	17	76	7
The single market programme has been a success for your firm	33	40	27	16	63	21
The single market programme has been a success for your sector in your country	25	44	31	16	62	22
The single market programme has been a success for your sector in the European Union	29	51	20	15	71	14

Source: Eurostat, European Commission

or high price and quality shirts). This type of trade had grown from 35 per cent of total manufactured trade in 1985 to 42 per cent by 1994. In the same period intra-industry trade in products with similar price and quality characteristics remained constant at about 20 per cent of the total of manufactured trade. Inter-industry trade declined in all member states, but was still over 60 per cent of the total for Greece, Portugal, Ireland and Denmark (*European Economy*, 1996).

The SEM programme appears to have made a significant contribution towards the growth of intra-industry trade based on products that have different price and quality characteristics. The more developed member states have tended to specialise in higher priced and quality products while the less developed countries have concentrated on the lower priced and quality products. Germany tended towards the top of the price/quality spectrum whereas Benelux, France and the UK were more towards the medium end. Spain and Portugal were clustered around the lower end of the spectrum. However, Greece and some of the poorest regions of the EU (notably Southern Italy) had not developed a significant specialisation based on intra-industry trade (*European Economy*, 1996).

The observed growth in intra-industry trade based on price and quality differences is not unexpected as this is the fastest area of growth of trade for countries that have similar levels of development (Krugman and Obstfeld, 1993). What is surprising is the growth of such trade in Spain and Portugal. This may indicate that these countries are catching up with the more developed countries of northern Europe. However, in Spain and Portugal the focus is on the lower end of the price and quality spectrum. This may have implications for income growth as the production systems associated with such products tend to have lower value added characteristics than higher price and quality goods.

The argument that economic integration between countries of different levels of development will force less developed countries to specialise in inter-industry trade based on labour-intensive production is not borne out by the cases of Spain and Portugal. An even more remarkable case is provided by Ireland where substantial growth of intra-industry trade has been achieved, some of which may be attributable to the SEM. However, the Irish economy also seems to have benefited from its strongly market-orientated economic system and from the nature of its institutional system that has encouraged the changes necessary for growth (Monti, 1996). Nevertheless, the cases of Greece and Southern Italy indicate that membership of a regional economic agency such as the EU is not sufficient to develop the type of industrial structures that can deliver high value added production systems. Furthermore, the cases of Spain and Portugal suggest that adjusting to trading with countries with higher levels of development can be a long and painful business. These cases provide important lessons for the development potential of those Central and Eastern European countries that are allowed to join the EU.

The competitive environment and price convergence

The Review discovered that because of a substantial increase in mergers and acquisitions (many of which were cross-frontier) some industries had experienced a significant increase in firm size and a consequent rise in market concentration. However, in most cases this had not led to a decrease in competition as measured by price-cost margins (*European Economy*, 1996). This evidence supports the view that, to reap economies of scale, enterprises have been involved in mergers and acquisitions but the liberalisation of markets caused by the SEM programme has ensured that these benefits have been passed on to consumers by lower prices.

However, the evidence on price dispersion indicates that significant differences remain in prices across the member states (see Table 1.6). This evidence suggests that the longer a member state has been in the EU the lower are the price differences. It would seem that time is necessary to develop knowledge of price differences and to allow for the emergence of distribution systems that permit traders to take advantage of price differences.

The Review found evidence that price dispersal and price-cost margins in some industries indicated that the desired effects of the SEM had not been forthcoming (Monti, 1996). These industries were often those that had high levels of state aid and/or where the liberalisation process had been slow to take effect – for example, airlines, telecommunication services, energy, and industries with strong reliance on public contracts. However, in some of these cases there had been a marked increase in market concentration. This implies that consumers have been harmed by the willingness of national governments to provide state aids and to slow down liberalisation programmes while allowing enterprises to engage in merger and acquisition activities.

Table 1.6   Coefficients of price variation for selected groupings (based on prices including and excluding VAT)

	1980		1985		1990		1993	
	Inc. VAT	Excl. VAT	Inc. VAT	Excl. VAT	Inc. VAT	Excl. VAT	Inc. VAT	Excl. VAT
EU-6								
Consumer goods	15.9	15.7	14.2	14.2	13.5	13.4	12.4	12.6
Services	22.7	23.1	23.9	24.6	20.0	20.2	21.3	21.7
Energy	18.4	17.2	12.5	10.4	19.4	18.8	24.3	23.4
EU-9								
Consumer goods	19.9	18.8	19.1	17.7	20.3	18.5	18.0	16.6
Services	25.2	25.7	25.6	25.2	24.6	23.7	23.4	23.3
Energy	22.1	20.5	16.1	13.3	24.7	22.6	30.6	27.4
EU-12								
Consumer goods	—	—	—	—	22.8	21.8	19.6	18.4
Services	—	—	—	—	31.8	30.9	28.6	28.4
Energy	—	—	—	—	28.0	26.8	31.7	24.7
EU-15								
Consumer goods	—	—	—	—	25.9	24.6	19.6	18.4
Services	—	—	—	—	35.9	37.4	28.1	28.4
Energy	—	—	—	—	27.5	26.3	31.9	30.7

Source: Eurostat, European Commission

Accumulation effects

The short period that has elapsed since the beginning of the SEM programme made it difficult for the Review to estimate any growth effects. Moreover, significant shocks to the economic systems of the member states have occurred in this period – German reunification, the end of communism in Central and Eastern Europe, and the move towards EMU. Nevertheless, the Review estimated that an additional boost to growth of between 1.1 and 1.5 per cent of the GDP of the EU had occurred due to the SEM programme. This was thought to have generated some 300,000 to 900,000 extra jobs. Furthermore, the SEM programme is credited with reducing inflationary pressures associated with growth because of the supply-side improvements that have resulted from the establishment of free movement (Commission, 1996b). These estimates are subject to a considerable degree of possible error because of the problems outlined above. However, they are significantly lower than the estimates given by the Cecchini Report (see Table 1.2).

The low level of extra growth that can be attributed to the SEM programme may arise from deficiencies in the legislative programme that have limited the establishment of effective free movement. The special circumstances that were experienced in the early 1990s in Europe may also have contributed to the relatively poor growth performance of the EU. It is also likely that the Cecchini Report overestimated the likely growth potential from the establishment of the SEM. Nevertheless, it has been argued by some economists (see Fig. 1.11) that the Cecchini Report may have underestimated the possible growth effects.

Location effects

The growth of intra-industry trade has encouraged the development of geo-graphically based specialisation. The Review indicated that the member states had experienced a measure of convergence in levels of economic development that was at least partly attributable to the SEM programme (*European Economy*, 1996). Ireland and Portugal had made the most progress, but Greece and Southern Italy had not made significant progress towards closing the development gap. The heavy reliance by these areas on inter-industry trade, based on low labour costs, was held to be mainly responsible for the failure to improve the relative position of these economies (Monti, 1996).

However, reliance on inter-industry trade of itself is not a sufficient reason for the development gap. Denmark, for example, has a heavy reliance on inter-industry trade, but could hardly be regarded as a less developed economy. Ireland also had a strong reliance on inter-industry trade (although intra-industry trade grew rapidly in the 1990s). However, Ireland has been one of the success stories of development in the EU. Clearly, factors other than patterns of trade, free movement of capital and labour, and even access to the structural funds of the EU are important to the development process of the poorer member states. Modern theories of growth suggest that factors such as geography (Krugman, 1991 and 1995), institutional structures (North, 1990), the quality of factors of production (Romer, 1986), and the evolution of technology (Nelson and Winter, 1982) are crucial for the successful development of economies. In view of these considerations the Review indicates that the integration process *per se* is not harmful to the growth processes of the poorer member states, and it may contribute to successful development for those countries that have the appropriate conditions for sustained growth.

However, the tendency for integration to lead to specialisation based on intra-industry trade that is based on differences in price and quality factors may lead to concentration and locking into lower valued added activities. However, these forces may be at work in any system of international trade. Therefore, regional economic integration agencies such as the EU may only reinforce existing trends. The key to the development of high income economies appears to rest on the historical, geographical, institutional and technology conditions that prevail in the countries concerned.

Evaluation of the Review

The Review, like most Commission backed studies on the SEM, tends to paint a rosy picture of the effects of the integration process. Nevertheless, the Review was unable to confirm the estimates that were made by the Cecchini Report. In nearly every case the Review could not identify benefits of the magnitude that were suggested by the Cecchini Report. The difficulties of isolating those changes that are due to the SEM programme may account for some of the discrepancies in the size of the benefits. Those who considered that the Cecchini Report was an overoptimistic assessment of the effects of the creation of free movement can find some evidence for their view in the fairly low estimates of the benefits of the SEM programme that were found by the Review.

The Review highlights several areas where additional action by the institutions of the EU and by national governments is needed to improve the effectiveness of free movement. These deficiencies in the legislative programme and the need for stronger positive policies to create the conditions for effective free movement may be responsible for the relatively poor results that have followed from the SEM programme. However, the Review did find evidence that substantial changes had occurred with industrial structures, trading patterns and market conditions from the SEM programme. The Review does not indicate that the SEM programme has had no significant effects; rather it suggests that these have been fewer in number than was expected by the Cecchini Report.

The Action Plan to improve the operations of the SEM

The Commission has proposed a series of measures to improve the effectiveness of the SEM. These proposals have been outlined in an Action Plan (Commission, 1996c). The Action Plan identified four main strategic targets to achieve a more effective SEM.

1. Making the rules more effective by ensuring that legislation is properly implemented and enforced.
2. Dealing with market distortions by removing distortions caused by taxation differences, and anti-competitive actions including state aids.
3. Removing obstacles to market integration by the provision of positive policies to aid the integration of markets, for example R&D policies.
4. Delivering benefits from the SEM for all citizens of the EU by ensuring that consumer rights are guaranteed, protecting the social conditions of workers, and protecting the environment from unacceptable damage.

The Commission has proposed a plan in three phases to tackle these issues. The Action Plan hopes that these targets can be achieved by 1 January 1999. The Plan envisages the successful implementation of outstanding legislation together with any additional legislation that may be required to achieve effective free movement. A system of administrative cooperation between national governments and EU institutions is also thought to be necessary to ensure that EU laws are properly implemented and enforced, particularly in areas such as public procurement, mutual recognition, company law, intellectual property rights, and the remaining limitations to cross-frontier trade in financial services. The full liberalisation of the telecommunications services and the energy sectors is also given high priority in the Plan. Measures to remove distortions caused by different taxation systems and to tighten controls on state aids were also included. Very little is specified in the Plan on the means whereby the social conditions of workers should be enhanced or on the types of measures that are necessary to protect the environment. This probably reflects the growing disenchantment of many of the governments of the member states for this type of legislation.

The main thrust of the Action Plan is not new. The Sutherland Report of 1992 (Commission, 1992) contained many of the ideas that are central to the Action Plan. The Sutherland Report led to a large number of strategic documents (for example, Commission, 1993a and 1993b), most of which did not lead to any meaningful action. The Action Plan has also stimulated a considerable number of strategic documents from the Commission, most of which have not led to any significant changes (for example, Commission, 1996d and 1996e). The SEM programme has had a low priority in the Community since the move towards EMU assumed a dominant position occupying much of the attention of the institutions of the EU and national governments. Moreover, there has been a feeling among politicians and some business people that the SEM has been successfully completed and that the EU is now an effective free movement area. However, the Review and the Action Plan clearly indicate that the EU has many obstacles to overcome before an effective free movement area is in fact established.

The EU is also unsure about the type of free movement area that it wishes to create. The tendency has been towards creating a social market based system with strong legal conditions governing free movement. However, the poor employment creation potential of the European social market approach has led to some disillusionment with this system. Nevertheless, the EU has been unwilling to move towards a more American concept of free movement based on encouraging the development of competitive markets with only light legal control of market transactions. Moreover, the reluctance of the member states to surrender sovereignty in areas such as taxation, social security rights and company law has made it difficult for the EU to develop a social market type free movement area. The complexity that arises from the interplay between EU and national laws adds further to the problems of establishing a social market type system. The establishment of an American type of market-based system with light legal control of market transactions, but with strong laws on anti-competitive behaviour that limits inter-state trade, may be easier to implement in the EU than attempts to establish a social market approach. However, most of the member states are reluctant to travel along this path, but they are also unwilling to adopt a full-blown European social market approach. This confusion over long-term objectives is reflected in the problems that the EU has encountered in establishing an effective free movement area.

Conclusion

The attempts by the EU to integrate the markets of the member states have come a long way from the tentative beginnings of the ECSC. The formation of a CU and the SEM programme led to significant changes that have moved the EU towards greater free movement. However, the EU is not an effective free movement area in the sense that the USA or Germany are. The establishment of EMU may help in the move towards the creation of such a free movement area. However, the legal, institutional and economic conditions for an effective free movement area are not yet fully in place in the EU. Moreover, the EU is unsure of the type of free movement area that it wishes to create. The enlargement of the EU to include many of the Central and Eastern European countries is likely to complicate the process of establishing the free movement area still further. The long haul towards creating a free movement area that was started by the Treaty of Paris in 1951 still has a long way to go before the task can be finally completed.

References

Balassa B 1961 *The Theory of Economic Integration*, Allen and Unwin, London.

Balassa B 1987 Trade Creation and Diversion in the European Common Market, *The Manchester School*, Vol. XLII, No. 2, pp. 93–125.

Baldwin R 1989 On the growth effects of 1992, *Economic Policy*, Vol. 2, pp. 247–81.

Cecchini P 1988 *The European Challenge: 1992 The Benefits of a Single Market*, Wildwood House, Aldershot.

Commission 1985 *Completing the Internal Market: The White Paper*, Office for Official Publications of the European Communities, Luxembourg.

Commission 1992 *The Internal Market After 1992*, Office for Official Publications of the European Communities, Luxembourg.

Commission 1993a *Reinforcing the Effectiveness of the Internal Market*, COM(93)256 final, Brussels.

Commission 1993b *Making the most of the Internal Market*, COM(93)632 final, Brussels.

Commission 1996a *The Single Market Review, 38 Reports*, Commission/Kogan Page, London.

Commission 1996b *The impact and effectiveness of the Single Market: Communication from the Commission to the European Parliament and Council*, Brussels.

Commission 1996c *Action Plan for the Single Market: Communication from the Commission to the European Council*, Brussels.

Commission 1996d *Public Procurement in the European Union: Exploring the Way Forward, Green Paper*, Brussels.

Commission 1996e *Commercial Communications in the Internal Market, Green Paper*, Brussels.

Commission 1997 *The Competitiveness of European Industry*, Office for Official Publications of the European Communities, Luxembourg.

Cutler T, Halsem C, Williams J and Williams K 1989 *1992 – The Struggle for Europe*, BERG, Oxford.

Davies E, Kay J and Smales C 1989 *1992: Myths and Realities*, London Business School, London.

Dyker D (ed.) 1992 *The European Economy*, Longman, London.

Emerson M, Aujean M, Catinat M, Goybet P and Jacquemin A 1988 *The Economics of 1992*, Oxford University Press, Oxford.

Ernst & Whinney 1988 *The costs of non-Europe: An illustration in the Road Haulage sector*, Research on the Costs of Non-Europe, Basic Findings, Vol. 4, Office for Official Publications of the European Communities, Luxembourg.

European Economy 1996 Economic Evaluation of the Internal Market, Reports and Studies No. 4, Office for Official Publications of the European Communities, Luxembourg.

Featherstone M, Moore B and Rhodes J 1979 EEC membership and UK Trade in Manufactures, *Cambridge Journal of Economics*, Vol. 3, pp. 399–407.

Geroski P 1988 *Competition and Innovation*, Research on the Costs of Non-Europe, Basic Findings, Vol. 2, Office for Official Publications of the European Communities, Luxembourg.

Grahl J and Teague P 1990 *1992: The Big Market*, Lawrence and Wishart, London.

Group MAC 1988 *The costs of non-Europe in the foodstuffs industry*, Research on the Costs of Non-Europe, Basic Findings, Vol. 12, Office for Official Publications of the European Communities, Luxembourg.

Hansen D and Neilsen J 1997 *An Economic Analysis of the EU*, McGraw-Hill, London.

Herin J 1986 *Rules of origin and differences between tariff levels in EFTA and the EEC*, EFTA Occasional Paper No. 13, EFTA, Stockholm.

Hindley B and Howe M 1996 *Better Off Out: The Benefits and Costs of EU Membership*, Institute of Economic Affairs, London.

Jacquemin A 1982 Imperfect Market Structure and International Trade – some recent research, *Kyklos*, Vol. 35, pp. 75–93

Jacquemin A and Pench L 1996 *Europe Competing in the Global Economy*, Edward Elgar, Cheltenham.

Kreinin M E 1969 Trade creation and diversion by the EEC and EFTA, *Economia Internazionale*, Vol. 22, pp. 1–43.

Kreinin M E 1972 Effects of the EEC on Imports of Manufactures, *Economic Journal*, Vol. 82, pp. 897–920.

Krugman P 1989 Economic Integration: Conceptual Issues, in A Jacquemin and A Sapir, *The European Internal Market*, Oxford University Press, Oxford.

Krugman P 1979 Increasing Returns, Monopolistic Competition and International Trade, *Journal of International Economics*, Vol. 9, pp. 469–79.

Krugman P 1991 *Geography and Trade*, MIT Press, Cambridge, Mass.

Krugman P 1995 *Development, Geography and Economic Theory*, MIT Press, Cambridge, Mass.

Krugman P and Obstfeld M 1993 *International Economics: Theory and Policy*, Harper Collins, New York.

Lipsey R G 1970 *The Theory of Customs Unions: General Equilibrium Analysis*, Weidenfeld and Nicolson, London.

Mayes D 1978 The effects of economic integration on trade, *Journal of Common Market Studies*, Vol. 17, pp. 1–25.

Mayes D 1997 *The Evolution of the Single European Market*, Edward Elgar, Cheltenham.

McDonald F 1997 European Monetary Union: Some Implications for Companies, *Journal of General Management*, Vol. 23, pp. 47–64.

Meade J E 1955 The Theory of Customs Unions, North Holland, Amsterdam.

Monti M 1996 *The Single Market and Tomorrow's Europe*, Commission/Kogan Page, London.

Muller J 1988 *The benefits of completing the internal market for telecommunications services*, Research on the Costs of Non-Europe, Basic Findings, Vol. 10, Office for Official Publications of the European Communities, Luxembourg.

Nelson R and Winter S (1982) *An Evolutionary Theory of Economic Change*, Harvard University Press, Cambridge, Mass.

North D 1990 *Institutions, Institutional Change and Economic Performance*, Cambridge University Press, Cambridge.

Nugent N 1995 *The Government and Politics of the European Community*, Macmillan, London.

Pelkmans J and Vanheukelen M 1988 *The Internal Markets of North America, Fragmentation and Integration in the US and Canada*, Research on the Costs of Non-Europe, Basic Findings, Vol. 16, Office for Official Publications of the European Communities, Luxembourg.

Porter M 1990 *The Competitive Advantage of Nations*, Macmillan, London.

Pratten C 1988 *A survey of the economies of scale*, Research on the costs of non-Europe, Basic Findings, Vol. 2, Office for Official Publications of the European Communities, Luxembourg.

Price Waterhouse 1988 *The costs of non-Europe in financial services*, Research on the Costs of Non-Europe, Basic Findings, Vol. 9, Office for Official Publications of the European Communities, Luxembourg.

Resnick S A and Truman E M 1971 An empirical examination of bilateral trade in Western Europe, *Journal of International Economics*, No. 3, pp. 305–35.

Romer P. 1986 Capital Accumulation in the Theory of Long Run Growth, in R Barro (ed.), *Modern Business Cycle Theory*, Basil Blackwell, Oxford.

Schwalbach J 1988 *Economies of Scale and intra-Community trade*, Research on the Costs of Non-Europe, Basic Findings, Vol. 2, Office for Official Publications of the European Communities, Luxembourg.

Smith A and Venables A 1988 *The costs of non-Europe: An assessment based on a formal model of imperfect competition and economies of scale*, Research on the Costs of Non-Europe, Basic Findings, Vol. 2, Office for Official Publications of the European Communities, Luxembourg.

Tinbergen J 1954 *International Economic Integration*, Elsevier, London.

Viner J 1950 *The Customs Union Issue*, Carnegie Endowment for International Peace, New York.

Williamson J and Bottrill A 1971 The impact of customs unions on trade in manufactures, *Oxford Economic Papers*, No. 23, pp. 323–51.

Williamson O 1975 *Markets and hierarchies: analysis and antitrust implications, A Study in the Economics of Internal Organisation*, The Free Press, New York.

Winters L A 1987 Britain in Europe: A Survey of Quantitative Trade Studies, *Journal of Common Market Studies*, Vol. 25, pp. 315–35.

2 Macroeconomic policy coordination

Nigel Healey

Introduction

Growing economic integration increases the policy interdependence between countries. Only truly autarkic states are insulated from economic developments elsewhere. For countries linked by trade and finance, changes in demand and interest rates are quickly transmitted from one economy to the next. The external debt crises experienced by many developing countries following the 1980–82 recession in North America and western Europe, which cut the developed world's demand for basic commodities, remain among the most dramatic examples of this interdependence. More recently, the October 1987 stock market crash (and the smaller, but more virulent, crash of October 1997) bear testament to the speed with which developments in one financial market can be transmitted to the rest of the globe's financial centres.

Within the EU, four decades of economic integration have deepened and strengthened the economic linkages between the member states. In 1997, intra-EU trade had reached 14.1 per cent of EU GDP, compared with 8.5 per cent for extra-EU trade (see Table 3.1, Chapter 3). Cross-border investment, including mergers and acquisitions, as well as transnational movement of labour, have been systematically promoted through, *inter alia*, the single market programme. While the need for greater policy coordination has increased in line with closer economic ties, member states were, until the mid-1980s, reluctant to act cooperatively in setting macroeconomic policy. The pursuit of national self-interest led to countries pursuing divergent fiscal and monetary policies, which interacted across the EU to produce economic and financial instability.

The establishment of the European Monetary System (EMS) in 1979 offered member states which participated in its Exchange Rate Mechanism (ERM) an opportunity to coordinate their macroeconomic policies more effectively. After a spate of early realignments, the ERM successfully provided a framework for policy coordination between 1983 and 1992. Inherent weaknesses in the system, which were brutally exposed by the exchange rate chaos of 1992–93, led the EU to seek an alternative arrangement in the form of economic and monetary union (EMU) (see Chapter 3). This chapter examines the need for macroeconomic policy coordination within the EU and assesses the role of the ERM in promoting policy cooperation between the EU member states since its establishment in 1979 (see also van der Ploeg, 1991).

Policy interdependence between member states

The countries of the EU are primarily linked via the balance of payments (Cooper, 1968). Any change in macroeconomic policy within one country changes aggregate demand (and so its demand for other countries' exports) and its interest rate; and with flexible exchange rates, changes in interest rates mean a change in relative exchange rates vis-à-vis other member states, with further knock-on effects for aggregate demand in all countries. The induced effects and the path back to equilibrium depend upon the nature of the initial change in macroeconomic policy. Figs 2.1 and 2.2 show that changes in fiscal and monetary policy affect trading partners in different ways: with flexible exchange rates, an expansionary fiscal policy tends to 'spill over' and stimulate activity in other states; an expansionary monetary policy, on the other hand, has the opposite effect, increasing demand in the originating state (which benefits from an exchange

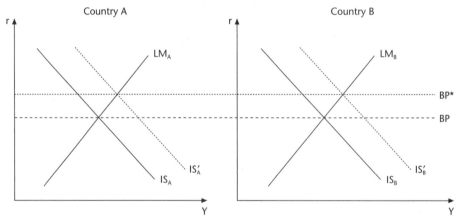

Figure 2.1   A fiscal expansion in country A (floating exchange rates)

Figure 2.1 shows the standard IS-LM model for a two-country world. The interest rate is on the vertical axis, with output on the horizontal axis. IS_A, LM_A represent goods market and money market equilibria in country A, and IS_B, LM_B represent goods and money market equilibria in country B. There is perfect capital mobility, which means that interest rates must be harmonised, here along the BP schedule.

Suppose that in country A the government increases government spending, shifting IS_A to the right to IS_A'. This fiscal expansion puts upward pressure on interest rates in country A and causes a capital inflow, leading to an appreciation of the exchange rate vis-à-vis country B. Part of the fiscal expansion is 'crowded out', limiting the rightward shift in IS_A. In country B, the fiscal stimulus on country A, taken together with the *depreciation* of its exchange rate vis-à-vis country A, leads to an induced shift to the right of its IS_B curve to IS_B' and upward pressure on interest rates in country B. Equilibrium is finally restored when interest rates have risen in both countries, shifting the BP function to BP*.

The final result of the fiscal expansion in country A is to increase output and interest rates in both country A and country B and cause the exchange rate of country A to appreciate vis-à-vis country B. As a consequence, the structure of demand in countries A and B is altered. In country A, government spending and imports are higher and (interest-sensitive) investment is lower. In country B, government spending is unchanged, investment is lower, but exports are higher.

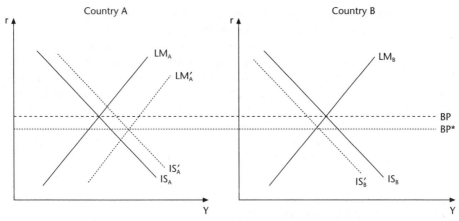

Figure 2.2 A monetary expansion in country A (floating exchange rates)

Figure 2.2 shows the effect of a monetary expansion in country A, shifting LM$_A$ to the right to LM$'_A$. This has the effect of increasing demand in country A and putting downward pressure on interest rates, inducing a capital outflow and a depreciation of the exchange rate vis-à-vis country B. This has the knock-on effect of shifting IS$_A$ to the right to IS$'_A$. In country B, the increase in demand in country A for its exports is more than offset by the appreciation of the exchange rate, shifting IS$_B$ to the left to IS$'_B$ and putting downward pressure on interest rates in country B. In equilibrium, output increases in country A and falls in country B, with interest rates falling. This effect is often known as 'exporting unemployment' by engineering a competitive depreciation. The pattern of demand is altered in country A (with consumption, investment and exports higher) and country B (with consumption lower and investment and imports higher).

rate depreciation), but reducing activity in the other countries (which suffer an exchange rate appreciation).

The speed and scale of the external effects of macroeconomic policy also depend upon the degree of economic and financial integration (Buiter and Marston, 1985; Hodgman and Wood, 1989). The greater the integration of goods markets (i.e. the openness of economies), the greater the extent to which changes in demand in one country will spill over to its trading partners. And the more integrated the financial markets, the greater the extent to which international capital will move across the foreign exchanges, changing exchange rates and driving together interest rates. The EU is highly integrated in both senses. The single market programme completed the elimination of non-tariff barriers to trade in goods and services, while also dismantling the remaining exchange controls that had previously allowed partial isolation of national money markets.

The discussion outlined in Figs 2.1 and 2.2 highlights the externalities involved in macroeconomic policymaking for interdependent countries. Under flexible exchange rates and with perfect capital mobility, part of the benefits of a fiscal expansion spills over to other trading partners, while a monetary expansion benefits the originating country at the expense of its partners. The terms of the 'share-out' in each case, however, depend upon the relative size of the countries involved. In the figures above, countries A and B are assumed to be of approximately equal size. Both share equally in the benefits of country A's fiscal expansion, while the proportionate boost to output in country A following its monetary expansion is broadly equal to the proportionate contraction suffered by B. If the countries are of unequal size, the share-out tips in favour of the larger country. For example, a large country will internalise most of the benefit of a fiscal expansion, while a small country will suffer most of the benefit spilling over to its larger neighbour. This issue of differing sizes is very important in northern Europe, where the German economy is very large relative to the smaller states (e.g. Denmark, Netherlands, Belgium/Luxembourg) with which it is most closely integrated. This question is re-examined in the discussion of so-called 'German policy leadership' later in this chapter.

The case for policy coordination

The existence of significant policy spillover effects raises the risk that, unless countries cooperate in setting policy, there may be significant inefficiencies (Cooper, *op cit*; Cooper, 1985). Consider first the case of fiscal policy under floating exchange rates. It has already been shown that, with perfect capital mobility, if a country pursues an expansionary fiscal policy, part of the expansionary effect will spill over to its trading partners. If all countries are seeking to reduce unemployment, smaller countries may be tempted to 'free ride' on the expansionary policies of larger countries. Table 2.1 summarises the impact of an expansionary fiscal policy on the initiating country, together with the induced effects on trading partners (free-riders). Significantly, both the initiator and the free-rider enjoy benefits in terms of increased output and employment. But the cost, in terms of a deterioration in the government's budget deficit and the current account, is borne by the initiating country, while the free-riders enjoy improvements in both sectoral balances (this is because for the free-riders the induced growth is 'export-led').

Table 2.1 suggests that countries have a strong incentive to free-ride on the expansionary fiscal policies of their larger trading partners. This tendency was in evidence during the mid-1980s (Ishii *et al.*, 1985). After the election of President Reagan in 1981, the new US administration embarked on a series of deep tax cuts designed to stimulate the economy. Output and employment did begin to recover, but at the cost of a large budget deficit and, as the US dollar appreciated due to the high US interest rates, an unprecedented current account deficit. As the value of the dollar peaked in 1985, the US administration accused the EU and Japan of free-riding on its expansion, enjoying the benefits of recovery while leaving the United States to pay the cost in terms of its budget

Table 2.1   Effects of expansionary fiscal policy (floating exchange rates)

	Initiating country	Free-rider countries
Government budget balance	Worsen	Improve
Current account	Worsen	Improve
Output/Employment	Increase	Increase

Table 2.2 Current account (% of GDP)

	1981	1982	1983	1984	1985	1986	1987	1988	1989
European Union	−0.8	−0.7	0.0	0.3	0.5	1.2	0.6	0.0	−0.5
Japan	0.5	0.7	1.8	2.8	3.6	4.3	3.6	2.8	2.0
United States	0.3	−0.1	−1.0	−2.5	−2.9	−3.3	−3.4	−2.4	−1.7

Source: adapted from European Economy

Table 2.3 Effects of expansionary monetary policy (floating exchange rates)

	Initiating country	Free-rider countries
Government budget balance	Improve	Worsen
Current account	Improve	Worsen
Output/Employment	Increase	Reduce

and current account deficits. Table 2.2 shows the divergent current account performance of the United States on the one hand, and of the EU and Japan on the other, over the 1980s, illustrating the basis of President Reagan's charges of free-riding. Under the 'Plaza Accord', the United States managed to coerce the leaders of the other two G3 countries, Japan and Germany, to adopt more expansionary fiscal stances and the imbalances gradually eased thereafter.

The external effects of monetary policy under floating exchange rates give rise to a different problem when macroeconomic policy is not coordinated. Recall that the country initiating the monetary expansion effectively 'exports' its unemployment to its trading partners, by using a competitive depreciation of its exchange rate to increase output by boosting net exports (since this is symmetrical, a country could equally export its inflation, by using a monetary contraction and an exchange rate appreciation). In this case, the risk is not of free-riding, but rather of retaliation by countries adversely affected by the negative spillover effects. See Table 2.3.

Uncoordinated monetary policy and the prisoner's dilemma

It is clear that, under floating exchange rates, it is the uncoordinated use of monetary, rather than fiscal, policy which poses the greater problem (Canzoneri and Minford, 1989). If other countries retaliate against a competitive depreciation by switching to more expansionary monetary policies, then not only will this cancel out the original depreciation, but all countries will be forced to adopt more inflationary monetary policies for no gain in terms of higher output and employment or an improved current account. In this sense, monetary policy is subject to the 'prisoner's dilemma' problem, in which rational decision-making by individual states leads to a collective outcome which is sub-optimal for all participants (in this case, inflation).

Under floating exchange rates, countries concerned to increase their competitiveness and employment face a choice between engineering a depreciation (by adopting a more expansionary monetary policy) or pursuing an unchanged monetary stance. The decision is complicated by the fact that their trading partners face the same choice. The pay-off to country A is positive if it depreciates and its trading partner, country B, does not, but negative (due to higher

Table 2.4 Uncoordinated monetary policy as an example of the 'Prisoner's Dilemma'

		Country A	
		Depreciate	*Do Not Depreciate*
Country B	Depreciate	−5, −5	−10, +10
	Do Not Depreciate	+10, −10	0, 0

inflation, with unchanged competitiveness) if both attempt to depreciate at the same time.

Table 2.4 illustrates the matrix of pay-offs that face each country. The first figure in each cell represents the change in economic welfare for country A, and the second for country B, of each set of outcomes. Clearly, their collective welfare is maximised if neither country attempts to depreciate its currency. However, for each country, the decision to depreciate is 'dominant'. For country A, depreciation is welfare-increasing if country B does not depreciate and the least welfare-reducing if country B does depreciate. Because the exchange rate policy 'game' is symmetrical, country B will similarly always choose depreciation. The net result is that both countries depreciate, cancelling out each other's attempt to gain a competitive advantage and causing only inflation (the worst possible collective result).

Because lack of coordination in the area of monetary policy provides the greater risk of a sub-optimal outcome, almost all examples of international policy coordination have tended to focus on monetary, rather than fiscal, policy (Foreman-Peck, 1991). Examples include the Gold Standard (*circa* 1821–1913), the interwar Gold Exchange Standard (1925–31), the Bretton Woods system (1944–73), the EU's currency 'snake' (1972–79) and the G3's 'Plaza Accord' (1985) and 'Louvre Accord' (1987). These all represent attempts to coordinate monetary policy through a system of managed (or fixed) exchange rates. In the absence of capital controls or other obstacles to the free movement of international capital, pegging the exchange rate to that of another country provides a mechanism for automatically bringing about convergence in monetary policies. It is to a consideration of managed exchange rates as a solution to the prisoner's dilemma that the next section turns.

Monetary policy coordination through managed exchange rates

While managed exchange rates provide a framework for coordinating monetary policies across participating countries, such arrangements do not completely eliminate the problem of uncooperative policymaking. This is known as the 'N-1 problem'. Within a managed exchange rate system, the monetary policies of the members must converge on some 'average' policy. The crucial issue is how that average is determined. For a very small country, managed exchange rates provide a discipline which forces its monetary policy into line with that of the exchange rate bloc as a whole. However, for large countries, their monetary stance both contributes to, and is determined by, the average monetary stance of the bloc.

The monetary effects of the balance of payments

Before turning to these more complex issues, consider the basic principle underlying exchange rate management. The starting point is the money supply identity:

$$M = D + F \tag{2.1}$$

The money supply, M, comprises the sum of domestic credit, D (i.e. bank credit to the government and private sector) and foreign exchange reserves, F. In terms of first differences (i.e. changes):

$$\Delta M = DCE + \Delta F \tag{2.2}$$

and

$$\Delta F = BP$$

so that,

$$\Delta M = DCE + BP \tag{2.3}$$

where ΔM is the growth in the money supply, DCE is domestic credit expansion (net bank lending to the government and private sector), and the change in foreign exchange reserves, ΔF, is equal to the balance of payments (on current and capital account) financed by foreign exchange intervention, BP. If the exchange rate is floating, there is no foreign exchange rate intervention by definition and $BP = 0$. For example, if there is a balance of payments deficit, this implies that the private sector's demand for foreign currency (to buy imports and foreign assets) exceeds the supply (from sales of exports, etc.). To maintain the target exchange rate, the central bank must satisfy the excess demand for foreign currency by selling from its official reserves, thereby reducing the domestic money supply. These monetary side-effects must continue as long as the balance of payments is in deficit. Herein lies the automatic adjustment mechanism of a fixed exchange rate system: payments imbalances automatically lead to changes in the money supply which work to eliminate the cause of the imbalance. For example, a country may have a balance of payments deficit either because aggregate demand is too high or because it is uncompetitive (i.e. at the target nominal exchange rate, domestic wages and prices are higher than those abroad). The monetary contraction caused by the balance of payments deficit will deflate aggregate demand and put downward pressure on prices and nominal wages, improving its competitiveness, until the deficit is eliminated.

Figure 2.3 illustrates the monetary linkages between member states in an exchange rate bloc. It shows that monetary policy becomes partly endogenous through the foreign exchange reserves component of the money supply, but that it retains an exogenous component through domestic credit. For small countries, almost all monetary discretion is lost in an exchange rate system because most of any exogenous increase in the money supply will be 'exported'. Large countries, however, can continue to exercise some monetary sovereignty. For example, consider two members of an exchange rate system. For country X, its money supply is equal to 5 per cent of the money supply of the bloc as a whole, while country Y has a share equal to 50 per cent. This implies that, if country

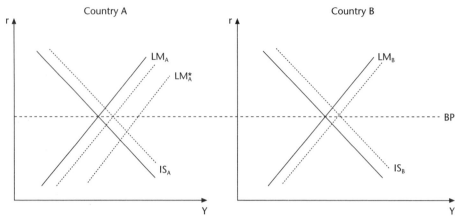

Figure 2.3 A monetary expansion in country A (fixed exchange rates)

In Fig. 2.3, country A pursues an expansionary monetary policy, shifting LM_A to LM_A^*. The result is a balance of payments deficit, which country A can accommodate in the short run by buying its own currency and running down its foreign exchange reserves. This foreign exchange rate intervention leads to a steady reduction in the money supply, gradually reversing the original shift in the LM curve. If country A is very small relative to the rest of the exchange rate bloc, then in time the monetary expansion will be completely reversed and the LM schedule will return to LM_A. Only the composition of the money supply will be altered (the domestic credit component will be higher and the foreign reserve element smaller).

The situation is altered if country A is large enough for the monetary spill-over effects to have an impact on monetary policy in other countries. In the figure above, the initial monetary expansion causes a rightward shift from LM_A to LM_A^* in country A, with a resulting balance of payments deficit. In country B, the increase in demand for its exports by country A leads to a rightwards shift in IS_B and a corresponding balance of payments surplus. For country A, the sales of foreign exchange reserves necessary to finance the balance of payments deficit gradually shift LM_A^* back to the left. But in country B, the purchases of foreign exchange reserves required to 'cap' its exchange rate in the face of a balance of payments surplus shift LM_B to the right. The resultant increase in output in country B feeds back to country A as higher demand for country A's exports, shifting IS_A to the right. Crucially, equilibrium is finally restored with output and the money supply higher in both countries. Country A has exported part of its monetary expansion to country B.

The significance of the relative size of the countries involved in an exchange rate system is clear. When one country adopts a more expansionary monetary policy, it increases the money supply of the exchange rate bloc as a whole. Because the countries are interlinked through the balance of payments, the money supply increase is gradually shared across all countries. For a small country, almost all the increase is 'exported', making monetary policy ineffective. For large countries, however, part of the increase is retained, giving them a residual power to use monetary policy for domestic purposes.

X were to increase its money supply by 10 per cent, 9.5 per cent of the increase would be 'exported' to the rest of the bloc. Across the exchange rate system as a whole, including in country X, the money supply would increase by only 0.5 per cent. For country X, its ability to pursue monetary policy would be effectively eliminated by its membership of the exchange rate system. For country Y, conversely, only half of an initial 10 per cent increase in its money supply would be 'exported'; that is, the money supply of the bloc as a whole, including country Y, would increase by 5 per cent, delivering a significant expansionary boost. For country Y, therefore, its domination of the exchange rate system allows it considerable residual monetary discretion.

The deflationary bias of managed exchange rates

Before considering the alternative ways in which the N-1 problem can be resolved, it is important to recognise a significant asymmetry in the monetary side-effects of exchange rate intervention. In the preceding discussion, it is implicitly assumed that all countries in the system, whether those with deficits or those with the offsetting surpluses, intervene to support or cap their exchange rates respectively and, crucially, that they allow the monetary consequences of this intervention to work its way through their economies. Consider, however, the situation faced by the two groups of countries. The deficit country will lose foreign exchange reserves for as long as the balance of payments deficits persists. The knowledge that, if its reserves run out before the deficit is eliminated, the country will have to either devalue or leave the foreign exchange system, means that countries with a deficit often take policy action to reinforce the automatic adjustment mechanism (for example, by reducing the domestic component of the money supply, tightening fiscal policy).

The surplus country, however, faces a different prospect. There is no limit to its capacity to accumulate foreign exchange reserves, while automatic adjustment implies allowing a monetary expansion to feed through to aggregate demand and increase prices and wages. There is a strong incentive for surplus countries, fearing the inflationary consequences of adjustment, to inhibit rather than supplement automatic adjustment. By selling, say, extra government bonds to its non-bank private sector, thereby reducing the domestic component of the money supply, a surplus country can 'sterilise' (i.e. neutralise) the monetary side-effects of its capping intervention in the foreign exchange market. That is:

$$\Delta M = DCE + BP \qquad\qquad\qquad (2.4)$$
$$\text{−ve} \quad \text{−ve} \quad \text{+ve}$$

In this way, a balance of payments surplus can be made consistent with an unchanged monetary stance, with the structure of the money supply shifting from domestic credit in favour of foreign exchange reserves. Clearly, if surplus countries sterilise their foreign exchange intervention, then the whole burden of adjustment to equilibrium must fall on deficit countries, which must adjust or leave the system.

This asymmetry is enormously important and gives surplus countries a powerful influence over the exchange rate bloc as a whole. In the absence of sterilisation, a country which increases its money supply 'exports' part of the increase to the rest of the bloc; conversely, a country which cuts its money supply can 'export' part of the reduction to the rest of the bloc. Sterilisation breaks the first of these links, but not the second. It prevents monetary expansions being exported and forces countries initiating monetary expansions to claw back the increase. But it still allows countries pursuing tight monetary policies to 'export' cuts in their money supply.

There are three possible solutions to the N-1 problem.

- Cooperative monetary policies, in which the members of the exchange rate system agree a common monetary stance, which is in the best interests of the bloc as a whole.

- Non-cooperative monetary policies, in which each country makes domestic monetary policy in its own self-interest, attempting to 'export' inflationary or deflationary monetary shocks. Given the deflationary bias due to sterilisation, the result will be that the low inflation members can pursue tight monetary policies, while the more inflationary members will be repeatedly forced to devalue or leave the system.

- Hegemony, in which the largest, low inflation member of the bloc dominates the rest, setting a tight monetary stance to which the others adjust.

This set of alternatives provides a useful way of categorising the operation of the EMS since 1979. Its architects set out to design a system built around monetary policy cooperation, in which symmetry was ensured and the participating member states would agree a common monetary policy. Its early operation, however, was marred by non co-operation, especially in the period 1979–83 and again in the period 1992–93. For the period in between, the EMS operated on a hegemonic basis, under so-called 'German policy leadership'. Since 1993, the EU has been attempting to build a new framework for monetary policy cooperation around a European Central Bank, issuing a single currency (see Chapter 3). It is to these issues that the next sections turn (see also Giavazzi *et al.*, 1988; Giavazzi and Giovannini, 1989; Portes, 1989; Artis and Healey, 1995; de Grauwe, 1997).

Monetary policy coordination through
the European Monetary System

The EMS began operation on 13 March 1979, with its membership comprising those countries which were then members of the EU. The core of the system, however, consists of those member countries which participate in the Exchange Rate Mechanism (ERM). The provisions of the EMS are basically fourfold and were originally designed to solve the N-1 problem through monetary policy co-operation rather than hegemony:

1. a set of provisions regarding exchange rates;
2. a supporting set of provisions regarding access to credit facilities;
3. a common currency of denomination, the European Currency Unit (ECU);
4. a framework for agreeing a common monetary stance.

The parity grid

The ERM is a system of fixed, but adjustable exchange rates. Its most important feature is the parity grid, which shows the central rates between each pair of member countries (see Table 2.5). The central parities can be realigned, but

Table 2.5 Central parities in the Exchange Rate Mechanism (October 1997)

	Sch	BFr	DKr	FFr	DM	I£	Fl	Es	Pta
Austria	100	293.163	54.2170	47.6706	14.2136	5.89521	16.0149	1456.97	1209.18
Belgium	34.1107	100	18.4938	16.2608	4.84837	2.01090	5.46286	496.984	412.461
Denmark	184.444	540.723	100	87.9257	26.2162	10.8734	29.5389	2687.31	2230.27
France	209.773	614.977	113.732	100	29.8164	12.3666	33.5953	3056.35	2536.54
Germany	703.550	2062.55	381.443	335.386	100	41.4757	112.673	10250.5	8507.18
Ireland	1696.29	4972.89	919.676	808.631	241.105	100	271.662	24714.5	20511.3
Netherlands	624.417	1830.54	338.537	297.661	88.7526	36.8105	100	9097.55	7550.30
Portugal	6.86356	20.1214	3.72119	3.27188	0.975561	0.404620	1.09920	100	82.9927
Spain	8.27008	24.2447	4.48376	3.94237	1.17548	0.487537	1.32445	120.493	100

Source: adapted from Eurostat, European Commission

only with the agreement of all other ERM members. Each member is required to maintain its currency's bilateral exchange rate against every other currency within a maximum permitted band of fluctuation around these declared central parities. The size of this band was ±2.25 per cent of central parity between 1979 and 1993. Exceptionally, countries could enter with wider transitional bands of ±6 per cent, which Italy, Spain, Portugal and Britain used before 1993. The standard band was increased to ±15 per cent in August 1993 following severe speculative pressures on some of the weaker currencies, although the Netherlands and Germany formally retained the previous narrow band for the guilder/deutschmark and Belgium/Luxembourg and Austria have informally respected the previous ±2.25 per cent band against the deutschmark (Collignon, 1994).

The present wide bands imply that, for instance, Germany must maintain its exchange rate vis-à-vis the French franc within a band FFr2.88810/DM–FFr3.89480/DM, buying deutschmarks when the lower band is reached and selling deutschmarks when the upper band is reached. Note that this obligation was intended to be symmetrical, applying equally to both weak and strong currencies. For the French central bank, its target band against the deutschmark is DM0.256750/FFr–DM0.346250/FFr, which is simply the inverse of the German bands. When the exchange rate reaches DM0.256750/FFr (i.e. FFr3.89480/DM), the French central bank must buy francs (using deutschmark reserves), while at the same time the German Bundesbank is required to sell deutschmarks, accumulating francs for its official reserves. Intervention is thus a collaborative effort, with the monetary authorities of the weak and strong currencies taking reinforcing action. Note, moreover, that in the absence of sterilisation such foreign exchange intervention will lead to a monetary contraction in the weak currency country and a monetary expansion in the strong currency country.

Credit facilities

As intervention in the foreign exchange markets is obligatory to prevent a currency from breaking through its bands, the ERM involves credit provisions under which the issuer of the strong currency is required to lend (without limit) to the issuer of the weak currency for purposes of intervention at the margin. The most important component of the credit mechanism is the so-called Very Short Term Financing Facility (VSTFF). Repayment is normally required within 75 days (45 days from 1979 to 1987), although revolving credits are possible. Finally, central banks also pool 20 per cent of their gold and foreign exchange reserves in exchange for ECU in a central fund, the European Monetary Co-operation Fund (EMCF), which has been superseded since January 1994 by the Frankfurt-based European Monetary Institute, the forerunner of the European Central Bank (see Chapter 3). This latter feature of the ERM has been used only infrequently in practice.

The ECU and the 'divergence indicator'

The identity of the EMS was enhanced by the provision for a common currency, the ECU. The ECU is a composite currency, consisting of a fixed quantity of

Table 2.6 European Currency Unit (October 1997)

	Amount in ECU	Weight in ECU (%)	Central rate/ECU
Belgian franc	3.43100	8.71	39.396
British pound	0.08784	11.17	
Danish krone	0.19760	2.71	7.2858
Deutschmark	0.62420	32.68	1.91007
Dutch guilder	0.21980	10.21	2.15214
French franc	1.33200	20.79	6.40608
Greek drachma	1.44000	0.49	
Irish punt	0.00855	1.08	0.792214
Italian lira	151.800	7.21	
Portuguese escudo	1.39300	0.71	195.792
Spanish peseta	6.88500	4.24	162.493

Source: adapted from Eurostat, European Commission

French francs (FFr1.33200), German deutschmarks (DM0.62420) and so on. The composition is chosen so that the respective currency weights in the ECU broadly reflect an average of their shares in the EU's GDP and trade. These weights are renegotiated every five years, with the next revision due in 1999. The ECU is used as the currency of denomination for EU transactions (e.g. for the EU Budget, farm support prices, etc.) and the central exchange rates of the ERM currencies are also expressed in ECU. Table 2.6 sets out the present composition of the ECU and the central rates for currencies remaining in the ERM.

Part of the rationale of the ECU was to prevent larger members of the ERM exporting inflation or deflation. The parity grid and credit arrangements *per se* would, by enforcing symmetry of adjustments, allow larger countries to influence the monetary stance of the ERM bloc as a whole. Given the scope for sterilisation, this meant in practice that the ERM faced the serious risk that the largest, low inflation country, namely Germany, would give the system a significant deflationary bias.

The architects of the ERM hoped that, by adding parities against the ECU to the parity grid and specifically limiting each currency's fluctuations against the ECU to less than the maximum permissible against other individual currencies, the system could prevent domination by large members. To illustrate the logic of this approach, consider a unilateral tightening of monetary policy by the German Bundesbank, which leads to the deutschmark appreciating x per cent against other member currencies. Because of the symmetrical nature of foreign exchange rate intervention, German open-market sales of deutschmarks (which, in any event, may be sterilised to prevent an increase in the German money supply) would be paralleled by open-market purchases of their own currencies by the N-1 other central banks, thereby allowing part of the German monetary contraction to be exported to the rest of the ERM bloc.

Against the ECU, however, the deutschmark will have appreciated by (1-wG)x per cent, where wG is the weight of the deutschmark in the composition of the ECU (approximately 35 per cent), while each of the other, smaller currencies, which have depreciated against the deutschmark but not against each other, will have depreciated by (wG)x per cent against the ECU. To illustrate this with some simple arithmetic, if the deutschmark appreciates 10 per cent against all other currencies, it will appreciate by 6.5 per cent against the ECU, while all other currencies will depreciate by only 3.5 per cent against the ECU. The ECU exchange rate therefore serves to identify currencies which are 'diverging', not simply from some other individual currency, but from all the others together.

The 'divergence indicator' was intended to impose a requirement for unilateral adjustment whenever a currency diverged from its central ECU rate by more than $0.75(1\text{-}wi)y$ per cent, where wi is the weight of country i in the ECU and y per cent is the maximum permitted deviation from central parities against other currencies (i.e. 2.25 per cent pre-1993, 15 per cent thereafter). The key point is that this threshold would be reached first by a currency moving out of line with the average, thereby forcing adjustment on countries pursuing a monetary policy at variance with its ERM partners. This concept of singling out a particular currency and forcing the presumption of adjustment upon it, whatever the direction of its deviation (i.e. weak or strong), was greeted as a radical innovation at the time of the inception of the system, promising a correction of the bias against weak currency (i.e. deficit) countries which tends to be endemic in fixed exchange rate systems. More directly, it was an attempt to free the EMS from German policy dominance, which had given a strong deflationary bias to earlier EU attempts at policy coordination.

Monetary policy cooperation

Having built in mechanisms to ensure symmetry of adjustment and to prevent individual countries 'exporting' inflationary or deflationary monetary policies, the architects of the EMS sought to solve the N-1 problem by cooperative making of monetary policy. Each month, the governors of the EU's central banks would meet to review economic conditions and revise their individual monetary policy targets, to ensure an internally consistent approach to fighting inflation and stabilising the real economy. In practice, however, the failure to prevent sterilisation by the surplus countries, a reluctance to use the divergence indicator as intended, and initially divergent views of the goals of monetary policy mean that the vision of cooperative policy making coordinated through the ERM was doomed from the outset. In the years that followed, non-cooperative policy making and the resulting exchange rate instability gave way to German hegemony.

Non-cooperative monetary policy making, 1979–83

The early years of the EMS can best be described as a period of non-cooperative monetary policy making and featured a number of realignments of central parities. Table 2.7 shows the dates and sizes involved of all the realignments undertaken between 1979 and the move to wider (15 per cent) bands in August 1993. It shows the frequent, generalised realignments which took place in the first four years of the EMS. The frequency with which realignments occurred provoked the description of the early EMS as a 'crawling peg' (e.g. Gros and Thygesen, 1992). This was a reference to the concept devised by Williamson in the 1960s

Table 2.7 Realignments within the Exchange Rate Mechanism

	B/L	DK	D	EL	E	F	IRL	I	NL	A	P	FIN	S	UK
24/9/79		−2.9	+2.0											
30/11/79		−4.8												
23/3/81								−6.0						
5/10/81			+5.5			−3.0		+3.0	+5.5					
22/2/82	−8.5	−3.0												
14/6/82			+4.25			−5.75		−2.75	+4.25					
21/3/83	+1.5	+2.5	+5.5			−2.5	−3.5	−2.5	+3.5					
22/7/85	+2.0	+2.0	+2.0			+2.0	+2.0	−6.0	+2.0					
7/4/86	+1.0	+1.0	+3.0			−3.0			+3.0					
4/8/86							−8.0							
12/1/87	+2.0		+3.0						+3.0					
8/1/90								−3.7						
8/9/92					Float									
13/9/92								−7.0						
16/9/92														Float
17/9/92					−5.0			Float						
19/11/92													Float	
22/11/92					−6.0						−6.0			
1/2/93							−10.0							
13/3/93					−8.0						−6.5			
2/8/93		Target	bands	widened	to	±15%								
6/3/95					−7.0						−3.5			

Notes: B/L = Belgium/Luxembourg; DK = Denmark; D = Germany; EL = Greece; E = Spain; F = France;
IRL = Ireland; I = Italy; NL = Netherlands; A = Austria; P = Portugal; FIN = Finland
Source: adapted from Eurostat, European Commission

(Williamson, 1983) of an exchange rate system in which real rates of exchange (i.e. nominal exchange rates adjusted for differential national inflation rates) are kept constant by periodically changing nominal rates in line with inflation differentials. Such a system allows countries to pursue quasi-independent monetary policies, while protecting their competitiveness (i.e. their real exchange rates). Between 1979 and 1983, inflation differentials were indeed high and member countries found it easy to resort to realignments to ape a 'crawling peg' arrangement.

This phase of the EMS proved temporary as countries began to adopt a more determined counter-inflationary policy stance. The pace at which countries adopted this new determination varied. For the system as a whole, the switch was gradual, but many commentators pick out the decision of the French government in early 1983 to adopt severe counter-inflationary measures as marking the end of the 'crawling peg' era (e.g. Sachs and Wyplosz, 1986). This convergence in policy objectives on the tough, anti-inflationary stance of the German Bundesbank made formerly expansion-minded countries like France and Italy more prepared to accept German hegemony. Thereafter, they increasingly allowed Germany to 'export' deflation and chose to follow the German policy lead, rather than seeking the soft option of devaluation. Paradoxically, the threat of German hegemony which had so preoccupied the architects of the EMS gradually came to be seen by its members as a positive strength in the mid-1980s, rather than a weakness (Wyplosz, 1989).

German policy leadership, 1983–92

The end of the 'crawling peg' period gave way to a period of German hegemony. Realignments became less frequent, as member countries consciously used their membership of the ERM as a means of disciplining inflationary expectations and achieving low inflation. The increased willingness of the other ERM members to accept German hegemony stemmed, in turn, from changing attitudes across the EU to the trade-off between inflation and unemployment. By the early 1980s, it was becoming increasingly accepted among EU governments that inflation is a 'monetary phenomenon' in the long run, so that higher inflation rates could not deliver sustainably lower levels of unemployment. It was the earlier belief in a stable trade-off between unemployment and inflation, and national differences over the point at which to strike a balance between these two social 'evils', which had resulted in the divergent national monetary policies of the 1970s. The gradual official conversion to the concept of a vertical long-run Phillips Curve (Friedman, 1968) persuaded many EU governments that price stability was the only sensible objective of monetary policy. In this new intellectual climate, the prospect of the ERM bloc being dominated by a low inflation Germany no longer caused the concern it had when the EMS had first been mooted.

Moreover, advances in economic theory suggested that, not only was German hegemony unlikely to impose long-run economic costs on other member states (in terms of permanently higher unemployment), but the ERM might actually reduce the transitional costs of achieving low inflation. The theory of 'reputational policy' (Barro and Gordon, 1983; Backus and Driffill, 1985) suggests that a country's ability to reduce its inflation rate and the cost in terms of higher unemployment of doing so depend on its 'reputation'. A government which is credible (i.e. has a good reputation) is able to make announcements about its counter-inflationary intentions which are believed and, because they are believed, inflationary expectations are reduced and the unemployment cost of getting inflation down is reduced.

The problem for the historically high inflation countries of the EU is establishing a reputation for pursuing low inflation, thereby reconditioning inflationary expectations in a way which makes disinflation less costly. ERM membership appeared to provide a solution: by maintaining an exchange rate fixed to low-inflation Germany, member governments were able to make a public commitment to price stability which was visible and easy for people to monitor and understand. For this reason, it became increasingly accepted during the mid-1980s that governments which participated in the ERM were able to 'import' the Bundesbank's anti-inflation reputation (de Grauwe, 1990; Weber, 1991). Shifts in governments' attitudes to the inflation/unemployment trade-off and widespread belief in the importance of reputation combined to make German hegemony not just acceptable, but positively desirable. Such was the transformation in government thinking over the 1980s that, by the time Britain joined in 1990, membership was publicly discussed almost exclusively in terms of the disinflationary benefits for Britain and hardly at all in terms of greater exchange rate stability on intra-EU trade.

During the period 1983–92, the evidence supports the thesis that German hegemony became established. For example, although all the formal provisions of the EMS are symmetrical, Germany sterilised the effect of foreign exchange intervention to a much greater extent than other countries, thus pursuing its own independent monetary policy. Foreign exchange intervention was almost always conducted 'intra-marginally' (i.e. before the exchange rate hit the band) and by countries other than Germany. Germany never devalued against any other currency in any realignment, and the divergence indicator fell into disuse (Mastropasqua *et al.*, 1988; Haldane, 1991). It is easy to see that, when the name of the policy game is the reduction of inflation, the divergence indicator would become useless (it would be inconsistent to ask Germany to raise its inflation rate towards the average in the name of symmetry when the overriding purpose of policy was to cut inflation).

The return of non-cooperative monetary policymaking, 1992–93

The phenomenon of high inflation countries choosing to follow Germany's anti-inflationary example, rather than devaluing against the deutschmark (or leaving the ERM altogether), was entirely unintended, but by the early 1990s had come to be regarded as the system's greatest attraction. Germany provided a strong, anti-inflationary anchor for Europe. By setting domestic interest rates at whatever level was necessary to maintain their exchange rates within their target bands against the deutschmark, other ERM states could effectively be guaranteed that their inflation rates would come down to low German levels. For countries (like Britain) which had unsuccessfully experimented with monetary targets and were left with no clear guide for monetary policy, ERM membership thus offered the prospect of both greater exchange rate stability and low and stable inflation rates.

However, while being one of its most attractive features, the German anti-inflation anchor also created a 'fault-line' in the system. The Bundesbank's hostility to unlimited intervention in support of weak currencies meant that currencies which fell to their trading floors were vulnerable to speculative attack. In other words, the ERM parities (and, indeed, the system as a whole) were simply not credible (Eichengreen and Wyplosz, 1993). During the 1980s, German policy leadership became steadily established, but the significance of the fault line was not fully realised for two reasons. First, until 1990 almost all the ERM members maintained some form of capital controls, which placed legislative restrictions on capital movements and artificially limited the scale of a speculative attack on a weak currency. Secondly, the business cycles of the EU economies were broadly synchronised during the 1980s, so that the policy adjustments necessary for other countries to follow the German lead and keep comfortably within their target bands against the deutschmark were relatively painless.

Tensions began to emerge almost immediately after German reunification in 1990. In order to control mounting inflationary pressures, the Bundesbank was forced to adopt a much tighter monetary stance, at a time when deflationary pressures were already intensifying in other EU states (notably Britain, France and Italy). The protection that capital controls had given to weak currencies was thus removed just as the costs (in terms of higher unemployment and lost output) of following the German policy lead were temporarily increased. Those countries which could not, or would not, continue to match German monetary policy accordingly became increasingly vulnerable to speculative attack, as high German interest rates forced their currencies towards their trading floors. For Britain in particular, international investors watched as growing political pressure to address the recession forced the Government into a series of interest rate cuts between October 1990 and September 1992, despite the fact that German rates were rising over the same period.

In the immediate run-up to sterling's withdrawal from the EMS clear signals given by the Bundesbank (to the effect that it regarded sterling as over-valued at DM2.95 due to a premature relaxation of British monetary policy) contributed to a massive speculative attack on sterling which (despite a 5 per cent interest rate rise on September 16, 1992) drove the pound below its floor and culminated in its formal suspension from the ERM. The Italian lira was forced out at the same time, and a series of devaluations by the remaining weaker currencies failed to settle the financial markets. Table 2.7 shows the spate of devaluations in the weeks following so-called 'Black Wednesday' on September 16, 1992. Eventually, with pressure refusing to abate, the EU was forced to introduce ultra-wide ±15 per cent bands in August 1993 to head off a politically embarrassing devaluation of the French franc. As de Grauwe (1997) notes, 'although in a legal sense the EMS remained in existence, for all practical purposes the system ceased to exist'.

Towards Economic and Monetary Union, 1993–99

The events of 1992–93 highlighted the inherent weaknesses that had been allowed to develop within the ERM. As originally designed in 1979, the system was secure against speculative attack. Provided that symmetry was maintained in foreign exchange intervention, the central banks of both the weak and strong currencies involved in a speculative attack must come to its assistance. While the capacity of the 'weak' central bank (which must use the strong currency to buy its own in the market) to support its currency is limited to its foreign exchange reserves and the amount it can borrow through the VSTFF, there are no such restrictions on the 'strong' central bank. The latter can sell its own currency in unlimited amounts to buy the weak currency and, in this sense, can always defeat any speculative pressure to force it into a revaluation of its currency.

German policy leadership and the deflationary bias of the ERM, however, turned on the Bundesbank's unwillingness to provide unlimited support to weak currencies, for fear of the inflationary consequences that the resulting monetary expansion would have caused in Germany. The growing commitment to low inflation across the EU and the broad synchronisation of business cycles during the 1980s allowed the fault line in the ERM to remain hidden, until it was brutally exposed by German reunification after 1990.

The travails of the ERM in 1992–93 have been interpreted in different ways (Svensson, 1994). One school of thought maintains that the speculative pressures of this period prove that the EU is unsuited to fixed exchange rates. If even a relatively modest arrangement like the ERM cannot work, in which there is a considerable margin for exchange rate fluctuations and scope to realign central parities periodically, then there is little point in further monetary integration. Within the core EU states, however, a different lesson has been learned. The disintegration of the ERM proves not that the original design was misconceived, but rather that German policy leadership was allowed to develop contrary to the intentions of its architects. Supporters of greater monetary integration point out that, had the system of monetary policy cooperation operated as intended, then the ERM could have provided a framework for low inflation without exposing the system to speculative attack. The German Bundesbank would have been able to support weaker currencies at times of speculative pressure, without having to worry that its long-run objectives of low inflation would be undermined by other states.

The EU's vision of economic and monetary union (EMU), which was incorporated into the Treaty on European Union and will be introduced in 1999, is the preferred way of reconstructing the EMS. Within EMU, exchange rates are irrevocably locked. Until national currencies are replaced by a common currency, the euro, in 2002, this implies that foreign exchange intervention to defend the central parities must be symmetrical and unlimited. At the same time, monetary policy will be set cooperatively. However, the decision-making body will not be a loose arrangement of national central banks, but a single European Central Bank (ECB) which is constitutionally bound to pursue low inflation and is independent from national governments. The ECB will provide cooperative policy making with a Bundesbank-like commitment to price stability, but will focus on the monetary situation across the euro zone, rather than exclusively in Germany. For the EU, therefore, the failure of the EMS has provided greater impetus for EMU, as a way of providing a more robust framework for coordinating monetary policy across member states. It is to the examination of the issues involved with EMU that Chapter 3 turns.

Conclusion

Increasing trade and financial integration has steadily increased the economic inter-linkages between the member states of the EU. As a result, fiscal and monetary policies pursued by one member state spill over and affect exchange rates, interest rates and economic activity across the rest of the EU. In the absence of formal mechanisms for coordination, fiscal and monetary policies have different external effects. With floating exchange rates, the external effects of fiscal policy tend to be positive: a fiscal stimulus in one country tends to boost output and employment in others. Monetary policy leads to more destructive 'beggar-thy-neighbour' effects: a monetary expansion 'exports' unemployment to other countries. Monetary policy is therefore plagued by 'prisoner's dilemma' considerations, with non-cooperation likely to lead to sub-optimal outcomes for all countries.

Managed exchange rate systems provide the most common solution to this problem. However, such systems can be dominated by their larger members. Moreover, given the inherently asymmetric nature of managed exchange rate systems and the scope for sterilisation of monetary inflows by low inflation countries, there is a danger of a deflationary bias. The architects of the ERM tried to prevent this bias by building in mechanisms to ensure symmetry and promote cooperative monetary policymaking. In practice, however, the ERM was overtaken by a shift in government attitudes to inflation, which encouraged other member states to submit willingly to German policy leadership, making the original design redundant.

The system as it evolved was flawed by a fundamental weakness. German hegemony was inconsistent with guaranteeing unlimited support to weak currencies. The price of the anti-inflation anchor was a 'one-way bet' for speculators, whose activities effectively destroyed the system in 1992–93. The EU's reconstruction of a monetary policy framework has been around EMU, in which a tough, independent ECB will provide the anti-inflation thrust, while ensuring that, until the Euro is introduced in 2002, foreign exchange rate intervention will be symmetrical and unlimited.

References

Backus D and Driffill J 1985 Inflation and reputation, *American Economic Review*, Vol. 75, pp. 530–38.

Barro R J and Gordon D B 1983 Rules, discretion and reputation in a model of monetary policy, *Journal of Monetary Economics*, Vol. 12, pp. 101–22.

Buiter W and Marston R C (eds.) 1985 *International economic policy co-ordination*, Cambridge University Press, Cambridge.

Canzoneri M and Minford P 1989 Policy interdependence: does strategic behaviour pay?, in D Hodgman and G E Wood (eds.), *Macroeconomic policy and economic interdependence*, Macmillan, London.

Collignon S 1994 *Europe's monetary future*, Pinter, London.

Cooper R 1968 *The economics of interdependence*, McGraw-Hill, London.

Cooper R 1985 Economic interdependence and the co-ordination of economic policies, in R Jones and P Kenen (eds.), *Handbook of international economics*: Vol. II, North Holland, London.

de Grauwe P 1990 The cost of disinflation and the European Monetary System, *Open Economies Review*, Vol. 1, pp. 147–73.

de Grauwe P 1997 *The economics of monetary integration: 3rd edition*, Oxford University Press, Oxford.

Eichengreen B and Wyplosz C 1993 The unstable EMS, *Brookings Papers on Economic Activity*, No. 1, Washington DC.

Foreman-Peck J 1991 Historical reflections in J Driffill and M Beber (eds.), *A currency for Europe: the currency as an element of division or a union of Europe*, Lothian Foundation Press, London.

Friedman M 1968 The role of monetary policy, *American Economic Review*, Vol. 58, pp. 1–17.

Gros D and Thygesen N 1992 *European monetary integration: from the European Monetary System to European monetary union*, Longman, London.

Haldane A 1991 The exchange rate mechanism of the European Monetary System: a review of the literature, *Bank of England Quarterly Bulletin*, February, pp. 73–82.

Hodgman D and Wood G E (eds.) 1989 *Macroeconomic policy and economic interdependence*, Macmillan, London.

Ishii N, McKibbin W and Sachs J 1985 The economic policy mix, policy co-operation and protectionism: some aspects of macroeconomic interdependence among the United States, Japan and other OECD countries, *Journal of Policy Modelling*, Vol. 7, pp. 533–72.

Mastropasqua C, Micossi S and Rinaldi R 1988 Interventions, sterilization and monetary policy in European Monetary System countries 1979–87, in Giavazzi F, Micossi S and Miller M (eds.), *European Monetary System*, Cambridge University Press, Cambridge.

Sachs J and Wyplosz C 1986 The economic consequences of President Mitterand, *Economic Policy*, Vol. 2, pp. 261–322.

Svensson L 1994 Fixed exchange rates as a means to price stability: what have we learned? *European Economic Review*, Vol. 38, pp. 447–68.

van der Ploeg F 1991 Macroeconomic policy co-ordination during the various phases of economic and monetary integration in Europe, *European Economy*, Special Edition, No. 1.

Weber A 1991 Reputation and credibility in the European Monetary System, *Economic Policy*, Vol. 12, pp. 57–102.

Williamson J 1983 *The exchange rate system*, Institute of International Economics, Washington DC.

Wyplosz C 1989 Asymmetry in the EMS: intentional or systemic, *European Economic Review*, Vol. 33, pp. 310–20.

Further reading

Artis M and Healey N 1995 The European Monetary System, in N Healey (ed.), *The economics of the new Europe*, Routledge, London.

Giavazzi F, Micossi S and Miller M (eds.) 1988 *European Monetary System*, Cambridge University Press, Cambridge.

Giavazzi F and Giovannini A 1989 *Limiting exchange rate flexibility: the European Monetary System*, MIT Press, Boston.

Kenen P 1989 *Exchange rates and policy co-ordination*, Manchester University Press, Manchester.

Obstfeld M 1995 International currency experience: new lessons and lessons relearned, *Brookings Papers on Economic Activity*, No. 1, Washington DC.

Portes R 1989 Macroeconomic policy co-ordination and the European Monetary System, *CEPR Discussion Paper*, No. 342, London.

Economic and monetary union

Nigel Healey

Introduction

Inspired by the early progress made in 'completing the single market' under the '1992' programme, in 1988 the European Union (EU) charged the then president of the European Commission, Jacques Delors, with preparing a blueprint for full economic and monetary union (EMU). Buoyed by rapid economic growth in the late 1980s and early 1990s, the EU quickly moved to ratify the so-called 'Delors Plan' (Delors, 1989), signing the Treaty on European Union (TEU), commonly known as the 'Maastricht Treaty', in December 1991 and setting a final deadline of January 1999 for the start of EMU.

Gathering recession across the EU and unsustainable tensions within the European Monetary System (EMS) following the reunification of Germany in 1990 quickly punctured the optimism that had surrounded the Maastricht summit. Nordic unease about the pace and shape of European integration (which eventually culminated in Norway's deciding not to join the EU in 1995) led Denmark initially to reject the TEU in a popular referendum. Within the crucial 'Paris-Bonn axis', the French left became concerned that the planned independence of a new European Central Bank (ECB) might give future monetary policy a deflationary bias, while in Germany there was electoral resistance to the idea of giving up the deutschmark. In Britain, monetary unification was widely written off as an unworkable 'grand design' along the lines of the EU's ill-fated Mansholt Plan (1968) and the Werner Plan (1970), while wrangles between supporters ('Europhiles', 'Euro-enthusiasts') and opponents ('Euro-sceptics', 'Euro-phobes') of EMU caused deep divisions within the Conservative Government, contributing to its electoral defeat in 1997. Enthusiasm across the EU for monetary union reached its lowest ebb in the mid-1990s, as recession, currency upheavals and the social costs of preparing national public finances for entry took their toll.

Preparations for EMU nevertheless continued. The European Monetary Institute (EMI), the forerunner of the ECB, began operations from its Frankfurt base in January 1994. The 'euro' was chosen as the name for the new single currency, which would have the same value as the ECU at the time EMU was created. Under pressure from the new left-wing French government, a greater emphasis was symbolically placed on the need to support growth, as well as achieving price stability after the start of EMU. And while the optional, early start date of January 1997 was missed, the accelerating recovery in continental Europe encouraged member states to reaffirm their intention to begin EMU on January 1, 1999. The European Council convened in May 1998 and decided which countries would be admitted to EMU in the first wave (all member states except Denmark, Greece, Sweden and the UK). EMU will begin the following January when exchange rates are locked. It is planned that the euro will replace national currencies through a monetary conversion on January 1, 2002 (see European Monetary Institute, 1997).

Eight years after the Delors Plan set the EU on the road to monetary union, opinions remain divided. As the British chancellor of the exchequer, Gordon Brown, recently wrote, 'the issues involved are complex and reasonable people may disagree about them' (in Currie, 1997). This chapter examines the underlying economic issues surrounding EMU and considers the prospects for future developments.

What is EMU?

Economic and monetary union, as the term suggests, involves the integration of both the real (economic) and monetary sectors of participating countries. For the EU, economic union has always been a central goal. During the 1960s and '70s, member states dismantled quotas and tariff barriers to trade between each other and set up central policy-making institutions for managing 'problem' industries like coal, steel and agriculture. In the 1980s, following the 1985 White Paper (Commission, 1985) and the 1986 Single European Act, the EU set about dismantling the remaining non-tariff barriers to the free movement of goods, labour and capital, and economic union was largely achieved by the target date of 1992. The Maastricht Treaty focuses on adding the missing component of EMU, namely monetary union. In technical terms, a 'monetary union' consists of an arrangement between participating countries in which:

1. bilateral exchange rates (i.e. the exchange rates between one member state and another) are permanently fixed, with no margins for permissible fluctuations;

2. there are no institutional barriers (e.g. legal controls) to the free movement of capital across national frontiers.

For a genuine monetary union, both of these conditions must be simultaneously fulfilled. For example, prior to German reunification in 1990, the currency (the ostmark) of the German Democratic Republic (East Germany) had been fixed at a 1:1 exchange rate against the German Federal Republic's deutschmark since 1949, but this arrangement did not constitute a monetary union. The exchange rate was entirely artificial and applied only to official transactions within East Germany; state regulations outlawed unofficial currency trading and prohibited the import or export of ostmarks. In West Germany, where illegally smuggled ostmarks could be freely traded, the market exchange rate averaged approximately OM5/DM1 in the year before reunification.

In addition to irrevocably fixed exchange rates and the abolition of all capital controls (which have already been removed under the 1992 programme (see Cecchini, 1988)), the form of monetary union agreed in Maastricht involves replacing national currencies with a common currency. Although monetary union technically requires no more than permanently fixed, bilateral exchange rates, moving to a common currency has the advantage of eliminating the transactions costs of switching between national currencies and making the prices of different products across the EU more 'transparent'. The adoption of a single currency also helps to make the monetary union more permanent, by increasing the costs to participating states of withdrawing from the arrangement (Delors, 1988). It is easy to overstate this argument, however: one of the first actions of the newly independent republics of the former Soviet Union after 1991 was to break away from the rouble zone and establish their own national currencies.

The benefits and costs of monetary union

Economics textbooks typically characterise exchange rate systems as 'fixed' or 'floating' and, on this basis, monetary union can be seen as the 'hardest' form of fixed exchange rate regime (that is, an arrangement in which the value of national currencies can neither fluctuate within bands nor be periodically realigned). To a large extent, therefore, the economic arguments for and against EMU are an extension of the long-running 'fixed versus floating rates' debate (e.g. Artus and Young, 1979; de Grauwe, 1988; Krugman, 1989), which turns on whether the economic benefits of stabilising the exchange rate (reduced exchange rate uncertainty) outweigh the costs of giving up exchange rate flexibility (sacrificing 'monetary sovereignty'). These costs, in turn, depend critically upon the characteristics of the national economies (e.g. degree of wage flexibility) and the linkages between the economies whose exchange rates are pegged.

The additional dimension of EMU is the transition to a single currency managed by an independent central bank, which promises extra benefits over and above reduced exchange rate uncertainty. As noted above, a single currency makes prices more transparent and underscores the permanence of the monetary union. Moreover, the ECB, which has a mandate to pursue price stability and built-in protection (in the form of the 'Growth and Stability Pact') from the inflationary effects of large budget deficits, should be able to deliver low inflation and low interest rates within the euro zone. The following sections examine the main benefits and costs of EMU in turn (see also Eichengreen, 1990; Begg, 1991; Barrell, 1992; Emerson, 1992; Ackrill, 1997; de Grauwe, 1997).

The economic benefits of EMU

The benefits of EMU are reasonably uncontentious. For supporters of EMU, the euro promises an end to exchange rate uncertainty on intra-EU trade, elimination of transactions costs on cross-border trade, greater price stability and a guarantee of future monetary stability through the commitment of the ECB to price stability.

Table 3.1   Intra-EU and Extra-EU imports (1995)

	Intra-EU imports (% GDP)	Extra-EU imports (% GDP)
Austria	21.4	8.4
Belgium/Luxembourg	40.2	12.8
Britain	12.9	10.6
Denmark	16.4	7.6
Finland	14.0	9.7
France	11.3	6.4
Germany	10.5	8.3
Greece	14.5	6.9
Ireland	27.5	21.7
Italy	12.0	6.2
Netherlands	26.1	14.2
Portugal	24.3	8.5
Spain	13.1	7.1
Sweden	17.7	10.6
EU 15	**14.1**	**8.5**

Source: adapted from European Economy

Reduced exchange rate uncertainty

EMU would clearly end the uncertainty that exchange rate fluctuations currently bring to intra-EU trade and investment. While it is true that increasingly sophisticated financial institutions provide a form of insurance against exchange rate uncertainty, these 'hedging' facilities are not costless and their cost reflects the potential savings to the EU of adopting a single currency. Moreover, for long-term horizons, so-called 'forward' facilities are not universally available. Such considerations have a special importance for members of the EU, the raison d'être of which is to facilitate cross-border movements of goods, services, labour and capital. Advocates of EMU argue that the potential gains from membership of the EU cannot be realised in the long term unless countries are able to fully exploit their own, unique comparative advantages (Jenkins, 1979; Brittan, 1991). To achieve this, economic resources (land, labour, capital and enterprise) must be transferred from relatively less, to relatively more, efficient sectors and the commercial decisions which make such reallocations possible depend critically upon expectations of the future. Since uncertainty about the future course of intra-EU exchange rates may inhibit the restructuring of production by which the potential gains from greater trade are translated into reality, EMU should therefore accelerate economic integration within the EU (Emerson, *op cit*).

Critics of EMU point out that, while a single currency will eliminate exchange rate risk from intra-Euro zone trade, the euro itself will still be prone to fluctuations against other major trading and investment currencies, notably the US dollar and the Japanese yen. Table 3.1 shows that, for each of the member states, trade with other EU countries dominates their trade with the rest of the world. For the EU as a whole, intra-EU trade (measured by imports) amounts to an average of 14.1 per cent of GDP, with extra-EU trade amounting to 8.5 per cent of GDP. While the euro will benefit, and increase over time, intra-EU trade, whether EMU succeeds in reducing exchange rate risk overall will depend on the stability of the euro vis-à-vis the dollar and the yen, and the

Table 3.2   Average price differences (net of taxes) of same automobile

	1993	1995
Belgium	116	122
Britain	120	120
France	121	121
Germany	124	128
Ireland	115	112
Italy	100	102
Netherlands	115	121
Portugal	108	108
Spain	108	105

Source: adapted from European Commission

way in which the ECB manages its cooperation with the US Federal Reserve Bank and the Bank of Japan.

Transactions costs

Business and leisure travellers are all too familiar with the transaction costs involved in changing currencies. These charges are made by banks to reflect their deployment of resources (e.g. personnel and equipment), as well as the opportunity costs of holding stocks of foreign exchange (i.e. the interest forgone). For tourists dealing in small retail amounts, these charges can easily amount to 10 per cent of the value of the currency changed. For large, multinational businesses, however, the transaction costs of switching between currencies are much smaller (typically less than 1 per cent). Small and medium-sized companies (SMEs) which lack sophisticated treasury departments are likely to benefit more from the euro than larger multinational companies. Early estimates suggested that, for the EU as a whole, eliminating transaction costs by the adoption of a single currency would yield savings of between 2 and 3 per cent of total EU gross domestic product (e.g. Artis, 1989), but it is now widely agreed that the more likely savings will be between 0.25 and 0.5 per cent of GDP.

Transparent prices

After 2002, when national currencies are replaced by the euro, there will be common currency prices throughout the euro zone. This means that consumers and corporate buyers will be able to compare prices across national markets, in the same currency, thereby enabling them to identify unjustified price differences and switch to more competitive suppliers. Average price differentials for automobiles are shown in Table 3.2.

Low and stable inflation

The ECB, as designed by the architects of the Maastricht Treaty, should be a guarantor of low, stable inflation across the euro zone. Table 3.3 shows the average inflation rates over the last four decades. It reveals that Germany has successfully achieved low inflation over the period since 1961 and that those countries (Netherlands, Belgium, Luxembourg, Denmark, Austria and, more

Table 3.3 Average inflation rates

	1961–70	1971–80	1981–90	1991–97
Austria	3.5	6.3	3.6	2.6
Belgium	3.1	7.2	4.6	2.4
Britain	3.9	13.3	6.0	3.7
Denmark	5.8	10.4	5.8	1.9
Finland	4.7	11.5	6.4	2.5
France	4.3	9.8	6.2	2.1
Germany*	2.8	5.2	2.6	3.0
Greece	2.5	13.2	18.3	11.9
Ireland	5.1	14.0	7.1	2.2
Italy	3.8	14.6	10.0	5.0
Luxembourg	2.5	6.5	5.0	2.4
Netherlands	4.1	7.6	2.3	2.3
Portugal	2.8	17.3	17.3	6.1
Spain	5.8	15.0	9.3	4.8
Sweden	4.1	9.6	8.2	3.8
EU 15	**3.9**	**10.6**	**6.5**	**3.6**

* West Germany only 1961–91
Source: adapted from European Economy

recently, France) which have pegged their currencies to the deutschmark, thereby effectively using the Bundesbank to set their national monetary policies, have 'imported' a similar inflation performance. In contrast, countries like Britain and Italy, together with Spain, Portugal and Greece, have suffered persistently poor inflation records and EMU offers a way to break with their inflationary past.

High inflation rates impose costs on economies in several ways. First, there are 'menu costs', which arise from companies and retailers having to change their price lists continually. Second, high inflation implies high (nominal) interest rates. The 'Fisher effect' highlights the link between real interest rates (r), nominal interest rates (i) and expected inflation (e), where:

$$i = r + e \qquad (3.1)$$

In steady state, nominal interest rates move to compensate lenders for expected inflation, thereby maintaining the real interest rate. High inflation countries have high nominal interest rates, and *vice versa*. High nominal interest rates give rise to 'shoe leather costs'. By raising the opportunity cost of holding (non-interest bearing) cash, inflation encourages individuals and companies to economise on holdings of cash, resulting in small, more frequent withdrawals from banks. High nominal interest rates also distort the way that companies repay loans, by bringing forward capital repayment and shortening the acceptable lifetime of a loan. This may inhibit investment, even though the real interest rate is not affected. High inflation also tends to be more volatile. Because changes in relative prices are the 'invisible hand' which coordinates economic activity in a democracy, high and variable inflation may introduce 'noise' into the 'broadcast' made by changing relative prices, preventing the efficient working of a market economy.

Real interest rates may also be lower in member states of the monetary union that have had a record of high and unstable inflation. In such countries a risk premium is applied to interest rates to compensate for erratic changes in nominal rates caused by high and unstable inflation. If the ECB delivers low and stable inflation, the real interest rate may decline in those member states that have faced relatively high real interest rates (Emerson, 1992). However, if the ECB delivers higher and more unstable inflation than has been experienced in some member states in the monetary union, they will face an increase in real interest rates.

The economic costs of EMU

It is the costs of monetary union that have proved so controversial. EMU entails the 'pooling' of 'monetary sovereignty' (that is, transferring the power to change interest rates and the exchange rate from national governments (where it can be used with exclusive reference to national economic conditions) to the ECB (where it will be used to set policy for the euro zone as a whole). Experience suggests that the monetary stance appropriate to any single member state may not coincide perfectly with the stance appropriate to the euro zone countries as a group. The Stability and Growth Pact (Commission, 1997) also places limits on the extent to which governments may use the other instrument of stabilisation policy, fiscal policy, since budget deficits for participating member states may not normally exceed 3 per cent of GDP. The clear risk is that by taking away one instrument (monetary policy) and restricting the use of the other (fiscal policy), EMU may prevent governments from adequately stabilising their national economies in response to economic shocks.

This issue is considered in detail below. It is important at the outset, however, to draw a distinction between stabilisation policy and growth (or supply-side policy). It is now widely accepted by economists that 'inflation is a monetary phenomenon' in the long run. Under certain circumstances, monetary policy can be used to stabilise output and unemployment about their trend paths in the short run, but the trend paths themselves are determined by supply-side factors (e.g. rate of capital formation, investment in human capital through training and education, technological progress, size of the labour force, etc.) (see Fig. 3.1). Monetary policy cannot, in the long run, alter real economic variables.

Real economic convergence?

It is often asserted that EMU will be doomed because there is a lack of 'real' convergence across the EU: that is, large differences in real magnitudes such as unemployment, per capita GDP and economic growth. Table 3.4 confirms that there are indeed marked differences in the real economies of the EU. Unemployment in 1997 varied from 3.3 per cent in Luxembourg to 21.3 per cent in Spain, while per capita GDP (EU = 100) ranges from a low of 46.3 in Portugal to a high of 175.4 in Luxembourg. Average annual economic growth rates over the period 1980–97 show considerable variation, from 1.5 per cent per annum for Sweden to 4.7 per cent in Luxembourg (the richest state in the

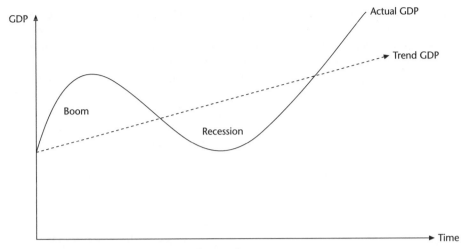

Figure 3.1 Stabilisation versus trend growth

The broken line shows the trend rate of growth of GDP over time, while the solid line shows the cyclical fluctuations in actual output about the underlying trend. Periods during which actual output exceeds GDP are typically termed 'booms', with 'recessions' characterised by episodes when actual GDP is below trend. Turning points in the economic cycle are signalled by the rate of growth of GDP rising above trend (the start of a recovery from recession) or falling below the trend rate of growth (the end of a boom and the onset of recession). The role of supply-side policy is to increase the underlying trend rate of growth of GDP. The purpose of stabilisation policy is to minimise fluctuations around trend GDP.

Table 3.4 Selected real indicators

	Unemployment, 1997 (% labour force)	Per capita GDP, 1997 (EU = 100)	Annual change in real GDP, 1980–97 (% pa)	Gross fixed capital formation, 1980–97 (% GDP)
Austria	4.2	113.7	1.9	23.1
Belgium	9.5	109.0	1.7	17.5
Britain	6.8	97.6	2.2	16.8
Denmark	5.1	142.3	2.1	17.0
Finland	14.0	104.8	2.1	21.7
France	12.5	111.7	2.0	19.8
Germany	9.7	120.3	2.2	20.8
Greece	8.9	52.6	1.7	22.5
Ireland	11.7	93.8	4.7	17.8
Italy	12.0	92.4	1.7	19.3
Luxembourg	3.3	175.4	4.7	21.6
Netherlands	6.0	106.8	2.3	19.9
Portugal	7.0	46.3	2.5	26.4
Spain	21.3	62.7	2.5	21.2
Sweden	9.9	118.4	1.5	17.8
EU 15	**10.6**	**100.0**	**2.1**	**19.7**

Source: adapted from European Economy

EU) and Ireland (the fourth poorest state in 1980, with a per capita GDP only marginally higher than Spain and Greece). Over the same period, one of the key supply-side factors contributing to growth and development, gross domestic fixed capital formation (over the period, 1980–97), also shows sustained variation from 16.8 per cent of GDP for Britain to 26.4 per cent for Portugal.

In the context of EMU, however, concern over the variance in real economic performance across the EU is largely misplaced. Monetary policy *per se* cannot permanently raise economic growth or reduce structural unemployment. These are supply-side problems which can only be effectively tackled by reforms to goods, labour and capital markets and by restructuring tax and social security systems. It is true that the transitional costs of establishing monetary union will be lower if business cycles among participating states are broadly synchronised (which implies a convergence of cyclical, rather than structural, unemployment and output gaps – the output gap being the difference between trend (or full-employment) output and actual output). This is discussed further below. However, focusing attention on the disparities in per capita GDP, for example, is misleading. Many unitary states have prosperous regions co-existing alongside highly depressed areas. Per capita income in northern Italy, for example, is among the highest in the EU, while the southern Mezzogiorno is plagued by high unemployment and widespread poverty; in Britain, there has been a 'north-south divide' for decades, with per capita incomes in the service-based south-east far above those of the declining areas in the north of the country. These differences reflect deep-rooted structural differences which monetary policy is powerless to affect in any sustained way.

The costs of pooling monetary sovereignty

The real costs of EMU lie in giving up the ability to use monetary policy to stabilise the national economy around its trend growth path. The power to make monetary policy will be transferred to the ECB, which will set a common interest rate and issue a single currency. National central banks will simply become the regional agencies of the ECB, with no independent power to alter local monetary conditions. The obvious danger is that the monetary stance (and the implied common inflation rate) chosen by the ECB may be inappropriate for certain member states. A useful starting point is to identify the conditions under which EMU would not result in greater variability of national output and employment about its trend path. Pooling monetary sovereignty will be costless if the following four conditions hold.

1. The business cycles of member states are synchronised and the objectives of the ECB are shared by each member state and the effects of the common monetary policy made by the ECB are the same on each state.
2. Fiscal policy (either by inter-temporal transfers or inter-state transfers) can be used to adjust demand differentially in member states.
3. Prices and wages within member states are perfectly flexible.
4. Goods and labour markets are perfectly integrated across the euro zone.

If condition 1 is fulfilled, it makes no difference whether monetary policy is pursued centrally by the ECB or independently by national governments. If condition 1 is not fulfilled, then EMU may still be costless provided that at least one of the alternative adjustment mechanisms set out in conditions 2–4 is available; that is, either demand can be stabilised by fiscal, as opposed to monetary, policy or asymmetric shocks to demand in member states can be absorbed through changes in real wages or movements of labour from areas of high to low unemployment.

'One monetary policy fits all'

Condition 1 is sometimes known as the 'one monetary policy fits all' requirement. If it is fulfilled, then the monetary policy stance taken by the ECB will be identical to, and as effective as, the policy response that each national government would choose in isolation. For example, in response to an inflationary shock, the ECB would raise the interest rate and reduce aggregate demand. If the inflationary shock is common to all member states and the interest-sensitivity of demand is the same in each country, and if member governments have the same aversion to inflation as the ECB, then it makes no difference whether the optimal policy response is taken by the ECB (on behalf of all member states) or by member governments individually.

In practice, business cycles across the EU have been rather desynchronised during the 1990s, in part due to the asymmetric shock to Germany (and, as a knock-on effect, to its smaller neighbours) from reunification in 1990. The federal budgetary outlays associated with reunification led to an inflationary boom in Germany, just as more peripheral states were moving into recession. Economic theory suggests that, with growing economic integration and a common monetary policy stance, business cycles should be broadly harmonised and, prior to reunification, there is some evidence that this was happening within the ERM countries (Artis and Zhang, 1995). While it seems likely that the EU will start EMU in 1999 with participating countries at different points in their business cycles, harmonisation should occur in the long run.

A major threat hanging over EMU, however, is that, even if business cycles do become harmonised over time, 'asymmetric' economic shocks (that is, supply-side or demand-side shocks which disproportionately affect one country more than the rest) may lead to sharp divergences in the future. The economic structures of member states are not identical; a sharp rise in the price of oil, for example, will deliver a positive boost to Britain as a net oil-exporter, but a negative shock to the rest of the EU. Moreover, further economic integration is likely to increase national specialisation in production. In the United States, which is widely taken as a model for the EU, individual states are much more specialised than is currently the case in Europe. The danger of asymmetric shocks causing business cycles to become desynchronised may actually increase, rather than fall, in future (Minford and Rastogi, 1990; Bayoumi and Eichengreen, 1992).

For pooling monetary sovereignty to be costless, it also requires that the objective functions of the ECB and the member states coincide. The constitution and statutory objectives of the ECB closely approximate those of the German

Table 3.5   Homeowners as a percentage of total households, 1994

Britain	France	Germany
66%	54%	40%

Source: adapted from Council of Mortgage Lenders

Bundesbank, which has a strong reputation for pursuing low, stable inflation (see below). Historically, the western (Ireland, Britain, France) and southern states (Portugal, Spain, Italy, Greece) have adopted a more expansionary approach to monetary policy, tolerating relatively high rates of inflation in the 1970s and early 1980s. However, there is now a widespread view among policy-makers across the EU that, in the long run, there is no trade-off between inflation and unemployment (i.e. the long-run Phillips Curve is vertical) and that the optimal objective for monetary policy is price stability. The Maastricht Treaty setting out this goal for the ECB was designed and ratified by all member states, which have all since made reducing inflation a political priority, suggesting that the likelihood of conflict between the ECB and member governments after 1999 may not be as great as once feared.

For EMU to be costless, national economies must behave in broadly the same way in response to a change of monetary policy. Critics of EMU point out, for example, that the interest-sensitivity of demand in Britain is typically higher than elsewhere in the EU, because a higher proportion of the population has borrowed money at variable interest rates (e.g. Britton and Whitely, 1997). There are clearly historical, cultural and social differences between spending and borrowing patterns in different countries which will mean that the interest rate chosen by the ECB is not optimal for every state, even if each were at the same point in the business cycle. On the other hand, increasing integration in the financial sector is likely to lead to convergence in borrowing and saving behaviour over time. It is also significant that the high levels of home ownership in Britain (see Table 3.5) are, partly at least, a rational response by individuals to monetary mismanagement by successive British governments in the 1970s and 1980s, when housing provided a tax-efficient hedge against high inflation.

On balance, it seems clear that condition 1 is not satisfied. Although business cycles are likely to become more harmonised, there is a real danger that asymmetric shocks will periodically cause a schism in the economic conditions of different groups of member states, making it impossible for the ECB to find a 'monetary policy that fits all'. Moreover, while all member states now share a broad commitment to price stability, national differences in financial behaviour may also mean that the interest rate appropriate to deliver low inflation differs from one country to the next, even if business cycles were synchronised. For these reasons, it is important that at least one of the alternative shock absorbers set out in conditions 2–4 can help to stabilise national output and employment.

Fiscal policy

In the short run, fiscal policy provides an alternative instrument to monetary policy for stabilising demand. In just the same way that individuals smooth their consumption over their lives, by borrowing in their earlier years to finance house purchases and saving in their middle years to provide income in retirement, so governments can borrow against future tax revenue to stimulate aggregate demand during a recession and repay past borrowing to depress aggregate demand during a boom. Moreover, economic theory suggests that fiscal policy may be more powerful with fixed exchange rates (or a monetary union) than with floating exchange rates. This is because government borrowing tends to raise interest rates and, with flexible exchange rates, the exchange rate will appreciate, crowding out net exports and dissipating the expansionary effects of the original fiscal stimulus. After EMU, governments will be able to borrow on a unified EU capital market, meaning that the deficit financing associated with attempts to stabilise demand within one country will have only a marginal impact on the EU interest rate, and so the value of the euro, and no impact on intra-EU exchange rates.

In this sense, national fiscal policy should, after EMU, provide a powerful replacement for monetary policy. However, the architects of the Maastricht Treaty were fearful that the increased ease of borrowing to finance budget deficits might lead some governments to pursue unsustainable fiscal policies. The Growth and Stability Pact imposes a limit of 3 per cent of GDP on the size of the budget deficit, although larger deficits are permitted to combat severe downturns (defined as four successive quarters in which the economy contracts at an annualised 2 per cent per year). Provided that member states plan for structural (i.e. full-employment) budget balance (or surplus), then a deficit ceiling of 3 per cent of GDP need not be unduly restrictive. However, given the structural deficits with which almost all member states approach EMU, the fiscal retrenchment needed to allow cyclical stabilisers to work fully within the 3 per cent ceiling is likely to be very painful.

An alternative way in which fiscal policy within the euro zone could replace the stabilising role of monetary policy would be through transfers between states, rather than between generations within one state. In a unified state, if one region suffers an asymmetric shock then demand is partially stabilised by a change in the net balance of fiscal transfers to other regions. For example, following the collapse of oil prices in 1985, Texas suffered a severe negative shock, which led to a sharp fall in income and employment. Federal tax payments, however, fell to reflect the lower level of activity, while federal disbursements increased to compensate for the greater poverty and unemployment. This shift in the balance of payments and receipts served to stabilise the fall in demand within Texas.

MacDougall (1977) explored this issue at great length in the context of the EU. Clearly, for inter-country transfers to play a significant stabilising role after EMU, the EU's central budget would have to be much larger than the present 1.38 per cent of GDP. The design would also have to alter. Although the EU has fiscal instruments like the European Social Fund and the European Regional Development Fund, these account for less than 25 per cent of total spending (which is dominated by the Common Agricultural Policy) and are, in any case, directed towards equalising structural differences in living standards rather than correcting short-term fluctuations in income and employment. The challenge would be to build into the central budget which transfers funds from countries with above trend output to those with below trend output, independently of per capita income.

In nation states, fiscal stabilisers play the role of redistributing income and stabilising demand. At a structural level, the fiscal system redistributes income from richer to poorer citizens. At a cyclical level, when a region suffers recession, its citizens become poorer and receive fiscal transfers from those in relatively richer regions. For the EU, given its large disparities between per capita income levels (see Table 3.4), a central budget which conflated the redistribution and stabilisation roles would be unwieldy and politically unacceptable. MacDougall (*op cit*) estimated that, by focusing on the stabilisation role, a fiscal system for the EU9 could have been constructed with a budget of 7 per cent of GDP. Currie (*op cit*) suggests an even lower figure of 4 per cent of EU GDP. Whether the poorer states would accept the principle of making fiscal transfers to rich northern states in recession is questionable, however. Without the redistribute dimensions, the moral imperative for fiscal transfers is greatly weakened.

On balance, with the Growth and Stability Pact restrictions on national fiscal policy and the low probability that member states will agree to the changes and expansion in the EU budget necessary to provide inter-country transfers on a sufficient scale to stabilise national demand, EMU seems likely to result in greater instability of aggregate demand within member states. The greater the differences between a member state and the 'average' EU state in terms of economic structure (and risk of asymmetric shocks) and responsiveness to changes in interest rates, the greater the instability. In the absence of the stabilisation provided at present by monetary and fiscal policy, adjustment will fall on either wages (condition 3) or labour migration (condition 4).

Wage flexibility

The foregoing discussion suggests that EMU may mean that centrally made monetary policy is periodically inappropriate to the needs of individual economies, while at the same time restricting the ability of national governments to use fiscal policy for stabilisation purposes without providing any increased fiscal transfers through the EU budget. The need for active stabilisation policy stems, in turn, from the inflexibility of labour markets. Clearly, if nominal (and real) wages were highly flexible, economic shocks (whether demand-side or supply-side) could be absorbed by changes in wages, rather than changes in employment and output. To illustrate the point, consider a simple case where there is a structural shift in demand across the EU, with consumers switching their preferences from French goods to German goods. In France, aggregate demand will fall, while in Germany aggregate demand will increase (see Fig. 3.2).

The time it takes for equilibrium to be restored depends critically upon nominal wage flexibility. If the excess supply of labour in France, and the excess demand for labour in Germany translate quickly into decreases and increases in nominal wages respectively, then the adjustment to the original demand-side shock will take place without serious dislocation to the real economies of the two countries. *In extremis*, if nominal wages are perfectly flexible, the two economies will simply slide down and up their respective long-run supply schedules (LRAS).

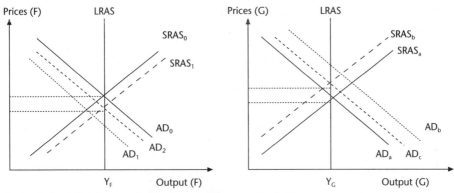

Figure 3.2 Adjusting to shocks by use of wage flexibility

In France, there is a fall in the aggregate demand from AD_0 to AD_1. If nominal wages are sticky, the economy moves down the short-run aggregate supply schedule, $SRAS_0$, and output falls below its trend or natural rate, Y_F. Prices fall, but with nominal wages sticky, real wages must increase and unemployment rises. Conversely, in Germany, aggregate demand increases from AD_a to AD_b and, again if wages are sticky, the economy moves up $SRAS_a$. In Germany, output increases above Y_G, prices rise and real wages fall, so that unemployment falls below its natural rate. For adjustment to long-run equilibrium, unemployment in France must push down nominal wages, shifting the short-run aggregate supply schedule down from $SRAS_0$ to $SRAS_1$. In Germany, the upward pressure on wages forces the short-run aggregate supply schedule upwards from $SRAS_a$ to $SRAS_b$. Falling French wage costs and rising German wage costs alter the relative price of French and German goods, leading to an offsetting shift in demand which increases aggregate demand in France from AD_1 to AD_2 and reduces demand in Germany from AD_b to AD_c. In final equilibrium, aggregate demand, prices and wages fall in France and rise in Germany, with both economies eventually returning to full employment.

If, however, there is nominal wage resistance, which is particularly likely in France where workers must take a cut in money wages, then the adjustment process will be more protracted and painful.

Figure 3.2 can be used to illustrate the alternative adjustment mechanism which EMU either closes off or restricts. The first, which is precluded by definition, is that the two governments could alter their nominal exchange rates to restore equilibrium. If the French and German governments could agree to realign their exchange rates following the demand shock, a devaluation of the French franc vis-à-vis the German deutschmark will restore the demand for French goods (shifting aggregate demand in France from AD_1 back to AD_0) and curb the demand for German goods (shifting aggregate demand in Germany from AD_b back to AD_a). Equilibrium can thus be restored without the need for output and wage adjustments.

Secondly, if the two governments agreed to coordinate fiscal policy in order to restore equilibrium, the French government could adopt a more expansionary policy (shifting aggregate demand in France from AD_1 back to AD_0), and the German government could pursue a more restrictive fiscal policy (shifting aggregate demand in Germany from AD_b back to AD_a). The difference between this policy response and devaluation is, of course, that such fiscal activism is only appropriate if the demand shock is thought to be transitory. If the demand shift

Table 3.6 Centralisation of wage bargaining

Low centralisation	Intermediate centralisation	High centralisation
United States, Canada, Switzerland, Japan	Germany, Netherlands, Belgium, France, Italy, Britain, Australia	Norway, Austria, Denmark, Sweden, Finland

Source: adapted from Calmfors and Driffill (1988)

is permanent, then eventually the French government will be forced to allow wages to adjust to achieve a sustainable equilibrium.

In the absence of either adjustment mechanism, the ability of member states to deal with economic shocks after EMU thus hinges on wage flexibility. The available evidence suggests that, while labour market institutions vary across the EU, in general European labour markets are much less flexible than, say, the United States (e.g. Heylen and van Poeck, 1995). The responsiveness of nominal wages to shocks is not, however, a linear function of the degree of trade union monopolisation, as many politicians suppose. As Calmfors and Driffill (1988) show, when wage setting is very decentralised (in the limit to company level), workers and their employers can observe the effects of their wage bargains on their competitiveness, so that wages tend to adjust more quickly to external shocks. The same is true for highly centralised, corporatist systems, in which national employers' federations negotiate directly with national unions. In this case too, unions and employers can take full account of the implications of their wage-setting behaviour for competitiveness and employment. It is in countries where there is partial centralisation that wages tend to be most unresponsive. Where trade unions represent only a proportion of workers in an industry and negotiate only with a proportion of the employers, it is difficult for wage bargainers to gauge the impact of their settlements on the employment prospects of the workers affected. The tendency is for unions to fight for wage increases and resist cuts, in the knowledge that their rivals are doing the same.

Table 3.6 shows the estimates made by Calmfors and Driffill (*op cit*) of the degree of centralisation of wage bargaining arrangements in different countries. It suggests that countries in the intermediate centralisation category are likely to suffer most from future asymmetric shocks after EMU, since it is this group which experiences the greatest nominal wage rigidities. This classification was based on labour market institutions before 1988 and places Britain in the intermediate group. It is likely that the reforms undertaken by the Conservative Government over the period 1979–97 have pushed Britain towards the low centralisation group, so that Britain may actually be better placed than Germany, France and Italy to deal with future economic shocks.

Labour mobility and optimum currency areas

In the absence of monetary or fiscal stabilisation, labour mobility provides an alternative to wage flexibility as a way of absorbing asymmetric shocks (Mundell, 1961; McKinnon, 1963). Refer back to Fig. 3.2. Suppose that, following the demand shock, workers were free to move between France and Germany. With wages sticky, French workers would become unemployed, while there would be excess demand for labour in Germany. If the unemployed workers move to take new jobs in Germany, the short-run and long-run aggregate supply schedules in France would shift to the left, and those in Germany to the right, until long-run equilibrium was restored at the intersection with the new aggregate demand schedules, AD_1 and AD_b. Labour migration thus provides a buffer in lieu of wage flexibility (Gros, 1996).

In contrast to the United States, where large-scale movements of labour have taken place in response to the changing economic fortunes of different regions, labour mobility in Europe is more limited (de Grauwe and Vanhaverbeke, 1991). Although the EU's 1992 programme to complete the single market abolished many legislative obstacles to the free movement of labour, different national languages and social and cultural traditions restrict the ability of workers to move to jobs. Moreover, it is highly doubtful if the EU has the political will to increase inter-country labour mobility seriously. The prospect of large numbers of unemployed, unskilled southern labour moving to take jobs in the richer northern states of the EU, placing demands on social welfare systems and creating ethnic tensions, is not appealing to many politicians. Indeed, the EU has always preferred to use regional policy initiatives to 'take work to the (unemployed) workers', rather than the reverse, fearing the social consequences of unfettered labour migration. It does not seem likely that labour mobility will provide a significant alternative to greater wage flexibility in the foreseeable future.

Predictable benefits versus uncertain costs?

On balance, it is clear that from an economic perspective the benefits of EMU are reasonably predictable and fairly modest, although to the extent that the euro stimulates more rapid integration they may be cumulative over time. Far more contentious are the economic costs of EMU, which are uncertain and unquantifiable. It seems likely that, although there are pressures leading to greater convergence of business cycles, the EU may be plagued by asymmetric shocks to different member states. Pooling monetary sovereignty necessarily means that the less integrated countries may be disadvantaged by a 'one monetary policy fits all' rule after EMU and fiscal policy will be unable adequately to take over a stabilising role, either at national or EU level. Adjustment will be thrown more heavily on wage flexibility and, to a much lesser extent, labour mobility. All of the major EU states (Germany, France, Italy and, to a lesser extent, Britain) are characterised by rigid labour markets, and major structural reform of labour market institutions may be necessary if EMU is not to lead to greater national instability.

The Maastricht Treaty and the road to EMU

The Maastricht Treaty set out the framework for achieving EMU by January 1999 and the constitution of the ECB. Under the terms of the Maastricht Treaty, the forerunner of the ECB, the European Monetary Institute (EMI), was set up in Frankfurt in January 1994. The ECB system is a two-tier central bank system:

- The ECB, which will have a president and an executive of six members appointed by the European Council for eight-year terms, and a governing council (the executive plus governors of the national central banks from participating member states).

- The European System of Central Banks (ESCB), consisting of participating national central banks, which will act as regional agents in carrying out the policy instructions of the ECB.

In drawing up the blueprint for the ECB, the Delors Committee and the European Council were greatly influenced by the economic literature on central bank independence, which suggests that governments can achieve low inflation by delegating control over monetary policy to an autonomous central bank (see Alesina and Grilli, 1992; Alesina and Summers, 1993; Healey, 1996). The German Bundesbank provides an exemplar of an independent central bank and, as Table 3.3 shows, it has consistently achieved the lowest inflation rates in the EU. The ECB was accordingly closely modelled on the Bundesbank, being forbidden to finance the budget deficits of national governments directly or take instructions from any political institution. Moreover, since the ECB will embrace, and operate through, national central banks, the Maastricht Treaty requires that central banks become fully politically and economically independent from their national governments before they may be admitted to the ESCB.

The convergence criteria

The Maastricht Treaty set out five 'convergence criteria' which member states must satisfy before they can accede to EMU in 1999. These convergence criteria fall into two categories: inflation criteria, which are designed to ensure that the transitional costs of joining are tolerable; and fiscal criteria, which are intended to guarantee that the ECB will not find its commitment to price stability undermined by profligate governments (Healey and Levine, 1992). Both categories have attracted intense criticism. The convergence criteria are outlined in Box 3.1.

Box 3.1   Convergence criteria

1. Successful candidates must have inflation rates no more than 1.5 per cent above the average of the three EU countries with the lowest inflation rates.

2. Long-term interest rates should be no more than 2 per cent above the average of the three countries with the lowest rates.

3. National currencies must not have been devalued and must have remained within the normal (15 per cent) bands of the EMS for the previous two years.

4. National budget deficits must be less than 3 per cent of GDP.

5. The national debt must be less than 60 per cent of GDP.

As noted above, if countries enter EMU at different points in their business cycles, adherence to a common, low inflation monetary policy will cause recession in the higher inflation countries. The three inflation criteria (items 1 to 3 in Box 3.1) are intended to provide a guide to the extent to which such convergence has taken place. The logic of these conditions is that, if satisfied, the short-run costs of pooling monetary sovereignty will be modest and, by implication, outweighed by the likely benefits.

With the exception of 2, these three criteria are self-explanatory. The significance of 2 lies in the fact that long-term interest rates provide a guide to the financial markets' expectations of inflation in the longer term. Put simply, today's long-term interest rate is a weighted average of expected future short-term interest rates. If investors expect inflation to be high in the future, they will expect short-term interest rates to be correspondingly high in the future as well. Today's long-term interest rate will accordingly be higher than in a country where inflation is expected to remain low in the future. Critics of the inflation criteria point out that inflation is only one dimension of the business cycle. The level of cyclical unemployment, the size of the output gap or the scale of the cyclical budget deficit all provide additional information about the extent to which business cycles are, or are not, harmonising across the EU. More seriously, by concentrating on nominal indicators, there is a danger that member governments seeking admission to EMU will focus their policy efforts on reducing inflation, at the expense of risking unsustainable real pressures (e.g. higher unemployment) to develop.

The rationale for the fiscal criteria (items 4 and 5 in Box 3.1) stems from the implications of creating an independent ECB with a statutory responsibility for maintaining price stability for national governments. An independent ECB would also constrain national public finances in two ways (see Healey and Levine, *op cit*). First, the right to issue 'fiat' money (i.e. notes and coin) is to be transferred from national governments to the ECB, so that 'seigniorage' profits would be lost to member governments (Grilli, 1989; Drazen, 1989). Such seigniorage profits stem from the fact that governments at present 'sell' newly created currency to their national banking systems for its full face value, while the actual production costs of printing notes and minting coins are much lower.

Table 3.7 shows that the southern Mediterranean countries (Greece, Portugal and Spain) would be particularly adversely affected by the loss of seigniorage profits. At present, these countries have relatively undeveloped financial systems, which means that their currency ratios (i.e. currency as a proportion of the money stock) are higher than in northern states. This region also suffers relatively high inflation rates, which continuously erodes the real value of currency in circulation, obliging the private sector to hold ever larger cash balances for transaction purposes. However, increasing financial integration and converging inflation performance should reduce seigniorage profits in the southern states as the deadline for EMU approaches.

The second implication of EMU for national public finances is that the requirement of economic independence for the ECB will deny governments the right of automatic, unlimited access to central bank credit. In contrast to the present

Table 3.7   Seigniorage revenue as a percentage of Gross Domestic Product

Country	Seigniorage revenue, 1994
Belgium	0.60
Britain	0.30
Denmark	0.32
France	0.40
Germany	0.57
Greece	1.37
Italy	0.74
Ireland	0.47
Luxembourg	0.16
Netherlands	0.60
Portugal	1.63
Spain	1.07

Source: adapted from Bank for International Settlements

arrangements within many member states, national governments will no longer be able to finance budget deficits (or refinance maturing government debt) by selling bonds to their central banks and increasing the money supply. To the extent that both the loss of seigniorage revenues and the ending of automatic credit facilities will make it more difficult for national governments to finance large budget deficits and refinance large national debts (i.e. as fixed-term bonds mature), the Maastricht Treaty requires that member states should control their budget deficits (limiting them to not more than 3 per cent of GDP) and stabilise their public debt:GDP ratios (at or below 60 per cent) prior to joining EMU.

The fiscal criteria, and their incorporation in the Growth and Stability Pact, have been strongly criticised (e.g. Buiter *et al.,* 1993). As discussed above, the need to use fiscal policy more actively will increase, not reduce, after EMU, since governments will need a replacement for the present stabilisation role played by monetary and exchange rate policy. However, while the fiscal convergence criteria appear very clear cut, the architects of the Maastricht Treaty provided room for discretion in their interpretation, which suggests that they may not prove excessively binding in practice. Article 104c of the TEU states that the European Commission 'shall examine compliance with budgetary discipline on the basis of the following two criteria:

1. Whether the ratio of the planned or actual government deficit to gross domestic product exceeds a reference value (i.e. 3 per cent), unless either the ratio has declined substantially and continuously and reached a level that comes close to the reference value; or, alternatively, the excess over the reference value is only exceptional and temporary and the ratio remains close to the reference value.

2. Whether the ratio of government debt to gross domestic product exceeds a reference value (i.e. 60 per cent), unless the ratio is sufficiently diminishing and approaching the reference value at a satisfactory pace.'

Table 3.8   Convergence criteria and outturns in 1997

	Inflation rate, 1997 (%)	Long-term interest rate, 1996 (%)	Debt ratio, 1997 (% GDP)	Budget balance, 1997 (% GDP)
1997 Criteria	2.9	8.2	60.0	−3.0
Austria	2.1*	6.3*	68.8	−3.0*
Belgium	1.9*	6.5*	126.7	−2.7*
Britain	2.3*	7.8*	54.7*	−3.5
Denmark	2.3*	7.2*	67.2	0.3*
Finland	0.9*	7.1*	59.2*	−2.2*
France	1.6*	6.9*	57.9*	−3.0*
Germany	1.9*	6.2*	61.8	−3.0*
Greece	6.0	—	108.3	−4.9
Ireland	2.0*	7.3*	68.3	−1.0*
Italy	2.7*	9.2	122.4	—
Luxembourg	1.7*	6.3*	6.7*	1.1*
Netherlands	2.4*	6.2*	76.2	−2.3*
Portugal	2.5*	8.6	64.1	−2.9*
Spain	2.4*	8.7	68.1	−3.0*
Sweden	1.6*	8.1*	76.5	−2.9*

Note: *denotes convergence criteria met
Source: adapted from European Economy

The outlook for EMU

In May 1998, the European Council convened to decide which of the 15 EU member states meet the convergence criteria. Of the 15, Britain and Denmark exercised their right to 'opt out' of the first wave of EMU, Sweden also did not wish to join (and was ruled out because of failure to keep the exchange rate critieria), and it was decided that Greece did not meet the convergence criteria. Of the convergence criteria, the provisions for exchange rate stability have been overtaken by events. In August 1993, following a long period of speculative pressure on the foreign exchange markets which drove the British pound and the Italian lira out of the ERM and forced Ireland, Spain and Portugal to devalue, the EU decided to widen the target bands from (±2.25 per cent to ±15 per cent, making depreciations of up to 30 per cent technically possible within the 'normal' bands of the ERM. It seems unlikely that the European Council would be able to exclude countries formally outside the ERM (like Britain) which have nevertheless 'shadowed' the ERM and maintained their exchange rates, albeit informally, within the new, wider bands.

Table 3.8 shows the state of the EU15 countries with reference to the other four quantitative convergence criteria in 1997 (see European Monetary Institute, 1996). Only Finland, France and Luxembourg unequivocally fulfil these four conditions for entry. The room for manoeuvre built into the fiscal criteria at Maastricht means that Germany, Denmark, Austria, Sweden, Ireland and the Netherlands (and with a generous interpretation, Italy and Belgium) are likely to satisfy the caveat requiring that 'the ratio [for public debt to GDP] is sufficiently diminishing and approaching the reference value at a satisfactory pace'.

Of the remaining member states, Britain, Portugal and Spain are close to satis-fying the convergence criteria. Only Greece, which is compromised by decades of fiscal mismanagement, appears isolated from EMU in the medium term.

Conclusion

The business cycles of the EU member states are desynchronised and their re-sponsiveness to the guiding hand of monetary policy is variable. The Maastricht Treaty restricts the ability of member governments to use fiscal policy to stabilise demand, and a centralised budgetary system capable of making significant inter-state transfers is many years away. Many of the most important EU states are characterised by labour market rigidities and labour mobility is limited in comparison with mature, federal monetary unions like the United States. While the introduction of a single currency would greatly benefit the EU by eliminat-ing exchange rate risk and promoting international trade and investment between member states, there is a significant threat of greater, rather than reduced, volatility in national economies. The key problem is that, while the Maastricht convergence criteria will reduce the transitional costs of 'settling into' a future EMU (by forcing convergence before, rather than after, monetary unification), there is a strong likelihood that the 15 member states will continue to be buf-feted by asymmetric stocks after the introduction of a single currency.

In the presence of wage 'stickiness', the sacrifice of monetary sovereignty implied by EMU means that participating member states will have to give up an import-ant 'shock absorber'. Since the EU is still far from being an optimum currency area and fiscal transfers between states at different stages in the economic cycle are negligible, there is no obvious substitute for the stabilising role currently played by national monetary policies. Yet despite the economic caveats, EMU is about much more than a simple calculation of economic costs and benefits. For the EU, economic integration has always been a means to political unification, rather than an end in itself. The commitment of the key member states to the ideal of political union means that EMU must be seen as part of a wider com-mitment to a unified, peaceful Europe rather than a limited exercise in trading off economic costs for economic benefits.

References

Ackrill R 1997 Economic and monetary union, *Developments in Economics*, Vol. 13, pp. 1–20.
Alesina A and Grilli V U 1991 *The European central bank: reshaping monetary politics in Europe*, CEPR Discussion Paper Series, No. 563, Centre for Economic Policy Research, London.
Alesina A and Summers L 1993 Central bank independence and macroeconomic performance: some comparative evidence, *Journal of Money, Credit and Banking*, Vol. 25, pp. 151–62.
Artis M 1989 *The call of a common currency*, The Social Market Foundation, Paper No. 3, London.

Artis M and Zhang W 1995 *International business cycles and the ERM: is there a European business cycle?*, CEPR Discussion Paper, No. 1191, Centre for Economic Policy Research, London.

Artus J R and Young J H 1979 Fixed and flexible exchange rates: a renewal of the debate, *IMF Staff Papers*, Vol. 26, pp. 654–98.

Barrell R 1992 *Economic Convergence and Monetary Union in Europe*, Sage, London.

Bayoumi T and Eichengreen B 1992 *Shocking aspects of European monetary unification*, CEPR Discussion Paper, No. 643, Centre for Economic Policy Research, London.

Begg D 1991 European monetary union – the macro issues, in *The Making of Monetary Union*, Centre for Economic Policy Research, London.

Brittan L 1991 *European monetary union: what money for Europe?*, TSB Forum, London.

Britton E and Whitely J 1997 Comparing the monetary transmission mechanism in France, Germany and the United Kingdom: some issues and results, *Bank of England Quarterly Bulletin*, Vol. 37, pp. 63–84.

Buiter W, Corsetti G and Roubini N 1993 Sense and nonsense in the Treaty of Maastricht, *Economic Policy*, Vol. 16, pp. 57–100.

Calmfors L and Driffill J 1988 Bargaining structure, corporatism and macroeconomic performance, *Economic Policy*, Vol. 6, pp. 13–61.

Cecchini P 1988 *The European challenge: 1992 the benefits of a single market*, Wildwood House, London.

Commission 1985 *Completing the Internal Market: The White Paper*, Office for Official Publications of the European Communities, Luxembourg.

Commission 1997 1997 Broad economic policy guidelines: the outcome of the Amsterdam European Council on stability, growth and employment, *European Economy*, No. 64.

Currie D 1997 *The pros and cons of EMU*, HM Treasury, London.

de Grauwe P 1988 *Exchange rate variability and the slowdown in growth of international trade*, IMF Staff Papers, Vol. 35, pp. 63–84.

de Grauwe P and Vanhaverbeke W 1991 *Is Europe an optimum currency area? Evidence from regional data*, CEPR Discussion Paper, No. 555, Centre for Economic Policy Research, London.

de Grauwe P 1997 *The economics of monetary integration: 3rd edition*, Oxford University Press, Oxford.

Delors J 1988 *Report on economic and monetary union in the European Community*, Committee for the Study of Economic and Monetary Union, European Commission, Brussels.

Drazen A 1989 Monetary policy, capital controls and seigniorage in an open economy, in M De Cecco and Giovannini, A (eds.), *A European central bank? Perspectives on monetary unification after ten years of the EMS*, Cambridge University Press, Cambridge.

Eichengreen B 1990 *Costs and benefits of European monetary unification*, CEPR Discussion Paper, No. 435, Centre for Economic Policy Research, London.

Emerson M 1992 *One market, one money: an evaluation of the potential benefits and costs of forming an economic and monetary union*, Oxford University Press; summarised in European Commission (1990) One market, one money, *European Economy*, No. 44.

European Monetary Institute 1996 *Progress towards convergence 1996*, Frankfurt.

European Monetary Institute 1997 *Annual report 1996*, Frankfurt.

European Monetary Institute 1997 *The single monetary policy in stage 3: specification of the operational framework*, Frankfurt.

Grilli V 1989 Seigniorage in Europe, in M De Cecco and A Giovannini (eds.), *A European central bank? Perspectives on monetary unification after ten years of the EMS*, Cambridge University Press, Cambridge.

Gros D 1996 *A reconsideration of the optimum currency approach: the role of external shocks and labour mobility*, Centre for European Policy Studies, Brussels.

Healey N M and Levine P 1992 Unpleasant monetarist arithmetic revisited: central bank independence, fiscal policy and European monetary union, *National Westminster Bank Quarterly Review*, August, pp. 23–35.

Healey N M 1996 What price central bank independence?, *The Review of Policy Issues*, Vol. 2, pp. 3–14.

Heylen F and van Poeck A 1995 National labour market institutions and the European economic and monetary integration process, *Journal of Common Market Studies*, Vol. 33, pp. 573–95.

Jenkins R 1979 European Monetary Union, *Lloyds Bank Review*, No. 127, pp. 1–14.

Krugman P 1989 The case for stabilising exchange rates, *Oxford Review of Economic Policy*, Vol. 5, pp. 61–72.

MacDougall D 1977 *Public finance in European integration*, Commission, Brussels.

McKinnon R 1963 Optimum currency areas, *American Economic Review*, Vol. 53, pp. 717–25.

Minford P and Rastogi A 1990 The price of EMU, in R Dornbusch and R Layard (eds.) *Britain and EMU*, Centre for Economic Performance, London.

Mundell R A 1961 A theory of optimum currency areas, *American Economic Review*, Vol. 51, pp. 657–64.

4 The budget of the European Union

Keith Penketh

Introduction

The budget of the EU has characteristics that distinguish it from national budgets, both in the identification of revenue and also of expenditure. It is far from being a mirror image of national budgets. Differences in the nature of the EU budget compared with national budgets relate principally to matters of size and composition.

One way of judging the significance of a budget is to consider its size. In an absolute sense, the EU budget appears to be large. In 1993, the utilisation of appropriations stood at ECU 63 milliard (thousand million). However, the size of a budget is normally related to the size of GDP. In relation to the EU12, the EU budget amounted to just 1.2 per cent of their combined GDP.

This figure may also be compared with the size of national budgets of countries within the EU. Across all members of the EU in 1993 general government expenditure was 51.7 per cent of EU GDP. Thus, the EU budget is relatively small (Eurostat, 1996). Largely omitted from EU budgetary appropriations, but significant in national budgets, is expenditure on social security, law and order, and education. At a national level these policies absorb the lion's share of budgetary expenditure. It is sometimes claimed that, whilst the EU budget is relatively small, it has nonetheless been rising at an excessive rate. A judgement on this assertion can be made by comparing the growth of EU expenditure with the growth at a national level of general government expenditure or national GDP. In Table 4.1 these growth rates are compared.

Table 4.1 Comparative growth rate EU budget/EUGDP/UK budget (%)

	EU final appropriations	EU12 GDP	UK general govt expenditure
1991–92	9.2	4.2	11.4
1992–93	9.3	0.52	7.3
1993–94	2.3	3.8	4.5
1994–95	10.4	3.7	6.8
Average annual growth rate (%)	7.75	3.05	7.5

Sources: Eurostat 1995, *Europe in Figures,* Office for Official Publications of the European Communities, Luxembourg

It cannot be claimed that, compared with the growth rate of UK general government expenditure, the growth of EU budgetary appropriations has been much higher. Both budgets, however, exhibit significantly higher growth than the growth rate of the GDP of the EU.

Of considerable economic significance is the so-called 'rule of equilibrium' which governs the balance of the EU budget. This implies that budgetary revenue must be equal to expenditure. In practice, the outcome for a given year may reveal a surplus or a deficit. An adjustment is made to the budget in the subsequent year. When a surplus arises it is entered on the revenue side of the budget in the following year and serves to reduce the call for finance in that year. Should a deficit arise, it is entered on the expenditure side of the budget in the following year and hence increases the call for finance.

The effect of this rule is to deny the use of the budget for fiscal fine-tuning in a traditional demand management sense. Any budgetary adjustment to the macroeconomy has to come principally by attempts to use EU expenditures to improve supply-side factors, for example the Structural Funds to invest in infrastructure and to help overcome obstacles to development in the poorer regions. These issues are discussed in Chapter 8.

The structure of the budget

Prior to 1975, power over the budget was vested solely in the Council of Ministers. This avoided conflict between the various institutions of the EEC. In 1975, under Article 203 of the Treaty of Rome, budgetary power was shared between the Council and the European Parliament. Parliament was given the right to reject the draft budget, and to have the last say, subject to a constraint, on non-compulsory expenditure. Expenditure was divided between 'compulsory' expenditure and 'non-compulsory' expenditure. The former consisted of 'expenditure necessarily resulting from the Treaty' and related mainly to agricultural expenditure and expenditure on third countries; the latter principally covered the structural funds. Parliament had the authority to increase non-compulsory expenditure by up to one half of the 'maximum rate'. This 'maximum rate' was the arithmetic mean of: the trend of GNP of EU countries; the average rise in member states' budgets; the trend in the cost of living.

The years from 1975–88 were marked by conflicts about the budget between European Parliament and the Council. However, the Brussels Inter-Institutional Agreement of 1988 secured a financial perspective for the period 1988–92 between Parliament, the Council and the Commission. At the Edinburgh European Council of December 1992 changes were made in the composition of budgetary expenditures that altered the financial perspective of budget. This perspective not only constrained the earlier proposals of the then President of the Commission, Jacques Delors, but also set limits to the growth of finance required to support current and projected policies. Table 4.2 illustrates the relative importance of EU policies in the period 1993–99.

It is clear from the table that planned CAP expenditure will continue to dominate expenditure appropriations in 1999. However, the share that this policy

Table 4.2 Financial perspective 1993 and 1999

	1993	*1999*
1. Common agricultural policy	50.9	45.2
2. Structural operations	30.8	35.6
3. Internal policies	5.7	6.4
4. External action	5.7	6.9
5. Administrative expenditure	4.8	4.7
6. Reserves	2.1	1.2

Source: adapted from European Commission (1995)

absorbs is falling, and the share that is allocated for structural operations will rise. These two policies continue to account for over 80 per cent of the budget of the EU.

The principal problems of the EU budget

There are a range of problems that beset the EU budget. These problems relate to the expenditure and revenue sides of the budget, and to the redistribution effects of the budgetary process.

The expenditure side

The principal appropriations of the EU budget, namely agriculture and structural operations, have both been subject to modification as new constraints have arisen. Up to the early 1990s, budgetary expenditure on agriculture developed rapidly. An important aim of policy was to reduce the secular decline of agricultural incomes within the EU. The price support mechanism was one of the ways used to achieve this particular objective. Recently there have been changes partly as a result of internal frictions, but principally from commitments entered into under the Uruguay Round Agreements. The price support measures have been weakened by changing methods of protection on the import side under a policy of tarification. Additionally, cuts in tariffs are scheduled to come into operation up to 1999. Cuts in agricultural subsidies are also promised on agricultural exports. However, the anticipated net effect is to reduce budgetary expenditure more than budgetary revenue.

A further impetus to change is the effect upon the budget of the anticipated membership of the EU by some of the CEECs (Central and Eastern European Countries), in the early years of the millennium. A policy of 'no change' in agriculture would have had serious budgetary implications for the present members of the EU. The policy of decoupling payments from production and hence hopefully of reducing costs has been given added impetus by this prospect. A review of the reforms to the CAP is provided in Chapter 11, and the implications of enlargement to include some of the CEECs are discussed in Chapter 13.

The issue of regional imbalance within the EU has figured prominently among the problems to be addressed. Some of the legislation that emerged from the Single European Act and the Maastricht Treaty exacerbated the problems of curbing regional imbalance within the EU. Reforms affecting the budget established during the meeting of the Brussels European Council of 1988 included significant changes in structural operations. Guidelines were set out for use in determining funding decisions relating to structural operations. These were modified by the Maastricht Treaty with the adoption of a Cohesion Fund and the expansion of the European Social Fund (ESF), to support the Social Policy objectives outlined in the Social Protocol. Other funds concerned with regional operations were the European Regional Development Fund (ERDF), the guidance section of the European Agricultural Guidance and Guarantee Fund (EAGGF) and the financial instrument for fisheries guidance. At Maastricht the objectives of the funds were re-cast and funding allocations were modified to meet these changed objectives. At least 74 per cent of the Structural Funds were to be allocated to objective 1 areas, thereby focusing on developing the poorest regions of the EU. The rest of the funding was allocated to combating long-term unemployment, youth unemployment and social exclusion, helping workers to adjust to changes in industry, and the promotion of rural development. Issues related to the use of the Structural Funds are discussed in Chapter 8.

As agricultural and structural appropriations absorb so much of the total, less than 20 per cent is left to the other policies requiring finance. The relative significance of all appropriations for 1995 is given in Table 4.3 below.

Table 4.3　Breakdown of expenditure (1995)

	%
1. EAGGF – Guarantee	47.5
2. Structural operations	32.9
3. Training, youth culture, information	0.9
4. Energy, nuclear safeguards, environment	0.3
5. Consumer protection, internal market, Trans-European networks	1.0
6. Research	3.7
7. Cooperation with developing countries	6.3
8. Common foreign and security policy	0.0
9. Repayments and reserves	2.3
10. Administrative expenditure	5.0
	100.0
	(ECU 80,893 million)

Source: adapted from Official Journal of the EC L301, Vol. 39, 25 November 1996

The revenue side

Before 1971 the EU budget was financed by contributions from member states based upon their relative GDP. A decision was made to introduce an own-resources system which came into operation in 1971. Tax revenues, therefore, identified more with EU as opposed to national policies, were earmarked for EU use. The revenues from customs duties and agricultural and sugar levies were switched from national to EU use. Revenue derived from a common VAT base, where VAT was applied at a rate of 1 per cent, was also transferred. Joining countries were obliged to adopt VAT.

The method of financing EU expenditure from own-resources was not entirely satisfactory. They did not prove to be sufficiently buoyant to meet growing calls for expenditure especially during the 1980s. It became difficult to control agricultural expenditure, which largely depended upon world food prices and the value of the dollar. Extra ERDF financing was scheduled, new policies had been launched – research, fisheries and the integrated Mediterranean programme (IMP) – and Greece, Spain and Portugal joined the Community. All three countries were net beneficiaries from the Community budget.

Reasons for the slow growth of own-resources were not difficult to pin-point. GATT negotiations had led to cuts in tariff rates and hence in tariff revenue. In agricultural products the EU was moving to self-sufficiency under the protective shield of CAP. Lack of buoyancy in the revenue from these sources was not compensated by the growth of revenue from the 1 per cent VAT levy on national revenues.

When expenditure outran revenue during the 1980s, transitional solutions were applied outside the own-resources ceiling. They usually took the form of intergovernmental loans. At the Fontainebleau summit an agreement was reached to increase own-resources by raising the VAT levy to 1.4 per cent. Revenue from VAT was not based upon any inter-country evaluation of ability to pay; indeed it was a regressive form of taxation. Nor was the budget as a whole based upon any principle of *juste retour*. It was simply a matter of raising revenue based upon the Communities' own-resources. The increase in the VAT rate to 1.4 per cent emphasised the regressive nature of this form of taxation. Suggestions that the VAT rate would eventually have to be increased to 1.6 per cent did not in effect materialise.

At the Brussels European Council of 1988 a further attempt was made to solve the problem of shortage of finance. Financial discipline was injected into the growth of EU expenditure and, in addition, the problem of the regressive nature of VAT was tackled. The outcome of the main characteristics of the new budget system is shown in Box 4.1.

The Brussels Agreement laid the foundation for a 25 per cent rise in the resources available to the EU (Commission, 1989). A rise in the VAT levy to around 1.9 per cent would have been required to produce a similar expansion of the revenue of the budget. Of considerable conceptual significance was the increasingly important role attached to the GNP aggregate in the system of Community finance. It was being used not only for the purpose of capping contributions from the VAT levy but also as a ceiling to define overall revenue available for the Community's budget.

The next significant step in the transformation of the budget arose out of the Edinburgh European Council 1992. The Edinburgh Council reform was based on consideration of the proposals put forward by the Commission – the so-called 'Delors II Package' (Commission, 1992). The main points that emerged from the Edinburgh Council are outlined in Box 4.2. The Edinburgh Agreement is especially significant because it limited the role of VAT in the finances of the EU and put more emphasis on the principle of ability to pay – the fourth resource.

Box 4.1   The Brussels Agreement on Reform of the Budget

- The VAT resource base was to be capped at 55 per cent of GNP at market prices, with the maximum call-up rate of 1.4 per cent.

- A ceiling was set on revenue between 1988 and 1992 equal to 1.2 per cent of Community GNP by 1992.

- The growth of agricultural expenditure was set at 74 per cent of the rate of growth of Community GNP.

- A revenue compensation scheme to be established to contend with unexpected additional expenditure occasioned by a weakening of the US dollar. This reduced the non-dollar price of agricultural output and increased the amount by which agricultural stocks had to be depreciated to make them competitive in world markets. A reserve equal to ECU 1000 million is to be entered in the budget each year.

- Production targets were to be set in agriculture. Extra co-responsibility levies were to be introduced to dissuade farmers from breaking the targets set. If expenditure targets were breached, a 3 per cent cut was to be applied to minimum guaranteed prices the following year.

- A set-aside scheme was instituted whereby farmers received compensation for taking arable land out of production.

- A new category of revenue reflecting the principle of ability to pay. This was the fourth resource based upon member states' relative GNP. It was seen as a balancing revenue item to bridge any shortfall between appropriations and other sources of revenue.

The redistributive aspect of the budget

Given that the EU is committed to economic convergence, it would seem inconsistent if economic divergence was reinforced rather than reduced as a result of the operation of the budget. Initially, almost the entire focus of the budget was on matters of resource allocation. Equity was not an issue that was given serious consideration. However, it was realised that on the accession of the UK to the EU a disproportionate financing burden would fall on that country.

For the UK throughout the 1970s, gross contributions were high relative to economic prosperity. There were two reasons for this. First, the UK's extra-EU import trade was high and hence dutiable imports were high, as were extra-EU agricultural imports. Secondly, UK contributions coming from the application of the 1 per cent VAT rate were also large, because of the relatively high levels of consumption expenditure to GNP.

In 1975 a 'financial mechanism' was introduced providing for refunds of excessive gross contributions. The conditions established as a qualification for a refund were somewhat restrictive, and no refund was secured through this mechanism prior to 1980. The situation for the UK would have been rendered more

Box 4.2 **The Edinburgh Agreement on Reform of the Budget**

- Between 1993 and 1999 the budget was assigned a maximum of own-resources starting at 1.2 per cent of Community GNP in 1993 and rising to 1.27 per cent of Community GNP in 1999. In an attempt to minimise qualitative differences between countries in the calculation of GNP the European System of Accounts was developed in 1995. This is to be applied to data published in 1999. (Official Journal of the European Communities, L310 Vol. 39, 30 November 1996)

- Within global budgetary limits, restrictions were placed on the principal appropriations in the budgets of 1993–99.

- The common VAT base was to be limited to 50 per cent of GNP for countries where GNP was less than 90 per cent of the Community average. For the other countries the threshold was to fall from 55 per cent of GNP in 1995 by equal stages to 50 per cent in 1999.

- The VAT levy was to fall from 1.32 per cent in 1995 in equal steps to 1 per cent in 1999.

- Two additional reserves were instituted to be covered by specific provisions. They were a Loan Guarantee Fund and Emergency Aid for non-member countries.

acceptable if high gross contributions had been offset by high gross receipts. This was not the case for the UK, where the amount of agricultural production qualifying for EAGGF (Guarantee) expenditure was relatively small. Hence high contributions were only partly offset because receipts were comparatively low.

The effect was to make the UK the second largest net contributor to the budget in the 1980s. Agreements to secure refunds were obtained covering the years 1981–83, but a more permanent solution was sought. However, the UK was given a larger budget share in the Regional and Social Funds, thus placing the emphasis upon an expenditure solution to the UK's budgetary problems. Given the limited nature of the Regional and Social Funds relative to the agricultural budget, the benefits were not substantial.

In an attempt to resolve the problem of equity and efficiency, the Spinelli Report commissioned by the European Parliament was published in 1980. The report proposed that a progressive element could be applied to contributions. One part would be based on GDP per capita relative to the EU average; the other part would be based on an index of population. Countries with relatively low per capita incomes and also relatively low populations would benefit. Although the report did not propose radical changes in contributions it was not adopted. There is no doubt that there are common features in the Spinelli Report and the Brussels Agreement, which was adopted eight years later.

The Fontainebleau Agreement of 1984, in addition to enhancing the resources of the EU by increasing the VAT ceiling to 1.4 per cent, addressed the issue of equity in relation to the UK's net contribution (see Denton, 1983). Here it is useful to distinguish between the 'allocated' expenditure of the EU budget and the 'non-allocated' expenditure. Allocated expenditure is that which can be identified as being used for the benefit of a particular country within the EU. Conversely, non-allocated expenditure cannot be identified as earmarked for the use of a particular member. The EAGGF Guarantee and Guidance expenditure can be allocated, but administrative expenditure on the institutions of the EU, or aid to Third World countries, cannot be allocated to particular EU members. Hence the net contribution that a country makes to the EU budget is simply the difference between total financial contributions and total allocated expenditure. Thus, it is possible to compare a country's relative contribution to the EU budget with its share of allocated expenditures. The introduction of a mechanism for refunding the UK for the gap which existed between payments by the UK of own-resources to the EU budget, and allocated receipts, was an innovation of Fontainebleau. It was to be financed by those countries that received more from the budget than they paid into it. In the event, the gap was not measured by relative own-resources and allocated EU expenditures, but by relative VAT payments and allocated EU expenditures. This had the effect of reducing the gap for the UK.

The significance of concentrating upon the difference between UK VAT payments and UK budgetary receipts in the calculation of the abatement may be appreciated by contrasting the gap to be financed with the size of the gap that would have arisen had agricultural levies and customs duties paid by the UK also been included. In 1995 for instance, when all payments are included, the gap to be financed was ECU 4720 million. If only VAT and GNP related payments are included, the gap to be financed falls to ECU 2043 million.

The UK secured an abatement because the framework of EU revenue and expenditure had led to an unwarranted financial burden upon that country. This alleged inequity is not solely a British problem. The largest net contributor, Germany, is fourth from the top of the per capita league table. This ranking is, however, based upon the omission of the three most recent members of the EU. Had all 15 members been included, Germany would rank sixth. The most prosperous member of the EU, measured in terms of GDP, is Luxembourg. However, Luxembourg ranks fifth in the order of net recipients. Likewise Denmark, the second most prosperous member of the EU, is a net recipient from the EU budget.

The UK, which is the second largest net contributor, is ranked eighth in GDP per capita and eleventh in relation to the EU15. Belgium, which appears to be slightly more prosperous than the UK, has actually received a small positive net transfer. Details of contributions and receipts are given in Table 4.4.

However, as the budget of the EU reflects the policies of the EU that are not solely egalitarian in principle, it is hardly surprising that inequities are revealed. Given the GDP rankings, the UK bears the biggest burden. Given the size of its net contributions, Germany can hardly be pleased with the situation today. Whatever the objective of the EU, it is difficult to support a system whereby residents of a relatively poor country provide financial benefits to residents of a relatively rich one. Moreover, the proposed enlargement of the EU to include countries with significantly lower GDP per capita than the richest member states has increased the pressure to reform the budget to allow for a more equitable

Table 4.4 Budgetary contributions and receipts

Rank order of net contributors to EU budgets, 1991–95 (Mio ECU)		Rank order of net recipients from EU budgets, 1991–95 (Mio ECU)		Per capita GDP (purchasing power standard 1993)	
D	57392	E	18461	L	25422
UK	12057	GR	18010	DK	17813
F	9266	P	10372	F	17434
I	6572	IRL	10209	D	17143
NL	6528	L	1768	NL	16308
SWE	937*	DK	1504	I	16228
A	904*	B	21	B	15956
FIN	164*			UK	15690
				IRL	12833
				E	12330
				P	10934
				GR	9999

Note: *1 year's figures
Sources: adapted from Official Journal of the EC C330, Vol. 35, 15 December 1992; C327, Vol. 37, 24 November 1994; L301, Vol. 39, 25 November 1996
Eurostat 1995, *Europe in Figures*, Office for Official Publications of the European Communities, Luxembourg

system of raising revenue and disbursing expenditures. The movement towards European Monetary Union (EMU) has also focused attention on the need for budgetary reform in order to help the poorer member states to adjust to the rigours of operating within a single currency area.

It is unlikely that the present situation will persist in the long run. A way forward would be to abandon own-resource funding and rely solely upon equal per capita contributions to provide the revenue. The expenditure side of the budget could then proceed without further intervention. Alternatively, a more radical solution would be to adjust relative income shares by a measure that reflected the relative prosperity of the member states. It would thus come closer to a system of progressive taxation imposed on the residents of a country by their respective governments.

The key to finding a solution to the contributions from the member states largely rests with German attitudes to budgetary reform. The relative position of Germany has shifted since unification from near the top of the GDP prosperity league to fourth position. In the period 1991–95, Germany contributed 83 per cent more than the combined contributions of the UK, France, Italy and the Netherlands. It is, therefore, unsurprising that Germany is pressing for a reform of the way that the EU budget is financed before the present agreement runs out in 1999.

Germany has proposed that a cap should be placed on member states' net contributions. The cap will be a certain percentage of the GDP of the member states. Payments in excess of the capped limits would have to be shared among those countries that had not reached the limits. The attitude of Germany to the EU budget has been influenced by the recession in the late 1990s. This has led Germany to adopt a more cautious approach to enhancement of EU expenditure and to develop a preference for reining in expenditure.

The future of the budget

Given the recent expansion in the range of policies that the EU has embraced and the concomitant need to finance these policies, the stage would appear to be set for further expansion, if only because a momentum of policy growth has been established. Furthermore, the prospect of membership by some of the countries of CEEC and Cyprus signals a larger EU budget in the future. In the short to medium term, however, there are strong grounds for believing that the budget will be constrained to the levels set by the Edinburgh Conference of 1992.

The Maastricht Treaty required that member states take steps to meet the convergence criteria before a country would be allowed to participate in the EMU – especially, but not exclusively, the provision that the budget deficit of a country must not be larger than 3 per cent of GDP. The anxiety that some countries have experienced, should they not qualify to participate in the monetary union, has influenced attitudes on the future of the EU budget. Some countries that have focused on restraining their national budgets are also looking towards the EU budget to exhibit restraint. Attitudes have hardened against the growth of EU expenditure, with cuts in contributions being sought by a number of member states, led by France and Germany.

There are further reasons why budgetary growth is unlikely to be rapid. In 1995 the EU underspent by ECU 9 billion, which was returned to contributors and which reduced the burden of contributions from countries in 1996. This underspending was the result of two factors. First, changes in the operation of the Common Agricultural Policy have reduced spending under CAP. Secondly, several countries have not taken up the regional aid that was allocated to them. Incredibly, in 1996 untapped credits for regional aid amounted to a ECU 20 billion. The principal reason for the shortfall in take-up appears to be the requirement of additionality, that is the requirement by members to match monies received for regional aid with additional monies of their own (see Chapter 8).

The consequence of the appearance of this surplus was a cut in the 1997 budget of ECU 2.5 billion. This is not to deny that there are significant pressures to increase spending in certain directions. The President of the Commission, Jacques Santer, has emphasised the need for more funding for trans-European networks and for EU research and development projects. The demands upon the agricultural budget are likely to rise from membership by CEEC states.

The Commission anticipates 2004 as the earliest date for entrance of the first batch of CEEC states to the EU. The PHARE aid programme has been scheduled to rise by 50 times. That this can be achieved in terms of a constant real growth budget in the next few years indicates that budgetary issues will be primarily in terms of re-allocation and redistribution, and not so much in terms of overall growth (Commission, 1996).

The debate over the appropriate budgetary system for the EU is likely to become more heated as the EU is enlarged. If the CAP and structural funds are not significantly reformed and if growth in the member states is low it is possible that the Community could encounter serious budgetary problems.

References

Commission 1989 *Community Public Finance*, the principal reference document of the 1988 Financial Reform, Office for Official Publications of the European Communities, Luxembourg.

Commission 1992 *Commission Communication, the Communities' finances between now and 1997*, 5201/2 COM(92)2001 final, Brussels.

Commission 1995 *General budget of the European Union for the financial year 1995*, SEC (95) 10 EN/January, Brussels.

Commission 1996 *Agenda 2000: For a stronger and wider Union*, Brussels.

Denton G 1983 *Budgetary problems and refund mechanics in reform of CAP and restructuring the EEC budget*, UACES, Secretariat.

Eurostat 1995 *Europe in figures*, Office for Official Publications of the European Communities, Luxembourg.

Eurostat 1996 *Europe in figures*, Office for Official Publications of the European Communities, Luxembourg.

Official Journal of the European Communities 1992 C330 Vol. 35, 15 December, Brussels.

Official Journal of the European Communities 1994 C327 Vol. 37, 24 November, Brussels.

Official Journal of the European Communities 1996 L301 Vol. 39, 25 November, Brussels.

Official Journal of the European Communities 1996 L310 Vol. 39, 30 November, Brussels.

Further reading

Ardy B 1996 The European Union Budget *The European Union Handbook*, Fitzroy Dearborn.

Bowles R and Jones P 1992 Equity and the EC budget, *Journal of European Social Policy*, Vol. 2, pp. 45–46.

Commission 1989 *Community Public Finance*, Brussels.

Costello D 1993 Redistributive effects of inter-regional transfers, a comparison of the European Community and Germany, in *European Economy*, 1993, *The Economics of the Community Public Finances*, No. 5.

Goodhart CAE and Smith S 1993 Stabilisation, in *European Economy*, 1993, *The Economics of the Community Public Finances*, No. 5.

Harrop J 1996 *Structural funding and employment in the European Union*, Edward Elgar.

Munk K J 1993 The rationale of the common agricultural policy and other EC sectoral policies. European Economy 1993, *The Economics of the Community Public Finances*, No. 5.

Spahn R B 1993 *The Community budget for an economic and monetary union*, Macmillan, London.

The European Union and competition policy

John Kemp

Introduction

This chapter surveys the status and workings of UK competition policy and explores the implications arising from the creation of the Single European Market (SEM). Initially, an economic rationale is presented for intervention in private industry, whether this is seen primarily as a policy to promote competition or as a corrective action for monopoly abuse. The next section provides a brief discussion of the alternative policy approaches and the subsequent section provides a review of the development of UK legislation and policy. This is followed by a section outlining current EU policy. Finally, an assessment is made of the effectiveness of current policy and, with the creation of the SEM, the important implications arising from the Treaty of Rome are considered in relation to the future direction of competition policy and proposals for change.

An economic rationale for intervention

Democratic nations, whether they have governments of the right or the left, usually have well articulated policies towards intervention in private industry. Such policies are designed to promote the efficient allocation of resources through the encouragement of competition, which is seen as the active progenitor of economic efficiency and welfare. They are, likewise, employed to limit the losses in efficiency that can arise from the presence of elements of monopoly. There is a clear underpinning economic rationale for competition policy and consequently the broad thrust of policy is rarely ideologically contentious. Thus, where disagreement does arise it is usually of degree rather than of substance, and is more likely to concern the detailed application of policy as opposed to general principles. It is currently fashionable to talk of 'competition policy' where one formerly talked of 'monopoly' or 'anti-monopoly policy'. The fact that this is partly a semantic change reflects the existence of an underlying consensus.

The relative efficiency of competition and monopoly

The results of this section depend upon a number of underlying assumptions. If any one of these does not hold, then the results cannot be upheld. First, it is assumed that consumers are utility maximisers and that producers are profit max-imisers. It is assumed that the price paid and received represent the value of the marginal unit traded both to the buyer and to the seller. Further, it is assumed that units of consumers' and producers' surplus can be added and subtracted, that is, a unit of surplus represents the same quantity of benefit irrespective of whether it accrues to the buyer or the seller.

If the objective of policy is to maximise economic welfare this implies that total surplus (that is, consumer and producer surplus) should be maximised. Thus, in comparing alternative economic structures, the most efficient is de-fined as the one that generates the greatest total surplus. This concentration on efficiency ignores altogether the important question of income distribution. As far as economic efficiency is concerned it is irrelevant whether surplus accrues to consumers or to producers. If a situation is deemed to be inequitable, then it is in principle possible to redistribute income according to some appropriate canon of equity. In other words, if we 'bake the biggest cake' it should be pos-sible to provide greater shares for all. This is not to deny that questions of income distribution are important, but they do not concern us here.

A comparison of the relative efficiency of perfect competition and pure monopoly demonstrates the inherent inefficiency of monopoly. The heart of the case against monopoly is that it reduces output, increases price and reduces wel-fare compared with perfect competition. This is a very powerful result. It means that it can be stated categorically that the effect of monopolisation *per se* is to reduce economic welfare. This result is illustrated in Fig. 5.1.

However, this result depends critically on the caveat that 'other things are equal'. In particular, subsequent monopolisation costs are unlikely to remain unchanged. Indeed, the argument is often advanced that mergers bring bene-fits through reducing costs of production because of the attainment of econom-ies of scale. It is undeniable that large-scale production can be technically more efficient. Following an analysis detailed by Williamson (1968) it is possible to consider how the previous result is affected if, after monopolisation, production takes place with lower costs. This analysis suggests that, if economies of scale are significant, it is possible that monopolisation will result in net benefits in terms of the relative welfare gains to losses. The conditions under which such an out-come is possible are shown in Fig. 5.2.

Empirical evidence on economies of scale across a large number of British industries suggests considerable diversity in their extent (e.g. Pratten, 1971; Silberston, 1972; HMSO, 1978). Thus, on the basis of empirical evidence about the nature of costs it is not possible to make a definitive statement of the effects of monopoly. It should, however, be noted that, while the analysis cautions against outright condemnation of monopoly and merger, the case against restrictive prac-tices and collusive agreements is not weakened. This is because after agreements, unlike mergers, individual firms maintain their separate existence. It is, there-fore, difficult to envisage how, under these circumstances, offsetting economies of scale could be attained without any rationalisation of productive units.

The analysis suggests that there is no theoretical justification for condemn-ing monopoly and/or merger outright, since the ill-effects of output restriction could be more than offset by reductions in costs. Under such circumstances

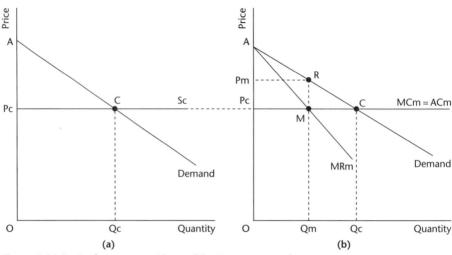

Figure 5.1(a)   Perfect competition   *(b)*   Pure monopoly

Purely for reasons of diagrammatic simplicity we assume that the perfectly competitive industry supply curve (Sc) is infinitely elastic and can be drawn as a horizontal straight line as in Fig. 5.1(a). This simplification does not in any way affect the qualitative nature of the results. Price (Pc) and output (Qc) are determined by the intersection of the supply and demand curves at C. There is no producer surplus, and total surplus is composed entirely of consumer surplus which is given by the area ACPc.

Suppose the industry is now monopolised with (unrealistically) no change in costs. That is, all productive units are merged into a single firm without any change in their numbers or their costs of production and, further, this newly created firm acts solely as a costless decision-making and coordinating mechanism for the activities of what were formerly the independent units. It follows that the supply curve (Sc) of Fig. 5.1(a) becomes identical to the marginal cost curve (MCm) of the monopoly firm. As such, it can be read horizontally across to Fig. 5.1(b). A consequence of the assumption of constant costs is that the monopolist's marginal costs are equal to average costs (ACm) as shown. There is no reason for consumers' tastes to have changed, and so the demand curve is unaffected. In Fig. 5.1(b) we can observe the changes due to monopolisation. Faced with the downward sloping market demand curve, the monopoly producer will maximise profits by producing where marginal cost is equal to marginal revenue at M, output will be cut back to Qm and price will be raised to Pm. Consumer surplus is now reduced to area ARPm. Surplus of PmRMPc has been transferred from consumers to producers and total surplus has fallen to ARMPc. There is, therefore, a net loss of surplus of RCM. Thus, economic welfare has unambiguously been reduced. With the important proviso 'other things equal', monopoly inevitably distorts resource allocation and is inefficient vis-à-vis perfect competition.

monopolisation would result in an increase in total surplus. Therefore, the policy implication that arises from theory is that in seeking to determine the effects of monopolisation it is necessary to weigh carefully the costs against the benefits, to examine the trade-off of one against the other. In these circumstances it is of crucial importance to have some means of measuring welfare changes. Clearly, this might not be a task that can be undertaken with any great degree of precision.

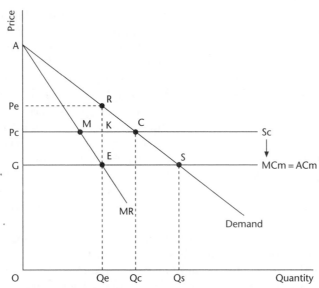

Figure 5.2 Pure economies of scale

In Fig. 5.2 price and output under perfect competition are, as before, at Pc and Qc. Suppose that, under monopoly, costs are lower, that is shown by the supply curve of competition (Sc) shifts downwards to form the monopolist's marginal cost curve (MCm). The monopoly equilibrium now occurs where the MR curve intersects this lower MC curve at E (as opposed to M). Thus monopoly price and output become Pe and Qe. Output has fallen and price risen, but not by as much as in the case depicted in Fig. 5.1(b).

Total surplus is now equal to AREG, of which ARPe is consumer surplus and PeREG is producer surplus. Compared with the competitive surplus of ACPc this change has been brought about by a loss of RCK, due to output restriction (i.e. monopolisation) and a creation of additional producer surplus of PcKEG, due to the ability of the enlarged monopolised firm to achieve lower costs. Area PeRKPc is simply a transfer from consumers to producers and can therefore be ignored. Thus, whether or not total surplus under monopoly (AREG) is greater or less than (ACPc) under perfect competition depends on whether the gain (PcKEG) is greater than the loss (RCK). There is no *a priori* justification for stating which will be the dominant effect. The net effect will vary according to the cost conditions within the particular industry under consideration, and within the real world we might expect considerable variation from one industry to another.

Some qualifications to the theoretical results

Economic theory suggests that monopoly leads to an inefficient allocation of resources in the sense that the level of output is restricted. There are a number of qualifications to this prediction, apart from the possibility of economies of scale. These are particularly important when considering the likely effects in the real world.

First, the analysis is entirely static, ignoring changes that may take place over time. Thus, any demonstrated effects on surpluses may be exacerbated or ameliorated as the industry progresses, and welfare losses which occur over time may cancel out immediate gains or *vice versa*. Further, this static analysis is cast in terms of certainty. Real firms have to make decisions within a climate of uncertainty, and market outcomes will differ according to their attitudes to risk.

Secondly, the competition of economic theory is cast solely in terms of price competition and narrowly defined profit maximisation. The foregoing analysis neglects the effects of firms' other competitive variables such as product quality, product range and product differentiation. Furthermore, if firms pursue objectives other than profit maximisation then the picture becomes even less clear-cut (Sawyer, 1979). For example, the theory of sales revenue maximisation (Baumol, 1959) assumes that managers pursue the objective of maximising revenue rather than profits. As a consequence, higher levels of output are predicted than under profit maximisation. The implication of this is that any policy proposal for a particular industry can be made only after an investigation of not only the structure of the industry, but also the objectives and conduct of the firms within it.

Thirdly, in economic theory it is presumed that any level of output is always produced at the lowest technically feasible cost. For the economist, inefficiency arises because the wrong level of output is produced. However, in the real world there is an additional concept of efficiency, which takes cognisance of the fact that real firms are never as technically efficient as the theorists' firm. This type of inefficiency arises because workers and management are often ill-equipped or lacking in motivation and so do not perform to the best of their abilities. Inefficiency of this sort, which involves a given level of output being produced at a cost which is higher than the theoretical minimum, is termed X-inefficiency. It is what the average person understands by 'inefficiency'. Clearly, such inefficiency is incompatible with perfect competition where the competitive threat would be sufficient to remove any less efficient firm. However, in monopoly markets X-inefficiency could arise because of the absence of competitive discipline. This would seem to strengthen the case against monopoly, for now there is reason to believe that a movement towards monopoly could lead to higher costs through the creation of X-inefficiency. This would offset, to some extent, any cost reductions due to economies of scale. The net effect on costs is therefore unclear, for the picture is now becoming highly complex. It is, however, evident that it would be necessary to weigh carefully all the costs and benefits before any categoric policy recommendation could be made (Rowley, 1973).

Fourthly, the theoretical proscription of monopoly has been arrived at by comparing the two theoretical extremes of perfect competition and pure monopoly. In the real world there is never a movement from one to the other, and it is correspondingly less clear what the implications for both allocative and X-efficiency are. For example, if a merger takes place between two firms in an industry of ten firms, so moving the industry apparently closer to monopoly, it is not at all apparent, *a priori* (even in the absence of any economies of scale), what the effects on either type of efficiency will be. Again, it would seem that this matter could only be resolved after a detailed investigation of the particular industry in question.

Fifthly, even if there are undisputed economies of scale so that there is a net increase in surplus, it can still be argued that there is a social opportunity loss.

Surplus could be increased further if the monopoly firm were required to produce where its marginal cost was equal to price. Thus in Fig. 5.2 an administered move from equilibrium at E to S would lead to an output of QS and price of G, with a further increase in total surplus to ASG.

Sixthly, and most importantly, the theoretical analysis normally used is entirely partial. That is, in considering the effects on one industry in isolation repercussions throughout industry as a whole have been ignored. Thus, an individual merger might be seen to be totally innocuous, but, if it is just one more merger among a spate, then the overall trend towards the monopolisation of industry in general may be worrying. This is rather like the problem of litter louts: one dropped piece of paper is harmless in itself, but the problem involves the total volume of litter!

Seventhly, Baumol *et al.* (1982) have argued that resources will be allocated efficiently (in the sense that prices will be equal to marginal costs) in industries which are perfectly contestable, and that this result holds irrespective of the number of firms in the industry (Button, 1985). A perfectly contestable industry is one which, in addition to free entry, is characterised by completely free exit. Thus, in the absence of any costs of leaving the industry, there will always be the incentive to enter, compete any profits away and then get out quickly without cost. The only protection against this potential threat of competition is afforded by firms charging prices equal to marginal costs and earning only normal profit. The implication is that large numbers of firms are not necessary to achieve economic efficiency, and so it is equally possible for oligopolies to attain an efficient allocation of resources. Thus, in this view, attention should be focused on the freeing of conditions of exit, rather than solely on encouraging actual competition from increasing numbers of firms.

Finally, the Austrian school of economics puts a different interpretation on the existence of profit. Competition is seen as a process, with profit representing both the spur and the reward of enterprise. Thus profit is a symbol of success, encouraging innovation and progressiveness, rather than being symptomatic of resource mis-allocation. Accordingly, this requires recognition of the dynamics of industrial change, which are often obscured by reference solely to comparative theoretical equilibria, as in the neoclassical tradition. Consequently, subscribers to the Austrian tradition would be somewhat less inclined to an actively pro-interventionist stance.

Ideally, all the above qualifications would need to be taken into account in any attempt to prescribe policy. The predictions of economic theory are not sufficiently clear-cut to permit us to proscribe monopoly outright. Theory does point to a clear suspicion that a lack of competition can, most certainly, lead to inefficiencies, but it also identifies possible benefits from the attainment of lower-cost production. An unambiguous policy recommendation would require evaluation of all these costs and benefits. Yet, given the qualifications noted above, this is clearly a daunting task. There have been a number of attempts to establish empirically whether any general conclusions can be drawn on the extent of welfare losses throughout the economy due to the presence of monopoly. If these could be found to be overwhelmingly large or small then the results could be of use in the framing of policy. However, no general consensus has emerged and the conclusions are no less disparate than those of theory (see Clarke, 1985, Hay and Morris 1991).

Empirical evidence of monopoly welfare losses

A number of attempts have been made to estimate the magnitude of the losses due to the presence of monopoly in the economy as a whole. An early attempt was undertaken by Harberger (1954), who calculated that, for US manufacturing industry, the resultant welfare losses were only of the order of 0.1 per cent of GNP. This is clearly very small and, if it were generally representative, then it would call into question the necessity for constructing any elaborate and costly policy to oversee monopoly, since the benefits gained would be unlikely to justify the costs of implementation. The way in which these estimates were obtained can be seen by reference to Fig. 5.3.

Harberger made two assumptions in order to calculate the welfare losses for a sample of 2,046 firms. First, he took the *average* rate of return in manufacturing industry as typical of the rate of return that would have been earned in competitive industry, and then took deviations from this as indicative of the size of the price-cost margin. Secondly, he assumed that the elasticity of demand was unity. Both these assumptions have been challenged on the grounds that they create downwardly biased estimates, and thereby the true losses would be understated. However, subsequent studies by Schwartzman (1960) and Worcester (1973) also showed low estimates of welfare losses and, despite a study by Kamerschen (1966) showing somewhat higher losses, the general consensus view was that monopoly losses were typically not very high for the US economy.

More recently, as a result of further studies of both the US and the UK economies, this consensus has been challenged. Posner (1975) has suggested that, in situations that are not perfectly competitive, firms engage in promotional activities and in attempts to create barriers to entry. To the extent that these activities raise firms' costs, it can be argued that they are wasteful and thus should be included as further elements of losses due to monopoly. If this is done then, clearly, much higher estimates of losses are obtained than those of Harberger. A difficulty is now apparent in that there is no clear criterion available for deciding everything that should or should not be included as elements of welfare loss. Inevitably, decisions on what to include and what to leave out are based on the value judgements of the researcher, and on practical considerations involving the limitations of available data. Consequently, it should not be surprising to find disparate estimates. Cowling and Mueller (1978) have produced estimates based on UK as well as US data, which suggest that welfare losses amount to as much as one half of monopoly profits – around 10 per cent of manufacturing output for the UK and 4 per cent for the USA.

Cowling and Mueller's methodology has been criticised by Littlechild (1981), and their estimates may, arguably, be biased upwards. However, their results along with Posner's have helped to dispel the previously held consensus view that monopoly losses were generally relatively small. This lack of any general conclusion from both theory and empiricism gives support to the piecemeal or cost-benefit approach to monopoly policy, whereby individual industries are

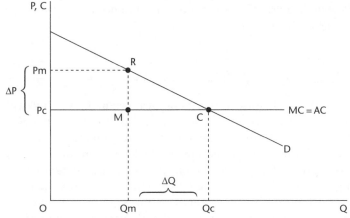

Figure 5.3 Welfare loss due to monopoly

In Fig. 5.3 the welfare loss is equivalent to the triangular area RCM. Thus, the size of this is given by:

$$D = 1/2\Delta P\Delta Q \qquad (5.1)$$

where ΔP is the difference between Pc and Pm, and ΔQ is the difference between Qc and Qm. The distortion of the monopoly price from the competitive price or the price cost margin (M) is defined as:

$$M = (Pm - Mc)/Pm \qquad (5.2)$$

but, since under perfect competition P = MC, Equation [5.2] can be written as:

$$M = (Pm - Pc)/Pm = \Delta P/Pm \qquad (5.2^*)$$

The elasticity of demand at R is defined as:

$$E = (\Delta Q/Qm)/(\Delta P/Pm) \qquad (5.3)$$

which on rearrangement gives:

$$\Delta Q = (E/Pm)\Delta PQm \qquad (5.3^*)$$

On substitution of Equation [5.3*] into Equation [5.1] and multiplication of the right-hand side by Pm/Pm (i.e. by unity)

$$D = 1/2(\Delta P/Pm)^2 PmQmE \qquad (5.4)$$

or

$$D = 1/2M^2SE \qquad (5.4^*)$$

which is negative (a loss), since with a downward sloping demand curve the elasticity of demand (E) is negative. Thus, the welfare losses are now computable in terms of (i) the level of sales revenue, S (i.e. PmQm); (ii) the rate of return M (i.e. $\Delta P/Pm$), which is the monopoly mark-up expressed as a ratio of the monopoly price; (iii) the elasticity of demand E. In principle, it is possible to make estimates of these magnitudes. The level of sales revenue is readily obtainable. Given constant average costs (for which there is considerable supportive evidence in manufacturing), it follows that marginal and average costs are equal. Hence, ΔP is the difference between price and average costs, since under perfect competition Pc = MC. Thus, industry rates of return can be estimated. The direct measurement of the elasticity of demand is not easy, and so an appropriate assumption has to be made concerning its magnitude.

evaluated on their merits. However, even this has not been a view acceptable to all, as is discussed in the following section.

Alternative policy approaches

In the light of this ambiguity in the theoretical predictions, allied with a lack of any clear empirical consensus on the extent of these losses and benefits, the question arises as to what form a pro-competition or anti-monopoly policy should take. The clear implication would appear to be that an individual cost-benefit approach is appropriate, with each monopoly situation being judged on its own merits only after a careful weighing of the gains and losses. Such an approach comes closest to the spirit of the pragmatic investigatory stance currently taken within the UK, where the Monopolies and Mergers Commission and the Restrictive Practices Court pronounce on individual cases. However, this *ad hoc* procedure has not been without its critics, largely because of doubts about whether it is possible to perform the exercise with sufficient precision to arrive at a clear-cut evaluation (see Crew and Rowley, 1970 and 1971; Howe, 1971 and 1972).

During the 1970s there was a vigorous debate surrounding the alternative approaches to UK policy. The issues raised are no less relevant to the formation of an appropriate EU policy, and so they are reviewed here. The main discussion and disagreements have centred around the appropriate policy for dealing with mergers. In the case of restrictive practices there is less contention. They are generally seen as anti-competitive and necessitating legislation to proscribe them, since they almost invariably create the detrimental effects of monopoly without engendering the benefits. In the case of single or dominant firm monopolies, while it is accepted that these may behave detrimentally to the public interest at large, few democratic governments have had, or are likely to have, the political will to intervene directly in their operation, particularly where their market positions have been legitimately attained and their activities are not overtly illegal. Usually the most that governments have been prepared to do has been to publicise their activities and/or to seek voluntary undertakings. Whether or not governments should take greater powers to break up already existing monopolies is an issue that is as much political as economic, for it involves issues of the freedom of the individual and the state. However, where attempts have been made to build up monopoly by merger there has been a heightened awareness of the inherent dangers, and governments have been more willing to take direct action to prohibit them.

Those who strongly doubt whether the cost-benefit exercise can be adequately performed are more inclined to a rules-based or structural approach. The major proponents of a rules-based approach in the UK have been Crew and Rowley (1970 and 1971). They argue that it is simply not possible to quantify all the costs and benefits involved, so any judgement must inevitably be inadequately based. In support of this they indicate that there have been worries about the ability of the Monopolies Commission to maintain consistency across its investigations. Thus, they claim that a climate of uncertainty is created which militates against the decision-taking ability of firms. On the other hand, they are not prepared to countenance the complete free rein of market forces, since the dangers of monopoly are well known. Consequently, they propose a policy more akin to that of the USA, based on rules which would automatically forbid mergers above a given size. This would remove the uncertainty and leave firms free to operate unconstrained within the legally created framework. They recognise that such arbitrary rules would result in some beneficial mergers being stopped, but argue that this sacrifice would be offset by the improvements in X-efficiency. In support of this approach they claim (contentiously) that economies of scale are, in general, only moderate, and also (on the basis of scant evidence) that the association between monopoly and X-efficiency is strong. Thus they contend that losses resulting from the automatic prohibition of mergers above a certain size are unlikely to be substantial, and are more than likely to be offset by the benefits arising from the creation of a climate of greater certainty and competition.

A *laissez-faire* approach of non-intervention has had few adherents in the past, since most economists have accepted that theory and evidence suggest that matters cannot be left entirely to the market. However, Beacham and Jones (1971) came close to taking this line on the grounds that it is not possible to perform the cost-benefit exercise well enough to obtain a soundly based conclusion. On the other hand, they could see little merit in a policy based on a rules approach, since rules are inevitably arbitrary and lacking in any underlying economic logic. As a result they have considerable doubts about the validity of the case for the control of mergers. More recently George (1989) has re-examined this approach, pointed out its drawbacks, and concluded that the balance of theory and evidence does suggest that there is a need for a mergers policy. In contrast, economists of the Austrian tradition (for example, Littlechild 1981, 1989) have come closer to the *laissez-faire* view, partly as a consequence of their different interpretation of profit. It is possible that they had some influence on the government of the UK during the 1980s, which was markedly less disposed to intervene directly in industry than its predecessors. However, most economists (and possibly politicians) accept that some form of control is required, and that this has to be exercised within one of the alternative frameworks.

It is the lack of clear and unambiguous predictions from both theory and evidence that is the source of the dispute over the nature of the approach to monopoly policy. However, on balance a majority of UK economists have appeared to favour the discretionary cost-benefit approach or have thought the rules approach too dogmatic (see Sutherland, 1970; Howe, 1972; Utton, 1975; Fleming and Swann, 1989; George, 1989), and have tended to argue for a continuation of the present investigatory policy with some considerable strengthening of procedures. Thus, UK policy continues to retain the character of discretionary intervention rather than moving towards that of North American rules-based approaches. In its overall approach to competition, EU policy is much closer in spirit to UK policy than it is to any of the alternatives discussed above, although there are some important differences of detail which are considered later. This in itself presents a powerful argument against fundamental change, for it is clearly desirable that national and EU policies should be broadly similar, if only because this is less confusing to the business community.

UK policy

Member states of the EU are free to determine their own policies towards competition within their national boundaries. However, in the case of matters affecting intra-Community trade, EU policy necessarily takes precedence. Historically, UK and EU policies developed separately, largely in isolation and over a different time-scale. Now, with the creation of the SEM it is clearly desirable that there should be a greater degree of harmonisation, without removing altogether the independence of national governments to deal with matters of internal trade. In order to clarify the relationships between UK and EU policy it is helpful, first, to outline the current framework of UK policy before discussing that of the EU.

There are three major strands to UK policy. These are the treatment of dominant firm monopolies, restrictive practices, and mergers. In 1973 the Fair Trading Act brought these together within the purview of a single body, the Office of Fair Trading, which is overseen by a civil servant, the Director General of Fair Trading.

Dominant firm monopoly

Where a firm or a group of firms acting collectively accounts for 25 per cent of the market or more, the Director General of Fair Trading can refer the industry to the Monopolies and Mergers Commission (MMC) for investigation. This body is then charged with providing a general report on the operation of the industry, and making recommendations for change where the public interest is seen to be compromised. The Minister at the Department of Trade and Industry then has complete liberty to accept or reject these recommendations, and to decide whether, and how, they should be acted on.

Since the 1980 Competition Act it is also possible for the Director General of Fair Trading to refer a particular practice of an individual firm to the MMC, where complaints have been received from supposedly injured parties, or the practice is suspected of limiting competition. In such cases a quick cost-benefit type appraisal and recommendation can be made. Where the practice is found to be anti-competitive the Minister can then accept voluntary undertakings from the firm to modify its practice or invoke extensive powers to proscribe the practice.

Restrictive practices

Restrictive practices, in the form of formal agreements between firms, are presumed to operate against the public interest. Hence they are pronounced illegal unless the parties to an agreement can set aside the presumption by 'proving' to the satisfaction of the Restrictive Practices Court that the agreement operates in the public interest. All agreements have to be registered with the Office of Fair Trading, where it is decided at what stage a registered agreement should be brought before the Court. The arguments that can be employed to defend an agreement are tightly drawn and defined in a series of 'gateways'. If an agreement successfully passes one or more of these gateways, the defendants still have to demonstrate that it passes a more general gateway or 'tailpiece' by conferring substantial benefits to the public interest, with the demonstrated benefits outweighing any detriments.

There is an important distinction between the approach to restrictive practices and that towards dominant firms and mergers. Restrictive practices policy is non-discretionary and purely legalistic, with issues to be resolved within the courts, as opposed to ministerial judgements made on the basis of administrative recommendations. Thus the element of political discretion has been removed.

The impact of the restrictive practices legislation has been such that many agreements were abandoned as firms were unwilling to incur the costs of defending an agreement within the Court, and also as firms gradually came to recognise the difficulties of overturning the presumption that an agreement operated against the public interest. Information agreements have been brought within the scope of the legislation because many firms circumvented the intentions of the legislation by forming agreements to swap information on, for example, proposed price changes. Clearly, if firms are predisposed to behave in mutually acceptable ways then such cooperation can be achieved simply through the dissemination of information and without the necessity to make a formal agreement. A major problem with the operation of restrictive practices legislation is that it is often difficult to capture secret or verbal agreements between firms. Also, because penalties in the UK, as opposed to the EU, have never been severe, firms have had contempt for the legislation. The whole procedure by 1988 was officially seen as no longer dealing adequately with the issues, as inflexible, slow, costly and in need of review (Department of Trade and Industry, 1988c). This led to proposals for a move to an EU type approach, which is discussed later.

Mergers

If a proposed merger is likely to lead to the merged firms having a market share greater than one quarter or alternatively involves assets in excess of £70 million, then it may be referred to the MMC. The MMC must then, within six months, carry out an investigation of the costs and benefits to determine whether the merger is contrary to the public interest. If the Minister accepts the report, he/she then has the power to prohibit a contrary merger from taking place. However, there is an important distinction to be made here, namely that, unlike restrictive practices, judgements about mergers possess an essentially political dimension. The appropriate minister retains complete discretion on whether or not to refer a merger to the MMC, and whether or not to accept any recommendation. In the past, ministers have been charged with failing to refer mergers which might have been politically sensitive, despite claims that a strong economic case existed for referral. As long as this element of political discretion remains, there is a potential source of dispute.

Throughout the whole of competition policy there is a presumption that intervention is justified in order to preserve the public interest. However, it is not always clear what the public interest is or what serves it. Who are the public? Are they producers, consumers, or both and, more importantly, what exactly is in their interest? The definition had been left somewhat vague in the legislation, although it was intended to embrace all relevant matters. Such imprecision creates the greatest problems within a legalistic approach to restrictive practices, where courts faced by inadequate definition have had to develop their own interpretations. However, in the 1973 Act the interests of consumers are stressed, and explicit reference was made, for the first time, to the necessity of 'maintaining and promoting effective competition'. Thus competition is singled out for the first time as the chosen mechanism for ensuring the public interest. Further informal articulation of this was provided by the 1984 guidelines, which indicated that in future greater attention would be given to competition aspects when deciding whether to make a merger reference. Thus, in the 1973 Act and in legislation since, it seems that the public interest almost becomes whatever it is that competition promotes. From this time on there was a shift in emphasis in official discussions from 'anti-monopoly' to 'pro-competition' policy. This was not entirely a semantic shift, and was to foreshadow a much wider change in attitudes to the relationship between State and Economy, which was to be felt throughout the 1980s and since, not only within the UK but within Europe and beyond.

Up to 1980 UK policy had been framed with scant reference to Community legislation. However, since then there have been further reviews and proposals which have had to take some cognisance of the creation of the SEM.

European Union competition policy

The EU has sought to develop a policy designed to secure the benefits that arise from a competitive market, since as national barriers to inter-state competition are removed there is a danger that these can be replaced by privately erected barriers. The competition policy of the EU stems from the Treaty of Rome and is mainly embodied in Articles 85 and 86. These were designed to ensure free competition within the EU, with the Commission being charged with the responsibility for applying the legislation. In the process of doing this the Commission has to work closely with national governments, and it is therefore clearly desirable that domestic and EU law should be mutually consistent. Individual states still retain the right to develop their own distinct policies on competition where trade is contained within their national boundaries. Therefore, even after the completion of the SEM, the provisions of UK competition policy remain unaffected, inasmuch as they concern internal UK trade. However, in terms of trade between member states, national legislation becomes subordinate to EU legislation.

Article 85 – Restrictive practices

Article 85 is concerned with the operation of restrictive practices, where they affect trade between member states. Thus, Article 85(1) prohibits agreements

'. . . which may affect trade between Member States and which have as their object or effect the prevention, restriction or distortion of competition within the common market . . .', and continues by listing specific types of agreement that are prohibited. The types of agreements which the legislation is designed to catch are precisely the same as those at which the UK legislation is aimed, namely price fixing, market sharing, restrictions on supply, etc. Article 85(3) grants exemptions in the case of beneficial agreements '. . . which contribute to improving the production or distribution of goods or to promoting technical or economic progress, while allowing consumers a fair share of the resulting benefit . . .', provided that such agreements do not impose any indispensable restrictions or provide the possibility of eliminating competition.

These exemptions may be granted either as block exemptions for certain categories of agreement (for example, cooperative research and development, exclusive distribution, exclusive purchasing) or on a case-by-case basis. While there is a clear similarity between the intentions of Article 85 and of UK restrictive practices legislation, in operation and emphasis the two approaches differ markedly. In the European legislation the emphasis is on the *effects* of a restriction, rather than the *form* of it as in the UK. That is, in the UK the requirement to register an agreement is based on the precise legal form of an agreement and not on its effects on competition. As a result many inconsequential or even pro-competitive agreements are caught up, while others that have anti-competitive effects may be drafted in a way designed to avoid the law. By contrast, within EU law it is the object or effect of an agreement that determines whether or not it is subject to the law. For example, in the *dyestuffs* case, the manufacturers did not admit to having formed an agreement but it was still possible to find them guilty of operating a concerted practice. On a number of occasions dyestuff producers had been observed to make simultaneous and similar price revisions. The producers did not admit that they were engaged in a concerted practice, but argued that the parallel price changes were simply a natural consequence of oligopolistic competition. Irrespective of this, their behaviour in making parallel price changes was found to have the *effect* of limiting competition, and consequently enabled the EU to find them guilty of operating a concerted practice for which they were substantially fined (Jacquemin and de Jong, 1977; Swann, 1983 and 1988). Such an effects-based approach is seen as being more efficient in that it is likely to capture for investigation a greater number of anti-competitive agreements and fewer of those that are innocuous.

Agreements that fall within the ambit of Article 85 are investigated by the Commission on the receipt of a complaint and/or request for exemption. The appropriate body within a member state (for example, DTI and/or OFT within the UK) is then consulted and assists in an advisory capacity, following which the Commission delivers judgement. Unlike the UK, where the Court, on declaring an agreement 'contrary to the public interest', has little power to impose effective penalties against offending firms, the Commission has considerable powers of enforcement and can fine firms up to 10 per cent of their turnover for operating an anti-competitive practice. Firms then have the right of appeal to the European Court of First Instance, and ultimately to the European Court of Justice (ECJ). The Commission's record on attacking cartels and concerted practices is impressive, as it has vigorously pursued and successfully secured the termination of a substantial number and variety of concerted practices. In particular, it has taken a strong line against price fixing (for example, dyestuffs, glass containers) and market sharing or quantity agreements (for example, cement) to the extent that such practices are now unlikely ever to be granted an exemption.

In the *glass containers* case of 1974, producers within five European countries were found to subscribe to an agreement to notify each other immediately of price changes, and also to align export prices with the domestic prices of the price leader within the importing country. The anti-competitive features of this practice are obvious and the Commission accordingly declared the system illegal (Swann, 1988).

The practice of exclusive dealing has also been the subject of investigation. If manufacturers appoint exclusive dealerships, then this could facilitate the division of the European market into sub-markets with restricted competition between and within them. In 1964 the *Grundig Consten* case highlighted this problem. The German manufacturer gave exclusive distribution rights to Consten for the sales of Grundig products within France, and forbade its non-French distributors from exporting into France. The effect of this policy was that prices in France were 20 to 50 per cent above those in West Germany. The Commission accordingly found this an infringement of Article 85.

Article 86 – Abuse of dominant market power

Article 86 is concerned with the behaviour of dominant firm or near-monopoly situations and bans the abuse of a dominant position where it affects trade between member states through the imposition of 'unfair' trading conditions. A non-exclusive list of examples of such abuses is included in Article 86.

- Directly or indirectly imposing unfair purchase or selling prices or other unfair trading conditions.

- Limiting production, markets or technical development to the prejudice of consumers.

- Applying dissimilar conditions to equivalent transactions with other trading parties, thereby placing them at a competitive disadvantage.

- Making the conclusion of contracts subject to acceptance by the other parties of supplementary obligations which, by their nature or according to commercial usage, have no connection with the subject of such contracts.

For Article 86 to be invoked there has to be an effect on trade, as it is not dominance itself that is contrary to Article 86, but the abuse of that dominance. Within the Article there is no definition of what comprises dominance in terms either of market share or of other criteria. This differs from, for example, the position in the UK legislation where dominance is arbitrarily equated with possession of a market share of 25 per cent or more. To some extent, this lack of guidance provides greater flexibility on the part of the authorities, who are not

> **Box 5.1   The United Brands Case**
>
> The company was found to have abused its dominant position in the market for bananas within the Community in four ways: (i) distributors and ripeners were prohibited from reselling green bananas; (ii) it refused supplies to distributors or ripeners who had participated in advertising campaigns for rival brands; (iii) different prices were charged according to the buyer's country, although there was no ostensible reason for this; (iv) unfair prices were charged in Germany, Denmark and the Benelux countries. The Commission fined the company and ordered it to cease the practices. The first three of these are clearly anti-competitive. However, it is not as easy to be objective about what are or are not 'unfair' prices, and on appeal to the European Court of Justice this charge was overturned for lack of proof.

constrained by a requirement to satisfy some precisely defined criterion of dominance as a precondition for investigation. Consequently, the conditions of dominance can vary from case to case. If an abuse is found to exist then, almost by definition, there must be some element of dominance, otherwise there would be no basis for that abuse. Indeed, it has been argued (Fairburn *et al.*, 1986) that the authorities, having found an abuse, have then adopted the device of contriving to define the market in such a way that the discovered behaviour of the firm becomes an abuse of a dominant position. Thus, dominance can be seen to arise where a firm has the power to behave independently of its competitors and customers, and this may result from a combination of a number of factors, none of which separately would necessarily imply dominance. This was the situation in the case involving *United Brands* (see Box 5.1).

The procedure for investigation and possible sanctions follows the same pattern as outlined earlier for matters dealt with under Article 85. Under Article 86, the Commission has dealt successfully with a number of abuses such as the granting of loyalty rebates (e.g. Hoffman-la Roche), refusals to supply (e.g. Commercial Solvents), and price discrimination (Chiquita) among others.

In the case of *Hoffman-la Roche* the Commission found that the practice of offering major buyers loyalty rebates in return for taking all their requirements from Hoffman-la Roche was an abuse of a dominant position, and thus incompatible with Article 86. The practice had the effect of restricting the buyers' freedom to take up alternative supplies and also acted as an entry barrier by making it difficult for new products to secure outlets.

The Commission held that refusal to supply, in order to eliminate competition, was contrary to Article 86 in the decision on *Commercial Solvents*. ZOJA, a major manufacturer of drugs for treating tuberculosis, had been the subject of a failed takeover bid. In response to this, the United States Solvents Corporation and its Italian subsidiary, Istituto Chimoterapico Italiano, decided to refuse ZOJA supplies of essential intermediate products for which they held a world monopoly. Additional steps were then taken to ensure that ZOJA could

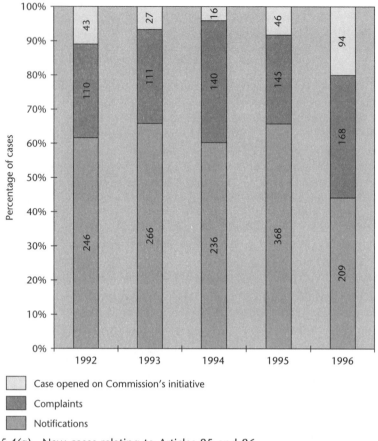

Figure 5.4(a)   New cases relating to Articles 85 and 86

Source: Annual Report on Competition Policy, European Community DGIV, 1996

not obtain supplies anywhere else on the world market. In the face of this attempt
to eliminate it from the market, ZOJA complained. The Commission imposed
fines and ordered the companies to resume supplies.

The levels of cases falling under Articles 85 and 86 are depicted in Figs 5.4(a)
and 5.4(b) for the period 1992–96. It can be seen that, despite a fairly high
and rising number of complaints and of cases opened on the Commission's
initiative (Fig. 5.4(a)), the vast majority of cases are able to be settled informally
and without necessitating a formal prohibition or fine (Fig. 5.4(b)).

Despite this, where serious abuse has been uncovered, the Commission has
not shrunk from imposing substantial penalties as evidenced in the case of *Irish
Sugar* (see Box 5.2).

It is important to emphasise again that it is not dominance in itself which is
contrary to Article 86, but the abuse of that dominance. This, combined with
the greater flexibility in defining dominance, leads to a European approach based
more on the *effects* of, rather than on the formal *structure* of monopoly, as distinct from the situation in the UK where structural criteria have to be satisfied
before investigation can proceed.

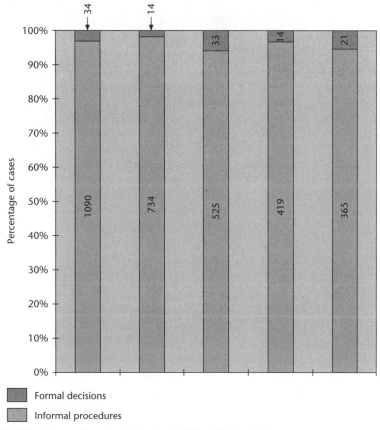

Figure 5.4(b) Cases closed relating to Articles 85 and 86

Source: Annual Report on Competition Policy, European Community DG IV, 1996

Mergers

Until 1990 there was no specific European legislation to deal with mergers. The only avenue for EU control was through the application of Article 85 and/or Article 86, which was only open to those cases involving the operation of restrictive practices and/or the abuse of a dominant position. Thus, if a merger was to lead to the creation of a dominant position and a consequent restriction of competition, this could arguably be classed as an abuse under Article 86. This procedural approach was successfully established by the Commission in the *Continental Can* case, where the merger further enhanced existing dominance, following the take-over of Dutch and German metal container firms by a Belgian subsidiary of Continental Can. This challenge was subsequently overturned by the ECJ in 1973, because the Commission had not demonstrated that competition had been sufficiently restricted.

However, the important general principle that Article 86 could be applied to mergers that restricted competition was accepted, although this power was weakened by the fact that the Article could only be applied to mergers *ex post*, that is to mergers already completed. Later, in the *Philip Morris* case of 1987 it

Box 5.2   The Irish Sugar Case

In May 1997, under Article 86 of the EC Treaty, the Commission found that Irish Sugar had infringed and abused its dominant position and it therefore imposed a fine of ECU 8.8 million on the company. Irish Sugar plc (a subsidiary of the Greencore Group) was the sole processor of sugar in Ireland with 95 per cent of the market, and had abused its dominant position since 1985 by seeking to restrict competition from imports and from small Irish sugar packers. It had done this by offering selectively low prices to the customers of an importer of French sugar, and also by offering selective rebates to customers who were geographically close to suppliers based in Northern Ireland. Rebates were also granted on purchases of bulk sugar by industrial customers who exported part of their final output to other member states. These rebates varied between customers without any systematic relationship to sales volumes or currency changes, and were seen as discriminating against customers who supplied only the Irish market. Irish Sugar had also sought to restrict competition from small sugar packers within Ireland by discriminating against them in the prices that it charged for bulk sugar, thereby placing them at a competitive disadvantage. Further, Irish Sugar had offered rebates to certain wholesalers and food retailers, making it difficult for smaller competitors to gain entry to the market. Through these diverse arrangements Irish Sugar had been able to maintain a significantly higher price level for packaged retail sugar in Ireland and for bulk sugar for 'domestic' Irish consumption compared with that in the other member states. This was to the detriment of both industrial and final consumers in Ireland. In setting the level of the fine the Commission took into account the fact that the infringements represented a serious breach of Community law, that they had been recognised as abuses of a dominant position by the decision of the ECJ, and that they had taken place over a long period of time.

was demonstrated that Article 85 had a relevance for merger control and could be applied where a firm acquired an influential shareholding in a competitor. However, given the growth of international competition and the emergence of the multinational enterprise, control of mergers through Articles 85 and 86 came to be widely recognised as too weak, particularly as leading up to 1992 the numbers of all types of mergers including cross-border mergers were increasing, although cross-border mergers did not appear to represent a rising proportion of the total (Geroski and Vlassopoulos, 1993). Thus, 'at best the existing rules were limited and technically inadequate for a proper merger control policy' (Brittan, 1992).

After a long period of drafting and redrafting, a European Merger Control Regulation (Council Regulation 4064/89) finally came into force on 21 September 1990. This now enables the Commission to investigate and control those 'concentrations' (i.e. mergers and takeovers) which have a 'Union dimension', while those mergers not having a Union dimension remain subject to domestic policies. Details on the Merger Regulation are given in Box 5.3. A critical evaluation of the Merger Control Regulation is given in Bishop (1993).

Box 5.3 **The Merger Control Regulation**

Mergers with a Union dimension are defined as those where the parties have an aggregate turnover in excess of ECU 5 bn, and where at least two of those parties have a Union turnover greater than ECU 250 m. If, however, each of the enterprises achieves more than two-thirds of its turnover within the same single member state, then the merger does not come under the Regulation. Special criteria apply for mergers between financial institutions. Mergers that are found to possess an EU dimension must be notified to the European Commission, which then carries out an investigation to determine whether they are 'compatible with the common market'. In phase I the Commission will decide, within a period of one month, whether there are any 'serious doubts' as to the merger creating or strengthening a dominant position to the likely detriment of effective competition. In the absence of such doubts the merger is permitted to proceed. If such doubts exist, then a phase II investigation is carried out over a maximum of four months to determine whether the merger should be prohibited or not.

A defence of the Regulation has been provided by a leading Commissioner (Brittan, *op cit*).

Table 5.1 displays detailed statistics on the operation of the Merger Control Regulation for the period from its inception. By the end of July 1997 the Commission had examined some 576 merger proposals. Of these, a majority of 538 were found to raise 'no serious doubts' and were cleared at phase I. Of these, 42 fell outside the Regulation, 474 were found compatible with the common market, 17 were found compatible with undertakings, and 5 were referred to a member state for their consideration. However, in 38 notifications 'serious doubts' were raised, and these were referred for detailed investigation in phase II. After investigation, nine of these were allowed to proceed without conditions, and nineteen were allowed to proceed with conditions imposed. In only eight cases was the merger prohibited, and in a further two cases effective competition was required to be restored.

Fig. 5.5(a) portrays the growth in merger decisions, and Fig. 5.5(b) shows the breakdown by type of operation. In all, only 5 per cent of mergers referred to the Commission were found incompatible with the common market and resulted in prohibition and/or the requirement to restore effective competition (Neven *et al.*, 1993).

The proposed acquisition of *Alfa-Laval* by *Tetrapak* is an example of a notification where initial 'serious doubts' were expressed, but which was then approved following the subsequent detailed investigation. Alfa-Laval was a major manufacturer of milk and juice processing machines, whereas Tetrapak had a dominant position in liquid packaging machinery. First indications were that the merger could create or enhance a dominant position. However, in the subsequent enquiry the markets for packaging and processing machines were found to be distinct, and so there would be no extension of dominance. Accordingly, the takeover was allowed to proceed unconditionally.

Table 5.1 Number and type of final decisions, European Merger Control, 21 September 1990 to 31 July 1997

Kind of decision: Phase I	1990	1991	1992	1993	1994	1995	1996	1997 to July	Total
6.1(a) Out of scope of the Control	2	5	9	4	5	9	6	2	42
6.1(b) Compatible with common market	5	47	42	49	77	90	109	55	474
6.1(b) Compatible with undertakings	*	3	4	*	2	3	*	2	14
6.1(c) Compatible & partial referral to member state	*	*	1	*	1	*	*	1	3
9.3(b) Total referral to member state	*	*	*	1	*	*	3	1	5
Total decisions in Phase I	7	55	56	54	85	102	118	61	538
Phase II									
8.2 Compatible with undertakings	*	3	3	2	2	3	3	3	19
8.2 Compatible without undertakings	*	1	1	1	2	2	1	1	9
8.3 Prohibited	*	1	*	*	1	2	3	1	8
8.4 Required to restore effective competition	*	*	*	*	*	*	*	2	2
Total decisions in Phase II	0	5	4	3	5	7	7	7	38
Total Final decisions Phase I and Phase II	7	60	60	57	90	109	125	68	576

Source: Competition Policy, European Commission, DGIV, 1996 http://www.europa.eu.int/en/comm/dg 04 home.htm

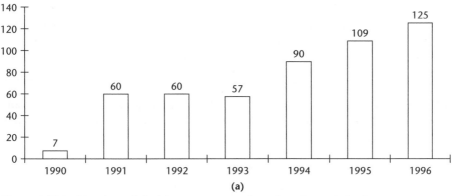

Figure 5.5(a) Number of decisions on cases referred to Commission's Task Force on Mergers

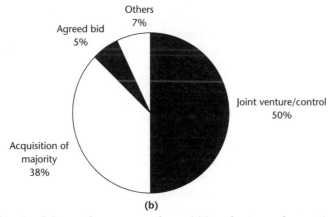

Figure 5.5(b) Breakdown of mergers and acquisitions by type of operation (total 1990–96)

Source: Annual Report on Competition Policy, European Commission DG IV, 1996

In the case of *Aerospatiale/MBB*, the proposed merger was seen to lead to a high market share in civilian helicopters. However, because of competition on the international market from manufacturers in the USA, such as Sikorsky and Bell, the Commission did not feel that the merged firm would attain a dominant position. No serious doubt was raised, and no further investigation was required.

However, this was not so in the disallowed merger of *Aerospatiale/Alenia/ DeHaviland*. ATR was the leading manufacturer of turbo-prop aircraft on the world market, and was jointly owned by Aerospatiale and Alenia. DeHaviland was the second major producer of turbo-prop aircraft, and Aerospatiale and Alenia were seeking to purchase it. Such an acquisition would have led to the creation of a firm with in excess of 50 per cent of the world market in turbo props, and in some sub-market categories considerably more than this. On examination, the Commission found that there was unlikely to be any competitive threat from other small-scale suppliers of turbo props, and that exit from the market was more likely than any new entry. Therefore the Commission decided to prohibit this merger.

In a number of instances where original merger proposals have been unacceptable, firms have had the choice of abandoning them or negotiating conditions for acceptance with the Commission. Typically, this has involved some divestment of existing activities. Thus, in *Accor/Wagons-Lits*, the Commission found that the combined firms would account for 89 per cent of motorway catering and 69 per cent of light meals. Also, the merged firm would have been some 18 times larger than its nearest rival in light meals, and any new entrants would face very high entry barriers. The market would have been clearly dominated by a single firm, and so approval was given only on condition that Accor divest itself completely of Wagons-Lits operations in France. This section will conclude with a look at some of the prohibited mergers.

A number of mergers have been prohibited by use of the Merger Control Regulation. Three of these cases are examined below.

If requested by a national authority, the Commission can investigate a merger even though it falls below the normal EC turnover thresholds. This was so in the *Kesko/Tuko* acquisition. In May 1996 Kesko acquired Tuko and attained a 55 per cent market share in retailing in Finland. In November 1996 the Commission declared the operation to be incompatible with the common market on the grounds that it had led to a dominant position and had significantly impeded competition in the Finnish retail and cash-and-carry markets. Additionally, it had affected intra-EU trade through its influence upon imports and the creation of barriers to entry from other EU states. Since the acquisition had already been completed before the investigation was initiated, the Commission set out measures in February 1997 to restore effective competition. These required Kesko to divest the daily consumer goods business of Tuko to a purchaser capable of acting as an active competitor to Kesko, and the appointment of an independent trustee to ensure compliance.

Another prohibited merger was that of *Gencor/Lonrho* which would have involved the merger of their platinum mining operations. Demand was growing, price was inelastic, and there was an absence of countervailing buying power. Supply was already highly concentrated in four suppliers, with Russian supplies expected to dry up, and there were high barriers to entry with high sunk costs. The merger would have led to a duopolistic position in the worldwide platinum and rhodium markets with no incentive for any post-merger competition. Thus, the merger was deemed to be incompatible with the sustaining of a competitive market.

A proposed joint venture involving the silicon carbide interests of *Saint-Gobain/Wacker-Chemie/NOM* was prohibited. The parties to the proposed joint venture were the technological leaders and would have gained a 60 per cent market share in the European silicon carbide market, with no other producers capable of providing the whole range of grades. The result would have been a lack of potential competition from other European producers or the rest of the world. The joint venture was accordingly declared incompatible.

The foregoing examples illustrate the breadth of the powers available to the Commission to deal with concentrations, and also the importance which the Commission attaches to actual or potential competition as mechanisms for delivering the public interest.

The future of EU and UK competition policy

In recent years there have been a number of wide-ranging official reviews of most aspects of UK competition policy, which have involved widespread consultations with academia, business and other interested parties. This consultative process has culminated in official proposals for change (Department of Trade and Industry,1997). While still maintaining an independent domestic policy towards competition within the UK, these latest proposals will have the effect of bringing that policy into greater alignment with the approach under EU policy. These will involve the abolition of the Restrictive Practices Court and the replacement of the Monopolies and Mergers Commission with a new Competition Commission. In the case of restrictive practices, the new proposals represent a major shift towards a European-type approach closely modelled on Article 85. Policy towards dominant firm monopoly and anti-competitive practices will also involve a shift to an approach closer to that of Article 86. However, in the case of mergers the proposed changes are largely procedural, and no significant re-orientation of present policy is envisaged.

Despite the early successes of restrictive practices legislation in combating collusive agreements, there is now a belief that within the present business climate the legislation possesses fundamental weaknesses. This belief was articulated within an official review of restrictive practices policy (Department of Trade and Industry, 1988c). The main problem is that the policy approach that has evolved is no longer seen as efficient. In particular, the deterrent effect is weak since the penalties for operating an illegal cartel are inadequate, and the Director General of Fair Trading has few powers to intervene and initiate investigations in situations where there is a suspicion that a secret cartel is in operation. A further difficulty is that the current legislation provides no means for combating the growth of the tacit or informal collusion which has come to replace the formal agreements of earlier years. In an attempt to deal with these inadequacies, proposals were put forward for a change from the present *form*-based approach to an *effects*-based approach, which would have involved almost the wholesale adoption of the principles and form of Article 85 (Department of Trade and Industry, 1989). In general, restrictive practices were to be banned. As in Article 85, an illustrative list of prohibited practices was to be published, which would include such specific practices as price fixing or any other practices which may be expected to have that effect. Collusive tendering, market sharing and collective refusals to supply were also to be included. As under Article 85, a facility for the block exemption of certain practices not seen as anti-competitive was to be incorporated.

The effect of these changes would have been to create a more relevant and effective policy, not only by creating greater harmonisation with EU restrictive practices policy, but also by strengthening domestic policy through the adoption of an approach designed to combat any practice which has the effect of restricting competition, as opposed to one that emphasises the form of an agreement, sometimes to the neglect of that effect.

A draft Competition Bill which recognises many of the weaknesses previously identified has been published (Department of Trade and Industry, 1997). This bill seeks to reform UK competition policy in a way that would move it closer to the approach taken by EU competition policy.

For many years there have also been worries over the increasing monopolisation of British industry through structural change, as evidenced by increased levels of both aggregate and market concentration, and of which there is little doubt that merger activity has, at times, been a major causal factor (see e.g. HMSO, 1978; Hughes, 1993). However, in the case of mergers there are no official proposals to change the orientation of policy, despite the concerns which have been expressed about the operation of present policy.

Though European and UK merger policies display a broad similarity in intent and approach, there is at least one important distinction. Within the UK it remains, and it seems will continue to remain, ultimately the prerogative of a politically accountable minister to decide, acting on the advice of the bureaucracy, whether to permit or to forbid a particular merger. By contrast, within EU policy the element of political discretion is much less, since the decision to permit or to forbid an investigated merger is a matter for the administration. Whether political or administrative accountability is the more desirable depends on one's view about the relationships that should exist between State and Society, but it is more likely that where decisions are made by political appointees there will be greater uncertainty, for such decisions then embody both a political and an economic dimension. For this reason EU merger policy *ought* to display less arbitrariness than has been the case within the UK. However, following the first takeover to be disallowed (Aerospatiale/Alenia/DeHaviland), some doubts were expressed over the abilities of Commissioners to submerge their national interests and remain free from political pressures. The potential for such conflict arises from the differing perspectives of industrial and competition policy. Some see the SEM as providing the opportunity for the restructuring of industry and the attainment of international competitiveness, while others see it as providing the opportunity to achieve efficiency by the creation of competitive conditions throughout the EU.

New European developments

Currently there are two new developments in European policy. In June 1997 a revision of the Merger Control Regulation was finally adopted which addresses issues detailed in a Green Paper (DGIV, 1996). In January 1997 the Commission published a consultative Green Paper setting out options for the treatment of vertical restraints (DGIV, 1997a).

Following the merger review it had become clear that many mergers with cross-border effects were not notified to the Commission since they did not meet the EU turnover criteria. However, many of these were being notified to multiple national competition bodies, thus creating unnecessary burdens on both businesses and regulators. Consequently, for mergers which involve activity in at least three member states, the turnover thresholds have been reduced. This should have the benefit of capturing smaller mergers, but with important cross-border effects. It will also simplify the process, and extend the 'one stop' principle by avoiding unnecessary duplication which occurs with referrals to multiple national authorities.

The review of vertical restraints is still at the discussion stage, but a number of issues are addressed. Currently vertical agreements have been considered on a case-by-case basis in accordance with the strict application of Article 85(1), but with block exemptions for exclusive dealing, exclusive purchasing and franchising under Article 85(3). However, the economic effects of vertical agreements are less clear-cut than those of horizontal agreements. The single market has provided opportunities for firms to enter new markets, and that process can be facilitated by the development of efficient distributive systems. Vertical agreements between producers and distributors can be pro-competitive where they enhance such market penetration. However, as with horizontal agreements, they may be used deliberately to restrict competition. Given that (i) the single market legislation is largely in place, (ii) the exemptions governing vertical restraints are shortly to expire, (iii) there have been major changes in distribution methods, and (iv) economic effects can be pro-competitive, the Commission is seeking consultations with a view to formulating a more coherent and consistent policy towards vertical agreements. If this were to lead to some liberalisation in the treatment of vertical agreements it would bring European policy closer to the most recent UK proposals where it is concluded that 'on balance, we believe that there are potentially significant benefits in excluding vertical agreements, so long as they are not price-fixing agreements, from the scope of the prohibition of anti-competitive agreements' (DTI, 1997, p. 1).

Conclusion

Throughout the debate and proposals on all sides it is the persistent emphasis on *competition* that has provided the continuing hallmark of policy. The current UK proposals represent one further stage in the piecemeal development of legislation, with a proposed move yet closer to the *effects*-based approach of the EU and away from the current *form*-based approach. If, as has been argued in this chapter, there are benefits from the harmonisation of policy, then it is clearly sensible to adopt an approach similar to that of Articles 85 and 86.

This slow convergence of EU and UK competition policy is to be welcomed, for with greater harmonisation of policies industry will be able to operate more efficiently through being able to plan within an environment of greater certainty, and will be more secure in the knowledge that its domestic and international operations are likely to receive compatible treatment from the respective authorities.

References

Baumol W J 1959 *Business Behaviour Value and Growth*, Macmillan, New York.
Baumol W J, Panzar, J C and Willig R D 1982 *Contestable Markets and the Theory of Industry Structure*, Harcourt Brace Jovanovich, New York.

Beacham A and Jones J C H 1971 Merger criteria and policy in Great Britain and Canada, *Journal of Industrial Economics*, Vol. 19, pp. 97–117.

Bishop M 1993 European or National? The Community's New Merger Regulation, in Bishop M and Kay J A (eds.), *European Mergers and Merger Policy*, Oxford University Press.

Bishop M and Kay J A (eds.) 1993 *European Mergers and Merger Policy*, Oxford University Press.

Brittan L 1992 *European Competitive Policy*, Brassey's, London.

Button K J 1985 New approaches to the regulation of industry, *Royal Bank of Scotland Review*, No. 148, December, pp. 18–34.

Clarke R 1985 *Industrial Economics*, Blackwell, Oxford.

Cowling K and Mueller D C 1978 The Social Costs of Monopoly Power, *Economic Journal*, No. 88, pp. 77–87.

Crew M A and Rowley C K 1970 Anti-trust policy: economics versus management science, *Moorgate and Wall Street Journal*, Autumn, pp. 19–34.

Crew M A and Rowley C K 1971 Anti-trust policy: the application of rules, *Moorgate and Wall Street Journal*, Autumn, pp. 37–50.

Department of Trade and Industry 1988c *Review of Restrictive Trade Practices Policy*, Green Paper Cmnd 331, HMSO, London.

Department of Trade and Industry 1989 *Opening New Markets: New Policy on Restrictive Trade Practices*, White Paper Cmnd 727, HMSO, London.

Department of Trade and Industry 1997 *A Prohibition Approach to Anti-competitive Agreements and Abuse of Dominant Position: Draft Bill*, August, DTI, London.

Directorate General IV 1996 *Green Paper on the Review of the Merger Regulation*, European Commission, Luxembourg.

Directorate General IV 1997a *Green Paper on Vertical Restraints in EC Competition Policy*, European Commission, Luxembourg.

Directorate General IV 1997b *European Community Competition Policy XXVIth Report on Competition Policy 1996*, European Commission, Luxembourg.

Fairburn J A, Kay J A and Sharpe T A E 1986 The economics of Article 86, in Hall G (ed.) *European Industrial Policy*, Croom Helm, London.

Fleming M and Swann D 1989 Competition policy – The pace quickens and 1992 approaches, *Royal Bank of Scotland Review*, No. 162, June, pp. 47–61.

George K 1989 Do we need a merger policy? in Fairburn J A and Kay J (eds.), *Mergers and Merger Policy*, Oxford University Press.

Geroski P and Vlassopoulos A 1993 Recent Patterns of European Merger Activity, in Bishop M and Kay J A (eds.), *European Mergers and Merger Policy*, Oxford University Press.

Harberger A C 1954 Monopoly and Resource Allocation, *American Economic Review*, No. 44, pp. 77–87.

Hay D and Morris D 1991 *Industrial Economics and Organization Theory and Evidence*, Oxford University Press, Oxford.

HMSO 1978 *A Review of Monopoly and Mergers Policy*, Green Paper Cmnd 7198, HMSO, London.

Howe M 1971 Anti-trust policy: rules or discretionary intervention? *Moorgate and Wall Street Journal*, Spring, pp. 59–68.

Howe M 1972 British merger policy proposals and American experience, *Scottish Journal of Political Economy*, February.

Hughes A 1993 Mergers and Economic Performance in the UK: a Survey of the Empirical Evidence 1950–1990, in Bishop M and Kay J A (eds.), *European Mergers and Merger Policy*, Oxford University Press.

Jacquemin A P and de Jong H W 1977 *European Industrial Organization*, Macmillan, London.

Kamerschen D R 1966 An Estimation of the Welfare Losses from Monopoly in the American Economy, *Western Economic Journal*, No. 4, pp. 221–36.

Littlechild S C 1981 Misleading calculations of the social costs of monopoly, *Economic Journal*, Vol. 91, pp. 348–63.

Littlechild S 1989 Myths and merger policy, in Fairburn J A and Kay J (eds.), *Mergers and Merger Policy*, Oxford University Press.

Neven D, Nuttall R and Seabright P 1993 *Merger in Daylight, the Economics and Politics of European Merger Control*, Centre for Economic Policy Research, London.

Posner M E 1975 The Social Costs of Monopoly and Regulation, *Journal of Political Economy*, Vol. 83, pp. 807–27.

Pratten C F 1971 *Economies of Scale in Manufacturing Industry*, Cambridge University Press.

Rowley C 1973 *Anti-Trust and Economic Efficiency*, Macmillan, London.

Sawyer M C 1979 *Theories of the Firm*, Weidenfeld and Nicholson, London.

Schwartzman D 1960 The Burden of Monopoly, *Journal of Political Economy*, 68, pp. 627–30.

Silberston A 1972 Economies of scale in theory and practice, *Economic Journal*, supplement, No. 82, pp. 369–91.

Sutherland A 1970 The management of mergers policy, in Cairncross A K (ed.), *The Managed Economy*, Blackwell, Oxford, pp. 106–34.

Swann D 1983 *Competition and Industrial Policy in the European Community*, Methuen, London.

Swann D 1988 *The Economics of the Common Market*, 6th edition, Penguin, London.

Utton M A 1975 British merger policy, in George K D and Joll C (eds.), *Competition Policy in the U.K. and E.E.C.*, Cambridge University Press.

Williamson O E 1968 Economies as an anti-trust defence: the welfare trade-offs, *American Economic Review*, Vol. 58, pp. 18–36.

Worcester D A 1973 New Estimates of the Welfare Loss to Monopoly, United States: 1956–69, *Southern Economic Journal*, 40, pp. 234–45.

6 Industrial policy in the European Union

Frank McDonald and Margaret Potton

Introduction

The 21st Report on Competition Policy of the EC (Commission, 1991a) defines industrial policy thus: 'Industrial Policy concerns the effective and coherent implementation of all those policies which impinge on the structural adjustment of industry with a view to promoting competitiveness. The provision of a horizontal framework in which industry can develop and prosper by remedying structural deficiencies and addressing areas where the market mechanism alone fails to provide the conditions necessary for success is the principal means by which the Community applies its industrial policy.'

This definition appears to include competition policy (to maintain a competitive environment), deregulation policies (to remove legal impediments that prohibit or limit competitive markets) and a wide range of social, regional and R&D programmes (to correct market failures). The EU has been active in all these areas. However, in the case of the EU it is not clear if these policies and programmes constitute an effective and/or coherent approach to industrial policy. Further, in some areas it is not clear that the EU is the appropriate agency to take the lead in industrial policy. The EU is hampered in devising a coherent industrial policy because of the very diverse approaches that the member states have adopted towards their national industrial policies (see Beije *et al.*, 1987; Woolcock, 1995). Nevertheless, the EU has developed a series of programmes that impact on a wide range of industries. Therefore, in a sense, the EU does have an industrial policy.

Rationale for industrial policy

Three main approaches to industrial policy can be identified:

1. market-based or negative industrial policy;
2. interventionist or positive industrial policy;
3. selective intervention or strategic industrial policy.

Market-based industrial policy is founded on the view that market mechanisms are on the whole effective in generating an efficient and vibrant industrial structure. This approach requires intervention only where there are significant cases

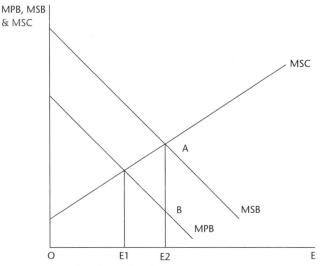

Figure 6.1 Externalities and industrial policy

MPB = marginal private benefit   MSB = marginal social benefit

MSC = marginal social cost   E = Expenditure on R&D

Maximisation of net benefits is where MSB = MSC (i.e. the marginal cost to society of R&D expenditures is equal to the marginal benefits to society). The optimal level of R&D expenditures is therefore E2. However, if the spill-over effects of R&D expenditures (i.e. the difference between MPB and MSB) are not taken into account, R&D expenditures will be sub-optimal (i.e. at E1 where MPB = MSC). In order to reach an optimal level of R&D expenditures, a subsidy of AB would be required to compensate the company engaging in R&D expenditures for the spill-over effects.

If governments do not estimate the size of the required subsidy correctly there would be either too little or too much R&D expenditure. This is 'government failure'. Another solution to the problem of sub-optimal R&D expenditures is to define intellectual property rights clearly such that the spill-over effects are captured by the company which engages in R&D expenditures. This would require the beneficiaries of R&D expenditures to pay the company for the benefits that are conferred on the rest of society from these expenditures, by for example the sale of patent rights. However, many of these expenditures are not amenable to such a property rights solution because of the difficulties of accurately defining intellectual property rights.

of market failure. Thus, if externalities lead to under-provision of R&D expenditures or training for labour there may be a case for government intervention to correct these market failures (see Fig. 6.1). However, many of the advocates of market-based industrial policies have reservations about the ability of governments to correct market failures successfully, and some argue that government intervention to correct for market failure often leads to a worse outcome than that which arises from the 'imperfect market process'. In other words, government intervention leads to greater inefficiencies than does market failure (see Buchanan, 1978). Therefore, in the market-based approach industrial policy is mainly negative, i.e. the prevention of abuse of market power and the removal of legal impediments to free trade. Hence, competition policy, the removal of state aids to promote competitive markets and deregulation programmes are regarded as the cornerstones of industrial policy.

Interventionist industrial policy is based on the view that market failure in areas such as R&D and labour training are important obstacles to the development of a dynamic industrial base. Social and regional considerations are also considered to be important factors in devising a 'good' industrial policy. Such social and regional factors are often considered to have important economic effects due to loss of productive potential and high public expenditures that arise from unemployment. Industrial policy that successfully improves the productive capacity of poorer regions or sectors of economies can increase employment levels and income (see Fig. 6.2). Positive action and financial support by governments to ensure adequate R&D and training expenditures and to provide aid to poorer groups and regions are considered to be an essential part of industrial policy. This approach tends to see a need for intervention in a wide range of industries and sectors covering both declining and emerging industries.

The selective interventionist approach to industrial policy takes a more strategic view of industrial policy. In this approach the main role for industrial policy is to aid the growth of emerging industries to replace those that are in decline. The need for such a strategic approach arises from the imperfect nature of the competitive environment, in particular in cases where there exist strong economies of scale and learning effects. In these cases selective help by use of state aids can give competitive advantages to companies. State aids can also be used to help companies to 'catch up' on foreign competitors that are established in the market (see Fig. 6.3). The theoretical benefits of this approach have been put forward by Krugman and Obstfeld (1991). However, Krugman is somewhat reluctant to advocate such an approach to industrial policy because of the risks of retaliation from competitors, and also because it is very difficult for governments to gather and assess the appropriate information that would allow them to choose potential 'winners'. However, the benefits of such strategic approaches seem to have been accepted by some American economists (Tyson, 1992), and the economic rationale for projects such as the European Airbus rests on strategic interventionist arguments. The arguments for and against an interventionist policy in the EU, in the light of the globalisation of economic activity, are examined in Nicolaides (1993).

In addition to these economic arguments a political-economic case can be put for industrial policy. Governments affect industry by their public procurement policies, subsidies, competition and regulatory frameworks, taxation systems, and other laws and policies that impact on companies. All governments exercise important influences on companies. As such, all governments have industrial policies or, more correctly, policies that have a significant impact on industry. Therefore, governments have no option but to have some kind of an industrial policy (Bangemann, 1993). However, an assessment of the economic arguments on the impact of government policy that affects industry may provide useful insights as to how wisely governments gear their policies with respect to the impact on industry. The general objectives of governments become important in what is regarded as good or bad industrial policy. Therefore, if the creation and maintenance of competitiveness of companies is a high priority, the current orthodox view is that a market-based industrial policy should be followed. However, the legacy of history is important. Decisions taken in the past

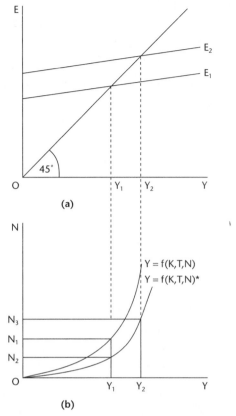

Figure 6.2 Industrial policy as a means of boosting employment

In Fig. 6.2(a) the level of national income (Y) is determined by national expenditure (E) at Y1. This will correspond to an employment level (with a given relationship between employment and income shown by the production function in Fig. 6.2(b)) of N1 on production function $Y = f(K,L,T)$. Where K = amount of capital, L = amount of labour and T = state of technology (the techniques that link capital and labour together in production processes). This production function is based on a fixed amount of capital and a given state of technology. If parts of the economy have poor levels of technology because of structural deficiencies such as low skill levels in parts of the labour force, it may be possible to improve technology in these areas by use of industrial policy (e.g. help with labour training). This will shift the production function to, say, $Y = f(K,L,T)^*$. In these circumstances, to produce an income level of Y1 would require employment of N2 (that is less than N1). Consequently, the first effect of this policy would be to reduce employment. However, the improvement in technology should lead to lower costs and therefore to lower prices for products. This will lower prices and therefore lead to higher expenditure. Expenditure would shift to, say, E2, leading to a higher income – Y2. This would require a higher employment level – N3. In this scenario a virtuous circle is created of improvements in technology leading to higher expenditures and thereby to higher employment levels.

The size of these effects depends on the scale of the shifts in the production function and the resultant effect on expenditure. The creation of the virtuous circle depends on the government accurately identifying the causes of the low technology in particular regions and sectors, and being able to rectify this at a cost that is less than, or equal to, the value of the benefits of any increase in employment. The potential for government failure in this area may be quite high. Moreover, the causes of the poor performance in the specified regions or sectors most be amenable to correction by government policies.

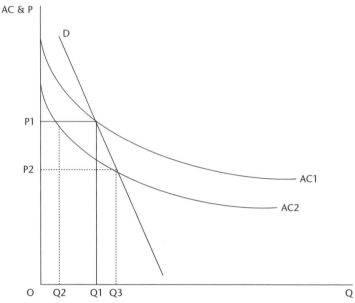

Figure 6.3   The strategic case for industrial policy

P = price   AC = average cost   Q = quantity

If a company establishes a plant in country A with average cost given by AC1, and it was the first company to produce the product, it would have a first mover advantage. The company will operate at P1:Q1 (assuming that the company sets price equal to average cost). Therefore, although the company in country B has lower costs than the company in country A (i.e. AC2 rather than AC1) it will not be able to enter the market because the company in country A has a first mover advantage. At the price P1 the company in country B cannot sell output at less than, or equal to, its average cost unless it enters the market with an output level of 0Q2 or above. To be able to realise such an outcome the company in country B would have to take market share from the first mover and it would make losses until it reached an output level of 0Q2. Moreover, as the company in country B entered the market it would put downward pressure on the market price and would therefore worsen its position with regard to the difference between price and its average cost.

   However, the government in country B could help the company to enter the market by strategic industrial policy. Thus subsidies could be given or other types of help to allow company B to offset the first mover advantage of the company in country A. If such help was given the company in country B would eventually replace the company in country A with price and output given by P2:Q3. This policy would be beneficial because it would allow the most efficient producer to supply the market and it would lower price and increase output (see Krugman and Obstfeld, 1991).

   The problem with this approach is that it assumes that government can select companies that would fall into this category and it also assumes that the government of country A would not retaliate in response to the loss of market share by its companies caused by the industrial policies of other countries.

to subsidise or favour particular industries often result in the creation of strong vested interests that can make it very difficult to alter existing policies. The member states have very different histories in their approach to industrial policy and this makes it very difficult to alter the direction of industrial policy.

Types of industrial policy

Industrial policy can be based on three different approaches.

■ Horizontal industrial policy
This involves the creation and maintenance of a competitive and regulatory framework for all industry that is compatible with the objectives of the government, for example, the promotion of competitiveness. Horizontal industrial policy can also include help to industry to help to achieve the objectives of governments, such as education and training policies that are geared to the needs of industry. These, however, are aimed at all industry, not at selected parts of the economy.

■ Vertical industrial policy
Vertical policy selects particular industries for special treatment. This type of policy is often related to help for declining industries and for those industries that are considered to be strategically important in terms of such factors as global competition or avoiding dependency on foreign technologies and products.

■ Mixed industrial policy
If governments select key industries for special attention in terms of creating and maintaining the conditions for good performance by modifiying competitive and regulatory frameworks and also by help in such areas as R&D, then a type of mixed industrial policy can be said to be in operation. This kind of approach is often observed in the IT and biotechnology industries.

Most countries take an eclectic view of industrial policy. Although the USA, Germany and the UK tend towards a market-based and horizontal approach, and France and Italy towards a more interventionist and vertical approach, these countries have a mixture of these types in their industrial policies. In a sense, the majority of countries adopt a mixed approach. However, in many countries there has been a pronounced shift towards a more market-based and hori-zontal approach to industrial policy. This movement can be seen in the dereg-ulation programmes in areas such as transport services, telecommunications services and airlines. The growth of privatisation programmes also bears witness to the move towards market-based industrial policies. Nevertheless, the large-scale protection of declining industries and the widespread used of state aids by many countries provide evidence that interventionist industrial policies are still a potent force in many economies.

EU Industrial Policy

The EU began with a significant interventionist approach in the areas of coal and steel with the Treaty of Paris which founded the ECSC. However, the EEC was more concerned with establishing free movement of goods, services, cap-ital and labour and the development of a strong competition policy. As the EU has developed, more interventionist and strategic approaches to industrial policy have arisen, for example, the growth of R&D programmes and policies to aid declining industries and poorer regions. Nevertheless, the EU has also engaged in significant deregulation programmes. For instance, a large part of the SEM programme was predominantly concerned with deregulation, and the Union has embarked on significant deregulation programmes in the telecommunication services and airline industries. The Commission is also encouraging the privatisation programmes that are taking place in many of the member states.

The debate over the characteristics of EU industrial policy has become an important issue due to the growth of Union policies and programmes that affect industry and because of the concept of subsidiarity. Three possible reasons for an EU industrial policy can be put forward – spillover effects related to externalities, creating the conditions for *free movement*, and promoting 'economic and social cohesion'.

In order for externality arguments to be a valid rationale for a common industrial policy for the EU, the member states of the Union would have to encompass most of the spill-over effects of R&D and training programmes. Given the lack of labour mobility in the EU, it is difficult to see a pronounced externality effect in labour training which would spill over to other member states. The position with regard to R&D programmes is less clear. However, given the increasing globalisation of business activities, it is not obvious that the EU is the appropriate agency to provide a coherent and effective R&D policy. The case for a European Industrial Policy on the basis of the spill-over effect is not very strong. However, if there is a case it would require a positive or strategic industrial policy.

The EU has a role to play in providing the conditions for *free movement*. The various industrial policies in the member states create the potential for the establishment of barriers to free movement and distortions to trade flows because of the use of state aids. The EU has played a significant role in reducing these barriers to free movement, but this involves primarily negative industrial policy. Indeed, the main requirements are related to competition policy, the control of state aids, and the creation and maintenance of legal frameworks that permit free movement.

The attractiveness of the EU as an effective agency for the provision of industrial policies to promote 'economic and social cohesion' would depend on the acceptance of this as an important goal for the Union, and also on whether this goal could be better met by promoting free movement in a predominantly market-based system. Nevertheless, this reason for industrial policy, if it were taken seriously, could involve a significant increase in EU programmes, many of which would be primarily connected to positive or strategic industrial policy.

Industrial policy as laid down in the Treaties

The first treaty provision for industrial policy was in the Treaty of Paris. The High Authority may 'facilitate the carrying out of investment programmes by granting loans to undertakings or by guaranteeing other loans'. It may also 'assist the financing of works and installations which contribute directly and primarily to increasing production' (Article 54). It can also ban loans if they are contrary to the Treaty. Article 55 says that the 'High Authority shall promote technical and economic research into the production and increased use of coal and steel'. The High Authority may 'initiate and facilitate such research'.

The High Authority also had the power to affect production (Article 58) if the Community 'is confronted with a period of manifest crisis'. It can establish a system of production quotas subject to Article 74. Article 46 established that the High Authority shall 'periodically lay down general objectives for modernisation, long-term planning of manufacture and expansion of productive capacity'. Thus the Treaty of Paris is quite *dirigiste*.

The Treaty establishing the European Coal and Steel Community was concluded in 1952 for a timespan of 50 years. As it is not going to be renewed in 2002, it has been necessary to start unwinding its financial activities. After 2002 industrial policy towards the steel and coal industries will be governed by the TEU. Three principal problems are being addressed to reduce the financial burden of supporting these industries.

1. Reduce the magnitude of the levies applied to protect the coal and steel sector.
2. Slowly reduce the number of borrowings contracted and loans granted by the ECSC. By 1995 the total amount of loans granted was already down by 40 per cent and this process will be escalated. For example, since 1 July 1994, the Commission has stopped accepting new applications for loans to encourage the consumption of steel.
3. Improve the coverage of the risks inherent in the financial transactions of the ECSC, by making greater use of standard provisions against risk. This is also in agreement with the recommendation of the Court of Auditors.

Combining these three principles should make it possible to run down the ECSC's financial activities gradually.

The Treaty of Rome scarcely mentions industrial policy. However, State Aids granted by member states are mentioned in Articles 92 and 93. Article 92 states that 'aid to promote the economic development of areas where the standard of living is abnormally low or where there is serious unemployment' is compatible with the Common Market, as is 'aid to promote the execution of an important project of common European interest or to remedy a serious disturbance in the economy of a member state' and 'other categories of aid as may be specified by decision of the Council acting by a qualified majority on a proposal from the Commission.' Article 93 is on the organisation of state aid. Section 1 says that 'the Commission shall, in cooperation with member states, keep under constant review all systems of aid existing in those states. It shall propose to the latter any appropriate measures required by the progressive development or by the functioning of the common market.'

At the time of the signing of the Treaty of Rome the industrial policies of France and Germany, which were the two dominant member countries at the time, were very difficult to align as they were very different. The French government believed in a *dirigiste* policy. There was a need in France for the government to have a strong influence on industrial development, if not to plan it centrally as in the then Eastern bloc. In Germany, on the other hand, there was, and still is, a reliance on a more *laissez-faire* regime wedded to market forces. In 1957 intervention in industry was not really an issue. The main aim was to set up a common market based on competition, and a healthy industrial structure was expected to follow.

Thus, up to the SEA, there was not much specifically laid down in the Treaties concerning industrial policy apart from the above-mentioned provisions in the Treaty of Paris regarding coal and steel. Article 23 of the SEA, however, modified the Treaty of Rome by adding Title V on economic and social cohesion which includes Article 130c on the ERDF, which 'is intended to help redress the principal regional imbalances in the Community through participating in the development and structural adjustment of regions whose development is lagging behind and *in the conversion of declining industrial regions*' (authors' italics). Title VI, which was also added to the Treaty of Rome by Article 24 of the SEA, is about research and technological development. Article 130f stipulates that the 'Community's aim shall be to strengthen the scientific and technological basis of European industry and to encourage it to become more competitive at international level'.

Thus research and technological development (RTD) programmes were to be implemented by promoting cooperation with undertakings, research centres and universities. Member states were to coordinate their R&D policies and programmes, and the Commission could take any useful initiative to promote such coordination (Article 130h). The Community was to adopt a multi-annual framework programme setting out all its activities. Thus guidelines for policy in research and technological development which were to become very important in later years were laid down in 1986 in the SEA.

The TEU amended the Treaty of Rome to include a section on industry, Title XIII, Article 130 (see Box 6.1). This article provided a foundation for the development of a treaty-based industrial policy based on creating the conditions that will encourage companies to pursue competitiveness.

A significant step was, therefore, taken in the SEA and the TEU to establish a firm basis for an industrial policy that is strongly focused on programmes for RTD. Therefore, by 1992 a clear, but limited, treaty foundation for an EU Industrial Policy had been established.

The development of the Community's Industrial Policy

Industrial policy has gradually evolved during the years through reports from Commissioners, summit communiqués, Green and White Papers and directives since its fragile start in the Treaty of Paris in 1951. Progress has finally been crystallised in the TEU after 40-odd years of piecemeal development.

Articles 92–94 of the Treaty of Rome on State Aid granted by member states were written so that state aids did not distort competition. In the 1960s state intervention was in the realm of regional aid. Therefore, the initial priority was to get member states to agree to guidelines on regional aid. Between 1968 and 1971 the Community's regional policy was developed. Different types of region

Box 6.1 **Key provisions in Article 130 on industrial policy**

1. The Community and the member states shall ensure that the conditions necessary for the competitiveness of the Community's industry exist.

   For that purpose, in accordance with a system of open and competitive markets, their action shall be aimed at:

   – speeding up the adjustment of industry to structural changes;

   – encouraging an environment favourable to initiative and to the development of undertakings throughout the Community, particularly SMEs;

   – encouraging an environment favourable to cooperation between undertakings;

   – fostering better exploitation of the industrial potential of policies of innovation, research and technological development.

2. The member states shall consult each other in liaison with the Commission and, when necessary, shall coordinate their action. The Commission may take any useful initiative to promote such coordination.

3. The Community shall contribute to the achievement of the objectives set out in paragraph 1 through the policies and activities it pursues under other provisions of this Treaty. The Council, acting unanimously on a proposal from the Commission, after consulting the European Parliament and the Economic and Social Committee, may decide on specific measures in support of action taken in member states to achieve the objectives set out in paragraph 1.

   The Title shall not provide a basis for the introduction by the Community of any measure which could lead to a distortion of competition.

   Article 130f of Title XV states that 'The Community shall have the objective of strengthening the scientific and technological bases of Community industry and encouraging it to become more competitive at international level, while promoting all the research activities deemed necessary by virtue of other chapters of this Treaty'. The Community is to encourage firms, research centres and universities in research and technological development activities, aiming to enable firms to 'exploit the internal market potential to the full' especially through the 'opening up of national public contracts, the definition of common standards and the removal of legal and fiscal obstacles to that cooperation'.

were classified, state aid 'ceilings' were established for different categories of region, and there were methods of ensuring that information and notification about regional aid were given to the Commission.

The Community's slow progress in RTD was recognised as early as 1967 when the EEC Medium Term Economic Committee set up a Working Party for Scientific and Technical Research Policy, or PREST. In this year it completed a report which proposed some ideas for encouraging research and innovation in the member states and in the Community. The first Council of Science Ministers was held in 1967 and made some resolutions. It noted that Europe needed to catch up with the USA and announced that the Community would establish a legal and tax framework that would encourage research. It furthered collaboration in the seven areas mentioned by the PREST working party, i.e. data-processing, pollution, telecommunications, meteorology, transport, the metallurgical industries and oceanography.

A new Directorate General XII for Research, Science and Education was founded at the Commission after the First Council of Science Ministers. Also, a new Directorate General III was established for industrial affairs in 1967. In 1970 the Council of Ministers established a forum called COST, i.e. European Cooperation on Scientific and Technical Research. Through this the Community collaborated with some non-member states.

In the 1960s and early 1970s the main thrust of industrial policy was to complete the internal market. Stress was put on the importance of eliminating non-tariff barriers to trade, reducing national preferences in government purchasing, and creating a harmonised tax, monetary and legal background for European industry. Industrial policy was primarily directed towards harmonising and controlling state intervention, especially by use of state aids.

By 1969, the 12-year transition period culminating in the completion of the customs union had ended and the Community could give its attention to new goals. Among these was industrial policy. In 1970 Guido Colonna, the Commissioner for DG IV, produced a 'Memorandum on Industrial Policy in the Communities', otherwise known as the Colonna Report (Commission, 1970a). It expressed the need to create a single European industrial system by enabling firms to function on a Community-wide basis and by creating a single European market. It stressed how important it was for companies to organise themselves on a European level, and that this would necessitate the provision of a European Company Statute, the harmonisation of company laws of member states, and the setting up of laws relating to corporate groups, and possibly new kinds of business networks. A need to eradicate taxation problems that affected cross-frontier mergers was also identified, because of the unfavourable effects of taxation systems on such mergers. The Commission perceived the transnational firm as a means to facilitate progress in technology. The concept of development contracts, which were to be given primarily to firms that were prepared to carry out technological development internationally, was originated. New kinds of industry based on technology were to be established to compensate for old industries which were declining. The need for mobility of labour and the use of the European Social Fund (ESF) in coping with declining industries was mentioned. In time the management of the vicissitudes of industries in decline was to become a main pillar of EU industrial policy. Most of the measures mentioned in the Colonna Report were adopted, in principle, by the Heads of State at the Paris Summit in 1972.

In 1973 an action programme on industrial and technical policy was put forward by the Commission under the influence of the Paris Summit communiqué. It was a subdued version of the Colonna Report. Two suggestions were made – first the harmonisation of company law in the member states, and secondly the creation of a European company statute. Also in 1973, a Commission memorandum establishing a scientific and technology policy programme was published.

In the first part of 1974 a programme of action on this subject was adopted by the Council of Ministers, mentioning the need for cooperation in science and technology, a free exchange of scientific and technological information, collaboration on projects of EU interest, the founding of an umbrella organisational structure, and forecasting about science and technology.

In 1975 the Colonna Report proposal for a European Company Statute was embodied in the *Proposal for a Council Regulation on the statute for European Companies* (Commission, 1975). This was a development from the *Proposal for a Council Regulation Embodying a Statute for European Companies* (Commission, 1970b). The proposal ran up against the problem of *Mitbestimmung* (the question of workers' participation in decision-making) in German companies not being accepted throughout the Community, and the problem of to what extent the European company should come under the aegis of the ECJ.

As a result of the Colonna Report's advocation of cross-frontier cooperation, there was a *Proposal for a Regulation by the Council on the European Cooperation Grouping (ECG)* (Commission, 1974). In 1972 the Business Liaison Office, as it was then known (now the Business Cooperation Office (BCO)), was founded by the Commission originally on a temporary basis for three years. It now provides a permanent service to companies on fiscal and economic problems in cross-frontier cooperation. It also facilitates the 'twinning' of SMEs and small banks. Also around this time the Community published two international patent conventions – the Munich Convention for the Grant of European Patents of 1973, i.e. the European Patent Convention, in conjunction with non-member states, and the Luxembourg Convention for the European Patent for the Common Market of 1975, i.e. the Common Market Patent Convention, in conjunction with the member states.

In the 1980s the Community became progressively more interested in the SME sector. This sector was identified as important because it was thought to be capable of generating jobs and of providing a stimulus to the innovative capacity of the economy of the EU. A European Year of Small and Medium-Sized Enterprises was organised in 1983 as the first measure establishing a Community Enterprise Policy. In December 1985 the European Council instituted an assessment of the impact of Community proposals on SMEs and planned to prepare measures to ease their tax, regulatory and administrative environment. Using Article 235 of the Treaty of Rome as a basis, these tasks were organised in two stages.

Stage One involved the establishment of the SME Task Force in June 1986. Two resolutions, one in November 1986, set up an action programme for SMEs and the other, approved in December 1986, contained measures which aimed to help SMEs by encouraging new enterprises and to increase employment in this sector.

Stage Two began in 1989 after the entry into force of the SEA when the Community agreed to give more resources to its Enterprise Policy. This resulted in the creation of a new Directorate General (DG XXIII) which took over the responsibilities of the Task Force for implementing Enterprise Policy as well as taking care of tourism, cooperatives and distributive trades. Another Council Decision, in July 1989, sought to improve the business environment and the

Box 6.2   Measures to develop the enterprise policy of the EU

- The White Paper on Growth, Competitiveness and Employment (Commission, 1993a) proposed a strategy to help enterprises, and especially SMEs, to ensure the appropriate mobilisation of economic forces for growth, competitiveness and employment.

- The Integrated Programme in favour of SMEs and the Craft Sector includes two types of action – (i) actions arising from Article 130 of the Treaty on European Union and aimed at furthering mutual consultation and coordination between member states, and (ii) the contributions the EU intends to make to the development of SMEs.

- Council Decision in 1996 (COM(96)98 final) for a third multiannual programme for small and medium-sized enterprises (SMEs) in the European Union (1997 to 2000) is based on the new thinking of the Integrated Programme and establishes a budgetary and legal basis for Enterprise Policy.

- A document from the Commission – 'Community Guidelines on State Aid for Small and Medium-sized Enterprises' (96/C 213/04) – calls for the development of a clear strategy for approving state aid for SMEs. This document also provides a definition of SMEs.

General definition of SMEs
Fewer than 250 employees and an annual turnover not exceeding ECU 40 million, or an annual balance sheet total not exceeding ECU 27 million.

Small enterprises
Fewer than 50 employees and an annual turnover not exceeding ECU 7 million, or an annual balance sheet not exceeding ECU 5 million.

To be defined as an SME they must be independent, that is, no more than 25 per cent of the capital or of the voting rights of the enterprise may be owned by another enterprise which does not meet the conditions for classification as an SME.

promotion of the development of enterprises, in particular SMEs. A subsequent Council Decision, in June 1993, developed a Multi-annual Programme of Community measures to intensify the priority areas and to consolidate policy for enterprise particularly for SMEs. For the period 1993–96 a budget of ECU 112.2 million was allocated to Enterprise Policy.

The TEU provided for Enterprise Policy in Article 130. This led the Commission to put a greater emphasis on cost-benefit analysis of the burden on SMEs of new EU laws. Since the TEU a number of resolutions and decisions have been made to develop the Enterprise Policy of the EU (see Box 6.2).

Industrial policy in the 1990s

In the 1990s the general position of the EU with regard to Industrial Policy was significantly influenced by two publications – *Industrial Policy in an Open and*

Competitive Environment: Guidelines for a Community Approach (Commission, 1990), and *An Industrial Competitiveness Policy for the European Union* (Commission, 1994), the so-called Bangemann Report. These documents reflect a significant shift in Community thinking on industrial policy. They sought to focus industrial policy in four main areas:

- to promote intangible investment;
- to develop industrial cooperation;
- to ensure fair competition;
- to modernise the role of public authorities with respect to industrial policy.

The overall view expounded in these documents is that industrial policy should be primarily horizontal, and focused on the development of competitiveness among European enterprises. The Commission has also encouraged greater use of IT to promote an 'information society'. A number of proposals relating to this were made in the Communication 'Europe's way to the Information Society. An Action Plan' – the follow-up to the Bangemann Report. These included: acceleration of the liberalisation of the telecoms sector; the establishment of a regulatory framework to promote effective interconnection of networks, and interoperability of telecommunications services and networks. The document advocates that particular attention should be paid to the SME sector, public administrations and the younger generation. The Bangemann Report argued for EU level frameworks to deal with the problems of the information society. Furthermore, each member state was encouraged to appoint a single minister to represent it in a Council of Ministers in matters related to the information society.

These developments moved the EU towards a more horizontal approach towards industrial policy. The use of protectionary policies and of subsidisation of national (European) champions is not regarded as a sensible approach to industrial policy. Nevertheless, the policy is confused. The use of a mixed approach in R&D policy and the highlighting of the importance of the IT and biotechnology sectors betray elements of a tendency to promote European champions. However, the need to develop free and competitive markets with the rest of the world is also prominent in the Community's new approach to industrial policy. How the potential inconsistencies in this approach will be overcome is not clear.

The EU has identified help with R&D as an important factor to help develop the competitiveness of European enterprises. R&D programmes are concentrated in the IT sector, telecommunications (equipment and services) and biotechnology. However, there are a number of R&D projects that extend beyond these areas (see Box 6.3). In an attempt to clarify and prioritise the objectives of the R&D programmes of the EU, the SEA called for the establishment of a multi-annual Framework programme. The Fourth Framework was agreed for 1994–98. The Framework identified the need to enhance the international competitiveness of European industry as the main objective of the Community's R&D programmes – 'to increase the economic spin-offs from Community research, in particular by concentrating on generic technologies which will enable European industry and its subcontractors to go back on the offensive in international competition.'

Box 6.3   European Union R&D programmes

During the 1970s and early 1980s there was a considerable increase in the number of Community organisations with a bewilderingly large number of acronyms. The main programmes included:

BRIDGE – Biotechnology Research for Innovation, Development and Growth in Europe 1990–94, continued as BIOTEC 2 – Research and Technological Development in Biotechnology 1994–98

BRITE – Basic Research in Industrial Technologies for Europe, developed into BRITE/ EURAM 3 – Research and Technological Development in Industrial and Materials Technologies 1994–98

DELTA – Developing European Learning through Technological Advance, continued as Area 4 of the Telematics Systems Programme – Telematics Systems in Areas of General Interest 1990–94 and then Telematics 2C Programme of Research and Technological Development in the Area of Telematics Applications 1994–98

ESPRIT – European Strategic Programme for Research and Development in Information Technology 1990–94, developed into ESPRIT 4 Research and Technological Development Programme in Fields of Information Technology 1994–98

EUREKA – European Research Coordination Agency founded in 1985 to coordinate collaboration between the member states in R&D programmes

RACE – Research and Development Programme in Advanced Communications Technologies for Europe 1990–94, developed into ACTS – Research and Development in Advanced Communication Technologies and Services 1994–98

STEP – Science and Technology for Environmental Protection 1989–93, continued in the Environment and Climate Programme

STRIDE – Science and Technology for Regional Innovation and Development in Europe 1990–93, incorporated into the Small and Medium-sized Enterprises Community Initiative.

(Commission, 1993b). The major focus of the available funds was on the IT and telecommunications sector, environmental protection technologies, and biotechnology.

The Commission has continued to focus on the need for industrial policy to help companies to develop competitiveness. A Green Paper on Innovation has been published which highlights some of the major shortcomings of European companies in the area of innovation, and also proposes some solutions to overcome these problems (Commission, 1995). The Green Paper states that the paradox about Europe is that it has an exceptionally able scientific base but is less successful than other developed countries in converting its scientific ability into new products, especially in high-technology sectors (see Box 6.4).

The Green Paper highlights some of the problems of the new approach to industrial policy. It is not difficult to highlight shortcomings in R&D expenditures

Box 6.4 Green Paper on Innovation

The Green Paper identifies a number of major problems that hamper the capacity of European enterprises to make best use of scientific and technological knowledge.

- Research and development expenditures are considered to be too low – 2 per cent of GNP in 1993 as against 2.7 per cent in the US and Japan.
- There are not enough scientists, engineers and researchers (4 per 1000 of EU workers as against 7 per 1000 in the US and Japan).
- Legal obstacles to the setting up of new companies – it can take as long as 300 days to set up a new company in Europe.
- There is a shortage of venture capital in Europe (compared with the USA), hampering investment in high technology and in young companies.
- The European Patent Convention is not yet ratified by all member states, leading to a heavy reliance on the use of the US patenting system.
- The cost of patenting is six times greater in Europe than in the US.
- Research, universities and industry and education and the business world are too strictly separate in Europe.
- Companies wishing to enter the European market are subject to too many national legal systems – the ability of enterprises to establish themselves freely in all member states is considered to be essential to encourage faster dissemination of new innovative technologies.

The paper recommends a number of requirements to help to promote greater innovation among European enterprises.

1. Better direct research efforts that help enterprises to be innovative.
2. Reinforcement of the human resources base for innovation.
3. Improving the financial conditions for backing innovation.
4. Reforming the legal and regulatory environment to suit innovation.
5. Developing helpful public attitudes to innovation.

The Green Paper led to the First Action Plan for Innovation in Europe: Innovation for Growth and Employment [COM(96)589 final].

and policies towards technological development by making comparisons with other developed economies. However, it is more difficult to decide what to do about these supposed shortcomings. Moreover, technological development is intimately connected with institutional, cultural and historical factors. Therefore, innovation processes are largely path dependent, that is, the overall nature and direction of change are significantly determined by the past history of societies (North, 1990). Hence what works in the US or Japan may not work in Europe. The member states have very different institutional, cultural and historical experiences, which makes it difficult to find innovation and technology policies that will be effective across all the member states. Furthermore, the use of competition and industrial policies that encourage the development of the competitiveness of enterprises are liable to lead to conflict with trade partners. Many of the problems in EU-US relations stem from disputes about the use of competition and industrial policies that encourage domestic enterprises (see Chapter 15). The OECD and the WTO are seeking to develop ground rules that will allow solutions to be found to conflicts of this type, and also to implement policies that will grant free access to markets (Commission, 1996; OECD, 1996; Falconer and Sauvé, 1996). The development of the Industrial Policy of the EU is, therefore, likely to become more and more linked to the common commercial and competition policies of the Community. This will require DG III (responsible for industrial policy) to work closely with DG IV (responsible for competition policy) and DG I (responsible for external relations) in the development of the EU's Industrial Policy.

The IT and biotechnology sectors

The EU has increasingly focused on development of the IT and biotechnology sectors as a major means of boosting the competitiveness of European enterprises. These sectors (particularly IT) are considered to provide enabling technologies that will have widespread spillover effects on the competitiveness of a wide range of industries.

A policy to help the IT sector, including a technological development policy, was advocated in *Industrial Policy in an Open and Competitive Environment* (Commission, 1990). It was deemed useful to employ this approach to the Community's electronics and information technology (IT) industries because they had serious structural adjustment problems in the early 1990s.

The Community's electronics and information technology industries have three main products – components, computers (i.e. hardware, printers, software, and optic and industrial automation applications) and consumer electronics. During 1990 the worldwide turnover of these industries was ECU 700 bn and the turnover in the Community ECU 175 bn. The market expanded rapidly in the 1980s, representing 5 per cent of GDP in 1990 and expected to rise to 10 per cent by the year 2000. These industries are normally regarded as very important as they provide the hardware, software and application systems which are used in practically all economic and social sectors. Industrial research and technological development work and many restructuring activities were pursued during the early 1990s, and major technological programmes were set up in the member states (see Box 6.5).

Biotechnology was another fast developing industry in the early 1990s and the Commission has signalled that it regards this industry to be strategically important (Commission, 1991b). In 1985 world sales of biotechnology-related products (excluding fermented foods and drinks) amounted to roughly ECU 7.5 bn. For the year 2000, estimates for the biotechnology industry vary between ECU 26 bn and ECU 41 bn (Marks, 1993). However, anxieties have been expressed about dangers inherent in biotechnological techniques and their implications

Box 6.5 The development of digital technology in Europe

Digital technology is concerned with the transmission systems used by broadcasting, computing and telecommunication networks. The older technology – analogue systems – have lower capabilities than digital systems in terms of the quantity and quality of data that can be transmitted. Many of the most exciting opportunities emerging from technological developments in the IT area are connected to the digital revolution. By linking information systems together, using digital technology, it is possible to generate new services (for example, selling systems that will permit individuals to specify their requirements directly to the producers of goods and services).

The development of High Definition Television (HDTV) illustrates one of the major failures of European technology policy in this important area. Three systems for transmitting for colour TVs emerged in the 1950/60s – NTSC in the USA and Japan, SECAM in France and Greece and PAL in most of the rest of the world. These systems were technically incompatible. The development of transfrontier transmissions by satellite, cable and telecommunications systems highlighted the problems caused by the lack of compatible transmission systems. Moreover, the analogue systems used in TV sets did not allow the quality of transmissions that would permit the development of new services.

In the 1980s programmes were started in Japan to develop HDTV that could receive clearer and more detailed colour pictures. The Japanese sought international agreement to fix a common standard for these HDTVs. The EU blocked this proposal and sought, via the EUREKA programme, to develop a HDTV system based on a European standard. The Japanese government sponsored its own R&D programme using a Japanese standard. The American government did not sponsor an R&D programme but encouraged companies (including European and Japanese based multinationals that operated in the USA) to compete to develop HDTV systems. Both the European and Japanese programmes encouraged the use of analogue systems whereas in the USA the winning system was based on the digital system. As digital technology has many advantages over analogue systems the US system was adopted as the global standard.

The failure by the Europeans and Japanese to develop the best technology because of state direct use of an inappropriate technology has meant that the technological lead in this important area has been taken by the USA. This experience also highlighted the dangers of seeking to encourage European standards instead of encouraging companies based in Europe (regardless of their home base) to compete to develop systems that are likely to confer the greatest commercial advantage.

for human and animal health. Technical advice should be available to the Commission in the area of ethics in biotechnology so that a common system of regulation could be developed that would be based on acceptable and agreed ethical standards.

The biotechnology industry is significantly affected by problems related to the protection of intellectual property rights. The economic importance attached to the protection of intellectual property in this field should not be under-estimated since firms will invest in long-term high risk projects only if they are assured of adequate returns from the results of their research. Trade barriers also influence the development of the biotechnology sector because of a host of different regulations and standards which often prevent or significantly limit trade in biotechnology products and services. The EU negotiated at the Uruguay Round to establish rules for trade in the biotechnology sector. The WTO is seeking to implement these rules but trade barriers still present significant problems for the development of international trade in this sector.

The successful completion of the SEM for biotechnology depends on two ele-ments – the legal framework for product authorisation and the development of standards. The regulatory system based on scientific analysis and evaluation covers worker protection and product legislation based on the three criteria of safety, quality and efficiency, which are also applied when assessing whether a product can be authorised for distribution on the open market. Standards are being developed by CEN and the International Standards Organisation.

Further action is proposed to develop the legal framework, the use of stand-ards, the protection of intellectual property, and financial support for research and development. Issues related to ethical problems raised by biotechnology and the impact on consumer information and choice also require attention if this sector is to flourish.

Problem industries

The recession in the mid-1970s in the aftermath of the doubling of the price of oil led to an intensification of the problems of Europe's older industries. This led to a policy in the Community of helping declining industries (as had been mentioned in the Colonna Report) specifically through the use of the ESF. A variety of programmes were established to help declining industries – RECHAR, RENAVAL, RESIDER and RETEX. The industries which were in decline at this time and showing structural problems were coal, textiles, steel and shipbuild-ing. These will be dealt with in turn in the following sections.

Coal

In 1991 the Commission noted that in spite of over 30 years of substantial state aid the coal industry was still in a critical condition (Commission, 1991c). Between 1986 and 1988 the EC12 paid an average of ECU 21,637 per worker in subsidies for coal mining. This aid was granted under Article 95 (providing for aid for regional and social considerations) of the Treaty of Paris. In Germany in the late 1980s about 80 per cent of electricity was generated by domestic coal which cost over three times the price of coal on the world market (Pearson and Smith, 1991). State aid for the coal industry has been substantial, but has not cured the underlying problems. Some member states, for example the

Netherlands and the UK, have cut their coal production and have been able to lessen their aid to the coal industry significantly. However, other member states, notably Germany, have continued to provide substantial aid to their coal industry.

The agreement by the EU to cut emissions of carbon dioxide to help to reduce the problem of global warming has also put pressure on governments to cut coal production that is used for generating electricity. In the Netherlands and the UK a significant shift towards the use of natural gas has helped to reduce the use of coal. However, some of the other member states continue to use substantial amounts of coal to generate electricity. The need to cut emissions of greenhouse gases and to curb the cost of state aid to the coal industry is putting pressure on these governments to adopt policies that will encourage the run-down of their coal industry. Nevertheless, the power of vested interest groups to resist such policies illustates the dangers of using vertical industrial policies to help particular industries – it is always easier to start state aid than to stop it.

The EU provides help to restructure areas affected by the decline of coal mining with the RECHAR programme. The programme was first approved in 1990 and has been extended to 1999. RECHAR funds can be used to help with environmental improvements and modernisation of social and economic infrastructures in coal mining areas.

Textiles

In 1971 the Commission produced a policy document on the rules for member states giving aid to the textile industry – *Framework for Aid to the Textile Industry* (Commission, 1971a). It stated that state aids should improve competitiveness and improve structure in the industry, and not simply fund inefficiency. As the industry consisted of a very large number of small-scale enterprises, this was difficult to supervise.

The late 1970s and early 1980s saw the Commission in conflict with the governments of member states, especially Italy. The Commission took a more protectionist point of view in the renegotiations of the Multi Fibre Arrangement (MFA) in 1977, and a system was developed whereby market quotas were guaranteed for developing countries, but which had the effect of restricting their exports.

The difficulties of the industry seemed to have eased by the mid-1980s and the policy of the Commission progressed from regulating aid from the member states to its elimination through modernisation and technical progress in the industry. This policy was continued with the establishment in 1992 of RETEX, a scheme to help regions with a high dependence on textiles and clothing industries. This programme was aimed at improving the quality, design and marketing of textile products, and at helping with the retraining and redeployment of redundant staff.

The need to modernise and rationalise this industry has been further strengthened by the Uruguay agreement whereby WTO will seek to remove progressively the protectionist effects of the MFA. This liberalisation of trade in textiles and clothing could lead to some problems for European-based textile companies, and it may increase the social and economic costs of the necessary rationalisation of this industry.

Steel

Under the 1951 ECSC Treaty the policies for steel have been more *dirigiste* than for most other industries. In 1975 the effects of the recession hit the industry. Output decreased by 20 per cent by 1977 and the industry was functioning on only 60 per cent of its capacity. A system of voluntary production quotas was started. Anti-dumping duties were fixed for steel imports under GATT rules and minimum prices were imposed. However, the decline continued. In 1980 a state of crisis was recognised. The production quotas were made obligatory. The Davignon Plan was conceived and a scheme for compulsorily reducing capacity was started. During the early 1980s quotas were rigidly adhered to. Pressure on imports was kept up, and the Commission made voluntary export restraint agreements with 15 non-Community countries affecting 75 per cent of the Community's imports. By 1988 the crisis had subsided and the Commission had calmed squabbles between member states. Collective bargaining power, as exemplified by the Commission, had a more incisive effect on the policies and prices of competing overseas countries than the member states could have sustained separately. Steel quotas were finally abolished in 1990.

However, by the early 1990s there was once again a crisis in the European steel industry. Considerable overcapacity existed and the growth of imports from the NICs and Central and Eastern Europe has made this problem even more severe. The EU instituted quotas against steel imports from Central and Eastern Europe and had disputes with the USA over state aids to parts of the European steel industry.

The decision in February 1994 to fine 17 steel companies for breaches of Article 85 led to strong criticism of the Commission. The 17 steel companies claim that the practices they were accused of (price fixing and market sharing) stopped in 1992, and that they were largely instigated by the Commission in attempts to deal with the crisis of the late 1980s. The Commission has also been attacked for its failure to reduce the level of state aids that are given by the Italian, German and Spanish governments. The 17 companies that were fined were particularly aggrieved by this, as they have no or very few state aids. These companies are also unwilling to cut back production, in accordance with the plans of the Commission, until these state aids are eliminated. The Commission therefore faces considerable difficulties with its policy towards steel, and the *dirigiste* approach that the Commission and some member states have taken towards the steel industry has contributed to these difficulties.

The Community established the RESIDER programme in 1988 to help in the process of combating the social and economic costs of steel plant closures in the poorer regions of the Community. RESIDER is limited to a 55 per cent share of the costs of job creation schemes and 50 per cent for projects to improve the infrastructure of regions affected by the closure of steel plants. Such rationalisation appears to be essential if the EU is to overcome the large over-capacity in the Community.

Shipbuilding

In 1969 there was a directive to harmonise all aid being given by the governments of member states to the shipbuilding sector. This was done to keep distortion of competition within the Community to the lowest possible level. The ultimate objective was to eradicate all state aids in the long run.

The oil crisis in the early 1970s resulted in 40 per cent less tonnage of ships being produced in Community shipyards by 1976. A directive in 1978 subjected state aids to shipbuilding to two tests: state aids should increase the efficiency of the shipyards; state aids should maintain or decrease capacity rather than increasing it.

In 1979 the Commission tried to encourage ministers to accept a policy whereby two tons of old ships would be scrapped for every ton of new ships built. Thus total capacity would decrease and employment would increase. This policy was not adopted. In 1986 there was a new directive to modernise the industry and aiming to eradicate state aids totally. In all there were six directives up to 1992 attempting to restrict state aid to shipbuilding. In 1990 aid was restricted to 20 per cent of the selling price of a ship.

In 1988 the Community began the RENAVAL programme to provide aid to regions affected by the decline in shipbuilding and ship repair activities. RENAVAL has similar objectives and conditions for applicability to RESIDER.

The list of problem industries in the EU grew in the 1980s and early 1990s. These industries have some common features: static or declining markets, significant import penetration and, in some cases, low productivity compared with the NICs, and high levels of state aids. The EU has generally adopted the view that these industries have to rationalise, modernise and move to higher added-value activities. In the case of the coal industry, a considerable reduction in the size of the industry is required in order to solve its long-term problems. Indeed, all of these industries will probably have to be downsized unless the Community is prepared and able to provide very substantial state aids and protection from foreign competition.

The EU has resorted to protectionist measures (particularly against Central and Eastern Europe) and has allowed some member states to continue to provide significant state aids to these industries. The Commission has also been active in the steel industry promoting collaborative arrangements between companies to achieve reductions in capacity in efforts to boost prices. However, the Commission has not always been careful to ensure that such reductions in capacity are based on economic criteria such as closure of high-cost plants.

This reluctance to take a tough stance seems to be partly based on regional policy and 'economic and social cohesion' considerations. However, reluctance to tackle the problems caused by state aids and capitulation to powerful interest groups may explain why the Commission appears to have an aversion to allowing market forces to achieve rationalisation of these declining industries. Nevertheless, this type of vertical policy has been considerably less important since the EU adopted a more horizontal and mixed approach to industrial policy.

Conclusion

The EU has developed a treaty basis for a limited role in positive industrial policies. Thus far it has had more economic impact on industrial structures by industrial policies linked to the creation of the SEM and the development of a common competition policy. The deregulation of the telecommunications services and airline industries is another area where the EU is significantly affecting the industrial structures of the Union by use of negative industrial policies. The role of the EU in positive industrial policies has been significantly less influential. Nevertheless, the EU plays an important role in the adjustment process of the declining industries of the Union. It is clear that the Commission would like a greater role in positive industrial policies to correct for market failure, and for strategic reasons. The EU is moving in the direction of a less interventionist industrial policy with less emphasis on a vertical approach. However, the desire of some member states to protect some of their industries, and the favoured status of what are regarded as key industries means that state aid and/or EU help plays an important role in many industries. Consequently, the move towards a more horizontal or mixed approach to industrial policy may not result in a lower level of EU influence on industry. The commitment to create and maintain a competitive and regulatory framework that seeks to promote competitiveness is likely to lead to increasing EU involvement in industrial matters. Furthermore, the policies to help companies in areas such as R&D and by specific help for sectors like IT and biotechnology are also likely to enhance the importance of the EU's industrial policy. Whether these actions and policies will be successful in attaining their goals is open to question.

References

Bangemann M 1993 *Meeting the Global Challenge*, Kogan Page, London.
Beije P R, Groenewegen I, Kostoulas I, Paelinck J and van Paridon C (eds.) 1987 *A Competitive Future for Europe? Towards a New Industrial Policy*, Croom Helm, London.
Buchanan J M 1978 *The Economics of Politics*, Institute of Economic Affairs, London.
Commission 1970a Memorandum on the Community's Industrial Policy, or The Colonna Report, *Bulletin of the European Community, Supplement 4/70*, Brussels.
Commission 1970b Proposal for a Council Regulation embodying a statute for European companies, *Bulletin of the European Communities, Supplement 8/70*, Brussels.
Commission 1971a *Framework for Aid to the Textile Industry*, Communication from the Commission (SEC(71)253), Brussels.
Commission 1974 Proposal for a Regulation by the Council on the European Cooperation Grouping (ECG), *C14/30, Official Journal*, Brussels.
Commission 1975 Proposal for a Council Regulation on the Statute for European Companies, *Bulletin of the European Communities, Supplement 4/75*, Brussels.

Commission 1990 *Industrial policy in an Open and Competitive Environment: Guidelines for a Community Approach*, (COM(90)556), Brussels.

Commission 1991a *The 21st Report on Competition Policy of the EC*, Brussels.

Commission 1991b *Promoting the Competitive Environment for the Industrial Activities based on Biotechnology within the Community*, SEC(91)629, Brussels.

Commission 1991c *Information Energy Europe*, EIE 91, Brussels.

Commission 1993a *White Paper on Growth, Competitiveness and Employment*, COM(93)700 final, Brussels.

Commission 1993b Second Commission Working Document concerning RTD Policy in the Community and the Fourth Framework Programme (1994/1998), Brussels.

Commission 1994 *An Industrial Competitiveness Policy for the European Union* (COM(94)319 final), Brussels.

Commission 1995 *Green Paper on Innovation*, COM(95)688 final, Brussels.

Commission 1996 *The Global Challenge of International Trade: A Market Access Strategy for the European Union*, COM(96)53, Brussels.

Falconer F and Sauvé P 1996 Globalisation, Trade and Competition, *The OECD Observer*, No. 201, pp. 6–9.

Krugman P and Obstfeld M 1991 *International Economics, Theory and Policy*, Harper Collins, New York.

Marks E 1993 Biotechnology, in Johnson P (ed.), *European Industries*, Edward Elgar, Aldershot.

Nicolaides P (ed.) 1993 *Industrial Policy in the European Community: A Necessary Response to Economic Integration*, Martinus Nijhoff, Dordrecht.

North D 1990 *Institutions, Institutional Change and Economic Performance*, Cambridge University Press, Canbridge.

OECD 1996 *Antitrust and Market Access: The Scope and Coverage of Competition Laws and Implications for Trade*, OECD, Paris.

Pearson M and Smith S 1991 *The European Carbon Tax: An Assessment of the Commission's Proposals*, Institute of Fiscal Studies, London.

Tyson L 1992 *Who's Bashing Whom? Trade conflict in high-technology industries*, Longman, London.

Woolcock S 1995 European Industrial Policy in the 1990s in A Cox and P Furlong, *The European Union at the Crossroads*, Earlsgate Press, Boston, Lincs.

Further reading

Commission 1997 *The Competitiveness of European Industry: A Key Issue for European Industry*, Office for Official Publications of the European Communities, Luxembourg.

Hayward J 1995 *Industrial Enterprises and European Integration*, Oxford University Press, Oxford.

Pelkans J 1997 *European Integration: Methods and Economic Analysis*, Addison-Wesley Longman, Harlow.

Social policy

Stephen Dearden

Introduction

This chapter outlines the evolution of the Community's social policy beginning with the social Articles of the Treaty of Rome, which included the establishment of the European Social Fund. Although a number of Directives were adopted in the 1970s on various aspects of employees' rights, it was the passing of the Single European Act that gave new impetus to the evolution of EU social policies, which continued with the Social Charter of the Maastricht Treaty on European Union.

However, central to these developments has been the debate as to whether action should extend beyond the immediate needs of the establishment of an internal market. Concern had been voiced that an unregulated internal labour market would undermine the competitive position of those member states that have relatively high wages and social security, and that the additional stresses of the structural transformation required by the Single European Market (SEM), both for individual employees and for industries, required an explicit commitment to policies necessary to maintain 'social cohesion'. The dramatic increase in unemployment across Europe that began in the late 1970s, and that has persisted ever since, has sharpened the polarisation between those who advocate the primacy of market forces and the need for flexible labour markets, and those who support an interventionist or corporatist approach to economic and social policy.

The chapter covers five main issues. It begins with a brief review of the major trends in the European labour market and then traces the development of EU social policy up to the Single European Act. It then examines the problem of social dumping and wage flexibility, and reviews those policies intended to foster 'social cohesion'. Finally, the chapter outlines the more recent developments of social policy, including those intended to enhance labour mobility and foster training across the Community.

The European labour market

In 1995, of the 372 million population of the EU some 148 million were economically active, either employed or unemployed. The overall labour force activity rate of 67 per cent has remained constant for 20 years and is lower than that of either the US or Japan at 77 per cent. However, trends in the activity rates of men and women have differed significantly. While male activity rates have fallen steadily from 89 per cent in 1975 to 78 per cent in 1995, female activity rates have risen over the same period from 46 per cent to 57 per cent (Commission, 1996b). The increased activity rates of adult women, combined with population growth, have led to the number of women in the EU labour force increasing by 2.5 million between 1990 and 1995, while the number of men fell by 1 million. Activity rates have fallen for both sexes for those younger than 25 years old, accompanied by higher rates of participation in education and training. By 1995, 85 per cent of 16 to 18 year olds were in some form of education, and 64 per cent of 19 year olds.

Over the period 1980–93 the number of jobs generated in the EU has increased by less than 0.5 per cent per annum (p.a.), compared with an increase in employment of 1.5 per cent p.a. in the US and 1 per cent p.a. in Japan. In the recession of the early 1990s, 5 million jobs were lost and it was not until 1995 that employment in the EU increased for the first time since 1991. By 1995 the employment rate (total employment as a percentage of the population aged 15 to 64) was 60 per cent, compared with 65 per cent in 1973, and in contrast to the 73 per cent employment rate in the US and 74 per cent in Japan. In common with other mature industrialised economies, most jobs created over the period in the EU have been in the service sector, especially personal and communal services (e.g. health, education and public administration). Other significant sectors of employment growth were in finance, distribution, hotels and catering. By contrast, employment in manufacturing declined by 0.2 per cent p.a. and agricultural employment by 0.3 per cent p.a., representing a loss of an average of 1 million jobs p.a. over the 13 years. By 1995 only 5.3 per cent of the labour force were employed in agriculture (1960: 23 per cent), 30.2 per cent in manufacturing (1960: 40 per cent), and 64 per cent in services (1960: 37 per cent) (see Fig. 7.1).

The rate of population growth, migration, changes in participation or activity rates, and the rate of net job creation will all have contributed to the observed unemployment trend. It is the deterioration in unemployment rates across Europe that has now become the major challenge to all EU governments. In 1970, EC12 unemployment was only 2.4 per cent; by 1994 it had reached 11.3 per cent in the EU15, with little improvement in 1996 (see Figs 7.2 and 7.3). Recovery from the recession of the early 1990s has not been fully reflected in employment growth. Unemployment is particularly concentrated among the young. While the difference between youth (16 to 25 years old) and adult unemployment rates narrowed in the 1980s, it widened again in the 1990s recession and is still double that of adults at 21.5 per cent (see Fig. 7.4). Moreover, half of those unemployed have been without work for more than a year – a similar percentage to that of ten years earlier. Unemployment also varies considerably from region to region, ranging from 3.5 per cent in Luxembourg in 1995, to 35 per cent in Southern Spain (see Fig. 7.5).

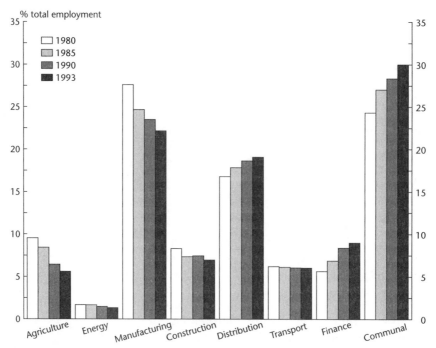

Figure 7.1   Employment by broad sector in the Union, 1980, 1985, 1990 and 1993

Source: Employment in Europe (Commission, 1996b)

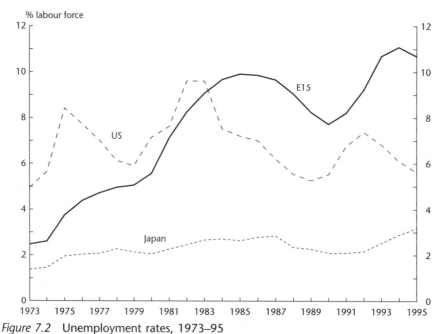

Figure 7.2   Unemployment rates, 1973–95

Source: Employment in Europe (Commission, 1996b)

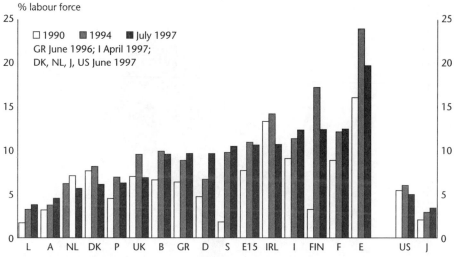

Figure 7.3 Unemployment rates in member states, US and Japan, 1990, 1994 and July 1997

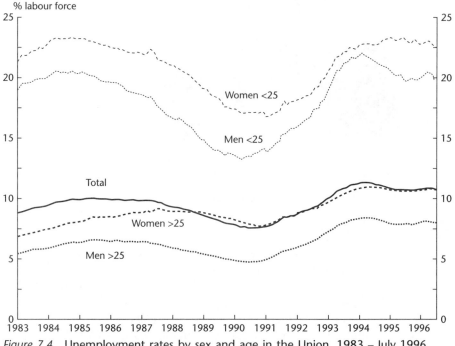

Figure 7.4 Unemployment rates by sex and age in the Union, 1983 – July 1996

Source: Employment in Europe (Commission, 1996b)

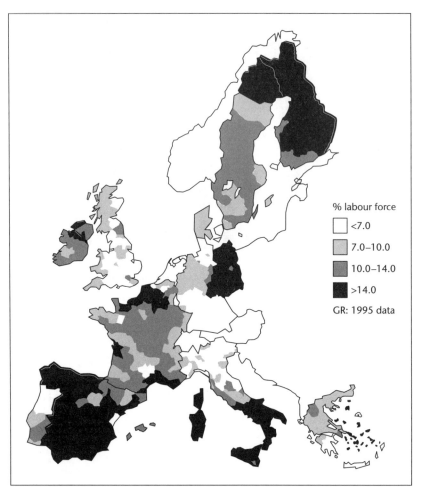

Figure 7.5   Unemployment rates by region, 1996

Source: Employment in Europe (Commission, 1996b)

The Treaty of Rome

The social provisions of the Treaty of Rome (1957) are relatively limited, and scattered throughout its various parts. Nonetheless, they extend to concerns beyond those necessary for the creation of a common market. The Treaty has binding provisions that seek to establish freedom of movement of workers (Articles 48 and 49), freedom of establishment (Articles 52–58), equal pay for men and women (Article 119), and rights to social security of migrant workers (Article 51). Non-binding provisions covered paid holidays (Article 120), commitments to improving living and working conditions (Articles 117 and 118), and the laying down of the general principles for implementing a common vocational training policy (Article 128). In addition, it established the European Social Fund (Articles 123–128).

The European Social Fund (ESF) was originally limited to localised retraining and resettlement, to providing financial support to the temporarily unemployed, and to issues associated with migrant workers. However, in 1971 the role and operation of the Fund underwent significant reform. Its financing was switched from levies on member states to the Community's own resources, and it was set two broad objectives – first, to address the employment problems arising from the implementation of Community policies and, secondly, to help overcome the structural problems experienced by certain regions or target groups, i.e. migrant workers, young job seekers, women and the handicapped. To achieve these objectives, 90 per cent of the Fund's resources were allocated to vocational training.

In response to the increase in unemployment in Europe in the 1970s the ESF was quadrupled. The increase in unemployment and the lack of a clear set of objectives led, in 1983, to a simplification and concentration of ESF activities. The measures to alleviate youth unemployment received 75 per cent of the ESF budget, and 40 per cent of the remaining general fund was allocated to the depressed regions of the Community, e.g. Greece, Northern Ireland, Ireland, Mezzogiorno. Other employment measures adopted during the 1970s included attempts to coordinate national employment policies, with the exchange of information and research, and Resolutions on training schemes for the young, information technology and vocational training. In 1975 the European Centre for the Development of Vocational Training (CEDEFOP) was created to disseminate information on training, and to promote good practice throughout the Community.

Harmonisation of working conditions

Although the remit of the Treaty of Rome was relatively narrow in this area a number of directives were adopted covering collective redundancies (1975); employee rights in the event of company takeovers (1977) or insolvency (1980); equal pay (1975); equal access to employment, vocational training (1976), and social security (1986). In 1974 an Advisory Committee on Safety, Hygiene and Health Protection at Work was established, leading to a series of Safety at Work Directives, and in 1975 the European Foundation for the Improvement of Living and Working Conditions was created to provide information on employment conditions. As with CEDEFOP it is administered by a quadripartite Board composed of representatives of the Commission, employers, workers and member governments. Non-binding recommendations for the introduction of a 40-hour week and a minimum four weeks' paid holiday (1975) were also adopted, together with a call for the examination of the potential for reorganising working time through early retirement and reduction in overtime working. However, the generally deteriorating economic situation, the widening of internal differences following the second enlargement of the Community, and changes in government (especially in the UK) led to a period of inactivity in the development of a Community social policy during the early 1980s.

The Single European Act

With the passing of the Single European Act (SEA) in 1987 much broader social issues were addressed, with a commitment to the harmonisation of national provisions with regard to health, safety, environmental and consumer protection (Articles 100a and 118a), and to policies fostering 'the economic and social cohesion of the Community' (Articles 130a–130e). Although Article 100a introduced Qualified Majority Voting (QMV) to overcome the blocking power of individual member states, this is confined to those measures essential for the establishment of the SEM, i.e. health and safety legislation. Thus proposals relating to the free movement of people and employees' rights remained subject to member state veto. Article 118a also restricted proposed legislation in that it required it to take into account existing national conditions and regulations, and to ensure that they do not impose administrative and financial burdens on enterprises. Article 118b also committed the Community to the encouragement of a 'social dialogue' between management and labour, i.e. the creation of a European dimension to industrial relations. This non-binding provision yielded little success, and underlined the difficulties of achieving progress in those social areas that went beyond the minimum conditions essential to the completion of the SEM.

The Single European Market

With the commitment to the completion of the SEM by 1992, and the passing of the SEA, interest was rekindled in the social implications of EU policies.

The movement towards the SEM was recognised as having implications for employment throughout the Community. Changes in costs and relative prices, stimulation of new technology and economic growth, were all factors which would determine the employment consequences of the Single Market. Econometric studies, although based on some heroic assumptions, suggested a positive impact upon most EU economies. However, the consequences for employment remained the most ambiguous. Nonetheless, a study by DG II did identify those industries and regions most likely to be affected by the completion of the SEM (Commission, 1988). The industries were usually characterised by state ownership or were dependent upon the state as principal customer. They included telecommunication equipment, computers and office equipment, shipbuilding, railway equipment, iron and steel, and pharmaceuticals. In the tertiary sector financial services were likely to be particularly affected by the development of a single financial market.

The SEM was also expected to have a differential regional impact (see Chapter 8). The expected enhancement of economic growth would not benefit all regions equally. Even before the structural changes arising from enhanced economic integration, regional disparities within Europe had increased. This had resulted from the general deterioration in employment conditions since the mid-1970s and from the second enlargement. A region's competitiveness is likely to be influenced by a number of factors – first, the qualifications and skill mix of the labour force, which might be undermined by outward migration and, secondly, the infrastructure, estimated to be 40 to 60 per cent below the EU average standard in some regions. Finally, labour costs – differences in labour productivity are often greater than differences in wage levels, and the further levelling up of wage levels with economic integration would continue to undermine the competitive position of some regions. Two types of area were therefore identified as being particularly vulnerable to structural problems – the underdeveloped mainly rural areas, and the regions where there was a concentration of declining heavy industries.

However, concern has also been expressed that particular social problems would emerge from the completion of the SEM across all of the EU. These arguments have focused upon two issues – illicit work (moonlighting) and social dumping.

Illicit work

Illicit work concerns work outside formal labour markets and tax and social security systems and is most frequent among those who are already employed. It is thought to be concentrated among the professions, domestic services, in agricultural work, vehicle repairs, and among skilled manual workers in construction. It is also estimated to be twice as prevalent in the southern states of the Community, reflecting differences in the structure of the local economies, levels of taxation, cultural attitudes and the effectiveness of official controls. Studies suggest that 25 per cent of Spain's labour force works in its informal or 'black' economy, 30 per cent in Greece, 18–28 per cent in Portugal, and 25 per cent in France. This is of concern within the single market since it distorts the operation of the labour market and competitiveness. Those firms within the Community that employ labour illicitly will reduce their labour costs and gain a competitive advantage, allowing them to displace those firms that finance the social security systems and adhere to established employment and safety regulations. Therefore the Commission has taken a number of actions to attempt to minimise the occurrence of illicit employment. It has sought effective compliance in public contracts to national and EU standards, close attention to sub-contracting arrangements, and the monitoring of cross-frontier activities. The Commission has also pursued the adoption of common administrative 'standards' for taxation and social security contributions across both regions and forms of employment (e.g. part-time, temporary workers).

Social dumping

Social dumping expresses the concern that employment will be lost in those states whose higher social standards are reflected in higher average labour costs. Faced with loss of market shares and firm relocation, there will be downward pressure upon social conditions (i.e. wages, social security, minimum labour standards, etc.). This fear has led to demands for minimum wage levels, social security provisions and minimum health and safety guarantees, to avoid competitive pressure reducing employment standards to unacceptably low levels. However, it has been argued that concern about social dumping is misplaced. It is pointed out

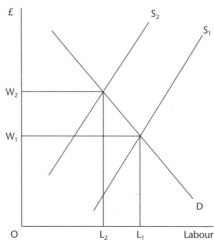

Figure 7.6 Social security financed by employees

Here all of the social security benefits are financed by payroll contributions by the employee. With employment at L_1 and wages at W_1, the imposition of a payroll contribution on employees is equivalent to a reduction in the net wage offered. This is equivalent to the vertical distance $S_1 S_2$. However, this fall in the net wage also shifts the supply curve of labour from S_1 to S_2. The equilibrium wage paid by employers now increases to W_2 and employment falls to L_2. But if workers regard the social security benefits that they now receive as part of their total wage package, and it is fully taken into account in their labour supply decision, then the supply curve will shift back to S_1, with wages and employment returning to their original level. Of course, not all social security benefits may be regarded as part of the remuneration package, e.g. maternity benefits to a single man, in which case the labour supply curve will shift only part of the way back to its original position. Nevertheless, the more inelastic the initial labour supply curve, the less impact this disregard of social security benefits will have on employment and wages.

that it is not a new phenomenon but predates the completion of the SEM. Wage costs are not the only determinant of competitiveness but must be considered within the context of relative productivity, with human and physical capital allowing high wage sectors to maintain their competitive advantage.

It can also be shown that, theoretically, high levels of social security contributions, by either employer or employee, need have no effect upon competitiveness as long as wages are completely flexible (see Figs 7.6 and 7.7.).

Wage flexibility

The only problem arises in a situation where wages are not downwardly flexible. Studies (Coe and Gagliardi, 1985; Dearden, 1995; Bean, 1994) have suggested that European labour markets tend to be characterised by a relatively high degree of real wage rigidity, and that this inflexibility has increased in the 1980s, despite increasing levels of unemployment. However, increasing economic integration, induced by the SEM, was expected by the Commission to enhance wage flexibility, as more competitive product markets increased the elasticity of firms'

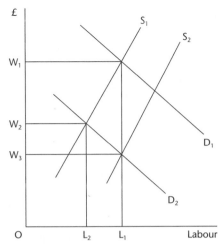

Figure 7.7 Social security financed by employers

In a social security system financed solely by employers we again begin with an equilibrium wage at W_1 and employment at L_1. Social security contributions are now imposed upon the employer equal to the vertical distance D_1D_2, reducing labour demand to D_2. With labour supply at S_1 the equilibrium wage falls to W_2 and employment to L_2. But again, if employees regard the social security entitlements as part of their total wages, they will respond by raising their total supply of labour in response to the increased value of their remuneration package, i.e. labour supply increases from S_1 to S_2. This returns employment to its previous level at L_1, and lowers the firm's wage rate to W_3. The difference between the original wage rate W_1 and the new lower wage W_3 is equal to the cost to the employer of the social security contribution. Thus the social security tax has been shifted on to the employee, and therefore the firm experiences no loss of profit, nor increase in total labour costs, and no change in its relative competitive position.

demand for labour. However, economic integration and monetary union may also increase workers' awareness of comparative rates of pay and conditions of employment across the Community. There is already some evidence that workers' expectations are rising in Spain, Greece and Ireland (Commission, 1991), while Portugal's 1991 'social pact' linked wage increases to the ECU value of the escudo and to the relative performance of productivity.

Real wage flexibility can also be achieved by increases in national price levels, while money wages remain constant; but this will undermine international competitiveness unless it is possible to devalue the currency. As the Community moves towards a full monetary union such adjustments will become impossible, and employment may shift to the low-cost regions of the Community, creating a competitive downward pressure upon all wages in the Community. This argument has been challenged on a number of grounds. It is argued that it is relative unit labour costs, which also reflect variations in the productivity of labour, that are more significant. Wage costs alone are unlikely to be the major factor in location decisions, except in the case of labour-intensive industries. It has also been pointed out that it is this very process of relocation to low-wage areas that is the market adjustment mechanism for spreading the benefits of economic growth throughout all of the Community.

Nevertheless, critics of the 'market forces' approach have also warned of the possibility of cumulative economic divergence as the poorer regions, especially in the Southern member states, find themselves specialising in labour-intensive, low-wage, low-productivity industries where they already face intense competition from the newly industrialising Asian economies.

The differences in labour costs faced by firms operating across the EU arise not only from differences in member states' social security systems, but also from the variation in other elements of the fixed labour costs that firms face. These non-wage costs include the extent of paid holidays, paid sick leave, benefits in kind (e.g. subsidised mortgages, canteens, sports facilities, cars) and redundancy pay. These emerge from collective bargaining, and express employees' preferences, and reflect the influence of such factors as the adequacy of state schemes, the structure of the national tax system, and the cultural characteristics of countries.

In 1992 non-wage labour costs in industry were approximately 30 per cent of total labour costs in France, Italy and Belgium, 25 per cent in Portugal, Spain and the Netherlands, but only 13 per cent in the United Kingdom, and 4 per cent in Denmark (Employment Observatory, 1995). High fixed labour costs create competitive pressures to substitute part-time workers when some of these fixed costs can be avoided. This has already been observed in the Northern member states of the EU. By 1995, 44 per cent of the women who were employed in the UK were working part-time, and 67 per cent in the Netherlands. However, female part-time working remains only 17 per cent in Spain, 13 per cent in Italy, and 8 per cent in Greece. Overall in the Community 31 per cent of women are employed part-time, in contrast to the 5 per cent of men (Commission, 1996b). To eliminate these 'distortions to competition' and casualisation of part of the labour force, the Commission has prepared a number of 'atypical workers' Directives, extending to employees on short-term and part-time contracts the same entitlements to holiday pay, redundancy pay, etc. as full-time workers.

Social cohesion

The negotiations leading to the adoption of the European Community Charter on the Fundamental Social Rights for Workers (the Social Charter) at the Strasbourg Summit in December 1989 brought into sharp focus the fundamental divisions between those advocating an interventionist regulatory role for the Community in the social area, and those who argue for the primacy of market forces and a *laissez-faire* approach (see Addison and Siebert, 1993 and Rhodes, 1992). The latter were most clearly represented by the UK government who failed to support the adoption of the Social Charter, and two years later demanded an opt-out from the Social Protocol of the Treaty on European Union (TEU). However, the Union of Industrial and Employers' Confederation of Europe (UNICE) has also resisted the extension of labour market regulation beyond that necessary to ensure fair competition under the SEM.

Proponents of unregulated labour markets, with freely negotiated labour contracts, regard them as providing both economic efficiency in allocating labour, and a wide variety of pay and conditions to meet individual workers' preferences. Attempts to impose uniform conditions, such as minimum wages, holiday entitlements, redundancy protection, etc., will impose additional costs upon firms. In response, companies will substitute capital, part-time workers, or more skilled workers for their low productivity unskilled employees whose employment costs have now risen, and whom such regulation was principally intended to benefit.

An alternative view is that such attempts at regulation will encourage the emergence of dual labour markets, a regulated high-wage high-productivity sector, and an unregulated low-wage unskilled sector offering unstable employment. This 'insider-outsider' problem is already found in many member states. In Spain and Greece high levels of youth unemployment and the increase in the amount of part-time employment are blamed upon the existence of tightly regulated procedures for the recruitment and dismissal of full-time workers. A recent study by Morton and Siebert (1997) of personnel policies in five multinational companies with plants across the EU found evidence that the plants in the more deregulated UK labour market employed workers with less prior experience, shorter tenure and more age variation. Although this suggested that in the UK employment was more open to 'outsiders' there was also evidence that employees in UK plants worked more overtime, had less generous holiday entitlements, and had a higher turnover. Regulation in the EU might thus only benefit existing workers at the expense of those wishing to enter the labour market.

The emergence of dual labour markets could become a major problem for ensuring fair competition across the Community. Already, member states vary in their ability and willingness to enforce Community, and even national, regulations, the enhanced competitive environment of the 1980s having encouraged a shift to deregulation. The simple 'social dumping' argument of differential social security provisions leading firms to relocate to the lower-cost regions of the Community can also be seen as a variant of the 'insider-outsider' phenomenon, as both employers and employees in the high cost member states, such as Germany, attempt to defend their existing conditions from competition. However, it has already been observed that increasing economic integration, far from encouraging such relocation to underdeveloped low-cost regions, may actually reinforce the advantages of the high productivity areas. Under these conditions of 'cumulative divergence' an interventionist social policy is more easily justified. It might be argued that such intervention should confine itself to the supply-side policy of enhancing vocational training, but the general conditions of employment that an employee faces are likely to influence the decision as to whether to invest in human capital. Improving conditions through EU regulation may raise employee morale and therefore productivity, and may also reduce staff turnover. High turnover imposes substantial recruitment and training costs upon firms and they will be unwilling to incur any additional costs, by further investment in their employees, unless there is an expectation of a long-term commitment by their labour force. Thus imposing improved employment conditions may complement, rather than inhibit, the transformation of the low productivity industries and regions of the Community.

Certainly the Commission views the creation of social cohesion as essential to realising the benefits of an integrated European economy. The Social

Charter represented a broad statement of the principles that were to achieve this objective.

The Social Charter

Building upon the objective of improving the living and working conditions embodied in the Treaty of Rome, and consolidated in the SEA, both the Economic and Social Committee and the European Parliament called for an explicit political commitment to fundamental social rights. Existing international agreements, such as the ILO Convention, have not been fully ratified by all member states, and are regarded as inadequate in providing for the needs of the successful creation of the SEM. Thus the Social Charter (see Box 7.1) both addressed the conditions necessary for the completion of the SEM, and attempted to create the social guarantees that the Commission regarded as essential to maintain broad political support for these developments.

Box 7.1   The Social Charter

The Social Charter includes the following commitments:

1. Improvements in Living and Working Conditions
   'The development of a single European labour market must result in an improvement in the living and working conditions of workers within the EC'. To avoid downward pressure on these conditions a number of issues must be addressed including the form of employment contracts (e.g. temporary, seasonal, part-time) and the organisation of working hours. There is a specific call for the establishment of a maximum working week. In addition, procedures relating to collective redundancies and bankruptcies should be addressed.

2. The Right to Freedom of Movement
   The establishment of the right to equal treatment with any other EC national with regard to the practice of any trade or occupation, access to training, rights to social security and residence.

3. Employment and Remuneration
   All employment must be fairly remunerated, established either through law or collective agreement, with particular attention to those workers not subject to the 'normal' employment contract of indefinite duration. Wages may not be withheld, except in conformity with national regulations, but 'in no case may an employed person be deprived of the means necessary for subsistence'.

4. The Right to Social Protection
   'Subject to the arrangements proper to each member state, any citizen of the EC is entitled to adequate social protection', i.e. social security or a minimum wage.

5. The Right to Freedom of Association and Collective Bargaining
   'Every employer and every worker has the right to belong freely to the professional and trade union organisation of their choice'.

This entails the right to choose whether or not to belong to a trade union and the right to strike. Procedures for conciliation and mediation between the two sides of industry should be encouraged, and contractual relations established at the European level if it is deemed desirable.

6. The Right to Vocational Training
   'Every worker has the right to continue his vocational training throughout his working life'. Both public and private bodies should establish continuing and permanent training schemes and provide leave for training purposes.

7. The Right of Men and Women to Equal Treatment

8. The Right to Information, Consultation and Worker Participation
   To be developed 'along appropriate lines and in such a way as to take into account the legal provisions, contractual agreements and practices in force in the member states'.

9. The Right to Health Protection and Safety at Work

10. The Protection of Children and Adolescents
    The minimum working age must be set at 16 years, and those over this age shall receive fair remuneration, and for a period of two years shall be entitled to vocational training in working hours.

11. Elderly Persons
    Shall receive an income that guarantees a decent standard of living.

12. Disabled Persons
    To ensure their fullest possible integration in working life, measures must be taken in respect of training, integration and rehabilitation, complemented by action to improve accessibility, mobility, transport and housing.

It should be noted that the Social Charter has no legal status, and many of the rights are qualified so as to accommodate existing national practices. Nonetheless, the Social Charter remains important in that it provided the underpinning for the implementation of a 47-point Social Action Programme (SAP) (COM(89) 568). However, of these 47 proposals only 28 involved binding Directives or Regulations – ten covering occupational health and safety, three improvements in living and working conditions, and two equal opportunities.

Many of the measures in the Social Action Programme were merely a continuation of existing developments aimed at fostering worker mobility within the Community, enhancing training provision, and establishing common health and safety requirements. However, some proposals were more controversial and faced strong opposition from the UK government and the European employers. These included three 'atypical' worker's Directives, extending to part-time and fixed-term workers the same entitlements as those enjoyed by full-time workers, namely a Directive establishing minimum employment conditions for young people; three Directives on collective redundancies, written contracts of employment and restrictions on working hours; and a Directive establishing minimum paid maternity leave.

In the case of the most controversial aspects of the Social Charter the Commission has proposed only non-binding Opinions and recommendations. Thus under the SAP the rights to freedom of association, collective bargaining and to strike have been compromised by being made subject to national 'traditions' (EIRR, 1990). Similarly, the discussion about the introduction of an EU-wide minimum wage has been replaced by reference to a Commission Opinion as to 'fair wages', i.e. a wage sufficient to maintain a satisfactory standard of living.

However, the Commission has made progress with the working hours, maternity and young workers Directives by a broad interpretation of the Health and Safety Articles of the SEA (Article 118a), allowing qualified majority voting to overcome UK opposition. After an unsuccessful challenge before the ECJ the Working Time Directive (93/104/EC) has been extended to the UK and now sets minimum daily and weekly rest periods, an entitlement to three weeks' annual paid holidays, and a limit of a 48-hour working week (except by voluntary agreement) across the Community. It currently excludes transport workers, seamen, and doctors in training, but the Commission intends to address their particular problems with separate proposals.

Of the three 'atypical' workers' Directives, the least controversial – extending health and safety protection to temporary staff – was accepted for implementation by the end of 1992 (91/383/EEC). The two remaining proposed Directives would have established equal treatment and set minimum standards for 'atypical' workers employed for more than eight hours per week with regard to access to vocational training, statutory social security, and occupational benefits, but they were initially blocked at the Council of Ministers.

Since 85 per cent of all part-time jobs across the EU are held by women, the employment conditions of 'atypical' workers and issues of sex discrimination have become intertwined. Thus a succession of ECJ decisions has established equal treatment for part-time workers in access to and benefits from occupational pension schemes, severance pay or sick leave schemes.

The Agreement on Social Policy

An alternative route for the development of social policy in the Community became available with the adoption of the Social Protocol, part of the TEU agreed at Maastricht in 1991. Within this Protocol is an Agreement on Social Policy, which allowed only 11 of the member states (excluding the UK) to adopt new procedures in the formulation and application of the EU's social policy. It extended qualified majority voting (QMV) to measures covering health and safety, working conditions, information and consultation of workers, equality, and the integration of the unemployed. Unanimity is still required for those measures affecting social security and social protection, redundancy, employee representation, immigrant workers, and the financing of job creation. The Agreement also provides for a central role for employers' and workers' organisations in the formulation of proposals for legislation (Article 4).

So far, the Agreement procedure has been used to adopt three pieces of legislation – the European Works Council, atypical work contracts, and Parental Leave Directives. The third of these emerged from negotiations between

UNICE, CEEP (European Centre for Enterprises with Public Participation) and the ETUC (European Trade Union Confederation) and offers unpaid leave, for both men and women, for a period of up to three months. Measures covering conditions of work and the burden of proof in relation to equal pay and conditions are still being considered under this procedure.

The Third Social Action Programme

Towards the end of the Social Action Programme (SAP) associated with the Social Charter, the Commission began a consultation process which culminated in the 1994 White Paper on Social Policy (COM(94)333). It did not propose a great deal of new legislation but emphasised the importance of implementing existing Community law effectively in the member states and of adopting the outstanding proposed legislation. It also raised the question of whether the Commission's powers to address discrimination issues should be enhanced and whether a Charter of social rights for non-workers should be adopted to complement that of the existing Social Charter. Subsequently, in March 1996, the periodically convened Social Policy Forum submitted to the Inter-Governmental Conference (IGC) the proposal that they should incorporate a Bill of Rights into the TEU, with right of appeal to an EU court composed of judges from member states' supreme or constitutional courts.

In April 1995 the Commission presented a third SAP (COM(95)134) to cover the period up to 1997. It was intended to achieve the objectives outlined in the White Paper and had five themes:

- Combating unemployment through improving the mobility and training of workers.
- Adopting outstanding legislation and ensuring its effective implementation.
- Ensuring equal opportunities for men and women.
- Enhancing the 'social protection' of disadvantaged groups.
- Carrying out a medium-term analysis of social needs.

In addition to the legislative programme (Box 7.2) the Commission intended to intensify its monitoring of employment trends and to encourage collaboration among the member states in their employment and social security policies. By the end of 1995 the Commission (COM(95)466) was outlining the issues that it believed the Community needed to address to finance its social security systems in the face of Europe's demographic changes, and the relationship between these schemes and the EU's employment objectives.

The social dialogue

The SAP associated with the Social Charter had sought the 'continuation and development of dialogue with the social partners' and consideration of the need for collective agreements at the European level. Nevertheless, there is debate about this need to establish a European framework for industrial relations.

Box 7.2 Third Social Action Programme legislative proposals

1. Transfer of pension rights, rights of residence, extension of mutual recognition of diplomas to skilled crafts, social security of migrant workers, cross-border health care, taxation of 'frontier workers', unemployment benefit and early retirement schemes.

2. Working conditions of 'atypical workers', working hours, home working, and a Fourth Programme on safety, hygiene and health at work.

3. Fourth Programme on equal opportunities, including a code of practice on equal pay and equal treatment in social security schemes.

4. Development of public health indicators.

5. Promotion of consultation with the 'social partners' and establishment of a European Training Centre for Industrial Relations.

As before, there is a conflict between the 'corporatists' who see it as an important dimension in the creation of 'social cohesion' at the European level, and those neo-liberals who see it as a threat to the economic efficiency of free labour markets. For the latter, efficiency demands flexibility for management in the determination of pay, employment contracts and hiring and firing, i.e. 'the right to manage'. UNICE has sought to defend this flexibility by opposing any EU measure which encourages the emergence of a European dimension to collective bargaining. In addition, they have emphasised the significant obstacles that the EU faces in this area, given the substantial variation in collective bargaining traditions across the member states. In particular, the frameworks of industrial relations in each state vary in their emphasis upon rights embodied in legislation or acquired through collective bargaining. Thus in the UK the existing legal framework is limited to immunities, not specific rights. With the loss of trade union membership and consequent weakening of collective bargaining, a highly 'flexible' labour market has been created. By contrast, West German industrial relations have remained 'corporatist', and in Italy large firms continue to face substantial legal constraints upon their hiring and firing activities.

However, both sides of industry have been involved in the development of Community social policy from its inception. Thus the Economic and Social Committee was established under the Treaty of Rome, although its influence to date has been limited as it covers too broad an area. Since 1972 the 189-member Committee has had the right to draw up opinions on all questions relating to Community economic and social policy, but it remains advisory. Nonetheless it is able to call upon independent experts and is often a source of technical expertise, and has occasionally, as in the Beretta Report on the social aspects of the SEM, made a significant contribution. Two further groups of Committees bring together employers and employees. The Advisory Committees deliver opinions before the Commission adopts a position. These Committees cover vocational training, freedom of movement of workers, social security for workers, safety, hygiene and health protection. The second group is composed of Sectoral Joint Committees and informal groups, covering industries such as railways, sea fishing, road and maritime transport. However, in 1996 the Commission (COM(96)448) was highly critical of the effectiveness of this group of Committees, finding the sectoral bodies rarely consulted and 'often unable to give their opinions until after the Commission has adopted the text in question'.

The ETUC began to press for the need for the development of an active social policy in the late 1960s and, in response, the first Quadripartite Conference, involving representatives of the Commission, Ministers of Labour, employers and employees, was held in Luxembourg in 1970. This led in turn to the creation of the Standing Committee on Employment, composed of representatives of the Commission, Council, employers and trade unions. From 1974 until 1978 Conferences were held annually, but at the 1978 meeting the ETUC expressed its concern at the lack of evidence of any positive results from the meetings. Although the Commission drew up proposals, adopted by the Council in June 1980, no conferences have been held since. Nevertheless, the Standing Committee on Employment continues to survive. Its deliberations precede decisions by the competent institutions, and it provides a forum for consultation and discussion between the Council, Commission and the two sides of industry. Until 1974 it focused upon reform of the ESF, but its agenda has now widened to include unemployment, reorganisation of working time, and youth unemployment. Since 1980 it has also considered new technology and long-run unemployment; however, the Committee remains purely consultative.

By the early 1980s the ETUC was expressing increasing dissatisfaction at this lack of progress, and the relationship between the employers and trade unions reached its lowest ebb when employers' opposition ensured the freezing by the Council of the 'Vredeling Directive' on worker consultation in 1986. This proposed Directive had already been substantially revised in response to the comments of the European Parliament and the Economic and Social Committee, and had begun its fruitless journey six years before.

An attempt was made to overcome this impasse by Jacques Delors, who presented an action plan, including the commitment to the completion of the SEM, at the 1984 Fontainebleau Summit. To revive the 'social dialogue' a meeting was held in November 1985 at Val Duchesse, which led to the establishment of two working parties, examining macro- and micro-economic issues. However the momentum was not maintained.

Under the influence of French national legislation, French multinational companies (MNCs) had been experimenting with European Works Councils (EWCs) (e.g. BSN, Thompson, Elf Aquitaine). This has been emulated by other European MNCs such as Volkswagen, Grundig and Volvo. These consultation arrangements, in turn, enhanced the role of the European trade union bodies. In some cases European company networks have emerged (e.g. Ford of Europe Workers' Committee), while in others more formal international bodies such as the European Metalworkers Federation and the European Confederation of Chemical and General Workers' Unions have been formed. Meanwhile, the

ETUC has been strengthened as the number of affiliated trade unions has grown, especially among 'white collar' workers. In October 1990 the first genuine European trade union was created by the merger of the 12 national airline pilots' associations.

More recently some dissent emerged among the national associations within UNICE as to its uniformly hostile approach to EU attempts at fostering a 'social dialogue'. Belgian, Dutch and Italian employers argued that an active involvement in European social policy-making would be more productive than outright hostility, especially when faced with the threat of Directives being imposed. As a result UNICE shifted its policy stance, and in November 1991 it reached agreement with the ETUC that they should participate in the Social Agreement consultation procedure. Under this Agreement the Commission was required to consult both sides of industry before submitting proposals in the social field. A member state could also entrust implementation of an EU Directive to management and labour if both 'social partners' requested it. However, most importantly, if the EU decides to legislate in an area, then UNICE, CEEP and the ETUC have a nine-month period in which to negotiate either a collective agreement on the matter or formulate a draft Directive for approval by the Council of Ministers. Further, the 'social partners' may themselves initiate negotiations on Community-wide contracts which, if they fall within ten policy categories defined in the Social Agreement, may be implemented by a Council decision on a proposal from the Commission.

However, some national employers' associations, such as the British CBI, continue to reject this agreement. It must also be recognised that the disagreement within UNICE may lie more in the means than in the ends – the ends being to ensure 'strict limits on the scope of EU intervention in this area, whether by law or agreement' (Secretary General of UNICE, *Financial Times*, November 1991).

Community policy

The Community's policy in the social area may be seen as seeking to fulfil three broad roles. First, harmonisation of national policies, especially in areas where it offers obvious advantages, e.g. labour mobility. Secondly, encouraging convergence, both through its own discussions and encouragement of inter-State cooperation. This approach is likely to be most appropriate where states are faced by similar problems, e.g. the impact of demographic changes upon social security systems. Finally, the Commission can act as a focal point for the spreading of innovatory experience throughout the Community. With the commitment to the completion of the SEM, added urgency was given to the Commission's 'watchdog' role in anticipating the social consequences of restructuring. However, the Commission is also a direct participant in fostering the necessary adaptability in the labour market. Thus the following sections will outline the broad areas of Commission activity, ranging from the more passive information role to its more controversial attempts at harmonisation through the Social Protocol and the proposed European Company laws.

Labour mobility

Although the Treaty of Rome had laid down the fundamental freedom of movement of workers (Articles 48–51) and the right of establishment in any economic activity across all member states, a succession of secondary legislation has been required to give concrete form to these principles. Any EU national may now reside in any member state to seek or take up employment, accompanied by his family (Directive 68/360/EEC), establish firms or provide services (73/148/EEC), and remain in that territory after having been employed in that State (70/1251/EEC, 72/194/EEC). In addition, any worker and his family should receive equal treatment in respect of social security, housing, access to education and training, etc., to that of any domestic national. Indeed, the Community has sought coordination of national social security legislation to facilitate mobility through Regulations 71/1408/EEC and 72/574/EEC. These Regulations establish three basic principles. First, the application of a single body of legislation in each case. Secondly, retention of all accumulated rights and entitlements (i.e. transferability). Thirdly, equal treatment between domestic nationals and citizens of other member states.

Nevertheless, some problems remain unresolved or unaddressed. Frontier workers, commuting from a country of residence to employment in another State, have a number of established rights, e.g. to social security benefits, but specific difficulties remain, particularly with regard to taxation. EU nationals seeking public-sector employment in other member states have faced restrictions. Although discrimination in employment is allowed on grounds of 'public policy, security or health, and exercise of public authority', this has been narrowly interpreted by the ECJ. The Commission therefore decided to take action to eliminate employment restrictions in the public utilities, health services, teaching and non-military research. The rights so far described are focused specifically upon the needs of workers and their dependants. Those who are not economically active continued to face residence restrictions, usually a test of 'adequate means' for intending migrants. To facilitate labour adjustment the Commission has proposed the transferability of unemployment benefit while workers seek employment in other member states. Although a proposed Directive granting a general 'right of residence' throughout the Community for students and the retired and other non-employed people faced substantial opposition from several member states, the Maastricht Treaty (TEU) created citizenship of the Union, with the right to freedom of movement and residence. However, the necessary measures for its realisation will still require unanimous agreement.

The Commission has also pursued a number of general policies aimed at enhancing worker mobility. In particular, it established comparability of vocational qualifications, beginning with hotel and catering, motor vehicle repairs, construction, electrical, agricultural and textile trades. Minimum skill requirements are being defined for training qualifications, with the assistance of CEDEFOP. The Commission has also been given responsibility for developing a broad Community recognised vocational training pass, but this will have to be built upon current activity in this area.

The Treaty of Rome had sought to enable professionally qualified people to practise anywhere within the Community (Article 57(1)) and the Commission had first addressed this problem of recognition by negotiations on a profession by profession basis. This proved a very slow process. It took until 1975 to achieve Community-wide recognition of doctors, followed by nurses (1977), dental practitioners (1978), veterinary surgeons (1978), pharmacists (1986), and architects (1985). Dissatisfaction with this approach led to the inclusion of a proposal to establish general mutual recognition as part of the programme to complete the internal market. By 1989 the Council had adopted the Diplomas Directive (89/48/EEC), to come into force from January 1991, which establishes mutual recognition of all the regulated professions' qualifications where study is of at least three years' duration. Safeguards remained in the provision of a period of supervised practice, aptitude and language tests.

However, its impact appears to have been limited. In the UK only 1046 applications were made for recognition of professional qualifications in 1992, 46 per cent of which were from teachers and 40 per cent from Ireland (Department of Trade and Industry, 1995). Criticism has been made that the Directive is imprecise and, as the professional institutes act as the competent authorities in assessing applicants, they are able to continue to discriminate against non-nationals.

The Community also established Sedoc (Regulation 68/1612), a European system of employment information exchange, but this remains inadequate and little used, with only 1000 job applications processed annually. Nonetheless, the Commission continues to foster a programme of exchanges and cooperation between national employment services focusing upon such topics as the frontier labour market, organisation of employment services, and labour market management.

Health and safety

The need to establish minimum European standards for health and safety has been accepted as essential to fair competition within the SEM. A good example of the approach now being taken is that of the Machines Directive, which covers over half of the total production of the European mechanical engineering industry. This Directive, based upon a Council resolution of May 1985, was innovative in that it only defines basic requirements, leaving detailed specifications to the individual standardisation bodies. The Commission invited representatives from industry, trade unions, European standardisation bodies (CEN and CENELEC) and member governments to be involved from the beginning. A tripartite structure of employers, trade unions and the Commission was created to oversee its practical implementation. This approach has been followed in the development of other health and safety Directives.

In 1995 a fourth action programme was adopted covering the period up to the year 2000. It has three themes. First, the effective dissemination of information with regard to the existing health and safety legislation, especially among small and medium-sized firms; this includes the ECU 1.5 million SAGE programme. Secondly, ensuring the national implementation of existing Directives, especially with regard to hazardous substances. Finally, providing a health and safety dimension in the development of other Community policies.

Box 7.3 **Structural Funds reform**

To be based upon four principles:

1. Concentration upon five objectives:
   a. Promoting the development and structural adjustment of the less developed regions.
   b. Converting the areas seriously affected by industrial decline.
   c. Combating long-term unemployment.
   d. Facilitating the occupational integration of young people.
   e. Promoting the development of rural areas.
2. Precise definition of the tasks of the Structural Funds in relation to these objectives.
3. An increase in resources.
4. Rationalisation of both assistance and management methods.

Structural Funds

In defining the role of the Structural Funds in facilitating the changes required by the accelerated economic integration of the SEM, the Commission followed two broad principles. Restructuring must coincide with the broader Community objectives, and Community funds must be matched by national funds. The Structural Funds – ESF, ERDF and EAGGF – have been supplemented by sectoral programmes aimed at restructuring the shipbuilding and steel industries. However, these *ad hoc* measures had created unnecessary complexity. In response, the Commission proposed reform of the Structural Funds in a draft regulation (COM(87)376 final/2) adopted in February 1988. At the same time the appropriation was doubled, in real terms, from ECU 7 bn per annum in 1987 to ECU 14 bn per annum in 1993. The Structural Funds now account for one-quarter of the Community budget and are expected to double again over the period 1994–99 under the financial arrangements of the TEU (see Box 7.3).

The ERDF now focuses on support for productive investment, modernisation of infrastructure, and studies of the potential for physical planning at the Community level (see Chapter 8). The ESF concentrates on assisting young people and the long-term unemployed, expanding general employment, and providing workers with vocational skills. Between 1989 and 1993 ECU 20 bn has been allocated to the ESF, with an expenditure of ECU 5.6 bn in 1995 alone, 90 per cent of the funds being spent on vocational training in the less developed regions of the Community (those with a GDP less than 75 per cent of the EU average).

Training

Ensuring the provision of adequate training of the labour force was seen as essential to achieve the structural adjustment necessary for the successful completion of the SEM. The process of creating the SEM required both new types of training, e.g. corporate planning for small and medium-sized firms, and the general expansion of education and training to create a European pool of skilled labour. The Commission sought to develop a strategy building upon discussions with both sides of industry, and focusing upon its three roles. First, the training of young people, building upon a Council Decision (December 1987) calling for the setting up of a system giving all young people the right to up to two years' basic training. Secondly, the Commission sought to improve comparability between national training systems. Thirdly, the Commission has fostered recognition of the importance of continuing and further training of the labour force by both industry and the State. These general principles have been given expression in the further development of a vocational policy required by Article 128 of the Treaty of Rome. The White Paper on the completion of the internal market (Commission, 1985) built upon this, calling for comparability of qualifications (Council Resolution, July 1985), a general system of recognition of higher education diplomas, and the introduction of a vocational training pass. Two programmes, Erasmus (1987) and Yes (1988) encouraged increased student mobility and youth exchanges respectively, while the Lingua (1989) programme aimed to foster students' knowledge of Community languages. Currently the main programmes for the period 1995–99 are Leonardo da Vinci and Socrates. Leonardo is focused upon improving the quality of vocational training policy and practice. Valued at ECU 620 million, it is funding pilot projects and exchange programmes for students and trainers. Socrates is a broader successor to the Erasmus programme and funds the exchange of students at both school and college levels.

Following from the White Paper 'Growth, Competitiveness and Employment' (COM(93)700) the Commission has recently presented another White Paper – 'Teaching and Learning: Towards the Learning Society' (COM(95)590). This attempts to identify the response that is necessary to meet the challenges presented by globalisation and technological change. It argues for the central role of education and training, and calls for recognition of the benefits of broad based knowledge and training that is relevant to employment. Specifically, it recommends the establishment of a network of EU research centres to identify skill shortages, and vocational training centres to meet this need. A Community accreditation scheme is suggested, with the development of personal 'skill cards'. The White Paper also proposes the development of a network of apprenticeship centres to encourage apprentice mobility along the lines of the Socrates programme for students in higher education.

For higher education it seeks to enhance mobility through ensuring the portability between member states of education grants and the mutual recognition of course credits through a European Course Credit Transfer Scheme. For schools the emphasis is upon multilingualism, with a 'School of Europe' quality label. To address the problem of 'school failures' concentrated in the Community's decaying urban centres, the Commission proposes redeploying funds to support national 'second chance' schemes that have been targeted at these groups. Finally, the Commission calls for the equal treatment of investment in physical and human capital in taxation and accounting terms.

European Works Councils

A central feature of the proposals for a European company law has been the desire to encourage worker participation, since the Commission believes this to be an important factor in firms' economic success. A number of proposals addressing this issue have been considered including the 'Fifth Directive' concerning company structures and the powers and duties of governing bodies. There has also been a proposed Regulation on the status of the European Limited Liability Company, first drafted in 1970, and the 'Vredeling Directive'(1980). This latter proposal specifically set out to be a piece of social legislation, concerned with information provision and consultation with the workforce in large, especially multinational, companies. This Directive was 'frozen' in the face of opposition from employers.

In June 1988 the Commission returned to this issue and submitted a new memorandum on the creation of a European Company statute. It proposed a simpler statute abandoning many aspects of the previous draft, and which would be optional. Firms could choose to operate under the new statute or retain their existing national corporate existence. In terms of worker participation, three options were available to a European company – a German model with workers represented on the management bodies; the Franco-Italian system of a works council separate from the management board; and the Swedish model, under which individual firms establish an agreement on participation with the workers. However, various safeguards were proposed. Prior agreement with the workforce on representation would be required before a European company could be incorporated, with a 'fallback' national standard model specified should there be a failure to reach an agreement. Any member state could also restrict the choice of model available. All three options would require quarterly reports on the company to the employees, and prior consultation with the workforce on decisions relevant to them. Despite its increased flexibility these proposals continued to face the implacable opposition of European employers (Union of Industrial and Employers' Confederations of Europe – UNICE) as part of their general hostility to the emergence of any European level of collective bargaining.

The Commission finally succeeded in establishing European Works Councils through decoupling them from the issue of a European Company Statute. It overcame the political opposition through the use of the Maastricht Social Agreement. A European Works Council Directive was finally adopted in 1994 (94/95 EC), to be implemented by September 1996. The Commission is to review the Directive, in consultation with the member states, employers and labour, by September 1999, including the issue of the threshold for its application (see Box 7.4).

Having achieved agreement on the EWC Directive, the Commission has returned to the stalled negotiations to establish a European Company Statute. However, the ETUC has observed that the issue is not just one of worker consultation but participation in decision-making, as is the case in Germany. Mutual recognition of the national registration of companies would result in firms merely seeking out those member states with the least demanding participation

Box 7.4   **The European Works Council Directive**

1. Applies to undertakings with at least 1000 employees, and at least 150 employees in at least two member states (Article 2).

2. A special negotiating body can be set up by management or at the request of at least 100 employees in at least two undertakings in two or more countries (Article 5).

3. The Directive outlines coverage, composition and how the EWC will operate (Article 6).

4. A default model is provided in the Directive if no agreement is reached between employees and management within three years (Article 8).

5. By agreement, alternative arrangements may be made for the establishment of an EWC (Article 6).

6. The Directive does not apply where there are pre-existing agreements in force (Article 13).

requirements. A European Company Statute must therefore specify a Community-wide standard of worker participation and this remains highly controversial.

Employment

The dramatic increase in unemployment across Europe during the 1980s and its persistence into the 1990s had moved this problem to centre stage. The recovery which had begun in 1994 lost momentum in 1995. Employment in 1995, at 148 million, was 4 million fewer than four years earlier. Unemployment averaged 10.7 per cent in 1996, only slightly below its peak of 11.3 per cent in April 1994, and the long-term unemployed now composed half of the total. Most of the new jobs created in the 1990s have been part-time, with 71 per cent of additional male employment being part-time in 1995, and 85 per cent of that for women. Similarly, almost all of the increase in employment for men was on temporary contracts, and just under half of that for women (Commission, 1996b).

The persistence of high unemployment levels had placed the conflict between the Euro-corporatist 'continental' tradition and that of the 'Anglo-Saxon' neo-Liberals in a new context. The argument for deregulation of the European labour market to increase its flexibility and generate employment, especially among the unskilled and semi-skilled, has been supported by the adverse comparisons that are made between the experience of the United States and the EU. Attempts to prevent 'social dumping' by an interventionist social policy are seen as contributing to the persistence of unemployment, and the policy debate among the member states appears to be shifting its ground.

In 1994, at the Essen Summit, unemployment had reached the top of the agenda. Five priorities had been identified – promoting investment in vocational training, increasing the employment-intensiveness of growth, reducing non-wage labour costs, improving the effectiveness of labour market policies, and helping disadvantaged groups. The Commission was to examine the impact of social security contributions upon employment, and during 1995 specifically addressed employment creation in its Recommendations on economic policy for the Community (COM(95)228). However, despite a succession of reports and opinions emanating from the EU institutions there was no real evidence of policy convergence among national employment policies.

The Essen Summit's employment objectives may influence the movement towards fiscal harmonisation. A Commission paper (SEC(96)487) has observed that between 1980 and 1994 the implicit tax rate on employed labour has grown by 14 per cent, while that on other factors of production has fallen by 20 per cent. Clearly, this is incompatible with the desired objective of increasing employment through reducing indirect labour costs.

Meanwhile, during the preparations for the 1997 Amsterdam Summit, the Commission's President, Jacques Santer, proposed a Confidence Pact on Employment. It focused on a number of areas – the adoption of coordinated macroeconomic policies favourable to employment creation; policies to encourage job creation in small and medium-sized enterprises; realising the potential of the internal market, and redirection of the Structural Funds towards employment objectives. After discussions with the ETUC, UNICE, CEEP and representatives of the member states, the European Council adopted the proposal in June 1996, but so far it has had little real policy influence.

The question of the importance that should be placed upon employment creation in future EU economic policy formation was one of the central issues discussed at Amsterdam. A 'Reflection Group' had argued that unemployment was now a central issue and that employment creation should be seen as one of the duties and tasks of the EU, not merely a side-effect of other policies such as the creation of the SEM and EMU. As a result, the Amsterdam Treaty includes an employment chapter committing the EU to achieving a 'high level of employment' and reasserting its intention to achieve improvements in workers' rights and social standards. However, no new money was to be allocated to achieving these objectives, although a £700 million programme of job-creating investment was to be funded by the European Investment Bank. Its remit was also to be extended from financing only commercial to 'socially useful employment' projects.

The continuing shift of emphasis to 'supply-side' policies was apparent at the special employment summit held in Luxembourg in November 1997. The member states resolved to create more flexible labour markets, lighten the burden of taxation, and promote business and training. However, the only real innovation was the acceptance of a commitment to submit annual national action plans for scrutiny by the other member governments. An employment objective of offering work or training to all under-25 year olds within six months of their becoming unemployed, and within 12 months for those older, was accepted by all the states except Spain. They also intend to offer training to 20 per cent of all of those unemployed within five years.

Conclusion

The problem of the Community's high rates of unemployment is starting to dominate the debate about the future development of the EU's social policy. Statistical studies have failed to identify any one cause for the persistence of the high levels of unemployment in the EU (Bean, 1994). Higher unemployment appears to have originated in the economic 'shocks' of changes in the terms of trade and the pursuit of deflationary policies to counter inflation pressures, although the employment 'cost' of these policies appears to have been much greater in the EU than in the US.

Rising unemployment and the challenge of 'globalisation' have shifted the balance of the argument towards those advocating neo-liberal labour market flexibility (see Addison and Siebert, 1994, 1997), and away from the preservation of the European neo-corporatist tradition, with its emphasis on 'social cohesion' and workers' rights. Wage flexibility will also be essential if the economies of the member states are to maintain their competitive positions after the abolition of internal exchange rates under EMU. Nevertheless, what composes labour market flexibility is open to a variety of interpretations. From a neo-liberal perspective, flexibility will be reflected both in variable wages and the right of managers to hire and fire easily. Policies should encourage geographical mobility, and there should be an emphasis on training and educational investment. However, the latter is common ground in the policy debate, with the increasing importance of flexible production underlining the need for employees who are multi-skilled and self-directed. This central role for investment in human capital requires the development of long-term relationships between employees and employers if the returns to such investments are to be realised (Dearden, 1995). However, such stable employment relationships, which may be reinforced by the Community's emphasis upon policies of 'social cohesion' and 'social dialogue', are regarded as anathema to those advocating the primacy of market forces.

In some areas of EU social policy there are, however, clear signs of a greater consensus. The end of the UK opt-out from the Social Agreement has allowed its incorporation into a revised TEU agreed at Amsterdam. At the same time the opposition of the employers' organisations has been overcome and they are now willing to participate actively in the 'social dialogue' approach to the development of EU social policy. Although this may have been a result of recognising the greater potential that this offers to shape the future direction of policy, in the face of an otherwise inevitable evolution of Community regulation demanded by the single market and EMU, it still represents a significant watershed in the development of EU social policy.

References

Addison J and Siebert W 1993 The EC Social Charter: The Nature of the Beast, *The National Westminster Bank Quarterly Review*, February.

Addison J and Siebert W S 1994 Recent Developments in Social Policy in the New European Union, *Industrial and Labor Relations Review*, Vol. 48, No. 1, October, pp. 5–27.

Addison J and Siebert W S 1997 *Labour Markets in Europe: Issues of Harmonisation and Regulation*, Dryden Press, London.

Bean C 1994 European Unemployment: A Survey, *Journal of Economic Literature*, Vol. 32, June.

Coe D and Gagliardi F 1985 *Nominal Wage Determination in Ten OECD Countries*, OECD Economics and Statistics Working Paper No. 19.

Commission 1985 *Completing the Internal Market: The White Paper*, Office for Official Publications of the European Communities, Luxembourg.

Commission 1988 *Social Europe, the Social Dimension of the Internal Market*, Brussels.

Commission 1991 Developments in the Labour Market in the Community: Results of a Survey Covering Employers and Employees, *European Economy*, No. 47, March.

Commission 1996b *Employment in Europe* (COM(96)485).

Dearden S 1995 Minimum Wages and Wage Flexibility in the European Union, *Journal of European Social Policy*, Vol. 5, No. 1, pp. 29–42.

Department of Trade and Industry 1995 Directive 89/48/EEC Article 11 Report, Report of the United Kingdom, London.

Employment Observatory 1995 Office for Official Publications of the European Communities, Luxembourg.

European Industrial Relations Review 1990, No. 1.

Morton J and Siebert S 1997 *Social Dumping and Insider-Outsider Distinctions in the European Union: Company Case Studies*, University of Birmingham, Mimeo.

Rhodes M 1992 The Future of the Social Dimension: Labour Market Regulation in Post-1992 Europe, *Journal of Common Market Studies*, Vol. XXX, March, pp. 23–51.

Further reading

Adnett N 1996 *European Labour Markets*, Longman, London.

Commission 1990–1991 *The Social Dimension*, Periodical 2/1990, Brussels.

Commission 1993 *White Paper on Growth, Competitiveness and Employment*, Brussels.

Commission 1994 *White Paper: European Social Policy: A Way Forward for the European Union*, Brussels.

Commission 1994 *An Industrial Competitiveness Policy for the European Union*, COM(94)319, Brussels.

Commission 1995 Employment Observatory Trends, *Bulletin of the European System of Documentation on Employment (SYSDEM)*, No. 21.

Commission 1996a *Commission Communication Concerning the Development of the Social Dialogue at Community Level* (COM(96)448).

European Industrial Relations Review 1990 Social Charter: Action Programme Released, *European Industrial Relations Review*, No. 192.

European Industrial Relations Review 1997 *The New Social Action Programme*: No. 257, pp. 12–19.

European Industrial Relations Review 1997 *Commission sets out the options for the future of the social dialogue*: No. 256, pp. 24–29.

Falkner G 1996 The Maastricht Protocol on Social Policy: Theory and Practice, *Journal of European Social Policy*, Vol. 6, No. 1, pp. 1–16.

Gold M 1992 Social Policy: the UU and Maastricht, *National Institute Economic Review*, February, pp. 95–103.

Gordon I and Thirlwall A 1989 *European Factor Mobility, Trends and Consequences,* Macmillan, London.

Hart R *et al.* 1988 *Trends in Non-wage Labour Costs and their Effect on Employment,* Commission of the European Communities, Brussels.

Majone G 1993 The European Community Between Social Policy and Social Regulation, *Journal of Common Market Studies,* Vol. 31, No. 2, June, pp. 153–70.

Molle W and Mourik A V 1988 International Movements under Conditions of Economic Integration: The Case of Western Europe, *Journal of Common Market Studies,* Vol. XXVI, March, pp. 317–42.

Read R 1991 The Single European Market, Does European Mobility Matter?, *International Journal of Manpower,* Vol. 12, No. 2.

Ulman L, Eichengreen B and Dickens T (Ed.) 1993 *Labor and an Integrated Europe,* The Brooking Institute, Washington.

Regional policy

Reiner Martin

European integration and the growth of regional heterogeneity

During the early years of what is now the European Union (EU), regional policy was not an important policy area. The founding members of the EU were a fairly homogeneous group of countries and the only area encountering major regional problems, such as low per capita income and high unemployment, was the southern part of Italy.

The 1973 enlargement, when Denmark, the Republic of Ireland and the UK joined the Community, increased regional disparities. Whereas Denmark did not deviate much from the original member states in terms of per capita income and regional balance, some of the UK regions, especially the North of England and Northern Ireland, were experiencing major unemployment problems and had a low level of per capita income compared with the rest of the EU. The third new entrant, the Republic of Ireland, was significantly poorer than the original member states. Its per capita income level in 1973 was just about half the EU6 average. The accession of Greece in 1981, and Spain and Portugal in 1986, all of whom had per capita income levels significantly below the average of EU6, finally established regional policy at the top of the European agenda. Although the richest parts of these countries were better off than the Republic of Ireland, they were still poor compared with the Union average. Moreover, the sheer size of the new 'poor' regions dwarfed the pre-1981 situation.

The two last accessions have also contributed to the regional problems of the EU, although to a lesser extent than the southern enlargement. The 1990 accession of the former German Democratic Republic (GDR) to the Federal Republic of Germany (FRG) added an area inhabited by 17 million people whose average income at the time was only 35 per cent of the EU average. The 1995 northern enlargement, which brought Finland, Sweden and Austria into the EU, was comparatively unproblematic, although large parts of Sweden and Finland have also become eligible for European regional support.

Over the years, the various enlargements have thus transformed the EU into a more and more heterogeneous group of countries with significant regional economic imbalances. In the next section these income and unemployment disparities are presented in greater detail.

Box 8.1   Defining regions

Eurostat, the statistical office of the European Commission, has defined various levels of regional disaggregation which are applicable in all EU member states. The so-called 'nomenclature des unités territoriales statistiques (NUTS)' has four main levels (NUTS 0-III), with NUTS 0 being the member states. In the UK, NUTS III is equivalent to counties and local authority regions, NUTS II to county/local authority groupings and NUTS I to standard regions (Eurostat, 1996).

Most analyses of regional disparities are based on the NUTS II level of regional disaggregation. Since NUTS II regions differ significantly in terms of size and population, a higher level of disaggregation would be desirable. However, data availability for regions below the NUTS II level is very restricted.

Regional economic disparities within the EU

In principle, the term 'region' can define any geographic entity, irrespective of whether this entity corresponds with national or sub-national boundaries or a group of countries. For regional policy purposes, however, regions refer to national or sub-national administrative areas. This symptom is known as 'nomenclature des unités territoriales statistiques (NUTS)' and is explained in Box 8.1.

Regional income disparities

Per capita income levels are the most commonly used indicator for differences in economic development. On a national, as well as a regional level, such income disparities are considerable within the EU. Fig. 8.1 shows the 1988 and 1996 per capita income of the EU member states relative to the EU15 average (100). In order to account for differences in relative purchasing power, income is measured in purchasing power standard (PPS) terms.

The figure indicates a narrowing of income disparities at the national level. The performance of Ireland in particular is remarkable. In terms of PPS, the country is now above the EU average per capita income. Portugal, Spain and Greece also made some progress, whereas some of the northern member states like Sweden, Finland and, due to reunification, Germany, experienced relative income decline. Luxembourg managed to increase its 'lead' vis-à-vis the EU average.

Income disparities are considerably wider at the NUTS II level of regions. The ratio between Luxembourg, the richest member state, and Greece, the poorest member state, was only 2.6 to 1 in 1996. The ratio between Hamburg, the richest NUTS II region, and its poorest counterpart, Ipeiros (Greece), however, is more than 4.5 to 1. Fig. 8.2 provides an overview of PPS per capita in 1994, the last year for which regional data are available.

Figure 8.2 shows a clear link between geographic peripherality and relative income. It also shows that most capital regions have a significantly higher level

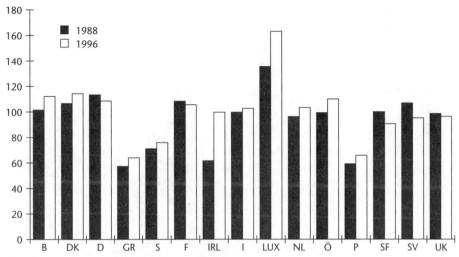

Figure 8.1 Relative per capita income in EU member states 1988 and 1994

Source: adapted from European Commission (1997a)

of per capita income than the other parts of the member states. Finally, significant differences in intra-national disparities emerge. Italy is characterised by a strong north-south income divide, and Germany by significant east-west disparities. The regional income distribution in the Scandinavian member states and France (outside Paris), however, is very balanced. The high values for eastern Scotland (Aberdeen) and the north-eastern part of the Netherlands (Groningen) are due to North Sea oil and North Sea gas which are brought ashore in these regions.

Unlike national income disparities, regional disparities have tended to widen during the last decade. In 1983, the 10 (25) poorest NUTS II regions had an average per capita income of 44 (53) relative to the EU15 average of 100. Figures in brackets refer to values measured in PPS. By 1993, these income values had increased to 48 (55). Relative income in the 10 (25) best-off NUTS II regions, however, has also increased, namely from 154 (140) to 158 (142). The standard deviation of income disparities at NUTS II level has also increased from 26.8 in 1983, to 27.2 in 1993. In terms of intra-national regional income disparities, the standard deviation has increased in 12 out of 15 member states. Only the Netherlands shows a decline in intra-national regional disparities, and the values for Finland and the UK remained constant (Commission, 1996).

Regional labour market disparities

Unemployment is another important indicator for the assessment of regional socio-economic disparities. Fig. 8.3 shows relative national unemployment rates for the EU member states in 1987 and 1996.

The most striking developments have taken place in Ireland, which managed to reduce its *relative* level of unemployment significantly, and in Finland, where

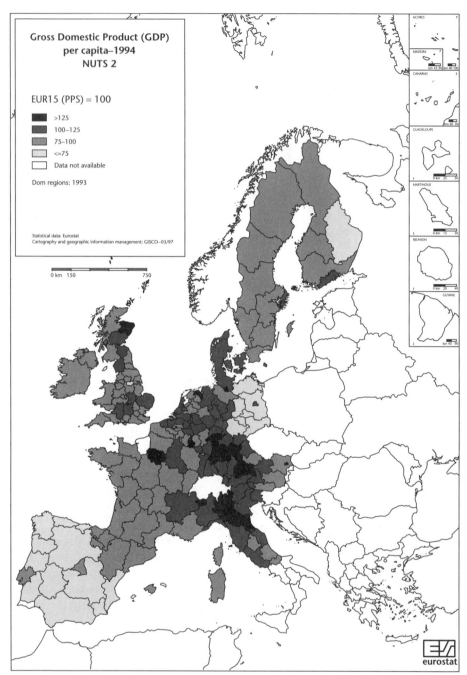

Figure 8.2 Gross domestic product (GDP) per capita – 1994 NUTS 2

Source: Regions – *Statistics in Focus*, Eurostat, 1997

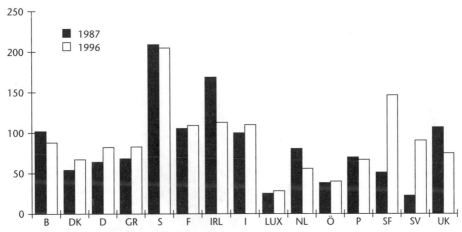

Figure 8.3 Relative unemployment in EU member states 1987 and 1996

Source: adapted from European Commission (1997a)

the opposite development has taken place. The relative performances of the Netherlands and the UK are also positive, although to a lesser extent than that of Ireland. It has to be kept in mind that the *absolute* level of unemployment in the EU has increased. The 1987 average of the EU15 was 9.8 per cent. The average value in 1996 was 10.9. The relative position of the 'poor' EU member states is quite mixed. Whereas unemployment seems to be less of a problem for Portugal and Greece, the unemployment rate for Spain is extremely high and shows little tendency to decline. However, the member states have different definitions for registered unemployment. For Greece and Spain in particular, unemployment figures are based on very restrictive criteria and this is likely to result in an underestimation of the actual problem (Commission, 1994). The regional incidence of unemployment in 1996 is illustrated in Fig. 8.4.

At the NUTS II level, unemployment differences are more pronounced than at member state level. In 1983, the Finnish region of Uusimaa had the lowest unemployment rate (1.7 per cent), a position that was taken over by Luxembourg in 1996 (3.2 per cent). The Spanish region of Andalucia was the poorest region in both years with an unemployment rate of 22.5 per cent in 1983, and 32.4 per cent in 1996. Regional unemployment disparities also tended to widen over time, with the standard deviation of all NUTS II regions increasing from 3.6 in 1983 to 6.0 in 1993 (Commission, 1996).

The regional income and unemployment data demonstrate clearly the existence of significant socio-economic disparities within the EU. These disparities exceed comparable values for the United States (Boltho, 1994). Moreover, in many 'poor' EU regions, low income coincides with high unemployment. Not only does Fig. 8.2 look in large parts like a mirror image of Fig. 8.4 but statistical analysis also shows a high correlation between relative regional income and relative regional unemployment. While these stylised facts are at the heart of EU regional policy, it is not clear whether regional disparities are likely to be permanent.

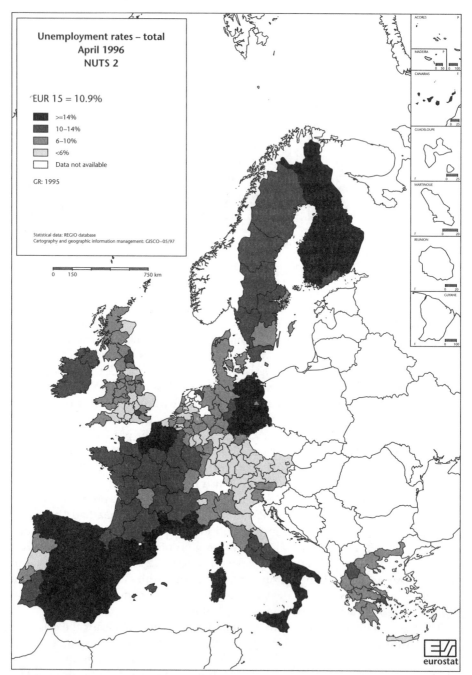

Figure 8.4   Unemployment rates – total April 1996 NUTS 2

Source: Regions – *Statistics in Focus*, Eurostat, 1997

Economic theories of regional disparities

Neo-classical economic theory predicts that factor incomes, i.e. wages and returns on capital, in all regions of an integrated economic area like the EU will eventually converge. This result depends on sufficiently strong adjustment mechanisms in the form of goods and factor movements within the integration area. This prediction is based on the argument that all regions have an optimal capital intensity. This outcome is based on an optimal mix between the factors capital and labour, which in turn is determined by the production technology that prevails in regions. According to the strongest form of convergence theory, integration will lead to identical production technologies in all regions. Thus, payments to labour and capital will equalise across all regions unless there are impediments to transfer of technologies. Conditional convergence theory relaxes this assumption and allows for differences in regional production technologies and, in consequence, regional differences in optimal capital intensities. Both forms of convergence theory argue that regional output and factor incomes will be below the utility-maximising level as long as the actual capital intensity in a particular region is different from the technologically determined optimal capital intensity. According to neo-classical theory a sub-optimal capital intensity can be altered by movement of goods and services and/or factors of production between regions, or by changes in the savings and investment rates relative to the growth rate of the population. Thus, relative disparities disappear as the competitive market process moves labour, capital, goods and services between regions. Therefore, neo-classical theory predicts that, in competitive markets, where there are no impediments to the free movement of goods, services, capital and labour, regional disparities cannot persist.

Divergence theory, however, leads to radically different conclusions. This strand of economic theory stresses the importance of technological differences, transport costs and the impact of differences in regional economic structures on regional growth. The importance of the growth of clusters because of agglomeration effects is also used to support the divergence theory. The link between economic integration and agglomeration effects is discussed in Chapter 1. Generally speaking, divergence theory predicts the development of a heterogeneous economic landscape with significant differences in the factor returns in central and peripheral areas. This in turn leads to substantial out-migration of mobile factors from poor to rich regions, which, in turn, widens the disparities even further. This cumulative causation view of regional disparities is discussed in Barro and Sala-i-Martin (1995) and Bradley *et al.* (1995).

Empirical observations provide partial support for both theories. Neven and Gouyette (1994), Armstrong (1995) and Martin (1997) find evidence in favour of income convergence among European regions. The convergence process has been fastest during periods of high growth although it has never been fast enough to allow for a significant reduction of regional disparities in less than a couple of decades. Moreover, the process has slowed down further during the 1980s. Empirical investigations of locational decisions point towards the importance of external and agglomeration effects as well as transport and transaction costs (Commission, 1990, 1993a). This supports the divergence point of view.

Furthermore, economists have stressed the importance of historical events and first-mover advantages like the location of important inventions as the key determinants of regional disparities (Rauch, 1993; North, 1994). There is certainly little evidence that lagging regions will benefit more from economic integration than the more advanced 'core' regions.

Supporters of divergence theory, as well as those convergence theorists that relax the assumption of identical technologies across all locations, argue that action by governments is required to bring about regional convergence. Nevertheless, it is not clear if interventions by governments can make a useful contribution to finding solutions to this problem. In particular, government intervention may improve equity but at the cost of hampering the quest for efficiency. Moreover, if the convergence theorists are correct, there is no need for regional policy. For these theorists, competition policy and the liberalisation of barriers to free movement are the routes to eliminating regional disparities.

Rationale for regional policy

The literature on the rationale for regional policy usually provides a blend of arguments, mixing social, political and economic reasoning (Armstrong and Taylor, 1993). The most frequently stated arguments for regional policy are:

1. the flattening of 'unjust' spatial income distributions (equity or fairness argument);
2. the easing of adjustment problems in economies undergoing major transformations or shocks;
3. reducing unemployed resources;
4. the optimisation of the spatial allocation of production by reducing congestion and other costs arising from the concentration of economic activity in rich regions.

A clear separation of the different rationales is often impossible. Literature on the growth effects of income distributions, for example, links the equity rationale with an efficiency argument by saying that there is a negative link between economic growth and inequality (Alesina and Rodrik, 1994; Galor and Zeira, 1993). The results of these studies, however, do not support traditional regional policy because they investigate the effects of inter-personal rather than inter-regional distributions. Henceforth, they are more suitable to provide support for social policy.

The rationale based on adjustment problems is essentially a socio-political argument, however. In the context of the EU, adjustment problems can become an obstacle for integration. A member state that is likely to experience a major rise in unemployment due to deeper integration because large parts of its industry are not competitive is unlikely to support further integration. In the light of this danger it becomes economically meaningful to compensate the country for its adjustment problems.

The last two points are economic arguments for regional policy. The 'employment of unused resources' rationale is based on an argument that, in some areas where economic activity is insufficient, this leads to certain factors of production, notably labour, being unemployed or under-employed. Regional policy may help to reintegrate these factors of production into the economic process, thereby increasing aggregate welfare. In principle, this argument can be used as an economic justification for state intervention. However, it requires two conditions to hold. First, that the surplus factors of production are too immobile to move to other parts of the integration area and, secondly, that the costs to activate them are lower than the welfare gains obtainable from their activation.

The first condition is, by and large, fulfilled in the EU. Despite the four freedoms, labour mobility in particular is very low. However, factor mobility, especially labour mobility, is frequently regarded as politically undesirable. Given the lack of political efforts to increase the spatial mobility of labour, factor immobility is to some extent politically determined rather than an unavoidable fact. Nevertheless, cultural and linguistic barriers also create barriers to large-scale labour mobility. The Commission has issued a communication 'Agenda 2000' in which arguments for policies to promote labour mobility have been strongly advocated (Commission, 1996).

The second condition is more difficult to achieve. In the absence of external effects such as congestion costs, and on the basis of the assumption of rational behaviour, the market outcome must be the optimal spatial allocation of resources. In the presence of externalities, however, private welfare-optimising behaviour is no longer equal to social welfare optimisation. A private decision to locate a company in the centre of a cluster, for example, can lead to negative side-effects like an increase in traffic congestion. The investor does not have to pay other economic subjects' costs due to the increase in congestion that his or her decision has caused. These costs are *external* to him or her. Most authors are very careful in assessing the welfare implications of regional market failures. 'It is not immediately clear whether they provide a case for regional policy. For example, if there are positive benefits from firms' agglomeration, this should not be discouraged, but it is easy to imagine situations where there is a case for policy' (CEPR, 1993).

Generally speaking, the welfare costs of regional policy interventions have to be weighted against the welfare gains. If a Pareto-optimal view of welfare is adopted, that is, no one may be worse off due to an aggregate welfare-increasing measure, regional policy is unlikely to be optimal because regional policy measures are bound to violate this criterion. However, by using the Kaldor-Hicks criterion, according to which total welfare gains have to exceed total welfare losses, it is possible to justify regional policy action. Most regional policy interventions cause direct costs, opportunity costs and efficiency costs, with the last of these arising due to the distortions of the market mechanism caused by the intervention. An attempt to improve the productivity of a lagging region by means of infrastructure investments, for example, is costly (direct costs), the money is no longer available for similar action in core regions (opportunity costs), and price signals in the economy are being distorted (efficiency costs).

In order to identify the preferable instrument, two general rules should be taken into account. First, measures that are trying to increase the underlying competitiveness of regions, like investments in human capital and infrastructure, are normally superior to measures that are directed at the firm level. Secondly, regional policy should aim at increasing the endogenous potential of lagging regions rather than diverting existing activities from one location to another (Temple, 1994).

The chances of regional policy increasing aggregate welfare by activating idle resources are very limited. Lammers (1992) argues that the marginal utility of factors of production in peripheral areas is by definition almost insufficient to generate a positive net welfare effect.

Regional policy measures to reduce allocative distortions due to external effects are normally a second-best solution. It is preferable to internalise external effects like environmental pollution and traffic congestion, for example by road use charges for private transport (see Chapter 10).

It seems to be fairly clear that there is not a good economic rationale in favour of regional policy. Equity arguments for regional policy are certainly more powerful than efficiency arguments.

European or national regional policy?

Most of the member states pursue some form of regional policy although there are significant differences in the form and scope of national regional policies across the EU. The need for an EU policy, given the existence of national policies, largely rests on equity arguments and its role as a lubricant to reduce friction caused by the integration process.

Four main reasons may be advanced to justify EU policy:

1. The 'financial targeting' argument is due to insufficient resources in the poor member states who are unable to target their regional problems themselves and therefore the EU has to provide the necessary resources.

2. The 'vested interest' argument is based on the belief that the solution of regional problems in one member state will be beneficial for other member states.

3. The 'effects of integration' argument is based on the assumption that the benefits of integration are not evenly spread across the EU, which in turn requires a central redistribution mechanism.

4. The 'effects of other EU policies' argument argues that, because the regional benefits of other policies like the Common Agricultural Policy (CAP) are not spread evenly, the relative losers therefore need to be compensated by means of EU regional policy.

The 'financial targeting' argument is relatively undisputed although empirical investigations of peripheral countries' expenditure patterns yield some surprising results. While it is true that Greece and Ireland, in particular, spend a larger percentage of their GDP on state aids than the EU as a whole (Martin and Schulze Steinen, 1997), the peripheral countries use a smaller share of their national income for important areas of investment like R&D and transport infrastructure. While *total* expenditures below the EU average are obvious, given the small size of the peripheral economies, lower relative expenditures are difficult to justify.

The 'vested interest' argument is also problematic. Rich member states do not necessarily benefit from the fact that other regions are made better off. In conjunction with the 'effects of integration' argument, however, it becomes more powerful. This line of reasoning argues that, without compensations for those regions which obtain less than their 'fair' share of the aggregate welfare gains, further integration would be impossible, which in turn would cause aggregate welfare losses. The question whether there are 'winners' and (relative or absolute) 'losers' of the integration process is hotly debated and the empirical evidence rather mixed. Lammers (1992), for example, stresses the probability that integration will reduce spatial disparities while Vickerman (1992) is more pessimistic concerning the divergence effects of the Single European Market. Regardless of the scientific debate, however, '... the division of costs and benefits is central to the political agreements needed to proceed with integration' (Begg and Mayes, 1993).

The 'effects of other EU policies' argument, finally, is frequently and, at least with regard to the spatial distribution of CAP payments, rightly mentioned in defence of regional transfers. It is mainly the better-off EU regions that benefit from expenditures under the CAP (European Parliament, 1991), although the EU has recently tried to reduce this bias (Commission, 1996). Another difficult area is the Trans-European Networks. While they are very likely to be beneficial for convergence at the member-state level, some peripheral regions of the EU will face a relative decline in accessibility (Bruinsma and Rietveld, 1997).

Why limits to regional policy transfers?

EU regional policy operates mainly on the basis of conditional transfers from the EU budget to specific areas within the member states. However, many commentators argue in favour of an alternative system based on unconditional financial transfers between rich and poor member states together with a 're-nationalisation' of regional policy. Various arguments are advanced in favour of a system of bounded transfers:

- The 'conditions of the donor' argument. The net contributors to EU regional policy want to make sure that the money is spent in order to improve the growth potential of those regions that are in greatest need for support.
- The 'insufficiency of regional authorities' argument. This assumes that regional authorities in most member states are unable to make sure that the 'right' measures to achieve regional convergence are pursued.
- The 'coordination' argument. Regional policy measures in one member state have spillover effects in other member states that are not sufficiently taken into account if regional policy is conducted on a national level.

- Purely national regional policy might lead to a wasteful subsidy race between different locations.

The first argument is the main reason for the current system of EU regional policy, namely the reluctance of the better-off member states to fund a fiscal transfer system without 'strings' for the recipients. EU regional policy is not officially designed as a system of fiscal federalism (Oates, 1972), contributing to convergence between the member states or to an equalisation of inter-personal income levels across the EU. Instead, its main purpose is to provide temporary support for those regions of the EU whose present level of competitiveness is insufficient. The net contributors to the EU budget would not have accepted the substantial increase in regional policy funding since the mid-1980s without having a substantial degree of central control over the use of structural fund resources for what they perceive as the 'right' measures for increasing regional competitiveness (CEPR, 1993; Folkers, 1995).

The second argument is essentially a rationalisation of the first argument. While the quality of regional authorities in some EU member states leaves much to be desired, it is obviously doubtful whether a central European administration is in a better position to design 'suitable' measures to increase regional competitiveness. In effect, information problems feature prominently among the difficulties created by the current centralised system.

An economic rather than a political argument for centralised regional policy is provided by the 'co-ordination' argument (Weise, 1995). Some regional policy measures, for example infrastructure investments that also improve international transport links, have cross-border repercussions (external effects). The same applies to human capital formation in conjunction with international migration although, as argued above, international migration within the EU is currently still very low.

As far as the fear of a subsidy race between different locations is concerned, efficient state aid control could prevent this outcome (Lammers, 1992). So far the efficiency of EU state aids control leaves much to be desired and on a per capita basis national regional aids in the supported parts of core member states like Germany and Belgium are usually far above corresponding values in the periphery (Marques, 1992; Martin, 1996). The weakness of competition policy, however, is a poor argument in favour of regional policy in general and even more so for centralised regional policy.

From the point of view of economic theory it is easier to find arguments against the current regional policy system than arguments in favour of it. Generally speaking, the preferable method of compensation in economics is lump-sum compensation. Since this form of compensation requires that the winners and losers are identifiable and that the sum to be transferred can be calculated, it is impracticable in its *perfect* form, although the sums to be transferred can be approximated in a bargaining process. After all, the funding actually used for European regional policy is also established in a bargaining process.

Among the most important reasons why direct transfers would be more efficient than the current system is the fact that, within the current system, distributional aims are pursued by means of allocational policy. Although EU regional policy is not officially designed as a re-distribute policy, it has significant re-distributive effects (Commission, 1996) and its distributional element can hardly be denied. This mix of aims and policies, however, is bound to lead to efficiency losses. From the point of view of economic theory, a system of direct or indirect transfers between the EU member states would clearly be preferable in order to fulfil the re-distribute function of EU regional policy (Strain, 1993).

Finally, the current system is not easily compatible with the subsidiarity principle. While some elements of regional policy, notably major infrastructure projects with inter-regional spillovers, are compatible with this principle, other forms of structural action undertaken by the EU, for example productive investment support in peripheral areas, might as well be performed by the member states. Therefore, political considerations of the kind described above prevent the realisation of an important principle of governance within the EU.

The development of European regional policy

The oldest elements of European regional policy are the European Social Fund (ESF), aimed at 'rendering the employment of workers easier and of increasing their geographical and occupational mobility within the Community' (Article 123, EEC) and the European Agricultural Guidance and Guarantee Fund, Guidance Section (EAGGF) (Article 40, EEC). Areas encountering economic problems could also obtain loans with below-market interest rates from the European Coal and Steel Community (ECSC) and the European Investment Bank (EIB). The geographical focus of early ESF activities was southern Italy, until the 1973 enlargement the unemployment hotspot of the Community. Funding from the EAGGF was mainly distributed to the better-off agricultural areas in the north of the EEC. In financial terms these instruments were very small and there was no clear strategy for promoting regional development (Kenner, 1994).

The 1973 oil shock and the first enlargement of the EEC eventually led to a strengthening of the Community's regional policy activities. Regulation 724/75, EEC ((OJ) L 73/8 1975) established the European Regional Development Fund (ERDF) which was later incorporated into primary Community law.

> The European Regional Development Fund is intended to help to redress the main regional imbalances in the Community through participation in the development and structural adjustment of regions whose development is lagging behind and in the conversion of declining industrial regions.　　　　(Article 130C, EEC)

ERDF resources were originally allocated to member states on the basis of fixed quotas. Member states had to co-finance ERDF-supported projects with national public funding – the principle of additionality. Up to 85 per cent of ERDF-funded projects during the 1970s and early 1980s were connected with infrastructure improvements. The design of EU regional policy during this first phase led to a number of serious problems. First, in order to make sure that the quota allocated to them was used up, member states frequently compromised the economic efficiency of ERDF-supported projects. Secondly, Community funding did not normally lead to additional projects but member states used the funding from Brussels in order to reduce national expenditures for projects which would have gone ahead anyway (Tsoukalis, 1997).

The European Commission made several attempts to reform this system of regional assistance. The aim of the Commission was to create a more encompassing regional policy that would have an increased role vis-à-vis the national authorities. In order to achieve this goal it was of crucial importance to move away from the member-state quotas for ERDF funds. In 1978 and 1985 the Commission launched attempts to scrap them, but the European Council left the quota system more or less intact. The member states were not yet willing to change a system that suited them well. They could use EU regional policy funds to reduce national expenditures and they were able to retain the initiative in regional policy making.

Probably the most important reason for the overhaul of the original system was the southern enlargement of the EU in 1981 and 1986. This not only increased regional disparities, but also led to demands by the existing southern member states to be compensated for their willingness to accept the widening of the Community. The so-called Integrated Mediterranean Programmes (IMPs) for Italy, France and Greece were designed in order to satisfy these demands. The IMP, launched in 1985, moved beyond the previous project-based approach and towards a more encompassing programme-type policy. They thus became 'pioneer' programmes for the large-scale 1988 EU regional policy reform (Bianchi, 1993).

Another reason for the reform was the Single European Market (SEM) project, launched by the Single European Act (SEA) in 1986. In the light of the uncertainty of the spatial economic effects of the SEM, the poorer member states demanded financial assistance from the EU in order to be able to increase their economic competitiveness. The richer northern member states were willing to satisfy these demands in order to make sure that integration would proceed. However, they wanted to make sure that this additional money was spent in a more effective way than previous ERDF funds. Their desire to ensure a more efficient use of the funds was even stronger than their reluctance to sacrifice the old system which, although operating on a smaller scale, had suited them well. As a consequence, the majority of the member states were willing to increase the influence of the Commission significantly and to scrap the fixed quotas. However, they were not willing to establish a system of unbounded fiscal transfers.

The increased European competence for economic and social measures was also manifested by the insertion of the Title 'Economic and Social Cohesion' (Article 130A – 130E, EEC Treaty) into primary European law.

> In order to promote its overall harmonious development, the Community shall develop and pursue its actions leading to the strengthening of its economic and social cohesion. In particular, the Community shall aim at reducing disparities between the levels of development of the various regions and the backwardness of the least favoured regions, including rural areas.   (Article 130A(1), EC Treaty)

Article 130B mentions the most important Community instruments to improve social and economic cohesion within the EU. The aims and organisation of the structural policy instruments as well as the coordination between these instruments and the European institutions concerned are regulated by Article 130C, EEC Treaty.

In terms of concrete policy changes, the Commission used the 'window of opportunity' created by the treaty changes to draw up a policy approach that was a dramatic departure from the previous system. The legal acts establishing the new system are outlined in OJL 374 1988. The reform affected not only the role and operations of the ERDF but also the other Structural Funds (SFs), namely the ESF and the EAGGF. The most important elements of the reform were arranged around four guiding principles, namely: programming, concentration, additionality and partnership. These principles will be discussed below.

Economic and social cohesion gained even more importance after the treaty revisions at Maastricht. According to the Treaty on European Union (TEU), improvements in cohesion among the member states shall foster balanced and sustainable economic and social progress. This in turn will pave the way towards the full implementation of the common market and, as the final goal, the creation of Economic and Monetary Union (EMU). Moreover, the idea of solidarity within the EU was emphasised (Marias, 1994). The treaties contain a clear obligation to use suitable policies in order to reduce socio-economic imbalances unless this reduction is likely to come about automatically and within a reasonable time period. Given the theoretical and empirical findings outlined above, however, this is very unlikely.

The TEU also led to a number of changes in the instruments of European regional policy. Two further cohesion instruments were created, namely the European Investment Fund (EIF) and the Cohesion Fund (CF). Both were designed to make the deepening of the integration process more attractive for the weaker partners in the EU. The EIF is a special credit facility, organically linked with the EIB. The facility is designed to ease the financing of projects in peripheral parts of the EU that involve a higher credit risk than the standard operations of the EIB. The CF is based on Article 130D(2) of the Treaty and provides additional funding for infrastructure and environmental projects in member states with a per capita GDP of less than 90 per cent of the EU average. At present, Spain, Portugal, Ireland and Greece are entitled to support from this facility. On top of the income condition, CF support requires the presentation and implementation of a national convergence programme in order to qualify for EMU. Given that the defining criteria are national rather than regional and in view of the fact that the CF is specifically designed to ease peripheral countries' transition to EMU, the Cohesion Fund is – strictly speaking – not comparable with the SFs. In the light of its declared aim to promote the economic development of the weaker member states, however, its inclusion in the list of SFs seems justified.

The sectoral instruments related to the fishing industry have been reorganised in the form of the Financial Instrument for Guidance in the Fisheries Sector (FIFG) adopted as Regulation EEC 2080/93 (OJ L 193/1, 1993). Whereas these instruments operated previously outside the scope of the Structural Funds, they have now become an integral part of the SF operations.

A final and potentially far-reaching change was the establishment of the Committee of the Regions (Article 198a-c). So far this Committee has merely advisory status, comparable to the Economic and Social Committee, and is serviced by the same secretariat. Regardless of its very limited power, the existence of a committee consisting of representatives of regional and local bodies reflects the growing importance of sub-national levels of administration within the EU. Whether the Committee will eventually become more influential for the decision-making process regarding EU cohesion policies than originally envisaged remains to be seen (Kenner, 1994).

Principles of European regional policy – A critical assessment

Concentration

One of the guiding principles of the 1988 reform was the concentration of regional policy on those parts of the EU that were in greatest need of structural support. Prior to the reform, areas eligible for national regional support qualified automatically for support from the European structural funds. However, the Commission developed its own regional policy 'objectives'. There are two main reasons for this change. First, the definition of eligible regions on a European level makes sure that member states do not unduly expand their national eligibility coverage in an attempt to maximise European structural support payments. Secondly, a European rather than a national perspective as to what constitutes a regional problem is useful for a policy aimed at the reduction of socio-economic disparities at Union level.

Since the 1988 reform, regional policy objectives have been developed. The first set of objectives prevailed from 1989–93, after which they were slightly modified to cover the operation of regional policy in the period 1994–99. Details of the objectives are given in Box 8.2.

The objectives can be divided into two different categories. In the 1994–99 period, Objectives 1, 2, 5b and 6 are 'regional', in that they refer to certain eligible regional areas. However, under Objectives 3, 4 and 5a, it is possible to fund activities that cover the entire EU.

In order to make the process for region-specific objectives more transparent, a set of designation criteria have been developed. The most precise criteria were set for the designation of Objective 1 regions. Per capita income in these regions, expressed in PPS, must be less than 75 per cent of the Community average for at least three consecutive years. Moreover, Objective 1 status can only be granted to NUTS II regions in order to prevent the 'creation' of low income regions by disregarding regional frontiers. However, the regulation allows for exceptions to these rules.

Designation criteria for the other objectives are less strict. In order to qualify for Objective 2 status, regions must have a greater unemployment rate and a higher share of industrial employment than the EU average. Moreover, industrial employment has to be in decline. These criteria must be satisfied for a couple of years but they are not clearly quantified in the regulations. In principle, the designation should be based on NUTS III regions but parts of NUTS II regions can also qualify.

Box 8.2 **European regional policy objectives**

1989–93 Period

1. Development and structural adjustment of lagging regions.

2. Conversion of regions or parts of regions seriously affected by industrial decline.

3. Combating long-term unemployment.

4. Occupational integration of young people.

5a. Speeding up the adjustment of agricultural structures.

5b. Development of rural areas.

1994–99 Period

1., 2. Not altered.

3. Combines former Objectives 3 and 4.

4. Facilitating structural change.

5a. As before but aid to the fisheries sector included.

5b. Aimed at the development and structural adjustment of rural areas.

6. Aimed at areas with very low population density (Nordic regions).

Source: Adapted from Commission (1993b)

The criteria for Objective 5b regions are a low level of socio-economic development, a high share of agricultural employment and a low level of agricultural income (Regulation (EEC) 2081/93). Once again, extensions of the eligibility criteria are possible and, as none of the criteria is quantified, this leaves a lot of leeway for 'political' designations.

Although it was an explicit aim of the 1988 reform to limit the geographical availability of EU regional assistance, more than 50 per cent of the EU population now lives in eligible areas. Moreover, the 1994–99 coverage ratio has gone up compared with the 1989–93 period. (see Table 8.1).

The quantitatively defined criteria for Objective 1 regions have been eroded. The 1994–99 additions to the Objective 1 list (Hainault in Belgium and France, Merseyside, and Highlands and Islands in the UK, and Flevoland in the Netherlands) neither correspond to NUTS II level regions nor is their relative per capita income below 75 per cent of the EU average. Moreover, the problem in all these regions is clearly not a lack of development, with the possible exception of the Highlands and Islands, but one of industrial decline. A designation as Objective 2 areas, however, would have reduced the available funding significantly compared with Objective 1 status.

During the 1989–93 and 1994–99 periods more than two-thirds of the available resources have been allocated to Objective 1 regions, arguably those parts of the EU that are in greatest need of structural support. The erosion of the

Table 8.1   Population covered by European regional policy objectives (%)

Objective	1 1989	1/6* 1994	2 1989	2 1994	5b 1989	5b 1994	Total 1989	Total 1994
Austria	n.a.	3.7	n.a.	7.5	n.a.	28.7	n.a.	39.9
Belgium	./.	12.8	22.1	14.2	2.7	4.5	24.8	31.5
Denmark	./.	./.	4.9	8.5	2.1	6.8	7	15.3
Finland	n.a.	16.7	n.a.	15.7	n.a.	21.6	n.a.	54
Germany	20.6	20.6	12.4	8.8	7.4	9.7	40.4	39.1
Greece	100	100	./.	./.	./.	./.	100	100
Spain	57.7	59.7	22.2	20.4	2.5	4.4	82.6	84.5
Sweden	n.a.	5.3	n.a.	11.5	n.a.	9.2	0	26
France	2.7	4.4	18.3	25.1	9.7	16.7	30.2	46.2
Ireland	100	100	./.	./.	./.	./.	100	100
Italy	36.4	36.7	6.6	11	5	8.3	47.8	56
Luxemb	./.	./.	38	34.6	0.8	7.9	38.8	42.4
Netherl.	./.	1.5	9.9	17.4	3	5.4	12.9	24.2
Portugal	100	100	./.	./.	./.	./.	100	100
UK	2.8	5.9	35.5	30.9	2.6	4.9	40.4	41.7
EU12/15	21.7	27	16.8	16.4	5	8.8	43	52.5

Note: *Objective 6 for Sweden and Finland, otherwise Objective 1
Source: European Commission (1996)

Objective 1 designation process is, therefore, particularly worrying. The effectiveness and efficiency of the use of the remaining third of structural fund money, however, is also put in question because the present Objective 2 and 5b designation policy is too soft.

Another example of the creation of area designation practice is the development of the Objective 6 areas in Sweden and Finland. These regions obtain EU structural support of a per capita magnitude that is comparable to some of the Objective 1 regions although they are well above the 75 per cent threshold. It is obvious that the main purpose of Objective 6 is to make EU membership in agricultural areas of Sweden and Finland more attractive. Prior to the accession of the Nordic countries to the Community these regions benefited from national agricultural support that was above EU levels. They thus suffered from the adoption of the CAP rules that in turn demanded some compensation in the form of structural aid.

The level of spatial concentration is frequently regarded as insufficient to have a real impact on the recipient economies (Bachtler and Michie, 1993). This is also recognised by the Commission. As will be shown below, the Commission aims to reduce the coverage ratio significantly after 1999.

Programming

Prior to the 1988 reforms, aid from the structural funds was granted predominantly on a project basis. The 'Framework' and 'Co-ordination' Regulations (2052/88 and 2082/88) changed this system into a programming approach. The major advantage of programming is that it allows the integration of different forms of regional support for a particular area into an all-encompassing development plan. The idea is to improve the coherence between the individual measures,

Table 8.2 Structural distribution of Objective 1 Structural Fund expenditures in Ireland, Greece, Portugal and Spain, 1994–99*

Type of expenditure	Ireland	Portugal	Greece	Spain
Productive environment	36.2	35.7	27.8	30.5
Human resources	43.9	29.4	24.6	28.4
Infrastructure	19.7	29.7	45.9	40.4

Note: *Figures in per cent
Source: European Commission (1996)

the evaluation of the policy, and the coordination between the different institutions involved at EU, member-state and regional level.

During the first phase of the programming, national regional development plans were drawn up by the national and/or regional authorities. There was a substantial amount of variation as far as these national plans are concerned. The most important differences were between plans for the different objectives. Plans for Objective 2 regions, for example, are obviously rather different from plans for Objective 5b regions. However, there are also major differences between regions covered by the same objective. This is partly because areas under the same objective may be very different. The problems of Basilicata in Italy, for example, are only to some extent comparable with those of Northern Ireland. Secondly, there are different national preferences for specific regional policy instruments. Some member states or regions put more emphasis on basic infrastructure or education: others prefer to support business-related infrastructures or productive investments.

On the basis of these national or regional plans, the Commission develops, together with the national or regional authorities, the Community Support Framework (CSF). The CSF is the second step in the programming process and provides more concrete information on the type and magnitude of the planned expenditures. During the 1994–99 period, the lion's share of CSF expenditures falls under the categories Productive Investment Support, Human Capital Formation, and Infrastructure Productive Investment Support. The first category includes support measures for industry and services, rural development, fisheries, tourism and agricultural structures. Human Capital Formation covers education, training, and research and development (R&D), and Infrastructure refers to areas such as transport, communication and energy, but also includes water, environment and health. Table 8.2 provides comparative data on the functional distribution of 1994–99 Structural Funds in the Republic of Ireland, Greece, Portugal and Spain.

The third step in the implementation process is the Operational Programmes (OPs). The figures given in the OPs come very close to the amounts actually paid out. The implementation of the OPs is mainly the task of the national and regional authorities within the member states. Intense consultations between national and European authorities take place during the planning and implementation process of the plans, and monitoring committees, made up of national experts as well as Commission officials, are set up for all CSFs and OPs.

This complex multi-stage programming arrangement has significantly increased the influence of the Commission in regional policy design. In fact, it is sometimes argued that it is now too strong (Bachtler and Michie, 1993). The changes for the 1994–99 programming period tried to accommodate this critique by introducing various simplifications into the programming process (Regulations 2081 and 2082/93). In particular, member states now have the possibility to submit a single programming document (SPD) replacing the CSF and the OP. A further streamlining of the administration of regional policy, however, remains high on the agenda.

The Community Initiatives

During the 1994–99 period the EU spent ECU 14 bn on Community Initiatives (CIs). The CIs are mainly designed to support regions that suffer from structural changes in specific industries, from their location along national borders, or the fact that they are located at the extreme periphery of the EU. The CIs are initiated by the Commission and implemented mainly by the regions. Although some of them have been received rather well, especially INTERREG, which aims to promote cross-border cooperation, the overall assessment of the CIs during the 1989–93 period was rather negative. In particular, the large number of CIs, the resulting lack of concentration and the administrative efforts they require were criticised.

During the 1994–99 period the CIs evolved around five core topics indicated in the Commission Green Paper on CIs of 16 June 1993:

- cross-border, trans-national and inter-regional cooperation and networks;
- rural development;
- assistance to the outermost regions;
- employment promotion and development of human resources;
- management of industrial change.

Within these fields, however, various CIs were launched and their total number did not decline very much (14 during the 1994–99 period *versus* 16 during the 1989–93 period) (Commission, 1996). For the period after 1999 a further concentration to three main areas of activity is envisaged.

Additionality

The additionality principle dates back to the pre-1989 period and was designed in order to ensure that EU funding actually increases total expenditures for structural purposes. In view of the negative experiences with additionality during the pre-1989 period the principle was explicitly incorporated into the Co-ordination Regulation.

> ... the Commission and the Member States shall ensure that the increase in the appropriations for the Funds (...) has a genuine additional economic impact in the regions concerned and results in at least an equivalent increase in the total volume of official or similar (Community and national) structural aid in the Member State concerned, taking into account the macroeconomic circumstances in which the funding takes place.   (Art. 9. Regulation (EEC) 4253/88)

Despite its increased legal profile it is still difficult to put the additionality principle into practice. In fact, it has become a cause for frequent disputes between the Commission and the member states during the 1989–93 period. A test case for the additionality debate was the struggle between the Commission and the UK government concerning EU funds for UK regions with a CI-developed programme under the RECHAR CI (McAleavey, 1993; Welfare and Beaumont, 1993). The UK government tried to deduct RECHAR funding allocated to 12 coal-mining areas in the UK from the global local authority spending ceilings for these areas. Since this was at odds with the additionality principle, the Commission withheld money earmarked for the UK under RECHAR until the UK government partly accommodated the Commission's objecting.

The revised Co-ordination Regulation (Regulation (EEC) 2082/93) requires the member states to provide more detailed financial information than before to ensure the implementation of the additionality principle. Nevertheless, it remains doubtful whether more subtle attempts to evade the additionality principle than that practised by the UK government in the RECHAR dispute will be detected.

The additionality rules are different for CF projects, where European funding can cover up to 85 per cent of the total project costs. This is in effect a departure from the principle of additionality, although an intended one. Since the CF was designed to enable poorer member states to improve their infrastructure endowments and to launch environmental projects without putting further strains on their national budgets in the run-up to EMU, this exception from additionality seems to be justified.

Partnership

The designers of the 1988 reforms realised that the successful implementation of EU structural policy depends on close partnership and cooperation between European, national and sub-national authorities in order to overcome the formidable information problems created by the involvement of various layers of administration as well as various sections within these layers.

Coordination has to take place between the different Structural Funds and between the SFs and related financial instruments of the EU like the EIB. Despite some coordination problems within the Commission this aspect of partnership does not seem to be a cause of major concern. The relationship between EU structural policies and non-spatial European and national policies, however, is much more difficult. The fact that CAP expenditures favour the core member states more than the cohesion countries is a frequently mentioned showcase for a non-spatial EU policy that compromises the efficiency of the regional policy.

The third and probably most prominent aspect of partnership concerns the links between the Commission and the national authorities and bodies. A definitive judgement on whether the partnership principle has been successfully put into practice is difficult to make. The complex programming system described above certainly creates a large potential for conflicts between the Commission and the member states that in turn is frequently mentioned as one of the main problems of EU regional policy. During the first few years after the 1988 reform, the absorption of EU commitments by the member states was in some cases rather low, particularly in Italy. This has been blamed partly on the lack of efficiency of the national administrations and also on the member states' unwillingness or inability to provide the necessary co-finance to match European commitments. However, it is important to keep in mind that a high level of absorption does not allow any conclusion about the efficient use of resources. There is evidence that some member states, for example, Greece, have shifted expenditures to easily realisable projects, with low returns, to enable high rates of absorption to be achieved (Tsoukalis, 1997).

Opinions as to how the present division of regional policy power should be altered are mixed. A large number of commentators argue in favour of a reduction of the Commission's influence and in favour of more subsidiarity (Roberts, 1993). However, a more vigorous application of the subsidiarity principle would face political resistance from the net contributors. Moreover, the Commission should certainly retain enough power to guarantee that EU regional policy is based on a proper 'European' perspective. In some cases it seems even desirable to grant more power to the Commission, for example, to prevent the inclusion of dubious Objective 1 regions like Flevoland.

An additional effect of the partnership approach in EU regional policy was the strengthening of the regions vis-à-vis the member states. The influence of regional authorities in the Structural Funds' implementation is greater than in most national regional policy schemes. This has been welcomed by most commentators as it brings more local knowledge into the regional policy process (Ryan, 1993; Roberts, 1993).

The spatial and functional allocation of Structural Funds support

The development of the financial allocations for European regional policy shows the increased importance of structural action within the overall framework of the EU. In the wake of the 1988 reforms, the available resources for the structural funds were doubled from ECU 7.2 bn in 1987 to ECU 14.5 bn in 1993. In relation to the EU budget this represents an increase from 20 per cent in 1987 to 35 per cent by 1999.

The latest increase was decided at the 1992 Summit in Edinburgh as part of the 'Delors II package'. It was agreed that 'the resources available for commitment from the Structural Funds and the Cohesion Fund shall be ECU 141.471 million at 1992 prices for the period 1994 to 1999' (Regulation (EEC) 2081/91, Article 12/1). In comparison with the 1989–93 period this represents roughly a doubling of the available resources.

During the 1994–99 period slightly more than two-thirds of the SF funding goes to lagging regions, and a further 11 per cent is earmarked for regions in industrial decline. The remaining 21 per cent is divided between Objectives 3 to 6. While Spain is the largest total recipient country, Ireland and Portugal have the highest per capita allocations under Objective 1 – ECU 262 million and ECU 235 million respectively. Per capita allocations for Objective 2 and 5b regions are mostly in the range of ECU 30 to 50 million, Objective 6 allocations around ECU 110 million. Details of the breakdown of the funds are given in Table 8.3.

Table 8.3 EU resources committed to structural action, 1994–99 – Breakdown according to member state and objective

	Obj. 1	Obj. 2[a]	Obj. 3+4	Obj. 5a[a]	Obj. 5b[b]	Obj. 6	Total
Belgium	730	341	465	195	77	./.	1808
Denmark	./.	119	301	267	54	./.	741
Germany	13640	1566	1941	1145	1227	./.	19519
Greece	13980	./.	./.	./.	./.	./.	13980
Spain	26300	2415	1843	446	664	./.	31668
France	2190	3769	3203	1936	2236	./.	13334
Ireland	5620	./.	./.	./.	./.	./.	5620
Italy	14860	1462	1715	815	901	./.	19752
Luxembourg	./.	15	22	40	6	./.	83
Netherlands	150	650	1079	165	150	./.	2194
Portugal	13980	./.	./.	./.	./.	./.	13980
UK	2360	4480	3377	275	817	./.	11409
Austria	162	99	389	388	403	./.	1432
Finland	./.	179	337	354	190	450	1503
Sweden	./.	157	342	260	174	247	1178
EC 12	92991	15352	15184	6155	6860	697	136395[b]
EC 12 (%)	68	11.1	11	4.4	5	0.5	100

Note: *Million ECU, 1994 prices
Source: European Commission (1996)

Table 8.4 Cohesion Fund resources, 1994–99

	Transport		Environment		Total
	Mio. ECU	%	Mio. ECU	%	Mio. ECU
Spain	3983	50.1	3967	49.9	7950
Portugal	1380	53.0	1221	47.0	2601
Greece	1235	47.5	1367	52.5	2602
Ireland	665	51.1	636	48.9	1301
EC 4	7263	50.2	7191	49.8	14454

Source: European Commission (1996)

Since 1993, additional funding for the four cohesion countries – Ireland, Spain, Portugal and Greece – is available under the CF. Funding from the CF is, by definition, earmarked for transport infrastructure and environmental projects. This has become a very significant part of the total assistance that the cohesion countries receive from the EU. As a proportion of total funding – SFs, CIs and the CF taken together – Cohesion Fund support is around 18 per cent for Spain and Ireland, and around 15 per cent for Portugal and Greece. Table 8.4 provides some illustrative data on how these funds were used.

Regional policy after 1999

In its Agenda 2000 Communication the Commission has responded to the critics of EU regional policy (Commission, 1996–97). Despite some apparently significant changes in the structure of the system, however, most of the existing features of regional policy will remain in place.

One of the key proposals of the Commission is a reduction in the number of Objectives from seven to three. The present Objective 1 would remain more or less intact although the 75 per cent per capita income criterion will be more strictly observed. The present Objective 6 regions should enjoy 'special arrangements' that may result in a special sub-Objective under the Objective 1 heading. The new Objective 2 for economic and social restructuring would encompass not only the present Objective 2 but also declining rural areas (the existing 5b), regions that are heavily dependent on fishing and, finally, urban areas experiencing socio-economic difficulties. The newly designed Objective 3 is supposed to focus on the development of human resources. It thus encompasses the old Objectives 3.4 and 5a in a very broadly defined framework.

Although the present regional policy objectives re-emerge in the Commission proposals, the Communication states the aim to reduce Objective 1 and 2 coverage from the present 51 per cent of the EU population to 35 to 40 per cent. In view of the previous experience with the principle of concentration this is a very ambitious aim. Although some of the present recipient regions, Ireland being the prime example, are by now far above the 75 per cent income threshold, it remains to be seen whether they will be removed entirely. Moreover, the phasing-out arrangements have not been decided. Also, the inclusion of urban problems in the list of SF tasks amounts to an invitation for demands for assistance from the largest share of the EU population unless some very clear definition of what constitutes a serious urban problem can be provided.

Besides improving the SFs in the present member states, the Commission also faces the challenge of including the likely new member states from Central and Eastern European countries (CEECs) in the EU regional policy arrangements while keeping the total costs of structural policies below the threshold of 0.46 per cent of the GDP of the EU.

For the total 2000–06 period the Commission foresees structural expenditures of ECU 275 bn at 1997 prices, ECU 45 bn of which are earmarked for the likely new member states (Poland, Hungary, the Czech Republic, Slovenia and Estonia) and the remaining five applicants from Central and Eastern Europe (the Slovak Republic, Rumania, Bulgaria, Latvia and Lithuania). The difference between the support earmarked for the prospective new member states (ECU 38 bn) and the remaining five CEECs (ECU 5 bn) has to be regarded with some concern since it may contribute to a stabilisation of the present economic differences within Central and Eastern Europe. A breakdown of the proposed expenditures from 1999–2006 is given in Table 8.5.

The Objective 1 share is supposed to remain at two-thirds of the total SF expenditures. In conjunction with reduced geographical eligibility this would result in a significant increase of per capita support in the new Objective 1 regions relative to the present per capita figures. For the new Objective 2 regions, however, the per capita figures would be slightly lower than during the 1994–99 period.

'Agenda 2000' makes the effects of Eastern enlargement on EU regional policy appear much less dramatic than sometimes prophesised. However, a lot of the assumptions on which these figures are based may turn out to be incorrect. A real EU growth rate of 2.5 per cent, for example, may be over-optimistic. Moreover, there will be a bitter struggle within the EU as to which areas will be

Table 8.5 Expenditures on structural operations, 2000–2006*

	1999	2000	2001	2002	2003	2004	2005	2006
EU15								
Structural Funds	31.4	31.3	32.1	31.3	30.3	29.2	28.2	27.3
Cohesion Fund	2.9	2.9	2.9	2.9	2.9	2.9	2.9	2.9
CEECs								
New member states		0.0	0.0	3.6	5.6	7.6	9.6	11.6
Pre-accession aid**		1.0	1.0	1.0	1.0	1.0	1.0	1.0
Total	34.3	35.2	36.0	38.8	39.8	40.7	41.7	42.8

Notes:
* ECU billion at 1997 prices
** In 2000 and 2001 for all CEECs, from 2002 onwards for the remaining candidates only
Source: European Commission (1997b)

removed from Objective 1 status after 1999. It may well be that at the end of the process there are not enough 'losers', which in turn will imply that the available resources have once again to be spread more thinly than anticipated.

Conclusion

An assessment of EU regional policy must take into account that the Community's structural action does not intend to provide a safety net against asymmetric regional shocks, and it does not work as such (Gordon, 1991). Unlike regional stabilisation systems like the German *Länderfinanzausgleich*, EU regional policy intends to improve the competitiveness and hence the long-term growth prospects of the supported regions.

Despite the official denial that EU regional policy is about redistribution, its redistributive effects are significant and comparatively easy to identify. Identifying long-run changes in the competitiveness of supported regions is a much more difficult task. Virtually all regional policy programmes are now subject to ex-ante, ongoing and ex-post evaluations but these evaluations suffer from massive problems (Bachtler and Michie, 1995; Cameron, 1990). Apart from the usual anti-monde problem of policy evaluation, the availability of regionalised data is still very poor. Another formidable evaluation problem is the short time-period during which the funds have operated in their present form. Finally, the variety in approaches towards evaluation has made the creation of a coherent picture even more difficult (MEANS, 1993). However, '. . . any search for an all embracing methodology applicable to all possible situations is equivalent to the search for the holy grail' (McEldowney, 1991; 264).

Ex-post evaluations of structural policy based on macro-economic models largely depend on the assumptions on which the model is based. There are therefore large differences in the estimations of additional growth that arises from the structural funds. The QUEST model estimates just over 1 per cent additional growth for Spain, and 2–3 per cent for Portugal, Ireland and Greece by the end of the decade. The HERMIN model, stressing the importance of supply-side improvements, predicts 9 per cent additional growth for Ireland and Portugal, and 4 per cent for Spain (Commission, 1996). Estimates of the job-creation effects are also varied but invariably positive. Whether the net welfare effect of regional policy remains positive if one takes the financial costs and the opportunity costs into account, however, remains an open question.

Suggestions for improvements of EU regional policy come under two different categories – first, improvements within the present framework and, secondly, more fundamental changes in the way in which regional economic imbalances are tackled.

As far as the first category is concerned, most analysts demand an increased level of concentration of regional assistance and a simplification of its procedures (Begg, Gudgin and Morris, 1995). These demands have been taken on board by the Commission; to what extent the critique will be accommodated remains to be seen. Another major area for improvements concerns the coordination between EU regional policy, national regional policy and non-spatial European and national policies. National regional support should in future be controlled more tightly, and cohesion countries should be strongly encouraged to invest more intensively in growth-conducive areas like education and infrastructure. If necessary, new elements of conditionality for Structural Fund support should be introduced.

Looking at the second type of recommendations, the link between factor returns and productivity should be monitored more closely (Dunford, 1996). To use an example, many EU countries have centralised wage-setting systems which do not allow for sufficient flexibility to take account of regional productivity differences. This, however, is bound to increase regional unemployment problems. Another way to improve intra-European factor allocation would be increased factor mobility within the EU. Labour migration in particular remains very low, which is likely to result in serious adjustment problems once monetary unification has been achieved. Finally, fiscal federalism on the EU level may be considered as a means of increasing the budget of the EU. Nevertheless, it could become a useful tool to counteract asymmetric shocks within EMU (Goodhart and Smith, 1993).

The accession of the CEECs shortly after the year 2000 will intensify regional disparities in the EU to an extent that has not been seen before. Especially in view of the challenges that enlargement will bring about, it is important to look also at alternative mechanisms to cope with the increasing regional heterogeneity of the EU.

References

Alesina A and Rodrik D 1994 Distributive Politics and Economic Growth, *Quarterly Journal of Economics*, Vol. CIX, May, pp. 465–90.

Armstrong H W 1995 Convergence among Regions of the European Union 1950–1990, *Papers in Regional Science*, Vol. 74, No. 2, pp. 143–52.

Armstrong H and Taylor J 1993 *Regional Economics and Policy, 2nd Edition*, Harvester Press, London.

Bachtler J and Michie R 1993 The Restructuring of Regional Policy in the European Community, *Regional Studies*, Vol. 27, pp. 719–25.

Bachtler J and Michie R 1995 A new Era in EU Regional Policy Evaluation? The Appraisal of the Structural Funds, *Regional Studies*, Vol. 29, No. 8, pp. 745–51.

Barro R and Sala-i-Martin X 1995 *Economic Growth*, McGraw Hill, New York.

Begg I and Mayes D 1993 Cohesion, Convergence and Economic and Monetary Union in Europe, *Regional Studies*, Vol. 27, pp. 149–55.

Begg I, Gudgin G, Morris D 1995 The Assessment: Regional Policy of the European Union, *Oxford Review of Economic Policy*, Vol. 11, No. 2, Summer 1995, pp. 1–18.

Bianchi G 1993 The IMPs: A Missed Opportunity? Leonardi R (ed.), *The Regions and the European Community*, Frank Cass, London, pp. 47–70.

Boltho A 1994 A Comparison of Regional Differentials in the European Community and the United States, Mortensen J (ed.), *Improving Economic and Social Cohesion in the European Community*, Macmillan, London.

Bradley J *et al.* 1995 *Regional Aid and Convergence*, Aldershot, Avebury.

Bruinsma F and Rietveld P 1997 The Accessibility of European Cities – Theoretical Framework and Comparison of Approaches, forthcoming in *Environment and Planning A*.

Cameron G 1990 First Steps in Urban Policy Evaluation in the UK, *Urban Studies*, Vol. 27, pp. 475–95.

Commission 1990 *An Empirical Assessment of Factors shaping Competitiveness in Problem Regions*, Office for Official Publications of the European Communities, Luxembourg.

Commission 1993a New Location Factors for Mobile Investments in *European Regional Development Studies*, Vol. 6, Office for Official Publications of the European Communities, Luxembourg.

Commission 1993b *Community Structural Funds 1994–99 – Regulations and Commentary*, Office for Official Publications of the European Communities, Luxembourg.

Commission 1994 *Employment in Europe 1994*, Office for Official Publications of the European Communities, Luxembourg.

Commission 1996 *First Report on Economic and Social Cohesion 1996*, Office for Official Publications of the European Communities, Luxembourg.

Commission 1997a AMEKO-Database, Directorate-General for Economic and Financial Affairs DG II, Brussels.

Commission 1997b *Agenda 2000 – Volume I – Communication: For a Stronger and Wider Union*, DOC/97/6, Strasbourg, 15 July 1997.

Centre for Economic Policy Research (CEPR) 1993 *Monitoring European Integration 4 – Making Sense of Subsidiarity: How Much Centralization for Europe*, CEPR, London.

Dunford M 1996 Disparities in Employment, Productivity and Output in the EU: The Roles of Labour Market Governance and Welfare Regimes, *Regional Studies*, Vol. 30, No. 4, pp. 339–57.

European Parliament 1991 The Regional Impact of Community Policies, Directorate-General for Research, *Regional Policy and Transport Series*, Vol. 17, Office for Official Publications of the European Communities, Luxembourg.

Eurostat 1996 *Regions – Statistical Yearbook*, Office for Official Publications of the European Communities, Luxembourg.

Eurostat 1997a *Regions – Statistics in Focus 1997–71*, Office for Official Publications of the European Communities, Luxembourg.

Eurostat 1997b *Regions – Statistics in Focus 1997–73*, Office for Official Publications of the European Communities, Luxembourg.

Folkers C 1995 Welches Finanzausgleichssystem braucht Europa? Karl H and Hinrichsmeyer W (eds.), *Regionalentwicklung im Prozess der Europäischen Integration*, Bonner Schriften zur Integration Europas Band 4, Europa-Union Verlag, Bonn, pp. 87–108.

Galor O and Zeira J 1993 Income Distribution and Macroeconomics, *The Economic Journal*, Vol. 106, pp. 1056–79.

Goodhart C and Smith S 1993 Macro-Stabilisation and Shock Absorption, *European Economy*, No. 5, European Commission, Brussels.

Gordon J 1991 Structural Funds and the 1992 Programme in the European Community, International Monetary Fund – Fiscal Affairs Department, Working Paper 91/65.

Kenner J 1994 Economic and Social Cohesion – The Rocky Road Ahead, *Legal Issues of European Integration*, No. 1, pp. 1–36.

Lammers K 1992 Mehr regionalpolitische Kompetenz für die EG im Europäischen Binnenmarkt?, Akademie für Raumforschung und Landesplanung (Hrsg), Regionale Wirtschaftspolitik auf dem Weg zur europäischen Integration, *Forschungs- und Sitzungsberichte* 187, Hannover, pp. 70–82.

Marias E A 1994 Solidarity as an Objective of the European Union and the European Community, *Legal Issues of European Integration*, No. 2, pp. 85–114.

Marques A 1992 Community Competition Policy and Economic and Social Cohesion, *Regional Studies*, Vol. 26, pp. 404–47.

Martin R 1996 *Regional Incentive Spending for European Regions*, Regional and Industrial Research Paper No. 19, European Policies Research Centre (EPRC), Glasgow.

Martin R 1997 *Regional Convergence in the EU – The Importance of Macro-Economic Policies and Regional Policy Variables* – HWWA Institute for Economic Research, Discussion Paper No. 43, Hamburg, March 1997.

Martin R and Schulze Steinen M 1997 State Aid, Regional Policy and Locational Competition in the European Union, *European Urban and Regional Studies*, Vol. 4, No. 1, pp. 19–31.

McAleavey P 1993 The Politics of European Regional Development Policy: Additionality in the Scottish Minefields, *Regional Politics and Policy*, Vol. 3, No. 2, pp. 88–107.

McEldowney J J 1991 Evaluation and European Regional Policy, *Regional Studies*, Vol. 25, No. 3, pp. 261–64.

MEANS 1993 *Methods to give meaning to the evaluation obligation: the conclusions of the MEANS programme*, MEANS/93/13/EN, CEOPS, Lyon.

Neven D J and Gouyette C 1994 *Regional Convergence in the European Community*, CEPR-DP 914, CEPR, London.

North D 1994 Institutional Competition, in Siebert H (ed.), *Locational Competition in the World Economy*, Tübingen: Mohr, pp. 27–37.

Oates W 1972 *Fiscal Federalism*, Harcourt Brace, New York.

Rauch J 1993 *Does History Matter only when it Matters Little? The Case of City-Industry Location*, NBER-WP 4312.

Roberts P 1993 Managing the Strategic Planning and Development of Regions: Lessons from a European Perspective, *Regional Studies*, Vol. 27, No. 8, pp. 759–68.

Ryan J 1993 The Regional Policies of the European Commission, the United Kingdom and Germany, *Journal of Regional Policy*, Vol. 13, Nos. 3–4, pp. 457–67 .

Strain J F 1993 *Integration, Federalism and Cohesion in the European Community: Lessons from Canada*, Policy Research Series Paper No. 16, The Economic and Social Research Institute, Dublin.

Temple M 1994 *Regional Economics*, St Martin's Press, New York.

Tsoukalis L 1997 *The New European Community – The Politics and Economics of Integration*, Oxford University Press, Oxford.

Vickerman R W 1992 *The Single European Market – Prospects for Economic Integration*, St Martin's Press, New York.

Weise C 1995 EU-Politik zur Steigerung regionaler Wettbewerbsfähigkeit, *Vierteljahreshefte zur Wirtschaftsforschung*, Vol. 64, No. 2, pp. 266–77.
Welfare D and Beaumont K 1993 All you ever Wanted to Know about Additionality but were Afraid to Ask, *European Information Service*, No. 142/1993, pp. 3–6.

Further reading

Armstrong H W and Vickerman R W (eds.), *Convergence and Divergence among European Regions*, Pion, London.
Biehl D 1991 The Role of Infrastructure in Regional Development, Vickerman R W, *Infrastructure and Regional Development*, London, pp. 9–35.
Bliss C and de Macedo J 1990 *Unity with Diversity in the European Economy: The Community's Southern Frontier*, Cambridge University Press, Cambridge.
Commission 1994 *Competitiveness and Cohesion: Trends in the Regions*, 5th Periodic Report on the Social and Economic Situation and Development of the Regions in the Community, Office for the Official Publications of the European Communities, Luxembourg.
Crafts N and Toniolo G (eds.) 1996 *Economic Growth in Europe since 1945*, CUP and CEPR, Cambridge.
de la Fuente A and Vives X 1995 Infrastructure and Education as Instruments of Regional Policy: Evidence from Spain, *Economic Policy*, April 1995, pp. 12–51.
Frazer T 1995 The New Structural Funds, State Aids and Interventions on the Single Market, *European Law Review*, Vol. 21, No. 1, pp. 3–19.
Hansen N 1995 Addressing Regional Disparity and Equity Objectives through Regional Policies: A Sceptical Perspective, *Papers in Regional Science*, Vol. 74, No. 2, pp. 89–104.
Krugman P 1991 *Geography and Trade*, LUP, Leuven, and MIT Press, Cambridge (Mass.).
Leonardi R 1995 Regional Development in Italy: Social Capital and the Mezzogiorno, *Oxford Review of Economic Policy*, Vol. 11, No. 2, pp. 165–79.
Mortensen J (ed.) 1994 *Improving Economic and Social Cohesion in the European Community*, Macmillan, Houndsmill.
Yuill D *et al.* 1994 *European Regional Incentives, 1994–95 – 14th Edition*, Bowker-Saur, London.

9 Environment policy

John Hassan

Introduction

The Treaty of Rome made no provision for a Community environment policy. When it became apparent in the early 1970s, however, that environmental problems might disrupt the Community's economic mission, the desirability of taking action in this field was recognised.

In 1971 the Commission made its first detailed Communication to the Council on the need for a Community policy. The impending oil crisis and pressures from environmentalists led Heads of State to agree on the adoption of a policy in 1972. The EU's environmental programmes now cover many fields, ranging from chemicals to climate change, but, briefly, the aims of the policy today are to protect the natural environment so as to contribute towards the realisation of sustainable growth and to bolster the single market. This chapter considers the case for an EU environment policy; it traces the development of Community actions, and illustrates the application of the policy with reference to traditional concerns in the fields of water and air pollution and waste management before, finally, assessing the impact of the policy.

The need for an EU environment policy

Three major factors have influenced the development of the environmental policy of the EU:

1. issues connected to transfrontier pollution;
2. determining the conditions for fair and free trade;
3. developing efficient and sustainable growth.

Transfrontier pollution

That the EU should have an environment policy can be argued on a variety of grounds. Environmental degradation might provoke economic or even ecological disaster. In the 1970s, a decade dominated by the oil shocks of 1973 and 1979, there were fears that resource shortages might destroy the world's economic prospects. Since the 1980s new concerns have developed especially about atmospheric pollution, which results in acidification, ozone depletion and global warming, and which therefore leads to climate change, threatening not just economic activity but the very existence of the human species. Such pollution does not respect national frontiers. The EU, with its unique supranational institutions and legal instruments, is well qualified to coordinate Europe-wide actions in the field.

Fair and free trading conditions

To fulfil the objectives of the Treaty of Rome and, in particular to realise a single European market, implies the implementation of common environmental policies by member states. The adoption by member states of different environment standards may lead to a form of social dumping where industries, in countries with lax regulations, by ignoring marginal environmental costs enjoy a competitive advantage. This leads them to overproduce and sell products at less than their true costs of production to the detriment of their trading partners (see Box 9.1). In these conditions the harmonisation of environmental policies and standards is necessary in order to ensure that neutrality of competition between members of the EU is achieved.

Economic efficiency and sustainability

The problem of selecting appropriate policy instruments to progress the aims of the EU's environment policy is related to the need to find efficient and sustainable economic growth. In principle, efficiency is promoted by requiring firms to internalise the external costs created by their polluting actions, so that output is set where price equals total costs. An effective method of achieving this, thereby curbing pollution, is through the use of market instruments, such as emission charges or, arguably, the theoretically even more desirable solution of tradeable instruments (see Box 9.2). However, in some countries, for example where municipal authorities are responsible for water quality management, there is a strong reluctance to replace traditional instruments of control with market-based methods of pollution control. In other cases a country, such as the Netherlands, may wish to retain tough regulatory controls in order to maintain world leadership in pollution abatement technology. There is a great deal of rhetorical support for market instruments in governmental and EU forums. However, as long as the relevant Community legal instruments prescribe only the ends, and not the means, of the environment policy, the pursuit of its objectives will remain contingent upon national factors. The incorporation of market-based methods into the EU environment policy therefore faces considerable obstacles, as the failure to agree on a carbon tax in 1993 illustrates. Consequently, traditional regulatory methods, such as setting quality standards for water and air, are likely to remain heavily relied upon for some time. While this pragmatism may not produce economically optimal outcomes, it is much better than no action, and can still contribute towards the realisation of the objectives of the EU's environment policy.

Empirical studies appear to demonstrate that non-action is costly. Environmental regulations may well increase industrial production costs. However,

Box 9.1   Environmental standards and fair trade

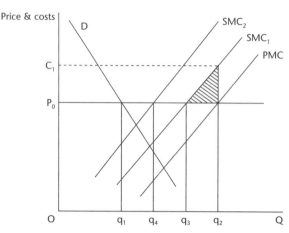

D = demand in the UK

P1 = ruling market price in both Germany and the UK

PMC = private marginal cost in the UK

SMC = PMC plus the marginal cost of the pollution associated with the production of output

SMC1 = social marginal cost in the UK

SMC2 = social marginal cost in the UK if German environmental standards are used

If no account is taken of the cost of pollution, UK companies would produce an output of 0q2. As demand in the UK is equal to 0q1, the extra output (i.e. q2–q1) would be exported to Germany. At this level of output the UK is not taking into account the pollution costs of producing the output. This imposes a cost (on the UK economy) shown by the shaded area (i.e. the area of social cost above the revenue received from selling output 0q2 at the price of P1). The UK could be accused of social dumping because it is not covering the social cost of the production. However, it should be noted that this cost falls on the UK economy. The unfairness on the German economy is that, if the UK covered the social costs of the pollution, it would have an output of 0q3, which would mean that exports to Germany would fall to q1–q3, thereby leaving more of the German market to their own producers.

However, if UK firms had to endure the social marginal costs of Germany when producing this output, production in the UK would fall to 0q4. Such an outcome would be inefficient because in this example the UK has lower social costs of pollution than Germany. Nevertheless, if Germany succeeded in having its views on the costs of pollution accepted by the EU, then UK companies would be treated unfairly. This example illustrates how environmental standards can be used to protect domestic markets. Moreover, in cases where the social costs of pollution differ between countries, the analysis indicates that environmental standards should vary according to the SMCs that prevail across countries.

Box 9.2   Efficient level of pollution

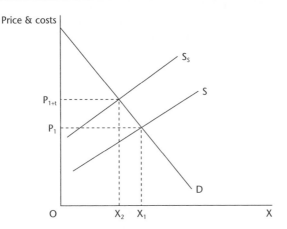

D = Demand for product X   S = Supply of product X

Ss = Supply of product X including social costs of pollution

P = Price

If there are no prohibitions on pollution associated with the production and consumption of X the price and output would be P1:X1. However, if the costs of pollution are taken into account in the production and consumption, the output should be 0X2. This output can be induced by a variety of means. Regulations could be issued to restrict output to 0X2. Alternatively, a tax could be placed on the good X until the price becomes P + t. A market-based solution would allocate permits to pollute up to the output level 0X2. If these permits were tradeable on markets, producers or consumers could purchase permits to pollute. In these circumstances those companies or consumers who obtain most benefit from the pollution (in terms of their valuation of the good X) would buy most of the permits. By this method the right to pollute would be given to those who put most value on this activity. The other two systems (regulation or taxation) may not achieve such an efficient outcome. However, if the distribution of income is not equal, the right to buy and sell the permits to pollute will reflect income differences as well as the valuation of the use of product X. The use of tradeable permits is often objected to on the grounds that they would reflect income differences more than the valuation that people place on the goods and services that pollute the environment when they are produced and/or consumed. For example, selling the right to pollute by driving cars would favour those who have high incomes. In these circumstances the use of regulation or taxes may offer a better solution.

pollution and corrosion cause damage to forests, agricultural land, buildings, equipment, and to human health and productivity. Public spending on environmental programmes in leading industrial countries in the 1980s was in the region of 0.8 to 2 per cent of GDP. To estimate the benefits of environmental protection policies is more problematic, and the methodologies chosen obviously have a major impact upon the findings obtained. The potential savings to the national economies vary, according to some studies, from 3.5 to 6 per cent of GDP (Commission, 1987; OECD, 1984, 1989).

Such findings support the thrust of much contemporary thinking that sustainable economic development and environmental protection are not competing but are, in fact, mutually supporting objectives. Most famously popularised by the Brundtland Report (World Commission) of 1987, this approach emphasises the interdependence of ecological and economic imperatives. These principles have been formally adopted by the EU, Article 2 of the Maastricht Treaty of 1991 committing the signatories to develop environmental policies which achieve sustainable growth.

The development of the Community's environment policy

After ministers had agreed to the adoption of an environment policy in 1972 an Environmental and Protection Service was established. This was elevated to full DG status in 1981. Once the decision had been made to add the environment to the Community's agenda it was not unnatural for attention to turn to the water environment where, at Europe's heart, there existed the apparently intractible problem of the grossly polluted River Rhine. The first Environmental Action Programme (EAP) covering 1973–77 stressed the need to reduce water pollution. In 1975 and 1976 as well as legislation specifying quality standards for different categories of water, agreements were also reached on smoke and SO_2 emissions and on waste management. Framework Directives were followed by Daughter Directives which prescribed detailed rules or standards in more narrowly defined areas.

EAPs set out a broad framework for Community policy. The first made a commitment to the 'polluter pays' principle and stressed the need for preventive rather than remedial actions. The second EAP (1977–81) extended and updated the first. Despite stated principles, actual actions taken during this period were reactive, and sought to redress urgent problems in specific sectors.

The limitations of this reactive approach were gradually recognised. It was realised that account should be taken of the interactions between polluting discharges and the environments which receive pollutants, and of the transfer of pollution from one part of the environment to another. In the third EAP (1982–86) environmental protection was viewed as a key factor in many fields, not just as a separate problem. An overall framework for policy development was proposed, which sought to encourage the integration of environmental considerations into the planning activities of other areas, including energy, industry and tourism.

Acknowledging the interdependency of environmental problems, agreement was reached on an Environmental Impact Assessment (EIA) Directive in 1985. It required member states to carry out assessments of the likely environmental effects of major industrial or infrastructure proposals before planning consent is given. Assessment has to be made of the probable polluting effects of planned projects, and of the impacts upon wildlife, natural resources and the cultural and archaeological heritage. Certain projects are exempted, and the EIA Directive does not apply to projects which are authorised by specific national legislation like the Channel Tunnel.

The growing importance of environmental protection to the Community was reflected in the agreement to the SEA of 1986. This measure was of fundamental importance for the development of environment policy. Hitherto Community action was based on a liberal interpretation of the application of the Treaty of Rome's omnibus clause, Article 235, to environmental issues. The SEA not only reiterated the goals of the Community's policy, but also explicitly confirmed for the first time, under Article 130, its competence to act in the field of environmental protection. Moreover, the power of the Council to take decisions by qualified majority voting (QMV) on environmental measures that bear on the single market was established. In addition, it was stated that: 'environmental protection requirements shall be a component of the Community's other policies'. Requiring that all other Community policies should take account of the environmental dimension is a unique clause in EC law. If fully enforced, it would have far-reaching implications for other policy areas, such as agriculture and transport. The Maastricht Treaty confirmed the commitment to such principles and reiterated the Union's competence in the environmental field.

Meanwhile, the fourth EAP (1987–92) continued established themes, but also reaffirmed the new emphasis upon integration in the Community's policy. As well as urging action in a number of sectoral areas, such as the use of agro-chemicals and the treatment of agricultural wastes, the need for measures to bolster the completion of the SEM was identified. Further, the necessity of improving the implementation of environmental Directives was a central theme of the fourth EAP.

The decision in 1990 to create a European Environment Agency (EEA) was an expression of the moves to promote integration, the preventive principle, and better implementation as core themes of the environment policy. The European Parliament (EP) wanted the Agency to have the power to enforce environmental law and to execute EIAs for EU-funded policies. However, wider disputes over the location of several EU institutions delayed the establishment of the EEA until 1994. It has been concerned primarily with monitoring the progress and impact of the environment policy and with improving the standardisation and exchange of environmental information.

The fifth EAP, entitled 'Towards Sustainability', was adopted in 1992 and covers the period from 1993 to 2000. To achieve the reconciliation of economic growth and environmental protection, it identified the need for a proactive approach in a number of areas, including the integration of environmental considerations into other policy fields, the broadening of the range of instruments, and the stricter enforcement of legislation. Reflecting major concerns over issues like global warming and the increased loads placed upon the natural environment, the fifth EAP called for specific action in a number of sectors, notably energy, transport, agriculture and tourism, and also adopted a number of targets for the reduction of polluting emissions by 2000.

Examples of EU environmental legislation

The EU has issued a number of Directives to help it to promote the objectives of the environmental policy. Directives have been issued in three main areas:

- the quality of water;
- atmospheric pollution;
- waste management.

Water directives

Measures to control water pollution have been so numerous for them to have been described as 'the jewel in the crown of the EU's environment policy' (Economist Intelligence Unit, 1989). If oversimplifying, it is convenient to distinguish three groups of water directives: those detailing quality standards applicable to specified categories of water, including bathing, drinking, shellfish waters and inland fisheries; those aiming to control the emission of dangerous substances; and those seeking to secure a greater protection of water resources as a whole.

The implementation of all these Directives has invariably provoked controversy. Since 1993 the Commission has developed proposals for an updating and simplification of the bathing and drinking water directives, but there is little prospect that this will lead to a dilution of EU water law. More specific daughter Directives, which followed the agreement on the parent dangerous substances Directive, have led in some cases to significant reductions in particular sources of pollution, notably mercury emissions. Nevertheless, the original ambition to extend such controls to 109 'black list' substances has now been abandoned, only 17 substances having been agreed to since 1976. The urban waste-water Directive, which will greatly reduce the sewage pollution of coastal waters from the late 1990s, and a nitrate Directive, which targets pollution from agricultural fertilisers, were both agreed to in 1991. They are illustrative of the Commission's attempt to achieve a more general protection of the water environment, which received fresh impetus with the issue of a Communication in 1996 on the need to develop a more flexible and integrated approach to the EU's water policy.

Atmospheric pollution

For a number of reasons, EU rules on air quality are less comprehensive and ambitious than those pertaining to water quality. However, from the 1980s those forms of pollution which contribute to acidification, ozone depletion and global warming have warranted more decisive actions. Nevertheless, EU moves frequently consist of endorsing broader international agreements.

Directive 88/609 was the first major attempt to tackle the problem of acid rain. It requires reductions of emissions of SO_2, NO_x and dust from power stations. This step has been followed by several others setting stricter standards for emissions from power stations and motor vehicles.

The Montreal Protocol of 1987 on ozone depletion has led to EU regulations being agreed to in 1988, 1991 and 1994, which have set progressively tougher targets with a view to achieving the virtual elimination of CFC gases in Western Europe by 2000.

The EU signed up in 1992 to a convention on climate change at the Rio de Janeiro conference. The chief method of squaring up to global warming has been to seek agreement on reductions of emissions of CO_2, the main greenhouse gas. In 1990 the EU had agreed to seek a stabilisation of CO_2 emissions by the year 2000 at their then current levels. However, attempts to progress this object-ive, especially through an energy tax, have not been successful.

Waste management

The Framework Directive 75/442 to promote the safe disposal of hazardous substances was one of the earliest pieces of EC environmental legislation. A pro-liferation of agreements have built upon this Directive, specifying detailed pro-cedures over the disposal of products like polychlorinated biphenyl, waste oils, liquid containers, sewage sludge and other toxic or dangerous substances.

While EU waste management policy has made progress in certain areas, such as the transboundary shipment of hazardous substances, other agreements, for example on recycling and the re-utilisation of waste, have made little impact. Policy statements in this area have done little more than piously extol good prac-tice rather than laying down regulatory standards. The need for more determined actions to harmonise the management and disposal of waste was implied by the disappearance of national border controls after 1992. Partly in anticipation of the single market a long-awaited Commission paper, 'A Community Strategy for Waste Management', was approved in 1990. By 1996 parts of the strategy had been realised, including agreements on landfills, incineration, packaging and eco-labelling. However, other, perhaps more significant elements, have not come to fruition, including the Commission's limited proposals for the reduction of wastes, the use of economic instruments, and measures to promote recycling.

Assessment

Environment policy was often regarded as one of the EU's major successes. Despite the lack of an explicit legal basis and unanimous voting being required, by 1986 some 100 Community texts in the environment field had been agreed to, and the number has continued to grow since then. In addition to this legislative achieve-ment, elaborate systems have been developed to gather and harmonise environ-mental data and to monitor the numerous initiatives which have been adopted under the environment policy. For some time, however, observers (for example, Klatte, 1986) have commented upon a marked discrepancy between the weight of environmental legislation and the effect it has exercised upon the natural environment.

Studies published in 1987 reveal ambiguous evidence regarding the policy's environmental impact (Commission, 1987; Weidner, 1987). In the 1980s declining emissions of smoke and SO_2 could be contrasted with growing emissions of CO_2 and NO_x. There was some evidence of an improvement in inland water quality, to be set against a continued loss of habitats in marine waters, dumping in coastal zones, and the gathering of a variety of pollutants in the seas, leading to a complex range of difficulties.

In the 1990s further reviews of the EU's environment policy were published (EEA, 1995a, 1995b, 1996; Commission, 1996). Their conclusions were that pressures on the environment showed little sign of abating and that there was a danger of critical loads being exceeded. Some progress towards achieving targeted reductions in polluting emissions by 2000 had been made, including CFCs and SO_2. However, disappointing trends in the 1990s were reported for a number of categories, from biodiversity and climate change to industrial accidents and urban noise levels. It appeared unlikely that objectives for the fifth EAP would be reached in such areas as acidification, nitrate emissions into groundwater, waste management, and NO_x emissions. A fall in CO_2 emissions in the early 1990s was due to unusual factors, such as the collapse of industrial activity in East Germany. It was probable that targeted reductions in CO_2 emissions by 2000, as part of the global warming strategy, would not be achieved and that, in fact, there would be an increase over the decade.

The implementation deficit

In reviewing the environment policy the Commission is wont to present a brave face and express 'cautious optimism' about the future. But it accepts that significant obstacles thwart the realisation of policy objectives and that the impact of the policy has been disappointing. As well as the emergence of disquieting trends as regards the meeting of sectoral targets, the Commission is equally concerned about the political problems which underlie EU policy formation. Where the EU had a 'lead role', by 1996 allegedly 70 per cent of the commitments envisaged by the fifth EAP had been achieved; but realisation had been much more problematic at the level of member states. For example, negligible progress had been made in broadening the range of policy instruments.

The fundamental reasons for the patchy impact of the EU environment policy lie with the long-recognised difficulties facing the implementation and enforcement of the policy. Several factors account for the 'implementation deficit'.

Insufficient resources

Given that it would not be legitimate to count Cohesion Funds as instruments of environment policy (Wilkinson, 1994), it may be argued that it is supported by insufficient resources. The proportion of the general budget dispensed through DG XI, the environment directorate, increased from 0.02 per cent in 1978 to only 0.05 per cent in 1994. With the limited staff at its disposal the Commission has left the initiation of complaints against contravention of the environmental rules to individual persons or organisations.

Policy conflicts

The pursuit and implementation of environment policy is undermined when its goals are in conflict with other EU policies. The pursuit of economic growth, the CAP and the energy policy, especially in its stress, for example, on the need to expand indigenous energy production, may all potentially lead to a worsening of water or air pollution. Recent attempts to seek an integration of environmental considerations into other policy fields have recognised this weakness, without necessarily resolving it.

Policy instruments

For many years member states seemed to approach their environmental commitments as if they were discretionary, rather than legally binding. This was encouraged partly by the non-coercive nature of the policy instruments. The Commission's EAPs were merely 'noted' by the Council of Ministers; they were not formally adopted. EIAs are compulsory for most major projects, but their conclusions may be ignored. The weaknesses of the EAPs were recognised in 1995 and 1996 when the Commission called for an 'acceleration' of the policy, and issued a proposal to supplement the EAPs with new Action Plans. The significance of this initiative would lie with the process leading up to the adoption of the so-called Action Plans, namely that compromises would be made in order to reach agreements on targets, which would then, however, become legally binding, whereas the EAPs set tough targets without legal obligations.

The principal instruments of the environment policy are Directives, and here lies the fundamental difficulty. They are technically binding as to outcome, but the choice of method to achieve the desired result is left to member states (a two-stage process involving legislative 'transposition' at the national level, followed by practical implementation). Delegation of responsibility to member states, and the sometimes ambiguous phraseology employed in the Directives, have permitted considerable scope for distortion, misinterpretation and delay. Klatte (1986) and Haigh (1987) noted how the environmental Directives were often badly implemented, incorrectly or not at all. A classic case of mischievous misinterpretation was the UK's initial designation in 1979 of only 27 bathing beaches under the bathing water Directive, in contrast to France's 3000 designated beaches, and even land-locked Luxembourg recorded 39.

The difficulties over non-compliance have been recognised, and enforcement was an important theme of the fourth and fifth EAPs. Since the late 1980s the Commission has been more ready to instigate legal proceeding against the governments of errant states. Even the threat of legal action can have an effect, encouraging the UK, for instance, to designate a further 326 bathing areas. However, the enforcement procedure available to the Commission has limitations. It is an extremely ponderous process and, moreover, the final decision whether to start proceedings is taken collectively by the Commissioners. It is, therefore, more a political than a legal decision, as is obvious when government ministers indulge in much publicised 'rows' over the environmental Directives that are clearly intended to influence the Commissioners' outlook. Dilatory application of EU environmental law by member states remains a serious weakness of the environment policy to this day.

Conclusion

It would be inappropriate, however, to conclude on too negative a note. Some of the weaknesses arising from policy contradictions or the devolution of responsibility for implementing Directives to member states are not peculiar to environment policy.

Despite the reservations made in this chapter, the policy has undoubtedly had major environmental, industrial and institutional effects. When it involves agreements to non-legally binding objectives or, as has been the tendency recently, takes the form of complex and ambitious goals in relatively elusive areas such as biodiversity, then assessment of the environmental policy's impact may conclude that it has been limited. Although this may not be the direction in which the Commission wishes to take the policy currently, however, when well defined standards are established for controlling the discharge of specified pollutants then its effect has been palpable.

Protestations by politicians and interest group spokespersons that the Directives are very costly to implement and undermine national sovereignty suggests that the environment policy does force changes in national behaviour. This was reflected by the vain hopes expressed in industrial and government circles in the UK in 1992–93 that the concept of subsidiarity and proposals to rationalise the water Directives would lead to a lessening of legislative and financial burdens. In fact, it is demonstrable that EU environmental law has led to several sectors undertaking multi-million, if not -billion pound investment programmes to improve pollution abatement methods. Examples include the requirement to reduce mercury emissions, the need to control discharges from power stations and motor vehicles, and the obligations under the bathing water and urban waste water Directives to control the effluent pumped from coastal sewage works into the marine environment.

Finally, the environmental policy has developed over time into a powerful and independent force in environmental politics and economics, representing not just a common denominator of national interests, but a factor that influences public opinion and empowers green pressure groups. It has required significant modifications to national practice being made in order to bring it into line with EU obligations. In the UK the Environmental Protection Act of 1990 provided for a multi-media, integrated approach to pollution control under a new environmental protection agency, and established air quality standards. These innovations were introduced to satisfy requirements which were established by EU environmental law. Such has been the impact of the environmental Directives that a number of scholars now argue that national environmental policies have been 'Europeanised' throughout the EU.

References

Commission 1987 *The state of the Environment in the European Community 1986*, EEC, Brussels.

Commission 1992 *The fifth Environmental Action Programme: Towards Sustainability*, EEC, Brussels.

Commission 1996 *Progress report on the implementation of the fifth Environmental Action Programme*, EEC, Brussels.

Economist Intelligence Unit 1989 *European Trends 1988–89*, London.

EEA 1995a *Environment in the European Union 1995: Report for the review of the fifth Environmental Action Programme*, EEA, Copenhagen.

EEA 1995b *Europe's environment: the Dobris assessment*, EEA, Copenhagen.

EEA 1996 *EEA Annual Report 1995*, EEA, Copenhagen.

Haigh N 1987 Assessing EC environmental policy, *European Environment Review*, Vol. 1, No. 2, pp. 38–41.

Klatte E 1986 The past and the future of European environmental policy, *European Environment Review*, Vol. 1, No. 1, pp. 32–7.

OECD 1984 *The macro-economic impact of environmental expenditure*, OECD, Paris.

OECD 1989 *Environmental policy benefits: monetary valuation*, OECD, Paris.

Weidner H 1987 *Clean Air Policy in Europe: A survey of seventeen countries*, Internationales Institut für Umwelt und Gesellschaft, Berlin.

Wilkinson D 1994 Using the European Union's Structural and Cohesion Funds for the protection of the environment, *Rectel*, Vol. 3, No. 2/3, pp. 119–26.

World Commission on Environment and Development 1987 *Our Common Future*, Oxford University Press. (Also known as the *Brundtland Report* after the chairperson.)

Further reading

Books

Andersen S and Eliassen K (eds.) 1993 *Making policy in Europe – The Europeification of national policy making*, Sage, London.

Haigh N 1984 *EEC environmental policy and Britain*, ENDS, London.

Haigh N 1992 *Manual of environmental policy*, Longman, Harlow.

Johnson S and Corcelle G 1989 *The environmental policies of the European Communities*, Graham and Trotman, London.

Liefferink J D, Lowe P D and Mol A J P (eds.) 1993 *European integration and environment policy*, Belhaven Press, London.

Lister C 1996 *European Union environmental law: a guide for industry*, Wiley and Sons, Chichester.

Stanners D and Bourdeau P (eds.) 1994 *Europe's environment: the Dobris Assessment – an overview*, EEA, Copenhagen.

Weale A 1992 *The new politics of pollution*, Manchester University Press, Manchester.

Articles

The *ENDS Report* is published monthly and is directed at a business readership, and provides detailed surveys and reports on current developments in environment policy.

European Environment appears every two months and contains articles which provide an accessible analysis of European environmental issues.

Guruswamy G, Papps I and Storey D J 1983 The development and impact of an EEC Directive: the control of the discharge of mercury into the aquatic environment, *Journal of Common Market Studies*, Vol. 22, No. 1, pp. 71–100.

Howarth W 1992 New strategies for water directives, *European Environment Law Review*, Vol. 1, No. 4, pp. 117–21.

Jachtenfuchs M 1990 The European Community and the protection of the ozone layer, *Journal of Common Market Studies*, Vol. 28, No. 3, pp. 261–77.

Semple A 1993 The implication of EC legislation and future water quality obligations, *Journal of the Institution of Water Officers*, Vol. 30, No. 2, pp. 14–17.

Sheate W R and MacRory R B 1989 Agriculture and the EC environmental assessment Directive lessons for Community policy making, *Journal of Common Market Studies*, Vol. 28, No. 1, pp. 68–81.

Taylor D, Diprose G and Duffy M 1986 EC environmental policy and the control of water pollution: the implementation of Directive 76/464 in perspective, *Journal of Common Market Studies*, Vol. 24, No. 3, pp. 225–46.

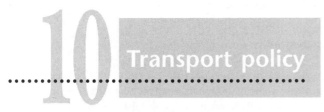

10 Transport policy

Stephen Dearden

Introduction

Transport, together with agriculture and external trade, was one of the few areas specified in the Treaty of Rome where the Commission was specifically required to develop a common policy (Articles 3, and 74–84). A Common Transport Policy (CTP) was expected both to contribute to European economic integration and to enhance economic development.

The adoption of a CTP was restricted to road, rail and waterways, but could be extended to marine shipping and aviation if decided by the Council of Ministers (Article 84). The CTP requires common rules for all cross-border traffic (Article 75), forbids discrimination in transport charges (Article 79) and called for reductions in the costs of crossing frontiers (Article 81). However, while prohibiting general subsidies to transport undertakings, the Treaty permits State subsidies for the coordination of transport or for public service obligations (Article 77), or as part of regional assistance (Article 80). Article 78 also states that any measures concerning transport rates and conditions 'shall take account of the economic circumstances of the carriers'.

Thus, from the beginning, transport policy has been an uneasy amalgam of two approaches:

1. The establishment of non-discriminatory competitive conditions in the European transport market.
2. The adoption of an interventionist and regulatory approach, based on the view that efficient transport is central to the functioning of modern economies and to the process of economic integration in the EU.

Given that individual member states gave a different priority to these two approaches, conflict and policy inertia were the inevitable outcome.

The development of transport policy

The first attempt to establish the general principles of a CTP was offered by the Schaus Memorandum (Commission, 1961) and embodied in an Action Programme which was to be implemented by 1970. Three alternative policy approaches were considered in the Memorandum:

1. A policy focusing on fostering competition.
2. The establishment of a common market in transport.
3. The pursuit of an active interventionist approach.

Although the last of these would seek to ensure that all transport modes faced harmonised conditions of competition, with a fair allocation of infrastructure costs, it was intended that capacity controls should be established to avoid the emergence of unstable market conditions. Regulations should also take into account the wider social and regional objectives of the Community.

The Council of Transport Ministers failed to reach any consensus upon either the Memorandum or the Action Programme. The Commission therefore prepared proposals in four areas. First, the control of road and inland waterway transport capacity with the establishment of common rules for entry into the industry. In particular, the Commission proposed the introduction of Community quotas of authorisation for inter-state road haulage. Secondly, the adoption of a 'forked tariff', setting upper and lower tariff limits to prevent operators exploiting dominant positions, or of creating destabilising cut-throat competition. Thirdly, to harmonise member state technical, tax and subsidy regimes in transport. Finally, to coordinate investment in transport infrastructure, and to ensure that each mode of transport contributes fairly to the infrastructure costs that it imposes.

However, because of opposition from the member states very little progress was made until a Council Decision in December 1967 established a timetable for implementing these proposals. Over the next few years a 'forked-tariff' regime was introduced in road haulage, together with common driving hour regulations, and competition rules and criteria were agreed for controlling rail subsidies. Nevertheless, overall the development of the CTP remained a hesitant affair. The entry of Denmark, Ireland and the UK in 1973 deepened the paralysis as disagreements emerged over adjusting the Community's road haulage quotas to accommodate the new member states, and over attempts to introduce new weight and dimension limits for commercial road vehicles.

The Commission attempted to stimulate development of the CTP by the publication of a policy statement and Action Programme in 1973. This was mainly a restatement of the 1961 Memorandum, with an emphasis on establishing the right to the freedom of Community transport operators to provide services throughout the EU and the creation of a harmonised competitive transport market across the Community. However, it also turned attention away from operational controls through quotas and regulated tariffs towards the planning and financing of an integrated Community transport network. This approach was reflected in the four priority areas selected in the Action Plan:

1. The creation of a Community network transport plan.
2. The development of criteria for the allocation of infrastructure costs between modes of transport.
3. Addressing the role of railways in the Community's transport plan.
4. Planning the development of the inland transport market.

Once more, resistance by the Council ensured that by the end of the 1970s little progress had been made in developing the CTP. Although the number of Community quotas for inter-state road haulage had risen over the years, they still represented only 5 per cent of all road haulage within the Community. Meanwhile difficulties remained in implementing Community regulations on road haulage drivers' hours. Nevertheless, pressure from the new member states, and a ruling by the European Court in 1974, extended the authority of the Treaty to marine and aviation transport.

In a further attempt to rouse the Council of Transport Ministers from its lethargy, the Commission, in October 1980, presented a list of 35 proposals for action over the next three years. The failure of the Council to respond to these proposals led the European Parliament to instigate action against the Council of Ministers in the European Court of Justice (ECJ) under Article 175 of the Treaty. The Parliament accused the Council of failing to establish a CTP as required by Articles 3 and 74 of the Treaty. In May 1985 the ECJ (13/83) ruled that the Council had indeed infringed the Treaty of Rome by 'failing to ensure freedom to provide services of international transport and to lay down the conditions under which non-resident carriers may operate transport services in a member state'.

This judgement, together with the accession to the presidency of the Commission of Jacques Delors in 1985 and the commitment to the establishment of the SEM, gave new impetus to the development of a CTP. Not only is the transport industry a significant part of the European economy but its efficiency is essential to the achievement of a successful SEM. Subsequently, in Articles 129b–129d of the Treaty on European Union the Community specifically committed itself to an active role in the development of trans-European transport networks. To achieve this objective it will foster harmonisation of technical standards, and contribute, through feasibility studies, loan guarantees and interest rate subsidies, to national programmes of common interest. Transport infrastructure projects will also be eligible for support from the Cohesion Fund that the Treaty established.

Infrastructure

Transport infrastructure is the fixed capital of any transport system and includes the provision of ports, airports, roads and railway lines. There are two aspects of Community interest with regard to transport infrastructure, namely pricing and the finance and coordination of investment.

Pricing

A correct pricing regime for the use of infrastructure is essential to ensure that users make the economically optimum choice of transport mode. To establish such a pricing regime and to secure a Community transport market that was fair and competitive, it was also necessary to ensure that State aids were clearly identified and subjected to Community controls. To this end, in 1970, a Regulation was introduced establishing a standard system of accounting for expenditure on transport infrastructure and, in 1971, a Memorandum was published containing the Commission's views on a suitable pricing regime. This was the result of six years of studies of infrastructure costs and benefits.

Economic theory suggests that charging for the use of infrastructure should reflect the equilibrium outcome in a perfectly competitive market, i.e. price should equal marginal cost. It also suggests that pricing should take account of any additional social costs that the market is failing to identify. These social costs, or externalities, include accidents, air and noise pollution. The Commission therefore argued that charges should reflect the marginal social costs that an additional vehicle would impose and they specifically recognised that congestion costs are an important externality. One additional vehicle on a congested road slows all other vehicles, increasing their travel time and therefore imposing a significant social cost. Therefore in cases where congestion exists the Commission argues for a fixed 'congestion tax' (see Box 10.1).

Infrastructure charging based on these proposals raised a number of serious practical problems. For the inland waterways, such a pricing regime would substantially raise freight rates since, historically, this mode of transport has made the smallest contribution to its infrastructure costs. For road transport, where the greatest social costs in terms of congestion and pollution are occurring, existing systems of fuel and motor vehicle taxes are incapable of reflecting the true marginal social costs. Although a 1968 Council Directive had suggested that commercial road vehicles should be taxed on the basis of the marginal costs they imposed on the road network, as determined by their axle weights, this failed to take into account the wider externalities of pollution and congestion. To reflect marginal social costs, more complex systems of road pricing would be required. The practical difficulties of adopting such a system, together with the reluctance of member states to lose control of an important source of tax revenue (which a harmonised Community pricing regime would imply), have ensured that little progress has been made in this area.

Finance and investment

It was recognised in the 1961 Memorandum (Commission, 1961) that the Community had an important interest in the coordination of infrastructure investment since investment decisions by member states were likely to reflect only national priorities. With increased intra-EU traffic it was essential that infrastructure projects were also assessed in their wider Community context, and if necessary funded by Community resources. The inadequacies of national transport planning were confirmed by preparatory studies by the Commission. Thus in 1965 the Commission proposed a programme of infrastructure work focusing on harmonising rail electrification schemes, identifying a strategic European road network, improving links between seaports and their hinterlands, and establishing links between the European waterway systems. In 1966 the Council instigated a system of Community consultation on transport infrastructure projects, but

Box 10.1   Congestion tax

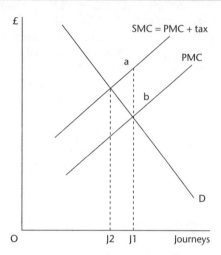

Fig. 10.1 Transport pricing with congestion costs

Drivers are faced with private marginal costs (PMCs) – e.g. wear and tear, petrol, travel time – which increase as the volume of traffic rises and congestion slows the journey. Faced with these costs, J1 journeys will be made. However, this represents over-use of this resource since the private costs faced by each driver are failing to reflect the full social costs they are imposing. Each additional vehicle not only experiences a slower journey, but slows all other vehicles on the congested road, imposing social costs. The imposition of a tax (ab) equal to these congestion costs reduces the volume of traffic to the optimum J2.

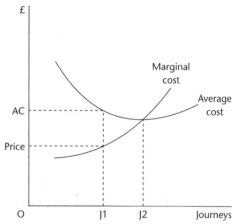

Fig. 10.2 Average cost pricing

However, charging each user the marginal social cost that they impose can result in insufficient revenue being raised to cover the costs of provision on the infrastructure. If the number of journeys being made (J1) is less than the optimum capacity of a road (J2), marginal cost pricing will not cover the average cost of each journey. Again the Commission recognised this problem and advocated imposition of a 'balancing charge' (AC = Price) to cover any remaining funding deficit.

resistance by the member states to the erosion of their autonomy undermined the effectiveness of this procedure.

However, in 1978 the Commission proposed the creation of a Transport Infrastructure Committee (TIC), composed of representatives of the member states, to consider national infrastructure programmes in the context of the development of a Community transport network. By the mid-1980s this had identified a core 24,700 mile trans-European motorway network requiring ECU 120 bn for its completion. Meanwhile the Commission continued the work begun in 1973 to identify the likely future transport needs of the EU up to the turn of the century. However, the Council continued to resist the development of a more active role for the Community in planning, evaluation and financing of projects of Community interest.

Having identified projects with an important Community benefit, the issue of Community finance was clearly crucial. In 1976 the Commission proposed a Regulation (OJ C 207, 2.9.1976, p. 9) identifying four categories of projects that were to receive financial support. These were:

1. Projects within a member state designed to eliminate bottlenecks in EU traffic.
2. Cross-frontier projects.
3. Projects fulfilling broad Community objectives.
4. Projects which standardise the EU transport network.

These were translated into a more detailed list of short- and long-term objectives including the upgrading of inter-city rail links (e.g. Amsterdam/Brussels/Strasbourg), links with peripheral areas (e.g. Dublin/Cork/Galway, East Anglia, Mezzogiorno), routes overcoming natural obstacles (e.g. Channel Tunnel, Appenine crossings), and bridging 'missing links' between transport networks (e.g. inland waterway link between Belgium and France). Qualifying projects would have been eligible for all forms of EU financial assistance, including EIB, ERDF and, since 1979, New Community Instrument loans.

In response to this Memorandum, the Council, in 1981, asked the Commission to evaluate the Community 'interest' in a limited number of specific projects. Subsequently the Commission presented a list of projects to form an experimental programme selected from among submissions by the member states. The total cost to the EU budget was to be ECU 968 mn to be dispersed over the years 1984–86, and was to offer a maximum support of 20 per cent of the cost of each project. Of the total, ECU 250 mn was to be spent on rail projects and ECU 550 mn on roads.

The European Parliament was critical of this road bias, and advocated instead an intermodal approach, and a greater attention to the needs of the inland waterways, ports and airports. In response, in 1983, the Commission proposed a multi-annual transport infrastructure programme (MTIP) (COM(83)474 final) to continue until the Council finally responded to the 1976 Memorandum. The MTIP would have provided a maximum of 70 per cent support for eligible projects which could have been combined with other sources of Community assistance. The MTIP was not realised, but the concerns of the

European Parliament were reflected in the shift of priorities expressed in the 1986 Medium Term Transport Infrastructure policy. Priorities were now to be:

1. Improvements in land-sea corridors.

2. Links to peripheral regions.

3. Construction of a high-speed rail network.

4. Reductions in transit traffic costs, including the development of combined transport (road/rail).

The modernisation of ports and airports was specifically identified as an important part of infrastructure policy, as were the demands created by the accession of Greece, Spain and Portugal to the Community.

The 1986 document also attempted to clarify the complex financial sourcing of infrastructure projects. It proposed concentrating funding under Specific Transport Instruments (STCs). However, the Council has resisted the establishment of a specific fund for transport. Nevertheless, in 1990 the Council of Ministers accepted an Action Programme designed to complete the single market (COM(90)585). This called for the creation of Trans-European Networks in telecommunications, energy and transport (3359/90). It also established the concept of a 'Declaration of Community interest', allowing up to 25 per cent of a project's total cost and 50 per cent of the cost of the feasibility studies to be funded by the EU. Subsequently, the Christophersen Group was formed to focus on the transport sector, while the Council of Economic and Finance Ministers (Ecofin) is examining the finance problem.

Over the period 1989–92 the EU has contributed ECU 702.7 mn to a transport infrastructure investment of ECU 11.2 bn by the member states (Vickerman, 1994). Over half of this expenditure is on rail projects. At the same time the ERDF has expended ECU 7 bn on transport developments in the Objective 1 peripheral regions. The EIB has also made loans for transport projects such as the Channel Tunnel, totalling ECU 12 bn over the period 1987–91 – 23 per cent of total EIB lending. However, a proposal, in 1993, for the EIB to raise ECU 5 bn from the international capital markets to provide soft loans for transport infrastructure projects was rejected by the member states. It must also be recognised that the EU remains very much the junior partner in transport investment compared with the national governments, providing only 6 to 7 per cent of national expenditures. These sums are also insignificant in relation to the estimated need for transport investment of between ECU 1000 bn and ECU 1500 bn for the period 1990–2010.

Finally, the position of Switzerland in relation to the development of the EU's transport network should be mentioned, lying as it does across the route from Italy to the northern member states. In 1992 a goods transit agreement had been made between Switzerland and the EU, addressing the problem of the Swiss 28-tonne heavy goods vehicle (HGV) limit. However, in 1994 a plebiscite decided to ban all foreign lorries from Swiss roads within ten years, forcing all international traffic to traverse Switzerland by rail. This will require bringing forward the ECU 14 bn Gotthard rail tunnel project and the improvements to the Simplon and Lotschberg links.

Table 10.1   Share of rail transport, 1993

	Route km	Freight '000 m.t.km	Passenger '000 m.p.km
Austria	5600	11798	9342
Finland	5885	9259	3007
Belgium	3410	7583	6694
Denmark	2349	1797	4700
France	32579	45033	58603
Ireland	1944	575	1274
Italy	15942	18792	47101
Netherlands	2757	2681	14788
Portugal	3063	1665	5397
Sweden	9746	18133	5830
Spain	12601	7558	15457
United Kingdom	16536	13765	30363

m.t.km = million tonne kilometres
m.p.km = million passenger kilometres
Source: Eurostat, *Basic Statistics of the EU*, Eurostat 1996

The railways

Across Europe the share of freight carried on the railways has been falling. In 1970, 31.4 per cent of freight was carried by rail and 54.9 per cent by road, but by 1980 the relative shares had changed to 23.2 per cent and 65.8 per cent respectively. In 1990 the railways' share had fallen further to 17.4 per cent, while Europe's roads now carried 74 per cent of all freight. Similarly, by 1990 the railways were providing only 6.6 per cent of passenger transport in the EU, and in none of the member states did they carry more than 9 per cent of passengers.

The railway systems of the EU vary considerably in their extent and importance in national transport (see Table 10.1). Although these characteristics are determined in part by the economic geography of each member state, they also reflect the transport policies pursued by the individual governments. Thus, in both Germany and France there was discrimination against road haulage for freight traffic beyond 150 km. These two countries, together with Italy, also share a commitment to the development of new high-speed rail lines, of which the French Train à Grande Vitesse (TGV) is the most well known. Over the years 1976–82 German railways invested ECU 9000 mn, French railways ECU 4500 mn, and British Railways (BR) ECU 3000 mn. In 1985 the German government approved a ten-year investment programme of ECU 17500 mn with a doubling of its high-speed network to 2000 km by the end of the century. In France, the completion of the South-East TGV to Marseilles and Switzerland was followed, in 1983, by the development of the TGV Atlantique to the South-West at a cost of ECU 1900 mn. In Italy, a new line has been constructed from Rome to Florence at a cost of ECU 2270 mn.

By contrast, in the UK the only major modernisation of the system, completed in the 1980s, was the electrification of the East Coast Mainline. BR has not only been constrained to relatively low levels of investment but has also been expected to cover a much higher level of its operating costs from its revenues – 76 per cent in 1990, compared with 31 per cent in Italy and 56 per cent in Germany. The level of State subsidies has varied significantly across the EU, ranging from 54.8 per cent of Belgian railways' value added to only 5.7 per cent in the case of the Netherlands (see Table 10.2).

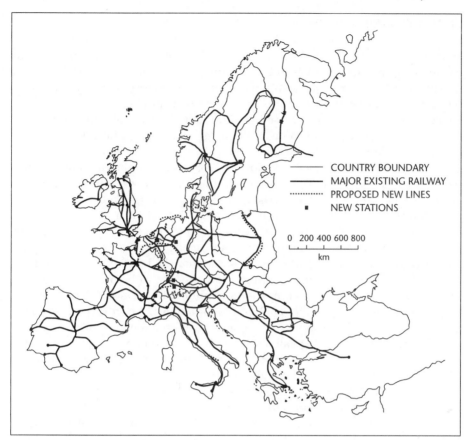

COUNTRY BOUNDARY
MAJOR EXISTING RAILWAY
PROPOSED NEW LINES
NEW STATIONS

0   200 400 600 800
km

Figure 10.3   Europe's railways

Source: derived from *Employment in Europe*

Table 10.2   State aid to railways

	Per cent of gross value added 1988–90
Belgium	54.8
Denmark	14.8
France	25.2
Germany	28.7
Greece	6.4
Ireland	14.6
Italy	6.9
Netherlands	5.7
Portugal	8.4
Spain	26.3
United Kingdom	5.9

Source: European Commission, *Second Survey on State Aids,* 1992

State subsidies

Despite this diversity in the railways of the EU they share a common problem in the need for state subsidies to cover continuing financial deficits. This arises in part from the requirements imposed upon the railways to maintain non-commercial services, and from state intervention in their pricing structures. A major concern of the CTP has therefore been to establish clear rules to regulate the level of such subsidies, and to ensure that they do not significantly distort the transport market of the Community.

This began with a Council Decision in 1965, which committed the member states to harmonising the rules governing the financial relations between governments and their railway undertakings. This was subsequently translated, in 1969, into two Regulations (1191/69 and 1192/69). These attempted to establish common accounting standards for the member states' railways, and allowed transport undertakings to apply to their governments for the removal of any public service obligation (PSO) which imposed a financial burden. If a government wished this PSO to be maintained, then the cost was to be borne by the state in accordance with common compensation criteria. Regulation 1107/70 sought to limit state aid beyond these PSO grants to help with coordination, research and development of transport systems, and for the elimination of excess capacity. Unfortunately these Regulations had only a limited impact as member states differed in the compensation offered to the railways for their PSOs, and the Regulations applied only to the mainline network services.

Thus, as early as 1971 the Commission was preparing further legislation to require railway undertakings to be given greater autonomy in their management and finance, with a clear definition of the responsibilities of the undertaking and the state. This proposal was embodied in a Council Decision (74/327/EEC) in 1975, which laid down a five-year legislative programme. At the end of this period the railways were expected to be operating in a commercial manner, except for their PSO activities for which they were to receive specific payments from the state. These subsidies were to be applied according to agreed Community rules. However, these further attempts to restrict the level of member state subsidies continued to be frustrated by the vagueness of existing EU Regulations and the difficulties of assigning railway costs.

In December 1989 the Commission again returned to these problems with a proposal for new PSO rules. Under the resulting 1991 Regulation, the existing systems of PSO grants were required to be replaced by a system of public service contracts agreed between the states and the railways but following a market approach. These grants can be retained for urban, suburban and regional services. The 1989 Commission proposals also raised again the issue of the separation of infrastructure management from service provision, and under Directive 91/440 separate accounts are now required for infrastructure and train operations. This separation was also intended to encourage competition through open access to the rail networks. In the late 1980s both Sweden and Switzerland had separated the control of the infrastructure from that of train operation, while the UK has gone further and privatised both its rail infrastructure, under Railtrack, as well as creating 25 train-operating companies.

The Commission, as has already been described, has attempted to remove distortions in the transport market by establishing clear common criteria for the allocation of infrastructure costs. In the case of the railways, it is argued that equality of treatment with the public road network would require the state to accept the financial responsibility for the infrastructure, with individual services being charged their marginal cost. This appears to offer an attractive means of alleviating the recurring financial deficits of railway undertakings. However, where marginal cost pricing is inadequate to cover average costs, additional charges must be made. Generally, governments receive more in road taxes than is spent upon road construction and maintenance, but overall railway revenues fail to cover their infrastructure costs. A transfer of responsibility for the infrastructure from the railways to the state would merely result in a reassignment of the underlying deficits. The core problem remains that of the nature of railways with their high fixed costs and economies of scale, which result in falling average costs as the volume of traffic increases. A more fruitful approach to improving the financial performance of the railways is likely to be found in focusing upon matching capacity to demand, and to achieving the potential productivity gains in their operation.

Integrating railway networks

The Commission also has responsibility for assisting in the integration of the Community's national railway systems. Although the rail systems of the EU share the Berne loading gauge (with the exception of the UK) and the core countries a common track gauge, this differs from that on the periphery in Spain, Portugal, Finland and Ireland. Their power and signalling systems also often differ. Thus the Channel Tunnel requires locomotives which can operate under three different electric power systems, and with the smaller rolling stock compatible with UK railways. There was also a preference for national suppliers for rolling stock and equipment, leading to high-cost products and excess capacity in the industry. The manufacture of railway equipment is one industry that is expected to undergo considerable rationalisation under the pressures of the single market, as seen with the creation of the Anglo-French company Alsthom and the Swedish-Swiss company ABB.

However, there is also a long history of cooperation between the railways of Europe through a variety of institutions, but especially the Union Internationale des Chemins de Fer (UIC). Its European Infrastructure Plan, adopted in 1973, has identified those lines whose development is necessary to the establishment of an integrated European network, based around the core of a Paris-Brussels-Cologne-Amersterdam link. As we have already seen, the Commission has also given priority in its infrastructure proposals to the development of a Community high-speed rail network. In 1990 the Commission submitted a plan (Commission, 1990), based upon national intentions, for a 35,000 km network to meet the needs of passenger traffic up to the year 2010. Subsequently, a working group has been established to examine the issues of funding and technical harmonisation.

The plan identified 14 key rail links, and one of these, and the most significant from a UK perspective, is the Channel Tunnel. Opened in 1994, at a final cost of ECU 12.5 bn, finance was provided by 210 commercial banks and the EIB, the largest single investor. Half of its capacity was to provide through-rail services, which were expected to carry 10.2 million passengers and 3.3 million tonnes (mt) of freight in its opening year, but only achieved 3 million passengers and 1.3 mt of freight. However, 5 million people and 4 mt of freight were moved on the Shuttle service, and by 1997 the direct rail service had captured 60 per cent of the London-Paris passenger market. The preference of the UK's government for private finance also led to delays in the construction of the London high-speed link. Work has recently been commenced by the private consortium which has been awarded the franchise, and it is hoped that the link will finally be ready in 2007. However, given this problem, and the competition from air services for those passengers travelling beyond London-Brussels-Paris, the Tunnel is likely to be of greater significance for road vehicles and rail freight than passenger services.

Despite the new-found enthusiasm of the Commission a number of difficulties are likely to face any attempt to establish a trans-European rail network. The principal problem lies in the national orientation of most railway policy. Route development is usually approached from the perspective of the needs of the domestic market, while high-speed train (HST) technology has been developed in competition rather than cooperation. Finance also remains problematic. Most countries' railways remain state-owned monopolies, characterised by inefficiencies and substantial accumulated deficits. The German railways alone had accumulated debts of ECU 37.8 bn by 1993. While the involvement of private finance will probably be essential, the Channel Tunnel experience illustrates the difficulties that this will involve. Private capital will require a return of 15 to 25 per cent upon its investment in contrast to the test rate of discount of governments of 8 per cent. Although some TGV routes are estimated to have returned 15 per cent, other projects, such as the Spanish Madrid-Seville AVE line, have been considerably less profitable. There is also concern that the demands of HST development have diverted funds from the needs of other areas of the rail system, some of which may be of greater social significance.

Combined transport

The Channel Tunnel has already proved of importance in the development of combined transport, with 75 per cent of freight trains being inter-modal. Combined transport is the carriage of goods that involves more than one mode of transport. It includes containers and 'piggyback' road/rail systems. Of these, containerisation is the most well established, with Intercontainer, a consortium of 23 railway companies, carrying over a million containers a year. Traffic is concentrated on Marseilles-Fos and Rotterdam, and is particularly important for German and French railways. The carriage of road vehicles or swapbodies by rail is less developed, with only half as many consignments carried by this means.

Germany has the largest volume of piggyback traffic for internal freight transport, and Italy for international trade.

Combined transport can be cost-effective over longer distances beyond 500 km, and offers environmental benefits if it can divert freight traffic from road to rail. It is also hoped that it may contribute to improving the financial performance of the railways. For these reasons the Community has been encouraging its development since 1975 when a Directive freed heavy goods vehicles (HGVs) from all restrictions if the trunk haul was by rail. In 1982 these exemptions were extended to road haulage combined with inland waterway carriage, and a scheme was adopted to reduce vehicle excise duties for HGVs for that part of journeys undertaken by rail. The Community has also offered financial assistance for the development of combined transport terminals, and recommended the adoption of competitive tariff structures that encourage combined transport.

A study by the Kearney Group of consultants for the Commission, completed in 1990, confirmed the economic advantages of combined transport and predicted a tripling of such traffic by 2005. It suggested that further improvements were possible through standardisation of equipment and organisational changes. In October 1990 a working party was formed with the specific remit of identifying those measures necessary for the establishment of a European combined transport network. By 1992 the Commission had outlined a network of rail and waterway routes, with road links for local haulage, that would cost ECU 2 bn to complete. However, the plan is merely indicative and, although some EU funding is available for the required infrastructure investment, most of the cost will fall upon the member states, who are likely to give priority to their national requirements.

In 1991 a Directive had further liberalised controls of the road element of combined transport, including allowing non-resident hauliers to carry out the road legs of the journeys, and exempted the road trip elements from any domestic tariff regulations. Directive 92/106/EEC extended the existing concessions for combined transport to all multi-mode unitised freight transport, and Regulation 3578/92/EEC renewed the existing provisions for state aid for another three years.

Road haulage

By 1990 road haulage accounted for 70 per cent of the movement of freight within the Community, 40 per cent of which was cross-border. It is therefore not surprising that the EU has had a far greater impact upon the operational environment of the road haulage industry than that of the railways. It has consistently pursued its objective of establishing a common competitive market in road transport, and to this end has sought the harmonisation of national regulations and the removal of restrictions. Road haulage has been subject to licensing in all of the member states at some time, leading to restrictions on entry to the industry or in the business for which road haulage can compete with rail. In the UK these controls had been abandoned by 1968, but by 1985 the UK and Sweden were still the only fully deregulated road haulage markets in Europe.

Complementing these domestic restrictions were licensing regimes for controlling road haulage between the member states. But these clearly conflicted with
the Treaty commitment to establishing the free provision of services (Article 52).

The Commission recognised that transitional arrangements would be necessary, and sought to achieve this by introducing a Community quota of licences
for intra-EU haulage. A hesitant start was made in 1968 with an experimental
three-year scheme, which was applicable only to cross-border traffic; only domestic haulage still required a national licence. These EU permits were shared
between each of the member states, and this allocation was to become a source
of considerable acrimony. A succession of Regulations extended the scheme, but
by 1983 only 5 per cent of all road haulage was under a Community licence.
In 1984, the Council decided to increase the EU quotas by 30 per cent from
1985 from their current 4038, and subsequently by 15 per cent in each of the
following four years. The commitment to the SEM increased the pace of deregulation. In 1988 agreement was reached to increase the EU quota by 40 per
cent for two years and, more significantly, to abolish all permit requirements
in January 1993.

Linked to the issue of intra-state road haulage have been the restrictions upon
cabotage – the carriage of goods for customers at any stage of a journey
between member states. This involves the opening up of the road haulage business of every member state to any EU operator. Article 75 of the Treaty requires
the Council to determine the conditions under which non-resident operators
may provide services within a member state other than their own. Despite a 1985
ECJ ruling, little progress was made on this sensitive issue until 1989 when
Regulation 4059/89 created an EU quota of 15,000 cabotage permits. In 1993
the number of permits was increased to 30,000, to rise annually by 30 per cent
until July 1998 when all quota restrictions were to be abolished.

Similar liberalisation has been taking place in the road passenger industry.
The EU has concentrated its attention upon international coach and bus services, leaving national services to be regulated by individual member states.
Although there were existing international regulations on which the EU could
build, it was a judgement of the ECJ in 1987 that forced the pace of liberalisation. It was not until 1992 that the Council finally agreed a Regulation abolishing licensing. They also agreed to allow cabotage on 'closed-door' tours, where
the same group of passengers stays with the same coach.

Complementing the liberalisation of the entry of operators into member states'
road transport markets has been the deregulation of tariff controls. As has already
been described, the issue of tariff controls illustrated the clear conflict of philosophy between those member states advocating the primacy of market forces,
and those attempting to avoid instability or the abuse of market power by maintaining regulation. The compromise that finally emerged in 1968 was the 'forked
tariff', setting compulsory maximum and minimum rates. This 'forked tariff'
was to apply only to international road freight traffic, and the rates were to be
set by agreements between the relevant member states. This system was never
adopted by Denmark, the UK and Ireland. In 1977 it was watered down by the
introduction of an alternative voluntary system of reference tariffs. Again the
choice was to be determined by mutual agreement between the member states

concerned with a particular traffic. This system clearly failed to establish a uniform Community common market in road freight traffic, and with the movement towards the SEM it was finally agreed that from 1 June 1990 all tariff controls would be abolished (Regulation 4058/89/EEC).

However, a truly fair and competitive transport market would also require a common vehicle taxing regime. In 1992 the national vehicle tax for a 38-tonne lorry varied from ECU 5314 in Germany and ECU 3824 in the UK to ECU 411 in Greece. In 1988 the Commission had proposed harmonisation of HGV taxation on the basis of a common method of infrastructure charging. Vehicles over 12 tonnes were to be taxed in their country of registration but on the basis of their use of the total road network of the Community. Germany sought upward harmonisation to protect its road haulage industry and linked the issue to liberalisation of cabotage, but faced stiff opposition from the Benelux countries who have significantly lower levels of taxation. The final compromise (Directive 93/89/EEC) recognised the burden on a particular country's transport infrastructure by allowing the introduction of a supplementary licence for the use of the motorways and principal roads of Germany, Denmark and the Benelux countries. This resulted in 73 per cent of the proceeds of these 'vignettes' being received by Germany. The member states also agreed upon a maximum annual vehicle tax of ECU 1250, reviewable every two years, and the harmonisation of fuel excise duty.

Differing vehicle technical specifications were also viewed as an obstacle to the efficient operation of HGVs, and to the development of the European vehicle manufacturing industry. A series of Directives had established common vehicle requirements covering safety features, noise, and air pollution standards. Finally, in 1992 the Council of Ministers agreed an EU vehicle 'type approval', allowing lorries constructed to this standard to operate throughout the Community. This replaced the national regulations from 1996.

Attempts to establish common weight limits for HGVs proved more controversial. These differences had arisen from the various national assessments of the trade-off between vehicle-operating efficiency and environmental damage. The member states also varied substantially in the standards applied to road construction and therefore to their vulnerability to particular vehicle weights. Axle weights in particular are crucial in determining the level of road damage that a vehicle can inflict, e.g. a 10-tonne axle weight does 17 times more damage than a 5-tonne axle. Attempts to arrive at a Community consensus proved extremely difficult.

It took ten years to achieve agreement among the original six members for a maximum axle weight of 11 tonnes and 40 tonnes overall. Unfortunately this was rejected by the new member states, Denmark, Ireland and the UK. In 1985 a compromise was finally reached, with a derogation for the UK and Ireland to continue with their lower limits of 32 tonnes. Following the Armitage Enquiry, in 1980 the UK government had raised the weight limit to 38 tonnes (see Dearden, 1990) under the derogation which will continue until 1999, but it has recently proposed falling into line with the Commission proposal for a uniform 44 tonne limit. Existing EU maxima only apply to international transport, and each country may also allow domestic operation of vehicles in excess of these limits.

Fair competition and road safety considerations have also led to a series of social measures controlling the working conditions of drivers. As early as 1969, a Regulation (543/69/EEC) established controls over driving hours. This was to be enforced through personnel log books, but the inadequacy of this method quickly led to a Regulation (1463/70/EEC) requiring the installation by January 1976 of automatic recording equipment (tachographs). The UK rejected this Regulation, but legal proceedings by the Commission forced compliance, and it was applied in the UK from January 1982. However, the EU recognised that the existing Regulations were too restrictive and, in 1985 (3820/85), revisions were made extending driving hours and increasing their flexibility. At the same time there was concern at the failure of all member states to enforce the Regulations fully. It has been estimated that half of the own-account vehicles in Portugal are regularly overloaded, and only 1 per cent have paid their vehicle tax. Consequently, in 1989 common enforcement standards were prescribed by a further Directive.

Inland waterways

The inland waterway network is an important mode of transport in continental Europe. It joins the Mediterranean to the North Sea, and extends from the Channel into Central and Eastern Europe. There are 27,382 kilometres of navigable waterway in Europe centred on two systems – the Meuse/Scheldt linking Belgium, France and the Netherlands; and the Rhine/Main/Danube (see Fig. 10.4). Of these two, the Rhine is the most significant, carrying 57 per cent of Europe's 50 bn tonne-kilometres of waterborne freight. However, it is an industry that has seen its share of freight traffic fall from 13.7 per cent in 1970 to only 8 per cent in 1990. It has consistently suffered from over-capacity, resulting in low returns to capital, with a consequent failure to invest in modern vessels. This problem has been exacerbated by competition from Eastern European boats operating at artificially low prices.

The Rhine navigation is governed by the long established Mannheim Convention (1848) and this has inhibited EU intervention in the inland waterways industry. Nonetheless, the EU has harmonised the technical specification of vessels (82/714/EEC) and established mutual recognition of navigation licences (76/135/EEC). In 1983 the Commission submitted five proposals to the Council, concerning entry to the industry, working conditions, introduction of a voluntary set of reference tariffs, cabotage, and access to the Rhine navigation. The subsequent Action Programme was more limited in scope, but included the preparation of a compensation scheme for scrapping vessels, combined with a ban on state aids for new vessels and an examination of the problems of infrastructure charging.

Aviation

Of all the modes of transport, aviation is the most highly regulated. The EU has to develop its policies within the context of well established international and

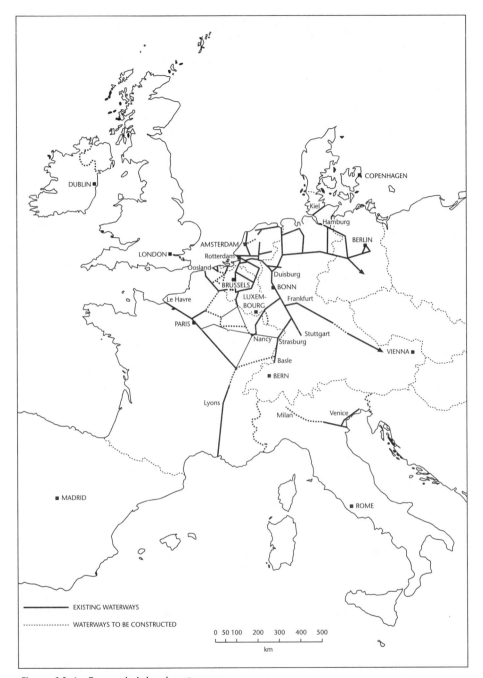

Figure 10.4 Europe's inland waterways

Source: derived from *Employment in Europe*

Box 10.2   The Chicago Convention

The Convention identified five air freedoms:

1. The right to overfly states' territories.
2. The right to land for technical reasons, e.g. refuelling.
3. The right to land to disembark passengers and cargo travelling from the country of an airline's registration.
4. The right to pick up passengers and cargo for journeys to the country of an airline's registration.
5. The right to transport goods and passengers between two countries other than the country of registration.

Signatories to the Convention granted the first two rights to all other signatories, but the remaining rights were determined by bilateral agreements (e.g. the 1946 Bermuda Agreement between the UK and US).

bilateral agreements. The foundations for the post-war system of international civil aviation were laid with the Chicago Convention of 1944 (see Box 10.2). Complementing the Convention was the creation in 1945 of IATA (International Air Transport Association), which organises a series of conferences at which fares are agreed for scheduled services.

The European civil aviation industry was characterised by relatively small, usually state-owned, national flag carriers. Scheduled services between states were usually restricted to the flag carriers, who were often entitled to 50 per cent of the traffic, with a revenue-sharing pool. In 1989, of the 750 non-stop short-haul flights in Europe, 71 per cent had only one carrier and a further 24 per cent only two (Pryke, 1991). Fares were agreed by the regulatory bodies of the two states. The high operating costs of many European airlines were sustained by this regime, producing fares 45–75 per cent above those in the US (McGowan and Trengove, 1986). Nonetheless, during the 1980s scheduled domestic air traffic increased by 65 per cent, and intra-European traffic by 31 per cent. Domestic flights account for approximately 11 per cent of European airlines' total revenue passenger kilometres (RPKs), and intra-European flights a further 20 per cent. However, only three airlines – Air France, British Airways and Lufthansa – account for 46 per cent of Europe's total RPKs.

Despite this highly regulated environment one of the earliest actions in the European aviation industry was an attempt to establish a European Civil Aviation Community. In 1958, Sabena, Lufthansa, Air France, KLM and Alitalia had discussed an agreement to foster cooperation and possibly a merger. The principal objective was to standardise their aircraft fleets, coordinate ground control, and pool traffic rights. Negotiations soon moved beyond the companies to involve their respective governments. In 1962 the companies and their governments signed an Air Union pact. Until 1965 inter-governmental negotiations continued between all of the original six member states, but outside the aegis of the Community. Meanwhile, the Commission attacked these activities as incompatible with the Treaty, and called for the development of a Community-based air transport policy.

Early attempts at liberalisation

In 1972 the Commission proposed action on air transport covering three main areas – improving regional scheduled services, developing a common approach to negotiations within IATA and to air links with non-Community countries. However, no significant progress was made until 1979 with the Commission's Civil Aviation Memorandum No. 1 (COM(79)311). Although this document suggested that freedom of entry into the industry was only a long-term prospect, it also represented the first clear commitment to the goal of establishing a competitive market environment. This shift had been encouraged by ECJ rulings in 1974 (167/73) and 1978 that the competition requirements of the Treaty (Articles 85, 86 and 90) also applied to air transport. It was also recognised that the move to a competitive environment would require a clear Community policy regulating the level of state aids to their national airlines. However, the endeavours of the Commission to establish a more liberal regime were frustrated by the Council, including its attempts to deregulate regional air services. Meanwhile Lord Bethell's action before the ECJ to force the Commission to intervene against the fare-setting arrangements in the industry failed.

However, the movement towards deregulation that had begun in the USA in the mid-1970s was beginning to influence the tenor of international negotiations. The apparently rigid regulatory regime of the Chicago Convention/IATA had always offered some scope for flexibility. The Convention had always excluded non-scheduled services from its ambit, and hence there was considerable growth of the charter market in Europe, encouraged by those states who wished to develop their tourist industry. By 1992, 60 per cent of European air traffic (passenger kilometres) consisted of charters. Most charter airlines are based in the UK and some are comparable to national airlines. Britannia Airways flew 14.1 bn RPKs in 1991, compared with Aer Lingus 4.1 bn, Alitalia 19.1 bn, and SAS 16.5 bn. Also the international regulatory controls had never applied to domestic flights, and offered considerable scope for liberalising bilateral agreements. Thus, in 1984, the UK and the Netherlands opened access on all their bilateral routes to all of their national airlines. Fare controls were removed unless both governments disapproved (double disapproval). Subsequently the UK extended such liberalising agreements to flights to Germany, Belgium and Ireland. This reflected the commitment of the UK to a liberal market environment in air transport, and followed the US government's radical experiment in domestic deregulation begun in 1978. The US applied its deregulatory zeal not only to its domestic air transport market, but also to its bilateral agreements and its dealings with IATA, assisted by the competitive pressures from Southeast Asian airlines who had remained outside the system. The beneficial results for passengers of the US experience increased the pressure upon the EU to curtail its protectionist regime.

Discussions within the Community moved slowly forward in 1984 with the Civil Aviation Memorandum No. 2 (COM 84)72 final). It introduced the concept of 'zones of flexibility' into fare setting. Governments would determine a reference tariff and a 'zone of reasonableness' in bilateral agreements. Within this zone airlines would be free to set fare levels, subject to country of origin approval or 'double disapproval', i.e. vetoes by both governments. The dominance of national flag carriers remained relatively unchallenged, although 50:50 traffic-sharing deals would be allowed to vary to 75:25. In return for this limited increase in flexibility the Commission was prepared to exempt fare setting, capacity sharing and revenue pools from the application of the competition rules of the EU for a period of seven years.

This proposal was overtaken by another landmark judgement by the ECJ in the Nouvelles Frontières case of 1985. This involved an attempt by the French regulatory authorities to prevent a travel agent from offering cut-price air tickets. Although the ECJ had already ruled on the applicability of the EU's competition rules, the 1985 judgement opened the way for parties to a dispute to force reference by national courts to the Commission's ruling on any restrictive agreement.

The first aviation package

This judgement forced the hand of the Council, and the result was a package of Regulations and Directives, accepted in 1987, which took the first positive steps towards deregulation. Regulation 3975/87 explicitly confirmed the authority of the Commission to apply the EU's competition rules. However, Regulation 3976/87 allowed the Commission to give block exemptions until 1991 to three categories of airline agreements:

1. Those concerning planning of capacity, revenue sharing and consultation on tariffs.
2. Those concerned with Computer Reservation Systems.
3. Those covering ground handling services.

These exemptions seriously undermined the immediate impact of the Regulation, but, being under the control of the Commission, created leverage in forcing the transition to a more competitive environment. This was indeed what was to occur.

The Council also accepted a Directive (601/87) which significantly reduced the ability of individual member states to control air fares. Although a government might still reject a proposed fare to prevent 'dumping' or predatory pricing, they were unable to reject fares on the grounds that they were lower than those currently offered. The Directive also specifically established the discounting of fares, within a broad range, as an automatic right. These arrangements were to apply for three years, after which further liberalisation was to take place. Similarly, greater access was to be allowed to new airlines, but in stages. Over the next three years member states were to allow traffic shares to move from 50:50 to 60:40, to accept additional airlines on routes (on a bilateral basis), and to introduce limited fifth freedom rights (cabotage).

The second and third aviation packages

The Second Aviation Package (1991) extended the right of the Commission to give block exemptions to airline agreements until the end of 1992, but it also committed the member states to ending the capacity-sharing arrangements from January 1993. From that date, scheduled fares were also to be allowed to match non-scheduled fare levels. This process of liberalisation was completed in the Third Aviation Package of three Regulations, which were also to apply from 1993. The Licensing Regulation introduced uniform criteria for the issue of an air transport operator's licence, to be recognised by all member states. The Market Access Regulation opened all EU routes to all licensed operators. Limited cabotage (i.e. the right to operate between two points within any country that is not the airline's home state) continued until April 1997, after which full cabotage became available. Finally, the Fares and Rates Regulation removed all controls on fare levels, subject only to safeguards against excessive tariffs. All remaining restrictions on non-scheduled services were also removed. These three Regulations finally established a single competitive air transport market within the EU. These conditions were extended to Norway and Sweden in an agreement signed in June 1992, and to the European Economic Area.

Industry restructuring

The final deregulation of the air transport market is by no means the end of the story. The problem of distortions arising from state subsidies and from the potential abuse of monopoly power remains. Indeed, European airlines have quickly responded to the changing transport environment by seeking partners. Following the US experience it is expected that only a few major airlines will dominate the market by the turn of the century. British Airways has made no secret of its global ambitions, and has swallowed British Caledonian (in 1988) and Dan Air (in 1992), and taken stakes in TAT and Air Liberté (French regional carriers), Delta Air (a German regional airline renamed Deutsche BA), and Qantas (the Australian national airline). Meanwhile, Air France has taken over UTA and Air Inter, and taken a 37 per cent stake in Belgium's Sabena Airlines, with Swissair taking another 49 per cent; SAS holds 25 per cent of British Midland; Lufthansa has acquired a 26 per cent stake in Lauda Air (Austria); and KLM has invested in Air UK, Transavia (Holland), Air Littoral (France) and Northwest (USA).

However, airlines have also followed the US companies in attempting to develop hub and spoke route networks. Dominating central hub airports creates the potential for the control of take-off and landing slots. With traffic growing at 7 to 9 per cent per annum, more than half of Europe's international airports are facing capacity problems. Flag carriers have traditionally retained their historic 'grandfather rights' to slots at their national airports, inhibiting competition and generating monopoly rents. The Commission has identified this problem, and a 1993 Regulation (95/93/EEC) establishes explicit rules for slot allocation. While recognising historic rights, under-utilised slots (those with less that 80 per cent usage) would be surrendered to a 'pool', which would also include newly created slots. Preferential rights to half of these 'pooled' slots would be given to new entrants. These 'pools' would only be created at 'coordinated' airports, to be designated by the national governments. Since this leaves discretion with the member states, dominant airlines might choose to utilise their existing slots, even at a loss, to avoid potential competition from new entrants. Therefore this Regulation may have only limited impact. However, the Regulation also requires reciprocity between states in slot access for airlines and provides for intervention by the Commission if the entry of new airlines appears to be being frustrated. Recently the Commission required Lufthansa and SAS to surrender, without compensation, slots at Frankfurt, Copenhagen and Stockholm. Nevertheless, the airlines regard these slots as valuable assets and a grey market has developed between airlines for their sale. The demand that BA surrender 168 slots at Heathrow, valued at £1 mn each, to obtain approval for its code-sharing with American Airlines, has brought this issue to a head.

The Commission has also taken action against Lufthansa and Aer Lingus for their attempts to place restrictions upon 'interlining', where passengers may exchange tickets between airlines serving the same route. Problems may also emerge with the ownership of Computer Reservation Systems (CRSs) by airlines. Such systems (e.g. Galileo), used by travel agents, provide the owning airline not only with the ability to give priority to its own services, but also with information as to the bookings of any other airline using the system. Attempts are being made to establish a Code of Conduct, but the issue of 'dehosting' – forcing companies that own CRSs to display their service information on competing companies' CRSs – is proving a major obstacle. These CRSs are likely to be closely monitored by the Commission, with the threat that the block exemption under the 1987 First Aviation Package (3976/87) could be ended. Similar problems may emerge with the use of code-sharing by airlines for through flights (e.g. between BA and American Airlines; Delta and Virgin Atlantic), or with agreements coordinating fares and services (e.g. between United Airlines, Lufthansa and SAS), marketing (e.g. Iberia and Alitalia), customer or ground services.

Evaluating liberalisation

An attempt has been made to assess the impact of EU liberalisation by the UK Civil Aviation Authority (CAA) (1995). It examined 500 intra-EU routes between 1992 and 1994 and found little evidence of increased competition. The number of routes served by more than two airlines only increased from 5 per cent to 7 per cent, while the proportion of monopoly routes increased from 57 per cent to 60 per cent. There also remains a variation in the degree of competition on routes between member states. Whereas the proportion of multi-carrier routes for France, Germany, Italy and Spain was between 4 per cent and 8 per cent, that for the UK was 11 per cent. The CAA also examined the trend in Fifth Freedom Rights (Box 10.2) and cabotage. In 1992, 19 Fifth Freedom services were in operation, and by the end of 1994 the number had only grown to 33. These services were dominated by national flag carriers. In the case of cabotage services, restrictions were still in force until 1997. Thus only five such services existed in 1992, doubling to ten by 1994.

The study also identified airport congestion as a major factor in reinforcing the dominance of the market by the national airlines through their control of slots. Nonetheless, the CAA recognised that the entry of new carriers since 1994 had reduced the market share of these flag carriers. There was also evidence of a significant increase in competition in the domestic markets of Germany, Spain and Italy, and more recently of France.

There is also concern about the declining international competitiveness of European airlines. A study found that European airline productivity is only 72 per cent of that of comparable US airlines, and labour costs of the US 'Big Three' (American, Delta and United) are only two-thirds of those of Alitalia and Lufthansa (McKinsey, 1992). On the highly competitive North Atlantic routes, by 1992 European airlines were offering only 44 per cent of the total capacity, compared with 50 per cent in 1978. With their lower fares, US airlines were also achieving higher payloads, carrying 71 per cent of passengers on US-France routes, and 61 per cent on US-Germany routes. Only on the US-UK route were shares roughly equal.

Unfortunately, external long-haul flights are particularly important for European airlines. In 1990 they accounted for 68 per cent of all mileage flown compared with only 34 per cent for the US airlines, and the North Atlantic represents a significant part of such traffic. In 1992 these routes generated approximately 20 per cent of the European airlines' total revenues and are of particular importance for BA, KLM and Lufthansa.

Air traffic control

The EU member states have an important role in the rationalisation of the highly fragmented system of air traffic control (ATC). In 1991 there were 44 control centres with 31 separate operating systems, and three-quarters of these centres were reported as having significant deficiencies. It has been estimated that inadequacies in Europe's ATC cost $4 mn in 1988 (AEA 1990) and that Europe's airways could accommodate 30 per cent more traffic with an integrated system. A European Organisation for the Safety of Air Navigation (Eurocontrol) was established as early as 1960, and in the 1970s it had launched an initiative to integrate European ATCs. Since this involved the loss of national sovereignty over the states' air space, little progress was made. Technical incompatibilities between national ATCs also raised serious obstacles to integration. The European Civil Aviation Conference in 1990 attempted to give new impetus to this process. It called for harmonisation of ATCs by 1998 to be implemented by Eurocontrol. The first major step has been a project to integrate the ATCs of Germany and the Benelux countries, while the organisation is also closely involved in all national ATC planning to ensure compatibility across Europe.

External relations

The Commission has also sought a role in the external relations of the EU industry with the rest of the world. Although as early as 1969 the Council of Ministers had adopted a proposal that member states should notify and consult the EU in the negotiations of their bilateral agreements with third countries, nothing happened. In 1990 the Commission reminded member states of this requirement and proposed that under Article 113 of the Treaty of Rome – the authority to negotiate matters related to the Community's common commercial policies – it should assume responsibility for external negotiations. It believed it was supported in this by the decision of the ECJ that its competition rules applied to air services between member states and third countries. It returned to this proposal in 1992, in response to the completion of the single internal aviation market, with the adoption of the Third Aviation Package, and the US-Netherlands bilateral Air Service Agreement. This agreement embodied an 'open skies' formula, allowing any US carrier access to any Dutch city for reciprocal access. In practice, it offered far more to the American airlines, giving access to a central European hub, and placed pressure on other European states for similar advantageous agreements. This 'divide and rule' strategy had been successfully employed by the US for a number of years.

The 1992 Commission proposal did not seek involvement of the Community in all external negotiations, but sought to identify those cases where Community involvement would give better economic results. It was particularly concerned to achieve more balance in the negotiations with the US and Japan. Negotiations were to be guided by an *ad hoc* Aviation Committee composed of two representatives from each member state. The benefits obtained from such negotiations were to be allocated at the discretion of a Management Committee for Air Transport, with decisions by QMV. Despite these attempts to reconcile the conflicting commercial interests of the member states, with their varying aviation policies and established rights under their bilateral agreements, the Council of Ministers strongly rejected any such role for the Community.

Despite this failure to find a role in external negotiations the Commission has successfully laid the foundations for the transition from a regulated to a competitive air transport market environment within the EU. The response of the airline companies will require careful monitoring by the Commission under its competition policy. The Commission will have the difficult task of ensuring that a balance is maintained between the achievement of economies of scale in operation through mergers and the potential abuse of monopoly power. Whether the consumer will experience the same gains in lower fares and improved services that were experienced with US deregulation, it is too early to say. The existence of competition from charter airlines, from new low-cost airlines such as Easyjet and Virgin Express, and from the high-speed rail network, may already have provided a stimulus to efficiency. But the major obstacle to realisation of a competitive common air transport market in the EU remains the existence of state subsidies. Since 1990, Sabena, Air France and Iberia alone have received more than $3 bn in state aid.

Maritime transport

The EU accounts for approximately 20 per cent of world trade, and 85 per cent of this trade is seaborne. Although declining, the merchant fleet of the

Community is still 25 per cent of the world total, earning \$9 bn per annum. Nonetheless, like aviation, maritime transport was initially excluded from consideration under the CTP. This arose from the 'continental' orientation of the original six member states, between whom sea transport was of little importance, and from the complexities of attempting to apply the Treaty within the context of a substantial number of existing international agreements.

In 1970 the Bodson report had first called for the development of a coherent Community approach to shipping under the powers of Article 84(2) of the Treaty of Rome. It identified a number of issues which needed to be addressed, i.e. agreements with non-EU states on cargo reservations and action on discrimination, a common approach to international negotiations, harmonisation of state aid and of crew conditions. Although supported by the Parliament, action under Article 84(2) required unanimity, and French opposition ensured that no progress was made until the 1974 ECJ judgement (ECR 631). This found that the competition rules of the EU also applied to air and sea transport, and arose from an action against France for maintaining rules which discriminated against non-French seamen. This judgement coincided with increasing concern in the UK, Netherlands and Germany about unfair competition from COMECON fleets, and from the French about the dangers of oil spillages. Thus from 1974 the Commission was to focus upon four issues:

1. Relations with the COMECON countries.
2. Organisation of liner shipping, and in particular the United Nations Conference on Trade and Development (UNCTAD) code of conduct.
3. The application of the EU's competition rules.
4. Marine pollution and safety at sea.

By 1976 the COMECON fleet accounted for 64 per cent of bilateral trade with the UK, 75 per cent with Germany, and 95 per cent with the Netherlands. In the international market it was also capturing an increasing share, with 25 per cent of North Atlantic trade. In 1978 the EU asked member states to monitor the freight liner trade (regular scheduled shipping services) with East Africa, Central America and the Far East, where competition with COMECON shipping was thought to be most acute. Member states could then apply to the Council for permission to instigate counter measures against countries where they believed unfair competitive practices were taking place.

More controversial was the debate within the EU on the ratification of the UNCTAD Convention on a Code of Conduct for Liner Conferences signed in 1974. This had arisen from political pressure by the developing countries for a greater share of the shipping between themselves and the industrialised world. Liner Conferences are composed of the shipping companies involved in a particular trade, and determine shipping rates and conditions of services. They usually cover between 50 and 70 per cent of total cargo shipments on any route. The crucial feature of the Code was the adoption of a 40/40/20 rule for participation in a trade. The national shipping companies of the two countries in the trade would each be reserved 40 per cent of the traffic, with 20 per cent open to 'cross-traders'. The USA was opposed to a further reinforcement of these shipping cartels. In the EU, Denmark and the UK, with their established fleets, also opposed ratification, while France, Belgium and Germany supported the Code. Disagreement focused upon two issues – the share to be allocated to non-EU OECD countries and the treatment of non-EU non-OECD carriers. The final compromise Regulation (954/79/EEC) that allowed ratification confined the 40/40/20 rule to those Conferences involving developing countries. Elsewhere commercial criteria were to apply in determining the shares of cargo traffic. The Code finally came into force in 1983. Some of the concerns about the consequences for EU shipping's share of liner trade may have proved well founded. The EU's share of world liner capacity fell from 45 per cent in 1983 to 38 per cent in 1992, while that of Far Eastern companies (excluding Japan) grew from 25 per cent to 34 per cent.

Although, contrary to expectations, the ratification of the Code did not require adaptation of the EU's competition rules in relation to Liner Conference agreements, the Commission remained concerned that they were compromising the Treaty. First submitted in 1981, a proposed Regulation sought to empower the Commission to enforce Article 85, against restrictive agreements, and Article 86, against abuse of dominant positions, with regard to sea transport. Block exemptions were to be given to the Liner Conference agreements, subject to certain conditions, since these were seen as contributing to a stable market environment. These conditions included non-discrimination in rates and conditions of carriage in services from different EU ports or users and consultations with customers. It was not until 1986 that this extension of the powers of the Commission was agreed under Regulation 4056/86/EEC.

The Commission remains concerned that Liner Conferences compromise the competition rules of the Community. In particular, it has focused on the issue of whether the fixing of multimodal rates (inclusive rates for both the shipping and road/rail components of a freight movement) under a Conference agreement is outside the block exemption that has been given. In 1995 a Committee of enquiry was appointed, the Multimodal Group under Sir Brian Carsberg, to establish whether the establishment of uniform rates by Conferences for multimodal transport was justified on efficiency grounds. Its interim report supports the critical position of the Commission (Multimodal Group, 1996). The Commission had already ruled in 1994 that the Trans-Atlantic Agreement violated the block exemption requirements, not only for setting multimodal rates, but also for establishing a capacity management programme and allowing differentiated pricing for individual shippers. The shipping lines involved have challenged this ruling before the ECJ and judgement is awaited. This is likely to follow the precedent established in a current reference to the ECJ from the English commercial court in the case of the Scandinavian UK North Europe Arabian Gulf Conference.

Regulation 4056/86/EEC was one of a package of four Regulations accepted by the Council to realise its commitment to establishing free and fair competitive conditions in shipping. A second Regulation (4055/86/EEC) prevented discrimination by a member state against the shipping companies of any other EU members in any of its trades. Existing unilateral cargo reservations were to be phased out by 1993. Similarly, cargo sharing agreements with third countries

Table 10.3 National fleets, 1994

	'000 Gross tons	% World
Denmark	5799	1.2
Finland	1404	0.3
France	4348	0.9
Germany	5696	1.2
Greece	30162	6.3
Italy	6818	1.4
Netherlands	4396	0.9
Sweden	2797	0.6
Spain	1560	0.3
UK	6520	1.4
USA	13655	2.9
Japan	22102	4.6
Panama	64170	13.5
Liberia	57648	12.1

Source: Eurostat, *Basic Statistics of the EU*, 1996

are now allowed only in exceptional circumstances. Attempts by third countries to impose such agreements can be met by countermeasures by the Community under the third Regulation 4058/86/EEC. Finally, Regulation 4057/86/EEC empowers the EU to impose compensatory duties on non-EU ship owners found to be engaging in unfair pricing practices. This Regulation was of particular relevance to the problem of competition from Central and Eastern European fleets.

These four Regulations created the foundations for a Common Shipping policy, and committed the EU to concerted action to combat protectionism by non-EU countries. It represented a significant transfer of power from individual member states to the Community. The EU, by combining the individual influence of the member states, will have a much greater impact upon the international negotiations that will determine the shape of this industry. Some rationalisation of the EU shipping industry is inevitable in the longer term. The EU still boasts 12 major shipping lines, compared with Japan's three and the US's two. But consolidation is more likely to occur through joint enterprises and the development of 'consortia', pooling shipping, than through mergers.

The Commission also attempted to address the problem of the major shift of registrations from EU national registers to the 'flags of convenience' such as Panama and Liberia (see Table 10.3). The extent of 'flagging out' by EU shipping companies varies from 25 per cent in France to 63 per cent in Denmark, with the UK at 50 per cent and Greece, with the largest fleet in the EU, at 43 per cent. This has a major impact upon operating costs. It is estimated that a 1500 gross ton container vessel with a third world crew costs $350,000 per annum, while a Dutch crew costs $1,286,000. This has not only distorted competition within the Community but has undermined the international competitive position of all Community shipping. It is also seen as compromising attempts to establish common and acceptable standards of operation.

In 1989 the Commission had proposed the creation of an EU shipping registry (EUROS) under an EU flag (COM(89)266). It would be open to any shipping company controlled by EU nationals, regardless of the company's domicile. Vessels were to be under 20 years old, on an EU national register, and had to employ EU nationals as officers and half the crew. It would have offered registered vessels cabotage rights within any member state, tax rebates on seafarers' earnings, and state aids. A number of problems have emerged with this proposal and it has yet to be adopted. In the event of accidents the law of the country of registration applies and as yet no similar body of EU law is available. The proposal would also exclude from the register ships controlled by non-EU nationals administered from within the Community. This is particularly a problem for the UK, with the large number of foreign shipping companies operating from London. However, most significantly it appears to offer little assistance in addressing the central problem of international competitiveness. Subsidies, to EU shipping companies to encourage investment in new vessels, are likely to be temporary and limited, while attempts to increase international competitiveness through a reduction in the tax burden on shipowners and seafarers, through the replacement of national taxes by a single EU tax linked to a vessel's age and tonnage, are likely to be frustrated by the limited competence of the Community in determining levels of direct taxation. It is resistance to the transfer of control of shipping industry subsidies from the national governments to the Community that has resulted in a compromise amendment that member states should have the option of whether or not their national shipping companies should join EUROS. At the same time the Commission is re-examining the proposal so as to increase the financial incentives for registration and to encourage investment.

Nonetheless, despite these limitations EUROS is seen as offering a potential contribution to meeting the concerns of some member states about operating standards and the threat of marine pollution. Concern had focused on this issue, in 1978, after the Amoco Cadiz oil spillage on the Brittany coast. In response to a Council request, the Commission had proposed a programme of action for the control of oil pollution, and also for Directives requiring member states to ratify a series of outstanding international agreements. These included the 1974 International Convention for the Safety of Life at Sea (Solas), the 1973 International Convention for the Prevention of Pollution from Ships (Marpol), and the ILO Convention 147 concerning minimum standards on merchant ships. Although the Council authorised a series of technical studies, it declined to impose ratification upon all member states; instead it merely agreed a Recommendation.

However, the Council did agree Directives on pilotage in the English Channel and North Sea, and for compulsory notification of potential marine hazards from oil tankers using Community ports. This failed to satisfy the European Parliament, which prepared its own critical report on what it regarded as the Council's inadequate response. In 1985 the Commission had reviewed its progress to date, together with outlining its future policy (COM(85)90/EEC). Although 'support for international efforts to maintain and improve maritime safety' had been identified as an important objective, so had the need to 'improve the commercial competitiveness of Community shipping'.

This conflict between the need to restore the international competitiveness of the EU's maritime industry and the desire to raise and harmonise operating conditions within the Community remains the central policy dilemma. Although the Commission has had very limited success in addressing the problem of European shipping's deteriorating international competitiveness, it has laid the foundations for fair competition within the Community. This culminated in 1991 with the agreement by the Council of Transport Ministers to maritime cabotage rights across the Community as part of the SEM (3577/92/EEC).

Conclusion

The Common Transport Policy differs fundamentally from the common policies for agriculture and external trade. In contrast to external trade policy, it has both an external and internal dimension, and unlike agriculture there has been no inclination to develop a highly interventionist regulatory regime. Indeed, the history of transport policy has been one of the gradual erosion of the influence of those member states attempting to sustain, at the Community level, their national interventionist traditions. However, the differing views as to the nature of a CTP, and the political debate about the appropriate boundaries for 'subsidiarity', ensured an impasse in its evolution for the first two decades of the Community. As in other areas of policy, it was the commitment to the establishment of the SEM that broke the log jam of policy development.

The success of the transport dimension of the SEM initiative has had a major impact upon the internal transport market of the EU, laying the foundations for fair and competitive market conditions. This enhanced internal competition may also produce the efficiency gains necessary to restore the international competitiveness of the European airline and maritime industries. Internally, the problem of funding major transport infrastructure investment remains, together with the failure to establish a clear system of infrastructure pricing that can take account of the social and environmental costs that each mode of transport imposes. Until this is achieved, significant distortions will remain, imposing substantial economic costs. However, since no member state has found this an easy issue to address at the national level, it would be harsh to condemn the Community for the lack of progress that it has made.

References

AEA 1990 Association of European Airlines, *Yearbook*, Brussels.

Civil Aviation Authority 1995 *The Single European Aviation Market: Progress So Far*, CAP654, London.

Commission 1961 *Memorandum on the General Lines of a Common Transport Policy*, Brussels.

Commission 1989 *Communication on a Community Railway Policy*, COM(89)238, Brussels.

Commission 1990 *Towards Trans-European Networks: For a Community Action Programme*, COM(90)585, Brussels.

Dearden S 1990 Road Freight Transport, Social Cost and Market Efficiency, *Royal Bank of Scotland Review*, No. 168, December.

McGowan F and Trengove C 1986 *European Aviation, A Common Market?*, Institute of Fiscal Studies, London.

McKinsey Global Institute 1992 Service Sector Productivity, Washington.

Multimodal Group 1996 Interim Report of the Multimodal Group, Commission, DG IV, Brussels.

Pryke R 1991 *American Deregulation and European Liberalisation in* Banister D and Button K *Transport in a Free Market*, Macmillan, London.

Vickerman R W 1994 Transport Infrastructure and Region Building in the European Community, *Journal of Common Market Studies*, Vol. 32, No. 1, pp. 1–24.

Further reading

Abbati C 1986 *Transport and European Integration: European Perspectives*, Brussels.

Bayliss B and Millington A 1995 Deregulation and Logistics Systems in a Single European Market, *Journal of Transport Economics and Policy*, Vol. 29, No. 3, pp. 305–16.

Bodson V 1970 Le Prospettive della politica commune dei trasporti: *Automobilismo e Automobilismo Industriale*, Nos 5–6.

Button K and Swann D 1989 European Community Airlines, Deregulation and its Problems, *Journal of Common Market Studies*, Vol. XVII, No. 4, pp. 259–82.

Gwilliam K 1997 EU Competition Policy and Liner Shipping Conferences, *Journal of Transport Economics and Policy*, Vol. 31, No. 3, pp. 317–24.

Papaioannou R and Stasinopoulos D 1991 The Road Transport Policy of the European Community, *Journal of Transport Economics and Policy*, Vol. 25, No. 2, pp. 201–08.

Ross J F 1994 High-Speed Rail: Catalyst for European Integration? *Journal of Common Market Studies*, Vol. 32, No. 2, June, pp. 191–214.

Stasinopoulos D 1993 The Third Phase of Liberalisation in Community Aviation and the Need for Supplementary Measures, *Journal of Transport Economics and Policy*, Vol. 27, No. 3, pp. 323–28.

11

The Common Agricultural and Fisheries Policies

John Gibbons

Introduction

For over 30 years the Common Agricultural Policy (CAP) has shaped the direction and structure of European agriculture. It has done so by means of an elaborate regime of financial rewards and penalties for its dwindling population of agricultural producers. In so doing, it has removed from the member states much of the burden of responsibility for agricultural decision making, but at a high price. The financial burden of the CAP on the EU budget has provoked much controversy throughout its history. Accusations of waste and fraud have abounded. Above all, the EU is seen to be financially constrained in its capacity to support policy initiatives in other policy areas, partly due to the huge commitments to CAP funding.

This is one reason why the issue of reform of the CAP has figured highly on the EU agenda, most notably in the 1980s and 1990s. The reform initiative has been driven by other factors such as international trade pressures, environmental and health concerns, and security issues arising from the collapse of the Soviet Union. A small trend in this reform process is towards the 'renationalisation' of responsibility for rural policies to member states. Were this to accelerate in years to come, it could mark the demise of the CAP.

The establishment of the Common Fisheries Policy (CFP) in 1971 followed the success of the Commission in obtaining agreement that Article 38 of the Treaty of Rome required the foundation of a fisheries policy for the Community. The CFP has proved to be a controversial policy area both with the member states and with third countries. Problems have arisen from the attempts to allow free access to Community waters and from the attempts to conserve fish stocks.

The Common Agricultural Policy

When the EEC was established in 1957, memories of food shortages were still fresh from the experience of the Second World War. Article 39 of the Treaty of Rome declared the objectives of a Common Agricultural Policy (CAP) as follows:

- to increase agricultural productivity;
- to ensure a fair standard of living for the agricultural community;
- to stabilise markets;
- to assure the availability of supplies;
- to ensure that supplies reach consumers at reasonable prices.

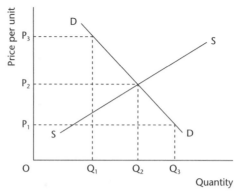

Figure 11.1   Supply and demand in agriculture

High price levels represented by P_3 occur as a result of shortages due to low production levels Q_1 such as those that result from poor weather conditions. Exceptional farming conditions generate high production levels Q_3 and low prices P_1. Equilibrium occurs at production levels Q_2 and price levels P_2. However, the price will fluctuate around this equilibrium level. The more price inelastic the demand curve, the greater will be the magnitude of these fluctuations. Agricultural products are also susceptible to price fluctuations arising from the fact that output cannot be immediately adjusted to current market prices: this can give rise to cobweb-type cycles.

To achieve these objectives the member states set up in the 1960s the European Agricultural Guidance and Guarantee Fund (EAGGF) to finance a price support system and the development of the structure of European agriculture. The Price Guarantee Section has operated by a series of target and intervention prices aimed at market stability. This is achieved by an annual price review, and by creating market intervention systems which vary from product to product. The Guarantee Section has also funded export subsidies when the price of EU farm goods set by the CAP is higher than world market prices. The Guidance Section of the EAGGF has funded improvements in rural infrastructure to help individual farmers and regions within the EU attain the goals set out in the CAP. The question arises as to why a common agricultural policy which is expensive and complex to operate was created, and why it is sustained in the face of strong criticism. Embodied in the objectives of the CAP were elements of the agricultural policies which already existed at national level in a number of member states. Agricultural protectionism had been established in many countries since the 1930s. The tradition of support for agriculture in Europe was also in part a recognition of the special problems of that sector. These included the impact of the vagaries of climate on planned levels of agricultural production, leading in a free agricultural market to extreme fluctuations between scarcity and over-supply, and consequent price fluctuations. These factors are illustrated by Fig. 11.1.

Other problems of the agricultural sector in Western Europe have included the low income elasticity of demand for agricultural products relative to many industrial sectors. Thus, as incomes have risen generally in Western Europe, demand for agricultural products has not risen as much as is the case for industrial products. Technological advances have increased the supply of agricultural goods, but because of decreasing returns to scale in agriculture, and the relative inflexibility of farm sizes, the rate of increase has been less than that experienced in manufacturing industry. The result of these and other economic problems which are peculiar to agriculture has led most governments (encouraged by agricultural pressure groups and in some cases fearful of the electoral revenge of the farming community) to intervene in markets with agricultural support measures. By one means or another these have been aimed at maintaining a constant supply of agricultural goods at stable prices and protecting farm incomes from severe decline.

The CAP system

A stylised version of the CAP pricing support system is illustrated in Fig. 11.2. This example is based on the market for wheat. The market for other agricultural products is somewhat different, but the general principles used here can be applied to many of the products which the CAP covers. The basic system operates by setting a target price which is normally greater than the equilibrium price. The system tends to generate excess supply which requires the authorities to buy wheat regularly to support the market price. This is the origin of the large stocks of foodstuffs which are associated with the CAP, and is the source of the large budgetary costs of operating the system.

An easy way to reduce the stocks of foodstuffs that result from intervening to boost the market price is to export the surplus stocks. However, this cannot be

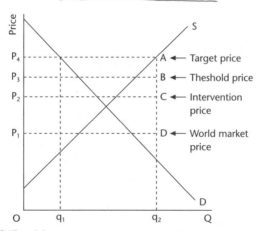

Figure 11.2 The CAP pricing system

A target price is set on a yearly basis to achieve a desired wholesale price in the city of Duisburg in Germany. As Duisburg is faced with poor levels of local supply of wheat, the price of Duisburg wheat is likely to be higher than the EU average. The target price is P_4. A threshold price is then calculated by allowing for transport and distribution costs of wheat from the port of Rotterdam. This is shown as the price P_3 in the figure. To ensure that imported wheat does not enter the EU at a price less than the threshold price, a variable import levy is imposed. This is equal to BD, i.e. the difference between the world market price P_1 and the threshold price P_3. The target price results in excess supply of the amount q_1–q_2. To keep the market price close to the target price, the authorities must remove this excess supply from the market by setting an intervention price, usually some 10 to 15 per cent below the target price – shown by the price P_2. If the market price of wheat falls to P_2 the authorities will enter the market and buy wheat to support the price.

done without an export subsidy to bring the price down from the intervention price to the world market price. An export subsidy (shown by CD in Fig. 11.2) is required in order for it to be possible to export this good. The use of such export subsidies by the EU has resulted in conflict with countries who are major exporters of agricultural goods, as they have rightly claimed that this is an unfair trading practice. It is an issue that lay at the heart of the Uruguay Round of GATT negotiations.

Problems with the CAP and possible solutions

While the objectives of the CAP were formulated mainly in recognition of the special problems in the agricultural sectors in Western European economies, they also took account of an additional political question, which was how to balance the national interests of the original six members of the EEC. In the case of the two major economies involved in the establishment of the EEC, West Germany was attracted by the opportunities of an industrial free trade area, while France saw market advantages for its relatively efficient agricultural industry. The establishment of the CAP brought about price levels in agriculture which were significantly higher than those prevailing in most member states before the introduction of the CAP. Under pressure from an electorally significant farm lobby the German government refused to open its borders to a free community agricultural market unless common prices for cereals were set at levels favourable to its own farmers. This set in motion a high-price policy in the CAP. It is perhaps not surprising therefore that a major factor in European agriculture since the early 1960s has been the steady increase in production, which in time went beyond self-sufficiency in many sectors and created an export potential. For example, in the early 1980s the Community became an exporter of beef and cereals, having been previously a net importer (Commission, 1987). From 1964, when common price levels for cereals were set at German price levels, the CAP has provided farmers with a strong incentive for expanding production (Hill, 1993). Through the EAGGF it has also absorbed much of the EU budget in support of those prices. This has generated debate outside the agricultural sector about the equity of such high levels of subsidisation for Europe's farmers.

There are theoretical solutions to these problems. If it is accepted that some sort of support for farmers is required because of the factors outlined above, and because of the strategic importance of food supply, then three possible solutions may be considered:

- a modified CAP system;
- a direct subsidy system;
- a direct income support system.

Assuming that there is a perfectly competitive market for agricultural products and considering only the partial equilibrium effects, then Fig. 11.3 can be used to illustrate the effects of these three possible systems.

The economic analysis in Fig. 11.3 suggests that the direct income support system is the least-cost method of providing support to farmers, particularly if income transfers were targeted at low-income farmers. Such a system is also likely

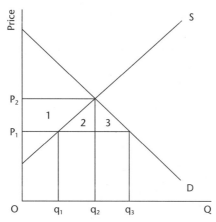

Figure 11.3 Welfare losses from different types of support systems

Modified CAP system

A world market price P_1 would result in domestic demand of q_3 and domestic production of q_1, the difference q_3-q_1 would be imports. The modified CAP system would operate by setting a target price of P_2, thereby eliminating the burden of intervention buying and the need to use exports subsidies to dump agricultural goods on the world market. This would be done by setting an import levy equal to P_2-P_1, leading to zero imports. The price rises from P_1 to P_2 will lead to a loss of consumer surplus shown by the areas 1+2+3. Area 1 is simply a transfer from consumers to farmers and is, therefore, not a net welfare loss. Area 2 is the cost of the resources used to produce the extra domestic production (i.e. q_1-q_2). This is a net welfare loss as these costs involve the use of resources which could have been used elsewhere in the economy. Area 3 represents the net loss of consumer surplus which follows from the fall in domestic demand from q_3 to q_2. Therefore, the modified CAP type system would lead to net losses equal to areas 2+3. If this system were to have lower import levy which allowed for some positive level of imports, the nature of the welfare losses would not change in character, but there would be a transfer from consumers to the government of the importing country from the revenues from the import levy.

A direct subsidy system

A direct subsidy system would operate by granting a subsidy to farmers of P_1-P_2 times $0-q_2$. With this subsidy domestic farmers would increase output to q_2. Domestic consumers would be faced with a price of P_1, therefore domestic demand would remain at q_3 and imports would fall to q_2-q_3. Farmers would receive a transfer of income equal to areas 1+2. Area 1 is a transfer from the government to farmers. Area 2 is the same as the area 2 in the modified CAP system outlined above and is, therefore, a net welfare loss. The direct subsidy system appears to have fewer welfare losses than the modified CAP system, as there is no loss of the area 3 in the subsidy system. However, taxes would be necessary to finance the subsidies. Economic theory suggests that nearly all taxes will have net welfare losses attached to them. In order for the direct subsidy system to have lower net welfare losses than the modified CAP system, it would be necessary for the welfare losses associated with the taxes to finance the subsidy to be less than area 3.

A direct income support system

A direct income support system would not affect price or quantities. The EU would simply transfer income to farmers to keep them involved in agricultural production. The welfare effects of this would depend on the size of the welfare losses associated with the taxes used to finance these income support schemes. If these losses are less than areas 1+2+3, then the income support system would have advantages over the other two systems.

to reduce the burden of the CAP for the budget of the EU. As is outlined below, the EU approach to agricultural support has begun to move in this direction. This change is linked to the various pressures which are being brought to bear on the CAP system.

The pressures to reform the CAP

Some agriculturalists respond to criticism of the CAP by blaming much of its high costs on the failure of the EU to achieve progress in integration in the other sectors of economic activity, and the absence of full economic and monetary union. Thus it is suggested that the links between the production, processing and marketing of agricultural products have not been helped by failings in transport policy and the absence of a common policy on food processing and of common efforts to improve the marketing of agricultural products (Commission, 1983). Currency differences between member states in the absence of monetary union also led to the system of expensive subsidies and levies called Monetary Compensation Amounts (MCAs). The significance of the system of MCAs is examined below.

The CAP has, however, not been immune to change. In order to explore some of the dimensions of this change, three areas are given particular attention:

1. The international pressure for change which has been notably channelled through the Uruguay Round of GATT negotiations.

2. An internal momentum which has come from within the EU for financial reform of the CAP, especially during the 1980s and early 1990s.

3. The impact of issues from the wider EU agenda on the CAP, notably the effects of the Single European Market (SEM), changing consumer attitudes, the prospect of enlargement of the EU to embrace the CEECs (Central and Eastern European Countries) and concerns about the agri-environment.

The global backdrop to change

The process of integration in European agricultural policy has taken place against the backdrop of a global impetus for change (Matthews, 1988). The impact of the Uruguay round of GATT negotiations on agricultural trade is an important factor. Agriculture was at the top of the Uruguay round, and posed a major challenge to the CAP. Previous GATT rounds achieved multilateral tariff cuts for industrial goods, but were less successful in dealing with agricultural goods. From 1986, when the Uruguay Round began, the USA and the 'Cairns Group' of agricultural exporters sought to bring about changes in international levels of agricultural support. Attention was focused particularly on the high subsidies given to European farmers granted by the provisions of the CAP. It was argued that these subsidies led to high prices, which in turn encouraged expansion in agricultural production. This transformed the EU from a major importer of agricultural goods into a major exporter. Particular opprobrium was directed at the EU regime of export refunds for agricultural exports which made high-priced

EU agricultural goods competitive on international markets. This led to unfair competition and lower prices for other countries who export agricultural products. At the beginning of the Uruguay Round, the USA, backed by the Cairns Group, demanded a *zero option* that involved the abolition of all supports within ten years and the introduction of free trade in agricultural goods. The *zero option* was revised to a demand for a 90 per cent cut in export subsidies and a 75 per cent cut in other supports. The EU committed itself to preserving the essence of the CAP market support system and argued that free trade in agriculture would lead to violent market movements, damaging to both farmers and consumers. It proposed an international policy of production quotas, and the setting aside of farmland from production. Furthermore, proposals for 'zones of influence' divided among agricultural exporting countries were suggested as a means of stabilising prices and reducing subsidies.

As the GATT talks continued unresolved into the 1990s it became clear that the size of the gap between the EU negotiating stance and that of the USA-Cairns Group on the question of reform of agricultural support in the EU was matched by the size of some of the divisions that were appearing between EU member states on this subject. Eventually after seven attempts to find agreement among the Trade and Agriculture Ministers of the EU on the issue of farm subsidies, an offer was made at the GATT meeting in Brussels in October 1990 of 30 per cent cuts in subsidies backdated to 1986 (a year in which support levels and rates peaked because of poor international market prices). This was equivalent to an offer of a reduction of support for farmers of 15 per cent between 1991 and 1995. In order to achieve agreement among the Trade and Agriculture Ministers of the EU on this negotiating position for the GATT meeting, various safeguards had to be included. These involved, at French insistence, protective measures against the dumping of products such as cereal substitutes on the EU market, and at German insistence a formula to allow almost limitless direct income aid to be paid to rural dwellers. The various negotiating positions of member states in their attempts to reach a common position for GATT were affected by the strengths of their respective agricultural lobbies. These included the formidable German lobby led by the German Farmers Union (Deutscher Bauernverband) and the importance of different agricultural product sectors in their agricultural economies, e.g. cereals in France, beef in the UK, and milk in Ireland.

The negotiating positions of those participating in the GATT talks were influenced by the different levels and forms of support for agriculture which operated in their countries and trading blocs. Thus countries such as Australia and New Zealand, with generally low levels of support, strongly advocated reducing the trade barriers to agricultural exports. By contrast, the USA and EU, with similar levels of agricultural support, disagreed about what were acceptable forms of support because of variations in their own policy mechanisms. In the case of wheat and maize, for example, 76 and 91 per cent respectively of the support in the EU came from 'market price support' (through minimum import and intervention prices), while in the USA only 17 per cent for wheat, and zero in the case of maize, came from this source. The USA had put much heavier reliance on direct payments to farmers (Coleman, 1990).

The suspension of the GATT talks in Brussels on 7 December 1990 was evidence of the large gap that existed between the EU negotiators and those of the USA and the Cairns Group. Despite the resumption of discussions in February 1991, the persistence of an atmosphere of brinkmanship in the negotiations was a constant reminder of the fragility of the Uruguay Round.

The renewal of talks after the suspension was partly a consequence of developments in the EU when new CAP reform proposals, which included the abolition and reduction of some export refunds (notably cereals) began to emerge. These are discussed in more detail below. However, 'the unwillingness of the EU to concede significant reform of the CAP was widely seen as a block to a successful outcome of the Uruguay Round' (Swinbank, 1993). That the European Commission was aware of this perception of EU policy abroad was revealed in the text of its CAP reform proposals of 1991 [the McSharry Reforms] when it noted that 'our trading partners are becoming decreasingly tolerant of a CAP whose surplus products weigh even more heavily on world markets' (*Agra Europe*, 1991a, p. 17).

From July 1991, the EU moved to discuss specific cuts in the three main areas of agricultural protection: export subsidies, support for farmers' incomes and market access. During the remainder of 1991 and the first half of 1992 the Community also undertook what was declared to be a major reform of the CAP (Commission, 1991a). The effect of these changes in the GATT talks was to offer a renewed possibility of overcoming the impasse between the USA and the EU on agriculture which was the biggest stumbling block in the way of concluding the Uruguay Round.

However, major obstacles remained. First, there were differences of substance. For example, in December 1991 the then GATT Secretary General, Arthur Dunkel, tabled a set of recommendations covering the main areas of dispute between the USA and the EU on agriculture. One of these recommendations was for a phased reduction in the volume of subsidised agricultural exports of 36 per cent over the years 1993–99. This was strongly rejected by the EU, as was a revised proposal for a 24 per cent reduction over the same period which the USA presented as its minimum negotiating position (*Agra Europe*, 1992a). Secondly, the negotiations during 1992 took place in a highly charged political atmosphere in the EU and the USA. The French referendum on the Maastricht Treaty on European Union in Autumn 1992 ruled out acceptance by France of any deal that could be interpreted by anti-Maastricht campaigners as a 'selling out' of its agricultural interest and what some regarded as its unique rural way of life. Also, the US Presidential race which climaxed towards the end of 1992 meant that the USA could not entertain second thoughts about its 'minimum' position of the 24 per cent phased reduction in the EU volume of subsidised exports (*Agra Europe*, 1992b).

Finally, there were frequent minor setbacks which seemed to cloud the main attention of the negotiations. For instance, the whole EU negotiating position seemed to be thrown into disarray when the Agricultural Commissioner, Mr McSharry, resigned as Joint EU negotiator at the GATT talks in protest against reported interference by Jacques Delors, the President of the European Commission, during talks in Chicago. Only after what seemed to be a humiliating climbdown by Mr Delors did McSharry resume his role in the negotiations (*Agra Europe*, 1992c).

Despite all these obstacles, a breakthrough seemed apparent in November 1992 when the EU and US negotiators struck a deal aimed at ironing out their differences on the issue of agricultural support. This deal is known as the Blair House Agreement, after the venue in Washington where the deal was struck. Compromise was reached on a number of issues including the vexed question of the volume of subsidised exports from the EU when a phased reduction of 21 per cent was agreed (*Financial Times*, 1993a).

Selling such a deal in Europe proved more difficult than could have been anticipated by the negotiators. National political interests hampered the attempts to reach a common position based on the Blair House deal. The French government argued that the USA-EU deal was not compatible with CAP reforms agreed in May 1992, and the EU negotiators in Washington had gone beyond the mandate set by the Council of EU ministers (*Financial Times*, 1993b). A general election in France in early 1993 produced a colourful rhetoric of opposition to the Blair House deal resulting in a demand for it to be renegotiated. French farmers took to the streets to air their opposition to the deal. Threats of US sanctions against EU products (including French wines) were turning the conflict into a card game with high stakes (*Financial Times*, 1993c and 1993d).

The brinkmanship continued until early December 1993, just over a week before the deadline of 15 December set by the GATT negotiators. However, the French gained a considerable number of concessions in the CAP reforms, (e.g. through extra direct income payments of cereal producers) and in the EU-USA negotiations after the Blair House Agreement (e.g. on the timing of the phased-in reductions in agricultural supports).

In conclusion, the Uruguay Round was important for European agriculture not least because it served as a stimulus for CAP reform. The implementation by 2000 of the agreed 36 per cent tariff cuts and the imposition of the 21 per cent reduction in the volume of subsidised exports have little effect on the CAP because of the many built-in safeguards won by the EU during the negotiations. However, the need for further reforms in international agricultural trade was recognised in the Uruguay Round Agriculture Agreement, and 1999 was designated as the year when further negotiations would begin. Those negotiations are likely to produce continued pressures for liberalisation from the US (where agricultural production levels are set to increase following a 1996 Farm Act) and from the Cairns Group (Grant, 1997). Such external pressures will inevitably have repercussions on the CAP reform process begun in 1991 with the McSharry Plan.

CAP reforms in the 1980s and 1990s

In 1987 the Commission described what it saw as the positive achievements of the CAP in respect of each of the objectives which had been spelt out in Article 39 of the Treaty of Rome (Commission, 1987). This report highlighted five major achievements of the CAP.

- a spectacular growth in agricultural production and efficiency;
- the protection of farm incomes from fluctuations in world market prices;
- a contribution to European external trade by encouraging exports;
- the security of supply of agricultural products;
- reasonable prices compared with food prices in other non-EC industrial countries.

Critics of the CAP focused particularly on the increasingly prohibitive budgetary cost of the policy, which rose from ECU 4.7 bn in 1976 to an estimated ECU 32.9 bn in 1991, by which time it absorbed over 60 per cent of the Community budget. Criticism was also levelled at the way that the budgetary costs of the CAP had been shared out among member states, with the UK in 1979 claiming compensation for what it saw as inequalities in the system of financing the Community Budget (see Chapter 4). Other criticisms included over-production leading to food surpluses, evidence of illegal and legal abuses of food subsidies, and damage to the environment. The CAP was also criticised for benefiting large farmers much more than small farmers, through a price guarantee system which ensured that the biggest windfalls from price increases were going to the biggest producers (Hill, 1993).

These criticisms led to some policy changes during the 1980s and 1990s. The dispute over Britain's budgetary contribution led to the publication of a number of reports by the Commission that eventually led to reform of the CAP in 1984. Production quotas were introduced to curb milk production in that year and did so successfully. They supplemented co-responsibility levies which were applied to milk from 1977, and were aimed at sharing the cost of surpluses in the sector between producers and the EU (Hill, 1993). In February 1988 the Council decided that the annual growth rate of EAGGF guarantee expenditure should not exceed 70–80 per cent of the annual growth rate of the GDP of the EU. Increases in cereals and oil seed surpluses generated a system of 'agricultural stabilisers' (a policy favoured by the UK government) whereby farmers were penalised by price cuts for excessive production, and the curbing of access to the intervention system of guaranteed prices. Other policies were introduced in the late 1980s and early 1990s such as diversifying farms into rural tourism or the craft industries, and the arable 'set-aside' policy whereby farmers are given direct area compensation payments to leave land fallow, and are offered large subsidies to encourage them to turn their land area to woodland (see Fig. 11.4). Farmers were also given a new role as stewards of the countryside (Swinbank, 1993).

In spite of these changes there was still a trend of continuing CAP surpluses and large budgetary costs. In January 1991, in response to the long-term pressures for change from within the EU, and against the backdrop of the suspended GATT negotiations, the Commission approved a discussion document by its Agricultural Commissioner, Mr McSharry. The McSharry Plan proposed radical cuts to agricultural subsidies and substantial reductions in quotas. This plan led, in July 1991, to a radical restructuring of the CAP (Commission, 1991b). Significant reductions in support for cereals in particular were anticipated. Most

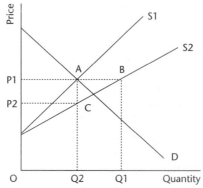

Figure 11.4   Welfare effects of set-aside

P = Price   D = demand in the EU   S = supply in the EU

If the CAP sets an intervention price equal to P1 with supply given by S2 an excess supply equal to AB would arise. The cost of the intervention buying would be ABQ1Q2 (i.e. the amount of the excess supply [Q1–Q2] times the intervention price).

If a set-aside system were introduced that led to a new supply of S1 by payment of subsidies and the intervention price was reduced to P2, the excess supply could be eliminated. The cost of set-side, if it were correctly determined, to reduce supply by the amount Q1–Q2 would be ACP2P1 (i.e. the amount that would induce farmers to reduce output such that total supply would be Q2 – no excess supply). This is lower than the cost of intervention buying, because the production costs of producing Q1–Q2 (BQ1Q2C) are no longer incurred. The production resources released by set-aside may not be employed elsewhere in the economy, thereby leading to problems of unemployment of agricultural resources. However, any system that deals successfully with the problem of over-supply in agricultural products will lead to a problem of transforming agricultural resources into other areas of work.

This analysis implicitly assumes that high-cost suppliers set aside their productive capacity. It is not clear that this will happen in the set-aside system. If low-cost suppliers set-aside, leaving high-cost suppliers in the market, the cost savings from set-aside may not materialise.

controversial were the proposals to create a two-tier EU farm policy that would target the CAP increasingly towards small and medium-sized farmers, a process referred to as 'modulation'. Critics of the plan argued that it placed a burden on efficient EU farmers to bale out 'inefficient small-holders' (*The Independent*, 1991). Moreover, the growth of third country food imports worried larger EU farmers who were also facing production cut-backs as a result of EU quota restrictions. Criticisms of the proposals stemmed mostly from Britain, Denmark and the Netherlands, who have larger and more efficient farm units. These divisions underlined the difficulty in forging a way ahead, but what seemed clear, as proposals to reform the CAP were debated in 1991, was a trend away from production-linked subsidies to income support paid directly to farmers.

The McSharry Plan was for the most part accepted by the Council of Ministers in May 1992, although proposed discriminatory measures between large and small cereals farmers were softened in response to the objections of large farmers. The main emphasis was on cereals for which measures were phased in from 1993. These included 'area aids' introduced to compensate farmers for losses in sales revenue for the cereals they were no longer producing in 'set aside' land. Price reductions of 29 per cent for 1995–96 were also agreed, with the expectation that by 1995 export refunds might no longer be required in this sector due to possible parity between EU intervention prices and world market prices (Swinbank, 1993). Such an anticipated outcome responded to the demands from the USA-Cairns Group and the GATT negotiators, as well as to concerns about the cost of the CAP budget.

The EU Farm Price Agreement of 1991–92 reflected the onset of an era of retrenchment and stocktaking of the CAP. Every year the Commission presents a proposal for agricultural support prices and related measures for the coming year. The Council of Agriculture Ministers is supposed to make a decision before the end of March, but in 1991 agreement was slow to emerge, requiring five sessions of talks between February and May. In order to hasten a decision the Commission invoked a clause of the 1988 Stabiliser Agreement, which states that, where there is a danger of a budget overrun, the Council of Agriculture Ministers must take a decision on the Commission's proposals within two months. The bitter pill of budgetary restraint was hard for some member states to take. While agriculture ministers from ten member states, led by France, lobbied to raise the agricultural budget ceiling, the Commission, supported by agriculture ministers from the UK and the Netherlands, rejected their arguments. On 24 May 1991 a budget was produced which, although not as severe as originally proposed, maintained expenditure below the overall budget guidelines and prepared the ground for the more fundamental reform of the CAP promised by the Commission in the McSharry Plan.

Opinions on the impact of the McSharry reforms have been mixed. However, they did enable the EU and the US to reach agreement on some of the trickier aspects of the Uruguay Round (Grant, 1997). Moreover, although the reforms did not represent a fundamental transformation of the CAP, which continued to dominate the EU budget, they did represent a first step on a path that will continue into the next century. In the short term, some of the best budgetary intentions of the McSharry reforms were undermined by the vagaries of the agrimonetary system.

The agrimonetary system

A system of border levies and subsidies known as monetary compensation amounts (MCAs) has in effect divided the EU into 12 national markets. It was introduced in 1969 when the French franc and the German mark were devalued and revalued respectively. The MCAs were created to ensure that French consumers and German producers were not penalised by the effects of the exchange rate changes on agricultural prices, and by speculators moving produce from one member state to another to gain advantage from exchange rate windfalls. Farm prices, levy and subsidy rates have been fixed in Brussels in ECUs but have been converted into national currencies by the Commission at fixed exchange rates called 'green rates' (*Agra Europe*, 1991b). Where the 'green rates' have been lower than the market exchange rates, MCAs have been charged as a subsidy on imports and a levy on exports. The system has applied to trade in most agricultural products. In recent years there has been a gradual trend towards the dismantling of the MCA system, not least because of the incentive it gave to smuggling and fraudulent activities. This was propelled by the establishment of the EMS in 1979 and the moves towards monetary union which tended to stabilise exchange rate fluctuations. In 1984 the process of eliminating the system was complicated by a new method of calculating MCAs. This included the creation of a device called 'switchover', mainly directed at helping German farmers whose price advantage was being threatened by a deutschmark rise in the ERM. 'Switchover' ensured that, if a strong currency (usually the deutschmark) climbed within the ERM against the ECU, the effect was not a revaluation of Germany's green rate but a devaluation of everyone else's. The result was 'that German prices expressed in deutschmarks would remain constant instead of falling, and prices expressed in all other national currencies would rise (*The Economist*, 1993). In July 1988, the Council of Agriculture Ministers and the European Commission declared that they intended to dismantle the remaining vestiges of the system by the end of 1992 and return CAP pricing to a 'real ECU' basis. In July 1990 it was reported that practically all British MCAs had been eliminated by the strength of sterling (*Irish Farmers Journal*, 1990). The Farm Price Agreement of May 1991 formalised this when it was decided to dismantle UK monetary gaps entirely. Only Greece, Portugal and Spain in July 1991 still had green rates which were not perfectly aligned with market rates. In the eyes of critics, what remained of MCAs was an important obstacle to the idea of a single market in agricultural products. However, it was expected that the success of the EMS and progress towards EMU would eventually eliminate this obstacle to an SEM throughout the EU.

The crisis that befell the ERM in the autumn of 1992 (see Chapter 2) showed how premature such expectations were. Nonetheless, the EU maintained its commitment to the goal of abolishing MCAs on 1 January 1993. It duly did so, but declared that it would retain the 'switchover' mechanism 'for at least a further two years' (*Agra Europe*, 1993). This was a costly decision taken by farm ministers for political reasons (with the main benefits going to German farmers) contrary to the recommendations of the Commission. The mechanism had led to price rises for most farmers of over 20 per cent since its inception in 1984, and with the currency turbulence it was estimated that the cost to the agricultural budget of this single item would be ECU 1.5 bn, leaving little room for manoeuvre in meeting additional demands such as those being made by the French government in its campaign against the Blair House agreement in the GATT round discussed already in this chapter (*Financial Times*, 1993d).

The near-collapse of the ERM in August 1993 led to further crisis and the consideration of further options to save the CAP pricing structure, but possibilities for action were limited. The availability of options was reduced on the one hand by commitments being entered into in the Uruguay Round of GATT negotiations as well as the McSharry Plan to cut subsidies to farmers in the EU, and on the other hand by the EU's own guideline on farm spending as a proportion of the total EU budget.

The solution arrived at in mid-1995 was to allow a partial introduction of national compensatory aid for farmers in those member states affected by the currency fluctuations of others (*Agra Europe*, 1995a). Meanwhile, hard currency countries, notably Germany, were still going to be able to protect their farmers' product prices by a variant of the switchover mechanism, a formula with a high price-tag attached. It was clear that, unless European monetary union came about soon and thus eliminated the need for such an expensive and complex agri-monetary system, the CAP might well disintegrate and some of its parts might be renationalised by the member states.

The CAP and the wider agenda of the EU

The CAP has significant effects on a number of major areas other than its impact on the agricultural industry and its relationships with trading partners. Three main areas are affected by the CAP – the SEM, consumer attitudes to food products, and the enlargement of the EU.

The effects of the SEM

By January 1993, a package of measures relating to the creation of the SEM in the agriculture and food processing sectors were set in place by legislation arising from the SEA. The resulting elimination of many physical barriers to trade simplified intra-Union transport of agricultural products: the elimination of most technical barriers to trade increased competition between member states for food products, and the elimination of some fiscal-related barriers to trade affected farm input costs such as farm machinery, fertilisers and feeding stuffs. The economic effects of these changes have not been felt uniformly across the EU and have depended among other factors on the structure, significance and efficiency of agriculture and food processing in particular member states (Grant, 1997). In this context, a north-south divide may be observed. At one extreme are those northern member states with relatively low levels of agricultural activity or with high levels of efficiency in their agricultural and/or food processing 'industries' – mainly Denmark, the Netherlands and the UK. At the other extreme are those mainly southern member states with less efficient agricultural and food processing sectors – Portugal, Greece and Spain. The SEM has enabled northern European agriculture and food processing industries to compete strongly against their southern equivalents. The large northern multinationals such as the French based Danone and Anglo-Dutch based Unilever have benefited most (Grant, 1997). They have expanded their operations into southern Europe during the 1990s through an active takeover policy of their weaker competitors. The SEM has contributed to the process of restructuring and consolidation in the agricultural and food manufacturing sectors in the EU.

It is not clear what the impact of the development of pan-European activities by multinationals such as Danone, Nestlé and Unilever will have on the agricultural sector. However, these companies have already been active in many of the member states for many years. Nevertheless, the growth of their activities by mergers and acquisitions may well encourage the agricultural industry to increase its supply of products of a better quality to ensure that they secure contracts from the large food processing companies. The expansion of nationally based supermarkets into European countries that have less well developed supermarket chains may also contribute to the pressure on the agricultural industry to improve the quality of its output. The potential for farmers to diversify into higher value-added products such as organically grown and reared products may also be enhanced by the growth of the effective distribution systems that supermarkets have at their disposal. However, developments along these lines may well require help from the EAGGF (Guidance section) for those agricultural areas that are not used to supplying the demanding conditions often specified by large supermarkets and food processors.

Changing consumer attitudes and the agri-environment

Over the years the EU has adopted legislation covering methods of producing, processing and marketing agricultural products and foodstuffs. This has been motivated by trade considerations as well as rising consumer expectations concerning food quality. In 1970 Community regulations relating to additives for animal feeding stuffs were issued. These were developed in 1976 when EEC legislation laid down maximum levels for pesticide residues and veterinary medicinal products in foodstuffs. The SEM hastened this process. Despite such controls, agricultural producers, driven by a market imperative, found ways to intensify production and reduce costs by use of intensive farming techniques. In at least one sector – beef – these practices had very serious implications.

The mounting evidence that there was a link between Creutzfeldt-Jacob Disease (CJD), which was becoming increasingly common in Britain in the 1990s, and the cattle disease bovine spongiform encephelopathy (BSE) prompted a collapse of consumer confidence that had repercussions for the beef industry across all EU member states and also for the CAP budget. Suspicion for cause of the infection of cattle with BSE was directed at the practice adopted, mainly in Britain, of using rendered sheep offal as foodstuff for cattle in the early 1980s. The sheep disease known as scrapie was suspected to have jumped species to become BSE in cattle and next, through human consumption of beef products, to enter the human system and become a new variant of CJD (Ford, 1996). Inadequate government response to the crisis, as more evidence of the effects of BSE became known in the 1980s and 1990s, led to an EU, and eventually, a world-wide ban on beef and beef product exports from the UK. The repercussions of the crisis were felt across the industry as a whole, as public confidence in beef throughout Europe suffered an enormous and seemingly irreversible set-back with more than a 10 per cent decline in EU beef consumption.

This crisis seemed to justify the analysis of those who were campaigning for a reform of farming and food policies that would make them more responsive to the environment. Central to the environmental perspective on agriculture is the view that intensive production methods have been encouraged by agricultural policy at the expense of the environment (e.g. soil erosion due to intensive hill farming) and public health (e.g. high levels of nitrates from fertilisers in drinking water). Extensive sustainable farming methods, rather than the intensive approach long encouraged by the CAP, are advocated by many environmentalists. The EU has responded to public concerns on the environmental impact of agriculture, for instance by introducing various measures concerning the use of nitrates. It also incorporated into the McSharry Reforms a package of 'accompanying measures' which have enabled member states to promote an environmental approach to agriculture, for example by providing subsidies for organic farming (*Agra Europe*, 1995b). However, these policy initiatives have been on the margins of the CAP and have not challenged the economic rationale of European farmers who invest in intensive agricultural production methods to reap the financial rewards of high EU subsidies and price guarantees.

Enlargement of the EU and the CAP

Proposals for the enlargement of the EU have provoked concern from at least some sections of the EU farming community. In the 1980s, the prospect of Spanish and Portuguese entry worried some French producers who faced the prospect of competition from their Southern neighbours. In the 1990s, it was the turn of the Spanish and Portuguese among others to express concern at the possible erosion of their bargaining power in CAP negotiations following the expansion of the EU northwards to Sweden and Finland, and eastwards to Austria (Middlemas, 1995).

The prospect of further enlargement of the EU to incorporate the CEECs is likely to be one of the issues that provokes very intense debate among agricultural policy makers in the early years of the next century. The wider political and international security impetus behind the movement to incorporate in the EU, for instance, the so-called 5-plus-1 countries (Czech Republic, Estonia, Hungary, Poland, Slovenia and Cyprus) creates profound economic questions, not least for the EU agricultural policy community. These questions include the cost to the CAP of the CEECs' entry, and the degree of compatibility with the EU necessary before entry for the CEECs' agricultural and food industry structures. The European Commission has prepared strategy papers on the issue of CEEC reform in which the need for structural reforms in the relevant agricultural economies is recommended and encouraged, and the prospect of accompanying reforms of the CAP is specified (*Agra Europa*, 1995c and Commission, 1996).

The proposed extension of the EU to include Hungary, Poland, the Czech Republic, Estonia and Slovenia will have significant implications for the CAP. This enlargement would lead to a 50 per cent increase in the agricultural land of the EU and it would double the size of the agricultural labour force (Commission, 1997). Agenda 2000 argues for the continued reform of the CAP to prevent serious problems if the present CAP system were to be extended to cover the proposed new member states. To avoid budgetary problems and the extension of surpluses the Commission argues for reductions in the intervention price of cereals (20 per cent), beef (20 per cent) and dairy products (10 per cent). An increased emphasis on structural adjustment in the agricultural sector and a more environmentally friendly approach are also advocated. The Commission believes that by 2006 such reforms will reduce expenditure on intervention buying by ECU 3.7 bn, but would add ECU 10.5 bn to direct income support and structural improvements expenditures. Agenda 2000 maintains that, if growth in the member states is in the region of 2.5 per cent, then the natural growth in the size of the budget will allow the extra costs of enlargement to be contained within the 1.27 per cent budgetary contribution of the member states. However, this rather rosy scenario assumes that the reforms to the CAP will be fully implemented and that the costs of the structural help are as estimated in Agenda 2000. Furthermore, other CEECs wish to join the EU, therefore the pressures on CAP of enlargement are likely to grow in the early part of the next century.

The Common Fisheries Policy

In 1966 the Commission argued that Article 38 of the Treaty of Rome required the establishment of a Common Fisheries Policy (CFP). Eventually the position of the Commission was accepted and the CFP came into being in 1971. The main principle of the CFP was that free access to Community waters should be established to allow for the creation of a single fisheries market. During the negotiations for the first enlargement a preliminary agreement was reached to create a CFP which granted free access, except for an exclusion zone of between six and twelve miles from the coasts of the major fishing nations of the Community. These exclusion zones were to be eliminated by 1982. The three new members reluctantly accepted this agreement. However, the seeds of future conflict between the major fishing nations were sown by this agreement. The need to conserve fish stocks added to the problems that arose from the need to grant access to foreign fishing fleets (see Fig. 11.5). When a system of curbing catches was introduced it required a restructuring of national fishing fleets. Further problems were encountered when free access permitted fishing fleets from other member states access to national waters. Therefore, although an agreement to reform the CFP was reached in 1983 it did not resolve these fundamental problems. The second enlargement in 1986 brought two new fishing fleets into the CFP and one of them (i.e. that of Spain) was large and was eager to take advantage of free access to Community waters.

In the years that followed, apart from the matter of exclusion zones, negotiations focused on a number of other issues and led to common measures being adopted in the agreement of 1983 for the production and marketing of fish. These were, first, the notion of a Total Annual Catch (TAC) aimed at overall fish stock conservation; secondly, a national quota system aimed at allocating the agreed TACs; thirdly, initiatives to improve the organisation of fish marketing; fourthly, schemes for fleet restructuring and investment and, finally, the negotiation of international agreements with 'third' countries, outside the EU.

Despite the adoption of these reforms to the CFP the sector has been beset by a series of crises during the 1980s and 1990s. The Commission has been inclined to blame the crises on fleet overcapacity, overfishing, low productivity and inappropriate marketing structures in the sector. Member states have preferred to blame each other or 'third' countries for the difficulties of their fisheries sectors.

One of the most serious disputes has arisen over the sale of UK quotas to Spanish based fishing boats. However, this problem largely arose from the

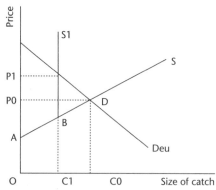

Figure 11.5   Regulation of fisheries

Deu = demand for fish

ABS = unregulated supply of fish

ABS1 = regulated supply of fish (a sustainable level of catches that allows the fish stock to reproduce such that fish stocks are constant)

P0:C0 = price and output with no regulation

P1:C1 = price and output with regulation

   If there is no regulation the catch will be at 0C0, leading to a depletion of fish stocks. If a system of quotas is issued to limit catches to 0C1 the problem of over-fishing will be solved. This
reduction requires the transfer of resources from fishing to other areas of economic activity. The
value of the resources to be transferred is shown by the area BDC0C1. However, the granting of
quotas gives a right to revenue from fishing. If quotas are given to all fishing boats in all member states the size of each quota may be too small to make fishing worthwhile. Consequently,
the initial allocation of quotas determines the right to earn revenue from fishing. If this quota
delivers a revenue below what the owners are prepared to accept they may sell (or trade their
quotas) if such trade is permitted. In these circumstances the quotas would be concentrated in
the hands of those who value them the most. However, quotas may end up being held by fishing
boats based in member states that do not have a coast line close to the main fishing waters (for
example, Spanish-based fishing boats fishing in the North Sea). This can lead to controversy with
fishing boats based in these main fishing areas that retained their quotas.

decision of the UK government to allow the sale of quotas to non-UK based boats
and the willingness of UK fishing companies to sell these quotas. Market forces,
that is, the sale of quotas, revealed that many Spanish fishing companies put a
higher value on UK quotas than did UK fishing companies. Nevertheless, the
UK fishing industry appears to be reluctant to accept the outcome of these market forces. This has been reinforced by the unwillingness of other member states
to sell their quotas to fishing boats that are not based in their countries.
However, if UK fishing companies were willing to sell their quotas, it is difficult
to argue that they have been forced to abandon their home fishing grounds by
the operation of the CFP. What has occurred is that they have been willing to
sell their rights to fish in Community waters to fishing companies which presumably valued these rights more highly than did UK companies. The major
problem is that what were formerly UK waters are now Community waters, and
the need to conserve fishing stocks has required the issuing of quotas. Many UK

based fishing companies decided that the best solution to this problem was to sell their rights to fish in Community waters. The remaining UK fishing companies then complained that other member states (mainly Spain) were depriving them of a living by fishing in UK waters by using UK quotas. Attempts to solve these disputes have normally involved proposals for a variety of administrative solutions such as a requirement to land fish in the member state that issued the quota. Such bureaucratic solutions may take some of the heat out of the disputes but they do not encourage the rational use of resources.

There has also been considerable controversy about the policing of the quotas across the member states. In 1994, Spanish fishermen conducted a so-called 'tuna war' in the Bay of Biscay over the use by France, Britain and Ireland of large drift nets. Irish and British fishermen, in turn, complained of illegal incursions by Spanish fishermen into their exclusion zones (Nugent, 1995). Disputes between Spain and Canada (a third country) also erupted in 1995 over the halibut TAC. After some diplomatic brinkmanship, resolution was eventually achieved by agreement on a new and reduced TAC and quota arrangement (Nugent, 1996).

Therefore, despite the tendency to blame others for the troubles besetting the fisheries sectors of individual member states, the EU collectively has been gradually, albeit reluctantly, facing up to the fact that fish stock supplies are in decline and, in the case of some species, seriously threatened (Nugent, 1997). From both an economic and an environmental perspective, continued reductions in TACs, national quotas and fleet sizes are unavoidable if the industry is to survive at all. The speed at which these adjustments take place depends to a large extent on member states' willingness to confront the domestic political backlash from their respective fishing communities.

Conclusion

Substantial reform of the CAP has been on the agenda of the Community for at least two decades. It has been kept there by pressure emanating from a variety of sources. These include member states (such as the UK) who have been critical of its share of the EU budgets. Pressure has also come from sources external to the EU, particularly the United States, for instance during the Uruguay Round of GATT negotiations. Factors such as the creation of the SEM as well as changing consumer preferences and environmental concerns have put further weight behind the reform process. Renewed GATT negotiations and the implications for agriculture of CEEC enlargement will continue to ensure that CAP reform figures prominently on EU agendas after 2000.

Although actual reform of the CAP has been somewhat piecemeal, limited policy trends are evident. The reforms are shaping an industry which is increasingly open to world market competition, which is supported less by EU production-linked subsidies and more by direct income support. Increasingly too, the industry is responding to the demands of environmental and consumer lobbies. There is also a tendency towards fewer but larger farms, and a corresponding exodus from the land of many smaller producers. More specifically, as a result of the GATT talks the reduction of export refunds for exporters of agricultural products exposes the highly priced products of EU farmers to greater competition in world markets. The gradual lowering of EU import thresholds enables more agricultural imports from other countries to compete with EU farmers in their home markets.

With the creation of the SEM the harmonisation of production processing and marketing standards is leading to more market integration, which has the effect of marginally lowering farmers' input costs, but certainly puts increased competitive pressures on the market for agricultural products and processed goods. In the CAP the freezing or reduction of common prices for agricultural products has also gradually pushed EU agricultural prices closer to world price levels. Added to this, 'set aside' schemes, agricultural stabilisers and quotas reduce the budgetary cost of the CAP but may also have the effect of reducing EU farmers' share of the European market in agricultural goods. The growing emphasis of EU policy makers on direct income support, however, maintains the principle that EU farmers should be protected. This may also be the method of protecting farmers which has the lowest budgetary cost. The efforts by policy makers to placate environmentalists by paying some farmers to be guardians of the countryside also offers a way of keeping some farmers in gainful employment. Finally, the renationalisation of many of these policies or the transformation of the CAP into a common rural policy are just some of the possible directions in which the EU could move as the original objectives laid out in the Treaty of Rome become increasingly obsolete.

The CFP has encountered difficulties with the member states and also with third countries. The pressure to conserve fish stocks and the need to address the problems caused to the fishing industry by the method of distributing quotas have led to a long series of disputes (particularly between the UK and Spain) over the CFP. However, as in the case of the CAP, it has proved to be easier to create a common policy than to find solutions to problems that arise from the distribution effects of such common policies.

A major lesson of the CAP and the CFP appears to be that policies that redistribute from consumers to producers (the CAP), or between producers in different member states (the CFP), can create major problems. Furthermore, these common policies encourage the development of strong vested interests among those who are affected by the redistribution who make it very difficult to reach economically rational solutions to the problems that arise from these common policies.

References

Agra Europe February 1991a Green Europe Supplement, p. 17, London.
Agra Europe 1992a, 3 July, p. 2, London.
Agra Europe 1992b, 10 July, p. 3, London.
Agra Europe 1992c, 6 November 1992, p. 3 and 13 November p. 1, London.
Agra Europe 1991b, 17 January, CAP Monitor, p. 201, London.
Agra Europe 1993, 27 November, p. 16, London.

Agra Europe 1995a, 23 June, p. 2, London.

Agra Europe 1995b, 10 March, p. 4, London.

Agra Europe 1995c, May 1995, p. 2, London.

Commission 1983 Implications for the agricultural sector of the lack of matching degree of integration in the other areas of Community Policy, *Green Europe*, Brussels.

Commission 1991a *The Week in Europe*, Brussels.

Commision 1991b *Green Europe*, January 1991, p. 15; Communication of the Commission to the European Parliament – The development and future of the CAP, Brussels.

Commission 1987 The Commission Agricultural Policy and its Reform, *European Bulletin*, Brussels.

Commission 1996 The CAP and Enlargement, *European Economy*, Report 2.

Commission 1997 *Agenda 2000: For a stronger and wider Union*, Communication from the Commission to the European Parliament, Brussels.

Coleman D 1990 *GATT Negotiations and their Likely Effect on British Agriculture*, Manchester University.

The Economist 1993, 25 September 1993, p. 54.

Financial Times 1993a, 21 November, p. 1.

Financial Times 1993b, 18 March 1993, p. 32.

Financial Times 1993c, 16 September 1993, p. 6 and 21 September, p. 1.

Financial Times, 1993d, 4 February, p. 30.

Ford B J 1996 *BSE: The Facts*, Corgi, London.

Grant W 1997 *The Common Agricultural Policy*, Macmillan, p. 197.

Hill B 1993 Agriculture, Johnson P (ed.) *European Industries*, Edward Elgar, Aldershot.

The Independent 1991, 5 February, p. 10.

Irish Farmers Journal 1990, 4 July, p. 9.

Matthews A 1988 *The Challenge of 1992 for the Rural Economy*, TEAGASC-AFDA Conference Paper, Dublin.

Middlemas K 1995 *Orchestrating Europe*, Fontana, London.

Nugent N (ed.) 1995 *The European Union 1994: Annual Review of Activities*, Blackwell, Cambridge.

Nugent N (ed.) 1996 *The European Union 1995: Annual Review of Activities*, Blackwell, Cambridge.

Nugent N (ed.) 1997 *The European Union 1996: Annual Review of Activities*, Blackwell, Cambridge.

Swinbank A 1993 CAP reform, *Journal of Common Markets Studies*, Vol. 31, No. 3, September, pp. 360–77.

Further reading

Commission 1994 *European Economy: Reports and Studies*, Office for Official Publications of the European Communities, Luxembourg.

Pelkans J 1997 *European Integration; Methods and Economic Analysis*, Longman, Harlow.

The Single Market Review 1997 *Processed foodstuffs*, Commission and Kogan Page, Brussels.

12

External trade policy

Keith Penketh

Introduction

The external trade policy of the EU is also known as the Common Commercial Policy (CCP). It does not, however, embrace all external economic relations of the EU. These may include overseas aid, foreign investment and business co-operation, where the trade effect is often indirect rather than direct. The focus of the CCP is upon the external trade of the EU. Article 113 of the Treaty of Rome defines the CCP as encompassing those external trade principles of member states that are common.

The following policy areas constitute the core of the CCP:

1. a common external tariff (CET);
2. establishing and managing trade agreements with the rest of the world;
3. the uniform application of trade policy instruments.

The implications of the use of the word 'common' require further explanation. It does not imply that in relation to the CET there is tariff uniformity across all imported commodities. The usage of the word common does not imply that trade agreements between the EU and countries outside the EU are identical. There are marked differences in bilateral agreements signed between the EU and other countries or groups. The use of the word common implies that there is a common application of the three practices constituting the CCP across all the members of the EU.

Significance of external trade

The relative significance of external trade can be gleaned from an inspection of Table 12.1 Clearly, intra-EU trade is of higher value than extra-EU trade.

A shift towards intra-EU trade and away from extra-EU trade has gradually taken place. There are several factors which have brought about this shift:

- The impact of the CET on intra-EU trade that arises from trade diversion/creation effects.
- Enhanced use of non-tariff barriers against external trade as distinct from internal trade.

Table 12.1 Relative significance of intra- and extra-EU exports (as % of GDP)

Country	Intra-Community exports	Extra-Community exports
EU 15 (1993)	13.1	8.0
UK (1993)	9.8	8.4
Germany (1995)	12.0	8.8
IRL (1995)	46.0	18.2
BEL/LUX (1995)	43.0	14.4

Source: adapted from *European Economy*, No. 60, 1995

- The SEM programme has reduced non-tariff barriers (NTBs) in the EU and thereby stimulated intra-EU trade.
- Growth of the EU from the original six members to fifteen members, producing the effect of internalising what had been external trade.
- Structure of EU external trade was not weighted sufficiently upon the commodities that had experienced the most rapid growth of world trade.

Aims of the Common Commercial Policy

The President of the European Commission, Jacques Santer, has defined the aim of the CCP as 'giving European exporters access to world markets through bilateral, regional and multilateral trade relationships' (Santer, 1995). However, this is only part of the effect of the CCP. In addition to the highlighted effect upon exports all three aspects of the CCP have implications for imports into the EU. The aim of the CCP appears to be to secure for the EU effects that are inimical to the development of a trade deficit between the EU and other contracting parties. The CCP is often viewed as mercantilist in approach, significantly distorting a trading order based upon comparative advantage. Employment protection has been a significant raison d'être of commercial policy as practised by the EU.

It can be argued that if the EU fully endorsed the principles of free trade then a re-direction of commercial policy in support of the objectives of the World Trade Organisation (WTO) would be needed. A global approach, where policy is shifted away from bilateral agreements and towards multilateral agreements, appears appropriate. If this is rejected then there must be features of bilateral deals which support an abrogation of free and open trade. It is possible to argue that the practice of free trade has deficiencies that call for a more measured approach (Krugman, 1988). Nevertheless, arguments have been raised against the development of movements such as regional trading areas that may limit the movement towards free trade. These movements are considered to lead to harmful effects in terms of the efficiency of resource allocation: 'Meddling with free trade or factor mobility supports an otherwise unsustainable productive specialisation which reduces welfare, re-distributes income from consumers to protected factor owners and in the long run stifles an economy's facility to adjust' (Boschek, 1996). Moreover, the intellectual case against free trade has been questioned: 'nearly all challenges to free trade are based upon fallacious reasoning' (Bhagwati, 1989).

Justification for protection in the 1970s and 1980s was based on arguments that there were significant differences that existed between private and social values and costs. Therefore, a case emerged to support policies that encouraged preferential trade because of market imperfections and externalities. Current arguments for fair trade, as opposed to free trade, come principally from those who allege that the international playing field is not level (Tyson, 1992). On the one hand, conditions of work and wages in developing countries are alleged to drive down wages and reduce the demand for labour in the developed countries. On the other hand, the associated costs of environmental protection observed principally by the developed countries are allegedly damaging to their balance of trade.

According to orthodox theory, in the long run beneficial patterns based upon comparative costs will prevail. However, in practice, there may be short-run dislocations, from beneficial trade patterns, caused by imperfections and rigidity in markets, for example monetary mechanisms that react slowly or inflexible factor price adjustment. Adjustment burdens associated with, for example, the costs of environmental protection may be placed upon developing countries, but they are least able to shoulder this burden. It is, in consequence, unsurprising that large parts of the underdeveloped world oppose the wholesale adoption of measures designed to promote 'fair' trade. The Commission has begun to discuss the use of 'fair trade' concepts with regard to the development of the CCP, particularly with regard to environmental conditions, working and employment practices (Commission, 1996b and 1997b).

A distinction can be made between a policy which constitutes 'protection' and a policy which reflects 'protectionism'. Protection is regarded as a legitimate policy to pursue because it is an attempt to protect domestic industry from unfair trade practices. Protectionism is an attempt to shield domestic industry from external trade which can be described as fair, and is hence a practice to be abjured.

Many disputes surround the designation of a trade practice with regard to whether they are fair or unfair. The distinction between the two practices is not clear-cut. For instance, retaliatory measures used against a country which has not implemented a certain environmental standard may be regarded as an act of protection by a developed country, but may be deemed an act of protectionism by developing countries.

Principal developments influencing EU policy

Two major developments have influenced the nature of EU commercial policy. First, the SEA changed the way in which control over commercial policy was shared between the nation states and the EU. Shorn of tariff-making powers under the Treaty of Rome, member states had turned to erecting NTBs against unwanted imports. Countries had negotiated Voluntary Export Restraints (VERs) with the aim of limiting the importation of 'sensitive' goods. Major commodities affected by these restraints were motor vehicles, steel, machinery, and electrical equipment. The passing of the SEA, which aimed to sweep away all internal barriers to trade, made national agreements of this nature redundant. The inability to

Box 12.1 Summary of the principal Uruguay Round agreements

Feature

1	INDUSTRIAL TARIFFS Average 5 per cent in 1993	Developed countries to cut tariffs on industrial goods by more than one-third.
2	AGRICULTURE High farm subsidies and cut price surpluses squeezing out more efficient producers	Subsidies to be cut over a six-year period and export subsidies reduced by 36 per cent.
3	SERVICES No international trade rules over services (banking, insurance, tourism, telecommunications, construction, accountancy and TV)	A basic MFN agreement signed.
4	INTELLECTUAL PROPERTY Ineffective enforcement of national laws	Governments are required to provide procedures and remedies under law to ensure that intellectual property rights can be enforced.
5	TEXTILES AND CLOTHING Quantitative restrictions and allegedly high import tariffs	MFA quotas progressively dismantled over ten years and tariffs reduced.
6	NON-TARIFF BARRIERS Extensive and serving to restrict fair trade	A series of measures designed to restrict the use of NTBs to unfair trade and not serve as a hindrance to fair trade.

Source: Based on *News of the Uruguay Round*, GATT 1994

enter the protected market of one country could now be overcome by exporting to member states that did not use VERs, once frontier controls were removed. In consequence, EU-wide agreements replaced national agreements. A well-known arrangement is the Community-wide understanding negotiated with Japan relating to motor vehicles. It is due to expire in 1999, after which vehicle imports from Japan are to be liberalised. A fuller discussion of this topic is given in Chapter 16 .

The second major influence on EU commercial policy was undoubtedly the GATT deal of December 1993, which marked the conclusion of the Uruguay round. This agreement established the WTO, which was charged with the task, among other things, of monitoring external trade policies. An outline of the main components of the Uruguay Round is given in Box 12.1. Some of the implications of the creation of WTO for developments in the external relations policy of the EU are discussed in Chapters 11 and 16.

Trade agreements

The treaty-making powers of the EU allow it to negotiate agreements with third countries which, when related to trade, go under the generic name of 'free-trade agreements'. Each agreement is negotiated with reference to the particular circumstances of the countries involved in the agreement. Therefore, although their application by countries of the EU may be common, their impact upon the individual countries of the EU or non-EU signatories and third countries is not of the same magnitude. A hierarchy of negotiated agreements exists, ranging from those that have few direct implications for trade to those that offer the most extensive of concessions.

Non-preferential trade and cooperation agreements have no direct implications for trade between the signatories. An agreement between the EU and the Gulf Co-operation Council signed in 1986 was of this nature. Cooperation and joint ventures in a number of fields were envisaged. Another example is the proposal that the EU concludes a cooperation agreement with Australia, covering investment, competition, consumer protection, education, information and culture. Further information on these and other non-preferential agreements can be found on the web pages of DG I (http://www.europa.eu.int/en/comm/dgol).

Two kinds of preferential agreements exist – reciprocal and non-reciprocal. With the former, reciprocity in trade concessions is required. Agreements with the EFTA countries were reciprocal; those with the Mediterranean countries are non-reciprocal. Where countries aspire to establish a free-trade area (FTA) with the EU, or indeed to seek eventual membership, then Association Agreements are signed. A summary of the Association Agreements of the EU is provided in Chapter 14.

The EU places special emphasis upon Mediterranean countries in an attempt, through trade, to secure stability in this region. The objective is to establish a Euro-Mediterranean free trade area by 2010 (Commission, 1997). A fuller discussion of existing relationships of the EU is found in Chapters 13 to 15.

Agreements with European countries

As a major supplier of EU imports and also a major recipient of EU exports, some of the EFTA countries felt dangerously exposed after the passage of the SEA. In 1994 agreement was reached to establish a European Economic Area (EEA) that included all member states of the EU and Austria, Finland, Iceland, Norway and Sweden. However, Switzerland remained outside the EEA and, because Liechtenstein was in a customs union with Switzerland, it could not join the EEA in 1994. The result of a referendum held in 1992 led to a rejection of EEA membership by Switzerland. The EEA established the SEM rules on free movement and the adoption of EU policies on competition, social, environmental issues, and Community rules on company law and consumer protection. There was no commitment for the EFTA countries to harmonise taxes or to adopt the CAP. The EEA shrank in number in 1995 when Austria, Finland and Sweden were admitted to membership of the EU. The Swiss rejected EU membership, as did the Norwegians.

On 1 January 1996 agreement was reached to establish a customs union between the EU and Turkey. Greek approval of Turkish membership was only secured when a timetable was agreed for the admission of the Republic of Cyprus to full membership of the EU. Turkey has a long-standing application to become a full member of the EU. However, concerns about the human rights record of Turkey and the economic costs of admitting such a large and relatively poor country have prevented any meaningful progress on the issue of full membership. The possibility of large migration from Turkey to the other member states (particularly Germany) has also made it difficult for the member states to agree on a viable way forward with regard to full membership. However, the willingness of the EU to enter negotiations for full membership with some of the CEECs while maintaining a distance from Turkey has caused considerable harm to relationships between the EU and Turkey. The member states have differences of opinion about Turkish membership. Greece is fundamentally opposed to full membership, Germany and France have strong reservations, but the UK is supportive of membership and favours developing close economic and political relationships as a means to achieve full membership. These differences of opinion among the member states and the political and economic problems that arise from Turkish membership are likely to have a strong influence on the development of the relationship between the EU and Turkey.

Bilateral or multilateral deals?

The widespread use of bilateral deals has led to debate on whether these deals are consistent with the obligations, specified in articles of the Treaty of Rome, to work towards global free trade. It is agreed that not only are bilateral deals unnecessary but that they are damaging to free trade on a global basis. This view is also held by some economists (Bhagwati, 1994 and 1996). However, Jacques Santer argued that bilateral deals help to open up world markets (Santer, 1996). Nevertheless, critics assert that bilateral deals enable the EU to protect sensitive industries such as agriculture, motor vehicles, steel, machinery and electrical equipment and thereby lead to accusations of protectionism. There has been criticism that the Commission neglects structural policy and simply reacts on a piece-meal basis to events. This view was evident when France opposed an agreement with South Africa because of a lack of consideration of the effects on the CAP. Indeed, farm ministers claim that they should play a greater role in setting the terms of any future trade agreements (*Financial Times*, 1996).

Views opposing bilateral trade agreements have been voiced by the USA. A former US ambassador in Brussels advised the EU not to sign any more trade agreements because they corrode the multilateral trading system (*Financial Times*, 1996). However, the US is seeking to promote its own regional trade agency NAFTA and is involved in discussions to found a Pacific Rim free-trade area (APEC). These developments indicate that the USA may be moving away from its postwar leadership of the free-trade movement. The EU may be seen as the natural successor to the USA in international trade negotiations. There are signs that the EU is taking a more active role especially in relation to such issues as labour standards, the environment, government procurement and investment (Commission, 1996b and 1997b).

It is possible that the WTO may extend bilateral free-trade deals made between the EU and other countries to other sectors such as agriculture. The possibilities of such developments have contributed to the reluctance to extend trade agreements and contributed to the decision, in 1996, to delay the finalisation of trade agreements between the EU and Mexico and South Africa. Opposition to trade agreements between non-EU countries has arisen from EU exporters who complain that, in the markets of Asia and North America, they are disadvantaged because of the existence of bilateral trade agreements in that area. However, the developing countries have opposed the insertion of social or environmental clauses in trade agreements. Instead, they pushed for more progress on textiles and agriculture. For all these reasons it is probable that the focus of the EU in the future will be to make more multilateral rather than bilateral agreements.

The WTO is making some progress in the negotiaions to liberalise trade in services (GATS) and in other areas. For example, at the Singapore Conference of the WTO in December 1996 a multilateral agreement by the EU, Canada, the US and Japan was reached to eliminate tariffs on products in international telecommunications and IT equipment by the year 2000. These developments have led some to postulate that multilateralism may become more important – 'discriminatory trade policies make no sense when production becomes increasingly globalised. With the WTO in place, multilateralism need no longer be discarded as unworkable' (Bhagwati, 1996).

Methods of protection against unfair trade

The CCP provides a series of measures to protect the member states from unfair trade practices: A variety of measures can legitimately be used by EU member countries against unfair trading practices by third countries. Details of the measures available under the CCP can be found on the web pages of DG I (http://www.europa.eu.int/en/comm/dgol). The following methods of protection may be adopted to inhibit an allegedly unfair flow of trade:

1. anti-dumping duties;
2. countervailing duties;
3. safeguard measures;
4. surveillance measures;
5. trade deflection measures;
6. the new commercial policy instrument;
7. counterfeit goods measures.

Dumping

To qualify for protection by the imposition of an anti-dumping duty, an imported commodity must satisfy two conditions. First, the good must be 'dumped' and, secondly, the import must threaten material injury to an established domestic producer (GATT, Article 6). Economists have not always been wholly condemnatory of the practice of dumping. For instance, dumping is harmful if it is not continuous. However, continuous dumping could produce consumer gains which exceeded producers' losses but sporadic dumping could displace domestic firms. If, after displacing domestic output, exporters were able to sustain a relatively high price, customers could suffer loss of consumer surplus.

Within the EU, anti-dumping rules apply to both agricultural and industrial goods. Whether a product is deemed to be dumped depends whether the price is considered to be lower than the normal value of a like product. The interpretation of 'normal value' gives scope for the use of creative accounting and gives rise to concern that anti-dumping duties are as much used for purposes of protectionism as they were for protection. After a complaint is lodged to the Commission, preliminary investigations may show that there is evidence of dumping and permit the imposition of a provisional duty. Ultimately, the Council of Ministers may impose a definitive duty. Anti-dumping duties are usually producer-specific and are subject to a 'sunset clause', i.e. they lapse five years after their imposition.

An exporter whose goods are subject to an anti-dumping duty may have an interest in circumventing the duty. Thus, part of the manufacture of a good may be diverted to a third country outside the EU, or indeed to a country within the EU. To meet this contingency the EU has devised Anti-Circumvention Measures. These consist of establishing the conditions under which the origin attributable to a particular good may be defined. The so-called 'screwdriver plants' in the EU, where the final assembly of a good takes place, are subject to a value-added proportion to avoid the incidence of an anti-dumping duty. For instance, if a good has more than 40 per cent local content then anti-dumping duties are not levied. There is, however, no uniformity of practice as it is not easy to secure the imposition of anti-dumping duties on products assembled within the EU. Conditions that must be satisfied have been designed to reduce overt interference with the inflow of foreign direct investment. Positive action against circumvention is likely to arise only under the following conditions:

1. there is an anti-dumping duty in force on imports of the finished product;
2. the assembly operation has to be carried out by a party who is related to or associated with the manufacture of the finished product;
3. the value of parts originating in the country of assembly of the finished product has to exceed by 50 per cent the value of all other parts and materials used;
4. account must be taken of the extent of research and development carried out by the assembler.

These conditions taken together are very restrictive. They make action to secure redress against 'screwdriver plants' unlikely except in a minority of cases. Obviously, this provides potential for friction within the EU, both at an intra-industry and at an inter-country level. Further discussion on the topic of screwdriver plants and FDI is included in Chapter 15.

Countervailing duties

These are authorised to neutralise the effect of subsidies under Article 6 of GATT. 'A countervailing duty may be imposed for the purpose of offsetting any subsidy bestowed directly or indirectly in the country of origin or export upon the manufacture, production, export or transport of any product whose release for free circulation in the Community causes injury'. Countervailing duties are not applied on the companies suspected of benefiting from subsidies but are imposed collectively on all imports originating from a particular third country. All countervailing measures have to be terminated within five years of their imposition. Tighter controls were imposed under the Uruguay Round, but generally the green light for limited subsidies was given where regional problems merited their use or where it was felt advisable to subsidise research and development costs. Additionally, in order to assist the transformation of centrally planned economies and LDCs, countries with less than $1000 per capita GNP are exempt from the Uruguay Round prohibitions on export subsidies.

Safeguard measures

An exception to the principle of not imposing quantitative restrictions on imports occurs where imports threaten to cause serious injury to domestic producers. If this is accepted by the Commission then safeguard measures can be imposed, consisting of quotas. The measures introduced must not exceed four years and are to be progressively liberalised. Under the Uruguay Round Agreement all existing safeguards, taken under Article 19 of the GATT, must be terminated not later than eight years after they were first applied. Steel, cotton textiles, and motor vehicles are industries subject to safeguards.

Surveillance

Unilateral action can be taken in matters of surveillance of exporting activities that may constitute unfair trading practices. Evidence may be gathered prior to the establishment of a case for Safeguard measures. Import licences may be required upon the importation of certain imports under surveillance which, nonetheless, are not subject to limitation. They merely provide the evidence from which to pursue, where appropriate, a redress to the alleged damage inflicted on the domestic industry. Since the coming of the SEM a more open trade policy has been adopted and surveillance measures have declined significantly.

Trade deflection measures

Where imported goods are subject to quotas (textiles and related products), an exporter subject to a restriction may attempt to gain access to an EU country through the unprotected market of another. Restrictions on deflected imports require application to the Commission and also authorisation.

Textiles are held to be most subject to Article 115 authorisations, which stipulate that the Commission shall authorise member states to take the necessary protective measures, the conditions and details of which it shall determine. Since the coming of the SEM with open internal borders, national restrictions hardly make sense and, in consequence, Community-wide restrictions were imposed.

New commercial policy instrument

Unfair trading practices are seen to relate not only to imports, but also to unfair competition with EU exports in third markets. Illicit commercial practices used by third countries were the reason why the CCP was extended in this direction. The Commission adopts an investigatory role but the Council of Ministers decides upon the nature of the retaliation. Measures can be quite wide in scope, varying from quantitative controls on the country's imports to import tariffs and the withdrawal of concessions granted in a trade agreement.

Counterfeit goods

Responsibility for action is here left with the national government. Where evidence is positive, the goods may be disposed of or other measures of equivalent effect taken. Threatened domestic industries often react by claiming that imports are counterfeit.

The unfair trading measures of the CCP may allow the EU to practise protectionist policies. There is evidence that the EU, together with other developed economies, uses trade regulation measures to protect its domestic market from what is considered to be unfair competition (Grimwade, 1996).

Conclusion

The two principal aspects of EU commercial policy are the regional dimension and the structural or fair-trading dimension. The EU maintains that the regional dimension supports deals that lead to a more rapid removal of barriers to trade. The WTO opposes this practice, as do the US and Japan. The argument is that weak countries are disadvantaged because sensitive sectors such as agriculture are often omitted from consideration or, when they are not, anti-dumping practices and other trade protection measures proliferate.

There is undoubtedly a shift from the bilateral to multilateral negotiations. The growth of regional economic associations such as NAFTA, APEC, Mercosur and AFTA may shift the EU towards multilateral negotiations with groups of regional trading bodies Additionally, the sectoral impact upon agriculture of many bilateral deals has resulted in internal criticism of the implications of these arrangements, with agriculture ministers in the EU often opposing the bilateral approach.

The eighth GATT round – the Uruguay Round – directly addressed a variety of trade practices that were used by countries to protect domestic industries. Their implementation by acceding parties will produce improved access to their markets. Whether, in the event, trade practices will match trade agreements, is a matter that only the future will reveal.

Attempts by the EU to advance conservation and social concern have run into some opposition, especially from LDCs who claim that the practice is simply a disguised form of protectionism (Wrighton, 1996). However, the operation and development of the WTO should give impetus to globally based discussions and shift the basis of agreement more towards the multilateral form of negotiation. Consequently, the CCP of the EU may become more and more concerned with relationships with WTO and with other regional trading bodies. However, important bilateral economic and trading relations with the US, Japan and the NICs are likely to continue because of the important trading interrelationship between these countries and the EU.

References

Bhagwati J 1989 Is free trade passé after all?, *Weltwirtschaftliches Archiv*, No. 125.

Bhagwati J 1996 The High Cost of Free Trade Areas, *Financial Times*, 30 May.

Boschek R 1996 Trade Policy of the EU, *Financial Times*, 8 March.

Brittan L 1996 New Tactics for EU Trade, *Financial Times*, 11 November. Cat. No. CF9295813END, Brussels.

Commission 1996b *The Trading System and Internationally Recognised Labour Standards*, COM(96)402, Brussels.

Commission 1997b *The Global Challenge of International Trade: A Market Access Strategy For The European Union*, Brussels.

Financial Times 1996 Leader The Road from Singapore, 16 December.

GATT 1994 *News of the Uruguay Round*.

Grimwade N 1996 Anti-dumping Policy After The Uruguay Round: An Appraisal, *National Institute Economic Review*, February, pp. 98–105.

Heidensohn K 1995 *Europe and World Trade*, Pinter, London.

Krugman P 1988 Is Free Trade Passé?, *Economic Perspectives*, Vol. 24, pp. 35–47.

Santer J 1995 *The Commission's Programme for 1996*: presentation to the European Parliament, 12 December.

Santer J 1996 *The Commission's Programme for 1997*: presentation to the European Parliament, 22 October.

Tyson L 1992 *Who's Bashing Whom? Trade Conflict in High-technology Industries*, Longman, London.

Wrighton D 1996 Social Clause in Trade Deals, *Financial Times*, 3 September.

Further reading

Allen D and Smith M 1996 External policy developments, *Journal of Common Market Studies*, Vol. 34, pp. 63–84.

Archer C and Butler F 1996 *The European Union: Structure and Process*, Pinter, London.

Commission 1995 Strengthening the Mediterranean Policy of the EU, *Bulletin of the EU*, Supplement No. 2.

Commission 1996a Trade Policy of the EC, *Bulletin of the EU*, Numbers 7, 8 and 9, Brussels.

Commission 1997a *The European Union and its partners in the Mediterranean*.

European Information Service 1996 *Fruitful discussions on external trade policy*, European Report No. 2167, 19 October.

European Information Service 1996 *Quad ministers narrow Singapore trade agenda*, European Report No. 2162, 2 October.

Falkenberg K F 1996 *The legal regulation of the European Community's external relations after the completion of the internal market*, Dartmouth.

Hindley B 1992 Anti-dumping policy after 1992, paper presented to CREDIT conference *European Trade Policy After 1992*.

Phinnemore D 1996 *The European Union and Nordic Countries*, Routledge, London.

Pinder J 1995 From Common Tariff to Great Civilian Powers in *European Community: the Building of a Union*, Oxford University Press, Oxford.

Van Bael I and Bellis J F 1995 *Anti-dumping and other trade protection laws of the EC*, CCH Editions, Bicester.

Woolcock S and Hodges M 1996 EU policy in the Uruguay Round, in H and W Wallace (eds.) *Policy Making in the EU*, 3rd edition, Oxford University Press, Oxford.

13 The EU and Central and Eastern Europe

Andrei Kuznetsov

Introduction

The Central and Eastern European countries (CEECs) share many similar features and face many similar problems inasmuch as their post-war political and economic development was influenced by the communist doctrine. The rise to power of Gorbachev in the Soviet Union in 1985, and the introduction of *perestroika* and *glasnost* movements, finally allowed the CEECs to escape from their Stalinist legacy. The collapse of communist rule in Central and Eastern Europe has triggered a very intensive process of economic restructuring in the ex-socialist countries. Post-communist regimes have generally demonstrated a willingness to break away from centrally planned models of economic development in favour of models in which market mechanisms are to play a prominent, if not a leading, role.

Developments in CEECs represented a challenge to the European Union. On the one hand, the EU sought to encourage reforms in CEECs and make them irreversible. On the other hand, the responsibility of the EU was to protect the interests of the member states in the face of a dramatic change in the political and economic situation on the European continent.

The legacy of communism

Political changes in Eastern Europe have triggered the process of marketisation, that is, the process of dismantling a Soviet-style economic mechanism and the restoration or, in some cases, the construction of a capitalist economy, with private property and market-based allocation of resources providing the basis for economic activity. Long before the initiation of reforms the European socialist countries experienced a protracted economic crisis. It existed mainly in repressed and hidden forms owing to an overwhelming state control of nearly all aspects of economic and political life. Its visible features were declining rates of economic growth, wasteful use of resources including labour and capital, a widening technological gap with advanced countries, persistent shortages on the supply side, and serious financial imbalances. The actual scale of deficiencies had not been clear until the change of political regime and elimination of central planning helped to establish the truth. The economies of Romania, Bulgaria,

Eastern Germany, Poland, the former USSR and, to a lesser degree, the former Czechoslovakia were revealed to be suffering from serious structural problems, they were badly managed, uncompetitive, and unresponsive to technological innovation.

The old central planning system has been analysed by Kornai (1986) using the concept of the 'soft budget constraint'. According to Kornai the planning system sought to maximise desired output and financial considerations were secondary to this. Efficiency in allocating resources could, therefore, not be achieved by financial criteria such as profit, as few prices were determined by market conditions, and differences between costs and the value of sales were covered by taxes and subsidies. There was also little effective competition between enterprises, and costs and revenues were determined in an arbitrary way by administrative discretion. Consequently, enterprises had little incentive to use resources efficiently, as they faced few financial pressures, that is, they operated with soft budget constraints. Indeed, the incentive was for the enterprise to acquire the maximum amount of resources possible in order to produce as much output as possible. This resulted in low productivity and a tendency to make poor quality goods. A secondary effect is that enterprise managers have little experience in setting prices, marketing and selling products, and financial control procedures.

These problems have been exacerbated by the control of foreign trade by the planning authorities. The linking of national economies to the world economy increases competition by extending sources of supply. The transfer of technical developments is also closely related to the openness of an economy to direct foreign investments, joint ventures, and licensing and patenting agreements. In Western economies the benefits of these factors have been acknowledged. In Eastern European countries under communism the costs of such a system were considered to be greater than the benefits. Trade and other economic transactions with the West were also hindered by the inconvertibility of currencies and the nature of the exchange rates. Most exchange rates were administratively determined and had little relationship to the true value of the currency. Eastern European countries also found difficulties in exporting to the West because of trade restrictions imposed on them and problems in penetrating Western markets because of the poor quality of their manufactured goods. The countries of Eastern Europe, therefore, have a legacy of poor integration into the markets of the West.

While the exact size of macroeconomic imbalances inherited by Eastern European countries is debatable, it is clear that they were serious enough to provoke an economic crisis. Hidden inflation in Poland, which existed in the form of a price gap between an official and a 'black' market, had already become hyperinflation under the last communist government, while in Romania stagnation and decay became evident in the early 1980s. However, the squeeze in the economies of Central and Eastern Europe in the 1990s would not have been so pronounced had there not been some important external shocks.

The ruinous impact of the decline in trade between the European ex-socialist countries must be placed first in the list of such shocks. Intra-COMECON trade was responsible for 40–50 per cent of their industrial exports. As COMECON collapsed at the beginning of the 1990s, East European producers, due to the poor competitiveness of their goods and also because of trade barriers imposed by the EU, failed to increase their share of Western markets quickly enough to compensate for the shrinkage in their traditional markets. Another consequence of the collapse of COMECON was the erosion of the financial position of ex-socialist countries which for years had benefited from implicit trade subsidies from the Soviet Union. Partly for political reasons and partly owing to inefficiency of the price mechanism, the Soviet Union sold its energy and non-food raw materials to Eastern Europe at prices below prevailing world market prices, and bought manufactured goods from Eastern Europe at prices above world prices. Experts estimate the amount of transfer to be billions of US dollars (Marrese and Vanous, 1988). Finally, the Gulf War of early 1991 not only disrupted trade with some Arab countries but also inflated world oil prices, thus aggravating the economic situation in Central and Eastern European countries, all of which depended heavily on imported oil.

The agenda for reforms

The task of marketisation has proved to be extremely challenging owing to the precarious state of the CEECs and the difference between the two economic models. Problems range from technical deficiencies, such as lack of functional capital markets and credit systems required for efficient capital formation and resource allocation, to a more general issue of changing prevailing behavioural patterns at all levels of society. They also involve finding the shortest ways towards creating jobs with high value added and wealth-generating capacities, improving labour productivity, and providing sustained technological innovation in order to increase national competitiveness in the face of the growing importance of international markets. What makes a systematic change of European Soviet-style economies particularly challenging is the fact that reformers cannot rely on any of the elements of the existing economic mechanism as being adequate to the standards of a market-based system. The task facing reformers is to redesign this mechanism, but at the same time to avoid a complete economic breakdown following from the progressive disintegration of their economic and political systems.

Although economies in the countries of Central and Eastern Europe basically imitated a Soviet pattern, initial economic conditions for marketisation were not identical across the region. Two countries, Hungary and Yugoslavia, had made some advance towards a decentralised open economy, while others had stuck to a conventional rigid central planning model. National peculiarities, in particular political constraints which were different in the different countries of the region, conditioned short-term policy choice and to a lesser degree long-term strategies. At the same time there appears to have been no great difference in opinion in the former socialist countries, as well as in the West, as to the nature of the essential stages of transition towards a market-type economy.

The first necessary stage is *economic stabilisation*, which implies the initial adaptation of the existing economic mechanism (prices, credit, money supply, wages) to the standards of the capitalist system. Macroeconomic stabilisation is essential in order to eliminate dangerous financial imbalances inherited from central planning and to kick-start the price mechanism which, under the market economy, facilitates the allocation of resources.

The second stage is a radical *institutional reform* aimed essentially at the restoration of private property and competition. Privatisation in the broadest sense is meant to eliminate the indeterminacy of capital ownership in the former socialist states, which was one of the main reasons for inefficient employment of capital assets in the period of the command economy. Privatisation is also expected to induce changes in entrepreneurial behaviour and to make enterprises profit-motivated. Microeconomic reform is also necessary to create a market relationship between the owners of capital and the manager of the firm which is more conducive to better performance by enterprises. This presupposes the adoption of new laws (for example, bankruptcy legislation), but no less important is the creation of an appropriate institutional environment, including investment banks, capital exchanges, auditing and consulting firms and other types of business services. Another important issue is to put an end to the monopolistic position of producers in the market by the break-up of large enterprises and through new business formation.

The third element, which is closely linked to the second, is *capacity restructuring*, that is, the shift of capital and labour from primary and machine-building industries to those producing consumer goods and high-tech products, and from industrial production to services. Moreover, integration of the ex-socialist economies in the international market is normally regarded as an important component of such a restructuring.

Early difficulties

The immediate consequences of marketisation have proved to be quite disappointing. From the outset a temporary deterioration of performance was regarded as an inevitable cost of transition. Indeed, marketisation in Central and Eastern Europe may be accurately described as a transition from one system of development with a related set of priorities and ruling principles, institutions and regulatory mechanisms to a completely different, if not an opposite, system. Such a profound qualitative change could not but provoke some drastic adjustments. However, the actual scale and persistence of the crisis vastly exceeded expectations, as a falling national output, growing inflation and unemployment and financial imbalances led to significant declines in output (Table 13.1). As the economic improvement expected from market reforms had been late to materialise, increasing scepticism with respect to the validity of the chosen strategy of change became noticeable by the middle of 1992. Characteristically, the UN Economic Survey of Europe in 1991–92 analysed the economic situation in Eastern and Central Europe with the heading 'Reform results to date: more pain than gain?'.

These new challenges, including devastating hyperinflation, growing shortages and deteriorating foreign debt position, required immediate action. This took the form of monetary and fiscal restrictions, price liberalisation, the devaluation of domestic currencies and wage guidelines. Because of the speed

Table 13.1   GDP growth

Year	Bulgaria	Czech Republic+	Hungary	Poland	Romania	Russia
1983–88	1.4	1.8	1.4	4.2	2.9	1.8
1989	−0.4	−0.7	−0.2	−0.2	−5.8	0.2
1990	−17.5	−1.5	−3.3	−11.6	−9.9	−2
1991	−25.7	−25.7	−10.2	−7	−13.7	−12
1992	−7.5	−7.5	−4	2.5	−9	−14
1993	−4.8	−2	−2	3.5	1	−10
1994	1.8	2.6	2.9	5.3	4	−12
1995	2.6	4.8	1.5	7	6.9	−4
1996*	−9	4	0.8	4.9	4.5	−4
1997**	−2	4	2.5	5.2	5	0

Notes:
+ Czechoslovakia prior to 1993
* estimate
** forecast
Sources: adapted from *PlanEcon* Report, No. 38–42, 1992, *Business Central Europe*, The Annual 1996–97

and radicalism of reforms this approach was dubbed 'shock therapy'. It had already been used in some developing countries. What made the difference was the swiftness of applying these measures and the fact that they were introduced for the first time in a non-capitalist economy characterised by the absence of a comprehensive banking system, labour and capital markets and developed taxation. Unlike most developing countries, the CEECs' stabilisation took place in a situation of social accord, as a new polity was enjoying enormous public confidence, permitting reformers to realise some very daring projects. This 'social pact' was based on the assumption that reforms would produce a swift result in the form of amelioration of the living conditions of the majority of the population. The Polish experience has demonstrated that 'shock therapy' was effective in eliminating pervasive shortages of consumer goods. At the same time, however, the extent of poverty has not diminished and may have grown, while a relatively small group of people with very high incomes has been emerging.

Currently, one can see that three very different Eastern European countries have the best prospects for fast recovery. These are Poland, Hungary and the Czech Republic. Since 1994 they have been showing growth rates well above the OECD average. It is also forecast that growth in Poland and the Czech Republic will remain strong in the next few years, while in Hungary it will be more in line with the area's average (OECD, 1997). Stabilisation plans pursued in these countries in the early 1990s included drastic price and trade liberalisation, targeting the real money supply and real interest rates, large devaluations and internal convertibility, extreme fiscal pressure on the state sector, rigid budget policy, wage restrictions and, in the longer run, large-scale privatisation. Nonetheless, nowhere in the CEECs was the course of economic austerity implemented consistently enough to claim that 'shock therapy' was fully applied. The actual practice of reforms has been very individual and, due mainly to social pressures, characterised by opportunism and manoeuvring not provided for in the theoretical schemes. This suggests that there are no generally valid recipes for success without reference to country-specific conditions. The more it became clear that the transformation was going to split the nation into losers and winners, the more important became the social and political dimensions of reforms. Governments were tempted to postpone unpopular decisions, introducing last-minute changes in already accepted policies or, in contrast, to rush into measures favourable to particular interest groups. This often distorted the contemplated effects of reforms and made the process of transformation more uncertain in terms of results.

It is important to realise the relative nature of recovery even in the most successful of transitional economies. The reform process is well advanced, but in 1997 Poland had only attained its 1989 level of GDP. Slovenia, the Czech Republic, Slovakia and Romania were edging towards the 90 per cent mark while at the other end of the spectrum countries like Lithuania and Ukraine were still struggling to get over the 40 per cent mark (Business Central Europe, 1997). As the social cost of economic reforms continues to be high it is not altogether certain that, in the case of quite a few countries, the most difficult stage of transition is behind them.

The challenges of marketisation

There are three major adjustment problems that have emerged with the onset of the reform programmes, namely inflation, unemployment, and deindustrialisation.

Inflation

There are some very strong arguments in favour of a price adjustment at an early stage of reform. First, there can be no market allocation leading to internal and external adjustment in the absence of reliable price signals but, if administered prices and market prices 'coexist', price indicators such as enterprise profits do not convey much meaning. Secondly, market-clearing prices are necessary to determine the real value of fixed assets (which under central planning were often given arbitrary evaluations), in order to help resume a normal investment process.

The problem with price liberalisation is that, in order not to allow a switch to market prices to be translated into sustained hyper-inflation, it is necessary to enact very firm anti-inflationary measures. However, such measures carry the risk of inducing recession. Stabilisation reforms succeeded mainly in establishing more realistic prices and exchange rates, the elimination of queuing, and in improving the quality of goods and services as a result of increasing foreign competition. A sharp price rise during the initial stage of stabilisation had been expected. However, many countries found themselves stuck in this stage for much longer than had been foreseen. Persistent double- to triple-digit inflation became a fact of life in most CEECs in the early 1990s and, with the exception of the Czech Republic, continued into the late 1990s. In 1996 in Bulgaria inflation was still in excess of 150 per cent. Even in Hungary and Poland, which belong to the leading group of transitional economies, the rate of inflation is four to five times above the average for the OECD countries.

Unemployment

Unemployment rates have risen dramatically during the transition, creating an uneasy situation in societies previously enjoying full employment. Registered unemployment leapt from almost zero to over 7 million in 1995, of which 40 per cent were out of work for more than 12 months (Eatwell *et al.*, 1995). The economic and political cost of unemployment is enormous, making it a serious obstacle to restructuring the transition economies, because substantial groups of the population lose hope of finding a job and become an under-class. This divides the society and creates social and political tension. Such 'transitional unemployment' has all the characteristics of a stagnant pool and, once in the pool, it is very difficult to get out of it (Boeri, 1997).

Governments are aware of the political discontent which growing unemployment may cause but have little to offer. Some palliative measures were introduced to relieve social tensions and introduce a social security net. They may make the governments look better in the short term but only steady economic growth will provide a long-term solution.

Deindustrialisation

Tight monetary, credit, fiscal and wage policies forced a collapse in demand which led to major problems for nationalised industries in transitional countries. In Poland, Bulgaria, Romania and former Czechoslovakia real wages dropped by 25–30 per cent and they have stayed low ever since, sometimes still below pre-reform levels. A rapidly shrinking economy drove up unemployment, which undermined demand even further. At the same time national markets were opened to previously unavailable foreign products. Local producers found themselves competing with leading international brands at the moment when they were least fit to do so. They were further disadvantaged by governmental policies that discriminated against state-owned enterprises (SOEs). Public enterprises found themselves deprived of traditional state subsidies, while the clear provisions of how the state sector was to be financed were generally absent. It was assumed that the enterprises would try to adjust to hard budget constraints by cutting costs. But macro-economic measures alone were not sufficient to bring about desirable responses. Many SOEs had a potential for market success, but could not realise it following the 'hands-off' attitude taken by governments in the CEECs in the early transition period, when assistance and protection were particularly important (Amsden, Kochanowicz and Taylor, 1994). As a result, even the most promising companies could not build upon their strengths and were overwhelmed by exposure to free-market forces to which they had no time and resources to adjust. In 1990–93 the average annual fall in industrial output for CEECs was close to 20 per cent, before eventually stabilising at levels far below those achieved in the 1980s.

Recovery of industrial production, which is the most important component of GDP, has been uneven, reflecting a generally poor investment situation. Securing investment growth has become a crucial issue, but the situation is not straightforward. Foreign investors show considerable interest in the region, but they tend to focus their activities on a very limited number of favoured destinations like Hungary and the Czech Republic. Most CEECs have to find ways to raise resources locally, which appears to be a serious obstacle to recovery considering the collapse of living standards and the inadequate development of the banking system.

Problems with privatisation

The privatisation of public property is universally regarded as another major issue in the post-communist transition process. In Eastern Germany the public sector included 8000 firms, in Poland about 7500, in former Czechoslovakia 4800, in Romania 4000, in Hungary 2500 and in Bulgaria 5000. The public sector accounted in each case for not less than 80 per cent of national value added (*The Economist*, 1991). By comparison, in the UK the much-heralded privatisation programme of the first Thatcher government involved only about 20 firms, accounting for a mere 5 per cent of value added.

All post-communist countries agreed on the need for a privatisation programme, but questions arose as to how to privatise, to what extent and how to treat the state sector in the meantime. Former Czechoslovakia provided a good example of the differences in approach to privatisation. While in the Czech Republic the political leadership put all its trust in the invisible hand of the market and started a large-scale privatisation programme, in Slovakia the government took a different approach and showed a willingness to preserve a considerable state presence in industry.

What made privatisation such a challenge were the specific features of public enterprises in socialist countries and the role they played in national economies. High concentration of production and employment in big enterprises was a general feature of socialism. In 1990, the share of industrial enterprises employing more than 500 people was 43 per cent in Czechoslovakia, 86.9 per cent in Poland, 74.5 per cent in Romania, and 72.1 per cent in Bulgaria. Also the enterprises were more narrowly specialised than is usual in the West, often with only one national producer of a particular product. The large scale of many state-owned companies aside, it was typical of state enterprises to be overmanned and to have a vast array of supporting services such as kindergartens, medical centres and holiday homes. It was obvious that they could not survive unchanged under any other conditions than those of a centrally planned economy. The economic recession has made things worse as enterprises have lost markets, reduced production, accumulated debt and discontinued their normal investment processes. As a result many enterprises seemed to be unsaleable unless a prior streamlining and financial restructuring was undertaken. However, the dominating belief has been that if large enterprises remained in state ownership they would not adapt to market conditions.

There are two principal ways of handling these problems. One reflects the perception that the duty of the government is to speed up the process, while a market mechanism is to be entrusted with the task of restructuring national property. Alternatively, microeconomic restructuring could precede or accompany the privatisation of state companies in order to increase their value and attractiveness as an asset.

The Czech Republic has chosen the first approach. There the voucher scheme has proved the most intriguing part of a large-scale privatisation programme. Each adult citizen was entitled, almost for free, to a voucher booklet allowing him or her to bid for the shares of privatised entities at public auctions. Over eight million people became owners of vouchers. In the first round of auctions, in 1992, corporate assets with a 'net book value' of about $9.3 bn were distributed to millions of new shareholders (Transition, 1992).

Nobody has yet had a chance to evaluate the full impact of voucher privatisation on the economy, but the implications of the scheme raised general scepticism outside the Czech Republic. Voucher privatisation is being blamed for lack of corporate restructuring and sluggish growth of industrial output (European Economy, 1997). Probably the main problem with this approach is that it does not provide any visible evidence that the change in ownership has promoted profit maximisation and business efficiency. As a rule, no new capital or expertise has been introduced into troubled companies. Furthermore, the individuals receiving a share in privatised enterprises, if ownership is broadly spread, do not have any influence over the specific competitiveness of the companies they come to own. The acquisition of assets involved a considerable element of chance, with some new owners discovering that their property was uncompetitive and unprofitable. In other cases enterprises, which were competitive in their operations, have fallen into the hands of incompetent individuals who lack the necessary entrepreneurial skills. As a result, business conditions in the country have remained uncertain.

The idea of prior restructuring of most enterprises is implicit in the privatisation programmes of Poland, Hungary and Bulgaria. However, financial and organisational restructuring takes time and money, and extends the period of transition during which public bodies continue to interfere with economic processes. To many this seems unacceptable. Only Germany provides an example of privatisation based on prior comprehensive micro-economic restructuring. In July 1990 10,500 East German enterprises, employing four million people, were put in the care of a government agency called the Treuhandanstalt. The Treuhandanstalt was entrusted with a mandate to maximise the returns on the sales of state assets while ensuring optimum employment. Its stated policy was to privatise quickly. However, if a company could not be sold the Treuhandanstalt's policy was to attempt to restructure it to salvage at least the core business or any other viable part. By June 1992 some 4803 companies had been privatised, 1209 closed down, and 5435 were still owned by the Treuhandanstalt (East European Markets, 1992).

Few Central and Eastern European governments are able to spare the resources and expertise that the Treuhandanstalt was able to lavish on state property. The apparent dilemma of privatisation programmes is that case-by-case privatisation by a central agency cannot accomplish much, given the resources available to be applied to this end. However, speedy mass privatisation may prove to be a shaky alternative unless supported by far-reaching institutional reform. The major flaw of any mass privatisation, as demonstrated by Czech and Russian experience, is that it fails to impose corporate governance on privatised companies. Hence the importance of regulations and institutions reinforcing the ability of asset owners to exercise control over their assets and persons entrusted with the task of managing them. So far mass privatisation of large enterprises changes little in managers' behaviour inasmuch as it does not expose them to new centres of control or provide them with means to restructure (Kuznetsov and Kuznetsova, 1998).

The reconstruction of Eastern Europe and the EU

As mentioned above, international factors have had a major impact on the dynamics of post-communist transition. The collapse of the intra-COMECON market in 1989–90 was responsible for much of the decline of industrial and agricultural output in the area. Foreign debt is another major issue. The communist governments of Eastern and Central Europe received loans from the West in the 1970s totalling $49.8 bn. These resources were generally misallocated and did not generate a flow of income in hard currency sufficient to repay them. By the time the CEECs started market reforms they had an enormous cumulative debt of $103.1 bn, putting a great strain on their economies, with Poland and Yugoslavia being in particular difficulties.

Unfolding marketisation boosted demand for foreign capital. Transitional countries sought financial credits to support structural adjustments and foreign direct investments to start up privatisation and modernisation of nationalised industries, and to make up for the chronic undercapitalisation which was typical of centrally planned economies.

The G24 countries and international institutions have made commitments to the CEECs amounting to $100 bn including food and medical aid, economic restructuring and technical assistance, export credit and investment guarantees, debt relief, and balance-of-payments support (Transition, 1992). However, only a meagre share of what the West promised has actually been delivered. A fraction of these funds was in grant form; the rest were loans and credit guarantees.

Economic difficulties in CEECs gave Western governments, international organisations and multinational corporations considerable leverage over Eastern and Central European governments. The EU insisted on measures leading to accelerated opening of the markets of the ex-socialist countries to Western products. The argument was that an end must be put to a situation in which CEECs were protected from competitive pressure of international trade which, in market economies, provided a strong incentive to improve efficiency. Transitional economies were called on to lift or restrict foreign trade control and facilitate access to foreign exchange resources for the residents by introducing internal convertibility of the national currency.

As a result, at the initial stage of transition the post-communist economies made a great stride towards openness when the slump in industrial production was at its deepest. Furthermore, although exports to the West increased they could not compensate for the collapse of intra-COMECON trade because Western governments were not ready to open Western markets to Eastern European goods. When Poland volunteered to drop all import restrictions the EU did not

Table 13.2   CEFTA countries: Key indicators, 1997*

Indicators	Poland	Hungary	Czech Republic	Slovenia	EU average
GDP (% growth)	5.2	2.5	4.0	3.5	2.9
Inflation (%)	18.1	18.0	10.8	8.5	2.2
Unemployment (%)	13.5	11**	3.8	13.8	10.8
Budget balance (% of GDP)	−2.8	−4.9	−1.1	−0.4	−2.5

Notes:
* forecast
** 1996
Sources: adapted from *Business Central Europe*, The Annual 1996–97, *European Economy*, No. 63, 1997

reciprocate. Soon Poland had one of the lowest tariff regimes in the world, but half of Poland's exports to the EU confronted some kind of restraint. In order to facilitate relations with the Community, Poland, Hungary, Czechoslovakia and Slovenia initiated the creation of a free-trade area in Central Europe under the Central European Free Trade Agreement (CEFTA) signed in December 1992. The countries involved in CEFTA have high growth rates but high unemployment with the exception of the Czech Republic (Table 13.2). The CEFTA was an attempt to help these countries to boost their trade, given the restrictions that existed for much of their trade with the EU. The CEECs obtained associated status with the EU, amounting largely to a promise of a ten-year transition to free trade. In the meantime the steel lobby ensured that the EU set an extremely low ceiling on East European imports – one per cent of total EU raw steel capacity. The EU also refused to relax restrictions on imports of food, textiles, clothing and chemicals. Together with iron and steel, these are the most competitive Eastern European industries (they account for 33–46 per cent of exports to the EU from the Czech Republic, Slovakia, Poland and Hungary).

The EU was concerned that cheap imports from CEECs, where labour costs were low, would adversely affect the employment situation and regional development in Western Europe. In particular, competition from Eastern Europe was feared in the markets for low value-added manufactured goods. Such industries are often located in the poorer regions of the EU, therefore trade liberalisation could well worsen the regional problems of the Community. These concerns, as well as problems with agricultural products, were limiting the access of the CEECs to the markets of the EU. In reality, as regards the four CEFTA countries, the trade balance has been positive for the EU ever since 1991. Even the traditional deficit in agricultural products turned into a surplus in 1993. This provided grounds for the claim that the total employment effect of the first tentative steps towards trade liberalisation was positive for the EU.

Following these results and the rapid progress of reforms in the CEFTA countries, the EU has taken a decision to speed up the liberalisation of the trade regime with CEFTA and with Bulgaria and Romania. By 1997–98 the EU's tariff barriers were to be eliminated for most of the exports coming from these countries. Nonetheless, the EU will still have at its disposal numerous measures restricting imports of industrial goods from the CEECs. Together these measures are known as 'managed trade' and include anti-dumping threats, safeguard clauses and voluntary export restrictions (Gabrisch, 1997). It is very difficult to control the application of such instruments by importing countries even within the framework of the rules of the World Trade Organisation. Restrictions on the part of the EU in relation to industrial products of the CEECs have been slow to disappear even after seven years of well publicised liberalisation campaigns. As far as agriculture is concerned, in the 1990s the EU market remained almost as closed to exports from the CEECs as in the previous decade.

Extending EU membership

In the long run the EU has much to gain from aiding the reconstruction process in Central and Eastern Europe. The CEECs have the potential for rapid growth as they progress towards the market economy. The demand for goods, services, capital and 'know-how' is likely to be very large. The EU is well placed to benefit from this growth in demand. The consumer market is also potentially very large, especially for consumer durables such as cars. Central and Eastern Europe may also provide a useful production base for many European firms seeking to supply this growing market and for exports to Western Europe.

Direct help by Western companies in the form of selling equipment and providing 'know-how' is a quick way of helping in the reconstruction process. Most CEECs welcome joint-venture enterprises. Some encourage direct investment either by buying existing enterprises or by establishing new enterprises. The privatisation programme could provide a quick method for Western companies to gain production plants in CEECs. Such companies could then transfer technology and processes at a very fast rate, thereby assisting in the transition process.

However, the troublesome heritage of centrally planned economies indicates that a great many long-term problems need to be solved before CEECs become an attractive area for many Western firms to operate in. The inflow of private capital has been below expectations and far below levels that policy-makers consider desirable. The largest amount of foreign investment has been recorded in Hungary. With $1272 of foreign investment per capita at the beginning of 1996 Hungary was far ahead of Poland and the Czech Republic, the other two destinations most favoured by Western investors. Ownership of productive assets by foreigners in Hungary was notably below the 20–25 per cent target set by the government. Private investors were mainly discouraged by high political and policy risks. In turn, the barriers to the export of products to the EU were important deterrents to some foreign investors, including firms from North America and the Far East, which would like to exploit location and cost advantages of the ex-socialist countries to compete in Western European markets.

Most Central and Eastern European countries and Baltic states have expressed a desire to join the EU. The CEFTA was envisaged as an integration 'exercise' by which the member countries could jointly build economic and legal institutions and regulations consistent with EU standards and requirements. In June 1997, at the summit in Amsterdam, the EU leaders considered the applications of ten CEEC nations, but only Poland, the Czech Republic, Hungary, Slovenia and Estonia were shortlisted. Negotiations are expected to start in 1998 and the first wave of entrants may take place as early as 2002 (Duff, 1997a).

Box 13.1   The Copenhagen Criteria

In June 1993 the European Council agreed a set of criteria for membership of the EU by the associate countries of Central and Eastern Europe. The conditions were:

- Stable and democratic institutions with the rule of law and respect and protection for minorities.

- The establishment of a functioning market economy with the capacity to compete within the EU.

- The ability to adhere to the obligations of membership including political, economic and monetary union.

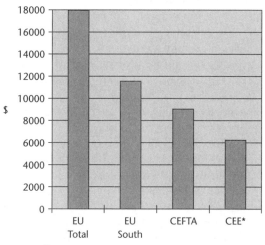

Figure 13.1   GDP per capita

* All European former communist countries excluding Russia and Bosnia-Hercegovina.
Source: The CIA World Factbook, 1996

However, the Commission, though acknowledging that enlargement enjoys a high political priority, made no secret of its opinion that no candidate yet met the entry criteria set by the EU's Copenhagen summit in 1993 (see Box 13.1).

It is the economic requirements that the Eastern European applicants find the hardest to comply with. In terms of economic performance the distance between the EU member states and CEECs is enormous, as is evident from per capita GDP figures (Fig. 13.1). In 1995, the EU average, according to purchasing power parities, was $21,353, while in the ten former socialist countries who applied for EU membership the per capita GDP average was only $5,876. Furthermore, CEECs are very different from EU's economies structurally, as far as production and distribution of goods and income are concerned. Most importantly, the Central European countries must secure economic growth if they want to be competitive within the EU.

Integration of new members from CEECs has put relations between the EU members through yet another test. The EU has difficulty in arriving at joint agreement on Eastern European matters, as member states have different perceptions. For Germany and Austria, relations with Eastern European countries have high priority, unlike countries like Greece, Spain and Portugal who fear increased competition from the CEECs in areas such as agricultural products and low value-added goods and services. Furthermore, granting membership to the CEECs would put pressure on the budget of the EU and could lead to a reduction in the share of the structural funds that are allocated to southern European member states (Duff, 1997b). The enlargement of the EU will require changes in the way decisions are taken within the organisation in such a way that majority voting will increasingly replace the principle of consensus. Some member states are worried that enlargement may reduce them to second-class members. It is also clear that, with the accession of new members, the degree of homogeneity within the EU is going to decline and a net transfer of resources in favour of newcomers will occur, in particular through structural funds and agricultural subsidies. It is obvious that some EU member states are concerned with the prospect of redistribution in funds allocation and growth of financial claims as a result of EU expansion. A much cited example is that of Poland which, if it were eligible for funds under the CAP, would cost the EU $30 bn a year or 40 per cent of the CAP's total budget.

Analysis shows that the volume of financial claims by Eastern European members on EU funds will be moderate compared with the immense boost to their economies which the provision of these resources is likely to give. This is possible because the size of the EU economy is so much greater than that of the CEECs. The combined GDP of the ten applicants is barely 4 per cent of the Union's present total. The anticipated transfer of EU funds will be below 0.5 per cent of the Community GDP, but for the recipient countries it will still represent a very hefty contribution. Poland alone, for example, is expected to receive a net transfer equal to 7 per cent of its GDP (Gabrisch, 1997). The potential impact of such a transfer becomes clear if one recalls the outcome of the Marshall Plan which amounted to just about 2 per cent of the recipient countries' GNP. At the same time accession to the EU may prove to be a painful experience for the applicants. To meet the entry criteria CEECs will need to implement rigorously certain policies which are likely to be unpopular with the public, by putting pressure on the standards of living in the countries concerned. More deregulation will be required, with the possible result that more national firms will have to close down or shed labour.

Agenda 2000

Jacques Santer presented Agenda 2000 (Commission, 1997) to the European Parliament on 16 July 1997. This agenda presented an assessment of the readiness of CEECs for membership of the EU. Ten CEECs were assessed for membership, and five were considered to fulfil the Copenhagen conditions (see Box 13.1) – Hungary, Poland, Estonia, the Czech Republic and Slovenia.

Conditions	Countries meeting conditions
Democracy and Rule of Law	All countries except Slovakia
Functioning Market Economy able to compete in EU	None (as of 1997) but Hungary, Poland, Czech Republic and Slovenia are deemed to be close to meeting this criterion. Slovakia is judged to be able to compete but not to have a functioning market economy.
Ability to adhere to EU obligations in Politicial, Economic and Monetary Union	None is considered to be able to join Monetary Union immediately on accession to the EU. Only Hungary, Poland and Czech Republic are thought to be able to implement the necessary legal changes quickly to conform to the obligations of EU membership. The other countries were considered to require significant changes before they can meet these obligations.

Figure 13.2   EU assessment of CEECs that have met the Copenhagen conditions

Box 13.2   Agenda 2000: For a stronger and wider Union

Agenda 2000 specifies three challenges for the Union with regard to enlargement:

- Reforming the Union's policies such that enlargement will help the EU to create the conditions for sustainable growth, high employment and improved living conditions.
- Preparing all applicant countries to meet the conditions for membership of the Union.
- Reforming the internal policies of the Union to ensure that enlargement does not result in financial problems for the budget of the EU.

These challenges are thought to require a number of reforms:

- Reform of the institutional structure of the EU.
- Development of policies to promote sustainable growth and high employment – complete the Single European Market, establish EMU, and improve R&D policies and Trans-European Network expenditures. Measures to improve employment and working conditions are also highlighted as important to meet the challenges of enlargement.
- A more effective use of the Structural Funds (see Chapter 8).
- Further reform of the CAP (see Chapter 11).

Negotiations with these countries began in 1998 with a view to accession by 2003. Bulgaria, Rumania, Latvia, Lithuania and Slovakia were deemed not to have yet fulfilled the Copenhagen conditions (see Fig. 13.2). Agenda 2000 calls for the institutions of the Community to help these countries meet the conditions to allow negotiations to begin early in the next century. An outline of the plans contained in Agenda 2000 is given in Box 13.2.

Estonia and Slovenia were judged not to have met the economic and legal conditions outlined in the Copenhagen Summit but they are to be permitted to join the negotiations for the first move of CEECs to join the EU. However, Slovakia, which is economically more able to cope with membership, is excluded from the first move because of its failure to meet the democratic conditions. This may reflect a strong political driving force behind the decision to expand EU membership to CEECs.

None of the aspiring members is currently deemed to fulfil important economic criteria – establishment of a functioning market economy and fulfilling the obligations for EMU. However, five countries are to be allowed to negotiate for membership by the early part of next century. This implies that these countries will very quickly be able to fulfill these economic conditions or, more likely, that the political objectives of the EU are taking precedence over more economic objectives. If this is the case, a series of significant economic problems may be encountered as a result of the pursuit of the political objective of integrating these CEECs into the EU.

The EU and Russia

Russia is a huge country rich in resources with outstanding industrial capacity. The population is large and well educated, and the country has a great tradition of scientific research and academic training. Yet the transition to a market economy has been extremely painful and slow. First attempts to modernise the Russian economy along the lines of marketisation can be traced back to 1985, when President Gorbachev inaugurated a programme of economic 'acceleration'. Under President Yeltsin some radical steps were taken towards dismantling the command economy and central planning which opened the way, in 1992, to a quick shift to a market-regulated system. It so happened that it also inaugurated a period of dramatic decline in the Russian economy and the quality of life of the population. By the end of 1996 the Russian economy, in terms of GDP, was only 61 per cent of its size when capitalist reforms began, shrinking to what it used to be in 1979. In 1997 industrial production was only 45–50 per cent of the pre-1992 level and continued to decline. Some 31.5 million Russians (21 per cent of the total population) had incomes below the official poverty line, while another 31 million were making just enough money to meet this minimal standard. The life expectancy was at its lowest for the last 20 years.

Whatever the explanations for this failure, the precarious state of Russian economy is a serious obstacle in the way of integrating this country into the European economy. Not surprisingly, Brussels showed little enthusiasm when the Russian prime minister V. Chernomyrdin made a statement in July 1997 that Russia would like to join the EU. A number of unresolved political issues, the confused legal environment, and growing protectionism leave a considerable gap between Russia and the economies of the EU member states.

A lot of contacts have, however, developed at the level of private companies. Russia is much more open than it used to be. Foreign trade and foreign capital have been growing in importance. Some $5.9 bn of foreign investments have been attached to Russia. This may be impressive on its own but it places Russia only in fourth place among former socialist countries after much smaller economies like the Czech Republic ($6.1 bn), Poland ($10.1 bn) and Hungary ($13 bn). The paradox of the situation is the fact that national capital flees the country on an unprecedented scale, vouching for the total lack of confidence by Russians in governmental policies. Even by modest estimates they have transferred abroad at least $100 bn (Voprost Ekonmiki, 1997). The only significant sector of the Russian economy generating profits is the natural resources industry, which accounted for 46 per cent of exports in 1996 (Business Central Europe, 1997). Understandably, natural gas, oil and metal extraction are the key targets of foreign investors in Russia. The government so far has failed to induce foreign capital to participate more actively in restructuring and modernising Russia's industrial structures. This contributes to the general wariness by the public about Western intentions vis-à-vis the regeneration of Russia through aid and investment.

The relationship of the EU with Russia will be very difficult to establish. Russia poses a greater problem for the EU than CEECs simply because of its great size. Russia has also preserved a high level of economic integration with other former Soviet republics. Bringing Russia into a closer relationship with the EU would mean that areas with very different economic, political and cultural characteristics would be drawn towards the Union. Only in the long run, when these countries have reconstructed their economic and political systems, would it be possible for them to establish close economic links with the EU. Given the nature of the economic and political crisis which faces the former Soviet Union, this is likely to take a considerable amount of reconstruction of all aspects of their societies.

Conclusion

The CEECs are undergoing a painful process of transition towards market-based economies. Most of the countries of Central and Eastern Europe wish to join the EU. The first wave of countries to join the EU may occur by 2003. However, this enlargement will pose many economic and political challenges for the EU and the new member states. Most of the countries that are not in the first wave appear to be determined to join the EU. Therefore, there is a good prospect that the EU will soon encompass all or most of the countries of Central and Eastern Europe. Such a change in the characteristics of the member states is bound to have significant implications for the future development of the EU. The relationship between the EU and Russia is also likely to develop. However, it is very difficult to evaluate the direction and significance of future EU-Russia relationships.

References

Amsden A, Kochanowicz J and Taylor L 1994 *The Market Meets Its Match. Restructuring the Economics of Eastern Europe*, Harvard University Press, Cambridge.
Boeri T 1997 'Heterogeneous workers, economic transformation and the stagnancy of transitional unemployment', *European economic review*, Vol. 41, Nos 3–5, pp. 905–14.
Business Central Europe 1997 The Annual 1996/7, in *European Economy* 1997.
Commission 1997 *Agenda 2000: For a Stronger and Wider Union*, Brussels.
Duff A 1997a *The Treaty of Amsterdam: Text and Commentary*, Federal Trust, London.

Duff A 1997b *Reforming the European Union*, Federal Trust, London.

East European Markets 1992.

Eatwell J Ellman M, Nuti M and Shapiro J 1995 *Transformation and Integration: Shaping the Future of Central and Eastern Europe*, Institute for Public Research, London.

The Economist 1991 *Survey on Eastern Europe*.

European Economy 1997 Annual Report, No. 3.

Gabrisch H 1997 Effects of EU Enlargement on New Members, *Europe-Asia Studies*, Vol. 49, No. 4, pp. 567–90.

Kornai J 1986 The soft budget constraint, *Kylos*, Vol. 39, pp. 27–39.

Kuznetsov A and Kuznetsova O 1998 Privatisation and Emerging Corporate System of Russia, in McDonald F and Thorpe R, *Organisational Strategy and Technological Adaptation to Global Change*, Macmillan, London.

Marrese M and Vanous J 1988 *Soviet subsidisation of trade with Eastern Europe. A Soviet Perspective*, University of California, Berkeley.

OECD 1997 *Transition Brief*, No. 6, Winter 1997, Paris.

Transition 1992 The Newsletter about Reforming Economies, Vol. 3, No. 7.

Voprost Ekonmiki 1997 No. 4.

Further reading

Calvo G A and Coricelli F 1992 Stabilizing a previously centrally planned economy: Poland 1990, *Economic Policy*, No. 14, pp. 175–208.

Dabrowski P 1991 East European trade (Part 1): The loss of the Soviet market, RFE/RL Research Institute, *Research on Eastern Europe*, Vol. 2, No. 40.

de Groote J 1992 Economic transition and western assistance to Central and Eastern Europe, *External Economic Relations of the Central and East European Countries*, NATO Colloqium 1992, pp. 59–78, Brussels.

Dobrinsky R and Landesmann M (eds.) 1995 *Transforming Economies and European Integration*, Edward Elgar, Aldershot.

Ellman M 1993 General aspects of transition, in Admiral P H (ed.), *Economic Transition in Eastern Europe*, Blackwell, Oxford.

Fry M and Nuti D M 1992 Monetary and exchange rate policies during Eastern Europe's transition: some lessons from further east, *Oxford Review of Economic Policy*, Vol. 8, No. 1, pp. 27–44.

Gowan P 1991 Old medicine, new bottles: Western policy toward East Central Europe, *World Policy Journal*, Vol. 9, No. 1, pp. 1–34.

Inotai A 1996 From association agreements to full membership? The dynamics of relations between the Central and East European countries and the European Union, *Russian And East European Finance And Trade*, Vol. 32, No. 6, pp. 6–29.

Kierzkowski H 1996 Central Europe Looks West, *The World Economy*, pp. 29–45.

Pinto B Belka M and Krajewski S 1993 *Transforming State Enterprises in Poland. Microeconomic Evidence on Adjustment*, Policy Research Working Papers: Transition and Macro-adjustment, Poland Resident Mission, WPS 1101, World Bank, Washington.

Rosati D 1992 The CMEA demise, trade restructuring and trade destruction in Central and Eastern Europe, *Oxford Review of Economic Policy*, Vol. 8, No. 1, pp. 58–81.

Welfens P J J 1992 *Market-oriented systematic transformations in Eastern Europe*, Springer-Verlag, Berlin.

14 The European Union and the Third World

Stephen Dearden

Introduction

The economic relationship between the EU and the developing world has been heavily influenced by the colonial histories of many of its member states. From the inception of the Community France sought the inclusion of its overseas territories in the customs union and special arrangements for Morocco and Tunisia. Italy sought similar concessions for Libya. Thus, under Articles 131–136 of the Treaty of Rome there was provision for 'association' status for non-European countries which had a 'special relation' with Community members.

Although the Yaounde Conventions, offering trade concessions and aid to some developing countries, began in 1964, it was not until the Maastricht Treaty on European Union (TEU) in 1993 that development cooperation became a shared European responsibility. Here, under Article 130u, the EU was to foster 'the sustainable economic and social development of developing countries, and their gradual integration into the world economy.' To achieve this, Article 130u states that development policy should be 'complementary to the policies pursued by the member states', while Article 130v requires the EU to take account of its development objectives in all its policies. This new explicit competence for the Community now gives the Commission the right to initiate new policies and programmes, and the responsibility to elaborate strategy. It also allows the Council of Ministers to make binding decisions by qualified majority voting rather than unanimity.

However, some 40 years after decolonisation, does 'dependence' still characterise the economic relationship of the Third World with the EU? Do these countries remain exporters of primary products and importers of European manufactures? For trade remains central to the long-term sustained economic development of less developed countries (LDCs), and is a barometer of the degree of their past success in achieving the necessary structural transformation of their economies.

Trade preferences

The pyramid of preferences

The pattern of trade preferences faced by exporters to the EU is a complex one and is illustrated in Fig. 14.1. Recent changes have undermined the distinction between the various levels of the pyramid of preferences but six broad categories can be identified:

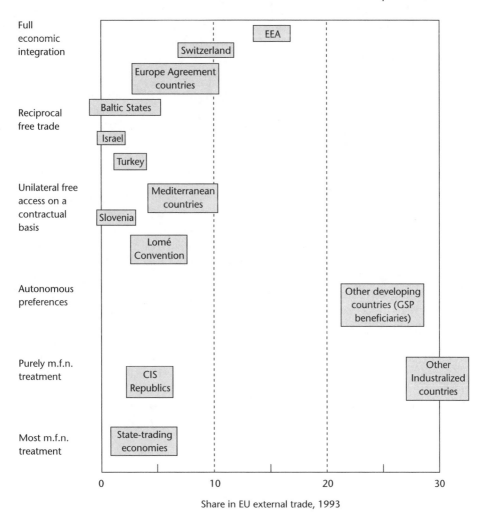

Figure 14.1 The EU preferential trade system, early 1995

Source: adapted from WTO Secretariat; and UNSTAT, Contrade database

1. Tariff-free Trade
   Member states and the EEA

2. Reciprocal Free Trade
   Baltic States, Israel

3. Non-reciprocal Free Access
   Mediterranean Countries and Lomé ACP (African, Caribbean and Pacific)
   states. Duty-free access for manufactured goods and most non-CAP
   agricultural products.

4. General System of Preferences
   Non-ACP LDCs. Offers similar preferences to Lomé but on a narrower range of products.
5. Most Favoured Nation
   CIS republics and most of the remaining industrialised countries.
6. State Trading Economies
   For example, Vietnam, North Korea.

The Lomé Conventions

The first Lomé Convention was signed in 1975, and replaced the Yaounde Conventions which had mainly benefited the ex-French colonies. Lomé was a response to the entry of the UK and the problem of preserving Commonwealth LDC trade preferences. Although it excluded many of the Asian Commonwealth countries, the number of associated states benefiting from Lomé now totals 71 – the ACP group (Africa, Caribbean and Pacific). Each Convention lasts for five years and has both an aid and a trade component. The current Lomé IV offers duty-free access for ACP exports of primary products and manufactures and most non-CAP agricultural products. Special arrangements exist for bananas, rum, beef and sugar, offering access for quotas from certain ACPs at higher guaranteed EU prices. Approximately 97 per cent of ACP exports enter the EU duty-free, but 63 per cent of ACP exports would have entered the EU duty-free without the Lomé Conventions. The greatest benefit to the ACPs from Lomé arises with products that would otherwise face substantial tariffs, and therefore command artificially high prices within the European market. Unfortunately, these comprise the smallest category of ACP exports to the EU and are being eroded. It has been estimated that only 7 per cent of ACP exports received this significant preferential margin in 1989 (McQueen and Stevens, 1989). In return for these tariff preferences the Community only requires that the ACP states do not discriminate in their own markets between EU member states.

The Mediterranean countries

Over the period 1988 to 1995 the share of EU imports met by the 12 LDC members (MCs) of the Euro-Mediterranean partnership remained stable at about 2.2 per cent, representing 9.1 per cent of the Community's LDC imports. However, the EU accounts for a substantial proportion of the export earnings of the MC states (see Table 14.1). But unlike relations with the ACPs through Lomé, those with the MCs lack any coherence or institutional framework, being embodied in a succession of individual association agreements. These began in 1962 with Greece, followed by Turkey (1963), Morocco (1969), Tunisia (1969), Israel (1970) and Spain (1970). The last two were particularly controversial and led to the offer to extend similar trade agreements to other MCs, including Egypt, Jordan and Syria.

However, as these agreements varied from country to country and required continual re-negotiation, in 1972 the EU proposed the development of a General Mediterranean Policy (GMP). It was intended to create a free-trade area

Table 14.1 Mediterranean exports to the EU (1995)

	% of total exports
Algeria	66
Cyprus	35
Egypt	49
Israel/Palestinian Authority	31
Jordan	6
Lebanon	21
Malta	71
Morocco	63
Syria	57
Tunisia	78
Turkey	51

Source: Direction of Trade Statistics Yearbook, IMF, 1995

in industrial goods, except for 'sensitive products', and to give preferential access to 80 per cent of the MCs' agricultural exports. Preferences were not as generous as under Lomé for 'non-traditional' fruit and vegetables, to protect EU suppliers. Reciprocity of the trade concessions had to be abandoned in the face of US opposition. The final outcome was little different from the preceding piecemeal agreements. The first unlimited duration agreement under the GMP was concluded with Israel in 1975.

In November 1995, at Barcelona, the EU launched the Euro-Mediterranean Partnership. This aims to create a free-trade area by 2010 and requires the MCs to give tariff- and quota-free access to EU exports of manufactured goods. At the same time the MCs are expected to remove duties on goods originating from other MCs. The Commission ultimately expects the MCs to adopt the EU's competition and origin rules. At the same time the EU is to increase its financial assistance to the MCs and has allocated ECU 4.7 bn from the general budget for the period 1995 to 1999.

The General System of Preferences

For those LDCs excluded from the Lomé Conventions, the General System of Preferences (GSP) introduced in 1971 is of significance. Originally conceived as a worldwide scheme, it was intended to offer duty-free access to developed country markets for LDC manufactured exports. The EU's GSP was instituted in 1971 and each scheme was intended to run for five years, but the Community's overriding commitment to the ACPs compromised the emergence of any comprehensive concession to LDCs.

Over its history the EU's GSP had become increasingly discriminatory, both by product and by country of origin. Thus, from 1986 the GSP was withdrawn from those countries' products where income per capita was greater than $2000, and where the country's share of EU imports of those products exceeded 20 per cent; in the case of textiles the share limit is 10 per cent.

Brazil, Hong Kong, China, South Korea and Singapore have all experienced the withdrawal of some GSP concessions, and some authors have concluded that GSP benefits were withdrawn from most LDCs' manufactured products that have penetrated EU markets to any significant degree. In addition, some 140 sensitive products, including textiles and clothing, were subject to tariff quotas or volume limits under the GSP. Once exports reached their tariff quota, further sales were subject to the higher 'most favoured nation'(MFN) tariff arrangements. These tariff quotas or volume limits were often applied by individual EU member states.

In January 1995 a new ten-year GSP was adopted by the EU. In order to maintain the LDCs' preference margins, the GSP concessions are to be expressed as a percentage of the MFN tariff. This is to be 85 per cent of the MFN for 'very sensitive' products, 70 per cent for 'sensitive' products (e.g. footwear, electronics, and motor vehicles), and 35 per cent for 'semi-sensitive' products, with other imports entering duty-free (Commission, 1994). A safeguard clause remains, allowing the reintroduction of duties should imports threaten to cause serious difficulties to an EU producer. There is also a 'graduation mechanism', providing for the exclusion of specific country-sector combinations from the GSP, depending upon the exporting country's overall level of industrial development and degree of 'export specialisation' as defined by the EU.

The Single Market

The movement towards the Single European Market (SEM) was an important development in EU-LDC relations. Although this was not an aspect that had been addressed by the Commission, a number of authors have attempted to evaluate its impact and it is best considered in terms of trade creation and trade diversion.

The Cecchini Report (1988) suggested a 4.5 per cent to 7 per cent enhancement of the growth rate as a result of economic integration, and this in turn was expected to increase demand for LDC exports. Matthews and McAleese (1990), assuming an extra 5 per cent growth of GDP for the EU, calculated that this would increase LDC exports by 6 per cent ($5.5 bn), although 75 per cent of this increase would be oil. For other products, especially manufactures, the efficiency gains of the EU's own producers arising from the SEM (for example, economies of scale) would lead to enhanced competition for LDC exports. The extent of this effect would vary from product to product, and would be expected to be most severe for LDCs where EU producers experienced the greatest efficiency gains. Thus LDC exports of steel and chemicals might have been particularly adversely affected. Although Davenport (1990) believed that on plausible assumptions trade creation for LDCs' manufactured goods would be approximately offset by trade diversion, Langhammer (1990) suggested a one-off reduction in EU demand for LDC manufactures of $2.3 bn.

For the LDCs the existing national preferential arrangements for their exports were often inconsistent with the 1992 programme, and many member state quotas, Voluntary Export Restraints (VERs) etc., needed to be replaced by EU arrangements. Under Article 115 of the Treaty of Rome member states had been allowed to suspend imports of goods from other member states where third countries were attempting to circumvent quotas through trans-shipment. Although this Article was restated in the Maastricht Treaty, with the ending of border controls it has not been employed since 1993. However, VERs were of more significance in limiting the volume of LDC exports and these survived 1992 on a Community basis. For although the Commission generally believes that many

Box 14.1 The Banana Protocol

Over the ten years to 1992 the EC12 imports of bananas from the ACP countries doubled to 0.7 million tonnes, worth ECU 413 million. The ACP's share of total banana imports had peaked at 25 per cent in 1986, but declined to 15.4 per cent by 1992. These are an extremely important source of export earnings and employment for a number of ACP island economies. For example, for St Lucia, St Vincent and Dominica they represent over half of export earnings and employ one-third of the labour force of the Windward Islands. However, they are in competition in EU markets with exports of 'dollar' bananas from Central and South America, where large plantations have a cost advantage. These 'dollar' bananas dominated the German market, which accounted for one-third of all EU imports. Special arrangements have therefore been made to preserve their traditional markets in the UK, France and Italy. But these arrangements were incompatible with the abolition of Article 115 restrictions on intra-Community trade. The Commission had proposed imposing an import quota on non-ACP bananas (COM(92)359). However, the GATT negotiations were seeking the abolition of non-tariff barriers to the trade in agricultural products. Thus, the new regime commencing in July 1993 established a tariff quota of 2 million tonnes for non-ACP banana imports. Up to this limit a duty of ECU 100 per tonne is imposed, increasing to ECU 850 per tonne on any additional imports – an effective tariff of 170 per cent. ACP banana imports continue to be duty-free, but the CAP was extended to include support for EU banana production.

However, it was challenged before the WTO by the US and four major multi-national banana producers. In 1997 the Disputes Panel issued its Interim Report, ruling against the size of ACP quotas and the guarantee of 30 per cent of the EU market. However, the report accepts the principle of preferential tariffs for ACP banana exports and the exemption of Lomé from the full force of WTO rules. Unlike GATT decisions the EU is obliged to accept these rulings, but further negotiations are likely.

industries should be able to withstand import competition after the restructuring following from economic integration, footwear, consumer electronics and ceramic tableware all continue to face quotas. Thus, VERs were required from South Korea and Taiwan for both footwear, where they supplied one-third of all EU imports in 1987, and consumer electronics.

The most significant VER affecting LDCs is the Multi Fibre Arrangement (MFA). Although MFA IV introduced a new mechanism whereby unused individual member state quotas could be transferred to other member states, in practice the total EU quota limit on LDC exports remained under-utilised. The elimination of individual member state VER quotas, as required by the SEM, offered potential benefits to LDC exporters. However, the future of MFA IV was bound up with the Uruguay Round negotiations of the General Agreement on Tariffs and Trade (GATT).

The move to a single market has also precipitated a major confrontation with the World Trade Organisation (WTO), the successor to GATT, over the Banana Protocol (see Box 14.1). This has thrown into doubt the whole future of trade concessions under Lomé.

Technical standards

The SEM also required the adoption of common technical standards. The mutual recognition of certification implies that any LDC export need only satisfy the conditions for any one member state, but certification may in some cases only be required for non-EU producers, which may create opportunities for discrimination. The close involvement of EU industries in setting Community technical standards may also offer further opportunities for deterring non-EU competition.

EU standards have existed for some time in relation to the health of plant and animal product imports. Since 1993 all inspections are carried out at the first port of entry, or in the exporting country, and Community-wide clearance is given. This may result in tighter standards being applied to achieve uniformity, with adverse consequences for particular LDC exports, for example planting materials and cut flowers. A Directive for meat products requires Community licensing of both slaughterhouses and processing plants for all non-EU suppliers, presenting problems for some African exporters. Another Directive setting standards of water quality may pose a threat to Southeast Asian shellfish exports.

Some aspects of EU-LDC trade relations were unaffected by the 1992 programme. For example, the national export credit agencies continued to operate independently. By contrast, 'tied aid' is required to be directed towards any EU exporter rather than exclusively at those of the member state granting the assistance. Of the $13.63 bn of bilateral aid of eight EU states in 1987, 57 per cent was partially or entirely 'tied'. This widening of the LDC recipient's choice of suppliers should significantly increase the real value of the aid, as enhanced competition should reduce prices.

The pattern of trade

In 1994 the EU imported goods to a value of ECU 160.7 bn from LDCs: 6 per cent of its total imports coming from both the Mediterranean and Latin American groups of countries, 13 per cent from the GSP Asian LDCs, and 2.8 per cent from the ACP states (Tables 14.2 and 14.3). In that same year exports to the LDCs as a whole totalled ECU 184.4 bn, of which ECU 14.9 bn went to the ACPs. Of the ACPs' total world exports, 41 per cent went to the EU, compared with 19 per cent to the USA, underlining the importance of the EU as both an export market and a source of imports for LDCs.

In real terms LDC exports to the EU have increased dramatically since its inception. In the 1970s the LDCs' export performance was particularly impressive, growing faster than that of either developed countries exports to the EU or intra-EU trade. However, in the 1980s the position reversed dramatically, with only the LDCs experiencing a reduction in their value of exports. In 1976 the LDCs accounted for 45 per cent of the EU's imports, but by 1990 their share had fallen to 31 per cent. This deterioration in export performance can be accounted for by two factors: the switch in oil imports away from LDCs and the fall in primary commodity prices.

Table 14.2 LDC-EU trade

	EU imports, ECU bn					
	1976	*1980*	*1985*	*1990*	*1992*	*1994*
ACP	10.5	19.4	26.8	21.9	18	18.6
Asia	6.7	16	26	50.9	66.4	84.3
Latin America	8.3	13.7	25.8	25.7	24.8	27.6
Mediterranean	9.6	16.4	32.3	29.8	30.3	30.8
All LDCs	70.7	114.3	128.9	143.8	145.6	160.7
Total EU Imports	157.7	269.9	399.7	461.5	487.6	546
	EU exports, ECU bn					
	1976	*1980*	*1985*	*1990*	*1992*	*1994*
ACP	9.6	15.7	17.4	16.6	17	14.9
Asia	7.5	13.1	29.4	41	47.1	70.5
Latin America	7.7	12	13.5	15.6	20.4	29.6
Mediterranean	13.3	19.8	29.8	28.5	28.6	33.1
All LDCs	550.9	83.4	121.7	134.2	153.1	184.4
Total EU Exports	141.3	221.1	380.8	415.3	436.1	539

Source: Statistical Yearbook 1958–94, External and Intra-European Union Trade, Eurostat

Table 14.3 LDC share of EU imports (%)

	1976	*1980*	*1985*	*1990*	*1992*	*1994*
ACP	6.7	7.2	6.7	4.7	3.7	2.8
ACP non-oil	6.1	5.3	4.8	3.5	2.9	
Asia	4.2	5.9	6.5	11	13.6	13.1
Latin America	5.3	5.1	6.5	4.6	5.1	5.4
Mediterranean	6.1	6.1	8.1	6.5	6.2	6.1
All LDCs	44.8	42.4	34.7	31.2	29.2	34.2

Sources: Statistical Yearbook 1958–94, External and Intra-European Union Trade, Eurostat

However, of greater long-term concern is the trend in manufactured exports. Although primary products dominate LDC exports, accounting for two-thirds of the total, it is the trend in manufactured products that would be expected to reflect the process of sustained economic development in LDCs. Unfortunately, the growth in manufactured exports has been confined to a very small number of LDCs. While the share of the ACP countries in manufactured exports to the EU fell from 6.6 per cent in 1962 to 1.5 per cent in 1987, that of the four Asian newly industrialised countries (NICs) – Taiwan, Singapore, Hong Kong and South Korea – demonstrated significant growth. In 1962 the Asian NICs accounted for only 1.7 per cent of EU manufactured imports, 16 per cent of the LDC total. In 1980 this share had reached 8.6 per cent of total EU manufactured imports and 60 per cent of the import of manufactures from the LDCs. By 1995 their share of LDC manufactured imports had risen even further to 83 per cent. Worldwide the NICs' share of the trade in manufactured goods was 21 per cent, which is comparable to the EU's 26 per cent, and Japan's 24 per cent.

The ACPs

Turning specifically to the ACP group among the LDCs, trends in their share of EU imports suggest that there has been little apparent benefit from the preferences given under Lomé. In 1976 the EU imported ECU 10.5 bn of goods

Table 14.4   ACP and LDC exports to EU

	EU imports 1993 (%)		Annual growth (1976–93)	
	Other LDCs	*ACP*	*Other LDCs*	*ACP*
Processed food	41.4	8.3	9.0	9.0
Chemicals	10.8	0.3	17.3	3.3
Textiles	45.1	2.3	11.3	9.4
Metal products	15.8	1.8	8.5	−3.8
Other manufactures	17.3	0.5	16.8	28.6
Total processed	21.7	1.1	13.0	4.4

Source: Eurostat

Table 14.5   % ACP exports to EU (1992)

	ACP exports to EU (%)
Nigeria	22
Côte d'Ivoire	9
Cameroon	6
Gabon	6
Mauritius	5
Angola	5
Zaire	4
Congo	4

	EU as % total export earnings
Cameroon	74
Central African Republic	82
Equatorial Guinea	99
Mauritius	80
Niger	80
Sierra Leone	73
Uganda	75
St Lucia	72

Source: Eurostat

from the ACP countries, giving them a market share of 6.7 per cent. Imports peaked in 1985 at ECU 26.8 bn but declined to 18 bn by 1992 (3.7 per cent); removing oil reduces imports to only ECU 12.3 bn (2.9 per cent). ACP exports to the EU continue to be dominated by primary products: 28 per cent of ACP exports between 1988 and 1992 were petroleum products and another 30 per cent were provided by eight other primary products. Although manufacture exports doubled between 1976 and 1992 they still accounted for only 29 per cent of total ACP exports in 1992. This performance is also significantly poorer than that achieved by the non-ACP LDCs (Table 14.4). Whereas these increased their processed goods exports by an average of 13 per cent per annum over the period 1976 to 1993 the ACP group only managed an increase of 4.4 per cent.

ACP exports are also dominated by a small number of countries. Eight countries account for 61 per cent of all ACP exports to the EU. Of these, Nigeria is by far the most important, with 22 per cent of ACP exports in 1992, principally oil. But for a number of other ACP countries the EU market dominates their export earnings (Table 14.5).

Although Lomé appears of limited value from the perspective of the overall performance of the ACPs, it may have been significant in fostering and protecting exports of particular products. However, this is difficult to demonstrate, as can be seen from Table 14.6. Here a comparison of ACP and total LDC shares in the growth of tropical products suggests a very mixed pattern. In the case of

Table 14.6 The European Union and the Third World

	EU import ECU m. 1986–87	Import Share 1986–87		Average growth 1978–89–1986–87		ACP tariff preference margin
		LDC	ACP	LDC	ACP	
Bananas, fresh	1266.1	100.0	23.4	1.6	3.4	20
Pineapples	121.9	99.1	92.6	9.0	8.8	9
Coffee beans	5364.0	99.2	41.4	3.4	4.7	4.5
Tea	489.0	88.5	44.9	0.2	3.4	0
Cocoa beans	1506.2	100.0	85.0	4.5	3.7	3
Tobacco	1745.2	50.4	15.9	0.4	7.0	7.5
Palm nuts/kernels	17.8	97.4	92.3	−3.4	−2.9	0
Palmoil	392.3	99.8	24.1	4.9	6.3	5.5
Oilcake, meal	112.8	99.8	8.6	14.1	−3.1	0
Raw sugar	674.2	99.6	81.7	−0.0	1.2	L
Crude rubber	768.0	99.6	15.8	27.4	6.9	0
Sisal etc.	29.6	99.5	39.4	−1.0	−7.6	0
Wood, rough	744.7	81.3	78.4	−2.9	−2.1	0
Weighted averages[1]						
all products	—	75.7	34.0	4.0	3.9	—
crude products	—	91.2	44.7	3.8	4.3	—

Notes:
([1]) Averages are weighted by 1986–87 total EU imports
L: Levy on non-ACP imports. The major ACP sugar producers have specific quantities of imports guaranteed at Community sugar prices
Source: Comext

coffee, tobacco and palm oil, where there are significant ACP preferences, these countries have gained market share relative to other LDCs. But similar gains have occurred with tea, where there is no ACP preference. Nonetheless, the ACP countries dominate in the supply of certain tropical products to the EU, including pineapples, cocoa beans, palm nuts, raw sugar and wood.

For some non-traditional non-primary products, McQueen and Stevens (1989) have suggested that the foundations have been laid for significant export growth. Although the absolute value of these exports is small, totalling only 6.9 per cent of non-fuel ACP exports to the EU in 1987, they have shown sustained growth. These products are based upon processing raw materials that increase the value added of previously exported primary commodities. It includes wood and leather products, cotton yarns, fabrics, clothing and canned tuna. In some cases, such as man-made yarns and veneers, this export growth has been associated with substantial ACP preferences over other LDC exporters, but this advantage has failed to produce gains in market shares in other products, for example tinned pineapples and wooden furniture.

Similarly, studies of export diversification in individual ACP countries (Riddell (1990) of Zimbabwe; McQueen (1990) of Mauritius; Stevens (1990) of Jamaica, Kenya and Ethiopia) suggest some contribution from Lomé preferences, but again there is no evidence that it was the decisive factor.

Causes of failure

In certain commodities, the ACP countries in particular, and the LDCs in general, have achieved an increased market share in EU imports. However, over the two decades of Lomé the ACP group have seen their share of EU imports halve, while studies of the impact of the GSP upon non-ACP LDCs (Langhammer and Sapir, 1987; Davenport, 1986) suggest that it has been of very limited value in stimulating exports. Several factors might account for this. First, it has been suggested that it reflects a deterioration in LDCs' internal supply conditions and therefore their international competitiveness. Overvalued exchange rates, rising wage costs, or capital shortages that lower productivity could undermine competitiveness. Similarly, poor infrastructure, an inadequate financial services sector or poor human capital may have been contributory factors. However, this does not explain the contrasting experience of LDC exports to the USA and EU. Whereas the value of EU imports has risen by only $4.1 bn over the period 1979 to 1989, US imports from LDCs increased by $36.9 bn.

Secondly, it is argued that technological change is undermining the comparative advantage of LDCs. Automation and the microchip revolution are challenging the advantage that LDCs have held in low labour costs for product assembly. Without this advantage production plants will tend to be located near their main markets, where design, marketing and production can be more easily integrated, and production made more responsive to changing market conditions. The new automated methods of production, essential to the new sophisticated products, also require the specialist support industries only found in the developed world. Although this may be a long-term phenomenon which may challenge the competitive position of LDCs in the export of manufactures, it is unlikely to explain the short-term deterioration in their export performance; and again is unable to explain their differential experience in the US and EU.

Finally, many commentators have suggested that trade preferences were of limited value to many LDCs. Small preference margins, quantitative limits and problems associated with 'rules of origin' are all regarded as serious limitations. Rules of origin specify the minimum level of domestic value added for a product to qualify as originating from a given LDC, and therefore to receive the appropriate trade concessions. It has been argued that these rules have failed to take into account the changes in the international division of labour, with the growth of outward processing and off-shore assembly. The Lomé Convention restricts non-ACP inputs to 10 per cent of the good's domestic value added for it to qualify for duty-free access. These restrictions are particularly onerous for the Caribbean and Pacific ACPs who look to the US and Japan for industrial partners (McQueen and Stevens, 1989).

More importantly, Lomé and the GSP have been compromised by other protectionist measures. Isolating the trends in the degree of protectionism by the EU presents a number of serious difficulties. These arise from the significance of non-tariff barriers to LDC exports, which take many forms, were often cumulative for particular products, and for which information was difficult to obtain. They were also applied at both the national and the EU level.

Tariffs faced by the LDCs rarely appear to have presented any serious obstacles to most of their exports since the Tokyo Round of tariff reductions (1973–79). For example, the non-agricultural 'most favoured nation' average tariff is only 4.7 per cent. However, certain products did face significant duties – textiles 10 per cent to 20 per cent, clothing 16 per cent, and agricultural products under the CAP regime, levies often exceeding 100 per cent.

In terms of the non-tariff instruments eight categories can be isolated – state aids to industries, public procurement restrictions, technical regulations, minimum import prices (under CAP), voluntary export restraints (VERs), quotas, anti-dumping duties, and surveillance. Public procurement restrictions, industry subsidies and technical regulations also distorted intra-EU trade and hence were a focus for harmonisation and EU control. Industry subsidies in particular have often inhibited LDC export growth, given their use in labour-intensive industries where LDCs might be expected to demonstrate a comparative advantage. However, perhaps the most important barriers are the five remaining non-tariff 'trade instruments'.

Turning first to quotas, it was only in 1982 that member states began to publish a general list of quotas. Interpretation of their impact is difficult given the level of aggregation, both by product and geographically – i.e. some member states applied quotas to individual countries, others to 'zones' of 30–50 countries. Although some quotas were not necessarily enforced, they remained available. Given these considerable qualifications there is still no evidence to suggest that the application of quotas had increased in later years, although France and Italy employed significantly more than other members of the EU.

However, the volume limits on LDC exports were more likely to arise under the more extensive VERs. There are two broad categories to consider – the Multi Fibre Arrangement (MFA) and non-MFA VERs. The MFAs, first established in 1974, run for four years and currently involve VERs negotiated with 25 countries. The ACP countries are exempt from the MFA and therefore gain a significant advantage over other LDCs. Although negotiated at the EU level they were subsequently expressed as national 'quotas'. Successive MFAs became increasingly restrictive until the mid-1980s, with both more LDCs and more products being subject to 'quotas'. By 1986, 60 per cent of LDC textile exports, and 78 per cent of clothing exports were facing non-tariff barriers in developed country markets. A review of non-MFA VERs is more problematic, but Pelkman (1987) concludes that they became popular in the late 1970s, and even more extensively employed in the early 1980s.

Short of VERs the EU may undertake surveillance of particular imports, i.e. the accelerated gathering of statistical information on imports from particular countries. This is not as innocuous a process as it might at first appear. It may require prior import documentation, which may be refused, or be used to inhibit LDC exports by threatening the imposition of other 'safeguards', should they exceed informally notified growth rate limits. Surveillance is central to triggering the MFA's 'safeguard options', and it occurred with all 159 'sensitive' products in Benelux, France, Italy and the UK, but only to a very limited extent in Germany and Greece, and not at all in Denmark. Pelkman suggests that the extent of surveillance increased over the period 1975–85, but since the early 1980s the Commission has attempted to reduce the number of approvals, requiring member states to make a more substantial case.

In contrast to the *ad hoc* approach taken to quotas and VERs, the EU has subscribed to the Anti-Dumping Code of GATT from 1980. Dumping is identified where the prices charged in export markets diverge from those charged for the product in the country's home market, i.e. a form of international price discrimination. Where there is evidence of dumping, and of a resultant 'material injury', an anti-dumping duty can be imposed. Although the EU subscribed to the GATT Code, the determination of 'normal prices' and the 'injury test' have led to accusations of hidden protectionism. The mere threat of investigation is often sufficient to ensure that small LDC producers accept 'price undertakings', i.e. raising their export prices. In the period 1980–84 the EU initiated 218 anti-dumping investigations, with LDCs' exports being involved in 25 per cent of this total. Of these 54 cases, 25 resulted in 'price undertakings' being given and 15 in anti-dumping duties being imposed. From 1989 to 1993 the percentage of EU imports subject to anti-dumping duties fell from 2.2 per cent to 1.3 per cent (OECD, 1996), but the prohibition of VERs under the Uruguay Round of GATT may lead to their more frequent use.

In general, over the decade 1975–85, Pelkman suggests that despite tariff liberalisation in the Tokyo Round, and some concessions on the GSP and Lomé, these have been more than offset by the increased protectionism of the MFA and *ad hoc* VERs. This conclusion is supported by the evidence of increased protectionism among all OECD countries in the early 1980s found by Balassa and Balassa (1984) and Page (1985). In particular, trade restraints have been targeted at a specific group of LDCs, the Newly Industrialising Countries (NICs), i.e. Taiwan, South Korea, Hong Kong, Brazil and Singapore; and have certainly focused on a particular group of 'sensitive' products, i.e. textiles, clothing, footwear, consumer electronics and steel.

Finally, it must not be forgotten that the CAP continues to represent a serious obstacle to the development of LDC agricultural exports – not only to the EU itself, but also through the competition on world markets presented by subsidised EU exports of surplus produce. The major losers from the CAP among the LDCs include Argentina and Brazil, efficient producers of cereals, meat and sugar, turkey, fruit and vegetables; and the Philippines and West Indies for sugar. Nonetheless, the LDCs' share of EU imports of fruit and vegetables has risen from 47 per cent to 63 per cent since 1976, although most of this increase has come from Asian and Latin American suppliers.

Future prospects

The future prospects for LDC trade with the EU will be determined by developments within the EU, its external policies and the world trade environment. In particular, the impact of tax harmonisation and the outcome of the Uruguay Round of GATT will be examined.

Tax harmonisation

As part of the single market programme, harmonisation of national tax regimes may occur. It has been proposed that all member states should set their VAT and excise duties within common bands, with excise duties limited to alcohol, tobacco and petroleum products. If adopted, this will have important implications for LDC exports of coffee, cocoa and tobacco. Currently coffee is subject to excise duties in many member states, for example Germany 41 per cent and Denmark 15 per cent.

Abolition of these duties would raise the value of EU imports by ECU 466 million (3 per cent), the main beneficiaries being Brazil, Colombia and Côte d'Ivoire. Similarly, the abolition of excise duties on cocoa and the imposition of a 5 per cent VAT rate would increase LDC exports by ECU 50 million. By contrast, an upward harmonisation of excise duties on tobacco within the EU would produce a 40 per cent price rise, with a consequent 10–15 per cent fall in LDC exports, worth ECU 50–80 million. Here the major losers will be Brazil, Zimbabwe, India and Malawi.

The Uruguay Round

The latest Round of the GATT was completed in 1994 and included the creation of the World Trade Organisation (WTO). It will affect LDC trade relations with the EU in a number of ways.

The trend towards increasing agriculture protectionism was challenged in the Uruguay Round by the thirteen-nation Cairns Group, which included both developed (Australia, Canada and New Zealand) and developing countries (Brazil, Chile, Philippines and Malaysia). This group pressed for the inclusion of agricultural products in the negotiations, a position supported by the US but opposed by the EU. Through the reduction in agricultural protectionism, the Cairns Group sought the eventual elimination of EU agricultural subsidies and the movement towards free trade, benefiting not only efficient LDC and developed country agricultural exporters, but also EU consumers. The reduction in agricultural subsidies was one of the major areas of contention between the US and EU in the GATT negotiations. The final agreement requires the substitution of tariffs for the existing complex system of quotas, VERs, controls and variable levies. The average tariff reduction will be 36 per cent over six years. However, as this was calculated on the basis of the large difference between Community and world prices in the years 1986–88, when tariffs were at a maximum, the real reduction will be considerably smaller. In addition, the EU will cut its agricultural export subsidies by 36 per cent over the six years from 1994. The overall effect will be to raise world food prices to the disadvantage of those LDCs who are net importers. It will also erode the market advantage enjoyed by those LDCs who had privileged access to the EU, and reduce EU prices. Overall, the ACPs are expected to see a deterioration in their trade balance of $226 million in temperate and $177 million in tropical agricultural products (Davenport *et al.*, 1995).

The preference erosion that will occur under the agricultural changes also applies to manufactures. For LDCs as a whole manufactures have become of increasing importance. In 1970 manufactures represented only one-third of their export earnings, but by 1992 this had risen to 75 per cent. By 1979 EU tariffs on manufactured imports were already low, with MFN tariffs at an average of 6.3 per cent. The LDCs enjoyed a further 2 per cent reduction under the GSP, and ACP manufactures entered duty-free. The Uruguay Round agreed a further reduction in MFN tariffs to 3.9 per cent, eroding the GSP and ACP preferences.

But these average tariffs disguise the discrimination against particular products. Clothing, leather, rubber, shoes and transport equipment all experienced small cuts on high tariffs. Unfortunately, it is these products that are of particular importance to some LDCs. However, overall, these changes are expected to cost the ACP countries only $317 million in lost exports.

Of more significance was the agreement to bring textiles back under the auspices of GATT. The MFA will be phased out over the next ten years, with tariffs replacing quotas, but these will remain relatively high at 12 per cent. An overall increase in textile and clothing exports to the EU of 20 per cent over ten years is expected. Efficient producers such as China, India and Pakistan are likely to gain at the expense of established exporters such as Jamaica and Mauritius. Other VERs must either conform with GATT rules or be phased out within four years.

The overall effect of the Uruguay Round on LDC world exports is mixed. The Overseas Development Institute (1995) has estimated that by 2005 Africa's exports will be reduced by 0.72 per cent on their 1992 figure, Latin America's will increase 0.62 per cent, and Asia's will increase 2.05 per cent. For the ACPs as a group, they will see exports fall 1.7 per cent. Indeed, the general benefits from the new GATT agreement will be received principally by the developed world. The OECD estimates that, of the $250 bn increase in world trade over a decade, three-quarters will accrue to the developed countries. The Asian NICs are expected to gain $7.1 bn – $3.3 bn from farm liberalisation, $1.8 bn from textile trade, and $1.1 bn from services. India is expected to gain $4.6 bn and South America $8.0 bn, but Africa as a whole is expected to lose $2.6 bn.

In terms of the ACPs' trade with the EU alone, export revenues are expected to fall by ECU 256 million (1.3 per cent of export earnings). The biggest losers are anticipated to include Ethiopia, Fiji, Trinidad and Tobago, Guyana, Mauritius, Senegal, Jamaica, Tanzania and Malawi.

Aid

Aid disbursements from the EU are provided from two sources – the European Development Fund (EDF), associated with the Lomé Conventions, and the general EU budget. The EDF constituted only 35 per cent of total EU aid in 1993 (Table 14.7) as there were no disbursements under STABEX, while food aid took over half of the remaining aid funded from the general budget. Assistance to the Asian, Latin American and Mediterranean LDCs has been taking a growing share in recent years. Under the New Mediterranean Policy (1989), ECU 4405 million of grants and loan were to be made available to eight Mediterranean countries over five years, half of which was to go to Morocco, Algeria and Tunisia. South Africa has received the largest non-ACP funding (ECU 60 million in 1993).

From 1984–93 the aid disbursed by the EU has been increasing at an average annual rate of 20 per cent. In 1994 aid totalled ECU 4.1 bn, making the EU the second largest multilateral donor after the World Bank. However, this represented only 17 per cent of the total official aid given by member states and was smaller than the bilateral aid budgets of France or Germany.

Table 14.7 Disbursements of EU aid, 1990–93 (ECU m)

	1990	1991	1992	1993
European Development Fund[a]	1256	1195	1942	1354
General EU Budget	953	1923	1553	1810
of which:				
Food aid	485	650	627	434
Asia and Latin America	245	253	319	354
Mediterranean	103	165	219	353
Humanitarian aid[b]	20	116	121	341
NGOs	85	87	101	129
Other	16	651	165	200
Total	2209	3118	3495	3164

(1 ECU = US$1.17 in 1993)

Notes:

(a) EDF disbursements fell in 1993 because there was no disbursement of STABEX funds (which took up 32% of EDF expenditures in 1992).

(b) Figures for humanitarian aid are not unambiguous due to the change in the statistical series used to calculate these figures.

Source: Aid Review, 1992–93 and 1994–95

Lomé

The Lomé Conventions are the basis of aid provision to the ACP countries. There is no requirement that the funds be disbursed within the period of any given Lomé convention. Thus by May 1989, 74 per cent of Lomé III funds had been committed, but only 11 per cent disbursed.

The aid is administered principally through the European Development Fund (EDF) which had been established under the Treaty. Subsequently, a separate EDF became associated with each Lomé convention. Thus, Lomé III, which commenced in 1986, was associated with the sixth European Development Fund (EDF6), disbursing ECU 7.4 bn. In addition, the European Investment Bank (EIB) made available to the ACPs ECU 1.1 bn. Eighty per cent of EDF6 funds were allocated to conventional aid projects (programmable), and 20 per cent to STABEX and emergency aid. STABEX began with Lomé I and provides partial compensation to the ACPs for falls in agricultural export earnings, either from a decline in commodity prices or from a fall in output; 48 'soft' commodities are now covered. Similar earnings support is offered to states dependent upon mineral exports under SYSMIN, created under Lomé II. There is also provision under Article 188 of the Treaty for assistance with the financing of imports during structural adjustment.

Programmable aid was divided, at the commencement of the Convention, into shares for each region and state. Each ACP government then negotiated a National Indicative Programme (NIP), setting out, in broad terms, the framework within which the aid will be spent. Within this framework specific projects were then planned.

Lomé IV

Although the economic situation of many ACP countries has deteriorated throughout the period of the Conventions, this deterioration became more marked during the period of Lomé III. Falling commodity prices, rising world interest rates and substantial borrowings resulted in a serious debt problem for many LDCs, especially the African states; for example, ACP African countries' debt had risen from $56 bn in 1980 to $128 bn in 1987.

Two major issues began to be addressed during Lomé III, and became a major focus of debate in the negotiations for Lomé IV: trade *versus* aid, and structural adjustment in the ACPs.

With regard to trade the Northern member states of the EU sought a further extension of trade preferences on temperate agricultural goods to ACPs rather than further increases in the volume of EU aid. However, they have faced opposition from the Southern member states, whose produce would face the enhanced competition.

The second major focus of debate within the EU had been the degree to which aid should be directed towards countries undertaking 'structural adjustment' policies, i.e. economic reforms involving cuts in government expenditure, removal of price controls, devaluation and privatisation. Initially, under the Conventions the ACPs were left with substantial freedom in deciding their aid priorities, but with Lomé III an attempt was made to influence ACP development strategies by stating EU preferences, for example, development of the food sectors, including drought and desertification control. Thus three-quarters of funds allocated under the National Indicative Programme were focused upon rural development, and the EU succeeded in establishing a 'policy dialogue' with each ACP government, asking them to indicate the range of policy measures they would take to support these priorities.

Nonetheless, in the negotiations over Lomé IV, some member states, especially the UK and the Netherlands, wished the ACPs to focus even more clearly upon structural adjustment policies by reallocating a greater proportion of EU aid funds away from conventional projects. The EU influence over the ACPs is clearly greater, the larger is the proportion of Lomé IV funds that have not been pre-allocated to countries under their NIPs. A further constraint on the ACPs arises with the issue of coordination of Lomé aid with IMF/World Bank funding, which itself is conditional on a commitment to structural adjustment. Again, the greater the proportion of Lomé aid dispersed under 'special structural adjustment' funds, the greater the potential for such coordination.

A structural fund was established under Lomé III of ECU 500 million during 1988 to provide import support for the poorest African states, in response to the STABEX fund becoming overdrawn. The eligibility criterion for drawing from this fund was that each LDC must have introduced appropriate economic policies, and agreements with the IMF/World Bank were taken as evidence of this. Thus, ACPs that have obtained a World Bank structural or sectoral adjustment loan (SAL/SECAL) may then apply for EU funding for a general import support programme. About half of the ACPs have sought adjustment credits from the World Bank. In the absence of World Bank support, the EU will make its own assessment as to a specific sectoral import support programme. However, fundamental disagreement with the IMF/World Bank may create difficulties for ACPs then applying to the EU.

Lomé IV was finally signed in December 1989 and, unlike previous Conventions, will run for ten years until the year 2000. The financial resources

Table 14.8 Volume of aid for the first five years of Lomé IV in comparison with Lomé III

	Lomé III Value (million ECU¹)	%	Lomé IV Value (million ECU)	%
Aid	4790	64.54%	6845²	63.38%
Risk capital	635	8.58%	825	7.64%
Stabex	925	12.50%	1500	13.89%
Sysmin	415	5.61%	480	4.44%
Structural adjustment support (SAS)	—	—	1150	10.65%
Soft loans	635	8.58%	—	—
Total EDF	7400	100%	10800	100%
EIB	1100		1200	
Total resources	8500		2000	

¹ 1 ECU = approximately £0.7 or 69 French francs (February 1990)
² Part of it can be used for SAS
Source: European Commission

allocated to the first five years of the Convention total ECU 12 bn, a 20 per cent increase in real terms over Lomé III (Table 14.8). Of this total, ECU 10.8 bn will be disbursed through EDF VII, and the remaining ECU 1.2 bn through the EIB. Recognising the increasing financial difficulties of the ACP countries, more of the assistance will be in the form of grants rather than loans, and EIB loans will be at lower interest rates (3 per cent to 6 per cent) than under Lomé III. Of the EDF funds, ECU 1.25 bn is set aside for assisting regional co-operation among the ACPs themselves, and ECU 1.15 bn has been allocated specifically to structural adjustment support (SAS). The Commission had proposed an SAS fund of ECU 2 bn and, in view of the smaller sums allocated, anticipates that only 30 to 35 ACP countries will benefit. These are most likely to be the countries already receiving IMF/World Bank approval. Thus, Lomé IV SAS may be regarded as merely complementary to IMF/World Bank funding.

In terms of trade concessions there was a reduction in restrictions on 40 agricultural products; the value of these concessions varies considerably. In the case of rum, all restrictions were abolished after 1995, but with other products concessions had been limited. For example, the ACPs sought an increase of 30,000 tonnes in the EU imports of rice and received an increase of only one-tenth of that. Critics suggest that it failed to provide the ACPs with the transparent trading regime for agricultural products that they needed. However, these agreements must be seen within the context of the wider GATT negotiations under the Uruguay Round which to a considerable extent have superseded it.

STABEX and SYSMIN have both been expanded and revised under Lomé IV. STABEX funding was increased by 62 per cent to ECU 1.5 bn in the face of falling commodity prices, and the threshold for assistance was lowered from a product contributing 6 per cent of an ACP country's total export earnings to a contribution of 5 per cent. STABEX transfers were also no longer repayable, but the EU had greater control of the use of the funds, directing them specifically towards greater diversification.

SYSMIN was increased to ECU 480 million with a change from loans to grants. It also now covered uranium and gold, as well as copper, cobalt, phosphates, manganese, bauxite and alumina, tin and iron ore. Any ACP where 20 per cent of export earnings is derived from these minerals could now seek assistance.

Finally, Lomé IV offered a crucial concession on the issue of rules of origin. If at least 45 per cent of the value added of a product can be shown to have been created within an ACP, it may be imported into the EU duty-free (compared with 60 per cent under Lomé III) as long as no market disturbance is entailed.

Lomé IV also emphasised the role of private-sector development within ACPs. This was to be encouraged with the provision of risk capital through the EIB, technical assistance and investment protection, environmental assessment of development projects, encouragement of 'micro projects' with non-governmental organisations, and the encouragement of active population policies.

The mid-term review

The mid-term review of Lomé IV began in May 1994 and had been intended only to consider the levels of aid to be given for the remaining five years, under EDF VIII. However, the international environment had changed significantly with the end of the Cold War, and the EU was increasingly dissatisfied with the lack of results from its long-term aid programme. Increasing emphasis was being placed upon the adoption of structural adjustment policies by the LDCs, i.e. devaluation, privatisation, free markets, tight monetary and fiscal policies, by all international aid donors. The EU sought to enhance its influence over the ACP governments to achieve these structural changes.

Administrative failings

In addition to these general criticisms, the actual operation of the Lomé Conventions had been subject to complaint. In particular, attention was drawn to the slowness of its disbursement of allocated funds. At the end of the third year of Lomé IV (EDF VII) only 15.5 per cent of funds had been paid, while in 1994 EDF V had finally closed, having disbursed only 87 per cent of its monies. STABEX was criticised for its lack of clear rules and failure to monitor the use of funds. In 1993 it had disbursed no funds at all, and in 1994 met only half of requests. SYSMIN was regarded as even more unsatisfactory; under Lomé III it had disbursed only 35 per cent of its funds.

The evaluation of EU project aid had also been regarded as inadequate, while the Commission itself recognises that one-third of projects are likely to have offered poor value for money. This relatively poor record has given weight to the arguments that greater emphasis should be placed upon macro-structural adjustment funding. Thus, project aid has taken a smaller share of EU aid recently, declining from 66 per cent to 42 per cent over the last ten years.

Concern has also been expressed about the role of the EU Humanitarian Office (ECHO), which was created in 1992 to coordinate emergency aid. EU emergency aid has been growing rapidly, and there is the possibility that funds will be diverted from long-term development assistance. This problem is exacerbated by the separation of the ECHO from the other EU Development Directorates and its poor coordination with them. Seen as bureaucratic and inefficient, it disperses most of its funds indirectly though international non-governmental (NGOs) and UN agencies.

The provisions

Despite an original Commission proposal of ECU 16.5 bn for EDF VIII and an increase in the number of EU aid donors from 12 to 15, the total value of Lomé IV aid for its final five years was pegged in real terms to ECU 14.96 bn. (see Table 14.9), including ECU 292 million of unutilised funds from previous EDFs. France became the largest contributor followed by Germany. The UK remains the third largest contributor but was the only EU member to cut its payments (see Table 14.10).

There was a 16 per cent reduction in tariffs on a number of products, including cereals, pork and rice, but sensitive products such as olives, wine and lemons were not included. The tariff quota on sheep, poultry, milk products and pears was doubled. More importantly, the rules of origin were relaxed. The limit on the non-ACP value of inputs for the product still to enjoy duty-free access to the EU was raised from 10 to 15 per cent of domestic value added. A further

Table 14.9 Financial Protocol, 1995–2000

	ECU million
EDF VIII	12967
of which:	
Risk capital	1000
STABEX	1800
SYSMIN	575
Structural adjustment	1400
Emergency aid	260
Interest rate subsidies	370
Regional cooperation	1300
Other	6262
European Investment Bank	1658

Source: The Courier, No. 155, European Commission January 1996

Table 14.10 Major contributors to the EDF

	ECU million	
	EDF VII	EDF VIII
Belgium	433	503
Denmark	227	275
Germany	2840	3000
Spain	645	750
France	2666	3120
Italy	1418	1610
Netherlands	609	670
UK	1791	1630
Austria		340
Finland		190
Sweden		350
EIB	1200	1658
Total	12140	14965

Source: The Courier, No. 153, European Commission September 1995

concession was given, allowing inputs from neighbouring non-ACP LDCs to be regarded as a part of the domestic value added.

To address the problem of slow disbursement and unallocated funds, and to enhance the influence of the EU in ensuring the commitment of ACP countries to structural adjustment programmes, aid was now to be phased. Only 70 per cent of a country's NIP aid is allocated for the first three years, the remaining 30 per cent being conditional upon satisfactory performance. Satisfactory performance will now include the issue of human rights, and Article 366 of the Convention will allow the EU to suspend aid if an ACP infringes these rights.

Private investment

The long-term success of LDCs' economic development depends crucially upon investment. Although this may be funded by aid, as both grants and loans, increasing emphasis is being placed upon the role of the private sector. Private investment is regarded as offering greater efficiency. It is more likely to identify commercially viable projects, implement them efficiently and provide essential complementary factors: for example, managerial skills, marketing and distribution. It is open to question whether this has been encouraged or discouraged by the creation of the single market.

In the 1950s the US had already begun to shift its focus of investment away from LDCs towards other developed countries, and this trend was followed in the 1970s by the UK, and in the 1980s by Japan (see Table 14.11). By this date most EU countries had already re-orientated their investment, for example, France and West Germany were directing only between 10 per cent and 20 per cent of their overseas investment to the LDCs. In 1983 direct investment in the LDCs had fallen dramatically to only $9 bn from $14 bn. However, during the 1990s there was a rapid recovery, with a five-fold increase between 1990 and 1995, averaging $25 bn per annum. The share of the LDCs in world foreign direct investment (FDI) had increased from 15 per cent in 1990 to 32.5 per cent in 1992. Part of this has been attributed, by the IMF, to debt equity swaps in Latin America, whose share in FDI had risen to 11.2 per cent. Japanese investment in Asia has increased substantially, raising their share of FDI to 18.6 per cent, with China an important recipient.

In 1996 it was estimated that private capital flows to the LDCs would be almost eight times the value of EU aid. Nevertheless, in the ACP countries private investment has been considerably smaller. Nonetheless, private flows have begun to assume much greater importance even here. By 1993 net private flows to the ACPs of ECU 1384 million were 16 per cent of the total flow of funds to these countries.

Six of the EU's member states account for the bulk of the Community's foreign investment (France, Germany, Italy, the Netherlands, Spain and the UK). In the mid-1980s their annual investment in the LDCs was averaging $4.5 bn, and by 1989 this had increased to $10 bn. However, this investment had been concentrated in the NICs (35 per cent in 1988–89) and Latin America (38 per cent). In 1990 this outflow fell significantly. Although this may be explained as

Table 14.11　Distribution of FDI inflows by region and country, 1982–92
(in percentages)

Country/Region	1982–87	1988	1989	1990	1991	1992
Western Europe	31.5	37.9	44.9	52.5	49.8	52.0
of which:						
EU	28.2	35.9	41.3	48.0	44.4	49.7
US	41.3	39.2	36.5	27.0	19.8	7.0
Japan	0.2	0.1	0.1	0.0	0.2	0.1
LDCs	21.8	17.5	14.0	15.0	24.1	32.5
of which:						
Africa	2.8	1.7	2.5	1.0	1.7	1.9
Latin America and Caribbean	8.9	5.7	3.2	4.2	9.3	11.2
East, South and South-East Asia	9.3	9.4	7.9	9.3	12.5	18.6
Total of above	94.8	94.7	95.5	94.5	93.9	91.6
Other countries	5.2	5.3	4.5	5.5	6.1	8.4
All countries (US$ billion)	67.5	159.1	196.1	207.9	162.1	158.4

Source: UN (1994), World Investment Report 1994, Transnational Corporations, Employment and Workplace

a response to the Kuwait crisis and to the onset of recession in Europe, it is also possible that the advent of the single market had an adverse impact.

To fully exploit economies of scale, cost reductions, market opportunities and the enhanced income growth of the single market, substantial restructuring and investment occurred throughout European industry. In addition, developments in Central and Eastern Europe have generated substantial demands for investment, and both historical ties and commercial advantage have produced a positive response from the Western European countries. The Community responded by initiating the foundation of the European Bank for Reconstruction and Development, with a capital of ECU 10 bn, one of whose principal aims was to act as a catalyst for private-sector investment in Central and Eastern Europe. By contrast, the poorer LCDs might appear a less attractive destination for corporate investment. Potential competition for FDI between Central and Eastern Europe and the LDCs of the Mediterranean basin has been highlighted, while, unlike all other LDC regions, Africa's share of FDI has failed to recover from its peak of $4.9 bn (2.5 per cent) in 1990.

Immigration

Finally, mention might be made of the impact upon immigration control policy of the creation of the SEM and the Treaty on European Union (TEU). So far, our discussion has focused solely upon the movement of goods and capital. However, for some LDCs, especially those of North Africa, the EU has been a significant destination for emigration. Faced with rapidly increasing populations, but limited employment creation, emigration has made some contribution to reducing these pressures, while remittances have been an important source of income. The creation of the single internal market entails free movement of labour and removal or minimising of border controls. In turn, this implies the need for the development of a common immigration control policy. Despite the increasing average age of Europe's population, labour shortages are more likely to be met by Eastern European migration and more capital-intensive modes of production, than by relaxation of EU controls on LDC immigration. Indeed, political pressure is likely to ensure that those countries that have traditionally adopted more liberal immigration controls, such as Italy, bring their policies into line with the more restrictive approach increasingly followed by the Northern member states. The TEU singles out immigration control as an area for a 'twin-track' approach of both inter-governmental agreements and Community law (see Geddes, 1995 and Baldwin-Edwards, 1991). It adopts cooperation provisions for the harmonisation of asylum policies and immigration controls, and amends the Treaty of Rome to allow the Community to establish common visa requirements. The draft Regulation on visa requirements, based upon the policies agreed by the Schengen group of EU countries, will require visas for most visitors from Third World countries.

Conclusion

In 1989 EU external assistance was ECU 2.3 bn, and by 1996 it had grown to ECU 5.5 bn. However, equally significant has been the change in its orientation. In 1989, 94 per cent of aid was directed at the ACP countries and Latin America, and by 1996 Central and Eastern Europe, Central Asia and the Mediterranean countries were taking almost half of EU assistance. This change resulted from two factors – first, the increasing concern over political instability in North Africa, Central and Eastern Europe, with the concomitant threat of mass immigration, and, secondly, the decision in 1992 that member states should contribute increasing amounts to the general EU budget for external assistance to non-ACP countries. This allowed funding of an aid policy aimed at meeting Europe's new political concerns but also placed traditional ACP aid through the EDF under pressure.

At the same time the EU was seeking greater effectiveness in its Lomé aid programme. Questions have been raised about both the number of aid schemes under Lomé and the role of the National Indicative Programme. The integration of aid that was the rationale for the NIPs has been compromised by the desire of the EU to have greater leverage over the LDC governments' use of funds; hence the proliferation of aid instruments such as the Structural Adjustment Facility. The EU's aid strategy has increasingly emphasised the enhancement of the competitiveness of the ACP economies and the development of their private sectors and international trade. To achieve this, the policy focus has turned to support for the mobilisation of private capital, the restructuring of the public sector, the development of infrastructure, and macro-economic stabilisation.

Discussion has also arisen as to the relative roles of the Commission and the member states' aid programmes. In May 1992 the Commission had set out its view of 'Development Cooperation Policy in the Run-Up to 2000' (Horizon 2000) which in part addressed the issue of operational coordination. Six pilot country aid coordination projects are now in progress. If successful, some member states, such as Belgium and Germany, favour particular donors or the Commission taking lead responsibility in a specific sector or area, particularly in its areas of strength, i.e. trade promotion, structural adjustment programmes or large project funding. Alternatively, some have argued that the EU should take prime responsibility for all EU development policy. However, reservations exist about the Commission's own capabilities, with major criticism of its organisational structure of five Commissioners responsible for external assistance, through four Directorates General, as well as the European Community Humanitarian Office.

More fundamental doubts have also been expressed as to the future of the Lomé Conventions themselves. Many commentators doubt whether any Lomé agreement will succeed the current Convention in the year 2000. The trade preferences given under Lomé may not be compatible with commitments made to the World Trade Organisation since they discriminate between LDCs and are non-reciprocal. Although Lomé currently has a waiver, this will end in 2000. The recent Green Paper on Lomé's future (COM(96)570) offers four main options for any new trade arrangements with the ACPs: the status quo, the replacement of Lomé preferences by the GSP, uniform reciprocity to meet WTO requirements, or differentiated reciprocity perhaps on a regional basis.

The ACP group of countries is also seen as the product of historic ties with member states rather than a coherent group. It excludes LDCs with lower per capita incomes, such as Bangladesh, and ignores the considerable variation in the situation and interests of the African, Caribbean and Pacific countries. The Green Paper offers four possible options: the status quo, a general agreement supplemented by bilateral arrangements to provide flexibility, splitting Lomé into separate regional agreements, or an agreement confined to the lowest income LDCs. There is a clear desire to increase the degree of differentiation in the EU's relationship with the LDCs, and regionalisation is emerging as the preferred outcome. However, this discussion is only just beginning.

References

Balassa B and Balassa C 1984 Industrial Protection in the Developing Countries, *The World Economy*, Vol. 7, No. 2, pp. 179–96.

Baldwin-Edwards M 1991 Immigration after 1992, *Policy and Politics*, Vol. 19, No. 3, pp. 199–211.

Cecchini P 1988 *The European Challenge: 1992, The Benefits of a Single Market*, Wildwood House, Aldershot.

Commission 1992 *Proposal for a Council Regulation (EEC) on the Common Organisation of the Market in Bananas*, COM(92)359, Brussels.

Commission 1994 *Council Resolution for applying a three year scheme of generalised tariff preferences (1995–97)*, COM(94)337 final, Brussels.

Commission 1996 *Relations Between the European Union and the ACP countries on the Eve of the 21st Century*, COM(96)570 final, Brussels.

Davenport M 1986 *Trade Policy, Protectionism and the Third World*, Croom Helm, London.

Davenport M 1990 The External Policy of the Community and its Effects on the Manufactured Goods of the Developing Countries, *Journal of Common Market Studies*, Vol. XXIX, No. 2, pp. 181–200.

Davenport M, Hewitt A and Koning A 1995 Europe's Preferred Partners? The Lomé Countries in World Trade, *ODI Special Report*, London.

Geddes A 1995 Immigration and Ethnic Minorities and the EU's 'Democratic Deficit': *Journal of Common Market Studies*, Vol. 33, No. 2, pp. 197–217.

Langhammer R and Sapir A 1987 *The Economic Impact of Generalised Tariff 1987, Preferences*, Thames Essays 49, Gower, London.

Langhammer R 1990 Fuelling a New Engine of Growth of Separating Europe from Non-Europe, *Journal of Common Market Studies*, Vol. 29, No. 2, December, pp. 133–55.

Matthews A and McAleese D 1990 LDC Primary Exports to the EC, Prospects post 1992, *Journal of Common Market Studies*, Vol. 29, No. 2, pp. 157–79.

McQueen M 1990 *ACP Export Diversification: The Case of Mauritius*, ODI Working Paper 41, London.

McQueen M and Stevens C 1989 Trade Preferences and Lomé IV; Non-traditional ACP exports to the EC, *Development Policy Review*, September.

OECD 1996 *Indicators of Tariff and Non-Tariff Trade Barriers*, OECD Publications, Paris.

Overseas Development Institute 1995 *Developing Countries in the WTO*, Briefing paper No. 3, May.

Page S 1985 *The Costs and Benefits of Protection*, OECD, Paris.

Pelkman J 1987 The European Community's Trade Policy Towards Developing Countries, *Europe and the International Division of Labour*, ed. C Stevens, Hodder and Stoughton, London.

Riddell R 1990 *ACP Export Diversification: The Case of Zimbabwe*, ODI Working Paper No. 38, June, London.

Stevens C 1990 *ACP Export Diversification: Jamaica, Kenya and Ethiopia*, ODI Working Paper 40, September, London.

Further reading

Commission 1990 Lomé IV, *Europe Information*, Brussels.

Davenport M 1992 Africa and the Unimportance of Being Preferred, *Journal of Common Market Studies*, Vol. 31, No. 2, June, pp. 232–251.

Davenport M and Page S 1989 *Regional Trading Agreements, The Impact of the 1989 Implementation of the Single European Market on Developing Countries*, ODI Report, London.

Overseas Development Institute 1997 *The Developing Countries and 1992*, Briefing Paper November, London.

Overseas Development Institute 1997 *Foreign Direct Investment Flows to Low-income Countries: A Review of the Evidence*: Briefing Paper, September, London.

Zimmermann K L 1994 Some General Lessons for Europe's Migration Problem, in *Economic Aspects of International Migration*, ed. Giersch H, Springer-Verlag, Berlin.

Zimmermann K F 1995 Tackling the European Migration Problem, *Journal of Economic Perspectives*, Vol. 9, No. 2, pp. 45–62.

15 The European Union and the Triad

Frank McDonald

Introduction

The Community has tended to regard commercial relationships with European countries as its top priority. This was reflected in the efforts that went into enlarging the EU, establishing trading agreements with nearly all European countries, and the emphasis placed on integrating the countries of Central and Eastern Europe into the EU's sphere of economic and political influence (see Chapters 12 and 13). In contrast, trade relationships with the USA, Japan and the newly industrialised countries (NICs) have tended to be lower down the list of priorities of the EU. Nevertheless, the emergence of a series of trade disputes between the EU and the US and Japan, and the development of the Asian NICs as major exporters have led to an increasing focus on commercial relationships with these countries.

Much of EU trade with Japan involves sensitive products such as cars and consumer electronic equipment. The high public profile of these sectors increased the importance that was attached to Japanese imports by many of the governments in the member states. The rapid growth of Japanese exports to the EU, combined with a persistent balance of payments surplus with the EU and accusations of protectionist restrictions on imports into Japan, increased tension in trade matters. Trade in agricultural products has been a major source of friction between the EU and the USA (see Chapter 11). The passing of the Omnibus Trade Act in 1988 and the LIBERTAD (Helms-Burton) Act in 1995 increased tension with the USA because of the attempts by the US to apply its laws to European companies.

The importance of the USA, and to a lesser extent Japan, in providing FDI inflows into the EU also increased the importance of relations with these countries. The creation of the SEM stimulated Japanese firms to set up production plants within the EU. Some member states regarded this FDI as a welcome contribution to boosting productivity and the quality of products. Others considered it a threat to the future of existing European-based companies.

The member states of the EU face growing penetration of their markets from the Asian NICs. Many markets in Europe are experiencing increasing competition from companies based in Taiwan, South Korea and Hong Kong. The countries of ASEAN (Brunei Darussalam, Malaysia, Philippines, Singapore and Thailand) are also seeking new markets in Europe. In many respects these countries are following the Japanese path. They have fast-growing economies and they base their expansion on export-led growth. The first markets they targeted were steel, shipbuilding, low value-added manufactured goods and chemicals. They had considerable success in these markets and are now turning to other, more high-technology sectors. Already companies such as Hyundai and Samsung are experiencing success in penetrating the European markets for cars and consumer electronics, and some of them have begun to engage in FDI activities in the EU. American and European multinationals have also established production plants in these NICs and are increasingly supplying the European market from these plants. The rapid growth of China has also led to increased penetration of EU markets by Chinese manufactured goods.

The Triad

The trade and business relationship between the USA, Japan and Europe is often referred to as the Triad – a term popularised by management theorists (Ohmae, 1985). The countries of the Triad are in effect the engine of the world economy. The economic relationships between the members of the Triad have a strong impact on the transmission of booms and slumps across the world economy. The mechanisms that link these economies in the economic cycle are not clearly understood, but the trading and FDI links play a key role in the process. Equally important, or perhaps more important, are the links created by international financial markets. The centres of these international financial markets are in the USA (New York and Chicago), Japan (Tokyo) and Europe (London). Changes in stock, futures and exchange rate markets in one of these centres are quickly picked up by the other centres, and funds flow freely between these markets in response to the changes. This process is of great importance in the transmission of cyclical changes in economic activity. The fairly minor effects of the financial crisis of 1998 among the Asian NICs on the economies of the member states indicate that the strength of the linkages between the EU, the US and the Asian economies is not symmetrical. The strongest links are between the USA and the EU, and the USA and Japan. The links between the EU and Japan are not as well developed as those with the USA, and the links to the Asian NICs are at an early stage of development. The linkages between these economies are further examined in Box 15.1.

Another reason for the importance of the Triad is that most of the large multinational companies have their base in one of the countries of the Triad. Many of these companies are also world leaders in their fields. In some industries Japanese companies are not important in terms of world market share relative to US and European companies, for example the food processing industry – Nestlé, Cadbury-Schweppes and Unilever in Europe, and Mars, Philip Morris and Coca-Cola in the USA, and personal hygiene products – Unilever and Henkel in Europe, and Proctor and Gamble and Colgate-Palmolive in the USA.

There is little doubt that, of the members of the Triad, the USA is the most important economy. The USA has the largest economy in terms of absolute and per capita GDP, the dollar is the most important currency in international trade, and the US is also the home base of many of the largest multinational companies

Box 15.1 Economic linkages in the Triad

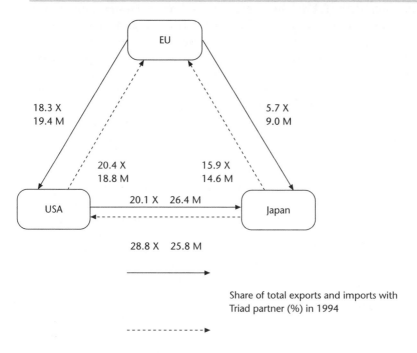

Share of total exports and imports with
Triad partner (%) in 1994

X = exports   M = imports

The size of trade flows indicates that the USA is a very important market (as a share of total trade) for both the EU and Japan, but that the USA is more important for Japan than it is for the EU. Japan has the highest dependency on trade within the Triad.

In terms of FDI flows the USA is the most important supplier and receiver of intra-Triad flows. In 1994 the outward FDI flows from the USA amounted to $45,640 million, compared with $38,108 million from the EU (i.e. excluding intra-EU flows) and $17,938 million from Japan. The stocks of FDI were USA $610,061 million, EU $579,900 million, and Japan $277,733 million. If intra-EU flows and stocks are considered, the Community has been the largest source of FDI stocks and flows since the early 1990s (Commission, 1996).

Trade with the Asian NICs is considerably less important than is trade with the members of the Triad. Only China is in the top five suppliers of EU imports (number five with 5.2 per cent of the total) and no Asian NIC is in the top five for EU exports (Commission, 1998).

in the world. About 32 per cent of the top 100 multinationals (as measured by size of foreign assets) are American, and 20 per cent are Japanese. However, European countries have the largest number of such multinationals, with 41 per cent, although there is only one European multinational in the top ten – Royal Dutch Shell which is number one. The US has five companies in the top ten; the rest are Japanese. Of the top five companies four are American (Commission, 1996). In many sectors US companies are among the world leaders, as measured by market share. Generally, US companies have a strong presence in a wide range of industries, for example information technology products (IBM, Hewlett-Packard, Intel, Netscape and Microsoft), vehicle production (Ford and General Motors), food processing (Coca-Cola, Mars, Philip Morris), aerospace equipment (Boeing), chemicals (Du Pont, Dow Chemicals and Union Carbide) and personal hygiene products (Proctor and Gamble and Colgate-Palmolive). The Europeans have few world leaders, but they are fairly strong in a number of sectors, e.g. telecommunications equipment (Siemens Alcatel Alsthom and Ericsson), food processing (Nestlé, Unilever and Cadbury-Schweppes), vehicle production (Daimler-Benz, Volkswagen and Renault) and chemicals (BASF, Bayer, Hoechst). The Japanese have some world class companies, but they tend to be concentrated in a smaller number of sectors, e.g. vehicle production (Toyota, Honda and Nissan), electronics (Hitachi, Matushita, NEC and Sony) and trading companies (Mitsubishi, Mitsui and Sumitomo).

The dominance of the USA in terms of economic size, world class companies and technological leadership is often overlooked in discussions on the Triad. The rise of Japanese companies and their successful penetration of the US market, particularly the car market, led to a view that the USA is in a period of relative decline and needs to restructure its economic base fundamentally to survive as a major economic power. This case is argued, with some force, by Thurow (1992).

This view of US decline is probably greatly overstated. As indicated above, the Americans are still the major players in many of the fastest growing markets in the world. There was evidence that, in the early 1990s, when views on the decline of the US were very popular, the USA was still the most productive nation in the world. A study by the McKinsey Global Institute (1993) discovered that, on average, the Japanese were 83 per cent as productive as the Americans, and the Germans (the most productive European country) were 79 per cent as productive. In some industries the Japanese were more productive than the Americans (cars and car parts, consumer electronics, metalworking and steel), while the Germans did not have higher productivity in any major sector and could match the Americans only in steel and metalworking. The USA has a decisive lead over the Germans in computers, cars and car parts, consumer electronics, soaps and detergents, beer and food processing. They have a clear lead over the Japanese in soaps and detergents, beer and food processing.

The 1998 World Competitiveness Survey, published by the International Institute for Management Development, ranked the US as the best country with regard to the ability of companies to develop competitiveness (IMD, 1998). In the 1990s the US has consistently come top of the World Competitiveness Survey. The Survey assesses a variety of factors that influence the competitiveness of companies, including quantitative data (for example, education expenditures,

GDP per capita, productivity) and qualitative data (for example, the impact of government regulations on companies). Among the member states the Netherlands was ranked fourth, Finland fifth, Denmark eighth, Luxembourg ninth, Ireland eleventh and the UK twelfth. Germany was ranked fourteenth, France was twenty-first and Italy thirtieth. Japan was ranked eighteenth and the Asian city states – Singapore and Hong Kong – were ranked second and third respectively. Of the other Asian NICs, only Taiwan reached the top 20 (ranked sixteenth). The World Competitiveness Survey cannot be regarded as an objective ranking of the effect of different economic systems on the ability of companies to operate effectively in competitive markets. However, it does provide a method, based on the gathering of a substantial amount of data, of comparing the effect of these different economic systems on company competitiveness. The presence of countries such as the Netherlands, Finland and Denmark in the top ten indicates that the methods used to rank countries does not depend on their having Anglo-Saxon type economic systems. The clear lead of the US in these surveys indicates that the American system is not in terminal decline.

The strong growth of the USA in the 1990s also focused attention on some of the strengths of the American economy – unemployment has fallen, inflation has remained low, and healthy growth rates have been maintained. This performance has been in marked contrast to most of the member states and Japan where unemployment has risen (particularly in continental Europe) and growth has been low. American companies have developed new technologies (especially associated with developments in IT, telecommunications and biotechnology). This has allowed the American economy to create a large number of private-sector jobs. The flexible nature of US labour markets, competitive and sophisticated capital markets, and the emphasis on shareholder value have been credited as the main reasons for this American 'success' story.

The establishment of EMU will affect relationships with Japan and the US. The emergence of the euro as a world currency will have implications for international money markets. Currently the international money markets are dominated by the dollar, with the DM and the yen having a lesser role. It is hard to see the dollar losing its dominant position in the near future. However, the introduction of the euro will affect the role of the dollar in the medium to long term. This will have important implications for relationships within the Triad.

American influence, therefore, arises not only from the size of the US economy and the important role that the dollar plays in world trade, but also from its relatively good economic performance in the 1990s. The political and military power of the US further adds to American dominance in most matters connected with international relations.

The development of economic integration in Europe and the creation of the North American Free Trade Area (NAFTA) between the USA, Canada and Mexico hold the prospect that the Triad may evolve into three trading groups, based on NAFTA, a 'Fortress Europe' and Japan (possibly with close links to the Asian NICs). Another possibility is the development of Asia-Pacific Economic Cooperation (APEC) as a free-trade area that would include the East Asian economies, the US and Canada (Funabashi, 1995). The Triad could develop into a complex set of relationships between regional trading blocs (see Box 15.2).

Box 15.2   The Triad and regional trade blocs

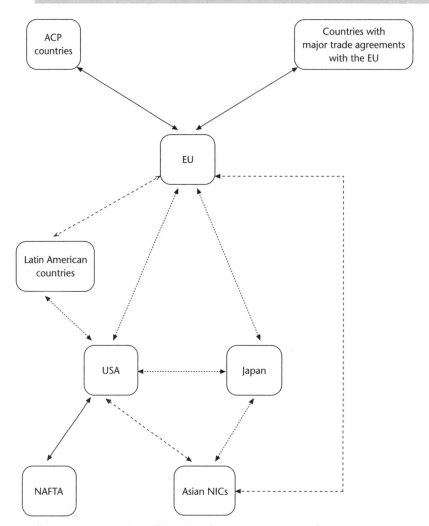

Asian NICs = Asean countries, China, South Korea, Taiwan and Hong Kong

Countries with major trade agreements with the EU – Turkey, most CEECs, Maghreb countries (Algeria, Morocco and Tunisia) and Mashreq countries (Egypt, Jordan, Syria and the Lebanon)

Key:

◄——► = institutional links with strong trading and business component
◄┄┄► = substantial trading links
◄--► = less substantial trading links

The links between the main members of the Triad and regional trade blocs mean that the bulk of world trade is connected with the economic relationships of the Triad.

Conflict between members of the Triad would raise serious difficulties for the world economy. Theory suggests that in such circumstances cooperation can result in mutually beneficial outcomes, whereas conflict can lead to all parties suffering losses. However, these theories also suggest that cooperation between such parties can be very difficult to achieve and maintain.

Cooperation or conflict?

The issue of cooperation versus conflict can be analysed using game theory. This theory is useful for analysing international relations as it provides a relatively straightforward method of investigating cooperative and non-cooperative behaviour between nations (see Nicholson, 1989). A simple example of the use of game theory to illustrate international trade liberalisation is given in Box 15.3.

The simple nature of these games (as illustrated in Box 15.2) tends to conceal some of the problems of using such models directly to explain real world behaviour. First, traditional economic theory suggests that unilateral trade concessions are better than no trade concessions. This follows from the gains

---

Box 15.3 Cooperation and conflict

Suppose that the EU and Japan are considering whether or not to grant trade concessions by easing or eliminating barriers to trade imposed on foreign firms.

		EU	
		A	B
	A	2,2	0,3
Japan			
	B	3,0	1,1

A = policy of granting trade concessions

B = policy of not granting trade concessions

If both parties adopt A, the outcome is a pay-off of 2 each. If they both choose B, the outcome is a pay-off of 1 each. If the EU chooses A, and Japan B, the pay-off becomes 0 for the EU and 3 for Japan (*vice versa* if the EU chooses B and Japan adopts A). This is the classic prisoner's dilemma game, where the outcome for a player depends on the choice of policy of the other player. Obviously, the best aggregate outcome is for both to choose trade concessions and adopt policy A. However, if one player chooses B, and the other player chooses A, the pay-off is 3 for the player who opts for B and 0 for the player who chooses A. There is therefore an incentive for both players to choose policy B, as by doing this the minimum pay-off is 1 and the maximum is 3, as opposed to a minimum pay-off of 0 and a maximum of 2 if policy A is adopted. In these circumstances a non-cooperative, or conflict, outcome prevails, even though the cooperative outcome yields the greater aggregated benefits.

to consumers of reducing trade barriers that lead to lower prices and higher output. In these circumstances it is not clear why the policy of not reducing trade barriers confers benefits to either party in the game. In the real world, however, trade concessions are often denied unless there is a reciprocal granting of concessions. In trade liberalisation in services and foreign investments, reciprocity is normally an important consideration. Even in the granting of trade concessions on goods, agreement on trade liberalisation packages is often dependent on reciprocal agreements to reduce barriers. The rationale for these actions may be based on placing consumer interests on a lower level than producer interests. It is also possible to provide a theoretical justification for this behaviour, as some of the new theories of international trade suggest that unilateral trade concessions are not necessarily beneficial. In a world of increasing returns to scale and imperfectly competitive market structures, there can be a sound economic case for providing strategic protection to allow domestic industries to reap advantage from economies of scale, and to benefit from the learning effects of expanding domestic production. However, the advocates of these new theories maintain that it is probably not possible to pursue such policies efficiently, and that the objective of free trade is on balance the best policy (Krugman and Obstfeld, 1993). Nevertheless, to engage in unilateral free trade while your trading partners are implementing strategic protection policies is likely to harm your economy. This suggests that the implementing of free-trade policies is best achieved by negotiations on some kind of reciprocal basis.

Another problem is the assumption that the games are played in isolation from each other, which implies that the players do not learn. If the non-cooperative solution emerges from several games, it might be expected that the players would learn how to make arrangements to allow for cooperative outcomes to be achieved. This can be analysed using the theory of supergames, where the same game is repeated a large number of times. The problems of playing supergames in international trade relations are discussed by Keohane (see Guerrier and Padoan, 1988). In such games problems arise with free riding, when some players in the game reap benefits from cooperative solutions without themselves granting concessions. This results in a sub-optimal outcome in the sense that the maximum possible benefits to the system as a whole are not reaped. It might be argued that Japan has done this by benefiting from trade concessions that have opened up the markets of the USA and the EU to foreign competition, without granting significant liberalisation of the controls on entry to Japanese markets. The solution to this problem revolves around various forms of reciprocity. In this respect the insistence by the EU and the USA on using the principle of reciprocity may be wise.

This does not mean that the way in which the EU is using this principle is useful in achieving a cooperative outcome. Indeed, Ishikawa (1990) maintains that the EU is adopting too rigid a concept of reciprocity in dealing with Japan and the USA. The main problem is the attempt by the EU to obtain 'mirror image' treatment. This involves the granting of very similar concessions by all parties, and presents problems in areas such as financial services where laws and regulations govern access to the market. In the past the EU has insisted that, in order for Japanese or US firms to gain equal access to the European financial services market, EU firms must face the same conditions in the Japanese or the

US market. This was asking Japan and the USA to adopt in their home markets the emerging EU rules and regulations governing access to a single European financial services market. This hard form of reciprocity is unlikely to succeed. The principle of equivalent but not identical access would seem to be useful to achieve a cooperative solution to this problem. The EU seems to have moderated its view on this issue in talks with the Americans, and seems to be adopting an approach based on equivalent access. The view taken by the EU in WTO talks on issues such as market access and international competition rules suggests that the Community is moving away from the use of hard reciprocity (Commission, 1997a).

These problems increase the need for the EU, Japan and the USA to find ways of playing these supergames in a manner that permits cooperative solutions to be found. This requires mechanisms to control free riding by utilising loose forms of reciprocity. Systems to reduce cheating and non-fulfilment of agreements are also needed. Keohane regards international institutional innovations as having an important role in this process. Institutions can monitor and publish data to identify, and therefore deter, cheating and free-riding behaviour. These institutional forums can also be used to forge issue linkages. This involves linking separate issues to reach agreement, so that, for example, the EU could grant access to US firms to the European financial services market in return for American concessions on agricultural problems. Hence institutional forums and agencies could play a key role in allowing cooperative outcomes to emerge. The Uruguay Agreement led to the creation of the WTO (Bourgeois, 1995) which is seeking to promote a more open trading environment and to liberalise trade, particularly in the area of services – General Agreement on Trade in Services (GATS). However, the WTO has a large number of members, and unanimous agreement is required to achieve settlements on trade liberalisation. Bilateral negotiations between the EU and the US and Japan, or Triad based talks may help to forge agreements that could form the basis for WTO agreements.

The existing institutional frameworks could hamper such developments. International agencies such as the IMF, G8 and the OECD have representation from member states rather than from the EU. Only in the WTO does the EU represent all member states. With the growing importance of EU-Japanese-US relations, it might help to achieve cooperation if the EU rather than the member states were the prime negotiator. The creation of the SEM added impetus to the role of the EU in these agencies. The establishment of EMU in the EU would seem to indicate that the role of the EU in the main international monetary agencies must grow. In the future not only trade issues but international monetary issues are likely to be within the competence of the EU, rather than the member states. In these circumstances good relations between the members of the Triad could become very important. This implies a need to change international institutional arrangements to allow the EU a greater role.

Trading relations with the USA

The USA adopted a benign attitude towards the EEC in the 1950s and 1960s. The demise of the Bretton Woods system and the increasing industrial power of the EEC led to a change in American attitudes towards the Community. The prime dispute has been over the CAP (see Chapter 11). The crisis in the world steel industry in the 1970s, 1980s and 1990s also led to some bitter trade disputes. Both parties were heavily involved in helping their steel industries, the Americans by the use of import quotas and the EU by a host of policies implemented under the ECSC. This led to both sides accusing each other of unfair trading practices, and to the implementation of a series of trade restrictions (Featherstone and Ginsberg, 1996).

The American insistence on trying to apply US law to foreign individuals and companies outside the USA has also caused friction with the EU. This is the so-called extraterritoriality problem. An early example of this problem was the US embargo in 1982 on the use by European firms of American goods, patents and licences to build the Siberian pipeline. This was a pipeline to carry natural gas from Siberia to Western Europe. The Americans regarded the pipeline as a threat to the independence of Western Europe, and the US government tried to take unilateral action to control the activities of European firms engaged in work for the pipeline. This action was deeply resented in Western Europe, and eventually the embargo was withdrawn.

The passing of the Omnibus Trade Act in 1988 led to a further deterioration in relationships. The Super 301 provisions of this Act required the US government to identify countries using unfair trading practices, and to take unilateral action to induce such countries to stop these practices. The EU maintained that such trading conflicts should be resolved by WTO rather than by unilateral action. No actions were taken against the EU under the provisions of Super 301, but the threat of action soured relationships between the US and the EU.

In the 1990s the LIBERTAD (Helms-Burton) Act and the Iran and Libya Sanctions Act (ILSA – commonly referred to as the 'D'Amato Act) provoked further tension by raising questions about the use of extraterritoriality powers by the US government. These Acts related to US foreign policy objectives to isolate Cuba (Helms-Burton) and Iran and Libya (ILSA – 'D'Amato). The US threatened to exercise Federal laws regarding investments in Cuba and trade with Iran and Libya, on foreign-owned subsidiaries in America and on executives of foreign companies who entered the USA. In October 1996 the EU began a disputes procedure with the US over the Helms-Burton Act and lodged strong opposition with the US government over the ILSA. An agreement was reached in April 1997 that allowed the US to preserve the letter of these Acts but guaranteed that they would not be enforced against EU companies (Commission, 1997b).

The trade disputes between the EU and the USA have been increasing. Both parties have issued complaints about the other's trading behaviour. The EU complained about US policies for public procurement contracts, as a host of federal, state and even local government rules and regulations control public procurement in the USA. Federal and state governments also operate 'Buy American' policies on many public procurement contracts. The EU is also concerned with the system of setting and maintaining technical standards in the USA. These standards are issued by a multitude of federal and state authorities, and often pay little regard to international systems of setting standards. This makes it difficult for EU firms to collect information to comply with US standards. Meanwhile, the EU is moving to a system of common European standards that will make it relatively easy for US firms to gather information on European standards.

The Americans have complaints about EU trading practices. The public procurement directives to open up public tendering within the EU discriminate against non-EU firms. A directive issued in 1989 called for most European television broadcasting to be domestically produced. The Uruguay Round was agreed only after this dispute over broadcasting was dropped from the negotiations. The Broadcasting Directive was clearly aimed at reducing American television programmes on European networks. There have also been complaints from the USA about the large subsidies from European governments for the European Airbus. As the USA is the only alternative source of such civil aircraft, this is regarded as a protectionist policy against the USA. The CAP provides a perennial source of American complaints about EU trading practices.

Disputes over regulations in health and safety and environmental standards have also soured EU–US relationships. The US has complained about EU regulations on beef hormones, the EU ban on the use of leg-hold traps in the fur trade, and eco-labelling. The EU has argued that US regulations in areas such as fuel economy standards, drugs inspections and an embargo on tuna caught without due considerations for possible harm to dolphins were types of NTBs that were being used to protect US companies from legitimate competition. It has been argued that differences in regulations are not being used primarily to protect domestic industries, but rather they reflect cultural attitudes, for example the ban on leg-hold traps (Vogel, 1997). Vogel argues that, because the EU and the US exercise a large influence in the development of regulations that are used to govern world trade, it is important that they find ways to cooperate in the setting and development of regulations. However, if cultural differences are the root of the diversity of regulatory systems, it will be difficult to reach agreement. Furthermore, Japan and the NICs are likely to be unhappy about accepting an EU–US arrangement for establishing trading rules. In these circumstances the prospects for WTO rules are bleak. The scene seems to be set for the continuance of disputes between the US and the EU over regulations that affect trade.

Trading relations with Japan

The post-war incorporation of Japan into the world trading system has been a difficult process. Although Japan applied for membership of GATT in 1952, it was not granted membership until 1955. Even then many West European countries refused to grant Japan MFN treatment, because of claims that Japan engaged in unfair export practices and that the Japanese domestic market was effectively closed to Western exports. Many Western European countries continued to apply quantitative restrictions on some Japanese exports. It was not until the mid-1960s that Japan was granted MFN treatment and admission to the OECD. Consequently, by the time the EU developed a common commercial policy the attitude of Western European countries towards Japan was one of distrust and suspicion.

It is difficult to find rational reasons for this attitude. There was a legacy of bad relations because of the export policies of Japan in the 1920s and '30s. In this period the Japanese had practised large-scale dumping of imitation Western products and had frequently ignored trademarks and patents. In the 1950s the experiences of the Second World War resulted in opposition from the UK and the Netherlands to granting Japan full rights in the world trading system, but these explanations seem inadequate to explain the hostile attitude of Western Europe towards Japan in the immediate post-war period. The cultural differences between Japan and Europe, and a marked lack of interest about Japan, may have contributed to this hostility. In this period Europe was preoccupied with the growth of the Cold War, and the early moves towards European Unity. When Europe finally began to take an interest in Japan, the dramatic growth of the Japanese export-led industries led to what might be regarded as a kind of paranoia. There developed a school of thought that regarded Japan as a country engaged in economic warfare to destroy Western industries. The persistent and growing trade surplus of Japan only added to this paranoia, particularly as Japanese exports in the 1960s and 1970s tended to be concentrated in sensitive sectors, such as shipbuilding, steel and textiles. During the 1970s and 1980s the growth of Japanese exports of cars and consumer electronics made further inroads into highly sensitive sectors. In the late 1980s Japan became a leading exporter of computers and other information technology equipment. The increasing dominance of Japanese exports in these sensitive areas has led to a continuing hostility towards Japan. This rather sad history of trading relations between Europe and Japan has had a powerful influence on the attitude of the EU towards Japan.

The EU has a variety of complaints about Japan's protection of its domestic market, in particular, impenetrable technical rules and regulations, exclusion from public procurement contracts, and heavily bureaucratic import documentation procedures. Ishikawa (1990) argues that these problems are also experienced by Japanese firms seeking to export to the EU. Nevertheless, the EU maintains that market access into Japan is hampered by complex regulations that are considerably more of a barrier to entry than the rules that govern entry into the SEM. The Commission has threatened to refer conflict over quotas on fish imports and the taxation systems for alcoholic beverages that discriminated against foreign produced products to the disputes procedures of the WTO.

The export of services to Japan is hampered by legal barriers, and the Japanese marketing and distribution system is complex and involves close collaboration between Japanese producers and wholesalers and retailers. This makes it difficult for EU companies to sell consumer goods in Japan, unless they have Japanese subsidiaries. The marketing and distribution costs which EU companies face in Japan are therefore likely to be higher than those costs for Japanese firms selling in the EU. Japanese companies have close collaboration with each other under the auspices of the Japanese Ministry of International Trade and Industry (MITI). Much of the collaboration which is encouraged by MITI would be illegal if carried out in the EU. The EU therefore maintains that this is tantamount to an unfair trading practice.

The Japanese government instituted a Deregulation Programme 1995–98, and in 1997 an Action Plan for Economic Structural Reform. The Commission submitted a list of 200 proposals to the Japanese government that suggested how the Deregulation Programme and Action Plan might improve market access for European companies. Attempts are also being made to complete an agreement with the Japanese government over mutual recognition of testing and certification procedures for EU- Japanese trade. The Commission hopes to obtain a similar agreement to those it has already reached with the USA, Canada and Australia. Talks are also being held to open up the Japanese market for services and for FDI inflows.

The Commission collaborated with MITI on an Export Promotion Programme (EXPROM) to help European companies to enter the Japanese market. The Gateway to Japanese Export Promotion Campaign is geared towards SMEs and is seeking to help European companies to take advantage of the liberalisation programme that is slowly opening up Japanese markets to foreign competition. Ten sectors have been identified as offering good potential for European companies – medical equipment, packaging machinery, internal moving equipment, food, waste management technologies, alcoholic beverages, marine equipment, and IT equipment and software. However, reducing the cost of exporting by removing NTBs is not sufficient to promote an increase in trade. A reduction in NTBs in Japan will stimulate an increase in exports to Japan only if companies can reap profits from exporting. This depends on the revenue and especially cost conditions that companies face (see Fig. 15.1).

The trade surplus that Japan has run with the EU has declined in the 1990s. In 1993 the trade surplus of Japan was ECU 119 bn. This had fallen by 1996 to ECU 66 bn. During this period the EU's trade surplus in services rose from ECU 37 bn to ECU 49 bn. The current account balance with Japan declined from a deficit of ECU 113 bn in 1993 to ECU 52 bn in 1996. The balance is forecast to move in Japan's favour in the late 1990s but this is largely because of the low growth in Japan which is reducing the demand for imports, and the depreciation of the yen which is boosting exports (Commission, 1998).

The efforts by the EU, backed by even greater pressure from the Americans, to improve market access to Japan seem to have lessened some of the problems with the trade surplus of Japan. The perceived success of the market access strategy, and the growing contact between the Commission and the Japanese government seem to have led to an improvement in EU-Japanese relationships from the rather frosty climate of the 1980s. Nevertheless, a series of major problems have still to be resolved, most notably with regard to NTBs in the services sector and with FDI inflows. Moreover, the difficulty of finding agreement on mutual recognition of testing and certification procedures indicates that the EU still has problems with the complex bureaucratic procedures that govern access to the Japanese market.

Trading relationships with the NICs and China

Relationships between the EU and the Asian NICs are not as developed as those with the USA and Japan. However, as the Asian NICs and China have increased their share of the EU market, the Community has extended its relationships with

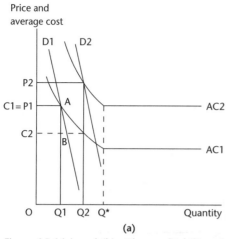

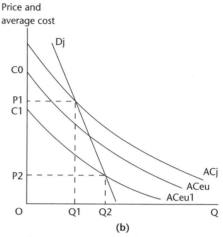

(a)

(b)

Figure 15.1(a) and (b)   The profitability of exporting

(a)

Q^* = minimum efficiency scale   D1 = demand in the EU

D2 = demand in the EU plus demand in Japan

AC1 = average cost (including normal profit)

AC2 = average cost including the cost of exporting

Cost of exporting = transport costs, transaction costs of fulfilling regulations, and exchange rate risk

If the market is competitive, P will equal AC. If there were no exports a price of P1 and output of Q1 would emerge and normal profits would be reaped. However, at P1:Q1 minimum efficiency scale is not reached. If the company took advantage of the possibility to export Q1–Q2 to Japan at a price of P2, the costs of exporting would be covered and normal profits would be reaped from the output that is exported. As output rises from 0Q1 to 0Q2 the average costs of producing output for the EU market falls from 0C1 to 0C2. This leads to an increase in profits (on EU output) shown by the area C2C1AB.

If the costs of exporting fall because of reductions in the transaction costs of complying with Japanese regulations, AC2 would move downwards, thereby increasing the volume of exports and further increasing the profits available from output for the EU market. However, when output reaches Q^* (i.e. minimum efficiency scale) no additional profits from EU output are available because in the example illustrated above the cost of producing output becomes constant after minimum efficiency

(b)

ACj = average cost in Japan

ACeu = average cost in EU plus the cost of exporting to Japan

ACeu1 = average cost in EU plus new lower cost of exporting to Japan

Dj = demand in Japan

scale output is reached. The incentive to export would then arise from the contribution to normal profit from exported output.

The costs of exporting mean that European companies can not enter the Japanese market at low levels of output because the costs of supplying the Japanese market (a cost close to C0) is greater than the price received (i.e. P1). However, if the cost of exporting fell such that the average cost became ACeu1, European companies could enter the market as the price is now higher than the cost of low levels of output (i.e. cost close to C1). It would now be possible for European companies to enter the Japanese market at low levels of output and gradually expand exports to the Japanese market, thereby moving down their AC. In these circumstances European companies would end up with the entire Japanese market with price of P2 and output of Q2. In this case, reducing the cost of exporting would allow European companies to exploit their comparative advantage.

The above examples illustrate that the incentive to take advantage of improved market access to Japan depends to a larger extent on the profitability of exporting, which is strongly influenced by production costs (level of output relative to minimum efficiency scale) and the costs of exporting.

these countries in efforts to find solutions to trading problems. In the early 1990s there were several visits by senior members of the Commission to the NICs in attempts to develop dialogue on trading matters. These efforts culminated in 1996 in the first meeting in Bangkok of the Asia-Europe Meeting (ASEM). The second meeting of ASEM was held in London in 1998. Economic and business issues form an important part of the work of ASEM as it provides an umbrella organisation for a number of specialised economic forums – Asia-Europe Business Forum, Investment Promotion Action Plan, and cooperation between customs authorities to develop better procedures for dealing with export and import documentation. The establishment of ASEM provides an institutional structure that allows the EU, the Asian NICs and China to discuss problems related to trading and business links. Therefore, the EU has a number of institutional frameworks that allow for discussions on trading problems with the Asian NICs.

In the main the EU takes the view that the NICs should be encouraged to liberalise their trading systems to grant companies in the EU easier access to their markets. Thus the Commission has complained about the close relationship between South Korean manufacturers and their subcontractors and distributors – the so-called 'chabeol' system. There has also been concern over the difficulties of tendering for public procurement contracts. The EU claims that these systems act like a series of NTBs, and that they are a significant barrier to entering the markets of South Korea. These complaints from the EU and the USA are very similar to those made about the difficulties of entering the Japanese market because of the system of 'keiretsu' (the collaborative relationships that exist between Japanese assemblers, suppliers and distributors, based on close financial links and technical collaboration). These problems have led the EU to embark on a process of seeking to promote 'fairer' market entry conditions and trading arrangements with South Korea and the other Asian NICs.

The Commission has imposed a number of anti-dumping measures on the NICs, for example on electronic weighing scales from Singapore and on microwave ovens from China, South Korea, Malaysia and Thailand. The Commission has imposed a large number of anti-dumping duties on Asian NICs. Very few non-Asian countries have been subject to anti-dumping duties. However, in the late 1990s China has attracted the largest number of anti-dumping duties (European Current Law Year Book, 1997). This is indicative of the problems that have arisen as China has begun to penetrate the EU market. European companies have also complained about access to the Chinese market. In efforts to overcome these problems the Commission has developed a strategy to improve relationships and to construct forums where trading problems can be discussed (Commission, 1998b).

The EU initially adopted a hostile approach to the rise of new low-cost Asian competitors in Community markets. The arrival of these new competitors has stimulated growing interest by the EU in the trading activities of the NICs. In some ways history is repeating itself, as the EU is taking a very similar approach to the NICs to that taken to Japan. The main complaints against the NICs are very similar to those levelled against the Japanese. In essence, these complaints are often based on accusations that these economies do not operate on European/ American models of company behaviour, and also that the state provides extensive help to protect their domestic industries. These factors are considered to make it very difficult for European/US economies to compete on equal terms. The solution to these problems, according to the Europeans and the Americans, is to encourage Japan and the NICs to transform their economies so that they become more similar to those of Europe and the USA. In some sectors of Japan and the NICs, this view is regarded as a type of cultural imperialism that has its roots in the failure of European and American economies to adopt new systems of management and production to enable them to compete successfully. However, pressures have arisen that are forcing some European and US companies to adopt some of the cost-saving and quality-enhancing procedures of Japanese and NIC production systems. These pressures have been brought to bear by the growing penetration of European and American markets by the Japanese and NICs, and by the expansion of Japanese FDI into the USA and Europe. Nevertheless, the Americans and Europeans still regard the domestic economies of Japan and the NICs as being very difficult to penetrate due to hidden forms of protection and, in the case of the NICs, high tariff barriers.

Macroeconomic cooperation within the Triad

The linkages that exist between the members of the Triad mean that macro-economic changes in one of the members of the Triad are likely to spill over to the other members. This leads to a coordination problem (see Chapter 2). The persistent recession in Japan in the late 1990s illustrated the nature of the spill-over effect. The Japanese economy experienced low growth in the late 1990s and the government was unable or unwilling to take appropriate macroeconomic policy measures to stimulate growth in Japan. This led to low growth of imports and contributed to the fall in the value of the yen. The latter effect led to a rise in Japanese exports and, in combination with the low growth of imports, contributed to the continuance of trade surpluses with the USA and the EU despite improved access to the Japanese market. This example illustrates that Japanese macroeconomic conditions have implications for trading conditions in the US and the EU, and also for those countries closely connected with the Triad.

The asymmetric nature of the linkages in the Triad (that is, the dominance of the USA) means that the spill-over effects do not have equal effect. Recession or booms in the USA tend to have more impact on trading conditions in the Triad than do such factors in the EU and Japan. The financial crisis in some of the Asian NICs in 1998 demonstrated the asymmetric nature of spill-over effects within the Triad and those countries that are closely associated with it. The crisis led to a marked fall in the price of financial assets and large-scale depreciation of the currencies of many of the Asian NICs. However, the crisis did not have very significant effects on the EU and the USA. The largest effects were experienced by Japan, but they were not sufficient to have any marked effect on economic conditions in Japan. The distribution of the effects of the crisis depends on the amount of trade and investments that companies had with the Asian NICs. The impact of a revival in the Japanese economy on the Asian NICs would be pronounced, and has been considered as the most useful contribution that could be made to help the Asian NICs to recover (*Financial Times*, 1998).

The institutional frameworks that exist among the members of the Triad and associated countries do not provide a suitable means of discussing problems that arise from macroeconomic factors (see Box 15.4). The IMF, BIS and G8 discuss these issues, but they are not specifically Triad based forums. Moreover, they do not provide the sort of practical arrangements that exist within the NTA, ASEM or APEC where forums have established structures to discuss issues related to trade, market access and FDI flows. However, macroeconomic problems are normally discussed in these forums only at formal and largely ceremonial meetings of the heads of government.

The establishment of European monetary union in 1999 may well lead to a very significant change in relationships within the Triad. The euro could become a major world currency, with a consequent increase in the macroeconomic linkages between the EU and the USA and Japan. These developments could have significant implications for the development of institutional frameworks within the Triad.

Box 15.4 Major institutional frameworks within the Triad

EU-US Transatlantic Agenda
The New Transatlantic Agenda (NTA) was established in 1995 when agreement was reached to develop the 1990 Transatlantic Declaration into a more work-like body. The NTA has four main objectives:

- Promotion of peace, stability and democracy.
- Cooperation on global challenges – environmental issues and organised crime.
- Promotion of economic relations and expansion of world trade.
- Building bridges between business, civic and academic communities.

The last two objectives have significant implications for trading and business links between the EU and the US. Cooperation between the EU and the US within the NTA was important in the securing of a WTO agreement to remove progressively all barriers to trade in the IT and telecommunications sectors. The Transatlantic Business Dialogue component of the NTA enabled an agreement to be reached to develop a system of mutual recognition of testing and certification procedures in EU-US trade. This is seen as an important step towards the objective of the NTA of establishing a Transatlantic marketplace – a type of single market for EU-US trade. The NTA has also provided a variety of forums where problems related to liberalisation of trade in services and the establishing of rules on foreign investment can be discussed. This has led to several proposals being made to governments and to the WTO on the best methods for promoting trade and of overcoming problems related to trading activities.

Asia-Europe Meeting (ASEM)
ASEM was inaugurated in 1996 at a meeting in Bangkok. This forum includes all of the Asian NICs and Japan. It provides a forum for sharing information and for discussion of economic relationships, development issues, environmental concerns, and educational and cultural matters. The second ASEM meeting was held in London in 1998. Much

of the work of ASEM has involved establishing bodies to gather and disseminate information on economic, business, environmental and cultural conditions and problems in the ASEM countries. The economic and business forums, especially the Asia-Europe Business Forum (AEBF), have identified a number of problems associated with trading and are working on ways to reduce the obstacles to trade that arise from tariffs and NTBs. However, ASEM does not have the same kind of practical agenda as the NTA. Moreover, the large differences in the cultures and economic development of the members of ASEM mean that it is very difficult for clear policy proposals to emerge from ASEM-based forums. However, ASEM may represent the beginnings of an institutional framework that could develop into a practical system of resolving problems connected to EU-Asian trade.

EU-Japan framework

A Joint Declaration signed in 1991 established the basis for an annual meeting between the Presidents of the European Council and the Commission with the Japanese Prime Minister as well as a variety of bodies to discuss particular areas of interest in EU-Japan relationships. The EU-Japan framework covers political dialogue, economic and trade matters, and global challenges (pollution and organised crime). The framework allowed the Commission to make a number of suggestions to the Japanese government on how the deregulation of the economy could be framed in ways that would facilitate attempts by EU companies to enter Japanese markets. The framework has also helped the Commission to collaborate with MITI to promote Japan as a market for EU-based companies. As well as these market access issues, the framework has also facilitated the development of cooperation schemes in the areas of R&D and environmental protection issues.

Asian-Pacific Economic Cooperation (APEC)

APEC was established in 1989 to promote economic integration of the countries of the Pacific Rim. In 1993 at an APEC meeting in Seattle, agreement was reached on a Declaration on APEC Trade and Investment Framework. This was followed at a meeting in Jakarta in 1994 to a commitment to create a 'free and open trade and investment area' – a type of free-trade area. The creation of this area requires the removal of tariffs and NTBs that affect trade in goods and services and that limit FDI flows. The area is planned to be completed by 2010 for the developed members of APEC, and 2020 for the less developed members. A large number of groups and committees have been formed to determine the conditions that are necessary for such an area. However, very few concrete steps have been taken to remove barriers to free movement among the APEC countries. There are also very different attitudes concerning the benefits of free movement and regarding the best way to establish such an area among the members of APEC. Nevertheless, APEC provides many specialist forums that facilitate the sharing of information and the pursuit of solutions for trading problems.

Members of APEC – Australia, Brunei Darussalam, Canada, Chile, China, Hong Kong, Indonesia, Japan, South Korea, Malaysia, New Zealand, Papua New Guinea, Philippines, Singapore, Taiwan, Thailand and the USA.

Information on the current activities of these bodies can be found on the web page of DG1 of the Commission (http://www.europa.eu.int/en/comm/dg01), US State Department (www.state.gov) and Jetro (www.jetro.go.jp).

The impact of European monetary union

The establishment of European monetary union is likely to have two main effects on relations in the Triad.

1. The introduction of a new currency that may become important for the finance of international transactions.
2. A change in the balance of power and influence in the international monetary system.

The first effect will alter the significance of the dollar as a means of financing international economic activities. This will have important implications for the development of financial and currency markets. The second effect could lead to significant changes to the main characteristics of the international monetary system.

Financing international business activities

International business transactions can benefit from the use of a currency that is widely used in world markets. Such currencies perform three functions.

1. A means of invoicing and for payments for international business activities.
2. A vehicle currency in the exchange markets.
3. The provision of financial assets to facilitate international capital activities.

The attraction of using a major world currency to finance international business activities follows from the lower transaction costs that are made possible by using such currencies. Buying and selling currencies to finance business activities involves transaction costs. If a large number of currencies are used, the transaction costs can be large. Furthermore, a measure of risk is involved when different currencies are used because of fluctuations in exchange rates and lack of detailed knowledge on the conditions that prevail in the home country of currencies. To fulfil the conditions for reducing transaction costs it is necessary for a currency to have both a wide and a deep market. A wide market means that a large number of different financial instruments exist that are denominated in terms of the currency, for example the currency itself, bonds, equities, derivatives and swap instruments. A deep market has a large number of traders in the primary and secondary markets (primary markets issue financial instruments and secondary markets provide a means whereby these instruments can be traded). In deep markets the competitive environment is likely to be keen, and hence the transaction costs of buying and selling financial instruments will be low relative to these costs in thin markets. The markets for dollars and dollar-denominated financial assets are wider and deeper than those for other currencies. Furthermore, the US economy is large, and information on conditions in the American economy and political system is easily available. The size of the US economy means that it is unlikely that dollars (held outside the US) could not be used to buy American assets, goods and services. In smaller economies the ability to convert the currency into assets, goods and services is limited due to the size of these economies. In these circumstances, holding large amounts of a country's currency poses a risk that holdings cannot be converted easily into tangible assets. The good access to information on the state of the American economy means that there is a low risk of large-scale unexpected changes in the value of the dollar. This gives the dollar advantages over most other currencies in terms of the transaction costs of using the currency to finance international business activities.

The deutschmark and the yen are also used as world currencies, but to a lesser extent than the dollar because the German and Japanese economies are smaller than the US and have less well developed markets for their currency. The DM tends to be used in European countries and the yen in Asia. However, even in these regions the dollar is the most important world currency.

Much of international trade is invoiced and paid for in dollars, for example all trade in crude oil, most primary commodities, and a substantial part of the ordinary trade of countries. The use of the dollar reduces the costs of invoicing and paying in a multitude of currencies. The significance of the use of the dollar as a means of invoicing and payment is shown by the proportion of world exports that is invoiced in dollars – about 45 per cent in 1987. This implies that a substantial proportion of the exports of countries is invoiced in dollars. In Japan in 1987 it was approximately 60 per cent of exports (Commission, 1990).

The dollar is also used as a vehicle currency in the exchange markets. Therefore, instead of exchanging Belgian francs for Spanish pesetas, Portuguese escudos and Swedish kroner, Belgian francs can be exchanged for dollars, and the dollars are then exchanged for the required currencies. The depth of the dollar markets means that there are lower transaction costs by using the dollar when converting into these minor currencies rather than using direct conversion from Belgian francs. In 1989, 89.4 per cent of trade that used a vehicle currency involved the dollar (Commission, 1990).

Dollar denominated assets are the most important means by which capital is recycled (across frontiers) from savers to borrowers. Capital markets are dominated by dollar denominated assets. For example, about 40 per cent of international bonds are valued in dollars, compared with 15 per cent in yen and about 10 per cent in DM (BIS, 1997). Most financial instruments that are traded internationally (e.g. equities, derivatives, swaps) are also denominated in dollars. Governments hold the majority of their foreign currency reserves in dollars. The dollar is, therefore, the most important currency in international capital markets and in the reserves of governments. This leads to a significant demand for dollars that are held outside the US. This role for the dollar leads to benefits to the US economy because of seigniorage effects.

Seigniorage effects arise because holding dollars (in currency form) does not yield a rate of interest. However, to obtain dollars it is necessary to exchange some kind of asset in return for the dollars – normally a financial asset that yields a rate of interest. The dollars that are obtained are a promise by the Federal Reserve Bank of America to pay an equivalent sum as stated on the dollar bill. This equivalent sum is paid in dollars – a dollar bill for $10 can be converted into another dollar bill valued at $10. Hence the Federal Reserve Bank of America obtains interest yielding assets in return for dollars that are non-interest bearing assets. This means that the Federal Bank receives an interest-free loan when it issues dollars. In periods of high inflation these seigniorage effects can be quite large because the holders of dollars have acquired a non-interest bearing asset in return for an interest bearing asset and, furthermore, the real value of their dollars is declining because of inflation. The benefits related to seigniorage are assumed to be fairly small (in a period of low inflation) but the large amount of dollars held outside the US indicates that the accumulation of these small benefits is not insignificant (Commission, 1990).

Effects of the introduction of the euro

The introduction of the euro will lead to a shift from the dollar in the invoicing and payment of international trade, as a vehicle currency, and in international capital markets. There may also be some shift from the dollar in government holdings of foreign reserves.

All intra-Union trade (except for crude oil and basic commodities) is likely to move to the use of the euro for invoicing and payment. Some of the countries that conduct the bulk of their trade with the EU may also move to the use of the euro in invoicing and payment. This will lead to a slight decline in the demand for dollars very soon after the establishment of monetary union.

The introduction of the euro will eliminate the use of the dollar as a vehicle currency for third-party exchanges that involve members of the monetary union, and perhaps for those member states that do not enter the first phase of the union (e.g. the UK). The euro may also be used as a vehicle currency for those countries that have significant trade with the EU (e.g. the CEECs). In the long run it is possible that the euro would be used as a vehicle currency throughout the world. This is likely to happen if the euro develops deep and wide markets that lead to low transaction costs compared with the dollar. Such developments could only happen over a fairly long period as the euro financial markets will have to develop. However, it is possible that the euro could become a serious competitor to the dollar in this area.

The denomination of government and private bonds in euros will create a very large euro bond market. This market could develop low transaction costs relative to the dollar markets and thereby lead to substantial movements from dollar assets to euro assets. Euro equity markets could also develop as serious competitors to the dollar dominated equity markets. Much will depend on how these euro markets develop. If regulatory systems are light but effective, and if the euro financial markets are stable, competitive and efficient, they could become lower-cost sources of international finance than the dollar markets. However, dollar financial markets have pronounced first-mover advantages and they are well developed in all of the major financial centres of the world. Furthermore, the US has well-developed regulatory frameworks that govern financial reporting requirements and the control of trade in financial assets. The euro market will have to be developed in a system where there are many different regulatory frameworks, and where international trade in financial assets is often governed by American rules. These benefits will make it difficult for the euro to replace the dollar quickly.

Governments may also wish to shift some of their foreign reserves from dollars and yen to the euro. Those countries that hold DM (and other currencies that will disappear when European monetary union begins) in their reserves are likely to convert them to euro holdings. Therefore, the euro will become a reserve currency very early in its history. Countries that have significant trade with the EU may also wish to hold a part of their reserves in euros. However, the euro bloc countries will have to increase their holdings of dollars and yen because they cannot convert their reserves of foreign currencies held in DM or other European currencies into euros because the euro will not be a foreign currency for such countries. These factors are likely, in the short term, to lead to only a very small shift from the dollar as the major reserve currency in the world. However, if the euro develops as a stronger currency than the dollar, because the ECB consistently delivers a better inflation record than the Federal Reserve Bank of America, the euro could develop into a major reserve currency.

The current dominance of the dollar and the need for euro markets to be firmly established and developed is likely to limit the shift from the dollar to the euro. The dollar has been in gentle decline as a world currency since the late 1970s as the DM and the yen became more important for international financial transactions. In these circumstances it is likely that the introduction of the euro will not have any significant effect on the use of the dollar in the short term. In the medium to long term the euro may slightly accelerate the decline in the use of the dollar. In this scenario the dollar would remain the dominant world currency for the foreseeable future (Commission, 1990). The main effect of the introduction of the euro in this case might be to undermine the use of the yen as a world currency, because the EU is a larger economy than Japan, and the financial markets for the euro will be larger and perhaps have lower transaction costs. However, if the euro develops quickly into a stable and strong currency with well-developed financial markets, the international monetary system could experience considerable turbulence as the euro displaces the dollar and perhaps also the yen.

If the introduction of the euro leads to a small and gradual decrease in the use of the dollar it is probable that euro-dollar-yen exchange rates will not be significantly affected by the shift to the euro. Moreover, the loss of seigniorage revenues will be low and should not cause undue problems for the USA. However, a large and rapid shift towards the use of the euro could have significant effects on the dollar exchange rate and on seigniorage revenues. In these circumstances euro-dollar-yen exchange rates could be very volatile, and co-operation between the members of the Triad may become difficult to maintain. Given the importance of the Triad for the stability and growth of world trade, such an outcome would be harmful to the well-being of the world economy.

New international monetary system

It is possible that the establishment of European monetary union will stimulate a greater degree of cooperation in international monetary and economic affairs. In particular, monetary union could lead to a tri-polar (USA, Japan and Europe) system of cooperation that could be more effective than the current G7 system in terms of creating the conditions that would allow for a more stable international monetary order (Alogoskoufis and Portes, 1990). Gains of approximately

0.5 to 1.5 per cent of the GDP of the members of the G7 have been estimated to be possible from effective coordination among the countries of G7 (Currie, Holtham and Hughes-Hallett, 1989). However, effective coordination may depend upon a hegemonic power controlling the process. This view, based on the importance of the hegemony of the USA in the post-war period, casts doubt on the possibility of a multi-polar system being able to generate stable coordination systems (Keohane, 1983). Therefore, it is possible that monetary union could further undermine the hegemony of the USA and thereby promote greater instability in international monetary markets. In this scenario, the creation of monetary union would lead to costs in terms of greater instability in exchange rate markets, leading to problems in finding cooperative solutions to macroeconomic problems within the Triad.

The euro may be a strong and stable or a weak and unstable currency. Whatever happens, the euro exchange rate is likely to have different characteristics from existing relationships between national currencies and the dollar and the yen. This has implications for the development of the competitiveness of companies. The euro-dollar-yen exchange rate will reflect the conditions between the USA, Japan and the European monetary union bloc. These conditions may be different from those that prevail in the current dollar-yen relationship of the member states. This could lead to euro-dollar-yen exchange rates that are significantly different from the rate that prevailed in the dollar-yen exchange rates of the member states before they joined the monetary union. It is possible that some member states could be faced with significant changes to their exchange rate against the dollar-yen. This will have important implications for companies that are based in these countries, who have large levels of extra-EU transactions.

If the international monetary system becomes more unstable as a result of a rapid and large decline in the use of the dollar, there may be significant implications for relationships within the Triad. A large shift out of dollars would lead to changes to euro-dollar-yen exchange rate parities. This would generate changes in nominal and probably real exchange rates, with a consequent effect on the competitiveness of companies. Large-scale changes would also affect seigniorage revenues and the size and importance of financial markets in the different parts of the Triad. A series of adjustment problems would arise from such large-scale shifts out of the dollar. Even if the changes are slow and minor it is likely that there will be problems in adjusting to the new environment.

The loss of hegemonic power by the USA may make it more difficult to achieve macroeconomic cooperation. In a hegemonic system power can be exercised on weaker partners to adjust their behaviour. This process has been identified as important in the early post-war experience in establishing the Bretton Woods exchange rate system, and in the early moves to liberalise trade by the GATT (Eichengreen, 1989). The decline of American hegemony has probably contributed to the difficulty of finding solutions to international problems because the US lacks sufficient power to force settlements to disputes. However, the continuing power of the dollar gave the Americans considerable influence in world financial matters. This power has been declining, but, because there was no serious competitor to the dollar, the Americans have retained considerable influence on international financial matters. The introduction of the euro may accelerate the decline of the dollar and lead to a new non-hegemonic international monetary system. In these circumstances new and effective institutional frameworks that can help to find solutions to international monetary problems may become necessary to avoid instability in exchange markets and recurrent financial crises.

Prospects for future relations

Relations in trade and business matters within the Triad have been characterised by disputes and conflict. The creation of the SEM and moves towards EMU make it important for all parties to improve this situation. The EU has been developing institutional frameworks as a means to finding solutions to these problems. The Community is placing a higher priority on relations with the USA, Japan and the NICs than it has in the past. The creation of the WTO also holds out the prospect for a more open and liberal trading regime, or at least for the development of institutional systems that can effectively find solutions to trading problems. However, the extension of trade to cover services and FDI flows is likely to increase the number and complexity of disputes. The role of bilateral arrangements between the EU and the major parties of the Triad may play an important part in the development of the world trading system.

All parties in the Triad have much to gain from creating a more liberal trading environment. The EU is the largest trader in the world and, together with the USA and Japan, it exercises enormous influence on the development of world trade. A more restrictive world trading environment would be harmful to the long-term interests of the EU. One of the main benefits of creating the SEM was to increase competition in order to induce lower prices and higher outputs (see Chapter 1). In principle, the opening up of the European market to US, Japanese and NIC competition should add to these benefits. Some European companies would suffer from increased competition from Triad countries, but this would also be true of increased competition from other member states. For a company operating within the EU it would not matter whether the increased competition came from a Japanese or a German source. The increase in competition would be painful for the company, and beneficial for the consumer. Companies that could not adjust to the new competitive environment would have to exit the market, leaving the more effective companies to operate in that market. This gives rise to structural and regional problems as the system adjusts to the new competitive environment. The EU has already accepted the need for such adjustment by agreeing to the creation of the SEM and is prepared to accept more structural change resulting from the creation of monetary union. Indeed, these structural changes are deemed beneficial for the economy and citizens of the EU. It is therefore difficult to see why opening up the EU economy to foreign competition, which would have much the same effects, should be deemed harmful to the EU.

If a very pessimistic view is taken of the ability of European companies to compete with the best American, Japanese and NIC companies, it might be beneficial to provide some temporary protection for European companies to allow them time to undertake the necessary adjustment, and to ease balance of payments problems. There may also be some strategic reasons to protect high-technology industries from being overwhelmed by US and Japanese companies. The danger with this approach is that 'temporary protection' is often extended to permanent protection and this is not normally conducive to an efficient and dynamic economy. Generally, the EU operates on the basis that competition is beneficial to the long-term interests of all Union citizens, so that to restrict such competition to European sources does not seem to have much of an economic rationale.

The EU has much to gain from adopting an open approach to the rest of the world, and to the USA, Japan and the Asian NICs in particular. In a few politically sensitive and strategically important areas it might be necessary for the EU to adopt a protectionist stance, but generally the EU is likely to adopt a fairly pro-competitive approach. However, as was indicated above, there are a host of unresolved problems between the EU and the USA, Japan and the NICs.

The establishment of European monetary union will bring a new set of problems to relations with the USA and Japan. The euro is likely to develop into a major new world currency and this will have significant implications for the role of the dollar, and to a lesser extent the yen. This makes it more urgent to develop effective institutional arrangements for the world international monetary system. If this does not occur, there could be an increase in instability in the exchange rates of the major currencies of the world. Provided that the euro is introduced within the context of a new and effective arrangement with the USA and Japan, the prospects for a mutually beneficial outcome may be good. However, the likely displacement of the dollar in some parts of the international monetary system, and the emergence of a new large financial market based on the euro may alter the balance of power and influence in the international monetary system. This could have significant implications for the development of good relationships between the USA and the EU, and could have some impact on relationships with Japan.

The prospects for the EU to establish good relations with the USA, Japan and the NICs depend to a large extent on the ability of governments to build effective institutional frameworks. However, problems with trade surpluses and large-scale adjustment costs to new trading patterns that emerge within the Triad could undermine the ability of even the must robust of institutional frameworks. Good relationships between the members of the Triad depend to a large extent on stable and healthy growth which increases income levels that can compensate for the adjustment costs that accompany growing trade and investment flows within the Triad. Institutional frameworks that can cope with pressures that arise from macroeconomic policy inconsistencies and monetary/exchange rate instability will be important to good relationships among the members of the Triad. The establishment of EMU may alter the balance of power in the Triad in these matters. Furthermore, the possibility of a substantial shift from the dollar to the euro in international financial markets may lead to instability in exchange markets that will require strong institutional frameworks to help to achieve co-operation among the members of the Triad. If such institutional frameworks are not developed, significant problems with macroeconomic policy inconsistencies may arise that could undermine the tendency for the Triad to open up their markets progressively and to develop trading and business links.

References

Alogoskoufis G and Portes R 1990 International costs and benefits from EMU, *European Economy*, The Economics of EMU, special issue.

BIS 1997 *Annual Report*, Bank for International Settlements, Basle.

Bourgeois J 1995 *The Uruguay Round Results*, European Interuniversity Press, Brussels.

Commission 1990 One market, one money, *European Economy*, No. 44, Office for Offiical Publications of the European Communities, Luxembourg.

Commission 1996 *Investing in Asia's Dynamism*, Office for Official Publications of the European Communities, Luxembourg.

Commission 1997a *The Global Challenge of International Trade: A Market Access Strategy for the European Union*, Communication from DG1, Brussels.

Commission 1997b *US Extraterritorial Legislation*, Facts Brief from DG1, Brussels.

Commission 1998a *EU-Japan economic and trade relations*, Communication from DG1, Brussels.

Commission 1998b *The EU's New Strategy Towards China*, Communication from DG1, Brussels.

Currie D, Holtham G and Hughes-Hallett A 1989 The theory and practice of international policy co-ordination: does co-ordination pay?, in *Macroeconomic policies in an interdependent world*, IMF and Brookings Institution.

European Current Law Year Book 1997, Sweet & Maxwell, London.

Eichengreen B 1989 Hegemonic stability theories of the international monetary system, in *Can nations agree? Issues in International Economic Co-operation*, ed. by Cooper R *et al.*

Featherstone K and Ginsberg R 1996 *The United States and the European Union in the 1990s*, Macmillan, London.

Financial Times 1998 *Special Issues on Asia in Crisis*, 12 to 16 January.

Funabashi Y 1995 *Asia Pacific Fusion*, Institute of International Economics, Washington DC.

Guerrier P and Padoan P C 1988 *The Political Economy of International Co-operation*, Croom Helm, London.

IMD 1998 *International Institute for Management Development: Annual World Competitiveness Yearbook*, IMD, Basel.

Ishikawa K 1990 *Japan and the Challenge of Europe 1992*, RIIA/Pinter, London.

Keohane R 1983 *After hegemony*, Princeton University Press.

Krugman P and Obstfeld M 1993 *International Economics, Theory and Policy*, Harper Collins, New York.

McKinsey Global Institute 1993, *Manufacturing Productivity*, Report of the McKinsey Global Institution, New York.

Nicholson M 1989 *Formal Theories in International Relations*, Cambridge University Press, Cambridge.

Ohmae K 1985 *Triad Power*, The Free Press, New York.

Thurow L 1992 *Head to Head: The Coming Economic Battle among Japan, Europe and America*, Nicholas Brealey Publishing, London.

Vogel, 1997 *Barriers or Benefits: Regulation in Transatlantic Trade*, Brookings Institution Press, Washington DC.

Further reading

Bergsen F and Il SaKong 1995 *The Political Economy of Korea-United States* Cooperation, Institute of International Economics, Washington DC.

Hufbauer G and Schott J 1993 *North American Free Trade,* Institute of International Economics, Washington DC.

Hufbauer G and Schott J 1994 *Western Hemisphere Economic Integration,* Institute of International Economics, Washington DC.

Hufbauer G and Schott J 1995 *Towards an Asian Pacific Economic Community,* Institute of International Economics, Washington DC.

Sazanami Y, Urata S and Kawai H 1995 *Measuring the Costs of Protection in Japan,* Institute of International Economics, Washington DC.

Material on issues connected to the impact of European monetary union on the international monetary system can be found on the Internet, http://www.ecu-activities.be and http://www.euro-emu.co.uk.

16 Foreign direct investment and the European Union

Adam Cross

Introduction

Foreign direct investment (FDI) occurs when a firm in one economy (the home country) makes a long-term investment in, and secures effective control of a company (the affiliate) resident in another economy (the host country). Such a firm is called a multinational enterprise (MNE), on account of its ownership of productive activities in more than one country (Casson, 1990). The affiliate may be a new firm that has been established from scratch by the MNE (a 'greenfield' investment), it may be a firm that has been merged with or acquired by the MNE, or it may be a joint venture which the MNE has set up with a partner firm.

The phenomenon of FDI has special relevance for the EU and European economic integration for a number of reasons. First, the EU is a major participant in the international flow of direct investments made by multinational firms. In the early years of the 1990s, the larger member states of the EU were donors for around half, and recipients of around two-thirds, of the annual global flow of FDI. A common indicator of the level of foreign involvement in an economy is the ratio of inward stock of FDI to gross domestic product (GDP). Over the last two decades, this ratio has increased for most nations of the world, reflecting the surge in global direct investment activity in modern times. However, this ratio has risen fastest for the EU, especially in the late 1980s. The Commission (1996) reported that the ratio of inward stock of FDI to GDP for the EU12 in 1992 was 11.5 – a figure which exceeded that of the developed countries as a whole (8.2), the rest of Europe (8.3), the United States (7.1) and Japan (1.1). It is probable, therefore, that FDI has more pronounced effects on the EU economy than on most other developed economies. MNEs, it follows, have had and will continue to have a critical role in determining the pace and structure of economic development across Europe (UNCTAD, 1996).

In order to realise many of the anticipated efficiency gains from the Single European Market (SEM) programme, economic activity needs to be redistributed across the EU, within and across industry sectors, geographical regions and member states. In today's global economy, MNEs and their trade and investment activities are the main instruments by which national economies are linked. As we shall see, multinational enterprises are contributing greatly to the process of redistribution as they react to the deepening and widening of the EU by establishing new operations and restructuring existing operations across national borders. Thus, MNEs from member states and other nations are not only responding to the process of European integration, but they are shaping it too. This role inevitably raises implications for policy, at the national as well as the pan-European level. Inward direct investment brings with it both benefits and costs to the home and host country, while MNEs' internal mechanisms and systems challenge the principles of pricing in free, or arm's length markets. As member states (and indeed regions within member states) compete to attract advantageous inward investment and manage the social costs of divestment, the question arises as to whether and to what extent the investment activities of MNEs in Europe should be monitored or regulated and, if so, by which authority?

This chapter is organised as follows. First, a theoretical framework is presented which suggests some predicted responses of both indigenous MNEs and non-member state MNEs to European integration. Secondly, patterns of FDI in the EU, from the early 1980s to 1995 are examined. Thirdly, and after highlighting certain methodological limitations, we relate observed patterns to that predicted by theory. Fourthly, we outline some of the benefits and costs associated with investment flows in and out of national economies. Finally, we describe some policy implications arising from, and concomitant governmental and Commission reaction to these investment flows, in the context of European integration and the economic development of the member states.

A theoretical framework

There are three dimensions to FDI and the European Union:

- *Intra-EU FDI* (when a firm from one member state invests in another member state).
- *Inbound extra-EU FDI* (when a firm from outside the EU invests in a member state).
- *Outbound extra-EU* investment (when a firm from a member state invests in a non-member state).

Given the special implications of FDI for European integration, this chapter focuses on inbound investment destined for a host member state – that is, intra-EU FDI and extra-EU FDI. For material on outbound European investment, see the Commission (1995) and UNCTAD (1996).

It is important to note that it is difficult, if not impossible, to assess fully the impact of European integration on the investment strategies of international firms (a point that is expanded upon later). The legislative programme of European integration, particularly with regard to the SEM, is highly complex. Much of this legislation is industry-specific and, therefore, affects most those industries where the incidence of technical barriers to trade is high, such as pharmaceuticals, automobiles, electronics and so on. Corporate objectives, of course, will also be critical in defining the investment strategies of individual firms. Nevertheless, despite such difficulties, we draw upon the work of Yannopoulos (1992) and Dunning (1993, 1997a, 1997b) to present a theoretical framework that considers the likely *a priori* responses of MNEs to European economic integration and the SEM programme. To simplify our analysis, we identify three generic strategies that motivate firms to invest in the EU, namely market-seeking, efficiency-seeking and strategic asset-seeking FDI. There is a fourth strategy, which is natural resource-seeking FDI. However, for the most part, the EU countries attract relatively little natural resource-seeking investment and, therefore, this is not considered here.

Market-seeking FDI

This type of FDI is defined as horizontal expansion by the MNE, whereby the MNE establishes a physical presence in particular countries or regions to facilitate the supply of products and services in these or adjacent markets (Dunning, 1993). The SEM programme is predicted to bring about two distinct types of market-seeking investment.

First, and for several reasons, the SEM programme is likely to hinder exporting to member states from a non-member state. The removal of physical barriers and the reduction in technical barriers within the EU have the equivalent effect to that of an internal tariff barrier reduction. Consequently, the SEM programme should benefit all firms servicing EU markets through exports. However, the reduction of trading and other costs by lowering these non-tariff barriers to trade is expected to be, on balance, greater for firms exporting between member states than for firms supplying EU markets from outside the EU. Firms that lack local production facilities and/or strong representation in the EU will also be disadvantaged by changes in external trade policy, such as policies which relate to nationally based and imposed voluntary export restraints, local content requirements, anti-dumping and other import trade restrictions. Outsider firms may also find it difficult to influence the development of product standards or the business environment in a favourable manner. Concerns such as these may combine to encourage many non-EU based trading firms to respond to the erosion by the SEM programme of their relative competitive positions by adopting a physical presence and producing from within the EU. This is *defensive import-substituting FDI*. It is used by MNEs to protect existing market shares in the EU previously achieved by exporting.

Secondly, the SEM programme is also expected to generate new market opportunities, improve market access and accelerate market growth across the EU. This will be most evident in sectors where market entry barriers had previously been substantial (such as banking and insurance) or where policy favoured local firms (such as in the public procurement of construction services). Both EU and non-EU firms (including those firms that had not previously serviced EU markets) may respond by undertaking in the EU *offensive import-substituting FDI*. In addition to access, this market-seeking investment strategy provides firms with proximity to pan-European markets, which lowers transportation costs and improves the flow of market knowledge and information to and from the consumer. Through direct investment, rather than licensing-out to EU firms, the MNE can retain and defend its market power by controlling the brand names, trademarks and other ownership-specific advantages it holds (Buckley and Casson, 1976).

Efficiency-seeking FDI

This type of FDI is undertaken by firms to restructure their existing resource-based or market-oriented operations. There are two types of efficiency-seeking investment strategy. First, the SEM programme is expected to intensify competition in the EU (especially in highly fragmented markets), and allow scale economies to be generated by those firms that can treat the member states as a single market. Consequently, cost reductions in intermediate inputs and final products may result. Firms, particularly those from outside the EU, may invest in the region to gain greater access to those industries generating such cost reductions. This is *rationalised FDI*. Secondly, the removal of some market entry barriers under the SEM programme should improve accessibility to low-cost production locations across member states. Multinational firms (both EU and non-EU) already active in the EU may respond to the competitive pressure faced in their domestic and other EU markets by restructuring their European operations. This type of efficiency-seeking activity is *reorganisation FDI*. Such reorganisation will involve the relocation of key stages of production to a limited number of sites from where multiple national markets in the EU can be supplied. Production is expected to relocate according to the comparative advantage of member states or regions – that is, to where it benefits most from local factor endowments (such as lower labour costs in the peripheral regions, for example). Firms undertaking reorganisation FDI should be able to generate scale economies, increase output, reduce X-inefficiency and spread risk across different production sites, resulting in lower costs and a more efficient operating position. These gains, in turn, should enable firms to compete more successfully in the SEM and beyond. If firms were previously obliged to produce inside fragmented national markets, such reorganisation will probably take the form of divestment from certain member states and a corresponding investment in others. However, it may also involve expansion, through mergers and acquisitions, to form larger and more competitive corporate entities. It has been noted that the locational strategies of efficiency seeking firms are less influenced by the size of local markets and more by the comparative advantage of a region arising through technological, transport and communication infrastructure. Thus, efficiency-seeking firms tend to be most footloose in their value added activities (Dunning, 1992).

Strategic asset-seeking FDI

This type of investment is typically used to complement the MNE's existing portfolio of assets in a manner intended to sustain or advance its international competitiveness vis-à-vis that of its competitors (Dunning, 1993). In so doing, the firm can achieve long-term strategic objectives. In the context of the EU, strategic asset seeking FDI is more likely to occur as a cross-border takeover rather than, for example, greenfield investment. This is because an international acquisition is an expedient method for gaining first mover advantage (or for later entrants, 'follow the leader' advantages) in opening markets previously closed to non-nationals. Acquisition is also an efficacious method for the acquiring firm to obtain the target firm's market knowledge and functioning distribution network when penetrating previously unfamiliar segments of the EU market.

Table 16.1 Share of FDI inflows (%) from all countries

	1982–87	1988–90	1991–93	1994	1995 (est.)
Developed countries	78.1	84.6	67.0	58.8	64.5
Developing countries	21.9	15.3	33.0	38.5	31.6
European Union	28.2	42.3	44.4	28.3	35.5
as a % of developed countries	36.1	50.0	66.3	48.2	55.0
United States	39.9	31.3	10.2	22.0	19.1
Japan	0.7		0.9	<0.1	<0.1

Notes: Figures for 1994 and 1995 are for the EU15
Source: adapted from UNCTAD (1996) and Commission (1996)

The European Union and patterns of FDI

Currently, around a third of the worldwide flow of FDI each year is directed at the member states of the EU15. As Table 16.1 shows, this share climbed throughout the 1980s and early 1990s, from just over a quarter in the first half of the 1980s, and peaking at 44 per cent of world flow in the period 1991–93.

The growth in the annual inflow of aggregate (intra and extra) FDI to the EU, in value terms, is illustrated in Fig. 16.1. Again, the sharp increase is revealed in the flow of FDI to the EU in the late 1980s and early 1990s, peaking at ECU 72 bn in 1990, before subsequently declining.

It has been estimated that, in 1995, over half (55 per cent) of all FDI inflows to the developed countries were directed towards the member states (UNCTAD, 1996). Even after normalising for differences in the growth of GDP between member states and the rest of the world, it is evident that the EU attracted a disproportionately high amount of global investment activity in the late 1980s and early 1990s (Dunning, 1997a). The current stock of investment in the EU reinforces this assertion. For example, by 1995, the EU12 was host to around half (50.4 per cent) of the stock of FDI in the developed countries and just over one third (36.7 per cent) of the worldwide stock of FDI (UNCTAD, 1996; Commission, 1996). Indeed, the ability of the EU as a whole to attract inward investment today exceeds even that of the United States, the single largest recipient country of inward investment (see Table 16.2). Although the level of global FDI bound for the USA has recovered from its low in 1991–93, the amounts witnessed in the 1980s have not since been repeated. Inflows of FDI to Japan, in contrast to the EU and USA, have consistently been virtually negligible.

In terms of the origin of this inbound investment, while estimates vary, it is thought that MNEs from outside the EU, mainly from the USA and, to a lesser degree, the European Free Trade Association (EFTA) countries, accounted for the majority, around two-thirds, of inbound FDI to the EU in the years 1957–84 (Dunning, 1997a). However, this share has since declined, primarily because of the growing importance in the EU of direct investment flows from other member states. From 41 per cent in 1984, intra-EU FDI rose to 55 per cent in 1986–90 and to over 60 per cent in 1991–93 (Commission, 1996). By comparison, investment from Japan into the EU over the same period has been relatively low, oscillating between 3 per cent and 8 per cent of the EU total of inbound FDI since 1984, with the largest inflow occurring in 1990.

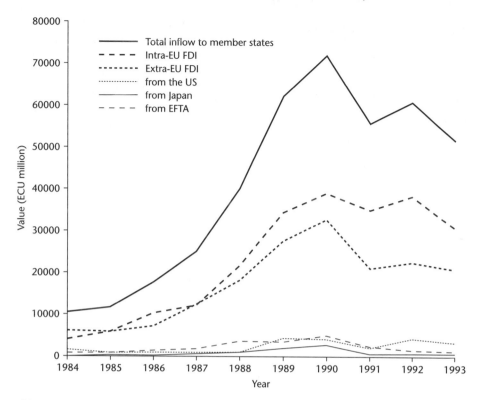

Abbreviations
EU   European Union
FDI   Foreign direct investment
GDP   Gross domestic product
MNE Multinational enterprise

Figure 16.1   EU FDI inflows from all countries

In terms of the destination of this inbound investment, prior to 1985 around 90 per cent of inbound FDI to the EU, from within and outside the EU, was concentrated in six 'core' member states, namely Belgium/Luxembourg, France, Germany, Italy, Netherlands and the United Kingdom. More precisely, Dunning (1997a) estimates that much of this, approximately three-fifths, was located within a 500-mile radius of Frankfurt. The major recipients of total inbound investment to the EU in the early 1990s have been the UK (with around 23 per cent of the total), followed by France (15 per cent), Belgium/Luxembourg (14 per cent) and Spain (12 per cent) (see Table 16.2). Given the size of Germany's domestic economy, its share of total inward FDI flow to the EU, averaging 8 per cent during the period 1990–93, is disproportionately low. Inbound direct investment, however, is not evenly distributed among member states with respect to the donor country. For example, as the dominant recipient of inbound FDI to the EU, the UK receives the majority of its inward investment from non-member states, primarily the USA and Japan. Between 1986 and 1992 the UK consistently received over 40 per cent of all extra-EU FDI inflows (Commission,

Table 16.2   Leading host economies for FDI based on cumulative inflows, 1985–95

Rank	Country	FDI (US$bn)	FDI per capita (& rank)	
1	United States	477.5	1820	(13)
2	*United Kingdom*	199.6	3410	(7)
3	*France*	138.0	2380	(10)
4	China	130.2	110	(20)
5	*Spain*	90.9	2320	(11)
6	*Belgium/Luxembourg*	72.4	6900	(2)
7	*Netherlands*	68.1	4410	(3)
8	Australia	62.6	3470	(6)
9	Canada	60.9	2060	(12)
10	Mexico	44.1	470	(17)
11	Singapore	40.8	13650	(1)
12	*Sweden*	37.7	4270	(4)
13	*Italy*	36.3	630	(16)
14	Malaysia	30.7	1520	(14)
15	*Germany*	25.9	320	(18)
16	Switzerland	25.2	3580	(5)
17	Argentina	23.5	680	(15)
18	Brazil	20.3	130	(19)
19	Hong Kong	17.9	2890	(9)
20	*Denmark*	15.7	3000	(8)

Notes: EU15 member states are italicised
Source: WTO (1996)

Table 16.3   Member states' share of FDI inflows, 1986–93

	Share of average intra-EU FDI flows to:			Share of average extra-EU FDI flows to:			Share of total FDI flows to the EU going to:		
	1986	1993	1990–93	1986	1993	1990–93	1986	1993	1990–93
Bel/Lux	7%	19%	17%	2%	16%	9%	5%	17%	14%
Denmark	0%	1%	1%	2%	4%	2%	1%	2%	2%
Germany	9%	7%	11%	3%	7%	5%	7%	7%	8%
Greece	1%	1%	1%	3%	0%	0%	2%	1%	1%
Spain	17%	13%	14%	15%	9%	9%	16%	11%	12%
France	14%	18%	15%	19%	14%	16%	16%	16%	15%
Ireland	1%	6%	7%	0%	6%	4%	0%	6%	6%
Italy	7%	7%	5%	–6%	7%	7%	2%	7%	6%
Netherlands	18%	16%	12%	13%	4%	10%	16%	11%	11%
Portugal	1%	2%	3%	1%	1%	2%	1%	2%	2%
UK	25%	9%	14%	47%	34%	37%	34%	19%	23%
Total	100%	100%	100%	100%	100%	100%	100%	100%	100%
Share of extra-EU flows to total				41%	41%	40%			

Source: Commission (1996)

1996). On the other hand, the UK is significantly less important as a site for FDI from other member states, absorbing less than 10 per cent of intra-EU FDI flows in 1993. Intra-EU FDI has tended to favour Belgium/Luxembourg and France, closely followed by Spain and then the UK (see Table 16.3).

The impact of this investment on the peripheral countries of the EU is reflected in figures for the ratio of FDI inflows to GDP (see Table 16.4).

These ratios of FDI inflows to GDP provide an indicative measure of the impact on the domestic economies of member states of inward FDI not captured by a

Table 16.4 Significance of the EU's FDI inflows to GDP by member state, 1986–93

Ratio of total FDI to GDP	1986	1993	1990–93
Belgium/Luxembourg	0.75	4.79	4.70
Denmark	0.23	1.04	0.89
Germany	0.13	0.22	0.37
Greece	0.86	0.56	0.64
Spain	1.20	1.32	1.75
France	0.38	0.78	0.89
Ireland	0.25	7.68	9.41
Italy	0.05	0.40	0.40
Netherlands	1.54	2.18	2.74
Portugal	0.65	1.47	2.64
UK	1.04	1.29	1.83
EU12	0.49	0.94	1.17

Source: Commission (1996)

simple analysis of the magnitude and destination of inward FDI in aggregate terms. For example, in the period 1990–93, inward investment had the greatest effect on Ireland, where the annual inflows of FDI were worth 9.4 per cent of GDP. This was followed by Belgium/Luxembourg with 4.7 per cent per year, then the Netherlands (2.7 per cent), Portugal (2.6 per cent), the UK (1.8 per cent) and Spain (1.7 per cent). Least affected by this measure are Germany (less than 0.4 per cent), Italy (0.4 per cent) and Greece (0.6 per cent) (Commission, 1996). These figures again illustrate the relative unattractiveness of Germany and Italy in particular as hosts for inward European investment.

Explaining FDI trends in the European Union

Evaluating the role of European integration, and in particular the SEM programme, in shaping observed trends in the investment behaviour of EU and non-EU MNEs is hampered by two major problems. First, there are limitations in the data. Data on FDI flows are rarely comprehensive and up-to-date, while the motives for individual investments are seldom recorded. Furthermore, many firms will have responded only relatively recently to the non-tariff barrier (NTB) reductions initiated by the SEM programme. As a consequence, current statistics on FDI into the EU will not embrace the full effect of the deepening of European integration on the investment strategies of MNEs. Secondly, isolating the role of European integration and the SEM programme from other factors that have helped to shape patterns of FDI across Europe is a formidable task. These factors include market size, market growth, relative factor costs, and so on. Moreover, not only does the process of integration itself exert influence on these factors, but it is also difficult to relate current investment patterns in the EU to the counterfactual – the level of investment that would have occurred if European integration had not taken place. In other words, patterns of FDI witnessed today in Europe may merely reflect broader trends within the global economy (Yannopoulos, 1992). However, despite such methodological limitations, it is possible to infer a number of responses of MNEs to the process of European integration, in terms of the investment strategy framework presented previously (see UNTCMD 1993; Yannopoulos 1992; Dunning 1997a, 1997b).

Market-seeking FDI

It is clear that the surge in inbound FDI from outside the EU in the early 1980s is attributable, at least in part, to the creation of the Customs Union (Dunning, 1997a). Many non-EU firms, particularly those from the US, undertook market-seeking investment in the EU for defensive import-substituting purposes (Balasubramanyam and Greenaway, 1991). By moving production to the EU, these firms responded to the trade diversion effects of the customs union and the common tariff (effectively a tariff wall) by 'tariff-jumping'. In so doing, they secured tariff-free access to the Customs Union, which helped them to protect market shares previously built up through exports. Nevertheless, because NTB distortions, especially those associated with marketing and service activities, still prevailed within the Customs Union at this time, many non-EU investors often continued to treat individual national EU markets as separate and distinct from each other. Latterly, in response to the SEM programme, and the market opportunities it presents, non-EU MNEs have substituted *offensive* import-substituting investment for defensive import-substituting investment (Buiges and Jacquemin, 1994; Clegg, 1995). This strategy reflects the relative attractiveness to non-EU firms of the single market vis-à-vis other investment opportunities worldwide in the 1980s. However, certain non-EU firms, most notably Japanese automobile manufacturers, continued to invest for defensive import-substituting purposes throughout the 1980s, while many Japanese suppliers to these manufacturers followed their principal customers to Europe for proactive market-seeking purposes.

Largely because of past import-substituting activity, US affiliates in particular are now well established in the EU. To illustrate, in the early 1990s nearly half of the total non-domestic assets of US multinationals were concentrated in the EU (Commission, 1996). Of the total market for US goods and services in the EU today, approximately 85 per cent is catered for by US affiliates in the EU, and just 15 per cent by exports from the US. This level of penetration has stimulated some commentators to state that it is 'quite possible that the world's third greatest industrial power after the US and Russia will not be Europe, but American industry in Europe' (UNCTAD, 1996, p. 419). As with extra-EU FDI in general, much of this US investment favoured the UK. Of course, the UK is one of the largest national economies in Western Europe, which in part explains its attractiveness to MNEs. However, Germany too has a large domestic economy, so clearly other factors are at work. For example, the UK's ability to attract inward investment may be due to the closer linguistic, cultural, legal and institutional ties between the UK and, especially, the USA, relative to the other core countries of the EU (Dunning, 1997a). In addition, by the late 1980s, the UK had a programme of deregulation and state sector privatisation that was relatively advanced, certainly more so than other member states in the EU. The UK also has a typical corporate structure that promotes take-overs (unlike several continental countries), and at times has had a comparatively weak currency (which lowers the purchase price of UK assets for firms from countries with stronger currencies). For these reasons, many UK enterprises will have proved enticing merger and acquisition targets for foreign firms looking to expand into the UK and beyond.

Turning now to the market-seeking activity of firms from member states, the creation of the Common Market and the removal of internal tariffs should have discouraged import-substituting FDI activity between member states. This is because lowering trade barriers within a customs union tends to promote the servicing of markets in member states by exporting directly from the home member country. During the 1970s and early 1980s, however, the continued existence of NTBs and the segmentation of national markets (at both individual member level and EU level) caused market-seeking direct investments between member states to replace a proportion of intra-EU trade. At first sight, the anticipated net effect of the SEM programme on aggregate FDI flows within the EU also appears ambiguous. On the one hand, if the SEM programme raises income levels and growth in the EU as expected, then offensive market-seeking FDI between member states would be expected to grow. On the other hand, to the extent that trade is facilitated by the SEM and plant-level economies of scale become available, import-substituting FDI in particular may no longer be necessary and net intra-EU market-seeking FDI may consequently contract. However, studies indicate that, to date, FDI outflows by EU member states are not found to be related to a corresponding decline in exports, nor have increases in exports led to a decline in intra-EU FDI (Commission, 1996; Pain and Lansbury 1996; Agarwal *et al.*, 1995). In fact, there is evidence that intra-EU FDI and intra-EU trade are complementary, with increases in exports proceeding FDI (Dunning, 1997b). These studies suggest that many EU firms have responded to the SEM programme by investing in member states for market-seeking purposes, presumably to complement their trade-related activities (for example, to be close to customers or to secure channels of distribution).

In general, the proportion of all FDI inflows into the EU contributed by member states has grown faster relative to extra-EU FDI, especially since 1988. Indeed, as Fig. 16.1 illustrates, the level of intra-EU FDI as a proportion of total FDI inflow to the EU more than doubled between the mid-1980s and the early 1990s (Dunning, 1997a). Since the mid-1980s, foreign investment flows between member states have consequently exceeded inbound investment from outside the EU for every year except one (1987). Two studies undertaken for the Commission indicate that this growth exceeded levels that would have occurred if the SEM programme had not taken place (Commission, 1996). This growth suggests that EU-specific factors, such as the SEM, have probably had a considerably greater impact on intra-EU FDI than on extra-EU FDI. However, the growth in intra-EU FDI probably results from the positive impact of the SEM programme on market size, income levels and the structure of economic activity across the EU rather than from the direct effect of the SEM programme itself (Dunning, 1997b).

Of course, both efficiency-seeking and strategic asset-seeking investment activity will have contributed a significant, although indeterminate, proportion of this increase in intra-EU FDI. However, before considering the effect of European integration on these investment strategies, it is worthwhile commenting on the decline in levels of inbound FDI to the EU since its peak in 1990 (see Fig. 16.1). The weakening of the relative locational advantage of the EU may have occurred for several reasons. For example, the recessions experienced by several larger member states in the early 1990s probably rendered them less attractive to inward market-seeking investors. Concurrently, the developing countries, notably China, became more successful at attracting direct investment, especially from Japan and the USA. In addition, many firms may have now realised their EU investment ambitions, while for others fears that the Common External Tariff (CET) would impede extra-EU trade have proved, for the most part, unfounded. These factors will also have had a negative influence on the level of inbound market-seeking FDI to the EU. Nevertheless, growth in the size of markets at the individual member level, and the deepening and widening of the EU at the pan-European level are likely to continue to promote market-seeking investments by non-EU firms through the 1990s and beyond.

Efficiency-seeking and strategic asset-seeking FDI

It is clear that much of the increase in intra-EU FDI took place as EU firms restructured their European operations following the SEM programme. To what extent such efficiency-seeking and strategic asset-seeking activities have contributed to the growth in intra-EU FDI is difficult to ascertain. However, data on European mergers and acquisitions provide some insights (see Table 16.5).

In recent years, the EU has become the focus of global merger and acquisition activity (WTO, 1996). Since 1989, of the global annual sales of assets by mergers and acquisitions, over one-third has consistently involved target firms located in the EU, reaching 48 per cent in 1991 and peaking at 56 per cent in 1992 (see Table 16.5). Within the EU, most acquired firms have been located in the UK (with asset sales valued at $24 bn in 1995 from $11 bn in 1994) and in France ($10 bn in 1995 from $8 bn in 1994). At the same time, of the global annual purchases of assets through mergers and acquisitions, around half have been made by acquiring firms from the EU. Most of these EU cross-border purchases were made by UK ($18 bn in 1995), German ($15 bn) and French firms ($7 bn). Intra-EU cross-border mergers and acquisitions increased from $20 bn in 1994 to $26 bn in 1995. By the mid-1990s, just under half of the total purchases made by EU firms were to acquire firms in other member states (WTO, 1996). Indeed, cross-border mergers and acquisitions are now the prime method of foreign market entry in the EU (Dunning, 1997a, 1997b). For both EU and non-EU firms, these mergers and acquisitions are examples of efficiency-seeking and strategic asset-seeking investments. They occur as firms seek to restructure their operations in order to strengthen their competitive position vis-à-vis US, Japanese and other European firms, to generate greater returns to scale in production and sourcing, and to reposition their business activities on a pan-European, rather than national level (WTO, 1996). Some Japanese firms have also acquired assets in the EU in industries in which they were comparatively disadvantaged, such as pharmaceuticals, or which offer complementary technologies or market access (Dunning, 1997b).

Table 16.5 Cross-border merger and acquisition sales and purchases (millions of dollars)

Economy	sales from								purchases by							
	1988	1989	1990	1991	1992	1993	1994	1995	1988	1989	1990	1991	1992	1993	1994	1995
All countries	**112544**	**123042**	**115371**	**49730**	**75382**	**67281**	**108732**	**134629**	**112544**	**123042**	**115371**	**49730**	**75382**	**67281**	**108732**	**134629**
of which:																
European Union	**29513**	**47107**	**43056**	**23984**	**42626**	**27134**	**38627**	**48604**	**64167**	**61286**	**65224**	**31756**	**30932**	**34658**	**51895**	**60953**
as a percentage of EU total:																
Austria	1	0	0	1	0	1	1	1	0	0	0	0	1	0	0	0
Belgium	1	3	2	5	1	1	2	3	1	3	0	0	3	1	2	6
Denmark	0	0	1	0	1	2	5	0	0	1	1	1	3	1	0	1
Finland	0	0	0	2	0	2	0	0	1	2	2	1	0	1	1	2
France	14	12	10	11	16	14	23	22	17	31	26	36	29	17	12	13
Germany	5	10	14	11	12	6	15	11	4	12	11	15	13	9	16	25
Greece	0	1	0	1	2	0	0	0	0	0	0	0	0	2	0	0
Ireland	2	0	1	1	1	5	0	0	2	2	1	2	1	2	4	2
Italy	11	4	9	5	7	10	8	5	2	3	6	7	20	2	2	5
Luxembourg	0	0	0	0	0	1	0	0	0	0	1	3	2	5	1	1
Netherlands	7	5	3	6	12	16	3	5	3	6	4	12	5	14	5	9
Portugal	0	1	1	0	1	1	1	0	0	0	0	1	1	0	0	0
Spain	3	4	9	14	8	4	7	2	0	0	3	1	2	1	1	2
Sweden	1	2	3	4	4	12	6	2	3	3	14	3	2	5	2	5
United Kingdom	55	58	47	38	35	26	28	48	66	36	31	19	20	41	52	30

Source: Commission (1996)

Theory predicts that, when undertaking efficiency-seeking investments, firms will relocate production to regions in the EU with relevant comparative advantage, and where capital will be employed most productively. What is the evidence that EU and non-EU MNEs have restructured their European operations in this way in response to the SEM programme?

In terms of industry-specific factors, following economic integration a geographical concentration of production in a few plants will most likely be observed in technology intensive industries, when plant economies of scale are most important. Such economies of scale would discourage dispersed production, especially when transportation costs are low (Dunning, 1997b). Conversely, less concentration of production activity in the EU would be expected in industries where products are more dependent upon the resource endowments of particular investment locations. In these industries, the pattern of FDI would reflect the comparative advantage of member states. To some extent, these predictions are observed in EU merger and acquisition activity. In northern member states, for example, cross-border manufacturing merger and acquisition activity is mainly in technology-intensive sectors such as engineering, transport equipment and machinery. By comparison, in southern member states, cross-border mergers and acquisitions are mainly in relatively basic products such as textiles, clothing, timber and wooden furniture (Commission, 1996).

In terms of location, there has been a trend for a proportion of manufacturing and distribution operations to relocate to an economic hub of the EU. This hub, which consists of Northern Italy, Northern Spain, Southern Germany, Central France and the South East UK, is a densely populated region, with large consumer markets and relatively low transportation costs to service these markets. The fact that intra-EU FDI in particular tends to prefer Benelux and France as investment locations may, in part, reflect a trend towards some geographic concentration of distribution and market seeking activity. A geographic concentration has also been observed in a few technology and information-intensive industries (Dunning, 1997b). For example, in the financial services industry (an information-intensive sector) the UK has maintained its comparative advantage as an investment location. This is due primarily to the continued, although declining, preference for US and Japanese MNEs to invest in, or acquire institutions in the City of London. A geographical concentration of investment activity has also been observed in the pharmaceutical industry (a technology-intensive sector). In this industry, some 91.3 per cent of the cross-border merger and acquisition activity in the EU between 1989 and 1994 involved the six core EU countries, particularly the UK and France (Dunning, 1997b). Some companies are also exhibiting a trend to relocate their headquarters to major financial centres such as Frankfurt, Paris, London and Brussels.

On balance, however, apart from these instances, there is little evidence of a general increase in the geographical concentration of FDI within the EU following the SEM programme. In fact, evidence from cross-border mergers and acquisition data indicates that there has been a slight *decrease* in the geographical concentration of FDI. For example, in technology and information-intensive sectors such as electronic components, office and computing machinery, industrial instruments and business services, there has been a trend for production to move away from the four largest EU countries, namely France, Germany, Italy and the UK (Dunning, 1997b). There has also been a modest decentralisation of investment in other sectors. These include auto-components and auto-assembly, with Spain becoming a major new production location for Japanese, EU and US companies and joint ventures, and chemicals, where production has moved from Germany and the UK towards the Netherlands and Spain (Dunning, 1997b).

It would therefore seem that peripheral countries such as Spain and Ireland, and certain regions of the 'core' countries, centred more or less around the Benelux countries, are indeed attracting greater inward investments. Much of this investment has come from other member states. As MNEs of all nationalities restructure their European operations, and move production to where it can take place most efficiently, the likelihood is that this process will promote economic redistribution in the EU and facilitate economic convergence. However, before this can be discussed, it is necessary first to evaluate some of the benefits and costs to countries that arise from inward and outward FDI.

Benefits and costs of FDI

Historically, the significance of the benefits and costs to both home and recipient nation of FDI has been a subject of fierce debate (an overview of this debate is provided by Dicken, 1998). Proponents argue that FDI is a vehicle for transferring technology to host countries, expanding trade, creating jobs and accelerating economic development. Detractors, however, charge FDI with creating balance-of-payments problems, permitting exploitation of host country markets and generally reducing the ability of host country governments to manage the domestic economy (WTO, 1996). For home countries, FDI has been thought to transfer jobs abroad and depress wages (WTO, 1996).

The current orthodoxy is that FDI is an important channel for technology transfers, including not only scientific processes, but also organisational, managerial and marketing skills. Indeed, it is the MNE's superior technology or innovative capacity that compensates for its cost disadvantage, relative to local firms, of engaging in foreign operations. This superior technology usually enables the MNE to exploit host country resources more efficiently than can locally owned firms. Technology transfer may be either a deliberate or a 'spill-over' effect. Deliberate diffusion occurs, for example, when the MNE licenses technology to local firms, upgrades the technological capabilities of local suppliers and customers to meet particular specifications, sells new products and processes in the local economy, or adapts existing products to suit local conditions. Technological spill-overs, on the other hand, occur when the MNE's technology is copied or learned by local competing firms. Indigenous firms may respond to the competitive pressure following an MNE's investment by upgrading their own technological capabilities and improving their own offerings and efficiencies. Incoming MNEs may also demonstrate new technologies, new modes of organisation and distribution, and train workers and managers who may later be employed by local firms (WTO, 1996). Inbound extra-EU FDI, from the US and Japan in particular, is seen by some as a very important vehicle for enhancing the technological capabilities of EU firms and distributing technologies across the EU. For example, the demonstration effect of Japanese management and labour practices on EU firms is widely recognised (Young *et al.*, 1994).

In terms of employment, again, the consensus is that the net employment effect of investment is generally favourable (Dicken, 1998). For home countries in the EU, the analytical tool to consider the impact of outward FDI on jobs is the linkage between trade and FDI. For example, the assumption can be made that production in foreign affiliates (outward investment) replaces home country production with exports and domestic consumption. The consequence is net job losses. However, empirical evidence does not support this notion (WTO, 1996). For example, a study of the trade-related impact of outflows of investment and employment in France found that outward investment by French firms during the period 1989–92 was carried out mainly by industries in which increased exports brought about net job gains (Messerlin, 1995). For host countries, whether inward investment in the aggregate increases or decreases net employment is also ambiguous. Clearly, inward 'greenfield' market seeking investment brings with it direct employment – workers employed directly by the MNE. To this figure must also be added the indirect employment created among firms with which the MNE has links. In addition, the salaries of MNE employees and those of linked firms will, if spent on locally produced goods, increase employment elsewhere in the domestic economy. On the other hand, against the number of jobs created in the local economy must be set the number of jobs displaced by any possible adverse effects on indigenous firms (Dicken, 1998). For example, local firms may be out-competed by the incoming MNE and new firm formation may be impeded. Furthermore, if the incoming firm is investing for efficiency-seeking motives, especially through acquisition, then direct job losses may occur as the acquiring firm 'down-sizes' the labour force or moves production away from particular locations or member states.

In recent years, most of the developed nations, including EU member states, have generally favoured the pro-FDI stance and adopted policies accordingly (a point which is returned to below). Both intra-EU and extra-EU FDI are considered important facilitators of economic convergence across the EU. Inbound extra-EU FDI, from the US and Japan in particular, is helping to enhance the technological capabilities of EU firms. Intra-EU FDI is important in creating competitive firms and promoting a reallocation of economic activity across the EU by restructuring activities on a pan-European as opposed to national basis. Regional development in particular benefits greatly from the growth in inward investment activities of MNEs to the peripheral member states.

Nevertheless, the gains from inward FDI remain equivocal. For example, some member states still harbour the view that extra-EU FDI, especially from Japan, is a threat to the future of existing European-based firms. In addition, some efficiency gains from intra-EU mergers and acquisitions may be dissipated by the problems associated with amalgamating two organisations with different languages, cultures, customs and business practices (Dunning, 1997b). Meanwhile, certain efficiency-seeking and strategic asset-seeking investments may merely involve a change in ownership, with no additional benefit to the host country firm or economy in terms of technology transfer or employment. There is also some evidence that, in intra-EU efficiency-seeking FDI, high value-added activities tend to remain in established clusters of activity in the core EU countries, while only lower value activities are relocating in response to the SEM programme (Dunning, 1997a). If this is the case, the net benefits of inward investment to the peripheral regions in particular may not be as great as presupposed. This brief discussion highlights the fact that FDI in the EU has non-trivial implications for the economic development of member states. Comparisons and contrasts in the policy reaction of Commission and member states to inward FDI-related issues are discussed in the following section.

EU policy towards FDI

Since 1973, and the publication of a document entitled 'Memorandum on Multinational Undertakings and the Community', the Commission has made no attempt to devise a comprehensive policy approach to MNE activity in the EU. It has failed even to present a general statement of philosophy or attitude to intra-EU and extra-EU FDI (Young *et al.*, 1994). Discussions on the implementation of the SEM programme, for example, avoided virtually any reference to MNEs and how their response, in terms of European investment strategy, would impinge upon the programme's objectives. Instead, the Commission seems to have adopted a tacit and benign policy founded on the perception that the advantages of inward investment outweigh the disadvantages. This policy stance probably owes its origin to the generally welcoming attitude of Europe towards foreign investments from the US in the 1950s and 1960s, which were concentrated in high technology and greenfield projects where the economic benefits in the form of new assets and capabilities were readily recognised (Young *et al.*, 1994). The Commission's policy at the time was to curb, through competition legislation, the potential monopoly power of US MNEs while simultaneously encouraging competitive European-based firms. Today, this tacit and benign policy stance is reflected in, for example, the adherence by the EU to the principles of national (or equal) treatment of EU and non-EU firms, and the support by the EU for the Organisation for Economic Co-operation and Development (OECD) and World Trade Organisation (WTO) multilateral rules and agendas intended to disencumber global FDI. In fact, today, many FDI issues are now under the discipline of the WTO, through its implementation of the General Agreement on Trade in Services (GATS) and Agreement on Trade-related Investment Measures (TRIMS), both of which impinge directly on the investment strategies of MNEs. Furthermore, the Commission tacitly encourages cross-border direct investment flows in the EU, under the assumption that this constitutes one of the prime mechanisms by which the gains from the SEM are to be realised. Confidence is placed by the Commission in competition policy being able to handle any distortions and counter any anti-competitive action by large foreign firms (Young *et al.*, 1994).

In the past, the EU member states have collectively had an ambivalent attitude towards inward FDI. In the 1960s and 1970s, for example, government attitudes among the 'core' member states were wide-ranging and divergent. At one end of the spectrum was France, which had the most explicit and restrict-ive policies towards inward FDI in order to inhibit any new investments that com-peted with local firms or interfered with government industrial policy. At the other end were Germany, the Netherlands and Italy. Since the Second World War these countries have more or less had an 'open door' attitude to foreign investment (although some sectors, for example telecommunications in Germany, remained subject to strict government control) (Dunning, 1992). The UK was located somewhere between these two extremes (Dunning, 1992). Although it generally welcomed inward investment, successive governments intervened to support indigenous firms in competition with foreign affiliates, particularly in the automobile, electronic and computer industries. During the 1960s and 1970s, attitudes also varied among the peripheral countries. Ireland and Belgium, for example, actively sought to attract efficiency-seeking and export-oriented inward investment as a means of fostering regional development. Consequently, they both have had very liberal FDI-related policies. On the other hand, prior to their accession to the EU, Spain, Portugal and Greece had many restrictions on inward investment and imposed strict vetting procedures in high technology and other sensitive sectors. They also had complex administrative procedures for most inbound direct investment. Moreover, all member states have, in the past, been generally sceptical about the benefits of foreign acquisitions and takeovers, prin-cipally on the grounds that these increased the concentration of foreign own-ership and reduced indigenous technological capacity (Dunning, 1992). Each member state, for example, has resorted to monopoly and anti-trust legislation at various times to thwart hostile take-overs by foreign firms.

From the mid-1980s, however, there has been a growing belief that inward direct investment can, by its provision of new assets, capabilities and organisa-tional direction, promote the competitiveness of indigenous firms. Member states have consequently relaxed their attitudes towards FDI and removed many of the obstacles to inward investment. Depending on the member state concerned, this has been manifested in a relaxation in export performance requirements; a sim-plification of administrative procedures (to merely notification and verification, with authorisation confined to only a few very large transactions); a reduction or elimination of all exchange controls on inward investment, and the reduc-tion or removal of many sectoral restrictions to foreign ownership (Dunning, 1992). The greatest liberalisation has occurred in the most restrictive eco-nomies, namely France, Spain and Portugal in the 1980s, and Greece in the 1990s.

A number of developments in the global economy over the past decade have led to calls from some commentators that the EU develop more explicit, detailed and consistent policies on FDI issues (see, for example, Brewer and Young, 1995; Young *et al.*, 1994). Competition to attract inward direct investment has intensified, as industries become more global in outlook and as investment pol-icies have become more liberal worldwide. While seeking to promote open access in world markets for EU firms, the EU is now finding itself in competition as an investment location not only with the developed countries but also, for ex-ample, with the emerging economies of Central and Eastern Europe and China. More significantly, perhaps, is that, as we have seen, FDI, and especially intra-EU FDI, is an important conduit for European integration, and in particular for the transfer of skills, technology and management culture across member states. Therefore, as firms relocate their market-seeking and efficiency-seeking activities, they influence the distribution effects of integration and generate adjust-ment costs associated with, for example, unemployment caused by divestment and 'down-sizing'.

It is, therefore, apparent that some coherent policy response towards FDI is required. However, this response is hampered by the division of competency between the EU and member states. EU policy authority, in general, stems from the 1957 Treaty of Rome, amended by the Single European Act (SEA) of 1986, and the Treaty on European Union (Maastricht Treaty) of 1992. As we will see, these provide the EU with partial competence in at least a number of areas relat-ing to FDI matters. However, these areas are administered by different Director-ates in the EU, which inevitably produces overlap, contradictions and gaps in policy coverage (Young *et al.*, 1994). Furthermore, the principle of 'subsidiarity', which appears in Article 3b of the Maastricht Treaty, provides member states with competency in several other areas relating to FDI policy, which these mem-ber states can unilaterally apply to attract inward investment. Thus, there exist in the EU certain dilemmas and conflicts of interest with regard to FDI policy which prevail among EU Directorates, between the EU and member states, and between member states themselves. Brewer and Young (1995) describe in detail a broad range of these dilemmas and conflicts of interest. For illustrative pur-poses, we highlight a few of the most significant problems relating to FDI in the EU that have arisen in the 1990s, in terms of the principal policy areas concerned.

Internal trade and factor movements

Although the EU has widespread competence derived from the Treaty of Rome and the Single European Act, individual member states are able to determine their own rules and regulations. This has caused conflict between the Com-mission and member states in several areas that impact on inward intra-EU and extra-EU FDI. For example, the pace of liberalisation of services in general has been slow in some member states, and national reciprocity agreements (that per-mission to invest depends upon reciprocity being granted by the home nation of the investing MNE) often still prevail, especially in banking and finance. In addition, despite Directives being passed, government procurement has often discriminated in favour of national firms and against the inward investor. More-over, some privatisations have restricted the level of foreign ownership allowed, while providing 'golden shares' for national government. Member states also determine their own fiscal regime (so that taxes could, until recently, be set at levels likely to attract inward investment), and they can press investing MNEs (often those from Japan) to accept informal performance and other require-ments before being awarded tax concessions or other incentives. Distortions in investment flows consequently follow.

Competition policy

The EU has competence under Articles 85 and 86 of the Treaty of Rome (relat-ing to restrictive business practices, cartels and the abuse of dominant position),

Council Merger Regulation (relating to concentrative joint ventures and oligo-polies) and Article 92(1) on State Aid. Respectively, the problems which affect inward direct investment as a result include the slow pace of decision-making under Articles 85 and 86; the uncertainty over which rules apply to joint ventures, and the fact that indigenous producers tend to be favoured by State Aid. Given the high levels of merger and acquisition in the EU, there is also a strong case here for centralised decision-making. For example, approval at the EU level can be granted for efficiency-enhancing mergers that have EU-wide benefits to consumers, shareholders and the workforce, which might otherwise be blocked by the particular member state with jurisdiction in the case (CEPR, 1993).

Trade and commercial policy

The EU has competence under Articles 110–115 of the Treaty of Rome, which permits it to establish a common commercial policy, including bilateral, multi-lateral and sectoral agreements, rules of origin and anti-dumping rules against MNEs. In the past, such rules have been centrally enforced. For example, in July 1991, the EU imposed quotas to peg the levels of automobile imports from Japan and it has implemented anti-dumping rules, primarily against Japanese and other Southeast Asian countries. These impositions stimulated a certain level of defensive import-substituting FDI. However, no evaluation of the impact of these decisions on the local industry or indigenous sub-contractors was carried out. For example, no effort was made to deal with circumvention strategies, for instance, when EU and non-EU based firms shifted production to low-cost third countries whose exports were not subject to anti-dumping duties and other protectionist measures in the EU. Moreover, little account was taken of the response by several Japanese firms to escape these protectionist measures by assembling products in the EU from kits exported from Japan. Such production involves limited transfers of technology and demonstration effects. This raises the concern that the EU may merely become a site for low value-added assembly plants servicing high value-added activities of the non-EU multinational. In the early 1990s, this concern led to a dispute between member states over the definition of 'EU production', with France in particular attempting to restrict exports of automobiles assembled by the Japanese producer Nissan in the UK.

Regional policy

The EU, under the terms of the Treaty of Rome, amended by the Maastricht Treaty, is permitted to vet the regional aid granted by member states under the European Regional Development Fund, taking account of regional differences. Under this scheme, grants and loans are provided to assist poorer peripheral regions and regions with above average unemployment to upgrade their infrastructure. Such regional aid is likely to attract capital-intensive, efficiency-seeking FDI and may consequently distort competition (Dunning, 1992). In addition, incentives offered at the regional level are thought to favour the inward investor and enhance the investor's bargaining position vis-à-vis the host member state. Together with unilateral investment incentives or 'beggar thy neighbour' policies used by individual member states to attract investment (such as taxation-related arrangements, labour-related subsidies and infrastructure improvements), the concern is raised that any net benefits that would accrue from a particular investment may be 'competed away' in the bidding process to attract it. The EU does impose ceilings on regional incentives to limit the intensity of competitive bidding. However, the Commission's role in defining priorities in the disbursement of regional aid has been disputed by some member states (CEPR, 1993), while the monitoring and enforcement of national and EU aid for specific MNE projects often lacks transparency. For example, disputes have arisen between member states over allegations of unfair levels of financial assistance offered to non-MNEs to sway their plant rationalisation decisions. In general, there is a strong need for the EU to promote transparency, provide greater guidance on acceptable forms of incentives, and reduce the overall level of incentives granted by member states for inward investment. This would benefit national taxpayers and lower the aid-related costs incurred by the EU.

Social policy

There is also a need for the EU to consider issues relating to the indirect effects of divestment and rationalisation of pan-European industry by the MNE. Such activity can result in unemployment and social unrest, highlighted in 1997 by the threat (which was subsequently withdrawn) of the French automobile manufacturer Renault to close its plant in Belgium and relocate production to France. Whether the member state concerned should bear the full social cost of divestment, or whether the EU or the particular MNE involved should bear a proportion of these costs, is open to debate. Other aspects of social policy also illustrate the difficulty (if not impossibility) of promoting a national policy towards MNEs while maintaining membership of an institution such as the EU. This point is highlighted, for example, by the impact on the UK of the Directive to establish Europe-wide Works Councils in MNEs active in Europe. In the mid-1990s, the UK was not obliged to adopt this Directive because of its opt-out from the agreement on social policy in the Maastricht Treaty. Nevertheless, the UK was forced to accept the policy 'through the back door' because many UK-based affiliates and firms voluntarily established European Works Councils as part of their pan-European investment strategy.

Industrial policy and research and technology policy

The EU has no direct competence for industrial policy outside the coal and steel industries, although it does have competence in certain research and development related matters, under Articles 130f–130p of the Maastricht Treaty, which seeks to avoid duplication and encourage coordination in such activities among member states. The lack of a centralised industrial policy with respect to MNEs highlights several major philosophical differences between member states regarding FDI. For example, France and southern European countries wish competitiveness to take priority over competition, which would mean the creation of pan-European champion firms through an accommodating mergers policy, sectoral targeting and a substantial increase in European R&D expenditure. This is a view resisted by, for example, the UK, which favours a passive industrial policy but strong competition policy to promote EU competitiveness. France and Italy have also tended to regard Japanese investment more as a Trojan horse than European or the US investments (Dunning, 1992). In particular, some concern has been shown towards several key sectors of the EU economy now dominated by Japanese and US companies, such as computer and information technology equipment sectors. Whether such foreign-owned firms should participate in EU research and development programmes such as ESPRIT has also been questioned (see Chapter 6).

It seems clear that the EU needs to develop more explicit, detailed and consistent policies on FDI issues (Brewer and Young, 1995). This could take the form of one single FDI policy, or a series of individual policies built around competition, industrial, regional development, trade and technology policies (Young *et al.*, 1994). However, the EU is currently a long way from establishing any coherent FDI-related policy of any sort. Consequently, some of the dilemmas and conflicts of interest highlighted above will prevail in one form or another between the Commission and individual member states, for at least the short term. At the beginning of the 1990s, Safarian (1991, p. 199) stated that it is 'difficult, if not impossible, for the EC to develop the kind of co-ordination needed . . . to assure net economic gain for the Community from strategic . . . investment policy.' Little has changed subsequently to invalidate this observation.

Concluding remarks and outlook

Prior to 1975, the creation of the Customs Union stimulated an inflow of market-seeking import-substituting investment. This was primarily defensive in nature and was made mostly by firms from the USA. Since then, and especially during the 1980s and early 1990s, there has been a shift towards greater efficiency-seeking and strategic asset-seeking activity in response to the SEM programme, particularly on the part of member state firms. There has also been a general widening in the source countries for this investment. Consequently, the EU is now the dominant recipient of global direct investment. Evidence suggests that much of this inward investment would not have occurred without the initiation of the SEM programme.

In many respects, the SEM programme has probably favoured the market-seeking and efficiency-seeking activities of non-EU multinationals (especially US firms) over their EU counterparts. In general, member state firms have been wedded parochially to their home markets, certainly in the early years of the SEM programme. By contrast, non-EU multinationals were generally unencumbered by entrenched market positions. Non-EU firms were consequently able to choose the most efficient production locations, as and when they became available, without regard for traditional national boundaries. They were also typically larger than their EU counterparts and, in the case of US firms, enjoyed greater organisational flexibility. As a result, many non-EU firms have been in a better position than most native EU firms to benefit from EU market integration (in attaining scale economies in production at the pan-European level, for example) and promote EU market integration. Indeed, Dunning (1997b, p. 201) observes that, even by the early 1990s, the European MNEs 'had still not geared up their European operations to meet the needs of the internal market'. However, the recent surge in intra-EU FDI suggests that many EU firms are now in the process of reorganising their European operations in order to compete successfully in the emerging EU business environment.

The next phase in inbound intra and extra-EU FDI will begin with the introduction, scheduled for 2002, of European Monetary Union (EMU) by some EU member states. Even before then, many EU and non-EU firms may incorporate into their EU investment strategy the benefits of locating part, if not all, of their production within the Single Currency Area. For market-seeking firms, these benefits might include the elimination of currency conversion costs, hedging costs and other financial control costs associated with trading in the Single Currency Area. Efficiency-seeking firms may benefit from greater access to cost reductions which, it is predicted, will be brought about by greater price stability and price transparency in the Single Currency Area (McDonald, 1997). By 1997, several large Japanese MNEs in particular had already articulated their desire to locate production facilities within the 'in' countries of Monetary Union, to the chagrin of 'opt-out' countries such as the UK and Denmark. Precisely how EU and non-EU MNEs will respond to a 'two-tier' EU consisting of countries with and without the euro remains to be seen. However, it is clear that the introduction of EMU will have a non-trivial impact on the evolving pattern of intra and extra-EU FDI. With the importance of FDI in facilitating the process of European integration, this is a development that policy-makers in the Commission and in member states would be ill advised to ignore.

References

Agarwal J P, Hiemenz U and Nunnenkamp P 1995 *European Integration: A Threat to Foreign Investment in Developing Countries,* Kiel Institut für Weltwirtschaft an der Universität Kiel, Discussion paper No. 246.

Balasubramanyam V N and Greenaway D 1991 Economic Integration and Foreign Direct Investment: Japanese Investment in the EC, *Journal of Common Market Studies,* Vol. 3, pp. 75–193.

Brewer T and Young S 1995 European Union Policies and the Problems of Multinational Enterprises, *Journal of World Trade,* Vol. 29, No. 1, February, pp. 33–52.

Buckley P J and Casson M 1976 *The Future of the Multinational Enterprise,* Macmillan, London.

Buiges P and Jacquemin A 1994 Foreign Investments and Exports to the European Community, in Mason M and Encarnation D (eds.), *Does Ownership Matter?,* Clarendon Press, Oxford.

Casson M 1990 *Multinational Corporations,* Edward Elgar, Brookfield.

Centre for Economic Policy Research 1993 *Making Sense of Subsidiarity: How Much Centralisation for Europe?,* CEPR, London, 1 November.

Clegg L J 1995 *The Determinants of United States Foreign Direct Investment in the European Community: A Critical Appraisal* mimeo, University of Bath.

Commission 1995 *Panorama of EU-Industry 95/96*, Eurostat, Luxembourg, pp. 41–53.

Commission 1996 Economic Evaluation of the Internal Market, *European Economy*, No. 4, Directorate-General for Economic and Financial Affairs.

Dicken P 1998 *Global Shift: Transforming the World Economy*, Paul Chapman Publishing, London.

Dunning J H 1992 Multinational Investment in the EC: Some Policy Implications, Chapter 12 in Cantwell J (ed.), *Multinational Investment in Modern Europe: Strategic Interaction in the Integrated Community*, Edward Elgar, Brookfield.

Dunning J H 1993 *Multinational Enterprises and the Global Economy*, Addison Wesley.

Dunning J H 1997a The European Internal Market Programme and Inbound Foreign Direct Investment, *Journal of Common Market Studies*, Vol. 35, No. 1, March, pp. 1–30.

Dunning J H 1997b The European Internal Market Programme and Inbound Foreign Direct Investment – Part II, *Journal of Common Market Studies*, Vol. 35, No. 2, March, pp. 189–223.

McDonald F 1997 European Monetary Union: Some Implications for Companies, *Journal of General Management*, Vol. 23, No. 3, Winter, pp. 47–64.

Messerlin 1995 *The Impact of Trade and Capital Movements on Labor: Evidence from the French Case*, OECD Economic Studies No. 1, pp. 89–124.

Pain N and Lansbury M 1996 *The Impact of the Internal Market on the Evolution of European Direct Investment*, NIESR, mimeo.

Safarian A E 1991 Firm and Government Strategies, in Bürgenmeier B and Muchielli J L (eds.), *Multinationals and Europe 1992*, Routledge, London, pp. 187–203.

UNCTAD 1996 *Transnational Corporations and World Development*, United Nations Conference on Trade and Development, Division on Transnational Corporations and Development, International Thomson Business Press, London.

UNTCMD 1993 *From the Common Market to EC92: Regional Economic Integration in the European Community and Transnational Corporations*, United Nations Transnational Corporations and Management Division, Department of Economic and Social Development, United Nations, New York.

WTO 1996 *Trade and Foreign Direct Investment*, World Trade Organisation Report, October 1996.

Yannopoulos G N 1992 Multinational Corporations and the Single European Market, Chapter 11 in Cantwell J (ed.) *Multinational Investment in Modern Europe: Strategic Interaction in the Integrated Community*, Edward Elgar, Brookfield.

Young S, Hood N and Hood C 1994 Transatlantic Perspectives on Inward Investment and Prospects for Policy Reconciliation, in Yamin M, Burton F and Cross A R (eds.), *The Changing European Environment*, Proceedings of the 21st Annual Conference of the UK Academy of International Business, March, pp. 1–34.

Further reading

Mason M and Encarnation D 1995 *Does Ownership Matter? Japanese Multinationals in Europe*, Clarendon Press, Oxford.

17 The importance of Germany in Europe: Trade and direct foreign investment

Heinz-Josef Tüselmann

Introduction

The importance of Germany for the other member states stems from the fact that it is the largest economy in the EU, the second largest world importer, for nearly every EU country the most important export market, and a major investor and net capital exporter for all Community members. On the other hand, Germany is the second largest world exporter, and the EU is the main outlet for German exports and accounts for over half of German Foreign Direct Investment (FDI) inflows. Therefore, EU countries are also of vital importance for the German economy. This high degree of interdependency has resulted in economic developments in Germany affecting the economies of the other member states and *vice versa*. The dramatic changes that occurred in the German economy throughout the 1990s, German reunification and serious supply-side problems, had a profound impact on German trade, FDI, economic growth and employment. However, they also had significant effects on the EU members' FDI and trade with Germany, which in turn had implications for their growth and employment performance.

The German economy exerts a powerful influence on the economies of other European countries in two main ways, by its role as the largest trading partner for most member states and by the significant FDI outflows from Germany. German policy also has considerable spill-over effects on the monetary conditions (and, therefore, general economic conditions) of the other member states. The latter issue is considered in Chapter 2; the former two issues are examined in this chapter.

Determinants and effects of trade and direct foreign investment

Exports are an important component of aggregate demand. Export growth boosts aggregate demand and national output via the foreign trade multiplier. It may, *ceteribus paribus*, raise investment in new machinery, equipment and plants, thereby enhancing the productive capacities and the growth potential of a country. Increases in exports may expand employment in the export industries, but also other industries, because of the additional employment impetus of the

multiplier effects. There are a number of factors that underpin the trade performance of a country. Export growth is to a large degree influenced by economic
growth and the business cycle developments of its main trading partners, and by
the price competitiveness of its exports, which in turn depends on the exchange
rate and the domestic production costs – especially ULCs (Unit Labour Costs).
Import growth is largely contingent on the economic growth and business cycle
developments of the domestic economy and the price-competitiveness of the
exports of its trading partners in relation to the domestic cost level. Given the
size and importance of the German economy, stable, growing and prosperous
Germany is thus of vital importance for the EU countries, and *vice versa.*

Although FDI is the result of location decisions of individual companies at
the microeconomic level, it does have an effect on macroeconomic performance.
On a first approximation it would appear the FDI inflows lead to an increase in
a country's GFCF (Gross Fixed Capital Formation), whereas outflows result in
lower domestic GFCF. Inward FDI may, therefore, make a positive contribution
to economic growth and employment, whereas outward FDI may have the
opposite effect. A country with a negative FDI balance is often assumed to experience lower growth rates and a net export of jobs. However, the connection between
FDI, trade, economic growth and employment is more complex. Location decisions of companies are influenced by a range of factors. On the one hand, these
include variables on the supply side of the economy. There are quantitative cost
and burden factors, such as labour costs and taxation, as well as qualitative variables, such as the skills level of the labour force, the density and tightness of
the regulatory frameworks at the goods and factor markets. On the other hand,
demand factors, such as market size and growth, as well as personal factors, such
as cultural affinity, can be identified. The weight and importance that companies attach to these variables depend on the underlying motive for carrying
out FDI, and determine the type of investment and subsequent impact on the
economies of the home and host country.

FDI may be market orientated, undertaken to cultivate, expand or open up
foreign markets, or to participate in the growth of the market. These investments
correlate closely with market size, growth and with the extent of the trade links
to the host country. A large part of FDI is thus linked to trade. This type of activity largely takes the form of distribution and marketing operations in the host
country. Market orientated investments are thus mainly complementary to the
home country's exports. This FDI may lead to direct employment creation in
the host country and make a positive contribution to its economic growth. Yet,
this type of investment, if it expands the size of the market and/or exploits the
market potential for the mother companies more fully, will boost exports from
the home country and may feed back into higher increases in investment, economic growth and employment in the home country. Thus, this type of investment is not only complementary to the home country's exports, but also to
domestic production and investment. However, this is not necessarily true for
all kinds of market orientated FDI. For example, local content rules may necessitate certain production activities being carried out in the host country. In this
case, FDI may in part substitute domestic production and investment.

If the FDI motive is based purely on financial considerations, companies may
establish holding companies in countries with favourable tax regimes, but leave

the location of production unchanged. Cost-orientated FDI, which leads to the relocation of production facilities, is to a large degree contingent on the level and development of the domestic cost and burden factors relative to those in other locations. By transferring production facilities abroad, these FDIs may substitute exports from the home country, as well as investment and domestic production. This can lead to job losses in the home country and job creation in the host country. However, the transfer of production facilities may not necessarily imply net employment gains in the host country if employees working for domestic companies lose their jobs because of increased competition in the host market from foreign-owned companies operating in the domestic economy. Provided that the labour market is sufficiently flexible, these workers can be employed in other sectors of the economy. Nevertheless, cost-orientated FDI can also be complementary to exports, domestic production and investment, possibly having positive employment effects in the home country. If the home country is a high wage/high skills location, companies may transfer the lower value-added parts of the production chain to lower wage countries in order to exploit international cost differentials and improve their competitiveness. This may lead to a larger market for the end-product at home and abroad because of lower production costs allowing for price reductions. Exports, domestic investment and economic growth may be spurred. The high skilled jobs in the home country may be safeguarded and/or expanded. The complex pattern and the interwoven nature of the determinants and effects of FDI have to be taken into account when assessing the investment relations between Germany and her EU partners (Dunning, 1994; Commission, 1993; OECD, 1994). A fuller treatment of FDI in Europe is given in Chapter 16.

The German export position in the global economy

Since reunification, Germany has retained her rank as the second largest exporter after the USA, with a world market share of roughly 10 per cent in 1996 (Deutsche Bundesbank, 1997). There are three indicators that are commonly used to assess the export position of a country: world market share, export performance, and a country's importance as a supplier of imports for other nations. Table 17.1 reveals that Germany has a mixed picture with regard to export performance.

Germany has lost world market share throughout the 1990s. During the immediate post-unification period there was negative export growth, partly as a result of the recession and weak economic growth rates of Germany's main trading partners, and the impact of unification on German trade. After this the positive export growth rates since 1994 were not sufficient to halt the slide in world market share. This may to a certain extent reflect the growing importance of the NICs and the emerging economies in world trade, which has led to a gradual loss of the industrialised countries' market share. Indeed, the share of the latter group shrank from 83 per cent in 1990 to 66 per cent in 1996 (Institut der deutschen Wirtschaft, 1997a). The regional structure of German exports may provide an additional explanation. Despite the growing importance of exports to Central and Eastern European Countries (CEECs), and the decreasing share of exports to the EU during the 1990s, the EU area continues to be the main outlet for

Table 17.1   German visible trade

	1990	1991	1992	1993	1994	1995	1996
Share on world exports (%)	12.2	11.6	11.3	10.3	10.1	10.4	9.8
Export performance (1989 = 100)	96.2	95.1	93.0	83.7	83.8	79.6	77.9
Export growth at constant prices, p.a. change (%)	−2.1	−0.5	−5.0	−9.8	7.0	5.0	3.0
Export growth to EU at constant prices, p.a. change (%)[1]	−3.1	−1.3	−4.5	−24.1	14.6	5.6	0.6
Import growth at constant prices, p.a. change (%)	7.4	11.1	−6.6	−14.0	6.0	3.8	1.6
Import growth from EU at constant prices, p.a. change (%)[1]	23.1	12.3	−6.4	−27.2	13.1	9.1	1.2
Visible trade balance (% GDP)	3.8	0.8	1.1	1.9	2.2	2.5	2.8
Visible trade balance with EU (% GDP)[1]	2.6	0.9	1.1	1.2	1.4	1.2	1.1
Current account balance (% GDP)	3.2	−1.0	−1.0	−0.7	−1.0	−1.0	−0.6

Note: (1) Excl. Austria, Finland and Sweden
Sources: Author's calculations based on:
European Economy, Annual Economic Report for 1996, No. 62, 1996
Euromonitor, *European Marketing Data and Statistics*, 1997
Deutsche Bundesbank, *Zahlungsbilanzstatistik*, various issues
Bundesministerium für Wirtschaft, *Wirtschaft in Zahlen*, various issues

Table 17.2   Distribution of German visible trade

	Regional Composition (%)				Export Structure (%)		
	Exports		Imports				
	1992	1996	1992	1996		1992	1996
EU[1]	54.3	48.0	52.0	49.2	Investment goods	57.0	56.0
ECE[2]	5.5	8.9	5.4	9.0			
USA	6.3	7.6	6.7	7.1	Consumer goods	12.7	12.1
Japan	2.2	2.7	6.0	5.0			
NICs	2.6	3.3	3.3	3.6	Basic and production goods	22.2	22.0
Others	29.1	29.5	26.6	26.1	Others	8.1	9.9
	100.0	100.0	100.0	100.0		100.0	100.0

Notes:
(1) Excl. Austria, Finland and Sweden
(2) Eastern and Central Europe
Sources: adapted from Deutsche Bundesbank, *Zahlungsbilanzstatistik*, November 1992,
September 1997

German exports (see Table 17.2). However, economic growth rates in the EU have been generally lower than those of the dynamic economies, such as South-East Asia, which still account for only a relatively low proportion of German exports.

The export performance indicator, which makes allowances for the regional effects, points to the under-utilisation of German export potential. This indicator, measuring the quotient of growth of German exports to the growth of German export markets, reveals that the German export performance has deteriorated by 22 per cent from 1989 to 1996 (see Table 17.1). German export markets grew more strongly (46 per cent) than the actual German exports to these markets (14 per cent). Other EU countries were either able to improve their export performance since 1989, such as Sweden, Austria and Spain, or experienced a less severe deterioration; examples include the UK or France (Institut der deutschen Wirtschaft, 1997a). At first glance, the third indicator appears favourable. Germany is the largest source of supply for 24 out of the 65 countries that account for 95 per cent of world trade (Institut der deutschen Wirtschaft, 1996a). However, in many of these 24 countries Germany lost market share between 1990 and 1996, including France, the UK, Italy, the Netherlands and Belgium (Institut der deutschen Wirtschaft, 1997b). Furthermore, market share has been lost in the USA, Japan and the NICs.

The combination of the powerful cost-push effects with the underlying appreciation of the deutschmark, compounded by the product range composition of German exports, would seem to be a major cause for the weakening German position in the 1990s. The bulk of German exports continue to be investment goods (see Table 17.2). The German export industries are specialised in high quality, high value-added, human capital intensive production within the medium technology range, and are competing in less price-sensitive markets. However, globalisation and the advance of the NICs in this product range imply that these markets are becoming more price sensitive and that German companies are less able to rely solely on the non-price factors to hold and/or expand their market share. Furthermore, Germany is losing market share in the rapidly expanding high technology areas, such as microelectronics, biotechnology and automated data processing machinery (OECD, 1994). This may point to weaknesses in the innovative capacities of German businesses and may carry the danger of Germany's falling behind in key technologies. Yet, the developments of traditional export markets seem to indicate that the high productivity and high skills levels found in German manufacturing are no longer sufficient to compensate for the high production costs.

Companies in Western Germany face one of the highest ULCs in the industrialised world. The accumulated ULC disadvantage between 1989 and 1995 amounted to 20 per cent relative to the average of Germany's main competitors (Institut der deutschen Wirtschaft, 1996b). Of this, two-thirds can be attributed to exchange rate effects because of the sharply appreciating – and overvalued – deutschmark in this period. However, since mid-1995 the deutschmark weakened considerably against the currencies of several main trading partners, such as the US dollar, pound and lira. This has helped to improve the price competitiveness of German exports from 1996 onwards. Nevertheless, one-third of the ULC disadvantage is of a domestic nature, reflecting labour cost increases, especially in the non-wage cost elements, above the level of productivity gains. ULCs rose particularly steeply during the early 1990s. This was in part the result of the post-unification boom that tightened labour market conditions in West Germany and pushed wage settlements well above productivity growth. Since 1993 wage increases have moderated considerably. Yet, the rising non-wage labour costs, totalling over 80 per cent of direct wages in 1996 (Institut der deutschen Wirtschaft, 1997a), seemed to have outstripped the benefits of wage constraint. In particular, the rapidly rising social security contributions, partly reflecting the continuing high net transfers to East Germany, bear a large part of the blame. However, given the depreciating deutschmark, the return to moderate wage settlements and the recent, though modest, reforms in the welfare system, Germany may regain price competitiveness and improve her position in the world export market.

Nonetheless, the pan-German export figures mask the poor export position of East Germany. The eastern region accounted, in 1996, for 24 per cent of the total population and for 10 per cent of the pan-German real GDP (Bundesministerium für Wirtschaft, 1996). The actual contribution to the German GDP is, however, lower because a large part continues to be financed by West German transfers (equivalent to 5 per cent of West German GDP), of which about 70 per cent are absorbed in consumption (mainly in the form of welfare benefits) (Neubaumer, 1996). Yet, the eastern region's share on German exports shrank from 5 per cent in 1990 to 2 per cent in 1996 (Bundesministerium für Wirtschaft, 1996). The collapse of the East German exports was due mainly to the disappearance of the traditional markets in CEECs, which formerly took over 70 per cent of her exports, and no corresponding establishment on western markets because of the weak competitive position.

The rapid decrease of the former GDR's exports to CEECs was masked by the German export growth to these countries (see Table 17.2) which was achieved mainly by West German companies. The competitive position of East Germany deteriorated from the beginning of the reunification process. The generous conversion rate of the Ostmark to deutschmark was above the market rate and led to a *de facto* revaluation of the Ostmark. The collective agreements on rapid wage convergence towards the western level produced wage rates far above the productivity level. Additional reasons were the largely obsolete capital stock and the production of outdated manufacturing goods. Because of the large gap between labour productivity and labour costs, ULCs in manufacturing were 55 per cent above the western level in 1991. However, the 1993 collective agreements provided for a slower pace in the process of wage convergence, and thus brought about lower annual wage increases than originally envisaged. Greenfield investments of western companies and rationalisation in the privatised companies, including massive lay-offs, are gradually improving labour productivity. Nevertheless, manufacturing ULCs were nearly 20 per cent above the western German level in 1996 (Deutsche Bundesbank, 1997h). Although the crumbling of East German exports seems to have come to a halt, the recovery of exports in 1995 and 1996 was on a very modest scale.

German trade and economic developments in the 1990s

The strong export orientation of the German economy means that one-third of all jobs in West Germany are dependent on exports (Institut der deutschen Wirtschaft, 1995). Germany is the second largest exporter, constituting over one-fifth of her GDP, of which one-half are intra EU-exports (see Table 17.2). Eight of the top ten destinations of German exports in 1996 were EU countries. France is the most important market for German exports (11.5 per cent), followed by the UK (8.8 per cent), USA (7.7 per cent), Italy (7.6 per cent), the Netherlands (7.5 per cent), and Belgium (6.3 per cent) (Deutsche Bundesbank, 1997c).

Throughout the 1980s the economic landscape in West Germany was characterised by relatively high growth rates, coinciding with price stability, low unemployment, external balance, and small but manageable public-sector deficits. Despite the traditional deficits in services and transfers, the relatively high trade surpluses led to current account surpluses, which peaked in 1989 at 4.8 per cent (Commission, 1993). However, unification led to a turn-around in German trade. After two years of rapid economic growth, and entering a third one in 1990, West Germany operated close to its potential output. Tendencies towards stagnation began to emerge slowly. Thus, unification took place right at the tail end of the boom. In East Germany, economic activities collapsed in the immediate post-unification period. Output had declined by almost 50 per cent by the beginning of 1992 (Statistisches Bundesamt, 1993). However, domestic demand increased because real incomes were boosted by the generous conversion rate of the Ostmark, and by the wage increases that followed. Furthermore, the release of the backlog of demand, accumulated during the communist era, and the new public-sector infrastructure programmes also explain why domestic demand in East Germany was twice as high as domestic production. The gap between aggregate demand and supply was filled mainly by large western transfers, which were financed by high public-sector deficits.

The large deficit spending programme prolonged the boom in West Germany and delayed the cyclical downturn. Given the high degree of capital utilisation in West Germany, the high demand in the western region was further increased by high eastern demand, and resulted in German demand outstripping supply. The gap was filled mainly by higher imports. The surge in imports (see Table 17.1), which was met to a large part by EU countries, and the diversion of West German production from exports to the enlarged domestic market, produced negative export growth rates (see Table 17.1), leading to a deterioration of the German trade balance. This caused the current account to move into deficit by 1991. However, the post-unification boom ran out in mid-1992 and by 1993 Germany was locked in a recession. Import growth slowed down and was negative from the second half of 1992 to 1993 (see Table 17.1). The slow-down of major European and the US economies, the marked reduction in price-competitiveness due to the appreciation of the deutschmark, and the high wage settlements during the post-unification boom all weakened demand for German exports. This resulted in a large decrease of German exports in 1993, especially to the EU (see Table 17.1), where the currencies of major German export markets, such as the UK, Italy and Spain, had weakened sharply against the deutschmark in the aftermath of the 1992 ERM crisis. The upshot was a continuation of the current account deficit.

By 1994, West Germany came out of recession, albeit with moderate growth rates between 1994 and 1996, and her main trading partners experiencing more dynamic growth. Since 1994, export growth resumed and has subsequently outstripped import growth rates (see Table 17.1). Although the current account stayed in deficit, trade surpluses increased continuously between 1994 and 1996. However, as discussed in the previous section, the export potential remained underutilised because of the loss in price-competitiveness. This may imply that economic growth and employment were lower than they would otherwise have been if price-competitiveness had been maintained. Nevertheless, because of the recent improvement in the price-competitiveness of German exports, a nominal export growth rate of 10 per cent and a recovery of the export performance have been forecast for 1997 (Institut der deutschen Wirtschaft, 1996c).

Furthermore, the economic growth potential in West Germany remains underexploited due to the weak domestic demand (investment and private consumption). Economic growth from 1994–96 can be attributed largely to growth in exports. Although one would have expected the export growth to translate after a time lag into higher investment, the growth of the productive capacities has actually weakened since 1993 (Sachverständigenrat, 1996). In addition to cyclical factors, investments are influenced by the cost of production. As discussed before, these rose sharply during the 1990s (especially non-wage labour costs). Recent forecasts predict an annual average growth rate in business investments of merely 2 per cent until the year 2000 (Institut der deutschen Wirtschaft, 1996d). This will not, however, be sufficient to solve the current unemployment crisis. By 1997, the unemployment rate in West Germany had reached 10.4 per cent, and the true rate in East Germany (taking into account the active labour market policy measures) stood at 26 per cent (Sachverständigenrat, 1996).

The weak investments and the high structural unemployment point to serious supply-side problems in the German economy, such as inflexible labour markets, high taxation and social security contributions to finance the generous welfare system. The cost of unification adds to these problems. Indeed, the budgetary transfers to the eastern region, amounting to an annual average of 130 billion deutschmarks between 1991 and 1996 (i.e. 5 per cent of the western German GDP per year), accounted for virtually all increases in the tax and social security burden during this period (Economic Intelligence Unit, 1997). Although East Germany has experienced positive GDP growth rates since 1992, growth started from a very low base after the collapse in 1990–91 and is heavily reliant on the construction industry, and still largely underwritten by western transfers. Convergence with the western level may still take many more years. This implies continuous pressure on the German budget, which is already struggling to meet the Maastricht deficit criteria, and on the welfare system, which is already strained by the demographic developments in Germany. Given the high labour costs encountered by companies operating in Germany, it seems clear that an overhaul of the welfare system, with a view to reducing non-wage labour costs, budgetary reforms and labour market reforms are vital to improve competitiveness, tackle the unemployment crisis and raise investments. Recent reforms such as the deregulation of atypical employment contracts, decentralisation measures in collective bargaining, and consolidation measures for social security spending have been first important steps in the right direction (Tüselmann, 1996). However, further and perhaps bolder reforms may be needed to bring the German economy back to the path of low unemployment, internal and external balance, as well as enhancing and fully exploiting her growth potential. With Germany as a major outlet for the exports of EU countries, the economic prosperity of Germany is also important for the economic growth of economies of the member states.

European Union countries' exports to Germany

The importance of Germany for the other EU members relies on the fact that it is the largest economy in the EU, making up over a quarter of EU GDP, and

Table 17.3 Exports of EU countries to Germany

	Exports as % GDP 87–95	% country's total exports			% country's GDP			Export/Import Ratio		
		87/89	90/92	93/95	87/89	90/92	93/95	87/89	90/92	93/95
B/L	57	19.1	22.6	21.3	11.8	13.3	10.3	75	89	84
DK	27	17.2	21.6	17.0	4.4	6.0	4.8	72	104	90
F	18	17.9	21.2	17.6	3.1	3.8	3.1	73	85	83
Gr	12	21.7	19.7	15.3	2.7	2.4	1.9	59	54	53
Irl	59	11.3	13.3	12.1	6.3	7.1	8.2	149	192	219
I	16	18.1	20.4	15.8	2.8	3.0	3.1	79	93	99
NL	46	25.8	27.6	20.2	11.6	12.5	9.7	95	108	101
P	23	16.5	19.8	19.6	4.2	4.3	4.2	71	79	94
Sp	13	12.8	16.8	14.4	1.5	1.8	2.1	51	61	78
UK	19	12.1	13.6	11.5	2.2	2.5	2.3	60	78	71

Note: (1) Until 1990 West Germany. East German trade with EU countries (excl. West Germany) before unification accounted for less than 2% of total East German trade
Sources: See Table 17.1

the second largest world importer, with imports equalling one-fifth of its GDP, of which approximately one-half are intra-EU imports (see Table 17.1). For all EU countries except Ireland and Spain, Germany is now the main export destination. Between 21.3 per cent and 11.5 per cent of the individual EU countries' exports is taken up by the German market, and exports to Germany constitute between 10.3 per cent and 1.9 per cent of the countries' GDP (see Table 17.3). The German market is of particular importance for the smaller, more open economies such as Belgium and the Netherlands, where exports to Germany accounted for about one-fifth of their total exports and one-tenth of their GDP. Even for the larger economies, such as France, the UK and Italy, the export share to Germany stands at 17.6 per cent, 11.5 per cent and 15.8 per cent, respectively, equalling 3.1 per cent (France, UK) and 2.3 per cent (Italy) of their GDP (see Table 17.3). This may already indicate the magnitude of the spill-over effects that economic developments in Germany may have on EU countries.

German unification serves as a useful example to demonstrate these effects. As previously discussed, German unification constituted a fiscal shock, resulting in all German demand outstripping supply, and the gap being filled by increases in imports. The surge in imports benefited the EU countries in particular (see Table 17.1). They were all able to step up their exports to Germany considerably, which is reflected by Germany's increased share in their total exports (see Table 17.3). The beneficial trade effect raised their aggregate demand and national output via the foreign trade multiplier. The cyclical downturn that began to emerge in most EU countries in 1990 was somewhat moderated by the impulse of German unification, which acted as a demand expansion programme for the EU. The beneficial trade effect increased GDP in the EU area by an estimated half a percentage point annually in 1990 and 1991 (Issing, 1993). Individual countries benefited to varying degrees, depending on the relative openness of their economies and the extent of their trading links with Germany. Belgium profited most from the trade effect, which made up one percentage point of GDP in 1990 and two percentage points in 1991 (Issing, 1993). For the UK, the stimulus on economic activity was roughly the same as the EU average. With export growth in Germany being flat, all countries apart from Greece were able to improve their traditionally negative bilateral trade balance with Germany (see Table 17.3). In 1992 the beneficial trade effect ran out. The German economy slowed down during the second half of 1992 and moved into recession by 1993. Import growth came to a halt and actually declined in 1993 (see Table 17.1).

The net effect of German unification appears, on balance, to be negative. The deflationary effects transmitted to EU members via the operation of the ERM seem to have outweighed the (short-run) beneficial trade effects (Englander, 1992). Confronted with inflationary pressures from the overly expansive fiscal policy and excessive wage settlements, the Bundesbank successively raised official interest rates between 1991 and summer 1992, causing the deutschmark to appreciate. With German *de facto* leadership in the ERM and the deutschmark as the anchor currency, the other ERM members had to tighten their monetary policy in order to maintain the parities of their currencies with the deutschmark within the fluctuation band. They shared the deutschmark appreciation and were faced with higher interest rates than would otherwise be the case. Thus, the tight monetary policy of the Bundesbank exerted deflationary pressures throughout the ERM area. However, business cycles were diverging. The boom period in West Germany was prolonged by the fiscal expansion, induced by unification, and economic activities slowed down only in the second half of 1992. In contrast, the other EU members were already experiencing low growth rates from 1990 onwards – though somewhat moderated initially by the rising German import demand. The deflationary effects of German monetary policy had thus led to a sharper slowdown of the economies of her partner countries than might otherwise have occurred.

However, after the 1993 recession, German imports picked up in 1994, but the import growth rates moderated continuously in the 1995–96 period, partly echoing the moderate economic growth figures in Germany. Nevertheless, the growth in imports from the EU was higher compared with total import growth, apart from 1996 (see Table 17.1). Although the share of exports to Germany dropped in every country after the end of the post-unification boom, and most countries saw their bilateral trade balance with Germany worsening, each country's bilateral trade balance was, however, more favourable than in the years preceding unification, except for Greece (see Table 17.3). In the aftermath of the 1992 ERM crisis the currencies of Spain, Portugal, Italy and the UK depreciated considerably against the deutschmark until mid-1995, thereby improving the price of competitiveness of these countries' exports to Germany. This may explain in part why Spain, Italy and Portugal, in contrast to the other EU countries, were able to improve their bilateral trade balance with Germany even after the post-unification boom, despite their rise in ULCs (measured in national currencies) not being significantly lower than the rise in West German ULCs. In the UK, ULC growth during the 1990s was even more pronounced than in West Germany, and the sharp drop in the value of the pound against the deutschmark could only partially offset the cost/productivity disadvantage. The bilateral trade balance deteriorated after the post-unification boom, though comparing more favourably with the balance of the pre-unification years (see Table 17.3).

Despite the widening of the fluctuation bands in the ERM to ±15 per cent, the currencies of the 'hard core' countries have not undergone significant changes vis-à-vis the deutschmark. The French, Dutch, Belgian and Danish bilateral trade balances with Germany followed the same pattern as the UK. Yet, their improvement compared with the pre-unification period is largely attributable to gains in price-competitiveness in relation to costs rather than depreciation. Their ULCs rose less steeply than the German ones. The currencies of these countries were also less affected by the appreciation of the deutschmark which occurred in mid-1995. However, the pound and the lira appreciated especially strongly against the deutschmark. This loss in price-competitiveness, if not off-set by ULC reductions, may result in these countries losing market share in Germany. With the German export market being vital for the economic per-formance of the EU countries, and in the light of increased exchange rate uncer-tainties in the run-up to EMU, the longer-term export prospects for EU members rest to a large degree on the extent to which reforms in Germany trans-late into higher German growth rates and their ability to hold down costs and/or improve productivity.

German direct foreign investment and

the *Standort Deutschland* debate

Throughout the 1980s and early 1990s, Germany was a net FDI exporter, with inflows amounting to just 20 per cent of outflows in both the 1985–90 and 1991–96 periods (see Table 17.4). German inward FDI stocks were nearly 40 per cent lower than outward stocks by 1995. Within the *Standort Deutschland* debate, it has become an orthodoxy to relate the negative balance of the German FDI flows to the vanishing international competitiveness of Germany as a location for busi-ness (Siebert, 1995; Beyfuß, 1995). It is often assumed that high and growing labour costs, inflexible employment and working practices (as a result of extens-ive and tight labour market regulations), and high corporate taxation, have led to international investors shunning Germany as a location for business. This is also thought to have led to the increased propensity of German companies to invest abroad, thereby contributing to the current unemployment crisis and weak domestic investment levels. However, the relationship between FDI and these effects is complex.

German outflows increased markedly from the mid-1980s, reflecting the worldwide trend in the rapid growth of FDI. Germany is the fourth largest provider of FDI flows, after the USA, Japan and the UK, accounting for 10 per cent of worldwide outflows (Bundesministerium für Wirtschaft, 1994). Some 2.8 million workers are employed in German companies' overseas affiliates (see Table 17.4). German outflows grew especially markedly throughout the 1990s. FDI outflows as a share of national GFCF grew from 5.4 per cent in 1985–90 to 5.9 per cent in 1991–96. As a percentage of GDP, they increased from 1.1 per cent to 1.2 per cent (see Table 17.4). Compared with other industrialised western countries, Germany occupies a mid-table position, as revealed by these indicators.

Empirical evidence shows that cost and the burden of legislation were of lesser importance for German outflows than market factors (Beyfuß, 1992; Ifo Institut für Wirtschaftsforschung, 1996). About two-thirds of all German FDI are aimed

Table 17.4 German foreign direct investment

	Outward FDI					Inward FDI				
	Outflows			Outward stock, 1995		Inflows			Inward stock, 1995	
	DM, bn	% national GFCF[2]	% GDP	DM, bn	No. employed (m)	DM, bn	% domestic GFCF[2]	% GDP	DM, bn	No. employed (m)
1985/90	113.6	5.4	1.1			22.0	1.0	0.2		
1991/96	198.7	5.9	1.2	375.8	2.8	41.6	1.0	0.2	232.3	1.6

Regional distribution – Flows %[3]

Outward FDI

	Europe	EU[4]	ECE[5]	USA	Japan	NICs
1985/90	55.6	48.5	0.3	35.0	1.4	1.1
1991/96	74.1	56.9	8.5	14.4	1.8	1.8

Inward FDI

	Europe	EU[4]	ECE[5]	USA	Japan	NICs
1985/90	77.3	58.2	0.7	-10.5	19.1	0.7
1991/96	66.3	53.6	5.0	5.5	7.0	1.2

Sectoral structure – Outward stocks (%)

1995

	All countries	EU	Non-EU
Manufacturing	38.5	29.8	49.5
Commerce	16.1	16.7	25.2
Financial sector	30.2	40.2	17.9
Holding companies	5.7	7.5	3.4

Notes:
(1) Data refer to West Germany before unification and the whole of Germany after unification
(2) Gross fixed capital formation
(3) A negative figure means repatriation of capital
(4) Excluding Austria, Finland, Sweden
(5) Eastern and Central Europe

Sources: Author's calculations based on:
European Economics, Annual Economic Report for 1996, No. 62, 1996
Bundesministerium für Wirtschaft, Runderlaß Außenwirtschaft, various issues
Deutsche Bundesbank, Kapitalverpflichtung mit dem Ausland, 1997

at expanding, cultivating or accessing foreign markets. The majority of these market-orientated FDI are linked to German exports. Indeed, the regional distribution of German FDI is largely identical to the regional distribution of German exports. (see Tables 17.2 and 17.4). As outlined before, this type of investment may boost German exports. It should therefore make a positive contribution to domestic production and investment, economic growth and employment. Furthermore, the internationalisation of the service sector, spurred by the SEM programme and the General Agreement on Trade in Services of the WTO, has led to the increased importance of financial service companies in the German outflows since the late 1980s. This is partly because the sales of financial products often require a local presence. This type of activity may have only a marginal effect on German jobs.

Although cost factors are of less importance as a motive for German outward FDI compared with market factors, recent studies reveal that their importance had nevertheless increased in the 1990s (Beyfuß, 1992). Labour cost considerations in particular have gained prominence in the light of the deterioration of the relative German labour cost position. However, just one-third of all German outward FDIs are cost motivated and associated with the transfer of production facilities. This part of outflows carries the potential of substituting domestic production and investment, and could lead to job losses in Germany. Yet, a significant proportion of German companies carrying out this type of FDI relocate only the intermediate production aspects of their production chain to lower wage countries (Institut der deutschen Wirtschaft, 1996e). This also explains the rapid growth of German FDI to the low wage CEEC region (see Table 17.4), and especially to the Visegrad countries, which accounted for roughly three-quarters of all German FDI into CEECs (Bundesministerium für Wirtschaft, 1997). By exploiting international labour cost differentials, German companies can improve the price-competitiveness of end-products, which in turn may lead to a larger domestic and foreign market. The upshot may be higher exports, domestic production and investment, as well as safeguarding or, under certain conditions, expansion of the higher skill/higher wage jobs in Germany. Indeed, empirical evidence suggests that FDIs into CEECs have safeguarded jobs in Germany (Institut der deutschen Wirtschaft, 1996e). Once this type of cost-motivated FDI and the market-orientated FDI are discounted, it appears that the negative effects of outward FDI on employment and domestic investment are less significant than often assumed. It could even be argued that, on balance, the overall effect may perhaps be one of net job creation, and the currently weak domestic investment levels may have been even more modest in the absence of the spill-back effects of outward FDI.

However, the concerns with regard to the low FDI inflows seem more justified. Although inward investment grew in absolute terms from the 1955–90 to the 1991–96 period, and affiliates of overseas companies employed some 1.6 million workers in Germany by 1995, the share of inflows on domestic GFCF and GDP remained stagnant at just 1.0 per cent and 0.2 per cent, respectively (see Table 17.4). In comparison with other western industrialised countries, Germany occupies a tail-end position for these indicators (OECD, 1996). This seems somewhat puzzling. Considering that Germany is the second-largest world importer, one would have expected correspondingly large market-orientated inflows. Germany also constitutes a large domestic market, which has been extended by unification. Moreover, Germany operates a very liberal FDI regime and occupies a key geographical position in the centre of Europe. The western region of Germany scores highly in international comparison for many of the qualitative (soft) location factors, such as the availability of a highly-skilled labour force, harmonious employee relations and a good infrastructure (Tüselmann, 1995). However, half of the FDI inflows are market-orientated, indicating that these qualitative factors are not sufficient to compensate for high costs. Foreign investors are indeed shunning Germany as a production base.

The comparison of the level and change of the quantitative (hard) location factors with the weighted average of the western industrialised world highlights the weaknesses of the German location. These factors rank particularly high in production-orientated location decisions. The level of effective corporate taxation, private environmental expenditure, plant utilisation, as well as wages, non-wage labour costs, and ULCs compare unfavourably with other locations. The relative West German manufacturing labour cost disadvantage is particularly pronounced. By 1995, hourly wages were 41 per cent, and non-wage labour costs 74 per cent, above the level of the average of the other industrialised countries. The relative labour cost disadvantage increased markedly in the 1990s, with the non-wage labour costs growing more steeply than the direct wage costs. Although the level of labour productivity in manufacturing is high by international standards, labour cost growth outstripped productivity gains, resulting in ULC increasing by more than in most other countries. Strict environmental protection legislation adds to the comparative cost disadvantage for companies operating in Germany. The short working hours, coupled with labour market regulations that impede the flexible use of labour and flexible working times, produced a comparatively low degree of plant utilisation and thus high capital unit costs. Furthermore, investments are hampered by the extent and complexity of government regulations. In particular, the long, bureaucratic planning and approval procedures hamper investments in greenfield sites.

In the light of the immense private investment needs in the eastern regions, FDI inflows into East Germany have been disappointing, despite the generous investment incentives. East Germany accounted for just 10 per cent of the German inward investments between 1991 and 1995. The per capita inflows were thus only 40 per cent of West German ones. However, given the grave labour cost and other disadvantages, this development is hardly surprising. East German manufacturing labour costs, though 40 per cent below the West German level in 1996, were 85 per cent higher than those in the advanced CEECs, well above the level of the Mediterranean EU countries and even above the US, UK and French level. With labour productivity being low, albeit gradually improving, the region remained grossly uncompetitive in ULC terms. The cost of cleaning up past ecological damage, bottlenecks in public administration, the inherited crumbling infrastructure, and the lower skills based compared with West Germany provide further explanations.

Nevertheless, this rather negative assessment masks the improvement of Germany as a business location that has occurred since the mid-1990s. Wage moderation in West Germany after the high settlements in the early 1990s, and cuts and freezes in collectively agreed non-wage benefits negotiated in many agreements have moderated West German labour cost growth in 1995 and 1996. The deregulation of atypical employment contracts, incentives to increase the uptake of part-time jobs, the replacement of the outdated working time laws, decentralisation trends in collective bargaining, and agreements on flexible working times were vital steps to improve the framework for more flexible working practices so that the degree of plant utilisation can be improved and capital unit cost reduced. Administrative barriers have been lowered lately by simpler planning and approval regulations. The company tax reform of 1994 cut corporate tax rates. In East Germany, productivity gains and the slowdown of the pace of wage convergence have already led to a narrowing of the ULC disadvantage. Administrative bottlenecks had been largely ironed out by 1997, and the public infrastructure programme, which is nearing its completion, will equip the eastern region with one of the most modern infrastructures in Europe. With further reforms of the welfare system, taxation and industrial relations on the horizon, Germany may in the future become a more attractive location for international production and FDI.

German direct foreign investment into European Union countries

The EU is the main recipient of German FDI, accounting for three-fifths of German outflows in the 1991–96 period (see Table 17.5). Germany is a net capital exporter and major investor in all EU countries. For example, Germany is the second largest investor in Belgium, the third largest in Denmark, and the fourth largest in Ireland, Italy, Spain and the Netherlands. German intra-EU FDI flows equated to 1.3 per cent of the GFCF of the EU in the 1990s, ranging from 5.1 per cent to 0.4 per cent in individual countries (see Table 17.5). These flows represented 0.2 per cent of the GDP of the EU, with national variations between 2.0 and 0.1 per cent. German affiliates in the EU area employed over 900,000 workers in 1995 (see Table 17.5). Once the indirect employment effects, which can arise from the positive spill-over effects of FDI on domestic companies (for

Table 17.5   German foreign direct investment flows into EU countries

	DM, bn		% Country's GFCF[(2)]		% Country's GDP		% German outflows		No. employed in German affiliates (000) 1995
	85/90	91/96	85/90	91/96	85/90	91/96	85/90	91/96	
EU[(4)]	55.2	112.9	0.7	1.3	0.1	0.2	48.5	56.9	922
B/L	8.5	18.0	2.8	4.2	0.5	0.8	7.4	9.0	97
DK	0.3	2.2	0.1	1.0	0.0	0.2	0.2	1.1	20
F	5.8	17.1	0.3	0.7	0.1	0.2	5.1	8.6	234
Gr	0.3	0.9	0.2	0.4	0.0	0.1	0.2	0.4	13
Irl	5.2	10.2	8.0	12.5	1.4	2.0	4.6	5.1	11
I	5.4	8.7	0.3	0.4	0.1	0.1	4.7	4.4	95
NL	7.0	16.4	1.4	2.6	0.3	0.5	6.2	8.2	91
P	0.5	1.6	0.4	0.7	0.1	0.2	0.5	0.8	44
Sp	5.5	10.2	0.7	0.9	0.2	0.2	4.8	5.7	152
UK	19.5	27.5	1.2	1.8	0.2	0.3	17.1	13.8	191

Notes: See Table 17.4
Sources: See Table 17.4

example, by creating business for domestic suppliers), are taken into account, the contribution to employment may be higher than the figure suggests. Whether German FDIs have led to net employment gains in the EU countries depends *inter alia* on the type of investment and the previously outlined competitive effects on the domestic industries.

In the run-up to the SEM, German FDI into the EU grew, accounting for the bulk of German FDI outflow growth. The EU's share of German outflows increased from 48.5 per cent in the 1985–90 period to nearly 57 per cent in the 1991–96 period (see Table 17.5). Because of the high degree of trade integration with the EU economies, German intra-EU FDIs are traditionally strongly market-orientated. Two-thirds of German outflows and stocks in the EU are concentrated in the four countries (UK, Netherlands, France, Belgium) which also account for two-thirds of German exports (see Tables 17.3 and 17.5). Yet, the SEM has increased the potential for a deeper integration of production between Germany and her EU partners. Nevertheless, leaving aside national variations, empirical evidence reveals that the surge of German intra-EU FDI was only in a minority of cases related to relocation or the establishment of production facilities in EU countries. These FDI outflows were driven mainly by market motives of financial considerations (Döhrn, 1994). The banking and insurance industries stepped up FDI in the light of the liberalisation of the financial service sector. A large part of the intra-EU FDI outflow growth has been in investment fund companies, capital investment companies and holding companies in countries with low corporate and capital gains taxation and/or in locations where favourable legislation with regard to the organisational structure of holding companies results in a low tax base for such companies. The comparison of the sectoral structure between German EU and non-EU FDI seems to confirm that FDI growth into the EU area had more to do with trade and financial integration, rather than integration of production and the transfer of production facilities (see Table 17.4).

The UK is the most important location for German intra-EU FDI, despite the reduction of its share in the 1991–96 period compared with the 1985–90 period. The UK is followed by Belgium/Luxembourg, France, the Netherlands, Spain and Ireland (see Table 17.5). For the UK, the Netherlands, Ireland and Belgium, the importance of FDI in terms of their GFCF and GDP is above the EU average. For the smaller German neighbours, such as Belgium and the Netherlands, with their relatively open economies and extensive trading links with Germany, these FDIs make a substantial contribution to their investment levels (see Table 17.5). Although German FDI into these countries is naturally mainly market-orientated, the dynamic FDI growth into Belgium and the Netherlands in the 1990s was largely accounted for by investments in holding companies (Löbbe, 1994). Both countries' business and tax regulations are favourable to this type of investment. For example, the share of holding companies, as a destination of the German outward stock in the Netherlands, reached 15.5 per cent by 1995 (Deutsche Bundesbank, 1997c). This is double the EU average (see Table 17.4). Furthermore, because of its advantageous ULC position, high degree of plant utilisation and geographical location, several German manufacturing companies have set up production facilities in the Netherlands.

German FDI into Ireland has grown dramatically since the second half of the 1980s. Although Ireland took only 1.0 per cent of all German exports to the EU, about 10 per cent of German intra-EU FDI was directed towards Ireland with German FDI amounting to 2.0 per cent of the Irish GDP in the 1991–96 period (see Table 17.5). The majority of these flows arose from financial institutions which established pension fund companies and capital investment companies in Ireland, because of low capital gains and corporate taxation, tax holiday incentives, and the extremely favourable double taxation treaty between Germany and Ireland (OECD, 1996). The relatively low labour costs of the Mediterranean countries, especially Greece and Portugal, would seem to make them the archetypal EU locations for German production-orientated FDI, particularly for the lower value-added and intermediate production aspects of the value-added chain. However, this region has attracted just 11 per cent of German intra-EU FDI since the mid-1980s, of which the lion's share (nearly two-thirds in 1985–90 and over three-quarters in 1991–96) went to Spain, where hourly labour costs are substantially higher than in Portugal and Greece (see Table 17.5). It would seem that, compared with Greece and Portugal, the Visegrad countries, and especially the Czech Republic and Poland, are more attractive locations for German manufacturers to transfer intermediate production operations. This is partly because of lower transport costs and the introduction of new production concepts and techniques, such as JIT production in the Visegrad countries. German FDIs into Spain, which increased from 4.8 per cent in 1985–90 to 5.7 per cent in 1991–96, are primarily market-orientated (OECD, 1996). However, there has also been some relocation of production to Spain, especially in the car industry.

The UK has remained the second-largest destination for German FDI and is the most important EU location. However, in the period 1991–98, the UK still attracted roughly the same amount of German FDI as France, Italy and Denmark together. The UK accounted on average for 8 per cent of German exports in the 1990s compared with an average of 14 per cent of German FDI (Bundesministerium für Wirtschaft, 1997). Thus, although a large part of the FDI has been export complementary, the UK has also attracted substantial German inflows into the financial service sector, as well as production-orientated FDI, especially into the car, chemical and electronics industries. While the UK would not seem particularly attractive for German manufacturers in terms of the aggregate ULCs for the manufacturing sector, the combination of deregulated, flexible labour markets (allowing for flexible staffing and working practices), and the availability of a suitably trained labour force allow investors to introduce modern production processes and techniques. This total factor productivity is relatively high, which combined with the relatively low labour costs may explain the attractiveness of the UK as a production location. Furthermore, corporate taxation and costs imposed by regulations, such as environmental protection legislation, are significantly lower than in Germany.

In summary, all EU countries, albeit to varying degrees, have benefited from the surge in German FDI. This has been mainly in the form of market-orientated investments and/or financial investments, but to a lesser extent in the form of production-orientated investments, with notable exceptions. However, the future prospects of most EU countries to achieve higher degrees of integration in production with the German economy are uncertain. On the one hand, the previously discussed recent and prospective reforms in Germany may lead in the longer run to a relative improvement in the cost and burden factors. This may result in a moderation of production-orientated outflows. On the other hand, international competition for German FDI is increasing. The continuation of the transformation process in CEECs will make this region increasingly attractive for the transfer of certain production operations (provided their relative cost positions are not exploding). The current efforts in the WTO and in the OECD to liberalise FDI regimes further may enhance the attractiveness of various non-EU countries as a location for German investments.

Conclusion

The economic landscape of Germany has undergone fundamental change since the turn of the decade. German unification and supply-side problems, especially on the cost front, have posed the greatest challenge. Combined with the appreciating deutschmark, these events brought about a weakening of the German export position in the world economy; negative export growth during the post-unification boom; export growth rates below the export growth potential thereafter; weak domestic investment and economic growth, as well as high unemployment. However, the price-competitiveness of German exports has improved somewhat since the mid-1990s. This was in part attributable to both the depreciation of the deutschmark since mid-1995 and the slow-down in labour cost growth, which resulted from wage restraint and moderate supply-side reforms. This development improved the framework for higher export, investment and economic growth. Nevertheless, East German companies are, in general, still uncompetitive in world markets.

The beneficial trade effect of German unification has meant that all EU countries stepped up their exports to Germany in the early 1990s, though to varying degrees. However, the net effect of German unification was negative because the deflationary pressures transmitted via the operation of the ERM outstripped the beneficial trade effects. Although the share of German exports dropped in all countries after the post-unification boom, their bilateral trade balances with Germany remained more favourable compared with the years preceding German unification. Whereas some countries, such as the UK and Spain, improved the price-competitiveness of their German exports on the basis of the devaluation of their currencies against the deutschmark in the aftermath of the 1992 ERM crises, others, such as the Netherlands and France, achieved this via lower increases in their domestic labour costs, rather than devaluation. The former group of countries saw their price-competitiveness deteriorate in the wake of the deutschmark depreciation since mid-1995.

The assessment of the development and effects of German FDI flows confirms, only in part, the concerns voiced in the *Standort Deutschland* debate. Outflows grew markedly during the 1990s, but were in the majority of cases related to market motives and may spill back into higher exports, domestic investment, economic growth and employment in Germany. Cost considerations were of less importance, although their importance is increasing. Lower than expected outflows were associated with the transfer of production abroad. Of these, a significant proportion was aimed at improving the competitiveness of German companies, which in turn may feed back into higher domestic production, investment and employment. However, the low level of German inward FDI throughout the 1990s could indeed be attributed in part to the relative disadvantage in the cost and burden location factors, such as labour costs, taxation and the costs imposed by regulations. The East German FDI performance was even more disappointing, but not surprising given the location disadvantages of the region. Recent reforms in the welfare system, industrial relations and taxation have somewhat improved the attractiveness of the German business location. In the run-up to the SEM, German FDI into the EU grew rapidly. Individual countries benefited to varying degrees. However, the surge in German intra-EU FDI was only in a minority of cases related to the relocation of production facilities, and was mainly driven by market motives and financial considerations. Nevertheless, some countries, especially the UK, have attracted significant production-orientated FDI from Germany.

Leaving aside future developments in business cycle and exchange rate movements, and assuming the continuation of the reform path in Germany, the outlook of German FDI and trade with the EU countries appears two-sided. Improved price-competitiveness of German exports may lead to higher exports to the EU countries, which in turn may increase German market-orientated FDI outflows. On the other hand, improvements in the German cost and burden factors may reduce production-orientated outflows and attract more inward FDI. For the EU countries, an enhanced framework for economic growth in Germany may translate into higher exports to Germany. However, a reduction in the relative price-competitiveness of their German exports may have the opposite effect. An increased price-competitiveness of German exports may raise the EU countries' imports from Germany. In turn, these countries may receive more market-orientated inflows from Germany. On the other hand, they may experience a decline in German production-orientated FDI if non-EU nations, such as the CEECs, attract more German FDI, and if the improvement in the cost and burden location factors result in a decrease of German FDI outflows. However, developments in the global economic environment and the pace of the catching-up process in East Germany add an extra dimension to the uncertainty surrounding these scenarios.

References

Beyfuß J 1992 Ausländische Direktinvestitionen in Deutschland – Bestandsaufnahme und Ergebnisse einer Unternehmensbefragung, in *Beiträge zur Wirtschafts und Sozialforschung*, 205/10, Deutscher Insitutsverlag, Cologne.

Beyfuß J 1995 Arbeitsplatzverlagerung ins Ausland: Standortschwäche oder Überlebensstrategie?, *IW Trends – Quartalshefte zur empirischen Wirtschaftsforschung*, Vol. 22, No. 3, pp. 93–100.

Bundesministerium für Wirtschaft 1997 *Wirtschaft in Zahlen.*

Bundesministerium für Wirtschaft 1994 *Neuere Entwicklungen und Perspektiven für Direktinvestitionen*, December.

Bundesministerium für Wirtschaft 1996 *Jahreswirtschaftsbericht*, pp. 124–25.

Bundesministerium für Wirtschaft 1997 *Wirtschaft in Zahlen*.

Commission 1993 *New Location Factors for Mobile Investment in Europe – Final Report*, Brussels.

Commission 1993 Annual Economic Report for 1993, *European Economy*, No. 54.

Deutsche Bundesbank 1997 *Monatsbericht*, January, Frankfurt.

Deutsche Bundesbank 1997c *Kapitalverpflichtungen mit dem Ausland*.

Deutsche Bundesbank 1997c *Zahlungsbilanzstatistik*, May.

Deutsche Bundesbank 1997h *Geschäftsbericht* 1996.

Döhrn R 1994 Deutsche Direktinvestititonen in der Europäischen Union: Produktions- oder Finanzintegration, *RWI Mitteilungen*, Vol. 45, No. 3, pp. 261–81.

Dunning J H 1994 Re-evaluating the benefits of foreign direct investment, *Transnational Corporations*, Vol. 3, No. 1, pp. 23–51.

Economic Intelligence Unit 1997 Report on Germany.

Englander A 1992 Adjustment under Fixed Exchange Rates: Application to the European Monetary Union, *OECD Working Papers*, No. 117, pp. 3–22.

Ifo Institut für Wirtschaftsforschung (1996) Umfang und Bestimmungsgründe einfließender und ausfließender Direktinvestitionen ausgewählter Industrieländer – Entwicklungen und Perspektiven, *Ifo Studien zur Strukturforschung*, Munich.

Institut der deutschen Wirtschaft 1995 *Informationsdienst*, No. 31, pp. 4–5.

Institut der deutschen Wirtschaft 1996a *Informationsdienst*, No. 19, p. 6.

Institut der deutschen Wirtschaft 1996b *Informationsdienst*, No. 28, p. 28.

Institut der deutschen Wirtschaft 1996c *Informationsdienst*, No. 26 p. 16.

Institut der deutschen Wirtschaft 1996d *Informationsdienst*, No. 27, p. 6.

Institut der deutschen Wirtschaft 1996e *Informationsdienst*, No. 40, pp. 4–5.

Institut der deutschen Wirtschaft 1997a *IW Trends – Quartalshefte zur empirischen Wirtschaftsforschung*, Vol. 24, No. 1, p. 7, p. 10 and p. 48.

Institut der deutschen Wirtschaft 1997b *Informationsdienst*, No. 36, p. 5.

Issing O 1993 *Deutsche Bundesbank – Auszüge aus Presseartikeln*, 4 April, p. 4.

Löbbe K 1994 Innovationen, Investitionen und Wettbewerbsfähigkeit der deutschen Wirtschaft, *RWI Mitteilungen*, Vol. 45, No. 16, pp. 135–45.

Neubaumer R 1996 Ostdeutschland – Erfolge und Probleme im deutschen Vereinigungsprozess, *HWWA Wirtschaftsdienst*, Vol. 76, No. 11, pp. 124–25.

OECD Observer 1994 No. 190, pp. 36–37.

OECD, 1995, *Foreign Direct Investment, Trade and Employment*, Paris.

OECD 1996 *Financial Market Trends*, June, Paris.

Sachverständigenrat 1996 *Jahresgutachten 1996/7*, November.

Siebert H 1995 in *Handelsblatt*, 13 December, p. 9.

Statistisches Bundesamt 1992 *Datenreport 1992*.

Statistisches Bundesamt 1993 *Volkswirtschaftliche Gesamtrechnung*.

The Economist Intelligence Unit 1997 *Country Profile – Germany*, London.

Tüselmann H J 1995 Standort Deutschland – is Germany losing its appeal as an international manufacturing location?, *European Business Review*, Vol. 95, No. 5, pp. 21–30.

Tüselmann H J 1996 Progress towards greater labour flexibility in Germany: The impact of recent reforms, *Employee Relations*, Vol. 18, No. 1, pp. 50–67.

Index

Index entries are to page numbers, those in *italic* referring to Boxes, Figures and Tables.

General Mediterranean Policy (GMP) 334–5
General System of Preferences (GSP) 335–6
George, K 137
Germany 407
  agriculture 284
  budgetary reform, attitudes to 125
  deutschmark 376, 411, 417
  East
    economic activities 413
    exports 412
    foreign direct investment inflows 420–1
    privatisation 322
  export position 409–12
  foreign direct investment *418*
    determinants and effects 408–9
    into EU countries 421–4
    inward 400
    and *Standort Deutschland* debate 417–21
  hegemony 87–9
  imports from EU countries 414–17
  industrial policy 163–4
  policy leadership 88–9
  productivity 360
  reunification 13, 209, 415–16
  trade 407–9, 412–14
Geroski, P 55, 146
Giavazzi, F 82
globalisation 206
Goodhart, C 234
goods, free movement 34, 50
Gordon, J 233
Grahl, J 59
Grant, W 194, 292, 294
Greece
  accession to EU 9, 43
  convergence in economic development 67
  economic integration 65
  foreign direct investment inward 400, 423
Grilli, V 111
Grimwade, N 311
Gros, D 86
Guerrier, P 364

Haigh, N 247
Haldane, A 89

Harbeger, A C 134
harmonisation 43, 166–7, 177, 185
Hay, D 134
Healey, N M 110, 111
health and safety 185, 200
hegemony 82, 87–9, 379
Henning, C 12
Herin, J 42
Heylen, F 108
Hill, B 284, 290
Hindley, B 56
Hodgman, D 75
Howe, M 136, 137
Hughes, A 152
Human Capital Formation 227

illicit work 187
immigration 353–4
inbound extra-EU FDI 385
income disparities 210–11, *211, 212*
industrial enterprises *63*
industrial policy 156–78, 403–4
industrial relations 195–6
inflation 88, 98–100, 104, 319
information society 169
information technology 172
infrastructure, transport policy 253–7
Infrastructure Productive Investment Support 227
inland waterways 252, 254, 266, *267*
innovation 170–2
institutional reform, CEEC 317
Integrated Mediterranean Programmes (IMP) 222
intellectual property rights, biotechnology industry 174
interest rates 99–100
intergovernmental agencies 8
Intergovernmental Conferences (IGC) 10, 14
interlining 272
intermodal transport 262–3
Internal Market 43–4
International Air Transport Association (IATA) 268, 269
International Convention for the Prevention of Pollution from Ships (Marpol) 278
International Convention for the Safety of Life at Sea (SOLAS) 278
INTERREG 227–8